Family Bonds and Gender Divisions:

Readings in the Sociology of the Family

Edited by Bonnie Fox
University of Toronto

Canadian Scholars' Press Inc.
Toronto

Family Bonds and Gender Divisions:
Readings in the Sociology of the Family

First published in 1988 by
Canadian Scholars' Press Inc.,
339 Bloor St. West
Suite 220
Toronto, M5S 1W7
Canada

Cover Design: Pixel Graphics Inc.

Canadian Cataloguing in Publication Data
Main entry under title:

Family Bonds and Gender Divisions

ISBN 0-921626-26-2

1. Family — History. 2. Sex role — History.
I. Fox, Bonnie, 1948- .

HQ503.F35 1988   306.8'5   C88-094647-4

 34   WC   92

Printed & bound in Canada by Webcom Limited

Bound to stay open

Publisher's Note
Otabind (Ota-bind). This book has been bound
using the patented Otabind process. You can
open this book at any page, gently run your
finger down the spine, and the pages will lie flat.

Table of Contents

Introduction

In public discourse, "the family" is equated with the intimate, caring relationships that sustain us. A product of the mass media which is used opportunistically by politicians, this image nevertheless reflects the personal experience of many of us. Yet for others of us, family life is the source of pain: its emotional dynamics can oppress us and its relationships can entrap us. Indeed, family life can involve psychological and physical violence as well as nurturance and support. For some people, the psychic damage from childhood — the constant sense of unfulfilled need or the unexplained sense of repressed anger — may prevent a healthy, happy adult life. All things considered, for nearly all people, family relationships and experiences have a profound impact.

The nuclear family — a man and a woman living with their children — continues to be the dominant popular image of family life. Indeed, many government policies and the structure of most housing assume the nuclear family (see Eichler 1988 on policy; Haydon 1984 on housing). Equating "family" with both loving relationships and nuclear form has an important consequence: the logical conclusion is that the nuclear family is *necessary* for supportive, intimate relationships.

Nevertheless, the composition, organization, and activities of families are changing dramatically. First, it should be recognized that in 1986 one in every four Canadian households did not consist of a family (that is, they involved neither a married or common-law couple nor a single parent living with children) (Statistics Canada 1987a: table 1). Nearly 12 percent of Canadians that year did not live in families — although no doubt many of these people were somehow involved with people they considered "family" (Statistics Canada 1987b: table 7).

Second, Canadian families exist in a variety of forms. Not all families contain children, and not all children are born to a married couple: in the 1980s, slightly fewer than one in five married women was childless; and approximately 17 percent of babies were born to unmarried women (Eichler 1988: 228). Since 1981, the majority of married women work outside the home, so men no longer bear the responsibility of financial support of their families (Eichler 1988: 192). While most families find two incomes necessary for living decently, other families contain only one adult — usually a woman. In 1986, 13 percent of Canadian families contained a single parent living with children. Eighty-two percent of these single parents were women (Statistics Canada 1987b: table 2). Finally, largely because the majority of women with young children now work outside the home (Statistics Canada 1985:

1

49), fewer than half of Canadian children under six years of age are cared for exclusively by their parents (Eichler 1988: 317).

In sum, what is clear from these few statistics is that the nuclear family in which the man is "the provider" and the woman primarily raises the children is a fairly uncommon type of family in Canada today. Aside from economic changes inducing women to work outside the home, and the mounting struggle of women to achieve equality with men, the rise in the divorce rate in the last two decades ensures change and diversity in the organization of families. In fact, there is such a variety of family types, it is inappropriate to think in terms of "the family." While change and diversity should be no cause for concern, because the nuclear family has come to represent both intimate relationships and (due to the opportunism of politicians) one of society's foundations, the recognition of change in family life often generates a sense of fundamental threat to intimacy and privacy.

At this juncture, social science has something important to offer. Information about different cultures indicates the variety of ways in which important activities such as child rearing can be successfully accomplished. And an appreciation of this flexibility in human nature is welcome during this period of rapid change. Moreover, knowledge about the social history of family life indicates not only how differently families can be organized but also what sets of factors produced the family features that are common today. In short, evidence from other times and cultures gives us some perspective on families today which is invaluable in the attempt to understand the changes they are undergoing, the problems many of us experience at home, and what is possible for the future organization of family life.

Sociology itself promises more: an understanding of those personal experiences and problems that large numbers of people have in common and which common sense (and psychology) cannot explain (Mills 1959). It does so by providing us with an idea of how "social structure," or social organization, shapes our life chances, constrains the choices we make, and creates stresses in family and personal life. In a culture that hosts the belief that we "make ourselves" — that is, that we freely choose how our lives will unfold — understanding social structure is critical for people perpetually confused by the failure of reality to match their expectations.

2

I. Conceptualizing "Family": Definitions and Theoretical Perspectives

The diversity of family types today makes clear the need for the student of family life to begin with a definition of "family." While dozens of such definitions have been formulated, that of George Murdock (1949) is perhaps most often used. According to Murdock and many sociology textbooks, "the family" is

> a social group characterized by common residence, economic cooperation, and reproduction. It includes adults of both sexes, at least two of whom maintain a socially approved sexual relationship, and one or more children, own or adopted, of the sexually cohabiting adults (Murdock 1949:1).

Unfortunately, this definition not only confuses family with household — the residential unit — it is also needlessly restrictive about family composition. In restricting "family" to those nuclear in form, this definition denies the reality of many current families.

One of the least restrictive definitions in the literature is that which Carol Stack (1974) derived after studying the domestic arrangements common in a poor black American community. Stack (1974: 31) defines "family" as "the smallest, organized, durable network of kin and non-kin who interact daily, providing domestic needs of children and assuring survival." Most useful in this definition is its focus on an activity and the relationships necessary to carry it out — though it is limited in its specification of family activities.

Perhaps the most useful conceptualization comes from anthropologist Rayna Rapp (1982), who defines "household" as the residential unit that pools material resources, and "family" as the sets of relationships that recruit people to share their resources. One might wish to add to Rapp's definition a list of activities that are commonly but not necessarily part of family life: sexuality, child bearing, child rearing, and the satisfaction of both subsistence needs and the need for intimacy. Rapp's definition, however, is useful in its focus on relationships, which can be organized in a number of different ways (e.g., hierarchically, or in an egalitarian manner), and its lack of restriction on the membership of those relationships. Unlike more precise definitions, this one encourages the assumption that there is adaptation and thus change in families. Adding to the definition a tentative list of probable activities — with child rearing uppermost on the list — could leave open the question *how* these activities are organized.

3

I. Conceptualizing "Family": Definitions and Theoretical Perspectives

Aside from definitional clarity, it is important when thinking about changes in families to work from a set of assumptions that are different from the commonsense notion that individuals simply *choose* how to live their lives. In directing attention to the social context, and specifically to *social structure*, the sociological perspective highlights the ways in which class and gender[1] especially represent differences in the opportunities and obstacles people face. The organization of society around such things as gender divisions entails similar organization in family life. For example, the responsibilities, if not the work, involved in raising children and managing a household typically are structured by a division of labour based on gender: they are still women's work. In turn, women's continuing disadvantaged position in the labour market is a consequence of women's historic attachment to domesticity.

Common patterns in family life such as the gender division of labour allow a "sociology of the family" and become our primary subject matter. And the fact that some problems in family life are experienced by very large numbers of people (e.g., women's dissatisfaction with the role of full-time housewife, violence against women and children) indicates that these patterns in the organization of family life are themselves primary causes of such problems.

Aside from a tentative definition of "family" and a sensitivity to social structure that comes with the sociological perspective, a more specific theoretical perspective is necessary to focus our attention and guide our study. The theoretical perspective that has dominated sociology of the family until recently is "structural functionalism," which involves a kind of systems analysis that takes the maintenance of the stability of a whole — whether that whole is society or an institution such as the family — as its primary concern. Structural functionalism assumes that the existence and organization of institutions such as the family are explained by the functions they perform to maintain society, or similarly that the characteristics of family life are accounted for by the functions they fulfil in maintaining families. The article by Morris Zelditch is a classic example of the structural-functionalist approach.

The most general argument that structural functionalists make about "the family" is the following: society requires that certain functions be fulfilled (e.g., reproduction and child care); the nuclear family fulfils these functions (and does so most effectively); therefore, the nuclear family exists. Implicit in this argument is the assumption that the

---

[1]While "sex" refers to biological differences between females and males, "gender" refers to everything that is a social product — although it should be remembered that biology and the social environment are in constant interaction, so the separation is a bit hazardous.

Introduction

nuclear family is best organized to perform crucial tasks such as child rearing, and that the nuclear family must exist in all human societies because it is essential for such tasks. Notice how close to commonsense conceptions this argument is. Notice also how ideological the argument is: it assumes that the nuclear family is the best family arrangement.

There are problems with such an argument. First, it confuses the current relationship between the organization of family life and the rest of society with the origins, or historical processes, that produced family as we know it. While it is important to understand the relationship between the organization (or structure) of society and the organization of families — and structural functionalism is useful for making this a central issue — the study of social history reveals a diversity of family forms. It also shows that a particular configuration of forces generated the privatized, small nuclear-family households characterized by a gender division of labour and gender inequality that are common in this century.

The second, most obvious problem with the structural-functionalist approach is its highly value-laden emphasis on the functional nature of arrangements that, from the vantage point of the individual (or at least some individuals) rather than that of the institution as a whole, are in fact dysfunctional and indeed harmful. Moreover, the failure to see dysfunction, conflict, contradiction, and tension in families produces a perspective that fails to predict, and can neither account for nor understand, change.

Finally, structural-functionalist arguments tend to be tautological. For example, it is common for such arguments to both define the nuclear family as the unit necessary to accomplish the task of child rearing and to use the current situation whereby families rear children to bolster an argument about the need for the nuclear family. The question of alternative arrangements for child care is not posed.

While there is no single unified theoretical perspective that has replaced structural functionalism, a general feminist approach has prompted a fairly thorough recasting of most sociologists' analyses of family life. An important insight coming from the feminist perspective is that women's and men's experience of family life is different, primarily because of the gender division of labour in families. Recognizing that gender, and other factors, shape people's experience means that at some point the study of family life should consider it from the various vantage points of different family actors — men, women, and also children. And feminist concerns urge a sensitivity to the differences in power of men, women and children.

The articles by Diana Gittins and Jane Collier, Michelle Rosaldo, and Sylvia Yanagisako provide a good introduction to the study of family life. Gittins effectively dispels the belief that biology determines family form: information about different cultures shows that there are no necessary social consequences of biology for the way in which family life is organized. Gittins declares "the family" to be a *social construction*, which means that the ways in which sexuality, child care, and other family activities are organized is a product of (collective) human decisions, or strategies of coping. Collier et al. take up Gittins' argument that "the family" is not a natural unit by arguing that it is a *social construct*. That is, "the family" is the product of a set of ideas — and consequent policies by the state — that arose out of the historical development of a separation of public and private life. While Gittins' main point is that family patterns are products of human history, Collier et al. are arguing further that "family" refers less to certain activities than to the beliefs we have about them. The point here is that actual social arrangements and ideas about them must be distinguished.

References

Eichler, Margrit.
1988. *Families in Canada Today*. Second Edition. Toronto: Gage.
Hayden, Dolores.
1984. *Redesigning the American Dream*. New York : Norton.
Mills, C. Wright.
1959. *The Sociological Imagination*. New York: Oxford University Press.
Murdock, George P.
1949. *Social Structure*. New York: Macmillan.
Rapp, Rayna.
1982. "Family and class in contemporary America: notes   toward an understanding of ideology." Pp. 168-88 in Barrie Thorne and Marilyn Yalom, eds. *Rethinking the Family*. New York: Longman.
Stack, Carol.
1974. *All Our Kin*. New York: Harper & Row.
Statistics Canada.
1985. *Women in Canada: A Statistical Report*. Ottawa: Ministry of Supply and Services.

_____.
1987a. *1986 Census*. Dwellings and Households: Part I (#93-104) Ottawa: Ministry of Supply and Services.

_____.
1987b. *1986 Census*. Families: Part I (#93-106) Ottawa: Ministry of Supply and Services.

Role Differentiation in the Nuclear Family: A Comparative Study*

Morris Zelditch, Jr.

Some early anthropological evidence suggested that there was unlimited variation in where the line between husband and wife activities was drawn. Professor Zelditch was led by theoretical considerations to predict the opposite: that despite variation in specific activities, there would be a general principle of differentiation of function between the sexes. In this selection, Zelditch reports the results of his test of this hypothesis on a carefully selected sample of 56 societies. The weight of the evidence, he finds, is strongly in support of the hypothesis.

The analysis of our own nuclear family structure reveals certain patterns of differentiation that we also see in other societies if we clearly distinguish the nuclear family from the extended kinship groupings in which, in a great many societies, they are incorporated. Parsons has pointed out that in this particular instance it is fruitful to begin analysis with the more highly differentiated social system of the United States, rather than the so-called "simple" non-literate societies, because in our society the nuclear family is structurally isolated from extended kin solidarities and functionally differentiated from other systems. But the nuclear family is not something characteristic only of our society. Murdock, for instance, has stated flatly that it is a discernible functioning group in all societies entering his sample; and there have been only one or two exceptions reported in the entire anthropological literature.[1]

In our system, the marriage pair is given precedence as a solidary unit over any link with the parents of either member of the pair. The so-called simple non-literate societies, on the other hand, often give precedence to solidarities with the family of orientation of one of the pair,

---

*Reprinted with permission of The Free Press, a division of Macmillan, Inc. from *Family, Socialization and Interaction Process* by Talcott Parsons and Robert F. Bales. Copyright © 1955 by The Free Press, renewed by Robert F. Bales and Helen W. Parsons.
[1]Most notably the Nayar. See, for instance, E.K. Gough, "The Traditional Kinship Systems of the Nayars of Malabar," prepared for the Social Science Research Council Seminar on Kinship (unpublished). Also, Gough, "Changing Kinship Usages in the Setting of Political and Economic Change Among the Nayars of Malabar," *Journal of the Royal Anthropological Institute*, Vol. XCII (1952).

or, in more complex forms, strong though differentiated obligations to both parental families. Even in the bilateral cases most closely approaching our own, the isolation of the nuclear family is not the distinguishing structural characteristic; rather a bilateral system generally functions to incorporate the nuclear family in a kin-oriented group, but one in which membership is fluidly structured from generation to generation.

Nevertheless, the nuclear family ordinarily can be distinguished, and does function as a significant group. This particular point, in fact, is responsible for a good many of the issues in the interpretation of matrilineal systems, which we will consider later, and a failure to distinguish the nuclear family from other kinship units in which it is incorporated is likely to confuse any sort of analysis of concrete kinship behavior.

The nuclear family in our society has a particular pattern of roles which we now suggest has a generic significance. There is, in other words, an underlying structural uniformity which gives a baseline for the analysis of the range of variation usually noted.

A statement of this sort, of course, can be only hypothetical at this point. It is the purpose of this paper, however, to indicate that it is not *only* hypothetical. On what basis can we argue that this uniformity occurs? A reference to Bales's and Slater's discussion[2] provides at least part of the answer. We argue, for instance, that it is essentially fruitful to consider the nuclear family as a special case of a small group and that the mode of differentiation observed in small groups has a genetic significance which extends to any of its special cases. The fact that Bales's experimental groups are ephemeral compared to nuclear families (even those which are terminated after only a few months of existence) does not imply that the conclusions reached from these groups are ephemeral.

More generally, a nuclear family is a social system, and the peculiar attributes which distinguish it from other systems (its particular age-sex structure and primary function, for instance) should be examined within this more general context. All groups are subject to certain imposed conditions of existence: not that all groups exist, but that all groups that do exist meet these conditions.[3] If we assume the existence of a nuclear family, therefore, we must inquire into the conditions of its existence. And certain of these conditions are common to all groups,

---

[2]In Chapter v of *Family, Socialization and Interaction Process.*

[3]The framework for this analysis is provided in T. Parsons, R.F. Bales, and E.A. Shils, *Working Papers in the Theory of Group Action* (Glencoe, Ill.: The Free Press, 1953); and Parsons, *The Social System* (Glencoe, Ill.: The Free Press, 1951).

appearing in such diverse forms as Bales's experimental groups and the family pattern of peasant Ireland.

Among the conditions of a system's existence is at least a certain degree of differentiation along lines imposed by the orbits of the system's movement. Consider first the general pattern of differentiation which in broad outline appears from the experimental small group. There is a tendency for a *task leader* and a *sociometric star* to appear. Although there is some problem in clearly isolating the complex factors defining the task leader, he seems to be associated with certain *behaviors* (in general terms, "task" behaviors; more specifically in giving suggestions, directions, opinions), and certain *attitudes* (involving, apparently, an inhibition of emotions and the ability to accept hostile reactions from others in the process of pressing a point, etc.). There are also, of course, reciprocal behaviors and attitudes on the part of other system-members toward the task leader. The sociometric star, although the term originally derives from attitudes taken toward ego by alters, also tends to show a certain pattern of behaviors and attitudes; namely, the *expression* of emotions, supportive behavior to others, the desire to please and be liked, and a more generalized liking for other members. The star may, of course, express negative reactions as well as positive supports; typically, these are significant in releasing negative reactions (often through humor) of the group as a whole, reducing, in consequence, the general tension level. (The difference between a "leader," here, and one who fails to become a leader may very well lie, in part, in the capacity to express reactions felt by the group as a *whole*.)

From a general theoretical point of view, this is *not* a fortuitous pattern of differentiation; it defines, in fact, the two basic conditions of the existence of a social system. In order to clarify and illustrate what we mean by this, we may take the nuclear family as a specific case; and it may be useful at the same time to begin with a differentiation logically prior to role differentiation itself.

Assume a time T_1 in which members of the nuclear family are dispersed somewhere in the external situation involved in devotion to the "task," or what we call "instrumental" activities. By either of these terms we mean here the manipulation of the object-world in order to provide facilities for the achievement of goals defined within the system. In our society, for instance, the husband typically goes to work in the morning, the mother shops or cleans up, the children go to school if they are old enough. In many other societies a similar dispersal, involving a departure of at least the husband-father (out hunting, or farming), often occurs. Now clearly, if there is no second occasion, T_2, during which the members of the system are *reunited*, the system will tend to disappear. It will no longer be identifiable as a system.

9

I. Conceptualizing "Family": Definitions and Theoretical Perspectives

There is then, a most primitive level of differentiation here in the simple presence or absence of members on two different occasions. From this, it is clear that one imperative of all social systems is integration, a coming together, which of course Durkheim emphasized a considerable time ago.

The other side of the coin, involving here a dispersal of members, introduces a more complex level of analysis. Although dispersal of system members is common during instrumental activities,[4] it is not necessary to define what we are talking about. We merely suggest this as a first point of purchase on the type of analysis involved. Typically, in fact, the mother and children remain at some location symbolically associated with the system's existence — the home is the crucial symbol, of course- and there is always a *latent* existence to the system (if it is to reappear). This function of symbols, in giving latent existence to systems, is of obvious importance as a basis for their physical reintegration.

What is significant in the differentiation of these two occasions, however, is not the states of spatial dispersion and integration, physically, but the difference in behavior and attitudes involved. The system may in fact always act in concert from the present point of view, and still show the differentiation we are here concerned with.

Reverting to our time period T_1, then, assume that all members are physically adjacent but devoted to instrumental or task activities. The entire family, say, is out farming in the fields. These instrumental activities involve, in gross terms, the manipulation of objects (plows or hoes, etc.), and an attitude composed of Parsons' pattern variables "specific, affectively neutral, universalistic, achievement-oriented," or in more gross terms a "rational" attitude toward the external situation, and an *inhibition* of emotions toward other members of the system. *In order for the system to continue as a system*, we now say, there must at some point be a change in attitude and behavior to integrative-expressive activities — to laughing, playing, release of inhibited emotions, the expression of affection for each other, a warmth and a symbolization of common membership through supportive, accepting behavior.

If we reverse our assumptions, we arrive at the same basic conclusion, something we were not able to do when we considered only physical presence or absence (we were not, that is, able to show why dispersion had to occur). Assume the time period T_2 in which all members are affectionate, responsive, emotionally warm and attached to each other, often symbolized in the meal-time break. The system *cannot*

---

[4]Because resources do not necessarily cluster around the immediate residence of the family, and typically a mother stays near the home partly, we may suppose, to symbolize the latent system.

continue in this state forever. It must, at some point, change to the necessary activities — and the associated attitudes — involved in manipulating the facilities of the object world so that the family has the food, shelter, fire, etc., which the external situation can provide. The family then becomes reinvolved in the *task*, which, no matter how much integrative behavior there was before or will be after — and perhaps also at breaks during the task — must concentrate on *getting the job done*. It must, that is, at least for the time being, devote its attention to instrumental acts.

A considerable refinement is involved in the further differentiation of the structure of *roles* in the system. One clue, perhaps, is suggested by the earlier peripheral comment that while husband-father is away at work or in the fields, the mother very often stays at home symbolizing the integrative focus of the system (even though her activities may be primarily instrumental during this phase of family activity). The fact that it is the mother who stays home is not, for the present, significant although shortly it will become so. What *is* significant, is that *someone* stayed, and that someone is in fact *more* responsible for integrative-expressive behavior than the person who went off to work.

Why after all, are *two* parents necessary? For one thing, to be a stable focus of integration, the integrative-expressive "leader" can't be off on adaptive-instrumental errands all the time. For another, a stable, secure attitude of members depends, it can be assumed, on a clear structure being given to the situation so that an *uncertain* responsibility for emotional warmth, for instance, raises significant problems for the stability of the system. And an uncertain managerial responsibility, an unclear definition of authority for decisions and for getting things done, is also clearly a threat to the stability of the system.

We can say, then, that the system must differentiate behaviors and attitudes in order to continue to exist as a system;[5] and that a further condition of stability is also that some specialization occur in responsibility for the attitudes and behaviors involved.

We actually want to examine two things in this paper. One is related to the generic significance of a certain pattern of differentiation. The relevant role-system, however, is indeterminate with respect to allocation when taken at this level. It is necessary to consider the nuclear family as a type of group peculiarly structured around age-sex differences

----

[5]There are several implicit assumptions here; for instance, that if you are inhibiting emotions in order to perform instrumental tasks, you cannot at the same time release them in integrative-expressive behavior. So that it is no solution to the problem to try to do both at once.

in order to arrive at a hypothesis concerning who plays the instrumental and expressive roles.

Now any system, it should be noticed first, has a problem often considered peculiar to families, that is, the processing of new recruits. While the "barbarian invasion" may be considered of special significance for the family, and thus to impose special conditions on its existence, the problem is in fact generic to all systems. Thus the family resembles other groups in this respect as well as in the more general terms discussed so far. What differs, and the difference is of crucial structural significance, is the age-sex matrix of the family and with it the situational reference points for the allocation of *facilities* in the performance of roles. At the grossest level of analysis, for instance, the father is stronger than the son, so that he, rather than the son, is allocated to leadership roles in instrumental activities (with the possible, and amusing, exception of the polyandrous Marquesas).

At least one fundamental feature of the external situation of social systems — here a feature of the physiological organism — is a crucial reference point for differentiation in the family. This lies in the division of organisms into lactating and nonlactating classes. Only in our own society (so far as I know, that is) have we managed to invent successful bottlefeeding, and this is undoubtedly of importance for our social structure. In other societies necessarily — and in our own for structural reasons which have *not* disappeared with the advent of the bottle — the initial core relation of a family with children is the mother-child attachment. And it follows from the principles of learning that the gradient of generalization should establish "mother" as the focus of gratification in a diffuse sense, as the source of "security" and "comfort." She is the focus of warmth and stability. Thus, because of her special initial relation to the child, "mother" is the more likely expressive focus of the system as a whole.

The allocation of the instrumental leadership to the husband-father rests on two aspects of this role. The role involves, first, a manipulation of the external environment, and consequently a good deal of physical mobility. The concentration of the mother on the child precludes a primacy of her attention in this direction although she always performs some instrumental tasks. In addition to the managerial aspects of the role, there are certain discipline and control functions of the father role. Consider, again, why two parents are necessary at all. The initial mother-child subsystem can do without the father (except that he provides food, shelter, etc., for this subsystem so that it need not split up to perform many of its own instrumental tasks). But some significant member of the nuclear family must "pry the child loose" from the mother-dependency so that it may "grow up" and accept its responsibilities as an "adult." There is necessarily a coalition of father and mother in this, or no stable socialization pattern develops. But the mother, by her special initial relation to the child is relatively more susceptible to seduction out of the coalition. We may note, for instance, that one of the pathologies of family dynamics may arise because the father tends to be susceptible to seduction by daughters; and the very fact of his relative power in the coalition makes this more of a threat to the family as a system. The problem of the "weak, ineffectual" father is more significant than that of the "weak, ineffectual" mother. (Conversely, of course, and quite as significant, the problem of the "cold, unyielding" mother is more of a problem than the "cold, unyielding" father.) If, therefore, the female is allocated the integrative-supportive role, there must necessarily be an allocation of authority for discipline and relatively "neutral" judgment to the husband-father.

We may summarize the hypothesis we have stated then, in this way. Because the nuclear family is a special case of the more general class of social systems, and because it must meet certain conditions of existence common to all social systems, we suggest that:

> 1. If the nuclear family constitutes a social system stable over time, it will differentiate roles such that instrumental leadership and expressive leadership of the system are discriminated.

Because the nuclear family, on the other hand, has certain peculiar features not common to all systems, we are further able to state a certain hypothesis about the allocation of these roles to system-members. This peculiar feature is the age-sex matrix of the nuclear family and the differential distribution of facilities for the performance of the fundamental roles. We suggest that:

> 2. If the nuclear family consists in a defined "normal" complement of the male adult, female adult and their immediate children, the male adult will play the role of instrumental leader and the female adult will play the role of expressive leader.

Summary and Conclusions

These hypotheses were tested on a sample of 56 societies drawn from a larger list of 75. An attempt was made to judge these societies by specific criteria but variations in the ethnographic materials made this difficult.

I. Conceptualizing "Family": Definitions and Theoretical Perspectives

While rather significant conclusions can be drawn, the crudeness of the method of verifying them makes them rather difficult to evaluate. This should be carefully considered in accepting the conclusions of the tests. In at least half of the cases, for instance, if "respect" and "affection" do not in fact indicate instrumental and expressive leadership (i.e., as defined in terms of actions of ego), then the hypotheses cannot be legitimately considered "proved" or "disproved." This chance was taken on the grounds that, having sacrificed the method of intensive analysis in the original conditions of the design, extensive replication was necessary. This demands numbers; and the number of monographs which provide evidence on the basis of direct designation rules is limited. Differences in rating might also be considered; although it may fairly be said for the differentiation hypothesis, at least, that the number of negative cases could have been increased by the equivocal cases finally judged positive and the hypothesis would still have held. The chief equivocal cases were the Lozi and the American middle-class family, which some raters might have treated as negative.

We may, as a matter of fact, consider the American middle-class case in reviewing the definitions we have given to instrumental and expressive leadership. From certain points of view, the American middle-class family approaches most clearly to equal allocation (or "no allocation") of instrumental and expressive activities. The universalistic value schema (in which women are "just as good as" men) coupled with the general attitude toward the explicit expression of authority ("I'm agin it") apparently constitutes the limiting case of no differentiation at all. Underlying this broad value-schema, however, a rather clear differentiation occurs.

In the distribution of instrumental tasks, the American family maintains a more flexible pattern than most societies. Father helps mother with the dishes. He sets the table. He makes formula for the baby. Mother can supplement the income of the family by working outside. Nevertheless, the American male, by definition, must "provide" for his family. He is responsible for the support of his wife and children. His primary area of performance is the occupational role, in which his status fundamentally inheres; and his primary function in the family is to supply an income, to be the breadwinner. There is simply something wrong with the American adult male who doesn't have a "job." American women, on the other hand, tend to hold jobs before they are married and to quit when "the day" comes; or to continue in jobs of a lower status than their husbands. And not only is the mother the focus of emotional support for the American middle-class child, but much more exclusively so than in most societies (as Margaret Mead has pointed out in her treatment of adolescent problems). The cult of the warm, giving "Mom"

14

stands in contrast to the "capable," "competent, go-getting" male. The more expressive type of male, as a matter of fact, is regarded as "effeminate," and has too much fat on the inner side of his thigh.

The distribution of authority is legitimized on a different basis in the "democratic" family than in the so-called "traditional" one; but the father is "supposed" to remain the primary executive member. The image of the "henpecked" husband makes sense only on this premise. His "commands" are validated on the basis of "good judgment," rather than general obedience due to a person in authority. But when the mother's efforts at "disciplining" fail, she traditionally tells the errant child, "Wait till Daddy gets home."

In generalizing this pattern, of instrumental leadership focused on the achievement of tasks and expressive leadership focused on emotionally-supportive behaviors, the most difficult problem of interpretation lies in clearly distinguishing the nuclear family from the descent groups which in some cases took precedence as solidarities over them. This may be discussed in terms of two rather unique cases. The Nayar (who do not appear in this sample) so completely incorporate the mother-child system in the matrilineage that no husband-father status exists in the sense usually given to this term. The males of the matrilineage take over the husband-father's functions, and to all intents and purposes no nuclear family exists. This is the limiting case in the incorporation of nuclear families in larger descent groups. It is, in a sense, the mirror opposite of the American isolated conjugal family; the same principle, applied in different ways is at stake. The question is simply the relative solidarity of two cross-cutting systems. In our society, the nuclear family is clearly a stronger solidarity than any other kinship based group and no corporate descent group exists. Among the Nayar, the matrilineage was the clearly dominant solidarity to the unusual extent of destroying the nuclear family as a continuously functioning group entirely. Somewhere in between these poles lie most of the cases known. The Trobriands approach the uniqueness of the Nayar, however, in giving the mother's brother more extensive obligations to and responsibility over the nuclear family of his sister than is common even in matrilineal societies. (It may some day turn out that many of these obligations are primarily symbolic and do not in fact take up as much of the mother's brother's productive activity as has been supposed.) The effect of this is to reduce the husband-father's role in the nuclear family, since he is a mother's brother in someone else's nuclear family and is occupied in task-functions outside his own nuclear family. Again, the basis of this is clearly the relative emphasis on the lineage as a solidarity.

Ordinarily, however, the solidarity of the lineage does not completely obscure the husband-father's instrumental role in his own nuclear family. The Trobriands, that is, is not the paradigmatic matrilineal case, any more than the Nayar is. And where the husband-father spends any time at all in his own nuclear family even in the matrilineal case he takes on significant defacto instrumental authority. To the extent, that is, that the nuclear family does function as a system, it differentiates in the direction expected.

In dealing with the allocation problem, it is apparent that the initial relation of mother and child is sufficiently important so that the mother's expressive role in the family is largely not problematical. It is particularly important to note that apparently no systematic principle, such as the impingement of descent groupings, tends to reverse her role, unless the Mundugomor can be taken as an instance. (It is likely that the problems of the Mundugomor arise because of the cross-cutting solidarities within the household group, and that it can best be described, not from the point of view of aggressive, dominant roles defined for the mother and father, but rather as a system subject to great tensions which are revealed in mutual hostilities.)

The allocation of instrumental leadership to the father, on the other hand, is only problematic in the sense that the interrelation of the nuclear family and the descent group may, in one class of cases, obscure the husband-father's role. And this we have already discussed. In the patrilineal cases, in which this particular problem raises fewer interpretative issues in concrete systems (except that, of course, there are important problems in the relation of a husband-father to his father), the role is reasonably clear. This is true also for bilateral systems.

On the whole, therefore, when the nuclear family can be clearly distinguished from incorporating solidarities, it differentiates in the direction expected and allocates the relevant roles to the persons expected. And the problems which are raised in interpreting the data do not arise so much from whether or not this is true, but rather from what effect the precedence of obligations to corporate descent groups may have. This becomes, stated in a general form, a problem of the relative authority of the husband-father compared to that of some person in the superordinate descent group; where this descent group is matrilineal, the problem is one of the relative authority of father vs. mother's brother. The effect on patrilineal systems is to confine the difficulties in this relationship within the corporate descent group; and eventually the husband-father achieves a role of dominance in the descent group as well as the nuclear family. The effect in matrilineal systems is different, since the father can never become a member of the matrilineage. He must validate his position through his contribution to the everyday life of the household group, and his position is much less stable. In a great many cases, nevertheless, he does become the significant instrumental figure in the household group; and always relative to mother this is the case. From the point of view of his legal status in the system, he is at the same time freed from certain obligations to his own family and denied certain rights in control of his own family; from the point of view of the general conditions for the existence of social systems as systems, however, he must accept some of these obligations and be allowed certain of these rights.

What is the Family? Is it Universal?*

Diana Gittins

Until recently most sociological studies of the family have been dominated by functionalist definitions of what the family is, and what 'needs'
it fulfils in society. Functionalists' theories of the family are treated
elsewhere at length (Morgan, 1975; Gittins, 1982), but it is worth
examining some of their main assumptions briefly.   Generally,
functionalists have argued that the family is a universal institution
which performs certain specific functions essential to society's survival.
Murdock, for instance, defined the family as a 'social group characterised
by common residence, economic co-operation, and reproduction.   It
includes adults of both sexes, at least two of whom maintain a socially
approved sexual relationship, and one or more children, own or adopted,
of the sexually cohabiting adults.'[1] The four basic functions of the family,
therefore, are seen as: common residence; economic co-operation;
reproduction; sexuality. Let us examine each of these in more detail.

Household is the term normally used to refer to co-residence.
Murdock's assumption is that it is also a defining characteristic of 'the
family', and vice versa. It is generally assumed that a married couple, or
parent and child(ren) will form a household, and that family implies and
presupposes 'household'. Yet this is by no means always so. Margaret
Mead (1971) showed how Samoan children chose the household where
they wanted to reside, and often changed their residence again later.
Sibling households — or frérèches — were common in parts of Europe,
and are a dominant form of household among the Ashanti (Bender, 1979,
pp. 494).

There are numerous examples in contemporary society of families
who do not form households, or only form households for periods of time.
Families where the husband is in the armed services, is a travelling
salesman or travels frequently abroad may only have the husband/father
resident for short periods of time. Families where partners have jobs
some distance away from one another may maintain a second household
where one of them lives during the week. Children who are sent to
boarding school may spend little more than a third of the year residing
with their parent(s).

---

*Reprinted with permission from *The Family in Question*, Macmillan, London and
Basingstoke.
[1]Murdock quoted in Morgan (1975). p. 20.

I. Conceptualizing "Family": Definitions and Theoretical Perspectives

Gutman (1976) found that it was common among black slave families in the USA for a husband and wife to live on different plantations and see one another for a few hours once or twice a week. Soliende de Gonzalez found this type of household very common in Black Carib society: 'there are groupings which I have called "dispersed families" in which the father, although absent for long periods of time, retains ultimate authority over a household for which he provides the only support, and where affective bonds continue to be important between him and his wife and children' (1965, p. 1544). Obviously people can consider themselves 'family' without actually co-residing, and can also co-reside without considering themselves to be 'family'.

On the other hand, households might be characterised by a shared set of activities such as sleeping, food preparation, eating, sexual relations, and caring for those who cannot care for themselves. Some have argued that household can be defined to some extent in terms of a range of domestic activities. 'Sharing the same pot' has traditionally been the boundary drawn by census enumerators for demarcating one household from another. Yet these activities need not necessarily, and often do not, occur within one household. Some members of a household may eat there all the time, while others only part of the time. Similarly, as mentioned before, some members may not always sleep in the household for a majority of the time. They may well consider themselves notwithstanding to be a family. Conversely, prisoners eat and sleep under the same roof, but do not consider themselves to be a family.

There is no hard and fast rule, much less a definition in universal terms, that can be applied to household in terms of domestic activities. Whether in modern industrial society or in Africa or Asia 'there is no basis for assuming that such activities as sleeping, eating, child-rearing and sexual relations must form a complex and must always occur under one roof' (Smith, 1978, p.339). Household is thus in some ways just as nebulous a term as family, although it lacks the ideological implications that 'family' carries.

Murdock further posits 'economic co-operation' as a defining characteristic of all families. This is a very broad term and can encompass a wide range of activities from cooking to spinning to resources in terms of people and skills. Economic co-operation is something which can, and does, occur throughout all levels of society and is not specific to the family. Economic co-operation frequently occurs *between* households as well as between individuals within households. Undoubtedly households do entail an economic relationship in various ways; in particular, they entail the distribution, production and allocation of resources. Resources include food, drink, material goods, but also service, care, skills, time and space. The notion of 'co-operation',

20

moreover, implies an equal distribution of resources, yet this is seldom so. Allocating food, space, time and tasks necessitates some kind of a division of labour; different tasks need doing every day and may vary by week and by season. The number of people living together will be finite but also changeable — not just in terms of numbers, but also in terms of age, sex, marital status, physical capacity.

All resources are finite and some may be extremely scarce; some form of allocation therefore has to occur, and this presupposes power relationships. Food, work, and space are rarely distributed equally between co-residing individuals, just as they differ between households and social sectors. Most frequently, the allocation of resources and division of labour is based on differences according to sex and age. Rather than using Murdock's definition of 'economic co-operation', it is thus more useful to understand families in terms of the ways in which gender and age define, and are defined by, the division of labour within, and beyond, households. These divisions also presuppose power relationships and inequality — in effect, patriarchy — rather than co-operation and equality.

Power relationships define and inform concepts of sexuality, Murdock's third defining category. His definition of sexuality is heterosexuality, although this is only one of various forms of sexuality. Presumably this is because the final — and perhaps most important — 'function' of families as seen by such theorists is reproduction, which necessitates heterosexual relations, at least at times. Sexuality is not something specific to families; rather, the assumption is that heterosexuality *should* be a defining characteristic of families. It also, according to Murdock, presupposes a 'socially approved relationship' between two adults.

Social recognition of mating and of parenthood is obviously intimately bound up with social definitions and customs of marriage. It is often assumed that, in spite of a variety of marriage customs and laws, marriage as a binding relationship between a man and a woman is universal. Yet it has been estimated that only 10 percent of all marriages in the world are actually monogamous; polyandry and polygyny are common in many societies, just as serial monogamy is becoming increasingly common in our own. Marriage is not always a heterosexual relationship; among the Nuer, older women marry younger women. The Nuer also practise a custom known as 'ghost marriages', whereby when an unmarried or childless man dies, a relation of his then marries a woman 'to his name' and the resulting children of this union are regarded as the dead man's children and bear his name (see Edholm, 1982, p.172).

Marriage customs are not only variable between cultures and over time, but also vary between social classes. Moreover, Jessie Bernard

21

I. Conceptualizing "Family": Definitions and Theoretical Perspectives

(1973) has shown that the meanings which men and women attribute to the same marriage differ quite markedly. Undoubtedly marriage involves some form of status passage and public avowal of recognising other(s) as of particular importance in one way or another, yet it does not occur universally between two people nor between two people of the opposite sex, nor is it always viewed as linked to reproduction. Marriage, in the way in which we think of it, is therefore not universal.

Similarly, definitions of sexuality with regard to incest have not been universal or unchanging. In medieval Europe it was considered incestuous to have sexual relations with anyone less than a seventh cousin, and marriage between cousins was proscribed. Now it is possible to marry first cousins. In Egypt during the Pharaonic and Ptolemaic period sibling marriages were permitted, and, in some cases, father-daughter marriages. This was seen as a way of preserving the purity of royalty and was not endorsed for the whole society — although it was permitted for everyone after the Roman conquest of Egypt.

Incestuous marriages were also permitted among royal families in Hawaii and Peru. The Mormons of Utah allowed incest (and polygamy) as a means of ensuring marriage within their church; this was not banned until 1892 (Renvoize, 1982, p.32). Obviously these examples are more related to marriage customs and inheritance or descent problems, but serve to illustrate that even an incest taboo cannot be taken as a universal defining characteristic of families: 'who could Adam's sons marry except their sisters?' (ibid., p.32). Nevertheless, the almost universal existence of some form of incest taboo is a useful illustration of the fact that all societies do, in a myriad of ways, have some form of social organisation of sexuality, mating and reproduction.

Murdock's definition does not take adequate account of the diversity of ways in which co-residence, economic relations, sexuality and reproduction can be organised. Various theorists have made amendments and refinements to Murdock's definition of the family, but all tend to make similar errors. In particular, they translate contemporary western (and usually middle-class) ideas and ideals of what a family should be into what they assume it is everywhere

Far more precise attempts at definition and analysis have been made by anthropologists who prefer the term kinship to that of family. A feminist anthropologist recently defined *kinship* as 'the ties which exist between individuals who are seen as related both through birth (descent) and through mating (marriage). It is thus primarily concerned with the ways in which mating is socially organised and regulated, the ways in which parentage is assigned, attributed and recognised, descent is traced, relatives are classified, rights are transferred across generations and groups are formed' (Edholm, 1982, p.166). This definition of kinship is a vast improvement on functionalist definitions of family because, first, it stresses the fact that kinship is a social construction, and, second, it emphasises the variability of kinship depending on how it is defined. The social nature of kinship has been stressed by many others elsewhere,[2] and yet there remains a strong common-sense belief that kinship is in fact a quite straightforward biological relationship. It is not.

We assume that because we (think we) know who our parents are and how they made us that kinship is therefore a *biological fact*. Consider, however, stories we have all heard about children who were brought up by parent(s) for perhaps twenty years, who all along believed their parents were their biological parents, but then discovered that they had in fact been adopted. Such people often suffer severe 'identity crises' because they no longer know 'who they are' or who their parents are. Their suffering is caused by the way in which we define kinship in our society, namely, in strictly biological terms, differentiating clearly between a 'biological' and a 'social' parent with whom a child should have the strongest ties and bonds. Knowledge of parenthood through families is the central way in which individuals are 'located' socially and economically in western society. This, however, is a culturally and historically specific way of defining parenthood and kinship. Other cultures and groups in modern society believe that the person who rears a child is by definition the real parent, regardless of who was involved in the actual reproduction process.

In many poor families in Western Europe and America well into this century it was not uncommon for children to be raised by a grandparent, other kin, or friend, and such children often thought of those who raised them as their parents, even though acknowledging that they also had biological parents who were different. R.T. Smith found such practices common in Guyana and Jamaica, and reports how 'close and imperishable bonds are formed through the act of "raising" children, irrespective of genetic ties...What is erroneously termed "fictive kinship" is a widespread phenomenon...while a father may be defined minimally as the person whose genetic material mingled with that of the mother in the formation of the child during one act of sexual intercourse the father "role" varies a good deal in any but the most homogeneous societies' (1978, p.353).

Others have shown the ways in which kinship is a social construction, and how those who are not biologically related to one another come to define themselves as kin: 'Liebow, Stack, Ladner and others described fictive kinship, by which friends are turned into family. Since family is supposed to be more reliable than friendship, "going for

---

[2]Notably C.C. Harris, J. Goody, W. Goode.

brothers", "for sisters", "for cousins", increases the commitment of a relationship, and makes people ideally more responsible for one another. Fictive kinship is a serious relationship' (Rapp, 1980, p.292). it is possible to argue that this is how all kinship began and becomes constructed. Kinship, whether we choose to label it as 'biological', 'social' or 'fictive' is a way of identifying others as in some way special from the rest, people to whom the individual or collectivity feel responsible in certain ways. It is a method of demarcating obligations and responsibility between individuals and groups.

It is thus essential to get away from the idea that kinship is a synonym for 'blood' relations — *even though it may often be expressed in those terms* — and to think of it as a social construction which is highly variable and flexible. Some anthropologists recently have argued that kinship is no more and no less than a system of meanings and symbols and that it is 'absolutely distinct from a biological system or a system of biological reproduction. Animals reproduce, mate, and undoubtedly form attachments to each other, but they do not have kinship systems' (Smith, 1978, p.351). Indeed, just as Marx argued that it is labour that distinguishes people from animals, it could equally be argued that it is kinship systems that do just that.

This is not to say that many kinship relations do not have some sort of biological base — many do — but the fact that not all of them do, and that the type of base is highly variable, means that it cannot be assumed that there is some universal biological base to kinship. There is not. As Edholm (1982, p.168) argues: 'notions of blood ties, of biological connection, which to us seem relatively unequivocal, are highly variable. Some societies of which we have anthropological record recognize only the role of the father or of the mother in conception and procreation...Only one parent is a "relation", the other is not. In the Trobriand Islands...it is believed that intercourse is not the cause of conception, semen is not seen as essential for conception...(but) from the entry of a spirit child into the womb...it is the repeated intercourse of the same partner which "moulds" the child.'

Because fatherhood is always potentially unknown, and always potentially contestable, it is therefore also always a social category. Motherhood, on the other hand, is always known. Yet apart from carrying and giving birth to a child, the biological base of motherhood stops there. The rest is socially constructed, although it may be — and often is — attributed to biology or 'maternal instinct'. Whether or not women breastfeed their children has been historically and culturally variable. Baby bottles are no modern invention, but were used in ancient Egypt and in other cultures since. Historians have noted the number of babies given to 'wet nurses' in earlier times in Europe as a sign of lack of love

24

and care for infants on the part of mothers. But we can never really know the emotions felt by people hundreds of years ago or their motivations for their practices. The most we can do is to note that their customs were different. To use our own ideology of motherhood and love and apply it universally to all cultures is a highly ethnocentric and narrow way of trying to understand other societies.

Notions of motherhood and 'good mothering' are highly variable:

> in Tahiti young women often have one or two children be-
> fore they are considered, or consider themselves to be, ready
> for an approved and stable relationship. It is considered
> perfectly acceptable for the children of this young woman to
> be given to her parents or other close kin for adoption...The
> girl can decide what her relationship to the children will be,
> but there is no sense in which she is forced into
> 'motherhood' because of having had a baby. (Edholm, 1982,
> p.170).

Who cares for children and rears them is also variable, although in most cases it is women who do so rather than men. Often those women who rear children may well claim some kinship tie to the biological mother — for example, grandmother or aunt, but this tie may simply be created as a result of rearing another woman's child. Motherhood, therefore, if taken to mean both bearing and rearing children, is not universal and is not a biological 'fact'.

Nor can it be argued that there is such a thing as maternal 'instinct', although it is commonly believed to exist. Women are capable of conceiving children today from the age of 13 or 14, and can continue to bear children approximately every two years until they are 45 or 50. This could mean producing around eighteen or nineteen children (although fecundity declines as women age), and this, of course, seldom occurs. Few women in western society marry before they are 18 or 19, and few women in contemporary society have more than two or three children. Contraceptives control conception, not instincts, and unless it were argued that women are forced to use contraceptives,[3] there is little scope to argue for such a thing as maternal instinct.

Consider further that women who conceive babies now when they are *not* married are not hailed as true followers of their natural instinct, but are considered as 'immoral', 'loose', 'whores', and so on. As Antonis (1981, p.59) notes: 'maternal instinct is ascribed to *married women* only.' That women can conceive and bear children is a universal phenomenon;

---

[3]For a full discussion of power relationships between men and women with regard to contraceptive practice see Gittins (1982).

that they do so by instinct is a fallacy. So is the notion that they always raise them. From the moment of birth motherhood is a social construction.

Sociological and historical studies of the family have tended to pay most attention to the vertical relationships between parents and children. Less attention is paid to the lateral relationships between siblings. Yet in other cultures, and in Western Europe in earlier times, the sibling tie has often formed the basis of households and may be seen as more important than that between parent and child. Among the poorer sectors of western society until quite recently it was common for the eldest daughter to take responsibility for supervising and caring for younger siblings from quite an early age, thereby freeing her mother to engage in waged or domestic work. This remains common in many contemporary societies. In Morocco, for instance, girls 'from the age of about four onwards look after younger siblings, fetch and carry, clean and run errands. The tasks themselves are arranged in a hierarchy of importance and attributed to women and girls according to their authority within the household...Boys tend to be freed from domestic tasks and spend their time in groups of peers who play marbles or trap birds' (Maher, 1981, pp.73-4).

The content and importance of sibling ties varies, and this is partly a result of different interpretations of reproduction. In societies where the role of the male is seen as peripheral or unimportant — or even non-existent — in reproduction, then his children by another woman are not seen as having any relation to those of the first mother, or vice versa if the mother's role is seen as unimportant. The salience of sibling ties also depends on the organisation of kinship generally. The relative neglect of studying sibling ties as an important aspect of — or even basis of — kinship betrays our own assumptions about the primacy of parenthood in families and, particularly, the assumption that reproduction is the 'essence' of kinship, with the mother and child forming the universal core of kinship. As Yanagisako (1977, pp.197-8) points out in writing about Goodenough: 'while he is undoubtedly right that in every human society mothers and children can be found, to view their *relationship* as the universal nucleus of the family is to attribute it to a social and cultural significance that is lacking in some cases.'

Implicit in definitions of kinship is a way of perceiving the social organisation of reproduction and mating, at the centre of which therefore is an organisation of relations between the sexes. The organisation of, and differentiation between, male and female takes many different forms, but all societies do have a social construction of the sexes into gender. Gender is an inherent part of the manner in which all societies are organised and is also a crucial part of the different ways in which

26

kinship has been constructed and defined. The social, economic and political organisation of societies has been initially at least based on kinship — and thus also on gender. Understanding society means understanding the ways in which a society organised kinship and gender, and how these influence one another. Gender and kinship are universally present — as are mothers and children — but the content of them, and the meanings ascribed to them, is highly variable.

The most basic divisions of labour within any society, as pointed out by Durkheim (1933) and others, are based on age and sex. While age as a category can eventually be achieved, sex is ascribed, permanent, and immutable. The biological differences between men and women are such that only women can conceive and lactate; only men can impregnate. In spite of these obvious differences, none of them is great enough to be adequate grounds for allocating one kind of work to women and another to men. Indeed, cross-culturally and historically there are very few jobs that can be claimed to be specifically and universally performed by either men or women. Women have ploughed and mined and still do; men have laundered, gathered fruit and minded children. Hunting and warfare have almost always been male activities, while care of the young and sick has usually been a female activity. But allocation of tasks is also strongly based on age, so it is important to remember that it may be young men who hunt and old men or women who care for children; old women may be responsible for cooking, while both young men and women may work in the fields or mines.

Age is an important factor to consider in trying to understand the organisation of kinship and households. Nobody remains the same age — contrary to contemporary images in the media of the 'happy family' where the couple is permanently 30 and the children forever 8 and 6. As individuals age, so the composition and structure of the unit in which they live change. Consider the ways in which the household composition and resources of a couple change as, first, aged 20, they marry and both work; second, aged 25, they have had two children and the wife has left the labour market for a few years to rear the children until they attend school; third, at 30, one partner leaves or dies and one parent is left with total care of the children; fourth, at 35, one or both may remarry someone who perhaps has three children from an earlier marriage, or may take in an elderly parent to care for, and so on. The number of wage earners and dependents changes over a household's cycle, just as it changes for the individuals within the household.

Thinking in terms of 'the' family leads to a static vision of how people actually live and age together and what effects this process has on others within the household in which they live. Moreover, the environment and conditions in which any household is situated are always changing, and these changes can and often do have important reper-

27

cussions on individuals and households. As Tamara Hareven (1982) points out, it is important when analysing families to differentiate between individual time, family time, and historical time. Thus in considering the structure and meaning of 'family' in any society it is important to understand how definitions of dependency and individual time vary and change, how patterns of interaction between individuals and households change, and how historical developments affect all of these.

The notion of there being such a thing as 'the family' is thus highly controversial and full of ambiguities and contradictions. Childbearing, childrearing, the construction of gender, allocation of resources, mating and marriage, sexuality and ageing all loosely fit into our idea of family, and yet we have seen how all of them are variable over time, between cultures and between social sectors. The claim that 'the family' is universal has been especially problematic because of the failure by most to differentiate between how small groups of people live and work together, and what the ideology of appropriate behaviour for men, women and children within families has been.

Imbued in western patriarchal ideology, as discussed previously, are a number of important and culturally specific beliefs about sexuality, reproduction, parenting and the power relationships between age groups and between the sexes. The sum total of these beliefs make up a strong *symbol-system which is labelled as the family*. Now while it can be argued that all societies have beliefs and rules on mating, sexuality, gender and age relations, the content of rules is culturally and historically specific and variable, and in no way universal. Thus to claim that patriarchy is universal is as meaningless as claiming that the family is universal.

If defining families is so difficult, how do we try to understand how and why people live, work and form relationships together in our own society? First, we need to acknowledge that while what we may thing of as families are not universal, there are still trends and patterns specific to our culture which, by careful analysis, we can understand more fully. Second, we can accept that while there can be no perfect definition, it is still possible to discover certain defining characteristics which can help us to understand changing patterns of behaviour and beliefs. Finally, and most important, we can 'deconstruct' assumptions usually made about families by questioning what exactly they mean. Before doing this, however, it is useful to attempt some definition of what is meant by 'family' in western society.

Problematic though it may be, it is necessary to retain the notion of co-residence, because most people have lived, and do live, with others for much of their lives. Thus 'household' is useful as a defining characteristic, while bearing in mind that it does not necessarily imply sexual or intimate relationships, and that, moreover, relationships *between* households are a crucial aspect of social interaction. 'Household' should not be interpreted as a homogeneous and undivided unit. Virtually all households will have their own division of labour, generally based on ideas and beliefs, as well as the structure, of age and sex. There will always tend to be power relationships within households, because they will almost invariably be composed of different age and sex groups and thus different individuals will have differential access to various resources.

Because the essence of any society is interaction, a society will always be composed of a myriad of *relationships* between people, from the most casual to the most intimate. Relationships are formed between people of the same sex, the opposite sex, the same age group, different age groups, the same and different classes, and so on. Some of these relationships will be sexual and sexual relations can occur in any type of relationship. Some relationships will be affectionate and loving, others will be violent or hostile. They may be made up of very brief encounters or may extend over the best part of a person's life-cycle. Thus while relationships are extremely varied in the ways in which they are formed, their nature and duration, *ideologically* western society has given highest status to long-term relationships between men and women, and between parents and children. Ideologically, such relationships are supposed to be loving and caring, though in reality many are not. They are presented as 'natural', but as we have seen, they are not. These ideals have become reified and sanctified in the notion of 'family', virtually to the exclusion of all other long-term or intimate relationships.

Ideas of family relationships have become enshrined in our legal, social, religious and economic systems which, in turn, reinforce the ideology and penalise or ostracise those who transgress it. Thus there are very real pressures on people to behave in certain ways, to lead their lives according to acceptable norms and patterns. Patriarchal ideology is embedded in our socio-economic and political institutions, indeed, in the very language we use, and as such encourages, cajoles and pressurises people to follow certain paths. Most of these are presented and defined in terms of 'the family', and the family is in turn seen as the bulwark of our culture. The pressures of patriarchal ideology are acted out — and reacted against — in our inter-personal relationships, in marriage and non-marriage, in love and hate, having children and not having children. In short, much of our social behaviour occurs in, and is judged on the basis of, the ideology of 'the family'.

Relationships are universal, so is some form of co-residence, of intimacy, sexuality and emotional bonds. But the *forms* these can take are infinitely variable and can be changed and challenged as well as embraced. By analysing the ways in which culture has prescribed cer-

29

tain, and proscribed other, forms of behaviour, it should be possible to begin to see the historical and cultural specificity of what is really meant when reference is made to 'the family'.

References

B. Antonis (1981) 'Motherhood and Mothering', in Cambridge Women's Study Group, *Women in Society*, Virago, London.

D.R. Bender (1979) 'A Refinement of the Concept of Household: Families, Co-residence and Domestic Functions', *American Anthropologist*, vol. 69.

J. Bernard (1973) *The Future of Marriage*, Souvenir Press, London.

E. Durkheim (1933) *The Division of Labour in Society*, Collier-Macmillan, London.

F. Edholm (1982) 'The Unnatural Family', in Whitelegg *et al.*, *The Changing Experience of Women*, Martin Robertson, Oxford.

D. Gittins (1982) *Fair Sex: Family Size and Structure 1900-1939*, Hutchinson, London.

H. Gutman (1976) *The Black Family in Slavaery and Freedom, 1750-1925*, Basil Blackwell, Oxford.

T. Hareven (1982) *Family Time and Industrial Time*, Cambridge University Press, New York.

V. Maher (1981) 'Work, Consumtion and Authority within the Household: A Moroccan Case', in Young *et al.*, *Of Marriage and the Market*, CSE, London.

M. Mead (1971) *Male and Female*, Penguin, Harmondsworth.

D.H.J. Morgan (1975) *Social Theory and the Family*, Routledge & Kegan Paul, London.

R. Rapp (1980) 'Family and Class in Contemporary America: Notes Towards an Understanding of Ideology', *Science and Society*, vol. 42.

J. Renvoize (1982) *Incest: A Family History*, Routledge & Kegan Paul, London.

R.T. Smith (1978) 'The Family and the Modern Woprld System: Some Observations from the Caribbean', *Jounal of Family History*, vol. 3.

S.J. Yanagisako (1977) Women-Centered Kin Networks in Urban Bilateral Kinship', *American Ethnologist*, vol. 4.

Is There a Family?
New Anthropological Views*

Jane Collier, Michelle Rosaldo and Sylvia Yanagisako

This essay poses a rhetorical question in order to argue that most of our talk about families is clouded by unexplored notions of what families "really" are like. It is probably the case, universally, that people expect to have special connections with their genealogically closet relations. But a knowledge of genealogy does not in itself promote understanding of what these special ties are about. The real importance of The Family in contemporary social life and belief has blinded us to its dynamics. Confusing ideal with reality, we fail to appreciate the deep significance of what are, cross-culturally, various ideologies of intimate relationship, and at the same time we fail to reckon with the complex human bonds and experiences all too comfortably sheltered by a faith in the "natural" source of a "nurture" we think is found in the home.

This essay is divided into three parts. The first examines what social scientists mean by The Family. It focuses on the work of Bronislaw Malinowski, the anthropologist who first convinced social scientists that The Family was a universal human institution. The second part also has social scientists as its focus, but it examines works by the nineteenth-century thinkers Malinowski refuted, for if — as we shall argue — Malinowski was wrong in viewing The Family as a universal human institution, it becomes important to explore the work of theorists who did not make Malinowski's mistakes. The final section then draws on the correct insights of nineteenth-century theorists to sketch some implications of viewing The Family, not as a concrete institution designed to fulfill universal human needs, but as an ideological construct associated with the modern state.

I. Conceptualizing "Family": Definitions and Theoretical Perspectives

Malinowski's Concept of the Family

In 1913 Bronislaw Malinowski published a book called *The Family Among the Australian Aborigines*[1] in which he laid to rest earlier debates about whether all human societies had families. During the nineteenth century, proponents of social evolution argued that primitives were sexually promiscuous and therefore incapable of having families because children would not recognize their fathers.[2] Malinowski refuted this notion by showing that Australian aborigines, who were widely believed to practice "primitive promiscuity," not only had rules regulating who might have intercourse with whom during sexual orgies but also differentiated between legal marriages and casual unions. Malinowski thus "proved" that Australian aborigines had marriage, and so proved that aboriginal children had fathers, because each child's mother had but a single recognized husband.

Malinowski's book did not simply add data to one side of an ongoing debate. It ended the debate altogether, for by distinguishing coitus from conjugal relationships, Malinowski separated questions of sexual behavior from questions of the family's universal existence. Evidence of sexual promiscuity was henceforth irrelevant for deciding whether families existed. Moreover, Malinowski argued that the conjugal relationship, and therefore The Family, had to be universal because it fulfilled a universal human need. As he wrote in a posthumously published book:

> The human infant needs parental protection for a much longer period than does the young of even the highest anthropoid apes. Hence, no culture could endure in which the act of reproduction, that is, mating, pregnancy, and childbirth, was not linked up with the fact of legally-founded parenthood, that is, a relationship in which the father and mother have to look after the children for a long period, and, in turn, derive certain benefits from the care and trouble taken.[3]

[1]Herbert Spencer, *The Principles of Sociology*, vol. 1, Domestic Institutions (New York: Appleton, 1973). Bronislaw Malinowski, *The Family Among the Australian Aborigines* (London: University of London Press, 1913).
[2]Lewis Henry Morgan, *Ancient Society* (New York: Holt, 1877).
[3]Bronislaw Malinowski, *A Scientific Theory of Culture* (Chapel Hill: University of North Carolina Press, 1944), p. 99.

In proving the existence of families among Australian aborigines, Malinowski described three features of families that he believed flowed from The Family's universal function of nurturing children. First, he argued that families had to have clear boundaries, for if families were to perform the vital function of nurturing young children, insiders had to be distinguishable from outsiders so that everyone could know which adults were responsible for the care of which children. Malinowski thus argued that families formed bounded social units, and to prove that Australian families formed such units, he demonstrated that aboriginal parents and children recognized one another. Each aboriginal woman had a single husband, even if some husbands had more than one wife and even if husbands occasionally allowed wives to sleep with other men during tribal ceremonies. Malinowski thus proved that each aboriginal child had a recognized mother and father, even if both parents occasionally engaged in sexual relations with outsiders.

Second, Malinowski argued that families had to have a place where family members could be together and where the daily tasks associated with child rearing could be performed. He demonstrated, for example, that aboriginal parents and their immature children shared a single fire — a home and hearth where children were fed and nurtured — even though, among nomadic aborigines, the fire might be kindled in a different location each night.

Finally, Malinowski argued that family members felt affection for one another — that parents who invested long years in caring for children were rewarded by their own and their children's affections for one another. Malinowski felt that long and intimate association among family members fostered close emotional ties, particularly between parents and children, but also between spouses. Aboriginal parents and their children, for example, could be expected to feel the same emotions for one another as did English parents and children, and as proof of this point, Malinowski recounted touching stories of the efforts made by aboriginal parents to recover children lost during conflicts with other aborigines or with white settlers and efforts made by stolen aboriginal children to find their lost parents.

Malinowski's book on Australian aborigines thus gave social scientists a concept of The Family that consisted of a universal function, the nurturance of young children, mapped onto (1) a bounded set of people who recognized one another and who were distinguishable from other like groups; (2) a definite physical space, a hearth and home; and (3) a particular set of emotions, family love. This concept of The Family as an institution for nurturing young children has been enduring, probably because nurturing children is thought to be the

33

primary function of families in modern industrial societies. The flaw in Malinowski's argument is the flaw common to all functionalist arguments: Because a social institution is observed to perform a necessary function does not mean either that the function would not be performed if the institution did not exist or that the function is responsible for the existence of the institution.

Later anthropologists have challenged Malinowski's idea that families always include fathers, but, ironically, they have kept all the other aspects of his definition. For example, later anthropologists have argued that the basic social unit is not the nuclear family including father but the unit composed of a mother and her children: "Whether or not a mate becomes attached to the mother on some more or less permanent basis is a variable matter."[4] In removing father from the family, however, later anthropologists have nevertheless retained Malinowski's concept of The Family as a functional unit, and so have retained all the features Malinowski took such pains to demonstrate. In the writings of modern anthropologists, the mother-child unit is described as performing the universally necessary function of nurturing young children. A mother and her children form a bounded group, distinguishable from other units of mothers and their children. A mother and her children share a place, a home and hearth. And, finally, a mother and her children share deep emotional bonds based on their prolonged and intimate contact.

Modern anthropologists may have removed father from The Family, but they did not modify the basic social science concept of The Family in which the function of child rearing is mapped onto a bounded set of people who share a place and who "love" one another. Yet it is exactly this concept of The Family that we, as feminist anthropologists, have found so difficult to apply. Although the biological facts of reproduction, when combined with a sufficiently elastic definition of marriage, make it possible for us, as social scientists, to find both mother-child units and Malinowski's conjugal-pairs-plus-children units in every human society, it is not at all clear that such Families necessarily exhibit the associated features Malinowski "proved" and modern anthropologists echo.

An outside observer, for example, may be able to delimit family boundaries in any and all societies by identifying the children of one woman and that woman's associated mate, but natives may not be interested in making such distinctions. In other words, natives may not be concerned to distinguish family members from outsiders, as Malinowski imagined natives should be when he argued that units of

---

[4]Robin Fox, *Kinship and Marriage* (London: Penguin, 1967), p. 39.

parents and children have to have clear boundaries in order for child-rearing responsibilities to be assigned efficiently. Many languages, for example, have no word to identify the unit of parents and children that English speakers call a "family." Among the Zinacantecos of southern Mexico, the basic social unit is identified as a "house," which may include from one to twenty people.[5] Zinacantecos have no difficulty talking about an individual's parents, children, or spouse; but Zinacantecos do not have a single word that identifies the unit of parents and children in such a way as to cut it off from other like units. In Zinacanteco society, the boundary between "houses" is linguistically marked, while the boundary between "family" units is not.

Just as some languages lack words for identifying units of parents and children, so some "families" lack places. Immature children in every society have to be fed and cared for, but parents and children do not necessarily eat and sleep together as a family in one place. Among the Mundurucu of tropical South America, for example, the men of a village traditionally lived in a men's house together with all the village boys over the age of thirteen; women lived with other women and young children in two or three houses grouped around the men's house.[6] In Mundurucu society, men and women ate and slept apart. Men ate in the men's house, sharing food the women had cooked and delivered to them; women ate with other women and children in their own houses. Married couples also slept apart, meeting only for sexual intercourse.

Finally, people around the world do not necessarily expect family members to "love" one another. People may expect husbands, wives, parents, and children to have strong feelings about one another, but they do not necessarily expect prolonged and intimate contact to breed the loving sentiments Malinowski imagined as universally rewarding parents for the care they invested in children. The mother-daughter relationship, for example, is not always pictured as warm and loving. In modern Zambia, girls are not expected to discuss personal problems with, or seek advice from, their mothers. Rather, Zambian girls are expected to seek out some older female relative to serve as confidante.[7] Similarly, among the Cheyenne Indians who lived on the American Great Plains during the last century, a mother was expected to have

[5]Evon Z. Vogt, *Zinacantan: A Maya Community in the Highlands of Chiapas* Cambridge, Mass.: Harvard University Press, 1969).

[6]Yolanda and Robert Murphy, *Women of the Forest* (New York: Columbia University Press, 1974).

[7]Ilsa Schuster, *New Women of Lusaka* (Palo Alto: Mayfield, 1979).

strained relations with her daughters.[8] Mothers are described as continually admonishing their daughters, leading the latter to seek affection from their fathers' sisters.

Of course, anthropologists have recognized that people everywhere do not share our deep faith in the loving, self-sacrificing mother, but in matters of family and motherhood, anthropologists, like all social scientists, have relied more on faith than evidence in constructing theoretical accounts. Because we believe mothers to be loving, anthropologists have proposed, for example, that a general explanation of the fact that men marry mother's brothers' daughters more frequently than they marry father's sisters' daughters is that men naturally seek affection (i.e., wives) where they have found affection in the past (i.e., from mothers and their kin).[9]

Looking Backward

The Malinowskian view of The Family as a universal institution — which maps the "function" of "nurturance" onto a collectivity of specific persons (presumably "nuclear" relations) associated with specific spaces ("the home") and specific affective bonds ("love") — corresponds, as we have seen, to that assumed by most contemporary writers on the subject. But a consideration of available ethnographic evidence suggests that the received view is a good deal more problematic than a naive observer might think. If Families in Malinowski's sense are not universal, then we must begin to ask about the biases that, in the past, have led us to misconstrue the ethnographic record. The issues here are too complex for thorough explication in this essay, but if we are to better understand the nature of "the family" in the present, it seems worthwhile to explore the question, first, of why so many social thinkers continue to believe in Capital-Letter Families as universal institutions, and second, whether anthropological tradition offers any alternatives to a "necessary and natural" view of what our families are. Only then will we be in a position to suggest "new anthropological perspectives" on the family today.

Our positive critique begins by moving backward. In the next few pages, we suggest that tentative answers to both questions posed above lie in the nineteenth-century intellectual trends that thinkers

---

[8]E. Adamson Hoebel, *The Cheyennes: Indians of the Great Plains* (New York: Holt, Rinehart and Winston, 1978).

[9]George G. Homans and David M. Schneider, *Marriage, Authority, and Final Causes* (Glencoe, Ill.: Free Press, 1955).

like Malinowski were at pains to reject. During the second half of the nineteenth century, a number of social and intellectual developments — among them, the evolutionary researches of Charles Darwin; the rise of "urban problems" in fast-growing cities; and the accumulation of data on non-Western peoples by missionaries and agents of the colonial states — contributed to what most of us would now recognize as the beginnings of modern social science. Alternately excited and perplexed by changes in a rapidly industrializing world, thinkers as diverse as socialist Frederick Engels[10] and bourgeois apologist Herbert Spencer[11] — to say nothing of a host of mythographers, historians of religion, and even feminists — attempted to identify any distinctive problems and potentials of their contemporary society by constructing evolutionary accounts of "how it all began." At base, a sense of "progress" gave direction to their thought, whether, like Spencer, they believed "man" had advanced from the love of violence to a more civilized love of peace or, like Engels, that humanity had moved from primitive promiscuity and incest toward monogamy and "individual sex love." Proud of their position in the modern world, some of these writers claimed that rules of force had been transcended by new rules of law,[12] while others thought that feminine "mysticism" in the past had been supplanted by a higher male "morality."[13]

At the same time, and whatever else they thought of capitalist social life (some of them criticized, but none wholly abhorred it), these writers also shared a sense of moral emptiness and a fear of instability and loss. Experience argued forcefully to them that moral order in their time did not rest on the unshakable hierarchy — from God to King to Father in the home — enjoyed by Europeans in the past.[14] Thus, whereas Malinowski's functionalism led him to stress the underlying continuities in all human social forms, his nineteenth-century predecessors were concerned to understand the facts and forces that set their experiential world apart. They were interested in comparative and, more narrowly, evolutionary accounts because their lives

---

[10]Frederick Engels, *The Origin of the Family, Private Property and the State*, in *Karl Marx and Frederick Engels: Selected Works*, vol. 2 (Moscow: Foreign Language Publishing House, 1955).

[11]Frederick Engels, *The Origin of the Family, Private Property and the State*, in *Karl Marx and Frederick Engels: Selected Works*, vol. 2 (Moscow: Foreign Language Publishing House, 1955).

[12]John Stuart Mill, *The Subjection of Women* (London: Longmans, Green, Reader and Dyer, 1869).

[13]J.J. Bachofen, *Das Mutterrecht* (Stuttgart, 1861).

[14]Elizabeth Fee, "The Sexual Politics of Victorian Social Anthropology," in Clio's *Banner Raised*, ed. M. Hartman and L. Banner (New York: Harper & Row, 1974).

were torn between celebration and fear of change. For them, the family was important not because it had at all times been the same but because it was at once the moral precondition for, the triumph of, and the victim of developing capitalist society. Without the family and female spheres, thinkers like Ruskin feared we would fall victim to a market that destroys real human bonds.[15] Then again, while men like Engels could decry the impact of the market of familial life and love, he joined with more conservative counterparts to insist that our contemporary familial forms benefited from the individualist morality of modern life and reached to moral and romantic heights unknown before.

Given this purpose and the limited data with which they had to work, it is hardly surprising that the vast majority of what these nineteenth-century writers said is easily dismissed today. They argued that in simpler days such things as incest were the norm; they thought that women ruled in "matriarchal" and peace-loving states or, alternatively, that brute force determined the primitive right and wrong. None of these visions of a more natural, more feminine, more sexy, or more violent primitive world squares with contemporary evidence about what, in technological and organizational terms, might be reckoned relatively "primitive" or "simple" social forms. We would suggest, however, that whatever their mistakes, these nineteenth-century thinkers can help us rethink the family today, at least in part because we are (unfortunately) their heirs, in the area of prejudice, and partly because their concern to characterize difference and change gave rise to insights much more promising than their functionalist critics may have thought.

To begin, although nineteenth-century evolutionary theorists did not believe The Family to be universal, the roots of modern assumptions can be seen in their belief that women are, and have at all times been, defined by nurturant, connective, and reproductive roles that do not change through time. Most nineteenth-century thinkers imagined social development as a process of differentiation from a relatively confused (and thus incestuous) and indiscriminant female-oriented state to one in which men fight, destroy their "natural" social bonds, and then forge public and political ties to create a human "order." For some, it seemed reasonable to assume that women dominated, as matriarchs, in the undifferentiated early state, but even these theorists believed that women everywhere were "mothers" first, defined by "nurturant" concerns and thus excluded from the business competition, cooperation, social ordering, and social change propelled and

---

[15]John Ruskin, "Of Queen's Gardens," in *Sesame and Lilies* (London: J. M. Dent, 1907).

dominated by their male counterparts. And so, while nineteenth-century writers differed in their evaluations of such things as "women's status," they all believed that female reproductive roles made women different from and complementary to men and guaranteed both the relative passivity of women in human history and the relative continuity of "feminine" domains and functions in human societies. Social change consisted in the acts of men, who left their mothers behind in shrinking homes. And women's nurturant sphere was recognized as a complementary and necessary corrective to the more competitive pursuits of men, not because these thinkers recognized women as political actors who influence the world, but because they feared the unchecked and morally questionable growth of a male-dominated capitalist market.

For nineteenth-century evolutionists, women were associated, in short, with an unchanging biological role and a romanticized community of the past, while men were imaged as the agents of all social process. And though contemporary thinkers have been ready to dismiss manifold aspects of their now-dated school of thought, on this point we remain, perhaps unwittingly, their heirs. Victorian assumptions about gender and the relationship between competitive male markets and peace-loving female homes were not abandoned in later functionalist schools of thought at least in part because pervasive sexist biases make it easy to forget that women, like men, are important actors in all social worlds. Even more, the functionalists, themselves concerned to understand all human social forms in terms of biological "needs," turned out to strengthen earlier beliefs associating action, change, and interest with the deeds of men because they thought of kinship in terms of biologically given ties, of "families" as units geared to reproductive needs, and finally, of women as mere "reproducers" whose contribution to society was essentially defined by the requirements of their homes.

If most modern social scientists have inherited Victorian biases that tend ultimately to support a view uniting women and The Family to an apparently unchanging set of biologically given needs, we have at the same time failed to reckon with the one small area in which Victorian evolutionists were right. They understood, as we do not today, that families — like religions, economies, governments, or courts of law — are not unchanging but the product of various social forms, that the relationships of spouses and parents to their young are apt to be different things in different social orders. More particularly, although nineteenth-century writers had primitive society all wrong, they were correct in insisting that family in the modern sense — a unit bounded, biologically as well as legally "inside" the home — is something that emerges not in Stone Age caves but in complex state-governed social forms. Tribal peoples may speak readily of lineages, households, and clans, but — as we have seen — they rarely have a word denoting Family as a particular and limited group of kin; they rarely worry about differences between legitimate and illegitimate heirs or find themselves concerned (as we so often are today) that what children and/or parents do reflects on their family's public image and self-esteem. Political influence in tribal groups in fact consists in adding children to one's home and, far from distinguishing Smith from Jones, encouraging one's neighbors to join one's household as if kin. By contrast, modern bounded Families try to keep their neighbors out. Clearly their character, ideology, and functions are not given for all times. Instead, to borrow the Victorian phrase, The Family is a "moral" unit, a way of organizing and thinking about human relationships in a world in which the domestic is perceived to be in opposition to a politics shaped outside the home, and individuals find themselves dependent on a set of relatively noncontingent ties in order to survive the dictates of an impersonal market and external political order.

In short, what the Victorians recognized and we have tended to forget is, first, that human social life has varied in its "moral" — we might say its "cultural" or "ideological" — forms, and so it takes more than making babies to make Families. And having seen The Family as something more than a response to omnipresent, biologically given needs, they realized too that Families do not everywhere exist; rather, The Family (thought to be universal by most social scientists today) is a moral and ideological unit that appears, not universally, but in particular social orders. The Family as we know it is not a "natural" group created by the claims of "blood" but a sphere of human relationships shaped by a state that recognizes Families as units that hold property, provide for care and welfare, and attend particularly to the young — a sphere conceptualized as a realm of love and intimacy in opposition to the more "impersonal" norms that dominate modern economies and politics. One can, in nonstate social forms, find groups of genealogically related people who interact daily and share material resources, but the contents of their daily ties, the ways they think about their bonds and their conception of the relationship between immediate "familial" links and other kinds of sociality, are apt to be different from the ideas and feelings we think rightfully belong to families we know. Stated otherwise, because our notions of The Family are rooted in a contrast between "public" and "private" spheres, we will not find that Families like ours exist in a society where public and political life is radically different from our own.

Victorian thinkers rightly understood the link between the bounded modern Family and the modern state, although they thought the two related by a necessary teleology of moral progress. Our point resembles theirs not in the explanations we would seek but in our feeling that if we, today, are interested in change, we must begin to probe and understand change in the families of the past. Here the Victorians, not the functionalists, are our rightful guides because the former recognized that all human social ties have "cultural" or "moral" shapes, and more specifically, that the particular "morality" or contemporary familial forms is rooted in a set of processes that link our intimate experiences and bonds to public politics.

Toward a Rethinking

Our perspective on families therefore compels us to listen carefully to what the natives in other societies say about their relationships with genealogically close kin. The same is true of the natives in our own society. Our understanding of families in contemporary American society can be only as rich as our understanding of what The Family represents symbolically to Americans. A complete cultural analysis of The Family as an American ideological construct, of course, is beyond the scope of this essay. But we can indicate some of the directions such an analysis would take and how it would deepen our knowledge of American families.

One of the central notions in the modern American construct of The Family is that of nurturance. When antifeminists attack the Equal Rights Amendment, for example, much of their rhetoric plays on the anticipated loss of the nurturant, intimate bonds we associate with The Family. Likewise, when pro-life forces decry abortion, they cast it as the ultimate denial of nurturance. In a sense, these arguments are variations of a functionalist view that weds families to specific functions. The logic of the argument is that because people need nurturance, and people get nurtured in The Family, then people need The Family. Yet if we adopt the perspective that The Family is an ideological unit rather than merely a functional unit, we are encouraged to subject this syllogism to closer scrutiny. We can ask, first, What do people mean by nurturance? Obviously, they mean more than mere nourishment — that is, the provision of food, clothing, and shelter required for biological survival. What is evoked by the word nurturance is a certain kind of relationship: a relationship that entails affection and love, that is based on cooperation as opposed to competition, that is enduring rather than temporary, that is noncontingent rather

41

than contingent upon performance, and that is governed by feeling and morality instead of law and contract.

The reason we have stated these attributes of The Family in terms of oppositions is because in a symbolic system the meanings of concepts are often best illuminated by explicating their opposites. Hence, to understand our American construct of The Family, we first have to map the larger system of constructs of which it is only a part. When we undertake such an analysis of The Family in our society, we discover that what gives shape to much of our conception of The Family is its symbolic opposition to work and business, in other words, to the market relations of capitalism. For it is in the market, where we sell our labor and negotiate contract relations of business, that we associate with competitive, temporary, contingent relations that must be buttressed by law and legal sanctions.

The symbolic opposition between The Family and market relations renders our strong attachment to The Family understandable, but it also discloses the particularity of our construct of The Family. We can hardly be speaking of a universal notion of The Family shared by people everywhere and for all time because people everywhere and for all time have not participated in market relations out of which they have constructed a contrastive notion of the family.

The realization that our idea of The Family is part of a set of symbolic oppositions through which we interpret our experience in a particular society compels us to ask to what extent this set of oppositions reflects real relations between people and to what extent it also shapes them. We do not adhere to a model of culture in which ideology is isolated from people's experience. On the other hand, neither do we construe the connection between people's constructs and people's experience to be a simple one of epiphenomenal reflection. Rather, we are interested in understanding how people come to summarize their experience in folk constructs that gloss over diversity, complexity, and contradictions in their relationships. If, for example, we consider the second premise of the aforementioned syllogism — the idea that people get "nurtured" in families — we can ask how people reconcile this premise with the fact that relationships in families are not always this simple or altruistic. We need not resort to the evidence offered by social historians (e.g., Philippe Aries[16] and Lawrence Stone[17]) of the harsh treatment and neglect of children and spouses in the history of the

---

[16]Philippe Ariès, *Centuries of Childhood*, trans. Robert Baldick (New York: Vintage, 1962).

[17]Lawrence Stone, *The Family, Sex, and Marriage in England 1500-1800* (London: Weidenfeld and Nicholson, 1977).

Western family, for we need only read our local newspaper to learn of similar abuses among contemporary families. And we can point to other studies, such as Young and Willmott's *Family and Kinship in East London*,[18] that reveal how people often find more intimacy and emotional support in relationships with individuals and groups outside The Family than they do in their relationships with family members.

The point is not that our ancestors or our contemporaries have been uniformly mean and nonnurturant to family members but that we have all been both nice and mean, both generous and ungenerous, to them. In like manner, our actions toward family members are not always motivated by selfless altruism but are also motivated by instrumental self-interest. What is significant is that, despite the fact that our complex relationships are the result of complex motivations, we ideologize relations within The Family as nurturant while casting relationships outside The Family — particularly in the sphere of work and business — as just the opposite.

We must be wary of oversimplifying matters by explaining away those disparities between our notion of the nurturant Family and our real actions toward family members as the predictable failing of imperfect beings. For there is more here than the mere disjunction of the ideal and the real. The American construct of The Family, after all, is complex enough to comprise some key contradictions. The Family is seen as representing not only the antithesis of the market relations of capitalism; it is also sacralized in our minds as the last stronghold against The State, as the symbolic refuge from the intrusions of a public domain that constantly threatens our sense of privacy and self-determination. Consequently, we can hardly be surprised to find that the punishments imposed on people who commit physical violence are lighter when their victims are their own family members.[19] Indeed, the American sense of the privacy of the things that go on inside families is so strong that a smaller percentage of homicides involving family members are prosecuted than those involving strangers.[20] We are faced with the irony that in our society the place where nurturance and noncontingent affection are supposed to be located is simultaneously the place where violence is most tolerated.

---

[18]Michael Young and Peter Willmott, *Family and Kinship in East London* (London: Routledge and Kegan Paul, 1957).

[19]Henry P. Lundsgaarde, *Murder in Space City: A Cultural Analysis of Houston Homicide Patterns* (New York: Oxford University Press, 1977).

[20]Ibid.

I. Conceptualizing "Family": Definitions and Theoretical Perspectives

There are other dilemmas about The Family that an examination of its ideological nature can help us better understand. For example, the hypothesis that in England and the United States marriages among lower-income ("working-class") groups are characterized by a greater degree of "conjugal role segregation" than are marriages among middle-income groups has generated considerable confusion. Since Bott observed that working-class couples in her study of London families exhibited more "segregated" conjugal roles than "middle-class" couples, who tended toward more "joint" conjugal roles,[21] researchers have come forth with a range of diverse and confusing findings. On the one hand, some researchers have found that working-class couples indeed report more segregated conjugal role-relationships — in other words, clearly differentiated male and female tasks, as well as interests and activities — than do middle-class couples.[22] Other researchers, however, have raised critical methodological questions about how one goes about defining a joint activity and hence measuring the degree of "jointness" in a conjugal relationship.[23] Platt's finding that couples who reported "jointness" in one activity were not particularly likely to report "jointness" in another activity is significant because it demonstrates that "jointness" is not a general characteristic of a relationship that manifests itself uniformly over a range of domains. Couples carry out some activities and tasks together or do them separately but equally; they also have other activities in which they do not both participate. The measurement of the "jointness" of conjugal relationships becomes even more problematic when we recognize that what one individual or couple may label a "joint activity," another individual or couple may consider a "separate activity." In Bott's study, for example, some couples felt that all activities carried out by husband and wife in each other's presence were similar in kind regardless of whether the activities were complementary (e.g. sexual intercourse, though no one talked about this directly in the home interview), independent (e.g. husband repairing book while the wife read or knitted), or shared (e.g. washing

---

[21]Elizabeth Bott, *Family and Social Network: Roles, Norms, and External Relationships in Ordinary Urban Families* (London: Tavistock, 1957).

[22]Herbert J. Gans, *The Urban Villagers* (New York: Free Press, 1962); C. Rosser and C. Harris, *The Family and Social Change* (London: Routledge and Kegan Paul, 1965).

[23]John Platt, "Some Problems in Measuring the Jointness of Conjugal Role-Relationships," *Sociology 3* (1969): 287-97; Christopher Turner, "Conjugal Roles and Social Networks: A Re-examination of an Hypothesis," *Human Relations 20* (1967): 121-30; and Morris Zelditch, Jr., "Family, Marriage and Kinship," in *A Handbook of Modern Sociology*, ed. R. E. L. Faris (Chicago: Rand McNally, 1964), pp. 680-707.

up together, entertaining friends, going to the pictures together). It was not even necessary that husband and wife should actually be together. As long as they were both at home it was felt that their activities partook of some special, shared, family quality.[24]

In other words, the distinction Bott drew among "joint," "differentiated," and "autonomic" (independent) relationships summarized the way people thought and felt about their activities rather than what they were observed to actually do. Again, it is not simply that there is a disjunction between what people say they do and what they in fact do. The more cogent point is that the meaning people attach to action, whether they view it as coordinated and therefore shared or in some other way, is an integral component of that action and cannot be divorced from it in our analysis. When we compare the conjugal relationship of middle-income and low-income people, or any of the family relationships among different class, age, ethnic, and regional sectors of American society, we must recognize that our comparisons rest on differences and similarities in ideological and moral meanings as well as on differences and similarities in action.

Finally, the awareness that The Family is not a concrete "thing" that fulfills concrete "needs" but an ideological construct with moral implications can lead to a more refined analysis of historical change in the American or Western family than has devolved upon us from our functionalist ancestors. The functionalist view of industrialization, urbanization, and family change depicts The Family as responding to alterations in economic and social conditions in rather mechanistic ways. As production gets removed from the family's domain, there is less need for strict rules and clear authority structures in the family to accomplish productive work. At the same time, individuals who now must work for wages in impersonal settings need a haven where they can obtain emotional support and gratification. Hence, The Family becomes more concerned with "expressive" functions, and what emerges is the modern "compassionate family." In short, in the functionalist narrative The Family and its constituent members "adapt" to fulfill functional requirements created for it by the industrialization of production. Once we begin to view The Family as an ideological unit and pay due respect to it as a moral statement, however, we can begin to unravel the more complex, dialectical process through which family relationship and The Family as a construct were mutually transformed. We can examine, for one, the ways in which people and state institutions acted, rather than merely reacted, to assign certain func-

---

[24]Bott, *Family and Social Network*, p. 240.

tions to groupings of kin by making them legally responsible for these functions. We can investigate, as Eli Zaretsky does in his essay in this volume, the manner in which the increasing limitations placed on agents of the community and the state with regard to negotiating the relationship between family members enhanced the independence of The Family. We can begin to understand the consequences of social reforms and wage policies for the age and sex inequalities in families. And we can elucidate the interplay between these social changes and the cultural transformations that assigned new meanings and modified old ones to make The Family what we think it to be today.

Ultimately, this sort of rethinking will lead to a questioning of the somewhat contradictory modern views that families are things we need (the more "impersonal" the public world, the more we need them) and at the same time that loving families are disappearing. In a variety of ways, individuals today do look to families for a "love" that money cannot buy and find; our contemporary world makes "love" more fragile than most of us hope and "nurturance" more self-interested than we believe.[25] But what we fail to recognize is that familial nurturance and the social forces that turn our ideal families into mere fleeting dreams are equally creations of the world we know today. Rather than think of the ideal family as a world we lost (or, like the Victorians, as a world just recently achieved), it is important for us to recognize that while families symbolize deep and salient modern themes, contemporary families are unlikely to fulfill our equally modern nurturant needs.

We probably have no cause to fear (or hope) that The Family will dissolve. What we can begin to ask is what we want our families to do. Then, distinguishing our hopes from what we have, we can begin to analyze the social forces that enhance or undermine the realization of the kinds of human bonds we need.

---

[25] Rayna Rapp, "Family and Class in Contemporary America: Notes Toward an Understanding of Ideology," *Science and Society* 42 (Fall 1978): 278-300.

II. The Social History of Family Life

If families do not naturally assume the nuclear form, then why is the nuclear family — built on the intimate relationship between a man and a woman — so common, and seemingly necessary? What social forces promote the nuclear arrangement? The most fruitful strategy for answering these questions seems to be an examination of social history. Studying the development of familiar characteristics of family life is an obvious way of determining what factors have shaped family patterns.

Social historians have discovered not only that the nuclear family is not universal in human history, but also that family organization did not simply evolve unilinearly through time in the direction of the nuclear form. At any point in time, family life has assumed different patterns in different places. Of course, the diversity has not been random: the way family life is organized has related to other aspects of social structure, such as the way production (or work) was organized. A review of some of the key features of family life in times past serves here as an introduction to the articles that follow.

Until the late nineteenth century, family membership was very unstable. One of the reasons was that by modern standards people had very short life expectancies (Gittins 1985). Children were very likely to die before reaching adulthood, and especially as babies; if they survived their first few years, they were likely to lose a parent — and acquire a stepparent — before reaching adulthood. These high mortality rates, which altered household composition yearly, affected all social classes.

Partly because short life spans meant that the lifetimes of three generations of kin were unlikely to overlap, extended-family households were never the common pattern. The nuclear family unit has been more common through human history. What is uncommon, and recent in history, however, is the *privatized* nuclear-family household, which stands on its own with respect to basic responsibilities (e.g., the pooling of material resources, child care), and is socially separated from the larger community and even the larger network of kin. In fact, in many societies the nuclear unit was so embedded in larger units that it did not have enough significance to be identified as "the family."

In the simplest human societies, those based on foraging (or gathering and hunting) for subsistence, it is the larger camp rather than the nuclear family that pools its resources and shares responsibility for all of its members, including children. Patricia Draper's article describes the absence of private family life among the !Kung of southern Angola, Botswana and South-West Africa, who are among the very few remaining foraging peoples. And the excerpt from Jean-Louis Flandrin's book,

II. The Social History of Family Life

Families in Former Times, makes clear that for all social classes, family life was not private even in recent European history — until the nineteenth century for the middle classes, and more recently for the working class.

The development of privatized family life was gradual. As Draper's article suggests, the change from nomadic foraging to settled agriculture entailed a subtle distinction between private and public spheres. With the later formation of the state, in agricultural societies, the seat of power left the kin group, and the split between the domestic and public spheres intensified. Yet, a clear separation between home life and public life came only with the development of industrial capitalism, when much work (especially men's) left the household.

Until the late eighteenth century, privacy was so alien to family life in England and France that "family" referred to either the household (that is, the residents of the household) or the wider kin group (Flandrin 1979). In turn, households usually contained people who were not related by blood to the married couple. Typically, besides the nuclear-family core, households included young "servants" and other people needed for the work they contributed (Flandrin 1979; Mitterauer and Sieder 1982). In fact, labour requirements were the primary determinant of household composition, aside from wealth and mortality. As labour requirements changed, household composition changed. What is most interesting from our vantage point is that no distinction was made between the people related by blood or marriage and others: everyone living under the authority of the household head was considered "family" and treated as such.

The households of wealthy couples were larger and more complex in composition than others. These couples had more children. They also took in more children from other households as "servants." Yet, being "in service" was common for youths of all classes: training for adulthood (i.e., learning to do domestic work, often learning a trade) typically took place in a household other than that of one's parents. As well, households incorporated adult labourers — journeymen weavers, tailors, and other skilled craftsmen, or farm workers — when the need arose. Peasant households, for example, relied on the farm labour of hired men when their children were either too young or gone from home.

Through history, until the development of industrial capitalism, the family/household has been the unit of production. Consequently, the requirements of survival took precedence over other matters in shaping most families. For the rich, the maintenance and reproduction of wealth took priority. Thus, the choice of marriage partner was based on practical considerations — the issue of alliances between families for the wealthy, and that of a man choosing an able reproducer and worker in the case of the peasantry — rather than physical attraction, compatibility, or emotional attachment. Even the needs of children were secondary to those of production: children were raised in and around women's other work.

In striking contrast with the way childhood is treated in western culture today, until recent centuries in Europe children were not assumed to need a tremendous amount of special attention (Aries 1962). Wealthy women sent their babies to "wet nurses" for the first few years, others had an older daughter or servant attend to most of the infant's needs. In England, only with the many changes associated with industrialization and urbanization did families begin to keep their children home until they grew up; only in the nineteenth century was motherhood defined as women's primary responsibility (Flandrin 1979). Earlier than recent European history, child rearing was not a privatized parental responsibility either: in the foraging societies of Africa that anthropologists have studied recently, even though children are highly indulged, the mother is not alone in providing care for the child (Lee 1979).

The transition in human history from foraging to agriculture meant (surprisingly) an increase in the work necessary to produce subsistence, as well as more complex social organization — the rise of social-class divisions, the development of the marketplace and the state, among other things. What is interesting is the attendant change in the relationship of the individual and larger social units. The uncertain struggle for survival among foragers produced a social organization based on cooperation and even communal living arrangements in many places. In turn, the need for cooperation and sharing by every member of society (for the sake of survival), coupled with every person's access to the means of subsistence, created a situation in which the individual was allowed considerable personal autonomy (Turnbull 1961; Lee 1979). Ironically, over the centuries, as communal organization eroded and the family/household progressively distinguished itself from the larger community, the interests of the individual were increasingly subordinated to those of the larger kin group initially, and to those of the household later — until recent times. And kin had ways of ensuring that individuals put collective (family) interests above their own (Haraven 1978). For example, the older generation in European peasant households, or on family farms in the British colonies of North America, typically obtained their grown children's labour with the promise of inheritance of the land (or a dowry, in the case of daughters).

There was a positive side to the priority that collective interests took over individual interests. Because "mutual help by family members was essential for survival" (Hareven 1978: 66), kinship entailed the expectation and obligation of assistance. The individual could rely on kin for support. This customary assistance was perhaps most apparent during the period of industrialization and urbanization in England: to cope with the general disruption, kin helped each other find jobs, shared housing, and otherwise aided each other (Anderson 1971).

There was a final, important change in family life over the course of human history. Just as the household, and the family within it, have been increasingly separated from the rest of the community, so too historical changes (especially the growth of industrial-capitalist society) brought about the segregation of family members by sex and by age. While the pattern in foraging societies was probably one of total absence of work on the part of children, in agricultural societies children's labour was needed. Consequently, after the historical transition to settled living, childhood became a fairly short period in the life cycle, and young children were integrated into adult patterns at very young ages. It was only in the nineteenth century that middle¬class children's lives became substantially different from adults, and a life cycle involving now-familiar stages developed (e.g., a period spent in school which preceded the assumption of an occupation) (Haraven 1978). Of course, that same century witnessed the horrible exploitation of working-class children by factory employers; only with mandatory school attendance and laws against child labour did working-class children acquire a childhood.

There was also a progressive segregation of the lives of women and men with the development of complex societies, until the twentieth century. The gender division of labour, which was so fluid in foraging societies, rigidified in societies based on agriculture and, later, commodity production. Nevertheless, in medieval Europe, where there were clear norms about women's work and women's subordination to men, the wife of a peasant or artisan often worked alongside her husband, doing work complementary to his (Clark 1919). The work that women performed did not restrict them to a private home either, since it frequently required activity in the public sphere and men's work occurred in a household that was open to customers and clients. Moreover, unmarried women — whether single or widowed — lived fairly unrestricted lives. For instance, they carried on business on their own account (Bennett 1987). With proletarianization and the need for individuals to stand on their own in the labour market, and the separation of commodity production and the household, women's work and men's work was increasingly segregated.

Relations between men and women also became more unequal over time, until recently. Foraging societies were egalitarian (Leacock

Introduction

1981; Anderson 1987). Horticultural[1] societies varied greatly, depending especially on whether they were matrilineal and matrilocal or patrilineal and patrilocal[2] (Martin and Voorhies 1975; Coontz and Henderson 1987). The article by Judith Brown describes the social position of Iroquois women: because the kin group organized social, political and economic life, and because the kin group was organized around women, there was no male dominance in that society (which is probably the most egalitarian of horticultural societies anthropologists have studied).

The slow erosion of the power of kin groups with the development of the state in agricultural societies, and the primacy of men's role in production when agriculture required the use of plows and domesticated animals, among other historical changes, meant that medieval European history involved a worsening of the position of the wives of peasants, artisans and even the nobility. Medieval women were subject to their father's and then their husband's authority (Bennett 1987). As capitalism developed, with proletarianization and the industrialization of work, women's economic dependence on men worsened, but the potential for gender equality was created as the power of families over their individual members eroded.

Overall, in terms of the quality of individuals' lives, historical changes in family organization have had mixed consequences. The collective interests of the family have weakened relative to the interests of the individual. This means that individual autonomy should have increased over time — though, as we saw, it was high in communal foraging societies. At the same time, however, the weakening of the collective accompanies an end to the embeddedness of the individual in a supportive kin group. Similarly, while personal needs have come to outweigh practical considerations (in matters such as the choice of a spouse), family relationships have gotten fewer and more intense: the individual depends on fewer and fewer people to meet his or her personal needs. And for women, the erosion of family control over behaviour has left the individual "free" to cope with a larger society that — like the family — is organized around gender divisions and gender inequality (e.g., as in the labour market).

---

[1]"Horticultural" societies are based on cultivation of the land, by means of hand tools and human energy. Anthropologists distinguish them from "agricultural" societies, which use plows and domesticated animals as the key energy source.
[2]"Matrilineal" societies trace identity and inheritance through generations of women (from the vantage point of the individual, these are traced through one's mother). "Patrilineal" refers to a tracing through the men. "Matrilocal" refers to the location of residence after marriage: the couple moves to live with the woman's kin group. "Patrilocal" entails living with the man's kin group.

51

II. The Social History of Family Life

When considering the history of family life, the aim should not be to attempt to reconstruct the details of changes over time. Instead, it is useful to examine different types of societies in order to derive some understanding of the "logic" of their organization — to understand the relationships among factors that in turn are related to the features of family life. The following articles will help in that exercise. Patricia Draper's interesting discussion of the lives of both foraging and settled !Kung suggests the complicated relationships in these communities among the organization of work, the arrangement of physical space, the form of households, the interaction of family and community, the position of women, and the degree of individual autonomy. Despite the negative consequences Draper finds accompanying settlement, Judith Brown's description of women's position in Iroquois society highlights factors that sometimes combined even in settled and fairly complex societies to allow women equality with men.

The excerpt from Jean-Louis Flandrin's book provides a vivid description of family life in recent European history; it is an interesting reminder of how different family life can be from the way it is now. The next two articles provide some description of Canadian family life in times past. Emily Nett's scholarly review of the literature indicates that despite a common pattern of nuclear-family households among European settlers, Canadian families were quite different even a century ago than they are now. Canadian patterns, in fact, were similar to many of the European patterns reviewed above. Finally, Bettina Bradbury's rich description of working-class Montreal families in the latter part of the nineteenth century shows the interplay between a family's economic condition, the health of its members, and its stability. Her argument highlights how profound the consequences of poverty can be, but also how strong families can be in coping with poverty. Bradbury's article raises the question of the need even in capitalist societies — in which domestic responsibilities such as child care are assumed to be privatized — for a socialization of some of these responsibilities.

References

Anderson, Karen.
1987. "A gendered world: women, men and the political economy of the seventeenth century Huron." in Heather Jon Maroney and Meg Luxton, eds. Pp. 121-39 *Feminism and Political Economy*. Toronto: Methuen.

Introduction

Anderson, Michael.
1971. *Family Structure in Nineteenth Century Lancashire*. Cambridge: Cambridge University Press.
Aries, Philippe.
1962. *Centuries of Childhood*. New York: Vintage Books.
Bennett, Judith.
1987. *Women in the Medieval English Countryside*. New York: Oxford.
Clark, Alice.
1919. *Working Life of Women in the Seventeenth Century*. London: Frank Cass.
Coontz, Stephanie and Peta Henderson, eds.
1986. *Women's Work, Men's Property*. London: Verso.
Flandrin, Jean-Louis. 1979.
Families in Former Times. Cambridge: Cambridge University Press.
Gittins, Diana.
1985. *The Family in Question*. London: Macmillan.
Hareven, Tamara.
1978. "Family time and historical time." Pp. 57-71 in Alice Rossi, Jerome Kagan, and Tamara Hareven, eds. *The Family*. New York: Norton.
Leacock, Eleanor.
1981. *Myths of Male Dominance*. New York: Monthly Review Press.
Lee, Richard Borshay.
1979. *The !Kung San*. Cambridge: Cambridge University Press.
Martin, M. Kay and Barbara Voorhies.
1975.*Female of the Species*. New York: Columbia University Press.
Mitterauer, Michael and Reinhard Sieder.
1982. *The European Family*. Oxford: Basil Blackwell.
Turnbull, Colin.
1961. *The Forest People*. Garden City: Doubleday.

Suggested Readings

Mitterauer, Michael and Reinhard Sieder.
1982. *The European Family*. Oxford: Basil Blackwell. A solid general overview of the social history of family life.
Stone, Lawrence.
1977. *The Family, Sex and Marriage in England 1500-1800*. New York: Harper & Row. A now-classic argument about historical changes in English family life.

II. The Social History of Family Life

Aries, Philippe.
1962. *Centuries of Childhood*. New York: Vintage Books. A fascinating description of changing ideas of childhood and family in European history.
Ryan, Mary.
1981. *Cradle of the Middle Class*. Cambridge: Cambridge University Press. A fine account of the origins of the middle-class family in nineteenth-century U.S.
Katz, Michael.
1975. *The People of Hamilton, Canada West*. Cambridge, Massachusetts: Harvard University Press.
A quantitative social historian describes changes in family life and social class in the latter part of the nineteenth century in Hamilton.

!Kung Women: Contrasts in Sexual Egalitarianism in Foraging and Sedentary Contexts*

Patricia Draper

Most members of the Harvard !Kung Bushman Study Project who have thought about the subject of !Kung women's status agree that !Kung society may be the least sexist of any we have experienced. This impression contradicts some popularly held stereotypes about relations between the sexes in hunting and gathering societies. Because sex is one of the few bases for the differentiation of social and economic roles in societies of this type, it has probably been attributed more weight than it deserves. The men are commonly depicted in rather romantic terms, striving with their brothers to bring home the precious meat while their women humbly provide the dull, tasteless vegetable food in the course of routine, tedious foraging. Contrary evidence is now emerging from several researchers that men and women of band-level societies have many overlapping activities and spheres of influence (Gale, 1970). The distinction between male and female roles is substantially less rigid than previously supposed, though there is variation among band-level peoples in the degree of autonomy and influence that women enjoy.

This paper describes relations between the sexes for two groups of !Kung: those living a traditional hunting and gathering life at /Du/da and those who have recently adopted a settled way of life in the !Kangwa Valley and who are now living by agriculture, animal husbandry, and a small amount of gathering.

The point to be developed at some length is that in the hunting and gathering context, women have a great deal of autonomy and influence. Some of the contexts in which this egalitarianism is expressed will be described in detail, and certain features of the foraging life which promote egalitarianism will be isolated. They are: women's subsistence contribution and the control women retain over the food they have gathered; the requisites of foraging in the Kalahari which entail a similar degree of mobility for both sexes; the lack of rigidity in

*From *Toward an Anthropology of Women*, ed. Rayna Reiter. Reprinted by permission of the Monthly Review Foundation. Copyright © 1975 by Rayna R. Reiter.

sex-typing of many adult activities, including domestic chores and aspects of child socialization; the cultural sanction against physical expression of aggression; the small group size; and the nature of the settlement pattern.

Features of sedentary life that appear to be related to a decrease in women's autonomy and influence are: increasing rigidity in sex-typing of adult work; more permanent attachment of the individual to a particular place and group of people; dissimilar childhood socialization for boys and girls; decrease in the mobility of women as contrasted with men; changing nature of women's subsistence contribution; richer material inventory with implications for women's work; tendency for men to have greater access to and control over such important resources as domestic animals, knowledge of Bantu language and culture, wage work; male entrance into extra-village politics; settlement pattern; and increasing household privacy.

Background to !Kung Research

The !Kung Bushmen of the Kalahari Desert are one of the better described primitive cultures, with the literature steadily increasing in the last twenty years. The work of Lorna Marshall, John Marshall, and Elizabeth Marshall Thomas gives a background to !Kung social organization and economy. The publications of the Marshall family concern primarily !Kung living in South-West Africa in the Nyae nyae area.

Since the early 1960s other researchers have entered the field of !Kung studies, in particular members of the Harvard !Kung Bushman Study Project. This team worked in western Botswana with populations of !Kung who overlap with the !Kung of South-West Africa first studied by the Marshall expedition. Members of the Harvard research team have focused on more narrow, specialized topics. Some of their publications have already appeared, and many others are currently in preparation (see Biesele, Draper, Howell, Katx, Konner, Lee, Lee and DeVore, Shostak, and Yellen).

Ethnographic Background to the !Kung: Traditional Population

The !Kung are a hunting and gathering people living today mostly on the western edge of the Kalahari sand system in what is now southern Angola, Botswana, and South-West Africa. The great majority of !Kung-speaking people have abandoned their traditional hunting and

56

gathering way of life and are now living in sedentary and semi-squatter status in or near the villages of Bantu pastoralists and European ranchers. A minority of !Kung, amounting to a few thousand, are still living by traditional hunting and gathering techniques. It is to these bush-living peoples and a few groups of very recently settled !Kung, that this paper refers.

The bush-living peoples subsist primarily on wild vegetable foods and game meat. They are semi-nomadic, moving their camps at irregular intervals of from several days to several weeks. The average size of individual groups (also referred to as bands or camps) is about thirty-five people, though the numbers range from seventeen to sixty-five people. Season and the availability of water are the chief factors affecting group size. During the rainy season (October to March), group censuses are lower due to the fact that water and bush foods are widely available in most regions of the !Kung range. Smaller numbers of people in the form of two- and three-family groups spread out over the bush. As the dry season approaches, the small, temporary water pans dry up and the people begin to regroup and fall back on the remaining water sources that continue throughout the dry season. As there are relatively few water sources in the heart of the drought, as many as two or three different camps may be found within one to three miles of the same water hole.

The rules governing the composition of these bands are extremely flexible. It appears there is no such thing as "band membership." Close relatives move together over much of the year, though individuals and segments of large kin groups frequently make temporary and amicable separations to go live some miles distant with other relatives and affines.

Material technology is extremely simple. Men hunt with small bows and arrows (tipped with poison) and metal-pointed spears. Women's tools include a simple digging stick, wooden mortar and pestle, and leather kaross which doubles as clothing and carrying bag. Both sexes use leather carrying bags, hafted adzes, and net slings made from handwoven vegetable fiber. Clothing, particularly among the bush people, consists of leather garments; in addition, various cloth garments are worn, especially by the settled !Kung, but also by the peoples of the bush.

Settled Population

As stated before, the great majority of !Kung-speaking peoples are settled around the villages of technologically more advanced peoples and have been there for as many as three generations. Among other !Kung, sedentarization is much more recent. In the case of the Mahopa people, in the !Kangwa area of Botswana, !Kung commitment to settled life is perhaps fifteen to twenty years old. I observed these people and the people of /Du/da for two years in 1968 and 1969.

About fifty !Kung lived in three separate villages around the permanent water hole at Mahopa. Bantu-speaking pastoralists also lived at Mahopa and watered their herds of cattle, horses, donkeys, and goats at the Mahopa well. These Bantu were chiefly of the Herero tribe and, like the !Kung, lived in about six villages, whose total population consisted of perhaps fifty people. Some !Kung lived in the Herero villages, but my research and remarks here do not refer to them.

The Mahopa people whom I describe lived in villages composed only of !Kung. The decision of the !Kung to avoid close proximity with the Herero is conscious, for relations between the two groups are not entirely amicable — Bantu of the area have a superior attitude and often (according to the !Kung) do not treat !Kung people fairly. Bantu see the !Kung as irresponsible, poor workers who are prone to killing occasional steers from Bantu herds.

The subsistence practices of the recently settled !Kung are mixed. The women continue to gather bush food, but not with the effort or regularity of the women of the traditional groups. Hunting by Mahopa men has virtually ceased. The people keep small herds of goats and plant small gardens of sorghum, squash, melons, and corn. For the most part, the Mahopa !Kung do not own their own cattle (at least, they did not during my fieldwork). Some !Kung women receive milk in payment for regular chores they do for nearby Herero women.

In the first discussion of !Kung women my remarks will pertain to women of the bush-living groups, unless otherwise specified. Description of the women's life in the settled Mahopa villages of the !Kangwa area will be handled second. The traditional, or bush-living !Kung lived in the /Du/da area, which straddles the border of Botswana and South-West Africa and stretches over a north-south distance of about seventy miles.

Self-Esteem Derived from Subsistence Contribution

Women are the primary providers of vegetable food, and they contribute something on the order of 60 to 80 percent of the daily food intake by weight (Lee, 1965). All !Kung agree that meat is the most desirable, most prestigious food, but the hunters cannot always provide it.

Without question, women derive self-esteem from the regular daily contribution they make to the family's food.

A common sight in the late afternoon is clusters of children standing on the edge of camp, scanning the bush with shaded eyes to see if the returning women are visible. When the slow-moving file of women is finally discerned in the distance, the children leap and exclaim. As the women draw closer, the children speculate as to which figure is whose mother and what the women are carrying in their karosses.

Often when women return in the evening they bring information as well as bush food. Women are skilled in reading the signs of the bush, and they take careful note of animal tracks, their age, and the direction of movement. On several occasions I have accompanied gathering expeditions in which, when the group was about thirty to forty minutes out of camp, one of the women discovered the fresh tracks of several large antelope. This find caused a stir of excitement in the group. Quickly the women dispatched one of the older children to deliver the report to the men in camp. In general, the men take advantage of women's reconnaissance and query them routinely on the evidence of game movements, the location of water, and the like.

A stereotype of the female foraging role in hunting and gathering societies (in contrast with men's work, which is social in character) is that the work is individualized, repetitious, and boring (Service, 1966: 12). Descriptions of the work of gathering leave the reader with the impression that the job is uninteresting and unchallenging — that anyone who can walk and bend over can collect wild bush food. This stereotype is distinctly inappropriate to !Kung female work, and it promotes a condescending attitude toward what women's work is all about. Successful gathering over the years requires the ability to discriminate among hundreds of edible and inedible species of plants at various stages in their life cycle. This ability requires more than mere brute strength. The stereotype further ignores the role women play in gathering information about the "state of the bush" — presence of temporary water, evidence of recent game movements, etc. On a given day, !Kung hunters consciously avoid working the same area in which women are foraging, knowing that movements of the women may disturb the game, but also knowing that the women can be questioned at the end of the day (Yellen, personal communication).

!Kung women impress one as self-contained people with a high sense of self-esteem. There are exceptions — women who seem forlorn and weary — but for the most part, !Kung women are vivacious and self-confident. Small groups of women forage in the Kalahari at dis-

59

tances of eight to ten miles from home with no thought that they need the protection of the men or of the men's weapons should they encounter any of the several large predators that also inhabit the Kalahari (for instance, hyena, wild dog, leopard, lion, and cheetah). It is unusual, but not exceptional, for a lone woman to spend the day gathering. In the times I observed at the /Du/da camps, the solitary foragers were either postmenopausal women or young, unmarried women who were still without children. Women with children or adolescent, unmarried girls usually gather bush food in the company of two or more other women. The !Kung themselves claim that lovers (as well as married couples) sometimes arrange to meet privately in the bush. !Kung sleeping arrangements may promote these tactics, for at night whole families sleep outdoors together gathered around individual campfires and within a few feet of other families sleeping at their own fires.

Similar Absenteeism for Men and Women

A similarity in the gathering work of women and the hunting work of men is that both activities take adults out of the camp, sometimes all day for several days each week. The pattern of both sexes being about equally absent from the dwelling place is not typical of most middle-range, agriculturally based tribal societies. In these latter groups one finds an arrangement whereby women, much more than men, stay at home during child tending, domestic chores, food preparation and the like, while the men are occupied with activities that take them outside the household and keep them away for many hours during the day. Frequent (daily) male absence may result in viewing men as a scarce commodity with higher value than women, who are constantly present in the household. If men in this sense are a scarce commodity, their homecoming must have greater significance to those who stay at home, and their influence even in the routine domestic affairs may be heightened simply because others are less habituated to their presence. Among the !Kung a case could be argued for the equal, or nearly equal, scarcity value of men and women. Both leave the village regularly, and the return of both is eagerly anticipated — as illustrated earlier in this paper with reference to women.

It seems likely that !Kung men and women have similar knowledge of the large hunting and gathering territory within their kin and affines range. Both men and women range out from the camp in the course of their subsistence work, and they are equally affected by group moves in search of bush food, game, and water. More recently, however, /Du/da men have gained larger knowledge of the "outside" world, for some young men have spent months, and even years, doing wage work at such towns as Ghanzi, Gobabis, and Windhoek. Women are less likely to have had these experiences. Henry Harpending (1972 and in press) has collected demographic data on the !Kung of the !Kangwa and /Du/da areas which shows that the space occupied over a lifetime does not differ for the two sexes. For example, the distribution of distances between birthplaces of mates and birthplaces of parents and offspring are almost identical for the two sexes, both currently and for marriages that took place prior to substantial Bantu contact in these areas.

The absence of warfare or raiding, either among !Kung themselves or between !Kung and neighboring Bantu, undoubtedly facilitates the freedom of movement of the women. If threat of enemy attack were a recurrent fact of life, many features of !Kung social organization undoubtedly would change, particularly in the area of political leadership, but probably in the area of sex egalitarianism as well. (See Murdock, 1949:205 for a discussion of conditions, including warfare, that increase status discrepancy between the sexes.)

Sexual Division of Labor

When asked, !Kung will state that there is men's work and women's work, and that they conceive of most individual jobs as sex-typed, at least in principle. In practice, adults of both sexes seem surprisingly willing to do the work of the opposite sex. It often appeared to me that men, more than women were willing to cross sex lines.

One afternoon while visiting in one of the /Du/da camps, I came across Kxau, a rather sober middle-aged man, industriously at work building his own hut. Building huts is predominantly women's work, and I had never seen such a thing. It happened that Kxau's wife was away visiting at another settlement many miles distant, or she would have made the hut. However, Kxau's daughter, an unmarried girl about seventeen years old, was in camp, and even she did not offer to make the hut or help him once he had started. Kxau proceeded to build the structure methodically and without embarrassment. I deliberately stayed in the vicinity to observe the reaction of other people. No one commented or joked with him about how his women were lazy.

Gathering is women's work, but there are times when men also gather (Draper, in preparation). Some married couples collected mongongo nuts together, but in my observation, the couples most likely to do this were elderly couples and a young couple who had been married

61

for several years but had no children. Water collection is normally considered to be women's work, particularly when the water source is close to camp, perhaps fifteen to twenty minutes' walk. However, when the people are camped several miles from water, men participate regularly in carrying water back to camp. In the months of August, September, and October of 1969, I observed two of the /Du/da camps where water was three miles distant. In this situation men and women both worked at bringing in water. Only on the occasions when several of the men were absent from camp for several nights on hunting trips did their wives collect water daily for the remaining members of the family.

I mentioned earlier that men seem more willing (or accustomed) than women to do work normally associated with the opposite sex. Gathering and water-collecting are outstanding examples of female tasks that frequently involve men. While there are undoubtedly sound economic and evolutionary reasons for the male monopoly on hunting (Judith K. Brown, 1970b), there is one aspect of male hunting tasks that could easily absorb female help but typically does not. I refer here to the job of carrying the meat back to camp from the kill site.

A common pattern among the hunters of /Du/da was for a group of three or four hunters to stay out three or more nights in a row. Frequently by the fourth or fifth day one of their number would appear back in camp with the news that an antelope had been killed and that volunteers were needed to carry in the meat. On such occasions the remainder of the original hunting party stayed with the carcass, cutting the meat into biltong and allowing it to dry and lose much of its weight and volume. Always the helpers recruited were men. Often, but not necessarily, they are young males in late adolescence who had not yet begun serious hunting. I personally never knew of a woman (or women) assisting in such a venture, and never heard of any woman having done it.

The !Kung recognize no taboo against women being present at a kill site. On the contrary, when one or two hunters have killed a large animal some distance from camp, one of the hunters will return to camp and bring back his own and the other hunter's family to camp temporarily by the slain animal. Quite possibly the !Kung could verbalize their feelings about why it would be inappropriate to ask women to carry butchered meat. Unfortunately, while I was in the field it never occurred to me to ask; such blind spots are apparently an unavoidable hazard of fieldwork. Professor Cora DuBois warned me of this problem a few months before I began my work in the Kalahari: "Beware that the scale of custom will form over your eyes and you will no longer see."

Child-Rearing Practices and Sexual Equality

As children grow up there are few experiences which set one sex apart from the other. Living in such small groups, !Kung children have relatively few playmates to choose from.[1] Play groups, when they do form, include children of both sexes and of widely differing ages. This habit of playing in heterogeneous play groups probably minimizes any underlying, biologically based sex differences in style — differences which in other societies may be magnified and intensified by the opportunity of playing in same-sex, same-age play groups.

The child nurse is a regular feature of many African agricultural societies. The custom of assigning child-tending responsibility to an older child (usually a girl) in a family is one example of sex-role typing which can begin at an early age. This responsibility shapes and limits the behavior of girls in ways not true for boys, who are usually passed over for this chore. The training a girl receives as an infant caretaker doubtless has benefits for her eventual role performance and more immediately for the family economy, since she frees the mother from routine child care and allows her to resume subsistence production. However, the typical nine-year-old who is saddled with carrying and supervising a toddler cannot range as widely or explore as freely and independently as her brothers. She must stay closer to home, be more careful, more nurturant, more obedient, and more sensitive to the wishes of others. Habits formed in this way have social value, but my point is that such girls receive more training in these behaviors and that they form part of the complex of passivity and nurturance which characterizes adult female behavior in many cultures.[2]

!Kung do not use child nurses of either sex on a routine basis; this fact follows from the long birth intervals and the pattern of adult subsistence work. The average birth interval is approximately four years (Howell, in press). !Kung mothers can and do give lengthy, intensive care to each child because no new infant arrives to absorb her attention. Such mothers are comparatively unpressured and do not need to delegate the bulk of child-tending responsibility to another caretaker. Naturally, older children interact with younger children and in the process give help, protection, and attention to them. But one

---

[1]The average size of camps in the /Du/da area was thirty-four persons of whom an average of twelve were children ranging from new-born to fourteen years of age.

[2]See Barry, Bacon, and Child, 1957, and Whiting and Whiting, 1973 for further discussion of cross-cultural regularity and variability in sex differences in nurturance training.

or more older children are rarely, if ever, the sole caretakers of younger charges for an appreciable length of time.

The rhythm of adult work also makes the role of child nurse unnecessary. !Kung adults work about three days per week, and they vary their time of being in and out of the camp, with the result that on any given day one-third to one-half of the adults are in camp. They can easily supervise their own children and those whose parents are absent. Older children are helpful in amusing and monitoring younger children, but they do so spontaneously (and erratically), and not because they are indoctrinated with a sense of responsibility for the welfare of a particular child or children.

A reflection of !Kung women's effectiveness in family life is the fact that a mother deals directly with her children when they are in need of correction. A different type of maternal strategy is common in cultures where women's status is clearly subordinate to that of the fathers and husbands. David Landy's study (1959) of rural Puerto Rican socialization techniques, Robert A. and Barbara LeVine's study (1963) of East African Gussi child training practices, and the L. Minturn and John T. Hitchcock study (1963) of child rearing among the Rajputs of Khalapur are particularly good examples of how a mother's ability to control her children is undermined by male superordinance, particularly when accompanied by patrilineal structures and patrilocal residence rules. Such mothers will hold up the father as the ultimate disciplinarian in an attempt to underscore their own power. !Kung women do not resort to the threat, "I'll tell your father...!"

Among the !Kung, both parents correct the children, but women tend to do this more often because they are usually physically closer to the children at any given time than the men. When such situations arise, a mother does not seek to intimidate the children with the father's wrath. In this milieu children are not trained to respect and fear male authority. In fact, for reasons which will be elaborated later, authoritarian behavior is avoided by adults of both sexes. The typical strategy used by !Kung parents is to interrupt the misbehavior, carry the child away, and try to interest him or her in some inoffensive activity.

This way of disciplining children has important consequences in terms of behaviors that carry over into adulthood. Since parents do not use physical punishment, and aggressive postures are voided by adults and devalued by the society at large, children have relatively little opportunity to observe or imitate overtly aggressive behavior. This carries over into relations between adult men and women in the society. Evidence from various sources is mounting in support of the notion that human males (and males of nonhuman species) are innately

64

more aggressive than their female counterparts (Bandura et al., 1961; Hamburg and Lunde, 1966; Kagan and Moss, 1962; Sears et al., 1957 and 1965). But among the !Kung there is an extremely low cultural tolerance for aggressive behavior by anyone, male or female. In societies where aggressiveness and dominance are valued, these behaviors accrue disproportionately to males, and the females are common targets, resulting in a lowering of their status. !Kung women are not caught by this dimension of sex-role complementarity. They customarily maintain a mild manner, but so do their men.

Relations of Men with Children

A further example of the equality between the sexes and the amount of overlap in their activities is the relationship between men and their children. In cultures where men have markedly superordinant status, women and children are expected to show deference to the male head of the family by staying away from him, observing routine formalities. !Kung fathers, in contrast, are intimately involved with their children and have a great deal of social interaction with them. The relation between fathers and young children is relaxed and without stylized respect or deference from the children. In fact, the lack of tact with which some children treated their parents was at first quite shocking to me.

As an example, I can relate an incident in which Kxau was trying to get his youngest son, Kashe, to bring him something from the other side of camp. Kxau was sitting at one edge of the village clearing with another man older than himself. Kxau repeatedly shouted to his son to bring him his tobacco from inside the family hut. The boy ignored his father's shouts, though !Kung camps are small, and the boy clearly could hear his father. Finally Kxau bellowed out his command, glaring across at his son and the other youngsters sitting there. Kashe looked up briefly and yelled back, "Do it yourself, old man." A few minutes later Kxau did do it himself, and Kashe received no reprimand.

Most fathers appear ill-at-ease when they hold very young infants, although by the time a child is nine or ten months old it is common to see the father playing with the child and holding it close to his face, blowing on its neck, and laughing. In the late afternoon and evening in a !Kung camp one often sees a father walking among the huts with a two- or three-year-old boy perched on his shoulder. The father ambles along, accepting an offer of a smoke at one hut, then moving on to squat elsewhere while watching a kinsman scraping a hide or mending a tool. At such times the father is mindful of the boy at his shoulder but pays him no special attention aside from now and then steadying the child's balance.

There are certain aspects of child care that men unanimously eschew. Most prefer not to remove mucous from the runny nose of a child. Most adults of both sexes have a rather high tolerance for this sight, but occasionally a man will see his child with an especially un-wholesome-looking smear on his upper lip, and will call out to his wife, "Ugh! Get rid of that snot." Men are also loath to clean up feces left by children. Usually the mother or an older child will scoop up the offending mess with a handful of leaves. If, however, a child's defeca-tion has gone unnoticed by all except the father, he will call out to his wife to remove it.

Effect of Group Size and Settlement Pattern on Relations Between the Sexes

!Kung camps are typically quite small; the average camp size at /Du/da was thirty-four with a range of seventeen to sixty-five. The small group size is related to the low order of specialization of sex roles. Given the rather small numbers of able-bodied adults who manage group life and subsistence in these camps, the lack of opposition (or specialization) of the sexes is highly practical. Especially in the rainy seasons when local group size falls to about fifteen people, it is useful and necessary for adults to be relatively interchangeable in function.

Observing the way people group themselves during leisure hours in a !Kung camp gives one a feeling for the tone of informal het-erosexual interaction. Men and women (children, too) sit together in small clusters — talking, joking, cracking and eating nuts, passing around tobacco. Individuals pass among these groups without caus-ing a rift in the ambience, without attracting attention. In general, the sexes mix freely and unself-consciously without the diffidence one might expect to see if they thought they were in some way intruding.

If there were a prominent opposition between the sexes, one would expect some expression of this in the organization and use of space within the !Kung camps. However, there are no rules and defi-nitions that limit a person's access to various parts of the village space on the basis of sex. The overall small size of the settled area almost removes this type of symbolism from the realm of possibility.

To an outsider, particularly a Westerner, the small size of !Kung camps and the intimate, close living characteristic of them can seem stifling.[3] Essentially, thirty to forty people share what amounts to (by our standards) a large room. The individual grass scherms, one to each married couple, ring an elliptical village space. The huts are often placed only a few feet apart and look a mere forty to fifty feet across the cleared, central space into the hearth and doorway of the hut on the opposite side of the circle. Daily life goes on in this small, open space. Everything is visible with a glance; in many camps conversations can be carried on in normal tones of voice by people sitting at opposite ends of the village. In this setting it is easy to see why the sexes rub elbows without embarrassment. In other societies, where sex roles and the prerogatives which attach to them are more exclusively defined, one generally finds architectural features used to help people manage their interaction and/or avoidance: walls, fences, separate sleeping and/or eating arrangements, designated spaced allocated to only one sex, etc.

In summary, many of the basic organizing features of this hunting and gathering group contribute to a relaxed and egalitarian relationship between men and women. The female subsistence role is essential to group survival and satisfying to the women. The foregoing remarks have illustrated a framework within which egalitarian relations are a natural or logical outcome. There are other issues bearing on the question of women's influence and control which are not answered here. Decision-making is one such issue. Leadership and authority are difficult problems to research in band-level societies generally, and in this one in particular. Still, the question of whether women or men more often influence group or family decisions is an empirical one, albeit one on which I have no data. Other areas that bear on the topic of women's influence and power are marital relations, access to extramarital relations, the influence of young women in determining the selection of their first husbands, changes in women's influence over their life cycles, etc.[4] So far as I know, these issues have yet to be researched in a systematic way among the !Kung.

The Sedentary !Kung of Mahopa

As stated earlier, my fieldwork was conducted in two areas of northwestern Botswana: the /Du/da area and the !Kangwa area. The second area was the locus of research similar to that conducted on the social life of the bush-living !Kung at /Du/da. Within the !Kangwa area (about seventy miles from the /Du/da water hole) I worked at Mahopa,

---

[3]For further discussion of living density of !Kung camps, see Draper, 1973.

[4]Some of these issues are discussed by Shostak, in press.

one of several permanent water sources in the !Kangwa Valley. Around Mahopa are various settlements, of which three were the focus of my study. The three settlements were composed almost exclusively of !Kung. (Of about fifty persons living there, only one was non-!Kung — a middle-aged Tswana man married to a !Kung woman.)

The Mahopa "well" forms a small pan, or pool of standing water, in the rainy season; but in the dry season it shrinks to a muddy, clay-ringed ditch. This ditch is dug out periodically during the dry season to ensure seepage of an adequate amount of water to supply the approximately one hundred human residents of the Mahopa area and the various domestic animals owned by !Kung and non-!Kung alike. Mahopa is like other settlements of the !Kangwa area such as !Goshi, !Ubi, !Kangwa, and !Xabi in these respects: It has the only permanent water source in its immediate environs, and it hosts a mixed population of !Kung- and Bantu-speaking pastoralists of the Tswana and Herero tribes. At all of these water holes a variety of villages are found, some having non-!Kung only, some having !Kung only, some having a mixture of both.

During my fieldwork at Mahopa I deliberately avoided those villages in which !Kung and Bantu lived. I was concerned with observing the effects of sedentism on a pattern of life which I had observed in the bush. I was not directly interested in the nature of !Kung-Bantu interaction. It goes without saying that in some respects (especially goat herding and crop planting) the local pastoralists were a model for the subsistence practices of the sedentary !Kung.

The additional question — whether or not Bantu sex-role ideals influence the changes in !Kung sex roles, especially in the direction away from egalitarianism — will not be answered in this discussion. Adequate handling of this topic would require greater knowledge of (particularly) Herero social organization and the dynamics of !Kung-Bantu acculturation than I possess. It remains, however, an important research question, both for the full description of !Kung sedentarization and for understanding general factors that accompany or produce shifts in status relations between the sexes. I will confine myself here to dealing with the sedentary !Kung and some of the changes in the relations between the sexes which appear to follow from the shift from nomadism to sedentism.

The Effect of Sedentism on Sex Egalitarianism

Stated most simply, my strong impression is that the sexual egalitarianism of the bush setting is being undermined in the sedentary !Kung villages. One obvious manifestation of status inequality is that at Mahopa sex roles are more rigidly defined, and at the same time women's work is seen as "unworthy" of men. In the bush setting, although adult roles are sex-typed to some extent — particularly with respect to the exclusive male hunting, and the fact that gathering is primarily done by women — men do not lose face when they do work typically done by women, such as gathering. But in the sedentary villages of Mahopa there is definitely a feeling that it is unmanly for a man to do the jobs that should be done by women. The following example is offered as an illustration of this and of how the community brings social pressure on women (not, in this case, men) to conform.

At the largest of the three Mahopa villages lived a wife, !Uku, about sixteen years of age, and her husband /Gau, about thirty. Like many first marriages of !Kung women, this union was not happy and had not been for some time. The primary source of discontent was the wife's refusal to do the normal domestic chores expected of her. Her husband ranted publicly, claiming that she refused to collect water for their household. !Uku in those days was looking sullen; she avoided her husband and refused to sleep with him. This kind of marital standoff was not unusual among any of the !Kung I knew. !Kung brides are notorious for being labile, uncooperative, and petulant. Young husbands, though usually five to ten years older than their wives, can also be fractious and emotionally ill-equipped to make a first marriage last. !Kung have an expression which invariably crops up when one or both partners to a young marriage sabotage domestic life. They say "Debi !oa kxwia //wa," which translates literally: "Children spoil marriage."

The atypical feature of the Mahopa couple's difficulty was that the husband made a continuing issue of it. He berated his wife's behavior loudly in public and enlisted her relatives to "shame" her into good behavior, etc. Though I never observed a precisely parallel episode in the bush, my prediction is that such a husband would have grumbled quietly, shrugged his shoulders, and either collected the water himself or tried to drink the water of friends and relatives. He also might have waited until his wife complained that he never provided her with meat and then reminded her that he could not spend all day hunting and still have to supply his own water.

By the time I was living at Mahopa and knew of this marital problem, it appeared to me that the elders of the village were working harder at trying to keep the couple together than would be usual in the bush. In the bush concerned relatives will work to keep a young couple together up to a certain point, but if the individuals themselves feel mismatched, there are few, if any, arguments that will persuade them to stay together. When (as often happens) the young couple divorces, no one loses a great deal — no property of any economic weight has changed hands, etc. If both the ex-spouses (together with some of the their respective kin) go their separate ways, their departure causes no special disruption in the context of routinely shifting residence patterns.

At Mahopa there were larger political factors at work in the village that may have accounted for the pressure on the couple to get along. Both spouses were related in different ways to the most influential couple of the largest of the three villages. The wife. !Uku, was indirectly related as "niece" to the man who was spoken of as the "owner" of the village. !Uku's husband, /Gau, was the actual brother of the village "owner's" wife. This older, influential couple needed to attract stable, permanent residents to their village. They were extremely "progressive" in comparison with other !Kung of the !Kangwa area. Both had had many years of experience living in various Bantu cattle camps but were now striving to maintain a separate community of sedentary !Kung who could live by agriculture and animal husbandry. Their village needed personnel; /Gau and !Uku were, in theory, ideal recruits to the village on account of their age and kin connections.

What is important for us here is that certain influential persons had vested interests in the success of the marriage, and that the bulk of social criticism was directed at the wife, not the husband. In this sedentary situation, various persons stood to lose a good deal in the event of a divorce. From the point of view of the village "owner" and his wife, a divorce might result in both young people leaving the village. This would be undesirable for reasons already stated. From the point of view of !Uku's parents, who also lived in this village — if their daughter divorced the brother of the "land-lady," then their own welcome in the village might become jeopardized.

Although social pressure was being brought to bear on !Uku, it appeared that these pressures were not having the desired effect. !Uku's mother told me privately that she was disgusted with her daughter, that she had tried to get her to change her ways, but that !Uku was obdurate and had even used insulting language to her. !Uku at this time seemed to go out of her way to irritate her husband, had seriously offended her mother, and appeared quite regressive in her behavior. For example, although she was then sixteen years old, she spent hours each day playing dolls with three other girls, ten, nine, and seven years of age. From the bush-living groups I was well acquainted with five adolescent females (both married and unmarried, and approximately the age of !Uku), but I never observed any of them playing so continuously and with such absorption with children five or six years younger.

In the sedentary situation individuals have a different kind of commitment to the place and the persons with whom they are living. People have invested time and energy in building substantial housing, collecting a few goats, clearing and planting fields, and processing and storing the harvested food. It is not easy for an individual to leave these resources behind merely because he or she is at odds with someone else in the village. The couple just described were aware of what they had to lose; the head couple needed neighbors and village mates, not only for the purposes of economic cooperation but because they wanted the human company that would come of a stable settlement around them.

The unhappy marriage remained with no solution or even the hint of one during the time I observed it. Neither party to the marriage appeared ready to leave, so their plight festered and spread into the lives of other people in the village. It was not clear to me why the greatest criticism was leveled at the wife. At sixteen, she was at least fifteen years younger than her husband (a greater age difference than is usual for !Kung couples), and as a juvenile she may have been an easier target than her mature husband. /Gau was known for his hot temper and generaly unpredictability. The concerned parties may have felt uneasy about urging him to a compromise. Such a marriage in the bush setting would have had a different history. !Uku would have left her husband long before, in all likelihood to spend another year or two in casual flirtations before marrying again.

Childhood Practices and the Greater Separation of Adult Sex Roles

Previously I have stated that in the bush children of both sexes lead very similar lives. Girls and boys do equally little work within the village. For similar reasons both girls and boys are not encouraged to routinely accompany adults of the same sex on their respective food-getting rounds. Children sometimes accompany the women on gathering trips (particularly in the rainy season when the women do not have to carry drinking water for them), but up to about twelve years of age the children make little or no contribution to the collected food which their mothers carry home. Children do, however, pick their own food and eat it during the trek.

In the settled life children continue to have a great deal of leisure, but there is a shift in the adult attitude toward a child as a po-

71

tential or real worker.[5] Boys, for example, are expected to help with
the animal tending.[6] They do not herd the animals during the day, but
at sundown they are expected to scout the outskirts of the village and to
hasten the returning animals into their pens. In each of the three
Mahopa villages there was one boy who was primarily responsible for
herding chores. In the largest village there were other boys also available, and these youths were frequently asked to help with the herding.
Girls were not expected to help in the animal tending, and they in fact
made no regular contribution.

An important feature of the herding work of the boys was that it
regularly took them out of the village, away from adults and out on
their own. There was no comparable experience for girls. They tended
to stay in or near the village, unless they were accompanying older
women to the water hole to collect water. On such occasions they
quickly walked the mile or more to the well, where they filled their
buckets and then returned more or less promptly to the village. In
contrast, the boys drove their animals to the water and then, their work
done, they lingered at the water hole. Herero men also came to the
well, driving animals to water. Herero and Tswana women frequently
came to the well to wash clothing. !Kung boys hung around the fringes
of this scene, listening and observing. Experiences like these are no
doubt related to the superior knowledge of Bantu languages which
!Kung men exhibit in comparison to !Kung women. Such experiences
must foster for boys a better and earlier knowledge of the greater !Kung
area and a more confident spirit when moving within it — or outside of
it, for that matter.

Women and girls appear to inhabit more restricted space — that
space being largely their own village or neighboring villages. The
Mahopa women gather wild plant foods, but they do this infrequently
and forage in an area much closer to the village and for shorter intervals as compared with the bush women.

Overall, the Mahopa women seem homebound, their hands are
busier, and their time is taken up with domestic chores.[7] A number of
factors enter into this change. Under settled conditions food preparation is more complicated, although the actual diet is probably less varied in comparison with that of the foragers. Grains and squash must

---

[5]The Barry, Child, and Bacon (1957) cross-cultural study reported this as a general
attribute to societies with a high degree of accumulation of surplus.

[6]See Whiting and Whiting (1973) for a discussion of factors that affect the
development of responsibility in boys.

[7]Unfortunately, during the period of study I collected systematic information on
adult work effort only at /Du/da and not at any of the settled !Kung villages.

be brought in from the fields and set up on racks to dry. Sorghum and corn are pounded into meal; squash and melons are peeled and then boiled before eating. Women do the greatest part of the cooking, and they also do most of the drying and storing.

The material inventory of the settled villagers is richer than that of the bush-living !Kung. People have more possessions and better facilities, and all of these things require more time and energy for maintenance. Housing, for example, is more substantial than in the bush. Round, mud-walled houses with mud thatched roofs are replacing the traditional grass scherms at Mahopa. More durable structures are a response to at least two changes. Once committed to settled life, it makes sense to build better and more permanent shelters. Also, the presence of domestic animals in and near the villages means that grass houses are either protected by barricades or they are literally eaten up. Most people believe it is easier to build the mud-dung earth houses and to close them with inedible doors, rather than being continually on the lookout against stock. These structures provide better shelter, but they also require more upkeep. The women periodically resurface the interior walls and lay new floors. The men do some domestic maintenance work, but it is more likely to be fencing, roof-thatching, and other nonroutine work. It appears that the Mahopa men are becoming peripheral to their households in ways that are completely uncharacteristic of the easy integration of bush-living men into their own households. More will be said about this later.

At Mahopa the work of adult women is becoming more specialized, time-consuming, and homebound, and these women are quite willing to integrate their daughters into this work. Girls have no regular chores to compare with the herding work of some of the boys, but their mothers give them frequent small tasks such as pounding grain, carrying away a troublesome toddler, fetching earth from termite hills to be used in making mud, etc. The little girls are usually on the premises and easy targets for their mothers' commands; little boys seem to be either gone from the village (on errands already described) or else visible but distant enough from the women so that their help cannot be enlisted conveniently.

Earlier in this paper I suggested that bush-living men and women are about equally absent from their respective households, due to the similarities in the location and frequency of their work. This is less true at Mahopa. Women are in the village a great deal. The greatest part of their work takes place there, and foraging occupies only a small part of their weekly work. Mahopa men are increasingly absent from the households as their women become more consistently present. There are tasks and activities for men in the village which

73

have already been described, though they are not routine. What work the men do often takes them away from the village. They water animals, and when the goats are giving birth to kids the men who own pregnant goats check on the grazing herd during the day to make sure the newborn are not lost or rejected by the mothers. During planting season the men clear the fields and erect brush fences around the gardens to keep out the animals. Some men leave home for several days at a time to do wage work for Bantu employers living at other settlements in the !Kangwa Valley.

It is difficult to specify precisely what effect this increasing male absenteeism had on family life or relations between the sexes. The activities of the sedentary men are different not only in form but in content from those of the women. They leave home more frequently, travel more widely, and have more frequent interaction with members of other (dominant) cultural groups. In their own villages the men carry an aura of authority and sophistication that sets them apart from the women and children. For example, occasionally some incident, such as a legal case pending before the Tswana headman at !Xabi, would attract attention in the !Kangwa area. In the afternoons I often saw a group of men composed of several !Kung and one or two Hereros sitting in a shady area of one of the !Kung villages. The men would be discussing the case, carrying on the talks in a Bantu language. Women never joined these groups, and even children seemed to give these sessions a wide berth.

What these episodes conveyed to me is that at Mahopa political affairs are the concern of men, not women. Why or how women have been "eased out" (at least in comparison with the influence they had in the bush) is not clear. The /Du/da people, so long as they remained in the bush, had only rare and fleeting contacts with members of different cultural groups. If one postulates that men are the natural political agents in intergroup contacts, then the /Du/da milieu would not elicit that potential of the male role. At Mahopa three cultural groups mixed. !Kung men, as already described, were more sophisticated than the women, and on those occasions when !Kung became involved in extragroup events, the !Kung men came prominently to the fore.

Organization of Space and Privacy in the Bush Setting

To recapitulate, in the bush, village space is small, circular, open, and highly intimate. Everyone in the camp can see (and often hear) everyone else virtually all of the time, since there are no private places to which people can retire. Even at nightfall people remain in the visually open space, sleeping singly or with other family members around the fires located outside the family huts (Draper, 1973). Elsewhere (Draper, in press), I have suggested that !Kung egalitarianism and commitment to sharing are more than coincidentally associated. The intensity of social pressure, in combination with the absence of privacy, makes hoarding virtually impossible, at least for individuals who wish to remain within the group. I am suggesting that the nature of village space in the bush acts as a "lock" on other aspects of culture that are congruent but capable of sliding apart. While it is true that !Kung values oppose physical fighting and anger, ranking of individuals in terms of status, material wealth, and competition, the context in which social action occurs is such that the earliest and subtlest moves in these directions can be perceived immediately by the group. Various forms of negative reinforcement can be employed by anyone and everyone, and the effect is to discourage anti-social behaviour, whatever form it may take.

Obviously a continuous socialization process is not unique to the !Kung. All of us experience our fellows shaping our behavior throughout our lives. What I would like to stress about the !Kung is that in this small, face-to-face society it is much more difficult to compartmentalize one's motives, feeling states, and (most of all) actions. In ways not true of our life. !Kung remain in continuous communication, though they may not be directly conscious of the exchanges of information that are occurring.

The potential for continuous socialization exists among the !Kung; if it works in the ways I have suggested, it need have no single effect on sexual egalitarianism among hunter-gatherers. There is, for example, abundant literature on other band-level peoples (notably Australian aborigines), where similar technology, economy, and settlement patterns produce at least formally similar settings for social action without attendant equality in male and female statuses (A. Hamilton, 1970; Hiatt, 1970; Peterson, 1970; White, 1970; Hart and Pilling, 1960). In the !Kung case, a number of factors appear to be working directly and indirectly to ensure high autonomy of females and immunity of females to subordination by males. Several of these factors have been isolated in the foregoing discussion in an attempt to "explain" sexual egalitarianism from inside the system — to show how sexual egalitarianism is a logical outcome given the realities of the !Kung life.

Looked at from the point of view of factors outside the normative system, another argument can be made for why an egalitarian, mutual interdependence prevails among these people. The nature and distribution of the resources used by the hunting and gathering !Kung probably have indirect consequences for potential competition between and within !Kung groups. Both vegetable and animal foods are thinly and unevenly distributed over the bush. This is particularly true of the large antelope, which move erratically and seldom in the large herds that are more typical in East Africa and Arctic North America. Under conditions as these, hunting success for a particular individual depends as much on luck as it does on skill. Among the !Kung, even the best hunters readily admit that there are times when game is unavailable or when conditions do not permit the stalk-and-close approach to game required by bow-and-arrow hunting. As a result, any individual man cannot count on success, and in this context sharing of meat is an essential form of social insurance — a way of distributing food to the have-nots against the time when their fortunes change. Not surprisingly, the rules about sharing meat constitute one of the most important values in !Kung culture. My guess is that in such a system where males are continually leveled and divested of their ownership of the single most valued item (meat), the potential male competition is largely removed. The strict sharing ethic, together with the values against interpersonal aggression described earlier, are checks on male agonistic behavior that leave the field open for female autonomy and influence.[8]

Organization of Space and Privacy in the Settled Villages

In the settled villages the organization of space and the notion of privacy have undergone some interesting changes. Instead of the circular, closed settlement pattern of the bush, the settled villages typically are arranged in an open crescent; individual households have moved farther apart; and household privacy is substantially increased, particularly for those people who have acquired more material wealth. With individual houses farther apart, the pattern of social usage of the village space is different. The average distance between interactive clusters of people also increases. In the settled village different activities are more typically separated in space, as contrasted with the bush setting where it is typical to find people carrying on a conversation and/or activity while sitting back-to-back with other people who are engaged in a wholly different enterprise.

---

[8]Lee (1969) provides a fascinating description of how an anthropologist's pride in making a gift of meat to a !Kung village was deflated by the !Kung expertise in putting down boastfulness.

At the time I was living at Mahopa a few families already lived in permanent mud-walled houses and some other families were in the process of building Bantu-style rondavels to replace their smaller grass scherms. Occupants of the completed rondavels build log fences around their houses; slender logs or poles are placed upright in the ground, reaching to a height of five to six feet, and spaced one to two inches apart. These fences encircle individual households and create an inner courtyard. Obviously, privacy is increased substantially by the changed house type, settlement pattern, and fencing.

When I asked settled villagers why people erected the fences, the typical response was that it is a means of keeping domestic animals away from people's living quarters. Goats, in particular, can be a nuisance. They steal food, knock over pots, even come into houses in search of food. Their fresh dung attracts flies which are also bothersome. If domestic animals entail a new style of building, the solid, roomy houses, fences, and more linear placement of separate households also change the quality of social interaction in the villages. There are internal boundaries within the village space, which people recognize and manipulate in ways completely foreign to the bush setting. In the bush people can see each other and determine, on a variety of grounds[9], whether it is appropriate or timely to initiate social interaction. In the Mahopa villages one heard such exchanges as "So-and-so, are you at home?" and "Shall I enter [your space]?"

There are differences in material wealth among the people of the settled villages that would not be tolerated in the bush. These differences are manifest in terms of household size and elaborateness of construction, unequal ownership of domestic animals, clothing, jewelry, and food reserves. The differences are not large in an absolute sense, but in comparison with the similar material wealth of individuals in the bush, the differences are impressive. Some !Kung live simply, still using grass scherms and owning few possessions; others are better off, though the men in particular seem to avoid some kinds of ostentation. For example, the two men who were the most influential males in their villages often dressed very simply and did not have the outward appearance of "big men."[10] Yet, if invited into their houses, one would see a remarkable collection of things: clothing, dishes, blankets, bottles, trunks with locks, etc. As a guest in such a house

---

[9]My impression while working in the field was that a student of proxemics would find a wealth of material in the area of nonverbal communication among the foraging groups of !Kung.

[10]Yet the middle-aged wives of these men often wore jewelry and clothing beyond the means of other women living in the settled villages.

one could sit on the floor, lean back against the cool, sound-deadening wall, and enjoy being alone with one's host while he or she made tea and murmured small talk.

Ranking of individuals in terms of prestige and differential wealth has begun in the settled villages. Men, more than women, are defined as the managers or owners of this property. One would hear, for example, such expressions as "Kxau's [a man's name] house" or "Kxau's village." Children are most often identified as being the child of the father rather than the child of the mother. Goats are also referred to as belonging to one or another adult male, though in fact a given man's herd generally includes several animals which in fact belong to his wife or other female relatives. These expressions can be heard in the bush setting, for individual ownership exists among the foragers as well, but the "owners" referred to are as likely to be women as men. At Mahopa this linguistic custom is being replaced by one in which the adult male stands as the symbol of his domestic group. It is a linguistic shorthand, but I believe it signifies changes in the relative importance attached to each sex.

Earlier I referred to the increasing peripheralization of males in the settled villages and the opposite centripetal moving of women to the local domestic sphere. As households and possessions become private, I believe women are becoming private as well. (Perhaps this is one reason the women can afford to be ostentatious of their wealth.) In contrast bush men and women are equally "public," mobile, and visible. I believe this exposure of women is a form of protection in the bush setting. For instance, residence choices of bush-living couples are such that over time the couples live about equally (often simultaneously) with the kin of both husband and wife (Lee, in press). (At present there is not even an ideal of patrilocal residence, so far as my own interviews could establish.) This means that the wife typically has several of her own close kin nearby. These people are already on the premises and can support her interests should they conflict with the interests of her husband or his close kin. When husbands and wives argue, people are at hand to intervene if either spouse loses self-control. Wife-beating in these settings is extremely difficult to effect.

Once, during my work in Mahopa, I had a conversation with two middle-aged women who lived in the largest of the settled villages where I was camped. I often asked !Kung adults about the Herero, what they thought of them, how they perceived the differences between the groups, mainly because for reasons already stated I seldom visited the Herero settlements and knew little from direct observation about the pattern of life there. In one such conversation I asked Kxarun!a, a woman of about fifty, "Who do you think has the better life — a !Kung woman or a Herero woman?" She answered in a serious, thoughtful way, "The !Kung women are better off. Among the Herero if a man is angry with his wife he can put her in their house, bolt the door and beat her. No one can get in to separate them. They only hear her screams. When we !Kung fight, other people get in between." The other woman sitting with us agreed earnestly.

It would be unwise to attach too much significance to this remark. People are always accusing the people "over there" of various dread offenses ranging from wife-beating to much worse practices. Still, the remark chilled me and I remember deliberately not looking at the Bantu-style rondavels which were going up in the middle of the village where we sat.

In this paper I have pointed out differences in sexual egalitarianism in the hunting and gathering groups versus the settled groups of !Kung. I have discussed factors in the bush setting which favor high autonomy for females and freedom from subordination by males. Once the !Kung shift their subsistence to animal husbandry and crop planting, a number of changes occur in the area of sex roles. A major aspect of this change is the decrease in women's autonomy and influence relative to that of the men.

References

Bandura, A., Ross, D., and Ross, S.A. 1961. "The Transmission of Aggression Through Imitation of Aggressive Models." *Journal of Abnormal and Social Psychology* 63: 575-82.

Biesele, Megan. 1972. "A !Kung Bushman Folk Tale." *Botswana Notes and Records*, vol. 4. Gaborone: Botswana Society.

Brown, Judith K. 1970b. "A Note on the Division of Labor by Sex." *American Anthropologist* 72: 1073-78.

Draper, Patricia. 1973. "Crowding Among Hunter-Gatherers: The !Kung." *Science* 182: 301-303.

Draper, Patricia. In preparation. "!Kung Subsistence Work at Du/da: Variation in Adult work Effort Among the !Kung."

Gale, Fay, ed. 1970. *Woman's Role in Aboriginal Society*. Austrialian Aborigin al Studies No. 36. Canberra: Australian National Institute of Aboriginal Studies.

Hamburg, David A., and Lunde, Donald T. 1966. "Sex Hormones in the Development of Sex Differences in Behavior." In *The Development of Sex Differences*, edited by Eleanor E. Maccoby. Stanford, Calif.: Stanford University Press.

II. The Social History of Family Life

Hamilton, Annette. 1970. "The Role of Women in Aboriginal Marriage Arrangements." In *Women's Role in Aboriginal Society*. Australian Aboriginal Studies No. 36. Canberra: Australian Institute of Aboriginal Studies.

Harpending, Henry. 1972. "!Kung Hunter-Gatherer Population Structure." Ph.D. dissertation, Harvard University.

Hart, C.W.M. and Pilling, Arnold R. 1960. *The Tiwi of North Australia*. New York: Holt, Rinehart, and Winston.

Hiatt, Betty. 1970. "Woman the Gatherer." In Woman"s Role in Aboriginal Society. Australian Aboriginal Studies No. 36. Canberra: Australian Institute of Aboriginal Studies.

Howell, Nancy. "The Population of the Dobe Area !Kung." In *Kalahari Hunter-Gatherers*, edited by R.B. Lee and Irven DeVore. Cambridge, Mass.: Harvard University Press.

Kagen, Jerome, and Moss, H.A. 1962. *Culture Theory*. Englewood Cliffs, N.J.: Prentice-Hall.

Katz, Richard. "Education and Transcendence: Trance-Curing with the Zhun/wasi." In *Kalahari Hunter-Gatherers*, edited by R.B. Lee and Irven DeVore. Cambridge, Mass.: Harvard University Press.

Konner, M.J. 1972. "Maternal Care, Infant Behavior and Development Among the !Kung Bushmen." In *Kalahari Hunter-Gatherers*, edited by R.B. Lee and Irven DeVore. Cambridge, Mass.: Harvard University Press.

Landy, David. 1959. *Tropical Childhood*. Chapel Hill, N.C.: University of North Carolina Press.

Lee, R.B. "Male-Female Residence Arrangements and Political Power in Human Hunter-Gatherers." Paper presented at the workshop in "Male-Female Behavior Patterns in Primate Societies" at the IV International Congress of Primatology. To appear as a special issue of *Archives of Sexual Behavior*, edited by Jane B. Lancaster.

Lee, R.B. 1965. "Subsistence Ecology of !Kung Bushman." Ph.D. dissertation, University of California, Berkeley.

Lee, R.B. and DeVore, Irven, eds. 1968. *Man the Hunter*. Chicago: Aldine.

LeVine, Robert A., and LeVine, Barbara. 1963. "Nyansongo: A Gusii Community." In *Six Cultures*, edited by Beatrice Whiting. New York: John Wiley.

Murdock, Goorge, P. 1949. *Social Structure*. New York: The Macmillan Co.

Peterson, Nicolas. 1970. "The Importance of Women in Determining the Composition of Residential Groups in Aboriginal Australia." In *Women's Role in Aboriginal Society*. Australian Aboriginal Studies No. 36. Canberra: Australian Institute of Aboriginal Studies.

Sears, Robert; Maccoby, Eleanor E.; and Levin, Harry. 1957. *Patterns of Childbearing*. New York: Harper and Row.

Service, E.R. 1966. *The Hunters*. Englewood Cliffs, N.J.: Prentice-Hall.

Shostak, Marjorie. " A Zhun/twa Woman's Memories of Childhood." In *Kalahari Hunter-Gatherers*, edited by R.B. Lee and Irven DeVore. Cambridge, Mass.: Harvard University Press.

White, Isobel M. 1970. "Aboriginal Woman's Status: A Paradox Resolved." In *Women's Role in Aboriginal Society*. Australian Aboriginal Studies No. 36. Canberra: Australian Institute of Aboriginal Studies.

Yellen, John E. "Settlement Pattern of the !Kung: An Archeological Perspective." In *Kalahari Hunter-Gatherers*, edited by R.B. Lee and Irven DeVore. Cambridge, Mass.: Harvard University Press.

Iroquois Women: An Ethnohistoric Note*

Judith K. Brown

My purpose is to investigate the relationship between the position of
women and their economic role. At least three possibilities are suggested
in the literature. Robert H. Lowie (1961:201) felt that the two were
unrelated, that in determining women's status, economic considerations
could be "offset and even negatived" by historical factors. On the other
hand, Bronislaw Malinowski (1913) maintained that the considerable
economic contribution of Australian aborigine women confirmed their
subservient position, since their labors were extorted from them through
male "brutalization." The opposite point of view is expressed by Jenness:

> If women among the Iroquois enjoyed more privileges and
> possessed greater freedom than the women of other tribes,
> this was due...to the important place that agriculture held
> in their economic life, and the distribution of labor...[which
> left] the entire cultivation of the fields and the acquisition of
> the greater part of the food supply to the women. (1932:137)

His explanation for the high status of women among the Iroquois
stresses the extensiveness of their economic contribution. A similar
position is taken by B.H. Quain (1961), who also states that matrilineality and matrilocality contributed to the position of Iroquois
women. (Stites, 1905; Murdock, 1949; Gough, 1961; Aberle, 1961;
D'Andrade, 1966; and Ingliss, 1970, among others, have suggested that
matrilineality and matrilocality are related to the subsistence role of
women.[1])

Thus the high status enjoyed by Iroquois women has been attributed to their considerable contribution to the subsistence of the tribe,
or to this in addition to the practice of matrilineality and matrilocality.
Closer examination reveals that neither was the case. As will be shown,

---

*From *Toward an Anthropology of Women*, ed. Rayna R. Reiter. Reprinted with
permission of the Monthly Review Foundation. Copyright © 1975 by Rayna R. Reiter.
[1]For the sake of brevity, I have oversimplified the relationship these authors suggest.
Thus for example, Gough (1961) does not imply that matrilocality and matrilineality are
necessarily based on current division of labor. She notes that descent and residence
may remain unaltered under certain conditions, in spite of changes in the division of labor.

it was the control of the economic organization of the tribe by Iroquois women that accounted for their high status.

The Position of Women Among the Iroquois

Most authors have described the Iroquois as if they had been a homogeneous group (see, for example, the ratings in the Ethnographic Atlas). They will be considered as such here, since the six member nations of the Iroquois Confederacy do not appear to have differed on the variables under consideration.

A further caution must be added. The accounts giving the fullest information describe the Iroquois during the eighteenth and nineteenth centuries. Although the data will be interpreted synchronically, certain historical factors should be kept in mind. The tribe was undergoing rapid change, and its economic organization and the status of its women did not remain constant. Cara Richards (1957) has pointed out the increase in the decision-making power of Iroquois women, and John Noon (1949) has noted the increase in their economic responsibilities in the early part of the period under consideration.

In dealing with the position of women, two aspects of status must be clearly differentiated. High status may be inferred from deferential treatment. However, as defined here, high status consists of an actual position of power over basic resources and important decisions. The two need not coincide and should be considered separately (D'Andrade, 1966).[2] Among the Iroquois, women were not accorded deferential treatment. Morgan (1962:324) noted with Victorian bias that such amenities signal the advance of civilization. He observed, "The Indian regarded women as inferior, the dependent, and the servant of man, and from nurture and habit, she actually considered herself to be so." However, the position of power that Iroquois women held has been pointed out by numerous authors, such as Beauchamp (1900), Carr (1887), Goldenweiser (1912), Hewitt 1933), and Randle (1951).[3] Murdock's statement (1934:302) can be taken as a summary: "Indeed of

---

[2]There is at present no consensus on an operational definition of women's status in society. For alternative definitions, the reader is referred to Oliver, 1972; Sanday, 1973; and Sacks, this volume.

[3]Beauchamp, Carr, and Hewitt published their articles over a span of nearly fifty years, yet all describe Iroquois "matriarchy." Carr's article contains the most documentation. Hewitt's information is somewhat idiosyncratic and contains no documentation. He ends his article with a paraphrase of Lafitau's (1724) famous passage, but does not attribute it to its original source.

all the people of the earth, the Iroquois approach most closely to that hypothetical form of society known as the matriarchate."

An early, detailed, and much-cited appraisal was made by Father Joseph Lafitau of the Society of Jesus.[4] Unlike other early sources, the account is not anecdotal but descriptive. The tone of the book is scholarly, and the information it contains is based on Lafitau's five-year stay in Canada, material supplied by another missionary who worked in Canada for sixty years, and material in the Jesuit Relations. According to Lafitau:

> Nothing, however, is more real than this superiority of the women. It is of them that the nation really consists; and it is through them that the nobility of the blood, the genealogical tree and the families are perpetuated. All real authority is vested in them. The land, the fields and their harvest all belong to them. They are the souls of the Councils, the arbiters of peace and of war. They have charge of the public treasury. To them are given the slaves. They arrange marriages. The children are their domain, and it is through their blood that the order of succession is transmitted. The men, on the other hand, are entirely isolated.... Their children are strangers to them. (1724:I:66-67; my translation).

This passage must be interpreted with caution. Lafitau does not specify in these often-quoted lines exactly which "Ameriquains" he is describing. It may be the Iroquois, the Huron, or both. The particular section from which this quotation is taken attempts to establish similarities between tribal customs and those of antiquity (foreshadowing much of late-nineteenth-century anthropology). Moreover, a number of the unusual powers enumerated were not vested in all Iroquois women, but only in the matrons, the elderly heads of households and work groups. However, such a position was achieved and could be aspired to by all women, as Martha Randle has noted. Unfortunately, there is no detailed description of how matrons were chosen. William Fenton's statement (1957:31), "the mild person who speaks easily and kindly succeeds to public roles which the women withhold from the over-anxious person," suggests that women made the selection on the basis of

---

[4]Lafitau's charmingly illustrated four-volume work carries the inscription "avec approbation et privilège du Roy," but no doubt helped to promote the revolutionary idea of the noble savage (Fenton, 1969).

personality traits. However, the author does not specify the sex of the would-be office holder. (Also see Quain, 1961:257.)

The evidence for statements such as those of Murdock and Lafitau must be evaluated by examining the role of Iroquois women in the political, the religious, and the domestic life of the tribe. In the political sphere, Iroquois matrons had the power to raise and depose the ruling elders, the ability to influence the decisions of the Council, and occasional power over the conduct of war and the establishment of treaties. Although women could not serve on the Council of Elders, the highest ruling body of the League, the hereditary eligibility for office was also largely controlled by them. Alexander Goldenweiser (1912:468) gives a retrospective account of the power of the matrons to raise and depose the ruling elders (whom he called chiefs):

> When a chief died, the women of his tribe and clan held a meeting at which a candidate for the vacant place was decided upon. A woman delegate carried the news to the chiefs of the clans which belonged to the "side" of the deceased chief's clan. They had the power to veto the selection, in which case another women's meeting was called and another candidate selected....

The actions of the new elder were closely watched, and if his behavior deviated from the accepted norms, he was warned by the woman delegate. If after several warnings he still did not conform, she would initiate impeachment proceedings.

It is surprising that Lewis Morgan, whose *League of the Ho-De'-No-Sau-Nee, Iroquois* stands as a classic to this day, should have taken no particular note of the political power of the Iroquois matrons. His account of the raising of the elders in *Ancient Society* (1963) differs in some details from the account given by Goldenweiser. Speaking of the election, he states, "Each person of adult age was called upon to express his or her preference" (ibid:72; italics mine). The right to depose "was reserved by members of the gens" (ibid.:73). Thus Morgan's observations do not contradict the fact that the matrons had a voice in these important matters. But for some reasons, he did not find this remarkable or did not choose to comment upon it. However, in a later work, Morgan (1965:66) quotes from a letter written by the Reverend Ashur Wright (who had been a missionary among the Iroquois for forty years) as follows:

> The women were the great power among the clans, as everywhere else. They did not hesitate, when occasion required, to "knock off the horns," as it was technically called,

from the head of a chief and send him back to the ranks of the warriors. The original nomination of the chiefs also always rested with them.[5]

Morgan's next paragraph begins, "The mother-right and gynecocracy among the Iroquois here plainly indicated is not overdrawn." He ends his paragraph with a footnote to Bachofen. It is therefore surprising when sixty-odd pages later he states:

> But this influence of the woman did not reach outward to the affairs of the gens, phratry, or tribe, but seems to have commenced and ended with the household. This view is quite consistent with the life of patient drudgery and of general subordination to the husband which the Iroquois wife cheerfully accepted as the portion of her sex. (Ibid.:128)

In his earlier work, however, Morgan (1962) noted that women had the power of life or death over prisoners of war, which must certainly be regarded as an influence reaching beyond the household. Furthermore, the women could participate in the deliberations of the Council through their male speakers, such as the Council of 1791 (Snyderman, 1951), the Council of 1804 (Beauchamp, 1900), and the Council of 1839 (Parker, 1916), and had a voice concerning warfare and treaties. Schoolcraft (1860:III:195-96) sums up these powers as follows:

> They are the only tribes in America, north and south, so far as we have any accounts, who gave to woman a conservative power in their political deliberations. The Iroquois matrons had their representative in the public councils; and they exercised a negative, or what we call a veto power, in the important question of the declaration of war. They had the right also to interpose in bringing about a peace.

It appears from the evidence (some of it Morgan's) that the political influence of the Iroquois matron was considerable. The nation was not a matriarchy, as claimed by some, but the matrons were an *éminence grise*. In this respect the Iroquois were probably not unique. What is unusual is the fact that this power was socially recognized and institutionalized.

---

[5]The letter was written in May 1879 and appears in its entirety in Stern, 1933. Another interpretation by Wright of the "knocking off of horns" appears in Fenton, ed., 1957.

II. The Social History of Family Life

In addition, Iroquois matrons helped to select the religious practitioners of the tribe. Half of these "keepers of the faith" were women and, according to Morgan (1962:186), "They had an equal voice in the general management of the festivals and of all their religious concernments." As Randle and Quain have pointed out, women's activities were celebrated in the ceremonial cycle, and female virtues of food-providing, cooperativeness, and natural fertility were respected and revered. Women might become clairvoyants or could join medicine societies; for several of the latter, women were managing officers (Quain, 1961).

Kin-group membership was transmitted through the mother, and since there were rules of exogamy, the father belonged to a kinship group other than that of his wife and children. Morgan (1962:84; 326-27) describes the rules of inheritance and succession as follows:

> Not least remarkable among their institutions, was that which confined transmission of all titles, rights and property in the female line to the exclusion of the male....
>
> If the wife, either before or after marriage, inherited orchards, or planting lots, or reduced land to cultivation, she could dispose of them at her pleasure, and in case of her death, they were inherited, together with her other effects, by her children.

Marriages were arranged by the mothers of the prospective couple, and they also took responsibility for the success of the union thus created. Both marriage and divorce involved little ceremony. The latter could be instigated by either the wife or the husband. In the case of a separation, the children usually remained with the mother (ibid.). Arthur Parker (1926) mentions that spacing the births of children was in the hands of the mother and there was greater delight at the birth of a daughter than at that of a son (Stites, 1905). The mother often had the power to confer a name on her child (Goldenweiser, 1912; 1914). Furthermore, Quain (1961:258) notes that "the women of the maternal line chose the child successors to a series of names which might culminate in high administrative titles of community or nation."

Crucial in consolidating the power of the women was the family longhouse. Traditionally this was a large structure of bark and wood containing many compartments and several fires, all connected by a central aisle. Each family occupied a compartment and shared a fire with several other families (Bartram, 1895:40-41). Rev. Wright is quoted by Morgan (1965:65-66) concerning the domestic arrangements of the tribe:

As to their family system, when occupying the old long-houses, it is probable that some one clan predominated, the women taking husbands, however, from the other clans; and sometimes, for a novelty, some of their sons bringing in their young wives until they felt brave enough to leave their mothers. Usually, the female portion ruled the house, and were doubtless clannish enough about it. The stores were in common; but woe to the luckless husband or lover who was too shiftless to do his share of the providing. No matter how many children, or whatever goods he might have in the house, he might at any time be ordered to pick up his blanket and budge; and after such an order it would not be healthful for him to disobey; the house would be too hot for him; and unless saved by the intercession of some aunt or grandmother, he must retreat to his own clan, or as was often done, go and start a new matrimonial alliance.

Two features of Iroquois domestic life deserve special mention. First, as noted by Murdock (1934), the authority over the household resided in the matron and not in one of her male relatives. Audrey Richards (1950) has identified as the "matrilineal puzzle" the reconciliation of matrilineal descent with the rule of exogamy, the reconciliation of descent traced through women with authority vested in men. The Iroquois suggest yet another solution to the domestic aspect of this dilemma. Authority over the household was not given to the matron's husband nor to her brother, but was exercised by the woman herself.

Second, as Randle has pointed out, the longhouse was the analogy on which the League was built. The Iroquois referred to themselves as the people of the longhouse. The figurative longhouse of the League was divided into geographical compartments, each occupied by a tribe. It is probable that this analogy helped to consolidate the considerable political power of the Iroquois matrons.

In sum, Iroquois matrons enjoyed unusual authority in their society, perhaps more than women have ever enjoyed anywhere at any time. The position of matron was open to all women who qualified. The matrons were socially recognized and institutionalized powers behind the throne (though one can hardly term the supremely democratic Council of Elders as a "throne"). Women were able to serve as religious practitioners, and the matrons helped to select all "keepers of the faith." Finally, the matron ruled supreme within the longhouse, and domestic arrangements were such that all women had dominant power within the household.

II. The Social History of Family Life

The Economic Organization of Subsistence Activities

Agricultural activities. The Iroquois supplemented cultivated foods with food gathered by the women, with meat hunted by the men (although women occasionally joined hunting expeditions), and with fish obtained by both men and women. However, the tribe depended upon shifting cultivation for the major portion of its food supply. Agricultural activity consisted of four stages: clearing the ground, planting, cultivating, and harvesting.

Men were in charge of preparing the fields, although Waugh and Quain claim that the women helped. Trees were girdled and allowed to die. The following spring, the underbrush was burned off (Parker, 1910). Planting and cultivating were conducted by the women in organized work groups. Elderly men occasionally helped, but for other men to do this work was considered demeaning. As Sara Stites has pointed out, the warrior in the field was always an assistant, never an owner or director. Men did join in the harvest, although this was occasionally done by women alone. Husking of the corn was a festive occasion, usually joined by the men. The work would be followed by a special meal and by singing and dancing.

Mary Jemison,[6] a white woman adopted into the Seneca tribe, offers a full description of the activities of the women's work group:

> Our labor was not severe; and that of one year was exactly similar in almost every respect to that of the others.... Notwithstanding the Indian women have all the fuel and bread to procure, and the cooking to perform, their task is probably not harder than that of white women, who have those articles provided for them; and their cares certainly are not half as numerous, not as great. In the summer

---

[6]Life of Mary Jemison: Deh-he-wa-mis was originally published in 1824 when Mary Jemison was about eighty. The book, written by James Seaver, is supposed to present her narrative, but it is written in a style that can hardly have been the idiom of a woman who spent most of her life as a Seneca. As it is the only source of its kind, it is quoted here. The edition used is that published in 1880 and contains chapters by a number of later authors. By 1924 the book had gone through twenty-two editions at the hands of four revisers, one of whom was Lewis Morgan. Any edition of the book is difficult to obtain today, even the 1961 paperback edition. Milliken (1924:87) writes of the first edition: "Published before the day of the dime novel, at a time when tales of adventure and romance were much less common than now and the thrillers of the silver screen were entirely unknown, it was circulated and read almost to complete destruction."

season, we planted, tended, and harvested our corn, and generally had all of our children with us; but had no master to oversee or drive us, so that we could work as leisurely as we pleased....

We pursued our farming business according to the general custom of Indian women, which is as follows: In order to expedite their business, and at the same time enjoy each other's company, they all work together in one field, or at whatever job they may have on hand. In the spring, they choose an old active squaw to be their driver and overseer, when at labor, for the ensuing year. She accepts the honor, and they consider themselves bound to obey her.

When the time for planting arrives, and the soil is prepared, the squaws are assembled in the morning, and conducted into a field, where each plants one row. [Note: The seeds were first soaked, and then planted in prepared hills.]

They then go into the next field and plant once across, and so on till they have gone through the tribe. If any remains to be planted, they again commence where they did at first, (in the same field,) and so keep on till the whole is finished. By this rule, they perform their labor of every kind, and every jealousy of one having done more or less than another is effectually avoided. (Seaver, 1880:69-71; see also Parker, 1910, and the footnote by Cornplanter in Quain, 1961:250).)

Loskiel (1794:part 1:16) emphasizes the toil of the women, adding, "Nothing but hunger and want can rouse the men from their drowsiness, and give them activity." Parker (1910) tends to agree with Mary Jemison that the work of the women was not hard.

The economic organization of the Iroquois was remarkable (and far from unique), for the great separateness of the sexes which it fostered.* [*This separateness of the sexes applied also to the child-rearing methods of the tribe.] In the words of Morgan (ibid.:325), "The care of their infancy and childhood was entrusted to the watchful affection of the mothers alone." This must have afforded the growing girl a reassuring continuity, but it contained inherent problems for the young boy. Men were often away on war parties for years at a time. Although wives or temporary wives, appointed especially for the purpose, occasionally accompanied men on the hunt, it wa was more usual for this to be a male pursuit. Even at the daily meal the sexes ate separately. It is no wonder that Morgan wrote:

II. The Social History of Family Life

Indian habits and modes of life divided the people socially into two great classes, male and female. The male sought the conversation and society of the male, and they went forth together for amusement, or for the severer duties of life. In the same manner the female sought the companionship of her own sex. Between the sexes there was but little sociality, as this term is understood in polished society. (1962:323)

Factors of production. In agricultural production, land constitutes the natural resource, seeds constitute the raw materials, and agricultural implements constitute the tools. The ownership of these factors of production — the land, the seeds, and the implements — among the Iroquois is difficult to establish from existing evidence. Goldenweiser (1912:469) offers the following information: "The husband, in ancient times, could regard as his own only his weapons, tools, and wearing apparel, his wife owned the objects of the household, the house itself, and the land."

It is also not entirely clear who owned the land. The importance of the fields can be deduced from the fact that village sites were chosen largely for the fertility of the surrounding land. As Randle has pointed out, these sites were changed as land became depleted, and not when an area had been hunted out. The extent of the cornfields can be estimated from the various accounts of their destruction at the hands of white war parties. In one such foray mentioned by Stites, it took the French forces about a week to destroy the fields of four Iroquois villages.

Morgan (1965) stressed that land was communally owned and that its individual ownership was unknown. Snyderman (1951) mentions the belief that land belonged to future generations as well as to the present generation. However, according to Randle, land was often registered in female names. Hewitt states that women owned the lands, the village sites, and the burial grounds. Nominal female ownership is indicated in the following statement by Red Jacket, speaker for the women at the Council of 1791: "You ought to hear and listen to what we women shall speak...for we are the owners of the land and it is ours" (Snyderman, 1951:20). In short, the lands of the Iroquois appear to have been communally owned, but held by the women.

The food produced. A great variety of corn was raised. Frank Speck (1945) estimates from fifteen to seventeen varieties, and it was prepared in numerous ways. Murdock (1834) suggests as many as fifty. Even the husks, silk, cobs, and leaves were used to make a number of useful articles (Parker, 1910). Beans were also a popular food — Speck

92

estimates that there were sixty varieties — as were squashes, of which there were eight varieties, according to Speck. All three of these foods were provided by the women and held in high esteem by the Iroquois. The foods were represented in their pantheon as "The Three Sisters," "Our Life," and "Our Supporters" (Morgan, 1962).

These staples were supplemented by foods gathered by the women — maple sugar, berries, wild fruit, nuts, roots, mushrooms, leaf foods — and by other cultivated foods, such as melons. Schoolcraft (1847) referred to the apple as "the Iroquois banana." The fruit was one of several introduced by the Dutch and the French. According to Parker (1910:94), during the Revolutionary War "General Sullivan in his famous raid against the hostile Iroquois cut down a single orchard of 1500 trees." Thus an impressive commissariat was supplied by the women of the tribe. The diet of the Iroquois was ample, varied, and nutritious. One is forced to agree with Morgan (1962), who considered the indigenous diet of the Iroquois far superior to that typical of the Europeans of pre-contact times.

Distributing and dispensing food. The generous hospitality that was customary among the Iroquois was probably the most salient feature of their food distribution. The rule of hospitality was perpetuated and its protocol codified by Handsome Lake, the early nineteenth-century prophet (Parker, 1913). Hospitality was extended to all strangers, and the stranger was to be fed before he was questioned about his mission (Lafitau, 1724). Hospitality was also extended to other members of the village, to the extent that no one went hungry (Parker, 1910). It is of interest to note Morgan's (1962:329) comment: "It [hospitality] rested chiefly upon the industry, and therefore upon the natural kindness of the Indian women." This statement demonstrates that the hospitality of the household reflected favorably on its women, not on its men. Furthermore, hospitality was motivated by generosity, which was valued in and of itself (Fenton, 1957).

There is conflicting evidence concerning the distribution of the fruit of the chase. Beauchamp says that the meat was given to the hunter's wife. Carr claims it was given to the hunter's mother-in-law. Lafitau mentions that the legitimate wife had a prior claim to that of the temporary hunting wife. (The Iroquois were not rigidly monogamous.) Hunting expeditions often lasted as long as a year, and if the hunter's wife refused to go, a special temporary wife might accompany him instead.

Stites cites one *Jesuit Relations* to the effect that one of the women's chief winter tasks was to go into the forest to bring home the deer their husbands had slain. Citing a different *Jesuit Relation*, however, she states that women were sometimes not given a share of the meat at all.[7] Wright, quoted by Morgan (1965), seems to suggest that the meat was contributed by the hunter to his wife's household. Morgan (ibid.:127) makes a similar statement himself, and this is probably the most correct description.

Thus the distribution of the food of the tribe, even the food procured by the men, appears to have been at the discretion of the matrons. By observing the rules of hospitality, the matrons made it possible for every member of the tribe and for visitors to obtain a share of the food supply.

The dispensing of food within the household also rested with the matrons. As Morgan (1962:327) observed, "The care of the appetite was left entirely with the women, as the Indian never asked for food." No author mentions any specified obligations which the matrons had to meet in performing this task.

The Iroquois had one meal a day, which was served in the morning. Lafitau (1724:III:79-80) offers a description of this meal. Morgan's (1965:65) later description is as follows:

> Every household was organized under a matron who supervised the domestic economy. After a single daily meal was cooked at the several fires the matron was summoned, and it was her duty to divide the food, from the kettle, to the several families according to their respective needs. What remained was placed in the custody of another person until it was required by the matron.... It shows that their domestic economy was not without method, and it displays the care and management of woman.

It was not only in the domestic realm that the matrons controlled the dispensing of food. By supplying the essential provisions for male activities — the hunt, the warpath, and the Council — they were able to control these to some degree. Thus Randle (1951:172) writes, "Indirectly, too, it stated that the women could hinder or actually prevent a war party which lacked their approval by not giving the supplies of dried corn and the moccasins which the warriors required."

Stites (1905:78) makes a similar assertion: "They also had control of the cultivated land and its produce, and gave support to the warriors only in return for their military services." This control was effected by

---

[7]This discrepancy demonstrates one of the difficulties in using the *Jesuit Relations*. The *Relations* cover an extended period of time and are anecdotal rather than descriptive. They are the work of many authors, whose prime purpose was to describe not the customs they found but their own missionary activities.

the monopoly that the matrons exercised on the staple food used on both the hunt and the warpath. According to Morgan (1962), this food was prepared while the warriors performed their dance. He gives the recipe for the dried corn-maple syrup provision (see also Bartram, 1895:71), and concludes, "The warrior could carry without inconvenience in his bear-skin pocket a sufficient supply for a long and perilous expedition" (Morgan, 1962:340). Further on he states, "This [the same recipe] was carried in the bear-skin pocket of the hunter, and upon it alone he subsisted for days together" (ibid.:373).

The importance of these provisions was also mentioned by Loskiel, who observed that hunting was not possible on the warpath for fear of giving warning to the enemy. He also describes the importance of the food provided by the matrons for the Council: "Provisions must always be in plenty in the council-house; for eating and deliberating take their turns" (1794:part 1:134; also see Bartram, 1895:58-63).

Iroquois women were in charge of the ingenious methods of preserving and storing the abundant food supplies. Corn, meat, fish, berries, squashes, and even fats were preserved. Some of these foods were buried in specially constructed pits, and some were kept in the longhouse. Stored food constituted one of the major forms of wealth of the tribe. Stites (1905:72) claims, "It was the women's organization which controlled the surplus and represented the owning class." Hewitt describes a tribal public treasury which contained wampum belts, quill and feather work, furs, and assorted stored foods. Its contents were scrupulously guarded by the matrons.

In sum, among the Iroquois, the distribution of food within the tribe was the responsibility of the matrons. They also controlled the provisions within the household, as well as those that made the major male activities possible. Some authors claim that the matrons also controlled the wealth of the tribe (much of it in stored food).

Summary

Iroquois women controlled the factors of agricultural production, for they had a right in the land which they cultivated, and in the implements and the seeds. Iroquois agricultural activities, which yielded bountiful harvests, were highly organized under elected female leadership. Most important, Iroquois women maintained the right to distribute and dispense all food, even that procured by men. This was especially significant, as stored food constituted one of the major forms of wealth for the tribe. Through their control of the economic organization of the tribe, Iroquois matrons were able to make available or withhold food for

II. The Social History of Family Life

meetings of the Council and for war parties, for the observance of religious festivals and for the daily meals of the household. These economic realities were institutionalized in the matrons' power to nominate Council Elders and to influence Council decisions. They had a voice in the conduct of war and the establishment of treaties. They elected "keepers of the faith" and served in that capacity. They controlled life in the longhouse.

The unusual role of Iroquois women in politics, religion, and domestic life cannot be dismissed simply as a historical curiosity. It cannot be explained by Iroquois kinship structure, nor can it be attributed to the size of the women's contribution to Iroquois subsistence. The powerful position of Iroquois women was the result of their control of the economic organization of their tribe.

References

_____. 1913. The Code of Handsome Lake, the Seneca Prophet. New York State Museum Bulletin 163. Albany: University of the State of New York.

_____. 1916. The Constitution of the Five Nations. New York State Museum Bulletin 184. Albany: University of the State of New York.

_____ 1847. *Notes on the Iroquois, or, Contributions to American History, Antiquities and General Ethnology.* Albany: Erastus H. Pease & Co.

_____. 1949. *Social Structure.* New York: The Macmillan Co.

_____. 1965. *Houses and House-Life of the American Aborigines.* Chicago: Chicago University Press.

Aberle, David F. 1961. "Matrilineal Descent in Cross-cultural Perspective." In *Matrilineal Kinship*, edited by David M. Schneider and Kathleen Gough. Berkeley: University of Califortnia Press.

Bartram, John. 1895. *Observations on the Inhabitants, Climate, Soil, Rivers, Productions, Animals, and Other Matters Worthy of Notice.* Reprint ed.: Geneva: W.F. Humphrey.

Beauchamp, William M. 1900. "Iroquois Women." *Journal of American Folk-Lore* 13 (April-June): 81-91.

Carr, Lucien. 1887. "On the Social and Political Position of women Among the Huron-Iroquois Tribes." Annual Report of the Trustees of the Peabody Museum of American Archaeology and Ethnology 3: 207-32.

D'Andrade, Roy G. 1966. "Sex Differences and Cultural Institutions." In *The Development of Sex Differences*, edited by Eleanor Maccoby. Stanford, Calif.: Stanford University Press.

Fenton, William N. 1957. "Long-term Trends of Change Among the Iroquois," Proceedings of the 1957 Annual Spring Meetings of the American Ethnological Society. Seattle.

Goldenweiser, Alexander A. 1912. "On Iroquois Work, 1912." *Summary Report of the Geological Survey of Canada*, Anthropology Division, sessional paper 26, pp. 464-75. Ottawa: Government Printing Bureau.

Gough, Kathleen. 1961. "The Modern Disintegration of Matrilineal Descent Groups." In *Matrilineal Kinship*, edited by David M. Schneider and Kathleen Gough. Berkeley: University of Califortnia Press.

Hewitt, John N.B. 1933. "Status of Women in Iroquois Policy Before 1784." *Annual Report of the Board of Regents of the Smithsonian Institution for 1932*, pp. 475-88. Washington: U.S. Government Printing Office.

Ingliss, Gordon. 1970. "Northwest American Matriliny: The Problem of Origins." *Ethnology* 9 (April): 149-59.

Lafitau, Joseph F. 1724. *Moeurs des sauvages ameriquains comparées aux moeurs des premiers temps*. 4 vols. Paris: Saugrain l'ainé.

Loskiel, George H. 1794. *History of the Mission of the United Brethren Among the Indians in North America*. Translated by Christian LaTrobe. London: The Brethren Society for the Furtherance of the Gospel.

Lowie, Robert H. 1961. *Primitive Society*. New York: Harper.

Malinowski, Bronislaw. 1913. *The Family Among the Australian Aborigines*. London: University of London Press.

Morgan, Lewis H. 1962. *League of the Iroquois*. New York: Corinth Books.

Murdock, George P. 1934. *Our Primitive Contemporaries*. New York: The Macmillan Co.

Noon, John A. 1949. *Law and Government of the Grand River Iroquois*. Viking Fund Publications in Anthropology 12. New York: Viking Fund.

Parker, Arthur C. 1910. *Iroquois Uses of Maize and Other Food Plants*. New York State Museum Bulletin 144. Albany: University of the State of New York.

Quain, B.H. 1961. "The Iroquois." In *Cooperation and Competition among Primitive Peoples*, edited by Margaret Mead. Boston: Beacon Press.

Randle, Martha C. 1951. *Iroquois Women, Then and Now*. Bulletin of the Bureau of American Ethnology 149: 167-80. Washington.

Richards, Audrey I. 1950. "Some Types of Family Structure Amongst the Central Bantu." In *African Systems of Kinship and Marriage*, edited by A.R. Radcliffe-Brown and Daryll Forde. New York: Oxford University Press.

II. The Social History of Family Life

Richards, Cara B. 1957. "Matriarchy or Mistake: The Role of Iroquois Women Through Time." Proceedings of the 1957 Annual Spring Meeting of the American Ethnological Society, pp. 36-45. Seattle.

Schoolcraft, Henry R.1860. *Archives of Aboriginal Knowledge*. 6 vols. Philadelphia: J.B. Lippincott & Co.

Snyderman, George S. 19512. "Concepts of Land Ownership Among the Iroquois and Their Neighbors." *Bulletin of the Bureau of American Ethnology* 149: 13-34.

Speck, Frank G. 1945. "The Iroquois, a Study in Cultural Evolution." *Bulletin of the Cranbook Institute of Science* 23 (Bloomfield Hills, Michigan).

Stites, Sara H. 1905. *Economics of the Iroquois*. Bryn Mawr College Monographs 1, no. 3.

The Material Context and the Ritual of Married Life*

Jean-Louis Flandrin

The castle and the cottage have left on the European landscape the imprint of the contrast between large and small households. Is it possible, in the same way, to rediscover the characteristics of family life in former times on the basis of what is known of the material environment? Evidence regarding the material life of our forefathers is, indeed, not lacking. We have the remains of the buildings of former times (particularly of the most beautiful, it is true, and of their external architecture rather than of their interior appointments); furniture and utensils preserved in our museums; paintings and interiors (unfortunately less plentiful and less realistic in France and England than in the Low Countries); inventories compiled after death containing detailed descriptions of the material context of the life of the deceased person; the mention, in some marriage contracts, of items of the bride's trousseau; and, finally, fleeting yet irreplaceable observations in the memoirs and novels of the period.

Interior architecture

First of all, let us attempt to summarize the excellent observations already made on this subject by Philippe Aries.[1] Both in the palaces and in the hovels, undifferentiation was formerly very much greater than today, and this hindered the development of modern family feeling. The poor were so uncomfortable in their own homes that they lived elsewhere as often as they could, and parents parted company with their offspring when the latter reached adolescence, sending them to work in someone else's house. As for the rich, their vast residences were crowded with domestic servants and visitors, which prevented them from living in privacy with their wives and children.

The changes in the internal organization of the great houses of the nobility or the bourgeoisie, which occurred in the course of the

[1]Philippe Aries, *L'Enfant et la vie familiale sous l'Ancien Régime* (Paris, 1973), pp. 441-61, and, for the iconography of family life, pp. 377-407.

eighteenth century, provide evidence of a quest for comfort and privacy. In the seventeenth century there were still large rooms, with no precisely defined functions, opening onto each other: people slept, ate and lived in them amid the coming and going of servants, children and visitors, the servants not hesitating any more than the children to take part in the conversation of their masters and the latter's friends, if one is to believe the evidence of the *Caquets de l'Accouchée*[2] or the comedies of Molière. At night, the servants slept near their masters, often in the same room, ready to answer their summons. At all times, privacy was unknown; each person, according to Philippe Ariès, lived 'in state' as at the Court of Versailles. In the eighteenth century, however, corridors were introduced and had the effect of giving autonomy to the rooms, which became specialized, more numerous and individual. The ladies, during the day, could shut themselves up in their boudoirs, or receive their close friends in small drawing-rooms. The servants were driven back to the kitchen, the servants' hall and the antechambers, and attempts were made to prevent the children from being too familiar with them. Within the confines of the great households, the modern 'family' began to achieve its independence.

After describing this development in broad outline, we must turn to the analysis of behaviour and the chronology of its evolution. Let us consider an anecdote reported by Longchamp, who was secretary to Voltaire after being *valet de chambre* of the Marquise du Châtelet.[3]

He tells us of the embarrassment that he felt when the Marquise stripped naked in front of him before getting into the bathtub and, in contrast to this, the unconcerned tone in which she had reproved him for his lack of attentiveness and his clumsiness when sprinkling her with the hot water. This certainly proves that, despite the greater privacy made possible by eighteenth-century interior architecture, some traditional customs took a long time to disappear. But how had these habits actually developed? Most of the commentators of Longchamp's account emphasize the contempt which such scenes implied on the part of the aristocrats — even those who were closest in outlook to the *philosophes* — towards those demi-men such as servants and others of the common people.[4] This, perhaps, became true in the eighteenth century; but was it also contempt for those who were present at his

---

[2]Les Caquets de l'accouchée (Paris, 1890); see, for example, pp. 14-15.

[3]S.G. Longchamp and Wagnière, *Mémoires sur Voltaire* (2 vols., Paris, 1826), vol. II, pp. 119ff., quoted in Franklin, *La Vie privée d'autrefois*, abridged edn. (Paris, 1973), p. 234.

[4]Norbert Elias, *La Société de cour* (Paris, 1974), p. 25, n. 1.

getting up, at his going to bed, and at his sessions on the lavatory-seat, that explains this kind of exhibitionism on the part of Louis XIV and of most of the other sovereigns? The reasons might simply be that Louis XIV on his lavatory-seat and Madame du Châtelet in her bath were not ashamed to carry out, in accordance with the ceremonial appropriate to their social status, the ordinary acts of human nature. When Philippe Ariès emphasizes the life 'in state' which was that of all the great nobles, he does so to contrast it with a need for privacy which cannot be proved to have existed before the eighteenth century, or with a sense of modesty which one might describe as neurotic had it become, in the eighteenth and nineteenth centuries, normal social behaviour.

It is still not known exactly how and why this need for privacy developed. One can, however, discern two elements which, directly or indirectly, are derived from the distrustful severity of the moralists of the Catholic Reformation and, indeed, the Protestant one. The communal living of earlier times had been accompanied by extremely rigorous sexual taboos: incest, adultery within the household, and the seduction of the girls of the house were punishable by death. The judicial records of the sixteenth and seventeenth centuries provide abundant evidence of this.[5] They also bear witness to the fact that, despite the rigour of the prohibitions, there were still dangers, which the militant Catholic reformers exerted themselves in trying to avert: not only did it become indecent to show oneself naked in front of the servants, but it became indecent to be in the nude by oneself, because nudity, even in solitude, involved the risk of inducing one to sin. Marie-Antoinette, brought up in accordance with these strict principles, avoided the immodesty of Madame du Châtelet not by bathing without witnesses, but by taking her bath dressed in a long flannel robe buttoned up to the neck. Moreover, while her two bath-attendants were helping her to get out of the bath, she insisted on a sheet being held in front of her to hide her from her women servants.[6] It was also Christian morality of the seventeenth century which multiplied the warnings against the bad influence on the children that might result from excessive familiarity with the servants. Finally, even though it was not possible to dissuade the masters of households and their grown-up sons from indulging in ancillary love-affairs, it became obligatory, on pain of public scandal

---

[5]Françoise Janihn, 'Crimes et délits sexuels dans l'ancien droit français, XVIe-XVIIIe siècles', unpublished M.A. thesis (University of Paris I, 1973), e.g. pp. 53-7.
[6]Mme. de Campan, *Mémoires* (3 vols., Paris, 1822), vol. I, ch. IV, p. 104, quoted in Franklin, p. 234.

and excommunication, to expel servant-girls from the house as soon as they became pregnant. This was one more way of keeping them in their place.

The desire of privacy seems to have been, at first, a reaction on the part of the libertines against the severity of this morality. It appears to have begun towards the end of Louis XIV's reign, when this moral code had become stifling, and it was a manifestation of the desire to lead a free life in a society extremely sensitive to scandal. Even after he had attained power, Philippe d'Orléans could not permit himself to do in public what he had been accustomed to doing on the occasion of his small intimate suppers. It was not until later, in the second half of the eighteenth century, that this desire for privacy came to be associated with the bourgeois joys of family life or the pastoral scenes of the Trianon. Before the triumph of the Catholic reforms, Henri VI had had no need to conceal himself in order to play with his children, legitimate or otherwise.

In the case of the popular sectors, it was the smallness of the dwellings that forced people into a communal life-style which to us appears intolerable, and their lack of comfort probably discouraged family reunions.[7] This, of course, is still the case in part of our western societies — from the shantytowns of Nanterre to the Harlem ghetto — to say nothing of the rest of the world. In the lowest levels of society, the history of family life corresponds to that of the standard of living, whereas among the elites, even as regards the most material aspects, it is a part of the history of culture. It is not, therefore, only because of the details revealed in historical documents that Philippe Ariès has described noble and bourgeois houses at greater length than popular ones: the principal reason is the decisive role played by the nobility and the bourgeoisie in the origin of our sentiments involving the family. Let us attempt, however, from the less genetic perspective that we are employing in this study, to imagine the domestic life of the masses in former times on the basis of what is known today about their material environment.

We are, in fact, beginning to acquire a more detailed knowledge of their habitat. In Lyons, in the eighteenth century,[8] nearly half the dwellings of craftsmen and workers had only one room. For example, Philippe Chalumeau, a journeyman-mason who died in 1780, lived in

---

[7]This idea has already been put forward by Ariès, pp. 443, 457-8, and by Bouchard, p. 236.

[8]Maurice Garden, *Lyon et les Lyonnais au XVIIIe siècle* (Paris, 1970), pp. 405-22, particularly p. 408.

one room which contained a bed and three couches. His widow explained to those who were compiling the inventory that these couches were let by the month to three journeymen-carpenters. Another example was that of François Gaillard, a master-tailor, who lived with his wife and two young children in a 'room' in which, at his death, there were his tailor's work-table, some shelves, a chest of drawers for his wife's clothes — he himself wore, according to her account, those of his customers — and a loft containing a bed and two couches. Such scantiness of furnishings was comparatively rare in the case of the master-craftsmen having their shops on the ground floor, but frequent among the workers living in the upper storeys. The silk-workers and most of the craftsmen of Lyons lived in two rooms, one being predominantly devoted to their occupation, and the other being used for living in and cooking. Often the shop, or the room devoted to the trade, included a loft where the beds were stowed away. Studies of Coutances,[9] Aix[10] and Marseilles[11] confirm the evidence obtained in the case of Lyons: the overwhelming majority of urban house-holds in the seventeenth and eighteenth centuries had only one or two rooms for accommodation and professional activities. In such material conditions, it was necessary either to get rid of the children — that is to say, not to lead what we would call a family life — or to live with them in an intolerable proximity. Usually, the youngest ones were put out to nurse and the adolescents sent to serve apprenticeships, while those between these ages — who might be numerous when, by good fortune, few of them had died in the nursing stage — spent the day at school or in the street, and only returned to their parents' house to sleep.

In the rural areas, the house of the poor or relatively poor peasant varied in size and appearance according to the region: in some places, the walls were of stone — although men were scarce where stone was abundant — and in others, of planks and daub; the roofs were most commonly of thatch, except in certain regions (the houses of the rich had roofs of tiles or slate); the floor was nearly always of beaten earth — soiled with refuse, among which the chickens scratched about — which in winter provided only poor insulation from the cold of the ground. In general, only one room was occupied and, in certain re-

---

[9] Richard Licl, 'Les Intérieurs domestiques dans la seconde moitié du XVIIIe siècle, d'après les inventaires après décès de Coutances', *Annales de Normandie*, 20th year, no. 4 (December 1970), pp. 291-316.

[10] J. Carrière, 'La Population d'Aix-en-Provence à le fin du XVIIe siècle', *Annales de la Faculté des Lettres d'Aix-en-Provence* (1958).

[11] Félix Tavernier, *La Vie quotidienne á Marseille, de Louis XIV à Louis-Philippe* (Paris, 1973), pp. 109-11.

gions, the people lived there in warm and malodorous proximity to the farm animals. The optimistic description which Noël du Fail has left us of the house of a worthy Breton peasant of the sixteenth century,[12] mentions only one inhabited room, separated from the stables — a 'roof for the cows' and a 'roof for the sheep' — by 'fine poles of hazelwood interlaced with subtle workmanship'. Similarly, the literary descriptions of the old-time English cottages, whether they are emphasizing their poverty or are couched in a facetious vein, mention only one inhabited room.[13]

Perhaps these literary descriptions give one a more accurate idea of the ordinary dwellings of the English cottagers and labourers than do the probate inventories, which were much more common among the rich than among the poor. Of a total of 3,600 rural inventories of the sixteenth and seventeenth centuries studied by a team of British historians,[14] only 300, i.e., 8 per cent, concern persons designated as *labourers* or *cottagers*, although these constituted 25 per cent of the population of England at the beginning of the sixteenth century, and 47 per cent at the end of the seventeenth century. This justifies the presumption that only the wealthiest fraction of this social category enjoyed the benefit of a probate inventory. An extreme example was that of Robert Wood, a 'peasant labourer' of Nuneaton — a parish in the forested part of the Midlands — whose 'farm' contained seven rooms and abundant, almost luxurious, furniture. This landless peasant was, in fact, a cheese-manufacturer on a large scale, and there must have been many others among those for whom an inventory of property was drawn up who were as unrepresentative of the typical condition of 'labourers'. Nevertheless, the fact remains that three-quarters of these inventories do not make any specific distinction between the rooms of the house, most probably because there was only one room.

These inventories also show how the value of the domestic property of these 'labourers' could vary in spatial and temporal terms: the average was £1-10s in the low-lying areas of the north of England, £3-

---

[12]Noël du Fail, *Les Baliverneries d'Eutapel* (1894), pp. 45-8; quoted by J.-L. Flandrin in Nouvelle histoire de France (36 vols., Paris, 1965-8), vols. XI, pp. 1298-9.

[13]Richard Carew, *Survey of Cornwall* (1602), p. 66; Robert Reyce, *Suffolk in the XVI century: the Breviary of Suffolk* (1618), ed. Lord Francis Henry (1902), p. 51; quoted in Joan Thirsk (ed.), *The Agrarian History of England and Wales*, vol. IV (Cambridge, 1967), pp.443-6.

[14]Thirsk, vol. IV; pp. 442-54, written by Alan Everitt, are devoted to the domestic life of the 'farm labourers'.

10s in the rural parts of the Midlands, £4 in East Anglia, £4-10s in the forested parishes of the Midlands, £6 in Somerset and £7-10s in Hertfordshire. In the low-lying parts of the north domestic property, which constituted on an average, 18 per cent of the inheritance at the beginning of the sixteenth century, came to constitute 29 per cent in the seventeenth century. During the same period, the proportion increased from 35 to 46 per cent in the open rural areas of the Midlands, from 59 to 69 per cent in Hertfordshire, and from 40 to 50 per cent in England as a whole. This would appear to signify, among that fraction of the 'labourers' whose property made it worth while compiling a probate inventory, an undeniable improvement in terms of comfort. From other sources, however, the evidence leads one to suppose that the other 'labourers', whose number increased continually, experienced a decline in their standard of living.

In France, the probate inventories of the peasants have not yet been the subject of comparable statistical studies. However, the few that have been published provide similar instructive information with regard to the communal style of domestic life. Let us observe, for a change, those referring to the better-off peasants and the rural 'bourgeois'. The house of a cooper in the Maconnais,[15] of which the inventory was compiled in 1674, contained only one room for living in, in which there were four beds in good condition and two not in use. That of a well-off farmer, described in 1723, consisted of a principal room, with a curtained bed, and a small adjoining room without a fireplace, with two uncurtained beds. At a still higher social level, one may observe as an example the house of the widow of an inspector of military finances, who died in 1780, leaving two unmarried daughters who had been living with her and three sons who had established themselves outside the house, one being a merchant in Lyons, the second a 'bourgeois' in Viviers and the third a master-surgeon. The house consisted of three inhabited rooms: one, which was a kitchen, dining-room and drawing-room, in which there were no beds although there were cupboards for clothes; one bedroom, with a curtained bed for the mistress of the house and a truckle-bed for the maidservant; and another bedroom for the two daughters, with two curtained beds. The specialization of the rooms is, therefore, more marked in this case than in the previous examples, and there is less communal living; this may be due to three reasons: perhaps the later date of the inventory; certainly, the higher social status; and, probably, the fact that the husband was already dead and the sons living outside the house

---

[15]According to Suzanne Tardieu, *La Vie domestique dans le Mâconnais rural pré-industriel* (Paris, 1964), pp. 47-55.

when the inventory was compiled. Support for this last hypothesis is found in the fact that in the attic there were the pieces of a fifth bed. However, even in this well-to-do house, apparently almost emptied of people, the mistress of the house still shared her bedroom with the maidservant.

Sleeping arrangements

In certain regions, it was common for families to sleep together. Thus, in the Queyras (Hautes-Alpes), according to an observer of about 1830: 'Families are large; all together in the cow-stables, on a rough bed covered with woollen sheets which are never washed.'[16] In the Loire-Inferieure, at the same period, an observer reported 'the well-nigh universal custom, in all families, of sleeping in the same room'. 'Six beds, hung with curtains of woollen serge and separated by only a narrow passageway, were in this room. When they told me that they were the beds of the boys and girls of the farm, I could not avoid showing my surprise.'[17]

In the homes of the peasantry in most regions of France, as in the houses of the great lords, the absence of privacy was partly offset by the enclosed character of the beds. Noël du Fail speaks of the bed, 'closed and shut, and standing fairly high', of the Breton peasant. The folklorists of the nineteenth century have also left us plentiful descriptions of such beds. Although they were perhaps less monumental in size in other regions, the beds of the peasantry — above all, the marital bed — were likewise closed. However, one should not too hastily abandon the hypothesis of communal sleeping: in the house of the Breton peasant, there was only one bed, and in such a curtained bed there often slept all the members of the household, including the servants, while sometimes passing guests were offered hospitality there. This appears to have been, at least, the customary situation in the Middle Ages.

"We forbid brothers and sisters or other kinsfolk of different sexes to sleep together after the age of seven years", wrote the Bishop of Saint-Brieuc in 1507; he was convinced that this practice 'gives rise to an infinite number of horrible sins, as has been reported to us by many confessors'. Despite the excommunication and the fine of ten livres with which he threatened those who infringed this ordinance, it may

[16]Hugo, vol. I, p. 154.
[17]Ibid. vol. II, p. 154.

be doubted that this practice ceased abruptly. Until the end of the eighteenth century the synodal statutes in all regions continued to complain about it. They also denounced, and with equal persistence, the practice of parents sleeping with their children in the conjugal bed. For example, in 1681 Mgr Le Camus, Bishop of Grenoble, wrote,

> we have ascertained in the course of our visits that one of the means which the Devil most commonly uses to make children lose their purity of soul by depriving them of that of the body, is the custom of many fathers and mothers of having their children sleep in the same bed with them...when they are beginning to have the use of reason.

He therefore ordered the parish priests to make every effort 'to remedy an evil so prevalent and so detrimental to the salvation of souls'. Yet how many beds could a poor peasant, if he was the father of a large family, both afford to buy and find room for in his house?

The fact that, in these complaints, reference is always made to 'kinsfolk of different sexes' merits our closer attention. The emphasis placed on the differences between sexes indicates that the secular clergy was more obsessed with the danger of heterosexual relations than with that of homo-sexuality. Though more culpable, the latter was, apparently, less frequent in France — unless it was merely practised more secretly. Moreover, was it because it was not often customary to sleep with the servants or with passing visitors, that no reference to them was ever made? Or did the complaints refer only to the parents because of an obsession with the gravity of incest?

It seems to have been customary to put together in the same bed persons of the same sex, whether or not they were related. In the legal action brought in 1533 by Marguerite, widow of Jean Jacomart, against her seducer Pierre Pellart, nicknamed Mordienne, a girl of eighteen testified 'that one night, when she was in bed with Marguerite in the latter's room, the accused came there and had carnal knowledge of Marguerite. She knows this because she was lying beside Marguerite and was touching her.'[18]

Towards the end of the fifteenth century and the beginning of the sixteenth, it also happened that adults of different sexes shared the same bed without any of them thinking ill of it. Others, it is true, were perhaps scandalized by the practice. Jeanne Jacquet, a girl 'aged

---

[18]Archives départementales de l'Aube, Inventory series G, vol. II, pp. 438-9.

twenty years or thereabouts', was, it seems, in bed with her mother and stepfather, when three young men knocked loudly at the door, crying out:

> 'Odds death! Odds flesh!...open the door, you whore!' The mother, hearing this noise, made her daughter get up and go up into the attic. Meanwhile, the three companions broke open the door...They came into the house and set about looking for Jeanne. They looked in the [only] bed, in the kneading-trough, in the oven, and, seeing that they did not find her they went up to the attic and there they found her.

It is just possible that the pretext for this attack followed by rape was, in fact, the cohabitation of the girl with her stepfather. However, the records of the trial make no reference to this.[19]

The allusions are more explicit in another case of rape, in 1516, where the victim was a woman called Perrette. She had gone to see her child, who was being nursed in the house of Jean Gauthier, a vine-grower at Barberey-aux-Moines, near Troyes. 'In the evening, after Jean Gauthier had already gone to bed, while his wife and Perrette were undressing in front of the fire' in order to go to bed too, two men knocked at the door on the pretext that they wished to buy larks. 'Boys,' said Jean Gauthier to them, 'I have no larks.' Then one of them said, 'Jean Gauthier, you have two women, and you do not need two. There is your one, and we need this one.' 'You shall have neither this one nor me,' answered the wife of Jean Gauthier. Finally, they went away, saying, 'others of us will come soon.' Thereupon *the wife of Jean Gauthier and Perrette went to bed, in the same bed in which Jean Gauthier and his manservant already were.* One or two hours later, the accused returned, accompanied by several accomplices. They broke down the door, and dragged Perrette off into the fields 'having no other clothes but her nightdress'. There 'they made her put on her petticoat which one of them had brought with him', then they raped her after thrashing her soundly.[20]

Although the presence of a woman in the house of a man who was neither her father nor her husband may have served as a pretext for some of these violent incidents — which were, in any case, common in those days — on the other hand, their sharing the same bed did not

---

[19]Ibid. p. 387.
[20]Ibid. pp. 385-6.

usually lead to this. No one remarked on it in the course of the legal proceedings, and no one seems to have been surprised by the fact that, for example, Jean Gauthier and his wife habitually slept with their manservant. However, from the sixteenth century onwards, even before the Council of Trent, this communal sleeping was a thing of the past among the well-to-do. Evidence of this is the dialogue of Noël du Fail:

> Do you not remember those big beds in which everyone slept together without difficulty?....Ever since people have worn shoes in Poulaine...the faith plighted by the women to the men was inviolable....As a result of this marvelous trust, there slept together all the married people, or unmarried ones, in a big bed made for the purpose, three fathoms long and nine feet wide, without fear or danger of any unseemly thought, or serious consequence; for in those days men did not become aroused at the sight of naked women...However, since the world has become badly behaved, each one has his own separate bed, and with good reason...One makes, by common consent, smaller beds for the benefit of some married men....Cursed be the cat, if he finds the cooking-pot uncovered, and does not put his paw in....[21]

Like the clergy, who tirelessly inveighed against the practice of the communal bed, it is for the sake of chastity that Noël du Fail here, somewhat facetiously, extols it. We, on the other hand, reject the communal living of former times less out of virtue than by reason of an instinctive repugnance.

We admit sexual contact only with selected persons. The warmth and the odour of another person, when they do not attract us, provoke our aversion. Is this due to a refinement of our sensibility, or of our modesty, that is the integration, at the most profound level, of taboos of which we are hardly conscious? It is, in any case, remarkable that in tracing the history of family feeling it is usually only those aspects of the communal living of former times that might run counter to our own family sentiments — the throwing open of the house, the room and even the bed to strangers — that have been emphasized. It has not occurred to historians to see in this practice one of the bases of the

---

[21]Noël du Fail, *Les propos rustiques de Noël du Fail* (1547), ed. Arthur de La Borderie (Paris, 1878), end of ch. V and beginning of ch. VI.

cohesion of the family in past times. There is, in our present-day delicacy, a sort of neurotic individualism that militates against the spontaneity of our relations with other people and, perhaps, with the members of our own reduced family. In the countries which, in principle, put conjugal love in first place, does not this delicacy go so far as to make married couples sleep in separate beds? We should, at least, admit the possibility that communal sleeping has been, among the peasants and other poor people in former times, one of the most interesting manifestations of the communitarian spirit, with the communal bed as one of the privileged places of family life, until, in the course of three or more centuries, the moralists obsessed with the sins of the flesh succeeded in abolishing it.

In any case, the communal bed was often the only meeting-place for poor families. The house was, above all, a refuge from the beasts and demons of the night-time. In summer, for pleasure or for work, both in town and country, people spent the whole day out-of-doors. In winter the peasants, ill-clad in cold hempen tunics, still needed energetic physical activity out-of-doors in order to get warm.[22] Fuel was, in fact, scarce and expensive in many parts of France and England, where there had been excessive deforestation. In addition, apart from cooking-stoves and ranges, heating systems were defective throughout France and in all sectors of society. The rich, sitting in front of their fireplaces, were roasted on one side and frozen on the other; the poor, with their wretched fires, sometimes situated in the middle of the room, got more smoke than warmth. To retain the heat, therefore, there was a preference for low ceilings, and apertures were reduced to the minimum. Thus, in Sologne, 'the inhabitants like to be able to touch the roof-beams of their rooms with their heads, which is a dangerous inconvenience for people of my height', the Prior of Sennely, who was not from Sologne, wrote at the end of the seventeenth century. 'They should open up [their houses] with big windows to let some air in, instead of which they are dark and more fitted to serve as dungeons for criminals than as the dwellings of free men.' These low and murky houses were lit by resin candles with hempen wicks which gave

---

[22]'Coarse linen, the clothing of many peasants, does not protect them adequately...but for some years...a much larger number of peasants have been wearing woollen clothes.' Fernand Braudel, *Capitalism and Material Life, 1400-1800* (London, 1973), p. 230. specimens of this coarse linen clothing can be seen in the Musée des Arts et Traditions Populaires. In this connection, see also Robert Mandrou, *Introduction à la France moderne* (Paris, 1960), pp. 35-43, particularly p. 42.

off a nearly unbearable smell.[23] In these conditions, there was little to encourage family reunions.

In these hovels, however, the inhabitants of Sologne had 'good feather beds', consisting of a wooden bedstead, a palliasse, the 'bed' itself — that is to say, a feather mattress — goose-feather bolsters, a drugget counterpane, curtains, cushions and festoons. The beds of the leaseholders were worth, on an average, 200 livres, those of the share-croppers 300, and even the poorest day-labourers had beds worth about a hundred livres. In a sample of fifty day-labourers, whose probate inventories have been studied, the bed always represents at least 40 per cent of the total value of the property.[24] There was, in short, a logical correlation between the discomfort of the house and the comfort of the bed. In this region, where wood was particularly scarce at the time, the only way to get warm, when one was tired of energetic physical activity, was to get into bed and draw the curtains to keep in the warmth of the body. In this warm intimacy in bed, did there not originate, among the members of the peasant family, a relationship as vital and as worthy of our attention as the rituals connected with our bourgeois homes?

Eating

In our traditional paintings of bourgeois interiors one of the great moments of family life is the family meal. The times of day at which these occurred and their degree of sacredness have all varied according to the historical period and the region concerned. In the French bourgeoisie of the nineteenth century, the ritual of the family meal seems to have been particularly important, and this probably has some connection with the high standard attained by French cuisine at that time, and the prestige, among Frenchmen today, of 'bourgeois cuisine'. Was this ritual as important between the sixteenth and the eighteenth centuries, and in which social spheres? In other words, did the act of feeding imply during that period the ritual reunion of all the family around the 'table', in that centre of the cult of the family which the 'dining-room' has become?

Among the rich, as Philippe Ariès has emphasized, the dining-room made its appearance at a late date. For a long time the table was set up only at the last moment, on trestles, in a room not assigned to

---

[23]Bouchard, p. 94.
[24]Ibid. p. 98.

any particular purpose.[25] This instability of the fundamental piece of furniture of our family life appears symptomatic of the lack of ritual importance in the daily meals and of the instability of the group that took these meals together. Our bourgeois tables, on the other hand — even if they are extended to cater for special celebrations — are normally adapted to the dimensions of a stable family group, and they remind old couples afterwards of the departure of their offspring.

Among the poor, the lack of any distinction between the kitchen, the dining-room and the bedroom is much less significant. What remains to be ascertained is what place the table had in the interior of humble dwellings. The peasants painted by Le Nain are sharing bread and wine with a visitor, on a makeshift table, while an enormous and ornate bed can be seen at the back of the room. There are texts describing identical scenes.[26] The inventory of the property of a day-labourer of Thil, near Bar-sur-Aube, compiled in 1744, mentions only two chairs, a bench and no table, which is surprising, considering the relative comfort indicated by the rest of his property.[27] However, the typical heavy tables of the peasantry do not date from the nineteenth century. One may observe, in the house of the Breton peasant described by Noël du Fail, 'the table of good material, without affectation, without decoration, but smooth'; or, in the inventories of the Maconnais, 'the table of walnut wood with its two benches' that one finds in 1674 in the house of a cooper, and the 'big table of walnut wood, with drawers, and flanked by two benches' belonging to a farmer in 1723.

The ritual character of the family meal was intensified by the recital of a prayer, the *Benedicite*. However, it seems that this prayer was not customary in all social spheres from the Middle Ages onwards, but developed, like other forms of worship within the family circle, only after the Protestant Reformation and the subsequent Catholic reforms. Philippe Ariès has observed that, in paintings, the theme of the *Benedicite* did not become frequent until the end of the sixteenth century.[28]

Among the peasantry, at what time of day did the whole family meet all together around the table?

---

[25]Ariès, p. 445.

[26]The peasants of Gascony, 'seated round the fire, are accustomed to eat without a table and to drink out of the same goblet,' wrote a sixteenth-century observer, quoted in Braudel, p. 212.

[27]Charles Kunstler, *La Vie quotidienne sous Louis XV* (Paris, 1953), pp. 337-8.

[28]Ariès, p. 401-4.

It had not been possible for Edme Rétif to impose a certain pattern in the day for prayers, or even for meals: the duties of the various persons employed were entirely different; it was only at breakfast, at five o'clock in the morning, that they were almost all gathered together; for in summer the cowherd and the shepherd had already gone off to the pastures. They said a brief prayer together, consisting only of the Lord's Prayer; then they went their ways, and did not meet together again until the evening. Then, however, everyone was present.[29]

Between these two meals, the workers made shift with a 'snack': 'they take bread, some nuts or a piece of white cheese for the snack'. And twice a week, when Barbe Ferlet, Rétif's mother, made bread, she 'made some very thin cakes, with butter and raised pastry, while the oven was getting warm, and she sent them, piping hot, to be taken by the servant-girls to the men who were at work'.[30]

For people to go from five in the morning until five in the evening with so little food, a substantial morning meal was needed.

In the house of our master, before we went off to the plough, we had a soup made from boiled salt pork, cooked with cabbages or peas, together with a piece of salt pork and a plate of peas and cabbages; or a soup made with butter and onions, followed by an omelette, or hard-boiled eggs, or green vegetables or fairly good white cheese.[31]

How fortunate were the domestic workers in good houses! The poor peasants in Burgundy usually ate only 'barley or rye bread, a soup made from oil of nuts or even hempseed' and drank 'a bad beverage, that is to say, water strained through marc, or just plain water'.[32] In other regions, the men often went off to work before daybreak, without eating anything. Then, after sunrise, they had a snack with what they had brought with them, or what was brought to them by a girl from the house. Sometimes they returned at midday. Elsewhere — or during other seasons of the year — they stayed in the fields until the evening. Some observers had reported that, in the Pyrenees, men and women,

---

[29]Rétif de la Bretonne, *La Vie de mon père*, ed. G. Rouger (Paris, 1970), p. 131.
[30]Ibid. pp. 191-2.
[31]Ibid. p. 191.
[32]Ibid. p. 191.

even when assembled, did not eat together.[33] However, in almost all parts of France, it seems that at least supper could be eaten together.

> Every evening, at supper, which was the only meal at which all the family could be gathered together, [Edme Retif] found himself, like a venerable patriarch, at the head of a numerous household; for there were usually twenty-two sitting at the table, including the ploughboys and those who tended the vines, who in winter were threshers, the cowherd, the shepherd and two servant-girls, of whom one helped to tend the vines and the other looked after the cows and the dairy. All these people were seated at the same table.[34]

This figure of twenty-two table companions is perhaps exaggerated, since six of the children of the first marriage had left Edme Rétif's house shortly after his second marriage, and those of the second marriage could not, as a rule, all be assembled together, but the interesting feature — because it was quite customary in the big farmhouses at that time — is the presence of the domestic servants at the family table.

Each person, however, knew his place.

> The father of the family was at the head, by the fire; beside him was his wife, ready to bring in the dishes to serve — for it was she alone who concerned herself with the cooking; the women servants, who had been working all day, were sitting and eating quietly; then there were the children of the house in the order of their ages, which alone determined their rank; then the oldest of the plough-boys and their companions; then those who tended the vines, after whom came the cowherd and the shepherd; finally, the two servant-girls concluded the number; they were at the foot of the table, opposite their mistress, from whom they could not hide any of their movements.[35]

---

[33]'The women eat once the men have been served', wrote Gaétan Bernouville in the twentieth century, in *Le Pays des Basques* (Paris, 1930). Moreover, one finds in the eighteenth century similar evidence regarding other Pyrenean regions, for example the notebook of the mountaineer and geographer Ramond.

[34]De la Bretonne, *La Vie de mon père*, p. 130.

[35]Ibid.

Blood, age, sex and the greater or lesser degree of honourability of occupations created among the members of the household distinctions and a hierarchy. There is no trace, however, of that gulf which, among the bourgeoisie of the nineteenth century, separated masters and servants.

It is true that it was customary in the eighteenth century to distinguish master and servants by the use of different bread and wine. In La Bretonne,

> everyone ate the same bread; the odious distinction be-
> tween white and whole-meal bread had no place in that
> house; besides, it would not have effected any saving,
> fairly rich bran being needed for the horses, the dairy-
> cows, pigs which were being fattened, and even ewes
> when they had lambed. As for the wine, since the father
> of the family drank little and had only adopted the habit
> late in life, he drank only old wine. The mother of the
> family drank only water, which her husband had some
> difficulty in persuading her to redden by adding only a few
> drops of wine. The children all, without exception, drank
> water. The ploughboys and the vine-tenders drank a wine
> which was much more agreeable to them than that of
> their master would have seemed: it was wine of the sec-
> ond pressing strained through odd remnants of crushed
> grapes. Everybody knows that the peasants like a wine
> that scrapes one's gullet; and this widespread taste is
> considerably intensified in Sacy, where the human species
> is of a coarseness and massiveness of which one can find
> few parallels, even in Germany.[36]

In the evening

In addition to being present at the table, the domestic servants in the large peasant households also took part in family prayers and in the after-supper activities.

> It was...after supper that the father of the family read
> from the Holy Scriptures: he began with Genesis, and
> read with unction three or four chapters, depending on

---

[36]Ibid. pp. 130-1.

their length, also making certain observations, which were brief and infrequent but which he considered to be absolutely indispensable. I cannot recall without a feeling of emotion the attentiveness with which that reading was received; how it communicated to all that numerous family a spirit of good-heartedness and brotherhood.

'In the family,' Rétif notes in an aside, 'I include the servants'; this interpolation shows that, to his readers, this was no longer taken for granted. In the rural areas, however, the servants were still the children of the master of the house, who was obliged to educate them like his real children. 'My father always began with these words: "Let us turn our thoughts to God, my children; it is the Holy Spirit that is going to speak." The following day, at work, the reading of the evening before formed the subject of conversation, especially among the ploughboys.' These social evenings after supper varied in length according to the season.

After the reading there was, in summer, a brief prayer together; then the children were made to recite a lesson from the diocesan catechism; then one went to bed in silence; for after the evening prayers, laughter and conversation aloud were strictly forbidden. In winter, when the evenings are longer in the country — for in town the time is always the same — after the reading and the lesson from the catechism, the father of the family told stories, both old and new; he introduced into them, at appropriate moments, the finest sayings of the ancient writers. This was our recreation. Everyone was eager to hear these instructive narrations, and since everyone could laugh and make comments, it was a delightful amusement for peasants and children who had never known more agreeable entertainments. These conversations and the reading must have pleased them greatly: we have often had in our house the sons of the best inhabitants as domestic workers; and when their parents asked them the reason for their eager desire to come to our house, the reason they gave was the reading and the conversations in the evenings.[37]

---

[37]Ibid. pp. 131-3.

It must not be thought, however, that Edme Rétif's house was exceptional in this respect. According to all the moralists of the seventeenth and eighteenth centuries, both in England and in France, the master owed to his servants and his children together the moral and religious instruction which he gave them. This subject will be dealt with more fully later. The profane stories which he told were a traditional feature of these social evenings. As early as the sixteenth century these stories were being told on winter evenings, in the big farmhouses of the Rennes basin described by Noël du Fail;[38] or in the house of the Sire de Gouberville, in his manor in Mesnil-au-Val, near Cherbourg, where he lived with two bastard children of his father, his own three natural daughters, nine male domestic servants and some female ones: 'On that day, the 6 February 1554, it rained without ceasing. Our people went to the fields, but the rain drove them home again. Later, throughout the evening, we read in *Amadis of Gaul* about his victory over Dourdan.'[39] It would appear, therefore, that from the sixteenth to the eighteenth century social evenings in the winter were, together with the evening meal and family prayers, one of the principal rituals of family life in the rural areas.

Nevertheless, a great number of other sources of evidence demonstrate that, among the humbler peasants, social evenings were only rarely family reunions. They generally, though not always, had a characteristic which is disappearing today: that of assembling in the same place men and women, young and old. They offered unmarried young people an opportunity of associating together, under the watchful eye of their parents.[40] However, precisely because they were meeting-places for young men and girls who could marry one another, these gatherings must normally have consisted of individuals living in different houses and often even in different villages. Let us note what Noël du Fail says of these occasions: 'There were meetings for spinning, which they call *veillées*, sometimes in La Valée, sometimes in La Voisardiere, in Souillas and other well-known places, where there met together from all the surrounding parts many young men and clownish youths, assembling there and playing an infinite number of games that Panurge never even thought of.'

In some mountainous parts of Auvergne these social evenings lasted almost the entire day, and their multi-family character stands

---

[38]Noël du Fail, *Les Contes et discours d'Eutrapel* (Rennes, 1603), ff. 52v-53v; quoted in J.-L. Flandrin, *Les Amours paysannes* (Paris, 1975), pp. 121-2.

[39]'*Journal du sire de Gouberville* (1553-1564)', *Mémoire Soc. Antiq. Normandie*, vol. XXXI (Caen, 1892).

[40]Flandrin, *Les Amours paysannes*, pp. 119-22.

in particularly clear contrast to the familial character of the meals and the sleeping arrangements. An observer at the beginning of the nineteenth century wrote, 'In the Planese, where there is absolutely no wood, the peasant would be horribly miserable during the winter and could not live there, if he had not discovered the means to do without wood to get warm: he does it by living in the midst of his farm animals.' After explaining why and how, in winter, these peasants carry their pallets to the cowshed, and how the men sleep late in the mornings while the women go out to look for water in the snow, light the fire, and cook the soup which is drunk at ten in the morning and then again at five in the evening, the observer finally describes these 'social evenings' spent in the day-time.

> It is rare for a family to spend the winter alone and isolated in its cowshed; neighbouring families assemble together spontaneously, and choose for the purpose the biggest and warmest cowshed. In the morning, after the soup, everyone hastens to join the group: they sit in a circle on benches, they chatter, they laugh, they complain about the taxes and the tax-collectors, they repeat the gossip that is circulating about the girls and young men, or they just sit and meditate. *At five o'clock they part company to go and have their meal,* then they return and continue chatting for a while, and *then each one returns to his own home to sleep.* [41]

Most of the descriptions of social evenings portray the women and girls working, while the men play cards or chat and the boys lark about. In this part of Auvergne, segregation of the sexes was carried even further.

> In all this only the men take part. The women, by reason of the inferiority of their species, are not admitted to the conversations of their lords and masters. However, as soon as the latter have gone, their reign commences, and the social evening, which for the men finishes at eight o'clock, does not end for the women until midnight or one o'clock in the morning; then they make up for lost time; but — and this is a detail characteristic of the thrift of this region — since it would not be just, when lending them a parlour, that the master of the house should provide

---

[41]Hugo, vol. I, pp. 237-8.

lighting as well, they have, for their private social evenings, a lamp for which the oil is paid for by all, from the modest earnings derived from spinning. Others, more economically, do without lighting, and the darkness does not prevent them from spinning or from talking.

More concerned to denounce the barbarity of these peasants towards their womenfolk than to comprehend the differentiation of the male and female roles in these mountain households, our enlightened bourgeois nevertheless does not conceal the fact that men and women did have activities in common.

In pious families, they have preserved the custom, in these winter reunions, of saying the rosary and of singing canticles. Others, more addicted to worldly pleasures, spend the evenings dancing. The man reputed to be the best musician stands up and sings; the women who are not dancing accompany him with their high-pitched voices, and all the rest skip and caper about, while the cattle chew the cud to the rhythmic beat of the sabots. Triumphant on these occasions are the national dances, the simple and figure bourrées. We have been present at some of the dances, and have noted that they take place to the accompaniment of authentic songs which, for the most part, are extremely satirical and refer to some scandalous incident well known in the district. The man who sings beats the time by striking the earth with a stick...A stove maintained at great expense would not give the cowshed as much warmth as it derives from this multitude of people and animals crowded together; the air becomes transformed into thick smoke, which one sees seeping in the form of vapour out of the apertures in the building; it becomes stifling, foul and unhealthy; it is one of the principal causes of the illnesses of those who live in the mountains.

In other regions of central France, it was not only within family dwellings that individuals drawn from several families assembled in winter to 'pass the time' together and escape from the cold, but also in outside dwellings, known as *écreignes*. We know about those of Burgundy, described in the sixteenth century by Etienne Tabourot, lord

119

of Les Accords.[42] They also existed in Champagne, particularly in the region of Troyes, as late as the eighteenth century. 'The *ecreignes*,' Grosley observes,

> are houses dug out below ground-level and covered with dung, where the women of the village assemble to spend a social evening and where work is seasoned with the delights of conversation....The interior is furnished with seats made of clods of earth, to seat all those present. In the middle there stands a small lamp, which gives light to the whole building....This lamp is provided, in turn, by all the people who come to the *ecreigne*. The village woman whose turn it is [to provide the lamp] makes sure to arrive first, so as to receive the others there. Each one arrives, carrying her distaff, with the spindle in the distaff, with her two hands on her sewing-kit and her apron over her hands, enters hurriedly and takes her seat without further ado. As soon as everyone is seated, the hands leave the sewing-kit, the latter is put in its proper place, *ad proprias sedes remeat,* the spindle is drawn from the distaff, the fibre is moistened with a bit of saliva, the agile fingers turn the spindle, and there is work under way....One knows...that prattling...is the purpose and the principal object of the *ecreigne*, and that work is merely the pretext. The conversation therefore becomes animated, always lively, always sparkling, and it continues without interruption until the time when the meeting breaks up.[43]

Besides being refuges from the cold, and places for work and conversation, the *ecreignes* were also places for *rendezvous*: 'In these assemblies of girls one finds a great number of young striplings and lovers,' wrote Etienne Tabourot, in the sixteenth century. In the diocese of Troyes, the same practice continued until, in 1680, a synodal ordinance promulgated by Mgr Bouthillier decreed excommunication for men and boys who went into the *ecreignes*, or waited for the girls at the door to take them home, and also for girls who admitted young men to their assemblies. In his pastoral letter of 1686 on the same subject, which included detailed instructions for the repression of these activities, the

---

[42]Etienne Tabourot, *Les Escraignes dijonnaises* (Paris, 1614), prologue; quoted in Flandrin, *Les Amours paysannes*, pp.120-1.

[43]Grosley, 'Dissertation sur les écreignes lue dans l'Académie de Troyes le 15 novembre 1743,' Mémoires de l'Académie de Troyes (1743).

reforming bishop asserted that it no longer concerned anyone except 'certain contumacious persons'.[44]

It seems that it is not by mere chance that these social evenings organized among neighbours and friends — in the home of one of them, in his cowshed or barn, or in an *ecreigne* shared by the girls of a village or of an urban district — are reported especially in the democratic and communitarian regions of the east and centre, rather than in southern France where the 'house spirit' predominated. In the study that he has recently devoted to social relations in Languedoc, Yves Castan does not mention these customs at all. On the contrary, he emphasizes the reluctance of the country people to permit any stranger to enter their homes, unless formally invited by the master of the house.[45] In the Pyrenees, where the social evenings in winter brought together, round the fireplace, neighbours and members of the family, the presence of the master of the house could never be ignored. He sat in the place of honour, in a wooden armchair; on his left were the women and girls busy with their spinning, on his right the older members of the family, while the boys — here, too, the indispensable trouble makers — found places wherever they could. Some evenings, the company listened to tales or 'true histories', often told by the shepherds; afterwards, the boys proposed games — 'hot-hand', blindman's bluff or all-in wrestling. On other evenings, at a signal from the master of the house, the assembled company turned round, with their backs to the fire: the evening was to be devoted to dancing.[46]

Long-term changes

Between the beginning of the sixteenth and the end of the eighteenth centuries, the material context and the ritual of family life changed. However, there were such great differences in the character of material existence and family ritual between the aristocracy, the urban and rural middle classes, and the peasants, and also such great differences from one region to another among the humbler peasants, that it is not easy to make an overall appreciation of these transformations. The segregation between servants and masters, which was far advanced in the towns at the end of the eighteenth century, was much

---

[44]Charles Lalore, *Ancienne discipline du diocèse de Troyes* (4 vols., Troyes, 1882-3), vol. III, pp. 257-8.
[45]Castan, *Honnêteté et relations sociales*, pp. 174, 236-7.
[46]Soulet, pp. 281-2.

less developed in the rural areas. It seems that it was first of all between parents and children — and, among the latter, between boys and girls — that the practice of sleeping in separate beds, or even separate rooms, became established, under the influence of the Catholic reforms, in so far as the standard of economic well-being made this possible.

This progress of individualism within the bosom of the family — of which one must not disregard the disintegrating effects, both among the peasantry[47] and among the aristocracy[48] — was, perhaps, offset by a development and an increased ritualization of family life which can also be attributed, in France at least, to the Catholic reforms. The religious education of the children by their parents, communal prayers, the more ceremonious character of the family meal, and the struggle waged by the Church against social evenings spent outside the home, became prevailing family concerns, until in the nineteenth and twentieth centuries religious events such as Christmas, the baptisms of new-born infants, or First Communions came to be family celebrations. Because it detected the odour of paganism and the grave risks of lapses from chastity in the old popular festivals and societies of young people, the Church seems to have preferred to abolish them, and to place the children more continuously than before under the watchful eye of their parents. One may observe, for example, the ferocity of the Church's battle against the apparently innocent meetings that took place in the *ecreignes* and at other social evenings; its denunciation of carnivals, torchlight processions and the Feast of Fools; and the ever-increasing distrust which is displayed towards popular pilgrimages, until the middle of the nineteenth century. While the strengthening of the framework of the family was a deliberate intention on the part of the Protestants in their struggle against the clericalization of the Church and the paganism of the traditional ceremonies, this policy rather imposed itself, less evidently, on the leaders of the Catholic reforms. Did they realize, then, that economic and social developments would in any case destroy the traditional structures? Or did they simply adopt a strategy which the Protestants had shown to be efficacious? It should probably be emphasized above all that the Catholic reforms, like the Protestant Reformation, were at first an urban phenomenon; and that they were the work of clerics reared in a culture based on book-learning and basically hostile to the 'pagan' traditions of the countryside. However, in order to evaluate more accurately the influ-

[47]Yves Castan, 'Pères et fils en Languedoc à l'époque classiqe', XVIIe Siècle, no. 102-103, pp. 31-43, especially pp. 40-1.
[48]Elias, ch. I.

ence of these clerics, whether Catholic or Protestant, on the formation of modern family feeling it is necessary to examine more closely their moral teachings with regard to domestic relations.

Canadian Families in Social-historical Perspective*

Emily M. Nett

Abstract. Published historical materials concerning Canadian families are examined, with a view to providing a select bibliography organized around some of the persistent "myths" about Canadian families in the past which are still found in the sociology of family literature.

Upon examination of the extant research findings, there is little support for beliefs about large and extended family households, low rates of geographical mobility for families, stereotypical roles of wives and husbands, or greater family stability and protection for children who grew up in the Canadian past.

Sociologists lag behind historians in making use of historical records and materials to learn more about Canadian families. Much research and theorizing remains to be done.

Introduction

Although there are no common goals among the numerous historians of the family, few sociologists interested in family issues (theoretical and practical) condemn the enterprise. Many praise it and some even do it. The new field of social history, however much its cross-disciplinary avenues have been touted, remains for the most part more frequented by historians than sociologists in Canada. For example, an article published in a Canadian history journal (Tepperman, 1978) stressing the importance of minimizing the distinctions between sociology and social history in general, preceded by two years a special social history issue of a sociology journal (Brym, 1979).

Why should Canadian family sociologists and students be interested in social history? Because, say some, it can dispel the favored myths of the past (Gordon, 1973); recreate more accurately the world we have lost (Laslett, 1972); and reconstruct the experiences of those who have gone before from their point of view, to help understand much about our own present (Roberts, 1978).

---

*Reprinted with permission from *Canadian Journal of Sociology* Vol. 6, 1981.
125

II. The Social History of Family Life

Grand in vision as the undertaking has been, however, and small as the actual number of scholars involved, the results of their efforts have been remarkable, both in research output (see Milden, 1977), and the infusion of vigor they have put into an area of family study forged by the crossing of the traditional boundaries of sociology and history (Gordon, 1973: ix; Graubard, 1977; Demos and Boocock, 1978).

The purpose of this paper is to examine some of the historical materials now available in published form on Canadian families, which might be useful in arriving at a fresh understanding of the family in Canadian society and the problems faced by Canadians in their daily experience of family life. The idea is to provide a selected bibliography, and to organize summary findings around some of the persistent myths about former Canadian families, indicating the nature and limitations of the available descriptions and analyses. It would be useful to end by assessing the current status of the social history of the family in Canada relative to other places.

The paper is divided into three parts. In the next section some of the "myths" will be examined. The evidence for or against these myths regarding households, marriage and children, roles and experiences of family members will be weighed. Finally, a summary follows of issues in an emergent social history of the family in Canada[1], relative to other Western nations, such as England, France, and the United States.

Family myths

Descriptions of families in the Canadian past are almost non-existent in the few works in family sociology published in this country.[2] However, lip-service is often given to the importance of the historical approach (Wakil, 1975:xii), of studying the family as an element in societal development (Ishwaran, 1971:8, 15), or of examining specific families at different points in time (Larson, 1976:13). The precedent established by Elkin (1968:11-13), however, of including a description of the family in Canadian history in a discussion of Canadian families has not been kept up by other writers, who have instead focused pri-

---

[1]To a large extent materials presented in this paper are those available to the English-reading academic. To the extent that French materials have been translated, they are included.

[2]An exception is an introductory sociology textbook by Himelfarb and Richardson (1979:297-301) in which are depicted three stages the family has gone through in the past 100-150 years, from preindustrial, to industrial, to symmetrical.

marily on the present situation (starting with 1931 census materials at the earliest). They assume that the contemporary pattern is different from a taken-for-granted, unified, former pattern of Canadian family life. Recognition that the model is not an accurate portrayal of family life in past centuries has been made by Jacobson (1971:33). She acknowledged (but without documentation for Canada) that based on the small amount of data available, the "classical family of western nostalgia" seems to be an exaggeration.

The elements in the stereotype which Goode (1970:6-7) tried to document as being at least partially incorrect in the image of the classical family are the following: the economic self-sufficiency of the farm family; large aggregations of kin who lived together in large houses or stayed together geographically; infrequent marital breakup; and general family stability and happiness. Whether due to sins of omission or commission, the literature on the Canadian family does little to set the story straight.

The most pronounced stereotype has to do with households. Elkin (1968:12) states flatly that families in the earlier days "were almost self-sufficient units of production and consumption." He is imprecise as to what were the living arrangements of French and British settlers and later immigrants. When, in his discussion of the westward move of the population and industrialization, he says that extended families "were split" by migration, the reader is left to decide whether the reference is to households or kin networks or both, and whether prior to this period such "splits" were rare. A more explicit statement of generationally extended household arrangements for earlier Canadians can be found in Irving (1972:4), who says, "In the colonial period, the family's activities were still home-centered and each member of the household, *including grandparents*, had tasks to perform which were vital to the maintenance of the family." (Emphasis mine.) Moving to a more recent but indefinite period, Boyd et al. (1976:13), in outlining the effect on the family within the last hundred years of urbanization, technology, and female employment, conclude that the most obvious change "is the transition of the family from both a production and a consumption unit to primarily a consumption unit." Only as an implied contrast emerges between various indicators of contemporary family organization and functioning, and that of the "former" model, does the image of former stability and solidarity coalesce in the latter. Comparing divorce rates today with those going back to 1921 and reviewing the predictions for the future, Ramu (1976:338) concludes that the increase from the earlier period in divorce rates suggests "a disorganization of familial life and family stability." The same conclusion is reached in most discussions of Canadian divorce rates (Boyd, et al., 1976:21-25; Himelfarb and Richardson, 1979:297-298; Ambert, 1980).[3] Family stability in the past, then, is implied by references to contrasting current rates of divorce and single parenting, high mobility and two-generation residence. Further assumptions are that "traditional" families were more integrated, more cohesive, and subsequently more moral. The failure to investigate the occurrence and frequency of illegitimacy, premarital and extramarital sex, alcoholism, rape, incest and child abuse occurring in families prior to the middle of this century has contributed to the myth of the happy family of the past.

What, then, is the truth about families in the seventeenth, eighteenth, and nineteenth centuries? And where does one go to discover it?

Sociologists and historians have been working for some years at reconstruction of family patterns in the past. The historian Masters (1958), relying on early literary accounts, briefly summarized social life in British North America, 1760-1867. These same first-hand materials were used by Burnet (1972) in her capsule of the family institution as basic in the social and economic organization of Upper Canada from 1790-1850. They continue to crop up as anecdotes in much of the recent social history of that period.

The adaptation of the French-Canadian family system to the conditions of North America initially and to the pressure for new land later constituted a problem for sociologists Gerin (1964), Garigue (1964) and Miner (1938), as did fertility patterns of New France and the cultural factors accounting for them, for Sabagh (1942) and Henripin, (1956). More recently, however, with increased interest in regional and developmental variance, cultural differences in colonizers and immigrants, the social class situation under a changing capitalistic economy, and the experience of women, many more threads have been added to the texture of the tapestry which Canadian social historians are weaving. More detail from all those sources will be included in the following brief discussions of households, marriage (formation, roles, and stability), and children.

---

[3]Disclaimers such as "divorce does not represent a radical change in the institution of marriage" (Ambert, 1980:252) seem to lack conviction without any other verification than high remarriage rates at the present time.

Evidence for and against the myths

Households

If the image is of large, generationally extended family households, economically self-sufficient, and representing stability and comfort for the individual, what can we say about the reality of households in the past?

It can be said with a fair degree of certainty that the type of household in which most Canadians resided, from the time of settlement in Acadia, New France, New England and later Upper Canada, was the nuclear, or "simple" family household. This was the case regardless of geographical locale or whether the residences were backwoods, settled farm, village, or urban. Neither the circumstances of settlement, migration, and economic opportunities of the frontier, nor the emerging ideology of independence would have conspired to alter an arrangement which scholars have shown had already become numerically normative by the seventeenth century in both France and England (see Katz, 1975, for a summary of the literature).[4] Quite the opposite might be expected.

The circumstances of settlement were different, of course, in New England and New France. Lineage and extended kin networks in New France were more important than in New England where the origins of the earliest settlers were more likely non-aristocratic and thus the household tradition more probably nuclear. In New France, however, early settlers were required to make adjustments to Native hostilities, which the New England colonists were fortunate to escape. Foulche-Delbosc's (1977) study of women in Three Rivers, Quebec, 1651-1663, is a surprising revelation of marriage and remarriage (and presumably the establishment of new households) in record-breaking sequence. Although the situation in families in Quebec and Upper Canada must have stabilized substantially after 1769, life expectancy was still sufficiently short at the age of marriage that three generations living under one roof was a possibility for only the most favored families, and then for no longer than a few years. There is nothing in the accounts to dispute the fact that the two-generation family household was the norm for most colonists and pioneers. Furthermore, in the research on the nineteenth century, there is remarkable consistency in the proportion of family households which fall into this cate-

---

[4]Gerin (1964:35) notes the irony in Gauldree-Boilleau discovering in 1861 in St. Irenee, Quebec what he mistakenly thought was the stem family of France at a time when LePlay's followers in Europe had already perceived that they had confused the particularistic family with the false stem-family.

gory. The figures found by Katz (1975) in Hamilton, Ontario between 1851 and 1861, and Medjuck (1979) in Moncton, New Brunswick, 1851-1871, and Gaffield (1979) in Prescott County, Ontario between 1851-1871 were remarkably close to each other and to those reported in subsequent census enumerations (Pelletier, 1942; Charles, 1948).

Considerable structural variation has been found, however, in particular families, depending on the internal family changes such as aging, death, and marriage of children, as well as societal ones like economic boom and recession. Over the life cycle of the average family there were brief periods when a newly married couple lived with the parents of one of the spouses, or when an elderly couple or parent shared the home of a married child. Indeed, among both English and French Canadians in rural Ontario, marriage was dependent upon the ability of a couple to establish a separate household (Gaffield, 1979). On the other hand, in the industrializing city of Montreal in 1871 over one-half of the working class couples began their married lives sharing a household, although not with kin but with unrelated families and couples (Bradbury, 1979). Similarly to Katz and Gaffield, Bradbury found household structure was closely related to the life cycle; unskilled workers' families were least likely to live in nuclear households at any stage. She concludes, however, that people were sharing houses not because they wanted to, but because they had to, and that the pattern was peculiar to a shortage of low cost housing.

Strong evidence exists that the family household until modern times was somewhat larger than it is today and that its character was significantly different. Declining birth rates alone, since the middle of the nineteenth century, would point to larger family size before that period (Henripin, 1972). Fertility rates and average completed family size of women in early cohorts, however, tend to exaggerate household size, since infant mortality rates were extremely high until about the eighteenth century. Also, the period of child-bearing for most women was their entire fertile period, so that some children were born after older ones had left home. The average number of children in Canadian families in 1971 was only about two fewer than in 1871, despite the fact that in 1871 each woman would have borne an average of between six and seven children in her life. Prior to modern times, however, family residences included non-family persons, particularly servants, but also youthful relatives. The proportions of households with relatives and non-related persons has been observed to have fluctuated with economic conditions (Katz, 1975; Medjuck, 1979), and immigration (Gaffield, 1979).

An additional difference in family residence today compared with the past is that prior to 1890 workplace and home were less often separate. Katz (1972a:408) estimates the proportion of households in Hamilton in 1850 which combined the function of work and residence for some of their members was at least four out of ten. Bradbury (1979:86-87) notes that absent from the statistics on industrializing Montreal, 1871, is the work done by wives in the working class homes: taking in washing, ironing, sewing, mending and babysitting, as well as doing work for the clothing trade which was "put out" from the factories. At the other extreme were the professionals, among them doctors, who in rural areas continued to practice out of their homes well after the first quarter of the twentieth century (see Peterkin and Shaw, 1976:4, for a description of the "permeability" of one Manitoba doctor's home; also see Goheen, 1970, on physicians in Toronto in 1860).

Somewhat larger average family sizes in the past did not necessarily result in larger houses. Crowded housing conditions have been documented from Montreal by Copp (1974), and Bradbury (1979). Modern patterns of residential differentiation in cities, based on socioeconomic criteria, evolved in both Toronto and Hamilton between 1850 and 1900 (Goheen, 1970; Davey and Doucet, 1975; Doucet, 1976). A pattern of higher house-to-land density existed in the areas of the Victorian city, where the poor resided in small houses in contrast to the substantial houses and grounds in the neighborhoods at some distance from the hazards of later urban development. It was the latter which were more likely to survive, as Goode has noted in explaining the myth of the big, old family home.

Was the earlier household solely a production unit? Was the family farm self-sufficient and a subsistence enterprise only? How far back does the consumer feature of domestic families extend? As Gaffield (1979) has described families settling in Eastern Ontario as late as the mid-nineteenth century, they produced their own food, yarn, fabric, clothing, rugs, and crops. Since the participation of women and children was crucial in survival, the farm economies were indeed family economies. Interestingly, the same situation has been described by Bradbury (1979) for Montreal in 1871. That is, the wages of working class urban men, women, and children alike were contributions to the family economy. On the other hand, the economic self-sufficiency of family households in the past has undoubtedly been exaggerated. The employment of paid servants in the households of New France, 1651-1663 (Foulche-Delbosc, 1977) indicate at least incipient consumption features in the earliest settler families. Furthermore, the more privileged European immigrant families in Upper Canada, in their journal accounts, reveal the family as consumer (Moodie, 1962). Backwoods families purchased furniture, some cloth, staple foods, and perhaps in the greatest quantity, alcohol. Consumption, of course, is essential in urban life; often ignored in the picture of the past is that not all families in Quebec were habitants, and not all in Ontario were "backwoods" or wilderness families.

That permanence of residence was no more a feature of past Canadian families than it is today is a conclusion which should follow logically from the facts of migration in the colonization of North America and the development of Canada as a nation, as well as the differential pull of economic opportunity at various historical periods. Yet the myth persists of a former age when families normally remained attached to a geographical place. This is somewhat remarkable in view of the striking example described by Gerin (1964) in his search for the supposed stem-family in St. Irenee. He relates that, by 1920, sixty years after Gauldree-Boilleau's false discovery of an inheritance pattern which should have kept at least one male member on their land indefinitely, the Gauthier family had completely dispersed, in the "hope of improving their circumstances." Demographic evidence has been amassed by Gagan and Mays (1973:35) which show that mid-Victorian rural Ontario was not, as has been imagined, "the stable society comprised of primarily permanent families attached, generation upon generation, to the family homestead." In fact, Gore Township, between 1851 and 1871, was the scene of soaring transiency, most of it including families rather than unattached persons.[5] In the nineteenth-century Canadian city as well, rates of geographic mobility were very high; between 50 and 75 percent of residents cannot be found there ten years later (Ornstein and Darroch, 1978:152).

In summary, then, the documentation suggests that, contrary to the implication, past households, although notably different in some respects from present ones, appear to have been for the most part two-generational, not much larger than current ones with members sharing small and somewhat crowded dwellings for all but the wealthy, not entirely economically self-sufficient, and experiencing frequent change of members and locale. Until recent times households were probably more "malleable," that is, they expanded and contracted to include more or fewer persons as circumstances required. Until the beginning of this century a fair proportion of them included other relatives as well

----

[5] Gagan (1976b) attributes the impermanence and instability in domestic arrangements, which affected all but a minority of nineteenth-century rural Ontarians, to the inheritance system. Bouchard (1977), who also found extreme instability among land-owning families in the north of Quebec 1851-1935, explains it in terms of the underlying family strategies and goals, rather than over-population or modernization.

as non-familial members, and some continued to serve as combined workplaces and residences.

Marriage

Less is known about marriage than about household in this history of the Canadian family. Fortunately, mystification of this area is less apparent. The task of the social historian is not so much to correct misperceptions as to complete the picture.

Mate selection. The marriage contracts of Three Rivers, 1751-63, point to the importance of the negotiating of property and monetary considerations through marriage. They also establish, as do the studies of New England marriage agreements (Kenkle, 1978:99-101), that although participants chose their own mates, romantic love was not the force that it was to become in the eighteenth century. In fact, according to Burnett (1972), even after the Loyalists and British immigrants moved into Upper Canada considerable emphasis was placed on pragmatics in the selection of a marriage partner. However, romance seems to have been well established by the end of the nineteenth century, at least among the leisure class (Cook and Mitchinson, 1976:65-69).

That marriage was a necessity for both women and men in the early years of the fur trade and settlement, and was considered desirable even after the political and economic situation had stabilized, is attested to by the marriage and remarriage rates. In both French and English colonies almost all young people married, and in New France a high proportion remarried. The persistent shortage of women and the pressures to populate the colonies kept the marriage rates high until at least the 1880s (Henripin, 1957), with the decline in Quebec at this time associated with the developing scarcity of land.

When compared with figures for the countries of origin of the settlers, age at marriage has been consistently young in Canada. Henripin (1957) reports a mean age of 22.4 for women and 26.9 for men founding families for the first time between 1700 and 1730. The modal age for women was 20 years, considerably higher than the most frequent age of 13 years in the contracts of Canadian-born women in Three Rivers some years earlier (Foulche-Delbosc, 1977:18). Using statistics based on the marriage registers of Wentworth County, Ontario, 1842-1869, Katz (1972a:415) found median ages for brides of 21.8 years and for grooms, 25.7. Regional and provincial variations in mean age at marriage were associated with ethnic composition in the census of 1871 (Tepperman, 1974:332-333). German and English married early relative to French and Irish who were intermediate, and Scottish married late; availability of land in the region of settlement in part accounted for the ethnic variation in age at marriage, as well as for variation in fertility rates. Economic circumstances were also factors in marriage formation for urban couples during that same period as reported by Bradbury (1979).

Tension between individual desires and official and informal community controls, with resultant adaptation, has been an ever-present feature of Canadian marriage. Relaxation of the rules against remarriage by the Catholic Church in New France as an accommodation to the fact of widowhood for many potential childbearers has been noted by Sabagh (1942) and Foulche Delbosc (1977). From the cases in Three Rivers where marriage contracts were drawn up for brides of twelve years and younger, it also appears that the Church abrogated the rule, rigidly applied in France, of sexual maturity as an absolute requirement for a marriage. Similarly, according to Van Kirk (1977:31), the Hudson's Bay Company later gave official status to marriage à la façon du pays (white trader taking a native woman for a wife) by the introduction of a marriage contract which emphasized the husband's responsibilities (i.e., made the woman a legal wife).

Marriage patterns within Wentworth County for the years 1842-69 were endogamous (Katz, 1972a:415). Few persons sought spouses who resided outside the county. Nevertheless, the majority of marriages involved persons who had both been born outside of Ontario, and indeed, outside of Canada. Moodie (1962:144-45) reports an incident of informal control in a protest organized against an interracial marriage in Upper Canada in 1833. A black man was killed by a group who enacted a "charivari" on the night of his marriage to a white woman. The existence of the ancient Southern European custom, by which the community expresses its collective opposition to deviant marriages, in predominately Anglo territory (the Scotswoman had never heard of it) is in itself an interesting fact.

Roles. Study of the role of women in earlier times and consequently of the division of labor by sex, and of the marriage relationship has thrown new light on the stereotyped notions of marital roles in Canadian history. It has become more apparent that current images of the colonial and pioneer home as women's exclusive place, emanating from nineteenth-century ideology, has obscured the contributions of married women to their communities and also the considerable variation in women's status over the years (Johnson, 1974).

Apparently women's community involvement in Acadia in the seventeenth century was taken for granted. Griffiths (1976:71) also reports a considerable degree of equality in family headship in this region. Nearby, in Three Rivers, Quebec, at approximately the same time, the relatively scarce women were able to incorporate their own interests into their marriage contracts (Foulche-Delbosc, 1977). The role of women in assuming responsibility for the family farm during the protracted absence of husbands has been noted by Fortin (1970:226-227), as well as depicted in the first-hand accounts of western pioneers in the last century, and the present one. In British Columbia in 1883 Susan Allison tended to the store, looked after the farm, taught her children and the Indian children in the area, in addition to keeping house during the frequent and long business absences of her husband (Ormsby, 1976). Some of the most vivid images of women's toil in the fields are found in descriptions of prairie families settled on marginal lands, well into the twentieth century (Potrebenko, 1977; Robertson, 1974)

Gainful employment of women occurred from the outset. The practice of bringing domestics from other countries began in New France. A common thread running through family experience in Acadia, New France, and Upper Canada until Confederation was the experience even of native-born Canadian young women spending some years in domestic service, except for those in the most fortunate circumstances in the towns and cities. Notwithstanding the high degree of selection and control over European women destined to become domestic servants, such employment provided other opportunities, not the least of which was marriage. Recognition that the search for servants abroad was also a search for Canadian mothers and wives seems to have reached its most conscious level during the period between 1888 and 1920 (Roberts, 1979:189), but the careful selection of, and control over, the first servants to New France leads one to suspect that this element was present from the start of immigration (Floulche-Delbosc, 1977).

Although gainful employment was associated with the single status of women and not with the wifely role, there were indeed married Canadian women in the labor force in the last century (see Bradbury, 1979:75, on women and children as a vital element in an industrial labor force in 1871). Women did not enter the labor force as early in the development of industrialization as men, and married women not as early as single women, but wives of working men did make excursions into the paid sector of the economy shortly after single women began to leave domestic service for factory work (see Leslie, 1974). Women and children made up nearly 42 percent of Montreal's industrial work-force in 1871, and the proportion in Toronto was 33 percent (Bradbury, 1979:75). Wives in paid employment were largely from the working class, employed by necessity, often in occupations that did not require full time absence from the home. With increased opportunities for higher education for women and training in the professions (Strong-Boag, 1979), some few higher status women remained in employment voluntarily, even after marriage and, presumably, childbearing. By 1921 one-quarter of the labor force was composed of women.

If the work roles of women and men have been more flexible historically than the Victorian middle class ideals specified, what can be said about the quality of the spousal relationship? There appears to be considerable inconsistency between the patriarchal model incorporated in some of the legislation and the teachings of the churches, on the one hand, and the more partner-like-situations created by the exigencies of outpost and frontier life, on the other. The words "egalitarism," used by Burnet (1972:54) to describe Upper Canada, 1830-1870, and "matriarchal" by Griffiths (1976) for Acadia, 1720, seem somewhat strong. The term "matricentric," applied to characterize the tradition of female dominance in the patriarchically organized rural family in Quebec, seems more apt. Until law reform in the married women's property acts in England in the middle of the last century, and until further reform in Quebec and other provinces in the first quarter of this century, women were extremely dependent upon the good will of their husbands and, in old age, their grown sons (McClung, 1972:91-92), which hardly fostered equality. Personal documents reflect little input from wives in major decisions, including family migration. The implication is that the role of wife was to be uncomplainingly supportive. The expectation of reciprocity along this dimension seems to be lacking particularly in descriptions of the treatment of women in childbirth and the reaction of men to the extreme loneliness women often experienced in the isolated spots to which they were taken (Potrebenko, 1977; Ormsby, 1976; Robertson, 1974). There are, of course, expressions of concern and understanding on the part of husbands (Robertson, 1974:56). How many couples felt compelled to accept unhappiness is difficult to estimate. An extreme case of husband-wife failure to communicate and support each other emotionally is described by Potrebenko (1977), whose Polish immigrant parents remained together despite their life-long incompatibility.

There are indications that role failure or role deviation was not uncommon. Native wives abandoned, following the arrival of white women at the Red River fur-trading post in 1830 (Van Kirk, 1977); deserted women homesteading on the prairies (Robertson, 1974); and

136

immigrant husbands unable or unwilling to support their wives (Ormsby, 1976) were the exception as they are today, but it did happen. Although the hardships were often great for such women, perhaps they were less in the first part of the last century than at its end for single mothers living in cities and trying to provide for themselves and their children (Klein and Roberts, 1974). There appears to have been not much censure of the man and very little stigma for the woman in the earlier period. Instead, it seems to have been accepted as one of the hazards of life, with the community rallying to aid the afflicted as much as possible. With this kind of aid, plus assistance from extended kin as well, a remarkable degree of success was achieved by Mrs. Moir whose second husband left her and her eighteen-year-old daughter penniless in Fort Hope, B.C. in 1864 (Ormsby, 1976). An early attempt at institutionalizing protection for deserted families, "turning off," is reported by Van Kirk (1977:20) in the Red River settlement in the 1830s.

Historical demographic analysis of aging as a part of the life cycle is not yet available for Canada, but, citing figures for the United States, Synge (1980: 137-138) concludes that there was no "empty nest" stage for women born even as late as the 1880s. Only half the women who married could expect to have their spouses survive until the children reached adulthood. The picture described by Katz (1975:225) of the married persons in the different age categories who became widowed between 1851 and 1861 in Hamilton, Ontario, substantiates his statement that widowhood was "a frequent experience." One out of four women and one out of ten men between the ages of 40-49 in 1851 were widowed by 1861, and the percentages increased to 34 for women and 15 for men at ages 50-59, and 54 for women and 32 for men who were 60-69 years of age. When marriage breakup due to the death of a spouse was combined with that due to desertion (which fluctuated with economic conditions), it undoubtedly affected at least proportionately as many children as a combination of divorce, death, and desertion did in the 1970s.

Sexuality

Sexual attitudes and behaviors prior to the 1890s remain in the realm of the unexplored (and perhaps unexplorable) in Canada. Exceptions are some data on premarital sex and illegitimacy, and on birth control. Premarital sex in early New France, similar to New England, appears to have been far from non-existent despite the rather strong proscriptions against it in the culture. Prenuptial conceptions for marriages celebrated between 1700 and 1730 were about 10 percent of first live births (Henripin, 1972). Most couples who conceived prior to marriage did marry legally before the child was delivered, however. As a consequence of this practice, illegitimacy was minor; less than 1 percent until after 1850, with the exception of 1741-1760, the years following the cession of Canada to England.[6] There has been fluctuation in the percentage of all births which are illegitimate, depending on societal conditions as well as demographic facts. The average for the period 1921-1925 of 2.2 percent and the high of 13 percent in 1978 are difficult to compare with earlier figures. As Henripin (1972:320) notes, a less crude and misleading index of the fertility of unmarried women would be rates based on the illegitimate births divided by the total number of women at risk (those in the childbearing years). Such computations might show that rates of illegitimacy have changed little over the years. On the other hand, it might show that as with fertility in general, they fluctuate with stressful economic conditions (Gagan, 1978:308-311; Katz, 1975:59).

As for birth control, McLaren's (1978) investigation of conditions at the end of the last century debunks the notion that married women were passive about their fertility during the Victorian period. On the contrary, he provides much evidence of their desire to limit births, and the considerable lengths they went to in order to do so. Acknowledging the impossibility of determining exactly the rate of abortion in Canada, he estimates that in 1896 between 17 and 34 percent of all pregnancies were aborted, and by 1922 the abortion rate (illegal) was somewhere between 7 and 14 percent. As he notes (1978:338), "the figure is remarkably close to that established once the practice was legalized and reliable statistics made available."

Attitudes of middle class Canadians of an earlier period about matters of their own sexuality are inferred by Bliss (1970) from best-selling English language manuals published between 1900 and 1915.[7] He concludes that the prevailing doctrine of creative sexual repression, including no masturbation, chastity before marriage, and limited sexual activity in marriage, was based on then-current mistaken medical knowledge about the physiology of sex which combined agreeably with the reformist zeal of the period. The result, he speculates, was high

---

[6]Foulche-Delbosc (1977:23) points out the greater deviance from "religious rectitude" in the more westerly and dangerous posts. For example, one illegitimate child among 674 births was found in a study of baptismal records of Notre Dame de Quebec from 1621 to 1661, extremely low.

[7]Bliss (1970) says the book reflected "sexual orthodoxy throughout much of the Western world and therefore I would be very surprised to find any significant variation of these attitudes in whatever literature in the French language on these questions that may have circulated in Canada."

anxiety in this social class, a generalization hard to dispute without further evidence. Rotenberg (1974) has called attention to the role of the double standard of morality in causing the "social evil" which prostitution represented at that time.

Summarizing the materials dealing with marriage, it appears there have been only minor changes in marriage formation and termination over the past 300 years, with considerably more modification in marital roles. The main new element which entered into mate selection prior to the nineteenth century was romantic love as an overlay to the more practical considerations of an early period. Age homogamy for first marriage increased, as a result of a somewhat lowered average age at marriage for men. There may have been fewer social pressures for racial and class homogamy in the years of the fur trade, rising during the middle of the last century and declining in this one. Whereas a tradition of Canadian husbands working away from their families began with the *coureurs de bois* in New France, it was only after industrialization that large proportions of husbands were employed away from home even in the cities. Toward the end of the nineteenth century women began entering the industrial labor force in order to contribute to urban working class family economies, just as rural women from the beginning had been totally involved in subsistence farm economies and farm enterprises as well as in paid employment as domestics. A matrifocal pattern of household relationships appears to have been not uncommon throughout Canadian history. Ironically, the middle class ideal of the Victorian lady exalted in motherhood, fully occupied with domestic matters, too delicate and emotional for participation in activities outside the home, and consequently represented by and protected by male dominance, emerged at the same time as increasing numbers of wives began assuming roles quite different from the ideal.

The stereotyped idea of wife-husband roles in the past has put too much emphasis on the confinement of women to the home-making role within the family and on their dependency. Indications are that much variation occurred, depending on cultural traditions, social class backgrounds, and the economic opportunities and circumstances of the particular historical period. Furthermore, the notion of fewer stresses and strains in marriage in the past does not seem warranted at this point. Desertion and the premature death of a spouse were likely disruptions of a high percentage of marriages in all earlier periods. Dependent children were frequently orphaned.[8]

---

[8]Uhlenberg 91980:315) calculates the probability of one or both parents dying before an American child reached age 15 in 1900 was .24 compared with 105 in 1976,

II. The Social History of Family Life

Children

It is only back to about 125 years ago that any image of children in Canadian families, other than their numbers, begins to materialize. Why were they not much noticed? What were they doing? Is the widely-held idea true that childhood was once a happier time and that it was more prolonged? Is it only in recent years that children have come to be looked after outside the home, and other agencies to become involved in their welfare?

Starting with the last question above, there is evidence that the contemporary institutionalized idea of the family as the guardian of minor children has not been much altered since the seventeenth century (Foulche-Delbosc, 1977:26). Not only did parents tend to the physical well-being of their children, but also financial responsibility upon the death of a parent was provided for in marriage contracts. On the other hand, Foulche-Delbosc hints at community involvement in child welfare in the following manner: "...in the early years of the colony, before families had many ramifications, we find outsiders devoting their time and energy to the interests of little children with praise-worthy zeal." Presumably she alludes to the nuns of the Catholic Church, who were on the scene in sizeable proportions (Sabagh, 1942:688) from the start. There has been a tendency to view the supports offered families by other institutions as novel to this century. History indicates otherwise.

Studies of families in the early years suggest that children were rather much involved in family and society in the same way as their parents, which may account for so few observations about them in accounts of early life. Prior to the middle of the nineteenth century "English-Canadians showed little awareness of children as individual persons; second, they saw nothing of the inner, emotional life of youngsters; third, young people played an important and often central role in rural and in family economies" (Sutherland, 1976:6-7).

As Gaffield (1979:57) describes the work of children in rural eastern Ontario in the 1850s and 1860s it paralleled that of adults. Accordingly, "Women organized this domestic industry on the basis of full participation by their sons and daughters." He attributes the lag in school attendance rates behind those in urban centres, like Hamilton, to the need for full participation in the family economy by children as soon as they were physically capable. Even in the working class sectors of the cities, however, child labor was a widespread practice, with

---

demonstrating that during this century orphanhood changed from a common occurrence to a rare event.

children's earnings being vital to family economies. Bradbury (1979:77-79) states that one out of four boys between eleven and fifteen years of age was reported in an occupation in the 1871 census of Ste. Anne. As Copp (1972:160) says, "With twelve as the minimum age for boys and fourteen for girls child labour was not only common, but legal." In that industrial section of Montreal, the larger a family, the more likely a young child would be sent out to work. Social class was the determining factor, with ethnicity also playing a part, since French-Canadian families were somewhat more likely to send their young children to work than other groups. Perhaps the cultural difference could be traced to family work patterns in subsistence agriculture in rural Quebec from where families had migrated.

Redefining the study of school attendance as a "record of family decision about formal education," Katz (1972b:433) documents the fact that poverty, rather than ethnic origins, kept children out of school. He found children of widows in Hamilton in 1851-61 particularly disadvantaged in attending school (Katz, 1978:S102). Obviously they had to work to help with family finances.

The research on attitudes toward children in families in English Canada suggests that the "twentieth century consensus" about children was "framed" in the industrializing and Victorian context (Sutherland, 1976). Houston (1972:256) traces the concept of "juvenile delinquency" to changes which occurred within middle class Victorian families. In this class children assumed a more conspicuous and integrated family role. The solution the reformers devised to deal with the new phenomenon of vast numbers of children of the urban poor on the city streets was "the creation of surrogate institutions for the lower classes appropriately analogous to middle-class family life." Glazebrook (1971:208) sketches the manner in which Ontario during this time attempted to deal with the requirements for social welfare. A number of moves were made for the extrafamilial protection of children, including the establishment of orphanages, hospitals for children, reformatories for boys and girls, the Humane Society, the Children's Aid Society, and of course, public schools. The provision of welfare facilities for children, as adjuncts to families, should not obscure the continuing role of nuclear families in looking after orphaned or deserted children, as the household figures indicate (Gagan and Mays, 1973:45). The lives of these children were often far from happy, as the cases of neglect, abuse, and exploitation of orphaned British children taken in by Canadian families in the period 1870-1930 demonstrates (Sutherland, 1976: Harrison, 1979).

The emergence of a new phase in the life cycle — a prolonged period of time spent with parents between puberty and marriage — is traced by Katz (1978) to the period of early industrialization in Canada. Modern patterns were already established by 1861 in Hamilton. For example, a drop occurred from a decade earlier in the large proportion (55 percent) of idle youths (13-16 years old) living with parents but neither in work nor at school, roaming the streets. Contrary to popular impressions, the problem of young people adrift in cities is not a recent problem. According to Katz it helped to make industrialization possible. The new phenomenon in western history of adolescent children living at home in the last century may have been responsible for the increase in working class home-ownership, according to Katz. He has also shown that young men in the early industrial cities of Canada did not follow in their fathers' trades to any great extent; they chose expanding sectors of the economy. On the other hand, the line between manual and non-manual occupations was fairly rigid, with most sons inheriting the manual and non-manual occupational world of their fathers. Unmarried girls, too, began seeking employment other than as domestic servants, and attending school. As Synge (1979:250) has observed, although the primary role of the working class adolescent in the early part of the twentieth century was of wage earner and contributor to the family income, the recent entry of married women to paid employment is in part a response to the withdrawal of teenage children from the labor force in this century.

Provision for child care outside the home appears to have been made in Canada as early as the middle of the last century, although not in name or intent. It appears from Katz's (1972b) investigations in Hamilton, 1851, that the "baby-sitting function" of the public schools served both the poor and wealthy families. Families with servants (an indicator of relative wealth) were more likely to send children to school early if there were large numbers of children in the family; in smaller families with servants, children were taught to read at home. Some slight proportion of children under five years attended school, although most entered at about age seven. As far as the first day-care facility, it may have been the East End Day Nursery, founded in Toronto in 1892 (Klein and Roberts, 1974:236) to deal with the problem of mothers being prevented from employment because of their maternal responsibilities. Government nurseries were established during the First World War in cities like Toronto (Ramkhalawansingh, 1974:292-293) as they were during World War II (Pierson, 1976:155).

To sum up the research on children in families in Canadian history, until the present century their experience corresponded to that of their parents and other adults. Children in earlier times were an important source of labor, both in rural Canada and in the cities during industrialization. Compulsory school attendance and the provision of other social welfare facilities in the last part of the nineteenth century changed that situation. During that same period, adolescence emerged as a new stage in the life cycle of individuals, which may have had profound effects on family and social life in the twentieth century. Little evidence can be found in the records that the childhood of the average Canadian in the past was either happier or that it lasted longer than that of contemporary children. Nor are there data to support the idea that nuclear families which had primary responsibility for child welfare in the past, much as today, were better equipped to provide children with greater stability or security.

The emergence of a social history of Canadian families

The brief summary of published literature made in the previous section of this paper has been the result of culling two kinds of sources: descriptive and explanatory materials. Some items, of course, included a combined approach. There are several different types of descriptive data: the literary reflections found in letters, diaries, and accounts of travelers, pioneers, and immigrants; official and unofficial records; and demographic materials such as censuses and vital statistics reports. Literary works have been much exploited by historians and a few have been frequently cited. They will continue to be used to gain clues about the phantom of the Canadian collective family past, and new ones will be undoubtedly forthcoming. Historians have made the best use of these materials (see Gagan, 1976a, on their limitations), but sociologists too have referred to them and will continue to rely on them. More familiar to sociologists are the demographic materials. One problem in their use is the discontinuity of time series, which makes for difficulty in relating changes to significant social and political events. The second kind of materials are the explanatory investigations. Generally sociologists who have explained trends in family indicators either correlate two or more items of family behavior, such as fertility and marriage rates, or they attribute patterns to broad societal processes, such as urbanization, industrialization, and modernization. The tendency of sociologists to generalize about the effects of such abstractly conceived factors as industrialization and modernization on family has obscured genuine understanding of developmental patterns. Fortunately the healthy concern with change, process, and content which illuminates much of the work of recent historians has provided accounts in which family patterns and experiences are related to specific social processes. Instead of dealing narrowly with structural changes in family over the entire 380 years of Canadian history, they investigate the interplay between family and social events within a specific time frame.

What do the selected references reported on in this paper represent in the overall development of family history in this country? Who is doing it? How does it compare with the American, British, and French enterprises? How far along is Canadian social history of the family? In which direction should it be heading?

Obviously the quantity of the research is not impressive, either absolutely or relatively. Of a total 430 entries in Milden's (1977) guide to the literature on family in history listed in the section on "The family in American history" (excluding the sub-section on the black family), nine were Canadian.[9] Seven of the nine Canadian listings were the published works of historians. Brym (1979:vii-viii) has given what he accurately refers to as a "not watertight" explanation for this state of affairs, namely the influence of the "static functionalism" of the American sociological tradition. Be that as it may, the Canadian situation of family study by sociologists does not appear to be much different from that described for the United States by Elder (1978:S23) who states that "genuine historical research on family and kinship is clearly not the vigorous industry...that we observe in...history."

In the several years since Milden's bibliography was published there indeed has been an acceleration in historical investigations of family life in Canada, and it appears that students have been encouraged to shift their inquiries in the direction of social history. In general, the cross-disciplinary nature of women's studies in the universities has given immense impetus to this development (see Prentice, 1978).

How far is the enterprise then? As this review of the literature indicates, the materials for Canada do not as yet lend themselves well to the kind of general history of the family which Shorter (1975), admittedly with "massive modesty," was able to undertake with "solid, primary evidence" mainly from France, starting with the sixteenth and seventeenth centuries. Nor does it seem possible to do as Stone (1977) did for England, between 1500, 1700, or Laslett (1972) for western Europe as a whole from the preindustrial to the modern era. Whether the applicable metaphor is the "turning point" (Demos, 1978), or the general direction is "up and left" (Brym, 1979) or "at the crossroads" (a pessimist might even say "at the starting line"), some momentum has

---

[9]Newton (1978) in a review, notes the flaws for Canadian researchers; lumping Canadian materials with the United States as "American," the absence of material on Quebec, and no mention of Native American families. The present article contains the latter omission as well.

been achieved. Family sociologists however, hardly seem to be aware of the archival studies of family relations, generations, and the life course that historians have turned their attention toward. In fact, sociologists seem far from being able to instruct those interested on how to do so (see, for example, Schulz, 1974). Most tellingly, they have yet to embark on any kind of intellectual exchange over social theory and its relation to the Canadian historical record; revisionist Marxist theory goes unchallenged. On the positive side, however, is the movement away from such abstract characterization of historical events ("modernization") and family experience ("systems" and "forms") to a focus on the historical world of families and the interaction between family members. This middle-level approach (between the general of sociology and the concrete of history) is what makes possible tie-ins with structural trends and specific processes of family change, or between various institutions.

What directions should sociologists be taking? First, needless to say, work that has begun should be continued, filling in materials for neglected timoo and regions and revising the interpretation as new data are uncovered and created. As the review in these pages indicates, several imbalances exist in the present accumulation of information: between urban and rural studies, between the relative opportunities for historical research in, say, Alberta (very poor), Ontario (good for the nineteenth century), Quebec (excellent), and the Maritimes (where virtually no work has been done), and between the various historical eras. Answers should be sought to questions suggested by discrepancies exposed in the "story"; every reconstruction needs to be challenged.

"Setting the record straight" is a basic and important task for historians, and their investigations into social conflicts and shifts have resulted in a rather substantial amount of family-related research which arises from other concerns (e.g., education). Furthermore, they have suggested (Armstrong, 1971) and demonstrated (Gagan, 1971) that the history of one family over many generations, or geneology, can "yield a rich harvest in Canadian social history."

For sociologists, however, much work lies ahead in identifying variables inside the family as an operating system, discovering methods of salvage, and determining the relationship between family life and societal events. There is at present only an insubstantial amount of research oriented toward life-cycle analysis. This is an area where very real opportunities exist for us, using either macro-level analyses based on published sources or creating our own micro-data for analysis."[10]

In conclusion, by addressing both issues — the one of families in societal context and the other of the experiences of persons in families and their meanings — a history of Canadian families would emerge. To paraphrase Kealey and Warrian (1976:8), in this enterprise the concern would be far from filling the interstices of the old theoretical tradition with odd facts and events that have escaped more conventional family sociologists; instead when established, it will constitute a new, distinctive and dynamic synthesis of knowledge about Canadian families, past and present.

References

Ambert, Anne-Marie.
1980 *Divorce in Canada*. Don Mills, Ontario: Academic Press.
Armstrong, F.H. 1971 "The family: some aspects of a neglected approach to Canadian historical studies," in *Historical Papers*, pp. 112-123. Canadian Historical Association.
Bliss, Michael.
1970 "Pure books on avoided subjects: pre-Freudian sexual ideas in Canada." In *Historical Papers*, pp. 89-108. Canadian Historical Association.
Bouchard, Gerard.
1977 "Family structure and geographic mobility at Laterriere, 1851-1935." *Journal of Family History* 2:350-369.
Bouvier, Leon F.
1968 "The spacing of births among French-Canadian families: an historical approach." *Canadian Review of Sociology and Anthropology* 5:17-26.
Boyd, Monica, Margrit Eichler, and John R. Hofley.
1976 "Family: functions, and fertility." In *Opportunity for Choice*, edited by Gail C.A. Cook, pp. 13-52. Ottawa: Statistics Canada in association with the C.D. Howe Research Institute.

---

[10]Of note in the latter category are the data bank on Quebec's early population created by Legare (1972; 1977) in order to "analyze deeply" the demographic behaviour of Canadian society under the French regime, the application of cross-section regression techniques to historical census micro-data by Denton and George (1970; 1973); and the techniques adapted to problems of data retrieval by Orastein and Darroch (1978). At another level, using oral traditions, Synge (1980) analyzes the experiences of persons in past families.

Bradbury, Bettina.
1979 "The family economy and work in an industrializing city: Montreal in the 1870s." In *Historical Papers*, pp. 71-76. Canadian Historical Association.
Brym, Robert J.
1979 "New directions in Anglo-Canadian historical sociology." *Canadian Journal of Sociology* 4(3):vii-xi.
Burnet, Jean R.
1972 *Ethnic Groups in Upper Canada*. Ontario Historical Society Research Publication No. 1.
Charbonneau, Hubert, Yolande Lavoie et Jacques Legare.
1971 "Le recensement nominatif du Canada en 1681." *Histoire Sociale* 7:77-98.
Charles, Enid.
1948 *The Changing Size of the Canadian Family*. 1941 Census Monograph. Ottawa: King's Printer.
Cook, Ramsay and Wendy Mitchinson, eds.
1976 *The Proper Sphere: Woman's Place in Canadian Society*. Toronto: Oxford University Press.
Copp, J.T.
1974 "The condition of the working class in Montreal, 1897-1920." In *Studies in Canadian Social History*, edited by Michael Horn and Ronald Sabourin, pp. 70-87. Toronto: McClelland and Stewart.
Davey, Ian and Michael Doucet.
1975 "The social geography of a commercial city, ca. 1853." In *The People of Hamilton, Canada West*, edited by Michael Katz, pp. 319-342. Cambridge, Mass.: Harvard University Press.
Demos, John and Sarane Boocock.
1978 "Sociology: introduction and overview." In *Turning Points: Historical and Sociological Essays on the Family*, edited by John Demos and Sarane Spence Boocock, pp. iv-xix. Chicago: The University of Chicago Press.
Denton, Frank T. and Peter J. George.
1970 "An exploratory statistical analysis of some socio-economic characteristics of families in Hamilton, Ontario, 1871." *Histoire Sociale* 5:16-44.
1973 "The influence of socio-economic variables on family size in Ontario, 1871: a statistical analysis of historical micro-data." *Canadian Review of Sociology and Anthropology* 10(4):334-345.
Doucet, Michael J.
1976 "Working class housing in a small nineteenth-century Canadian city: Hamilton, Ontario 1852-1881." In *Essays in Canadian Working*

Class History, edited by Gregory S. Kealey and Peter Warrian. Toronto: McClelland and Stewart.

Elder, Glen H., Jr.
1978 "Approaches to social change and the family." *American Journal of Sociology* 84:S1-S38.

Elkin, Frederick.
1968 *The Family in Canada*. Ottawa: The Vanier Institute.

Fortin, G.
1970 "Women's role in the evolution of agriculture in Quebec." In *Social and Cultural Change in Canada*, Vol. 1, edited by W.E. Mann, pp. 224-229. Toronto: Copp Clark.

Foulche-Delbosc, Isabel.
1977 "Women of Three Rivers, 1651-63." In *The Neglected Minority: Essays in Women's History*, edited by Susan Mann Trofemenkoff and Alison Prentice. Toronto: McClelland and Stewart.

Gaffield, Chad M.
1978 "Canadian families in cultural context: hypotheses from the mid-nineteenth century." *Historical Papers*, pp. 48-70. Canadian Historical Association.

Gagan, David.
1971 "The historical identity of the Denison family of Toronto, 1792-1860." *Historical Papers*, pp. 124-137, Canadian Historical Association.
1976a "The prose of life: literary reflections on the family, individual experience and social structure in nineteenth-century Canada." *Journal of Social History* 9:367-381.
1976b "The indivisibility of land: a microanalysis of the system of inheritance in nineteenth-century Ontario." *Journal of Economic History* 36:126-141.
1978 "Land, population, and social change: the 'critical years' in rural Canada West." *Canadian Historical Review* 59(3):293-318.

Gagan, David and Herbert Mays.
1973 "Historical demography and Canadian social history: families and land in Peel County, Ontario." *Canadian Historical Review* 54:27-7.

Garigue, Phillippe.
1964 "Change and continuity in French Canada." In *French-Canadian Society*, Vol. 1, edited by Marcel Rioux and Yves Martin, pp. 123-137. Toronto: McClelland and Stewart Ltd.

Gerin, Leon.
1964 "The French-Canadian family — its strengths and weaknesses." In *French-Canadian Society*, Vol. 1, edited by Marcel Rioux and Yves Martin, pp. 32-56. Toronto: McClelland and Stewart Ltd.

Glazebrook, G.P. de T.
1971 *Life in Ontario: A Social History.* Toronto: University of Toronto Press.
Goheen, Peter G.
1970 *Victorian Toronto, 1850 to 1900: Pattern and Process of Growth.* Department of Geography, University of Chicago. Research Paper No. 127.
Goode, William J.
1970 *World Revolution and Family Patterns.* New York: Free Press.
Gordon, Michael, ed.
1973 *The American Family in Social-Historical Perspective.* New York: St. Martin's Press.
Graff, Harvey J.
1976 "Counting on the past: quantification in history." *Acadiensis* 6(1):115-129.
Graubard, Stephen R.
1977 "Preface to the issue on the family." *Daedalus* 106:v-xiv
Griffiths, Naomi 1976 *Penelope's Web: Some Perceptions of Women in European and Canadian Society.* Toronto: Oxford University Press.
Harrison, Phyllis, ed.
1979 *The Home Children: Their Personal Stories.* Winnipeg: Watson and Dwyer Publishing Company.
Henripin, Jacques.
1957 "From acceptance of nature to control: the demography of French Canadians since the 17th century." *Canadian Journal of Economics and Political Science* 23:10-19.
1972 *Trends and Factors of Fertility in Canada.* 1961 Census Monograph. Ottawa: Statistics Canada.
Himelfarb, Alexander and C. James Richardson.
1979 *People, Power and Process: Sociology for Canadians.* Toronto: McGraw-Hill Ryerson Limited.
Houston, Susan E.
1972 "Victorian origins of juvenile delinquency: a Canadian experience." *History of Education Quarterly* 12:254-280.
Irving, Howard I.
1972 *The Family Myth.* Toronto: Copp Clark.
Ishwaran, K., ed.
1971 *The Canadian Family.* Toronto: Holt, Rinehart and Winston.
Jacobson, Helga E.
1971 "The family in Canada: some problems and questions." In *The Canadian Family*, edited by K. Ishwaran, pp. 23-38. Toronto: Rinehart and Winston.

II. The Social History of Family Life

Johnson, Leo.
1974 "The political economy of Ontario women in the nineteenth century." In *Women at Work: Ontario 1850-1930*, edited by J. Acton, B. Shepard, and P. Goldsmith, pp. 13-32. Toronto: The Canadian Women's Educational Press.

Katz, Michael.
1972a "The people of a Canadian city: 1851-52." *Canadian Historical Review* 53:249-401.
1972b "Who went to school?" *History of Education Quarterly* 12:432-454.
1975 *The People of Hamilton West: Family and Class in a Mid-Nineteenth Century City.* Cambridge Mass.: Harvard University Press.

Katz, Michael B. and Ian E. Davey.
1978 "Youth and early industrialization in a Canadian city." In *Turning Points: Historical and Sociological Essays on the Family*, edited by John Demos and Sarane Spence Boocock. Chicago: University of Chicago Press.

Kealey, Gregory S. and Peter Warrian, eds.
1976 *Essays in Canadian Working Class History.* Toronto: McClelland and Stewart Limited.

Kenkle, William F.
1978 *The Family in Perspective.* Fourth Edition. New York: Appleton-Century Crofts.

Klein, Alice and Wayne Roberts.
1974 "Besieged innocence: the 'problem' and problems of working women — Toronto 1896-1914." In *Women at Work: Ontario 1850-1930*, pp. 211-261, edited by J. Acton, B. Shepard, and P. Goldsmith. Toronto: The Canadian Women's Educational Press.

Larson, Lyle, ed.
1976 *The Canadian Family in Comparative Perspective.* Scarborough, Ontario: Prentice-Hall.

Laslett, Peter.
1972 *The World We Have Lost.* Second Edition. London: Methuen.

Legare, Jacques, Yolande Lavoie, and Hubert Charbonneau.
1972 "The early Canadian population: problems in automatic record linkage." *Canadian Historical Review* 53(4):427-442.

Legare, Jacques, Pierre Beauchamp, and Bertrand Desjardins.
1977 "Automatic family reconstitution: the French-Canadian seventeenth-century experience." *Journal of Family History* 2:56-76.

Leslie, Genevieve.
1974 "Domestic service in Canada, 1880-1920." In *Women at Work: Ontario 1850-1930*, edited by J. Acton, B. Shepard, and P. Goldsmith, pp. 71-126. Toronto: The Canadian Women's Educational Press.
McClung, Nellie 1972 *In Times Like These.* Toronto: University of Toronto Press.
McLaren, Angus.
1978 "Birth control and abortion in Canada, 1870-1920." *Canadian Historical Review* 59:319-340.
Masters, Donald C.
1958 *A Short History of Canada.* New York, Toronto: Nostrand Reinhold Company.
Medjuck, Sheva.
1979 "Family and household composition in the nineteenth century: the case of Moncton, New Brunswick 1851 to 1871." *Canadian Journal of Sociology* 4(3):275-285.
Milden, James Wallace.
1977 *The Family In Past Time: A Guide to the Literature.* New York: Garland Publishing Company, Inc.
Miner, Horace.
1938 "Changes in rural French-Canadian culture." *American Journal of Sociology* 48:365-378.
Moodie, Susanna.
1962 *Roughing it in the Bush.* Or *Forest Life in Canada.* Toronto: McClelland and Stewart Limited.
Newton, Jennifer L.
1978 "Review of James Wallace Milden. The Family in Past Time." *Canadian Newsletter of Research On Women* 7:101-102.
Ormsby, Margaret A.
1976 *A Pioneer Gentlewoman in British Columbia.* Vancouver: University of British Columbia Press.
Ornstein, Michael D. and A. Gordon Darroch.
1978 "National mobility studies in past time: a sampling strategy." *Historical Methods* 11(4):152-161.
Pelletier A.J. and F.D. Thompson.
1942 *The Canadian Family.* Sixth Census of Canada 1921. Ottawa:
Peterkin, Audrey and Margaret Shaw.
1976 *Mrs. Doctor: Reminiscences of Manitoba Doctors' Wives.* Winnipeg: The Prairie Publishing Company.
Pierson, Ruth 1976.
"Women's emancipation and the recruitment of women into the Canadian labour force in World War II." *Historical Papers*, pp. 141-173. Canadian Historical Association.

Potrebenko, Helen.
1977 *No Streets of Gold: A Social History of Ukrainians in Alberta.*
Vancouver: New Star Books.
Prentice, Alison.
1972 "Education and the metaphor of the family: the Upper Canadian
example." *History of Education Quarterly*: 12:281-303.
1978 "Writing women into history: the history of women's work in
Canada." *Atlantis* 3:72-84.
Prentice, Alison and Susan E. Houston, eds.
1975 *Family, School and Society in Nineteenth-Century Canada.*
Toronto: Oxford University Press.
Ramkhalawansingh, Ceta.
1974 "Women during the Great War." In *Women at Work: Ontario
1850-1930*, edited by J. Acton, B. Shepard, and P. Goldsmith, pp. 261-
308. Toronto: The Canadian Women's Educational Press.
Ramu, G.N.
1976 "Courtship, marriage, and family in Canada." In *Introduction to
Canadian Society: Sociological Analysis*, edited by G.N. Ramu and
Stuart Johnson, pp. 295-348. Toronto: Macmillan.
Roberts, Barbara.
1978 From memory into history: social histories and the shape of
women's lives. *Canadian Newsletter of Research on Women* 7:67-71.
1979 "'A work of Empire': Canadian reformers and British female
immigration." In *A Not Unreasonable Claim: Women and Reform in
Canada 1880's-1920's*, edited by Linda Kealey, pp. 185-201. Toronto:
The Women's Press.
Roberts, Wayne.
1976 *Honest Womanhood: Feminism, Femininity and Class
Consciousness Among Toronto Working Women, 1893-1914.* Toronto:
Hogtown Press.
Robertson, Heather.
1974 *Salt of the Earth.* Toronto: James Lorimer and Company,
Publishers.
Rotenbert, Lori.
1974 "The wayward worker: Toronto's prostitute at the turn of the
century." In *Women at Work: Ontario 1850-1930*, edited by J. Acton, B.
Shepard, and P. Goldsmith, pp. 33-69. Toronto: The Canadian
Women's Educational Press.
Sabagh, Georges.
1942 "The fertility of the French Canadian women during the seven-
teenth century." *American Journal of Sociology* 38:680-689.

Schulz, Patricia.
1974 "Research Guide." In *Women at Work: Ontario 1850-1930*, edited by J. Acton, B. Shepard, and P. Goldsmith, pp. 363-368. Toronto: The Canadian Women's Educational Press.
Shorter, Edward.
1975 *The Making of the Modern Family*. New York: Basic Books Inc., Publishers.
Smith, James E. and Barbara Laslett.
1979 "Introduction to the special issue on historical change in marriage and the family." *Sociology and Social Research* 63:325-431.
Synge, Jane.
1979 "The transition from school to work: growing up working class in early 20th century Hamilton, Ontario. In *Childhood and Adolescence in Canada*, edited by K. Ishwaran, pp. 249-269. Toronto: McGraw-Hill Ryerson Limited.
1980 "Work and family support patterns of the aged in the early twentieth century." In *Aging in Canada*, edited by Victor W. Marshall, pp. 135-144. Toronto: Fitzhenry and Whiteside.
Strong-Boag, Veronica.
1979 "Canada's women doctors: feminism constrained." In *A Not Unreasonable Claim Women and Reform in Canada 1880's-1920's*, edited by Linda Kealey, pp. 109-129. Toronto: The Women's Press.
Sutherland, Neil.
1976 *Children of English-Canadian Society: Framing the Twentieth-Century Consensus*. Toronto: University of Toronto Press.
Tepperman, Lorne 1974 "Ethnic variations in marriage and fertility: Canada 1871." *Canadian Review of Sociology and Anthropology* 11(4):324-342.
1978 "Sociology in English-speaking Canada: the last five years." *Canadian Historical Review* 59:435-446.
Uhlenberg, Peter 1980 "Death and the family." *Journal of Family History* 5(3):313-320.
Van Kirk, Sylvia.
1977 "The impact of white women on fur trade society." In *Essays in Canadian Women's History: The Neglected Majority*, edited by Susan Mann Trofimenkoff and Alison Prentice. Toronto: McClelland and Stewart Limited.
Wakil, S. Parvez, ed.
12975 *Marriage, Family and Society: Canadian Perspectives*. Toronto: Butterworth.

The Fragmented Family: Family Strategies in the Face of Death, Illness, and Poverty, Montreal, 1860-1885*

Bettina Bradbury

Working-class families in mid- to late-nineteenth-century Montreal lived in fairly constant contact with disease, poverty, and death. The newborn children of the poor were almost as likely to die as to live. Many families were fragmented by the death of a mother or father. Many more experienced periods when one or both parents or children were sick, perhaps hovering on death. The high incidence of disease coupled with the fragility of many a family's earning power presented constant challenges to basic survival and to family coherence and stability.[1]

As the city industrialized, families were increasingly dependent upon an uncertain and very seasonal labour market. Fathers were usually the primary wage-earners. In all but the most skilled of working-class households, however, additional wage-earners were necessary. Only seldom did a wife and mother work for wages. It was to their children that working-class parents turned for the necessary extra income. In addition, the family required the labour of the mother and, often, daughters in the home to make the necessary purchases, cook, sew, and clean to replenish the working members.[2]

Their family economy was a fragile one, changing over the life cycle, but always subject to sudden challenges. If either wage-earner

---

*From *Childhood and Family in Canadian History* by Joy Parr. Used by permission of the Canadian Publishers, McClelland and Stewart, Toronto.

[1] Philip Carpenter, "On Some of the Causes of the Excessive Mortality of Young Children in the City of Montreal," *The Canadian Naturalist*, New Series, Vol. 4 (1869), 198. Paul André Linteau, René Duroche et Jean-Claude Robert, *Histoire du Québec Contemporain* (Montréal: Boréal Express, 1979), especially Chapter 7 and pp. 175-9; Fernand Harvey, *Revolution industrielle et travailleurs, Une enqête sur les rapports entre le capital et le travail au Québec à la fin du 19e siècle* (Montréal: Boréal Express, 1978); Bettina Bradbury, "The Family Economy and Work in An Industrializing City, Montreal in the 1870s: Canadian Historical Association, *Historical Papers* (1979). On the need for several family members to work in a different city, see Frances H. Early, "The French Canadian Family Economy and Standard of Living in Lowell, Massachusetts, 1870," paper presented at the Canadian Historical Association Meetings, Montreal, June, 1980).

[2] Bradbury, "The Family Economy," 77-8, 86.

or mother became sick, families faced a temporary crisis. If either died, the crisis was more fundamental. Even at such times as pregnancy or childbirth the delicate balance of incoming wages and household management could be shattered. Only when both parents survived and several children reached working age was a degree of financial security ensured. While sons and daughters were too young to work parents had to seek other ways of stretching their incomes or minimizing necessary expenditures. When sickness, death, or loss of work shattered a family's precarious material security, help had to be sought from neighbours, kin, or charity.[3]

Working-class families dealt with such crises in a variety of ways. Some, when the future seemed particularly bleak and impossible, gave up their children permanently to kin, orphanages, or other institutions. Some shared housing with relatives or strangers. A few mothers took jobs that could be done at home; still fewer went out to work. Charity tied others over difficult times, while some placed their children temporarily in orphanages, taking them home again when the particular crisis had passed or when they were old enough to work.[4]

It is particularly with this latter strategy that this paper is concerned. The history of the use that parents made of one Montreal orphanage, L'Orphelinat St. Alexis, in St. Jacques ward, shows how some families responded to poverty, sickness, and death. The experiences of these children shed light more generally on family survival strategies.

The impact of poverty, sickness, and death upon working-class families cannot be understood apart from the context within which they lived. Throughout the nineteenth century, but especially after 1850, Montreal changed rapidly, if unevenly, from a city dominated by commerce to one in which industry held a central and increasingly important position. Children grew up in a world that was visibly changing and very different from that of their parents' youth. Parents raising their families in an industrializing city had to draw on both old traditions and new resources.

Since the 1850's industrial capitalists had persistently reshaped the nature of production and work. Their factories employed hundreds

---

[3]Jane Humphries, "Class Struggle and the Persistence of the Working Class Family," *Cambridge Journal of Economics*, I (1977), 248-9.

[4]Bradbury, "The Family Economy," 92, 86. On the semi-permanent giving up of children to orphanages in England, see Joy Parr, *Labouring Children* (London: Croom Helm, 1980), especially Chapter 4, "Family Strategy and Philanthropic Abduction."

of workers, drawing on an increasing proportion of the city's growing population. The pace and speed of change varied from trade to trade. Its fundamental result was the divorce of an ever-growing number of workers from ownership of their own productive units and from control over their work. The sons and daughters of both rural and urban producers became an urban proletariat. They formed families with no capital and no land to fall back on in times of crisis. Their survival depended on their ability to sell their labour power in an impersonal and changing labour market.[5]

The reorganization of work coincident with factory production was rendering old skills obsolete. "There is a considerable feeling of depression," explained a shoemaker in 1888, "because the working man has been replaced by a machine." Apprentices no longer learned how to make a commodity from beginning to end. They had become cheap sources of labour for employers interested only in maximum, rapid production. Women and children as well as men were drawn into the new and usually tedious kinds of jobs created by the mechanization of old processes. Skilled workers faced competition from unskilled workers and from women and children in jobs that might retain their old names but were fundamentally altered in their content.[6]

These changes in the nature of production had contradictory effects upon the families of the growing proletariat. Skilled workers' chances of being unemployed increased. A swelling body of unskilled workers would compete for jobs and depress wages, or at least prevent them from rising. On the other hand, with the growing demand for female and child labour, some other family members were more likely able to find work. While work by sons, daughters, or wives sustained the family income, it also perpetuated the low-wage system. The desire of capital for cheap workers, and of families for extra income, were

---

[5]Gerald J.J. Tulchinsky, *The River Barons: Montreal Businessmen and the Growth of Industry and Transportation, 1837-1853* (Toronto: University of Toronto Press, 1977), especially Chapter 12; Linteau et al., *Histoire du Québec*, especially Chapter 7; Joanne Burgess, "L'industrie de la chaussure à Montréal, 1840-1870 _ Le Passage de l'artisanat à la fabrique," *Revue d'histoire d'Amerique française*, 31 (Septembre, 1977).

[6]The Royal Commission on the Relations of Labour and Capital, Quebec Evidence, 1889, 369. These testimonies are particularly eloquent and explicit on the nature and meaning of these changes to the workers. On the work of women during this period, see Suzanne Cross, "The Neglected Majority: The Changing Role of Women in 19th Century Montreal," in Susan M. Trofimenkoff and Alison Prentice (eds.), *The Neglected Majority: Essays in Canadian Women's History* (Toronto: McClelland and Stewart, 1977).

thus inextricably linked. An economy built on wage dependence would be a shaky and unstable one for many families.

The growth of industry reshaped the geography of the city as it did people's work and lives. Areas took on specific characteristics. Ste. Anne in the west and Ste. Marie in the east became predominantly industrial, working-class districts. The old city became a centre of commerce, its residents gradually moving out to the old suburbs and to the newer wards. In St. Jacques ward in the east this transition was particularly evident. Artisanal workshops and small stores, often with dwellings above them, were interspersed among workers' housing. While most productive units in the area were small workshops with under five employees, the ward's three large factories employed more people than all other manufacturing units combined.[7]

In St. Jacques old and new were mixed, but newcomers and new ways were rapidly affecting the old. Migrants to the city mingled with established city dwellers. St. Jacques' population rose by over 12,000 between 1861 and 1881, an increase of 94 per cent compared to the 55 per cent by which Montreal as a whole grew over the same period. The 2,000 houses built in the ward during these two decades were not sufficient to keep up with the influx. The demand for cheap workers' housing was a boon to the owners of land and to builders and construction companies. Proprietors took advantage of the great increase in the value of land by cramming houses as close together as possible. Houses were rapidly and carelessly constructed. City regulations aimed to prevent fire hazards were avoided more frequently in St. Jacques than in any other city ward. Wooden houses, sheds, and stables remained unbricked despite a city by-law requiring the end of wooden housing. The building of houses neither kept up with population growth nor provided space at rates that the poorer families could afford. Families shared houses. Sometimes four to five families resided in "one small tenement house." Under half of the unskilled families of the area had a dwelling to themselves. St. Jacques had the highest population density of any area of town, with over 150 people per acre in 1877, 168 in 1884, and 235 by 1896. The increased density represented an increase in the number of people sharing houses, from 1.35 families per house in 1871 to 1.65 in 1881.[8]

---

[7]Industrial Schedules, Manuscript census, 1861, 1871, St. Jacques Ward.

[8]Montreal's population increased from 90,323 in 1861 to 140,747 in 1881. In the same period that of St. Jacques increased from 13,104 to 25,398. On the nature of this part of town, see Bradbury, "The Family Economy," 74; Census of Canada, 1861, 1871, 1881; "Mayor's Valedictory," *Reports on the Accounts of the Corporation of the City of Montreal, 1870* (hereafter *Montreal Annual Reports*), 90; "Report of the Inspector of

Crowding and high death rates went hand in hand. Throughout this period St. Jacques and Ste. Marie wards consistently had the highest death rates in the city. City records placed St. Jacques' rate at between 35 and 39 per 1,000 in the 1870's and around 30 in the 1880's. However, as a Dr. Fenwick pointed out in the 1870's, aggregate rates hide vast variations. He suggested that, "in certain unhealthy and overcrowded courts, or in certain crowded districts of this city" mortality rose "to 40, 50, 60 or 70 per 1,000" while "in the other more open, airy and well ventilated localities the death rate" fell to 10 or 20 per 1,000. Such an overcrowded area lay in the southeastern corner of St. Jacques ward, stretching east into Ste. Marie. There, where once there had been a swamp, the "largest proportion of deaths" in the city were found.[9]

The city's medical officer had no hesitation in attributing high death rates to overcrowding. In such parts of town the isolation necessary to prevent the spread of smallpox was impossible. The disease spread within the "most over-crowded parts of the city, among poor families located in small badly lighted and ill ventilated rooms." Certainly overcrowding, dirt, malnutrition, and ignorance were important factors. But these were the results of poor wages and lack of steady work, and especially of the poor condition of the housing built by the speculators of the city. "It is the duty of Council," Dr. Philip Carpenter argued in 1859, "to see that the wages of death are no longer wrung from the hard earnings of the poor, but that all who undertake to let houses shall be compelled to put them and their surroundings into a condition favourable to health and life." Housing continued, however, to be expensive, poorly constructed, and unsanitary.[10]

Death hit unequally. It was the children who were dying in greatest numbers and especially the children of the working class and poor French Canadians. Of the babies born in Montreal in 1867, for instance, "two out of every five died within the year." Used to death, some parents attributed "disease and misery to the Divinity which are rather the consequence of ignorance and often of unpardonable neglect.

Buildings," *Montreal Annual Reports*, 1873; "Report of the Medical Health Officer," *Montreal Annual Reports*, 1876, 10; Bradbury, "The Family Economy," 92; Jacques Bernier, "La condition des travailleurs, 1851-1896," in Noel Belanger et al., *Les Travailleurs Québécois 1851-1896* (Montréal: Les Presses de l'Université du Québec, 1975), 47.

[9] "Report of the Medical Health Officer," 1876-79; "Mayor's Valedictory," 1874, 15-16; "Report of the Medical Health Officer," 1879, 21.

[10] "Report of the Medical Officer," 1876, 10; Philip Carpenter, *On the Relative Value of Human Life in Different Parts of Canada* (Montreal: Lovell's, 1859), 15; "Report of the Medical Officer," 1879, 11.

II. The Social History of Family Life

Children are exposed to a contagious disease, they become affected and it is said that God ordained it so."[11] In the first year of life intestinal diseases and diarrhea were the major killers. These ailments were often the result of adulterated milk to which "chalk, starch and the brains of sheep" were added to increase the specific gravity. Mothers and producers added water to make milk go further, diluting away its nourishment. Had infants been breast-fed in the early months, many of these deaths might have been avoided. But weary, malnourished mothers make poor breast-feeders. "The majority of mothers living in cities" were reported to "believe themselves incapable of nursing their infants and have recourse to artificial alimentation which is one of the principal causes of the excessive mortality of children under 1 year of age."[12]

For children over one year of age, smallpox was the major cause of death. St. Jacques and Ste. Marie were areas where resistance to inoculation was especially strong. This opposition was not mere backwardness and suspicion on the part of the people. Some vaccines had been contaminated, and even with good vaccine the experience of inoculation was gruesome and did not guarantee immunity. Families hid their children and made a variety of excuses to avoid it. In 1878, 594 people refused or avoided inoculation. In these two wards were concentrated over half of the city's smallpox deaths, but only one-third of its population.[13]

Among adults and especially women between the ages of twenty and forty, phthisis or tuberculosis was the leading killer. Predisposition to phthisis was acquired, the city's medical officer explained, "by want of exercise, by occupations which confine the thorax, by impure air, and by insufficiency and bad quality of nourishment and above all anything that lowers morale." Childbearing, depriving themselves to feed the rest of the family better, and the exhaustion of child-rearing made mothers especially vulnerable to such disease. The sickness of a mother presented special problems to wage-earning families unable to pay for assistance.[14]

---

[11]Carpenter, "Excessive Mortality," 198.

[12]"Report of the Medical Officer," 1879, 19; 1876, 65; Georges Genier, *Quelques Considerations sur les causes de la Mortalité dans Enfants contenant des conseils aux meres sur les soins a doner aux enfants* (Montréal: Senecal, 1871), 9-10.

[13]"Report of the Medical Officer," 1878, 24, 18. It should be noted that such parents were not as remiss as we might think. Smallpox inoculations were gruesome and often dangerous during this period.

[14]"Report of the Medical Officer," 1877, 65.

Bradbury: The Fragmented Family

In this changing, growing, and probably bewildering city, keeping a family sheltered, clothed, healthy, and together was a difficult task. Some parents just could not cope. At all stages of a family's life cycle a few, seeing no way out, deserted their children on their spouse. Some parents, married or single, abandoned their newborn children at the doors of the city's founding hospital. These babies' chance in life was minimal. Of the more than 600 abandoned in 1863, for instance, only 10 per cent survived. Many were already dead by the time the Grey Nuns found them. Other parents relinquished all moral control over their older sons and daughters, allowing them to roam the streets by night and day, to the consternation of the upper classes. Such children moved effortlessly and almost naturally into delinquency and crime. In 1869 the Inspector of Prisons argued that abandoned children constituted the nursery from which three-quarters of the prison population sprung. It was hoped that schools of reform and industry would offer shelter to the "many poor, unhappy infants without parents, protectors or shelter." That year nearly 2,000 children under six teen went to prison.[15]

Other parents relinquished their sons and daughters permanently to city orphanages, hoping that, there, the children might escape their meagre and disorganized beginnings. By the 1860's at least twelve institutions run by six orders of nuns and various lay and Protestant groups cared for 750 orphaned youngsters annually. Some orphanages placed children out as apprentices, others had them adopted by good families. Still others retained them in the institution, giving them the education and skills necessary to make it on their own.[16]

---

[15]L.A. Huguet-Latour, *L'Annuaire de Ville Marie* (Montreal, 1863), 63. On a later period see J. Germano, "Histoire de la Charité a Montréal," *Revue Canadienne*, 32 (1896), 423-38; see also *The Municipal Loan Funds and the Hospitals and Charities of the Province of Canada* (Morning Chronicle, Quebec, 1864), 5; *The Saturday Reader*, Montreal, IV (1867), 22; "Rapport des Inspecteurs des Prisons," *Quebec Sessional Papers*, 1869, 2-3.

[16]Figures on the numbers of orphans were derived from institutions listed in Huguet-Latour, *Annuaire*, 57-103. The number (750) refers only to those in Catholic institutions; the real number, therefore, would have been considerably higher. For information on other orphanages see their annual reports, e.g., *Boys' Home Montreal, Annual Reports*, 1890; *Protestant Orphan Asylum, Annual Reports*, 1858-1869; *Protestant Infants' Home, Annual Reports*, 1870-1895. See also Alfred Sandham, *Ville Marie*, or *Sketches of Montreal Past and Present* (Montreal: Georges Bishop and Co.; 1870), 302-3; Marie-Claire Daveluy, *L'Orphelinat Catholique de Montréal*, 1832-1932 (Montréal, 1920); Janice Harvey, "Upper Class Reaction to Poverty in Mid-Nineteenth-Century Montréal: A Protestant Example" (M.A. thesis, McGill, 1978), 88-100.

II. The Social History of Family Life

But not all orphanages took children for indefinite periods. And not all demanded or expected parents to abandon their young. Several of the city's institutions consciously provided a short-term shelter where families could place their children during difficult times. Still others, while ostensibly caring for real orphans, welcomed youngsters who would sooner or later return to their own families. The St. Alexis Orphanage, located in St. Jacques ward, the area described above, was one such institution. The parents and children who used St. Alexis are interesting because they are typical of working-class families that fragmented temporarily in crisis, yet stayed together in the longer term.[17]

The St. Alexis Orphanage was officially founded in 1853. It was run by the Sisters of Providence, one of many orders created by Bishop Bourget. The mid-nineteenth century was a period when the Catholic Church throughout Quebec expanded its power, increased its personnel, and began to deal specifically with the problems of poverty and secularization accompanying industrial capitalist production. The Sisters had begun their work among the widows and the elderly. Their tasks rapidly expanded to include visiting the poor and sick in their homes, providing food for the hungry, teaching, and providing institutional care for orphans, widows, and elderly priests.[18]

Speaking in 1867 to the lay women who helped the Sisters raise money and visit the poor, Bourget pointed with evident fear to the rapid population growth and the miseries that would accompany it. He stressed that charitable institutions would have to be prepared to care for the existing wretchedness, for if they did not he believed they would be overwhelmed by it and it would recur in even more hideous form. Home visiting in the poorest neighbourhoods could prevent demoralization from devastating the lowest classes.[19] The Sisters and their lay

---

[17]The Protestant Infants' Home (founded 1870), the Montréal Protestant Orphan Asylum, and the St. Patrick's Asylum run by the Grey Nuns also took children on a short-term basis, returning them to their parents. More research is required to tell which other institutions did the same.

[18]Nive Voisine, *L'Historie de l'Eglise au Québec, 1608-1970* (Montréal: Editions Fides, 1971); Huguette Lapointe Roy, "Pauperisme et Assistance Sociale à Montréal, 1832-1865" (M.A. thesis, McGill University, 1972); Serge Gagnon, "Le diocese de Montréal durant des années 1860," in Pierre Hurtubise et al., *Le Laic Dans L'Eglise Canadienne-Francais de 1830 a Nos Jours* (Montreal: Fides, 1972); Leon Pouliot, "L'impulsion donnée par Mgr Bourget a la pratique religieuse," *Revue d'histoire d'Amerique Francaise*, 16 (juin, 1962); l'Institute de la Providence, Histoire des filles de la Charité. *Servantes des Pauvres dites soeurs de la Providence*, Vols. II, IV, VI (Providence: Maison Mere, 1940).

[19]*Histoire des Filles de la Charité*, VI, 168.

helpers would help to regulate families and keep the peace in households. They could thus instruct the ignorant, correct vices, suppress scandals, and encourage attendance at the sacraments and industry and economy among the poor.[20]

The Sisters' work in the orphanage thus blended with their work in the homes of the poor. Some families took their daughters to Sisters they had met through household visits. Sisters suggested that certain girls, especially those not receiving a Catholic upbringing at home, be sent to them. Pere Gauvin called upon the Dames de la Charité to help the Sisters to give youngsters spiritual guidance. Quoting Christ's "suffer the little children to come unto me," he suggested that the women assiduously seek out abandoned or deserted children for care by the consecrated daughters of the church.[21]

The proliferation of orphanages, schools, day nurseries, and kindergartens during this period brought more and more children into close and sustained contact with nuns and priests. They hoped through saving children to preserve the family and broaden Catholic social values. The orphanage and other charitable works were to counteract the evils of a rapidly secularizing city. Youngsters sheltered for a time in church institutions gained a religious education and the force of example to help them resist temptation when they returned home.[22]

To families, such orphanages offered pragmatic advantages. The placement of their girls temporarily in the orphanage offered parents the change to recover from sickness, bereavement, or unemployment secure in the knowledge that their children were being fed, clothed, and cared for.

Over 1,000 girls passed through the St. Alexis orphanage between 1860 and 1889. At first, parents from both rural and urban areas sheltered their children there. Increasingly over the period, however, the institution came to serve the people of Montreal and especially the families of the surrounding district of St. Jacques. By the 1880's over 80 per cent of the girls entering St. Alexis had parents who lived in Montreal.[23]

---

[20]*Histoire des Filles de la Charité*, VI, 191.

[21]Association des Dames de Charité de l'Asile de la Providence (Montréal: n.d.), 1.

[22]On schools, see Marta Danylewycz, "Through Women's Eyes: The Family in Late Nineteenth-Century Quebec," paper presented at the Canadian Historical Association meetings, Montreal, June, 1980.

[23]"Registre pour les orphelines de l'orphelinat St. Alexis" (hand-written register), Archives of the Sisters of Providence (hereafter ASP).

II. The Social History of Family Life

Nearly all these girls came from working-class families. Labourers, whose work was always temporary and poorly paid, were especially likely to send their daughters to St. Alexis. So, too, were shoemakers, men whose trade was rapidly being undermined by the reorganization of the work process, the elaboration of putting out, and the employment of women and children that accompanied industrial capitalism. The other girls' fathers were also from trades in which the pay was low, the work seasonal and especially vulnerable to cyclical variations in the economy. They were from families completely dependent on wages so low they allowed for no savings against crisis.[24]

Eighty per cent of the girls were first taken to St. Alexis when they were between the ages of four and eleven. The average age of entry was around eight, an age when children might cost as much to support in food and clothes as an adult yet were unlikely to contribute to the family income. Most children did not spend many years at the St. Alexis orphanage. The orphanage was, like the nineteenth-century city, a place of great mobility with children continually arriving and leaving. Ten per cent of the girls stayed one month or less, half for under one year. Between 1860 and 1885 the length of the girls' stays grew shorter. Increasingly, parents seem to have used the orphanage to solve short-term rather than long-term family crises. Thus in the 1860's, only one-third of the girls stayed under one year; in the 1870's 58 per cent, and between 1880 and 1885, 65 per cent. The mobility of the girls reflected that of their parents. Some were placed with the Sisters while their father or mother sought work away from Montreal. Nineteen per cent returned to families who had moved elsewhere in Quebec, three per cent to families in the United States, and one per cent to households in Ontario. Thus, of those who originally came from Montreal, a quarter did not return there.[25]

Some of the girls came to the orphanage for a second term, a few for a third. Charlotte Bolduc's stays in the orphanage, for instance, spanned eight years. She arrived first at age four in early 1873 and stayed for four months. Her mother then came and took her home but returned her a year later, this time for three years. At the age of eight she went home for five months but then returned to the orphanage for

---

[24]One hundred parents' occupations were found in the manuscript censuses and in the parish registers. 23 per cent were labourers, 19 per cent shoemakers, 9 per cent carpenters or joiners. 90 percent were in working-class occupations.

[25]This and following sections are based on the information given in the register on the 538 girls from the Montreal area who entered St. Alexis between 1860 and 1884. The register listed the child's name, her father's name, and her mother's maiden name as well as her age at entry, the dates of arrival and departure, and the person who collected her.

another four years. She left St. Alexis in 1881, old enough to be a valuable helper at home or to go out to work for wages.[26]

Of the 538 girls from Montreal who entered the orphanage between 1860 and 1885, half were accompanied, followed, or preceded by a sister. Most sisters came to the orphanage together (70 per cent), but some were brought at different times, perhaps years apart, sometimes only after an older sister had been taken home. The Feliatrault sisters, daughters of a blacksmith, present an extreme example. Albina, Alphonsine, and Maria were taken to St. Alexis by their mother, Emelie, on the 5th of January, 1871. They were aged 111/2, 9 and 6. Their older sister Fredoline, who was old enough to be helpful around the house, remained at home with her parents. Two years later the mother returned for Albina, six months later for Alphonsine, and finally three years later for Maria, now eleven years old. Maria had by then spent five years in the orphanage. In 1881 the four girls, then aged sixteen to twenty-eight, were still living with their parents, two of them working as seamstresses. Apparently their placement in the orphanage had not made them resentful of their parents, or eager to leave home. With three members at work, the family probably lived better in these years than it ever had before.[27]

The experience of the four Crepeau sisters was less happy. Their mother Celina died on the 22nd of March, 1870. That very day their father, Jerome, a forty-one-year-old labourer, took his two middle daughters to the orphanage. Seven-year-old Ernestine died there a year later. Undeterred by this sad event, Jerome took his oldest daughter to St. Alexis in 1872. She was soon apprenticed out, probably as a servant in St. Denis. Eight years later the youngest daughter came to the orphanage and was placed with a lawyer in St. Athanase. After the death of his wife, Jerome obviously tried to bring up his daughters but was forced to relinquish them one by one, until his family was scattered.[28]

Few of the St. Alexis girls were true orphans. Parents brought them to the orphanage, parents returned to take them home again. Over half of the girls whose families were found in the censuses of the

---

[26]The individual family histories were built up by matching the children to their families in the manuscript censuses of 1861, 1871, and 1881. Parish death registers were also checked to see whether their parents had died. The families of 104 girls (66 families) were found in the three censuses. "Registre" nos. 617, 675, 814.

[27]"Registre," nos. 543, 544, 545; 1881 mss. census, St. Jacques Ward, HH no. 187, Fam. no. 221.

[28]"Registre," nos. 509, 510, 608, 943; 1861 mss. census, St. Jacques Ward, no. 7865; 1871 mss. census, St. Jacques, 6, HH no. 109, Fam. no. 166.

II. The Social History of Family Life

St. Jacques area had two living parents at the time they entered St. Alexis. Probably one-third had only one parent. Three-quarters of the girls would be reclaimed by one of their parents, others were called for by kin. Only 16 per cent were adopted or apprenticed out to strangers.[29]

The death of a spouse was a common feature of married life in Montreal but a very different experience for men and women. For men it meant, indeed necessitated if there were children, hasty remarriage. For women, loss of a spouse was usually followed by years of struggle to bring up a family alone. Remarriage for widows was less likely than for widowers. If they did remarry, it was seldom soon after their first husband's death. As a result, at any one time widows always predominated over widowers. Thus, in St. Jacques ward in 1871, there were 565 widows, but only 177 widowers. Together they represented 13 per cent of all people over twenty years old. One-third of women over sixty-one were widows. Some of these lived in institutions, most tended to live alone or board with children or non-related families.[30]

For widows with young children, survival was especially precarious. Nearly all those under fifty began looking for work. Sickness or unemployment made continued care of the children extremely difficult. At least 15 per cent (thirty-four) of the girls arriving at St. Alexis had mothers who were widowed. Another three lost their fathers soon after, suggesting that their mothers had brought them to the Sisters during family illness.[31]

It was not the loss of a spouse that precipitated admission. Mothers did not place their girls in the orphanage immediately after the father's death. Rather, the death of a husband made survival more difficult for women lacking both skills and capital. Widows usually looked after their children for some time following their husband's death. They struggled to survive as best they could, working as seam-

---

[29]Estimates on how many children had one or two parents are based, first, on the families found in the three censuses and second on scrutiny of the parish registers between 1850 and 1875. The names of both parents of the girl were checked in the death registers. As the name of the spouse was given on death it was easy to be definite about matches. This method obviously missed any parents dying outside Montreal, thus underestimating the numbers with one or two dead parents. The fractions should be viewed only as reasonable approximations.

[30]For a recent review of widowhood and remarriage, set in one particular place, see Alain Bideau, "A Demographic and Social Analysis of Widowhood and Remarriage: The Example of the Castellany of Thoissey-en-Dombes, 1670-1840," *Journal of Family History*, 5 (Spring, 1980); Census of Canada, 1871. Material on living arrangements is based on analysis of a 10 per cent random sample of families living in St. Jacques, 1871.

[31]Ten per cent sample of St. Jacques, 1871. Orphans linked to death registers.

stresses, charwomen, or washerwomen. These jobs usually allowed them to work with their young children at hand. The girls were only placed in the orphanage when this new and more fragile family economy was upset by illness or loss of work. Most widows returned for their children. Indeed, widows' daughters stayed in the orphanage for less time and were more likely to be reclaimed than the girls of the orphanage as a whole. This was because widows needed help from their children. Such youngsters were much more likely than those with two parents to be sent out to work under the age of 15. They also appear to have stayed at home longer, supporting their mothers until they were late into their twenties.[32]

The fragility of a widow's survival is clear from the histories of widows Josephine Brousseau and Angelique Fauteux. Josephine lived on Amherst St., sharing a dwelling with a couple, a twenty-four-year-old widower and his one-year-old child. She worked as a washerwoman. In 1868 she placed eight-year-old Clara in the orphanage for a year. By the time Clara was twelve she was working with her ten- and fourteen-year-old brothers in the Macdonald's tobacco factory, the largest employer of the area.[33]

Angelique Fauteux had three daughters. In 1875 she took her nine-year-old Emelie to the Sisters. A year later she took her home but left the youngest sister Eugenie there. Eugenie, in turn, was taken home twice, then went back to the orphanage, the second time with younger sister Victoria. Finally in 1881, when Eugenie was thirteen and Victoria eleven, they all returned home. By then the girls were old enough to work or to provide vital help around the home.[34]

If it was difficult economically for widows to survive, the problems that faced widowers were of a different order. The sexual division of labour made men the wage-earners, and women, even when they worked for wages, the socializers and nurturers of children. Reproductive work, providing meals, shopping, doing housework, and raising children, was women's work. The death of a wife, therefore, thrust upon a man's shoulders a whole range of new experiences, ones that were difficult to perform while working. Those with a steady and reasonable income could engage a housekeeper. Those without sought alternate strategies. Relatives might help by taking the children or doing housework. Not surprisingly, more widowers than widows appear

---

[32]These two latter statements are impressions gained from material collected from the 1861, 1871, and 1881 mss. censuses but not yet statistically analysed.

[33]"Registre," no. 455; mss. census, 1871, St. Jacques, 6, HH no. 265, Fam. no. 446.

[34]"Registre," nos. 736, 774, 812, 921, 922.

to have taken their daughters to the orphanage at some point after their spouses' deaths.

About 20 per cent of the girls had only a father when they were placed in the orphanage, two more lost their mother three to four months later. More widowers than widows placed their daughters with the Sisters within a week of their spouses' deaths, others waited a month. Some supported them or had help from relatives and friends for up to seven years.

Widowers were somewhat less likely to return for their daughters than were other parents or widows. Men probably felt particularly inadequate for the task of raising daughters. For instance, Ubalde Mazurette, a watchman, kept his sons with him, following his wife's death, but relinquished charge of his daughters, first to the Sisters and subsequently to strangers elsewhere in the province.[35]

No record can be found of remarriages among the widowed mothers of orphans. At least seven of the twenty-eight identified widowers definitely remarried, usually within two years of their spouses' deaths. Remarriage does not seem to have led to the automatic withdrawal of the children. Some girls were taken home before their father remarried, more returned home between a month and two years afterwards. Eugene Laroche, for instance, lost his wife Priscille in August, 1862. This left him with one-year-old Elie and four-year-old Adelaide to look after. He managed somehow for seven months, then in March, 1863, placed his daughter at St. Alexis. She returned home two years later. In 1871 Elie, now aged ten, was working with his father as a shoemaker. Adelaide, now aged thirteen, was at home helping her stepmother keep house and looking after her new one- and two-year-old siblings.[36]

For couples, as well as for widows and widowers, poverty was probably a major reason for temporarily relinquishing children. This inability to provide for a family might result from the economic ups and downs characterizing the emerging world industrial capitalist system; from life-cycle-based poverty in families where children were too young to work and the father's wage insufficient and irregular; or from misspent wages, especially earnings dissipated on alcohol. In other families parents may simply have been fed up, exhausted, or temporarily unable to cope and so taken advantage of the service offered by the nuns to get a few days or months respite from care of some of their children.

---

[35]"Registre," nos. 575, 576, 577, 578; mss. census, 1881, St. Jacques, Lovell's City Directory, 1878.
[36]"Registre," no. 326; mss. census, 1871, St. Jacques, 5, HH no. 165, Fam. no. 220.

The economic depression that hit Quebec between 1874 and 1879 was soon felt by the families of St. Jacques. The Sisters running the local Salle D'Asile St. Vincent De Paul, a daycare for working mothers, reported an increase in the number of parents who could no longer pay for their children's care. In 1876 they commented on the arrival on Monday mornings of small boys, trembling with weakness, who had not eaten over the weekend. In the school within the orphanage the numbers of non-paying students who took advantage of free lunches offered by the Sisters increased. So, too, did the numbers of girls entering the orphanage. Thirty-five girls entered in 1873 compared to fifty-one in 1874. The numbers fluctuated but remained high until 1881, when the request for some payment deterred the most needy parents. That year the poorest children were refused admission and only those whose parents could pay the $2 to $3 a month were taken. This regulation was probably relaxed by 1887 when the numbers increased dramatically.[37]

Some parents had always sent a few dollars a year to contribute toward their daughters' upkeep. Most payments came from parents outside Montreal, from those who had apparently consciously given up their children forever, or from widowers, glad to contribute to their daughters' upkeep.[38]

Most parents did not and could not pay for their daughters, for the girls came from the class most subject to unemployment and low wages. Furthermore, they came from families at a stage of the life cycle when their children were in need of much care but too young to work for pay. Half the girls came from homes where all the children were under the age of eleven. Another one-quarter of the families had no youngsters over fifteen. This was clearly the critical stage of the life cycle. Families were at their largest but had the smallest number of wage-earners. In St. Jacques in 1871, 25 per cent of families in this situation shared with other families, more took to boarders. Unskilled workers were especially likely to share space. The girls at St. Alexis came from dwellings where up to four families resided. The placement of children in the orphanage was another method of dealing with

---

[37]"Notes pour les Chroniques de L'Asile St. Vincent" (handwritten), ASP, 1876, 30; "Chroniques de l'Orphelinat St. Alexis depuis l'Année 1854" (handwritten chronicles), ASP.

[38]"Recettes-Orphelinat St. Alex," ASP. These list the names of orphans whose parents paid pensions for their daughters between 1869 and 1874.

poverty and, especially, with this difficult period of the family life cycle.[39]

A complex variety of factors determined when parents reclaimed their daughters. The age of the girls, the time of year, the reestablishment of stability after sickness or loss of a job were all important. When life-cycle-related poverty had been a major reason for surrendering a daughter, arrival at working age might mean she would return home. Eliza Masson, for instance, spent just over four years in the orphanage between the ages of eight and twelve. When she was fifteen the census enumerator found her back with her family. She was working as a seamstress, adding to the shaky wages of her shoemaker father, while her younger sisters went to school. Eliza St. Germain, whose father was a barber, left the orphanage at the age of thirteen and joined her mother working as a seamstress, probably at home in the crowded building that they shared with three other families.[40]

Many of Montreal's leading industries relied on young workers, and wage labour by girls under sixteen was not uncommon. About 20 per cent of girls and 28 per cent of boys under sixteen years old worked in manufacturing establishments in 1871. More would have worked in commerce and especially as domestic servants. It is hard to know exactly why parents placed their daughters in the orphanage and even more difficult to determine why they took them home again. The immediate future of some girls can be examined. Of those found living with their parents after leaving St. Alexis, about one-quarter were working, mostly as seamstresses and factory hands. The Sisters tried to counteract the tendency of parents to reclaim girls the order considered too young to work or not ready for the world. In 1886 they established a workshop to give those over fourteen an apprenticeship in dressmaking. This program aimed to give girls a useful skill and to encourage them to remain longer in the convent "because the parents had been taking them out to send them to work for their profit."[41]

When parents did withdraw girls of working age their action was not merely mercenary. The placement of one or several daughters with the Sisters had reduced family expenditures during a troubled period. Once children had grown old enough to work they no longer needed to be separated from the rest of the family. They might pay for their keep and perhaps contribute additionally to the family income. If

---

[39]Mss. census, 1861, 1871, 1881, Linked families, St. Jacques; Bradbury, "The Family Economy," 23-4.

[40]"Registre," nos. 278, 464; mss. census, 1871, St. Jacques, 5, HH no. 309, Fam. no. 363; "Registre," no. 457; mss. census, 1871, St. Jacques, 5, HH no. 27, Fam. no. 50.

[41]"Chroniques de l'Orphelinat," 184.

parents were exploiting children for their wages, the reasons lay in the structure of an economy in which one worker's wage was insufficient to support a family. That many of the girls remained at home with their parents for many years after their period in the orphanage suggests that they did not think themselves exploited by the family they rejoined.

More children, it seems, returned home because particular family crises had passed. With some sort of family equilibrium re-established, daughters returned to school or to housework. More of them went to school after leaving than went to work. There they extended the education they had received in the orphanage, kept out of the mothers' way during the day, but were free to help at home at night. Other girls returned home and became their mothers' household help, especially when there were many younger siblings to be looked after.[42]

While some girls came from homes torn apart permanently by the death of a parent and others from families that fragmented through the difficult period of the family life cycle, yet others came to the orphanage because of sickness at home. Ill health, in this area of high morbidity and mortality rates, posed a constant problem, especially for those unable to pay for assistance. The high birth and infant mortality rates meant that mothers were pregnant almost every second year. Pregnancy, childbirth, and associated illnesses thus posed recurring challenges to family management. At the Protestant Infants' Home, the sickness of mothers was a major reason for children's entry. Its 1895 report stated of the children's families that "Many are too poor to pay anything — out of work — wife sick — seeking the benefits of the home for their little ones until such times as they can provide a home for them." In that home, 21 per cent of the 1895 "orphans" were sent to the home because their mothers were sick. Sick fathers explained only 2 per cent of the entries.[43]

These figures underline the importance of a mother's role in such working-class families. Where the mother was ill, care of the children, cooking, and housekeeping would not get done unless there were children of an age to help. Similarly, when a mother was sick during pregnancy or after childbirth, or when a new and demanding

---

[42]Census of Canada, 1871. Montreal had 6,117 girls between the ages of eleven and fifteen; 1,262 or 20 per cent of them worked in industrial establishments; only twenty-seven girls have been found in the manuscript censuses of 1871 and 1881 living with their families after their stay in the orphanage. Of these, eleven were at school, six were listed as working, and ten were not listed as doing either. The latter were all of an age to do odd jobs or to help with care of younger children or with shopping and housework.

[43]Protestant Infants' Home, *Annual Reports*, 1895, 6.

and often sick child arrived, care of older children became a problem. The relationship between the Masson family and the St. Alexis orphanage illustrates this dilemma well.

Louis Masson was a shoemaker. He lived, in 1871, with his wife Delphine at 456 Jacques Cartier, a few blocks away from the orphanage on St. Denis Street. In May, 1861, their oldest child, Eliza, then aged eight, was placed in the orphanage. She stayed there four years, returning home with her mother in 1865. Three years later, the third girl of this family of girls, Roseanne, went to the orphanage for five years. When she returned home Eliza was twenty and had been working for at least two years as a seamstress. The orphanage relieved this family of care of two of their five daughters at critical periods. Eliza's first stay coincided with the births of the third girl in 1861 and another the following year. When brought home at the age of twelve, Eliza was probably able to help look after the younger girls, until at some point she began to work as a seamstress, thus contributing to the family income. Roseanne's time in the orphanage coincided with the birth of the youngest child, Marie. While Roseanne was in the orphanage her two nearest sisters in age were able to attend school. Any equilibrium this family briefly attained was shattered shortly after the 1871 census had been taken by the death of the father. Roseanne remained in the orphanage for several years after his death. When she returned home, she, too, was old enough to work. The family at that time moved, probably to cheaper lodgings.[44]

Putting the children in the orphanage may well have been a last resort — something that was done only after kin had been turned to for help. Kin regularly took children who had been in the orphanage for some period of time, as in the case of Helene Girourd. The Girourd family lived in the same building as the Massons in 1871. Andre was a labourer and, like many of his neighbours, was illiterate. In 1865 their eight-year-old daughter, Helene, joined her neighbour Eliza in the orphanage, leaving her fourteen-year-old brother and two younger sisters at home. Six years later, her brother was working as a domestic servant, possibly contributing some money to the family or at least receiving support for himself. Helene, however, left the orphanage, not to live with her parents but with an aunt.[45]

Helene's experience was important. For some of the children, kin evidently took the place of parents, even when parents were living. While 70 per cent of girls whose future is known returned home with

---

44"Registre," nos. 278, 464; mss. census, 1871, St. Jacques, 5, HH no. 309, Fam. no. 363, Lovell's, 1871-2, 1873-74.
45"Registre," no. 366; mss. census, 1871, St. Jacques, 5, HH no. 307, Fam. no. 361.

one of their parents, 5 per cent were taken home by an aunt or uncle and 4 per cent by a grandparent or older sibling.[46]

Children truly orphaned were often taken into the families of kin. Widows frequently lived with married children. Young married couples moved in with their parents, and related people doubled up in the houses of St. Jacques. Living together they could provide support in times of need and share costs. Thus, the family in Montreal, as elsewhere, acted as a major source of welfare in a time before the state directly provided any such services. The church both complemented and competed with the family in this sphere, especially among the poor.[47]

For the church, orphanages and schools offered a chance to raise a new generation in the Catholic faith. Bourget's speeches and the actions of the Sisters suggest that their view of the family was similar to that held by reformers in Ontario in the same period. Children were to be taken from homes that did not offer a suitable, in this case, Catholic, environment. Orphanages were seen not simply as alternatives to the family, but as places where the omissions and failings of the family could be countered. Where family situations appeared inimical to a Christian and Catholic upbringing, the Sisters were only too happy to keep the children with them. The story of Céléste Bacon, who died in 1887 after eight years in the orphanage, is especially poignant. "Several hours after her death," wrote the Sister in the Chronicles,

>...we received a telegram from her father who, not believing she was gravely ill, was asking her to rejoin him in the United States. We thanked God...for having preserved this dear child from such a danger...The father could not raise her decently or in Christianity, because of defects in his character.[48]

Where parents were poor, but devoted, they were to be assisted in every way possible. The Sisters tried to help keep worthy families to-

---

[46]These figures are based on the 484 girls for whom the nuns recorded information about their future. For another fifty-four no information was available. Where girls returned several times only their final experience was counted. 16 per cent went to non-relatives; 6 per cent died while resident in the orphanage.

[47]Bradbury, "The Family Economy," 23. Priests, bishops, and sisters seem to have encouraged familial support only as long as the people involved were considered good practising Catholics. Where there was any question of Protestant influence or of slipping from Catholic principles, church institutions were seen as preferable to familial aid.

[48]"Chroniques de l'Orphelinat," 174.

II. The Social History of Family Life

gether. Occasionally mothers were taken in as residents in the orphanage so that they could be near their daughters. An unemployed
father was given work repairing the buildings while his daughters
were housed there. The line between the church and the family was
thus flexible. Did not the Sisters and the church offer a spiritual family for the girls? Care of the girls, in turn, offered the Sisters a chance
to mother the young, a role they clearly enjoyed and fulfilled with compassion.[49]

For the girls themselves, their parents' decision meant that for
varying periods they were separated from their family of origin.
Instead, they lived with up to 100 other girls in the two large dormito-
ries of the orphanage. There, they slept, took classes, helped with the
housework, and learned to sew and knit. There they received, if they
remained long enough, a solid grounding in the Catholic faith, a habit
of deference to the givers of alms and charity, and a free education.
They were taught what girls of their class were expected to know as
workers and mothers. Some of the girls became very fond of the nuns
and the priests who served the orphanage and returned later to visit
them. While in the orphanage, girls were probably better fed, clothed,
and cared for than they would have been at home in a time of crisis.
Life in the orphanage offered not only education, housekeeping, and
religious duties but also entertainments that most working-class families could not have afforded. The girls went on occasional trips to the
country and for day-time excursions, and they celebrated Christmas
and the New Year with festive dinners provided by their patroness.[50]

L'Orphelinat St. Alexis and similar institutions clearly served
primarily working-class families. They were probably a last resort for
those lacking either the money or the family and friends to enable them
to deal with crises in some other way. Obviously not all working-class
families placed their children temporarily or permanently in orphanages.[51] Highly skilled workers earned enough to support their families
adequately. Some families managed better on meagre incomes than
others. Some had friends and relatives more affluent than themselves
to whom they could turn. That some did need to place their children in
orphanages high-lights the fragility of the family economy based on
wage labour. Such orphanages were not a temporary or purely local

---

[49]Ibid., 57, 65, 67.
[50]Ibid., 1860-89.
[51]Cap. XIII, 35 Vict., 1871, allowed "any incorporated orphan asylum" to "apprentice
or place out under indenture to any respectable and trustworthy person, any child or
juvenile offender under their control....During the whole term of any placing
out...the rights, power and authority of the parents over...such child, shall cease."

phenomenon. Nor were they limited to St. Jacques ward or parish or to the French-Canadian working class. Both the Protestant Infants' Home and the Protestant Orphan Asylum run by the Grey Nuns provided mostly for Irish Catholic boys and girls. Parents made similar use of institutuions in eighteenth-century France and in nineteenth-century Ontario. Well into the twentieth century many of the Grey Nuns' day nurseries were still very much like St. Alexis. Sociologist Arthur St. Pierre suggested in the 1930's that true orphans constituted only a small body of the children in Quebec's institutions. Orphanages, he argued, helped to preserve the family "by giving shelter for a time to one whom it helps and who will later return to his home." Discussions of orphanages during that decade show social workers and Sisters aware that most of their charges had parents who used the institutions when they could not cope. Proponents of mothers' allowances in the 1920's argued that such payments would ease burdened institutions by enabling mothers and widows to support their children at home. Clearly, the orphanages of the recent past served both parentless children and those with living parents and thus acted as a prop to the families of the poor.[52]

In nineteenth-century Montreal, death, illness, and poverty regularly threatened working-class households. The temporary placement of children in institutions that separated parent and child, sister and brother, fragmented the kin group for a time, but in many cases ensured the family's survival.

---

[52]Susan E. Houston, "The Impetus to Reform: Urban Crime, Poverty and Ignorance, 1850-1875" (Ph.D. dissertation, University of Toronto, 1974), 281-5, 304-6; Cissie C. Fairchilds, *Poverty and Charity in Aix-en-Provence, 1640-1789* (Baltimore: Johns Hopkins University Press, 1976), 86-8; Micheline Dumont-Johnson, "Des garderies au XIXe siècle: Les Salles d'asiles des Soeurs Grises à Montreal," *Revue d'Histoire de l'Amerique Française*, 34 (Juin, 1980), 52-3; Terry Copp, *The Anatomy of Poverty: The Condition of the Working Class in Montreal, 1897-1929* (Toronto: McClelland and Stewart, 1974), 122; *L'Ecole Sociale Populaire, Nos Orphelinats* (Montréal, 1930), 3-4; Veronica Strong-Boag, "Wages for Housework: Mothers' Allowances and the Beginnings of Social Security in Canada," *Journal of Canadian Studies*, 14 (Spring, 1979), 32.

III. Family Today

Before examining the various activities that family life involves, it is important to consider recent trends that have shaped families. The key demographic changes involve longer life expectancies and lower birth rates. Since the late nineteenth century (in France, the eighteenth century), women in western Europe, England and North America have given birth to fewer and fewer children. The "baby boom" was an exception to this long-term decline in fertility. Child rearing is now a fairly small period in adult life. As a result, there is now a period in the life cycle — unique to the twentieth century — in which the married couple lives alone after their children have grown (Wells 1971; Beaujot and McQuillan 1982).

The trend toward a smaller and smaller *nuclear-family* household, which seems to fit well with an industrial-capitalist economy, has continued through the twentieth century. That is, the extra relatives, and especially the boarders that were common to working-class households early in this century, have disappeared from Canadian homes. While families were getting progressively simpler through much of this century, however, recently rising divorce rates have produced masses of "reconstituted," complex families — sometimes containing people related neither by blood nor marriage (e.g., the children of two different marriages). The likelihood that children will not be raised by both of their biological parents is now quite high. Consequently, individuals maintain fairly complicated sets of familial relationships, with people they may or may not be living with and may or may not be related to by blood. Thus, divorce has replaced death in breaking up old families and pushing adults to create new ones — and does so in approximately the same proportion of families as experienced the death of an adult in the nineteenth century.

Finally, the most apparent recent trend in family life is the steady increase in the involvement of women who are married, and even those with young children, in wage work outside the home. A majority of Canadian women with preschool children is now in the paid labour force.

There are many other trends in family life. And there are larger economic, social and political changes behind all these trends. Pat Armstrong's article reviews some of the economic and political currents affecting families in both Canada and Australia. She details the changes that families have experienced, and considers the probable implications of these for people's personal lives.

When considering family, it is important to understand that variety results from more than divorce and remarriage. As Bettina

177

III. Family Today

Bradbury's article made clear about the nineteenth century, for instance, differences in social class involve differences in family life. A decent, stable income is necessary for stable nuclear families. So, students should keep in mind social-class and other differences when they are examining overall trends and specific activities in family life.

References

Beaujot, Roderic and Kevin McQuillan.
1982. "Life in Canada before, during and after the demographic transition." Paper presented at the meetings of the Canadian Population Society.
Wells, Robert.
1971. "Demographic change and the life cycle of American families." Pp. 85-95 in Theodore Rabb and Robert Rotberg, eds. *The Family in History*. New York: Harper & Row.

Suggested Readings

Stack, Carol.
1974. *All Our Kin*. New York: Harper & Row. A very fine study of poor black families in an American community.
Rubin, Lillian.
1976. *Worlds of Pain*. New York: Basic Books. An insightful description of American working-class families which probes the significance of social class for personal life.
Young, Michael and Peter Willmott.
1957. *Family and Kinship in East London*. Baltimore: Penguin. A classic British study of a working-class community which focuses on family relationships; presents a traditional pattern of working-class family life.

The Marital System
Australian and Canadian Patterns

Pat Armstrong

The Marital System

Writing in the seventeenth century about Quebec's Montagnais society, Jesuit Paul Le Jeune complained that "The young people do not think that they can persevere in the state of matrimony with a bad wife or a bad husband." "They wish to be free and to be able to divorce the consort if they do not love each other" (quoted in Leacock, 1986:12). He objected as well to their acceptance of sexual freedom after marriage (Leacock, 1986:11). But divorce and open marriages were not the only seemingly modern practices that were evident from the earliest period of European settlement in Canada. Lone parent families headed by women were not uncommon, especially amongst the Native women who had married "a la façon du pays" to fur traders who returned to Europe, or amongst the European women married to men who went to seek furs. Nor were blended families — ones based on a second marriage and involving children from more than one marriage — uncommon, given the high death and remarriage rates. And many women and men avoided marriage entirely, lived communally and took vows as nuns or priests.

While variations in family forms have existed throughout Canadian history, the frequency, acceptability, structure and meaning of the variations have changed significantly over time. These changes reflect the complex interaction of economic conditions, ideas, biology, technology and collective actions. Consequently, family experiences vary not only with historical periods and from country to country but also with region and class. And they are different for women and men.

This chapter examines the recent and dramatic developments in the economy, women's labour force participation, and fertility and mortality patterns which have marked the transformation of the structures, activities and meanings of family life in Canada. It begins with a brief examination of the economy because it is assumed that what happens in the market sets the conditions for, but does not determine, what happens in households. Women's movement into the market has reflected emerging household requirements at the same time as it has influenced these requirements. Similarly, declining fertility rates are both cause and product of women's movement into the market and they, too, have an impact in family life as well as on the market. As more people survive through the early years and live well into old age, both households and economy are affected. In the process, marriage patterns have been altered. So have the laws related to the establishment and dissolution of families.

In tracing these developments, this chapter also draws out some comparisons with Australia — a country like Canada in its huge land mass, small population, British colonial past, and resource-extraction-based, foreign-dominated economy, but with a different history of collective action and state legislation. The contrast is designed to illustrate how the two economies have encouraged similar patterns, but how collective strategies have created somewhat different results.

Economic Conditions

The economies of Australia and Canada have been restructured since the second world war. While some jobs have disappeared, others have been created. New products, technologies and services have been introduced; old means of satisfying needs have been eliminated. These developing economic trends have produced new conditions for family life and have in turn been influenced by emerging patterns within households. Since the 1970s, deteriorating economies in both countries have placed additional pressures on family structures and relationships.

The economic boom that followed the war was characterized by the growth of giant, mainly foreign-owned, corporations and by the virtual disappearance of small, family-owned enterprises. The family farm and the family store became memories in most areas of Canada and Australia. As they entered the 1980s, few people worked together as a family in order to acquire the necessities of life and few lived in rural areas. Contrary to much popular myth, Australia and Canada are now highly urbanized and suburbanized countries.

The economic boom also created new urban jobs and helped keep unemployment low. So did union successes in winning better job security, vacations, hours and pensions. Demands from unions and other groups contributed as well to the expansion of state programs for health care, education, welfare, unemployment insurance, family allowances, and pensions, and to the reduction of the standard work week to forty hours. These developments also helped maintain relatively full male employment. The combination of income security programs, low unemployment and rising real wages contributed to high family consumptions levels. Reflecting these trends, jobs in health, welfare and education, and in clerical and sales work grew dramatically, while the

180

standard of living rose. The demand for female workers increased, as did the demand for workers with many years of formal education. Taxes also increased, as the state extended both regulation and services.

In Canada, differences in rates of unionizations, provincial governments, and resources meant that the benefits from this economic boom were not evenly distributed across regions and classes. And lower minimum wages for women, along with the sex segregation of work, meant that rewards were not equally distributed between the sexes. Nevertheless, most Canadians experienced improved material conditions, and educational and employment opportunities, for several decades after the war. In Australia, the boom created similar tendencies, although there were some important differences. Because half of Australian workers, compared to a third of Canadian workers, were unionized, and because many wage settlements were applied nationally, differences were smaller amongst industries and regions. But state sanction of a family wage, which set minimum male pay at what was argued to be sufficient to support a man and his family, helped keep women out of the labour force and helped maintain large pay differences between women and men.

Seeking to increase sales and to maintain wartime production levels, companies in both countries introduced a wide array of new products, appliances and services in the years following the war. Cake mixes and other partially prepared or frozen foods appeared for the first time, often at prices which made them cheaper to purchase than the raw materials required to make their equivalents at home. Automatic dishwashers, clothes dryers and washing machines, no-iron fabrics, self-polishing floors, oil and gas furnaces and power lawn mowers became available on the market. Fast food restaurants multiplied, as did dental services and television programs. Post-secondary educational institutions offering specialized training appeared overnight. New contraceptive techniques were developed and the rapid expansion of medical technology encouraged the growth of hospital-based health care. Many of these "luxuries" rapidly became necessities as their usefulness was demonstrated and as their alternatives disappeared. For example, Canadian winters and regulations restricting clothes lines mean that few people are willing or able to forgo the use of a clothes dryer. Television not only provides a less expensive alternative to many forms of entertainment, it also disseminates enormous amounts of information, much of which is now assumed by teachers. Once medical technologies and specialized educational institutions are developed, they become integral parts of the system. And automatically regulated gas or oil furnaces have become essential in Canadian households, because wood and coal are no longer delivered to the door and because they are much more convenient than constantly stoking a stove. With rising real incomes, households were able to purchase many of these new goods and services, in the process abandoning many of the alternatives and losing many of the required skills.

But by the end of the 1960s, there were clear signs that the boom was coming to an end. Seeking to reduce costs, employers introduced more technology and used more part-time workers. Unemployment rates began to rise significantly in the mid-1950s and they continued to grow. "Before 1958, postwar unemployment never reached 5.0 per cent; since 1970, it has never been that low" (Armstrong, 1979:70). Although Australian unemployment rates grew later and more slowly than those in Canada, they followed a similar, if less rapid, progression. Prices, too, continued to rise, and to do so more quickly than wages. The large increases were in loan and mortgage rates, housing and heating prices, taxes and transportation costs. There are few alternatives to these goods and services, they are difficult to do without, and they have to be paid for in cash. Like the benefits from the boom, the losses from the developing recession have not been evenly distributed across regions, classes or sexes, but few people in either Canada or Australia escaped feeling the pinch.

Female Labour Force Participation

These developments in the economy have set the stage for rising female labour force participation rates. More than four out of five people in both Canada and Australia are classified as belonging to families. For most of them, the family represents an economic collective, even if the economic resources are not evenly distributed or equally controlled (see Dulude, 1984; Edwards, 1981). In the 1950s, the majority of families depended on income received by the male "breadwinner" in order to purchase most of their market goods and services (Armstrong and Armstrong, 1984: Table 23). By the 1980s, this was the pattern in only a minority of households. A mere 16 percent of Canadian families had a husband as the sole income recipient in 1982 (Statistics Canada, 1985: 64) while, in the previous year, 22.5 percent of Australian families had one adult income earner, one adult not in the labour force and some children at home (Institute of Family Studies, 1985: 4).

The cause of this fundamental change in the family's economic base was, of course, the massive movement of married women into the labour force. With the boom still evident in the early 1960s, only 17 percent of married Australian women and 21 percent of their Canadian counterparts were in the labour force. By 1981, 42 percent of married

182

Australian women and 52 percent of married Canadian women were counted as having a paid job or actively searching for one (Armstrong and Armstrong, 1984: Table 20 and Edwards, 1984: Table 2.1). In recent years, even women with small children have been entering or staying in the market. A third of the Australian women with pre-school children and almost half of the Canadian mothers of children under 5 were participating in the labour force by 1981 (Statistics Canada, 1985: Table 49 and Edwards, 1984: Table 2.3).

Women responded to the rising demand for female workers primarily because their families needed the income. Few of the new goods and services that were becoming necessary could be produced by women working at home, and women's possibilities for making money within the household or reducing family need for income were declining. With inflation and rising unemployment, their economic needs became even more pressing. Research in both countries has demonstrated the consistent link between husband's income and wife's labour force participation, concluding that "the wives of men earning below or about average weekly earnings have a higher labour force attachment than the wives of men with higher earned incomes (O'Loughlin and Cass, 1984: 5). As one married woman recently interviewed explained, "All of a sudden...you found your husband's pay cheque wasn't adequate. Especially when the family was younger, there was always so many things they needed. When the necessities became hard to come by, then you knew that you had to go out to help" (Armstrong and Armstrong, 1983: 36-37). Women married to men in higher income groups have also been entering the labour force. But Australian research indicates that such women are more likely to work part-time or intermittently and when attractive jobs are available, while economic pressure pushes other women to take any job, full-time if possible (O'Loughlin and Cass, 1984).

New domestic technology and products increased the need for cash income in most households, especially as wages failed to keep up with prices. They also made domestic work both easier and more boring. Consequently, it became more possible and more desirable for women to leave their homes in search of a job.

At the same time, greater accessibility of higher education and the increasing demand for workers with more years of formal training encouraged women to stay longer in school. With more education, women had more employment opportunities and different attitudes about remaining in the home to do domestic work. Males, too, were staying in school longer. As a result, children of both sexes were spending more years as dependents in their parental homes, increasing the economic pressures on their families.

III. Family Today

Different rates of female labour force participation in Australia and Canada may be primarily explained by differences in wage rates and male unemployment levels. In Australia, strong unions representing the majority of workers and often served by Labour governments, helped maintain the purchasing power of male wages for a longer period of time. The economic boom lasted longer in Australia as well, ensuring more men had stable employment. Male attitudes may also be a factor in varying female labour force participation rates. It has been argued that Australian men display "suspicion, hostility and fear of women who step out of an essentially domestic role" (quoted in Dixson, 1976: 22). But other research suggests that men's attitudes towards their wives working in the labour force depend more on family need than on traditional values (Brewer, 1983: 10).

Although a growing number of women are working outside the home and although new technology has helped reduce the domestic workload, there is still a large amount of work to be done in the home, and it is still mainly done by women. Most of the personal service work for the majority of Canadians and Australians is performed within the domestic sphere. An Australian study published in the early 1980s found that the "average homemaker spent 69 hours per week 'on the job' of which 38 were spent devoted to housework and 31 hours to childcare" (Gowland, 1983: 36). The amounts of work done by women working full-time in the home varied little with family income or with women's education. In Canada, Luxton found that housewives averaged 28 hours a week in food preparation alone (1980: Table 153). When women take on a second job in the market, they reduce their hours of domestic work by working faster when they are at home, doing some chores less often and purchasing more goods and services. But Canadian women with paid work still spend an average of four hours a day providing childcare, doing housework or household maintenance tasks and shopping even when they also work for pay in the market (Statistics Canada, 1985: Table 20).

And while 70 percent of Canadians and 85 percent of Australians think men should help with the housework, men in both countries have increased their contribution only slightly as more of their wives enter the workforce and as male hours spent in paid employment decline (Gowland, 1983: 42 and Boyd, 1984: 39: Table 3). One Canadian study found that, in families with children, the husband's contribution to regular housework increased by an hour a week when their wives obtained paid employment (Meissner et al., 1975: 436). Another reported that the total time men devoted to childcare, housework, household maintenance and shopping averaged about half as much as their employed spouses (Statistics Canada, 1985: Table 20). Husbands

184

are helping more with household chores, especially with the more enjoyable tasks related to childcare, but they are not equally sharing the burden of domestic work (Luxton, 1983).

Women's responsibility for domestic work reinforces and is reinforced by their segregation in the market. In both countries, the majority of women do clerical, sales or service work and more than a quarter of them have only part-time jobs, mainly in these fields (Armstrong and Armstrong, 1984: Table 5: 15 and Eccles, 1984: Table 5.4). Segregated into low paying, frequently part-time jobs, women do not earn as much as men even when they are doing similar work. In 1984, women in Canada were paid just over 60 percent of what men receive. In Australia, the gap is significantly smaller, with women paid close to 80 percent of the male wage (Power et al., 1985: 58). The smaller gap reflects the abandonment, under pressure from women's groups, of the family wage policy in the early 1970s and the higher rate of unionization which made equal pay agreements more effective than the equal pay legislation in Canada.

The combination of higher male wages, female segregation and traditional attitudes towards men's labour force work means that men's jobs in the market take precedence over those of women. When families have to decide who will leave the market in order to care for children or elderly relatives, handle emergencies, or do regular domestic work, they usually choose to forgo the earnings of the person with the lowest wage and least interesting work. Although the number of househusbands may be growing slightly, Australian research indicates that this practice "is confined to professional couples drawing good salaries. In keeping with the majority of decisions about dual-working in lower income families the need to guarantee economic sufficiency is paramount" (Brewer, 1983: 7). Canadian research also suggests that few men interrupt their paid work in order to fulfill domestic responsibilities or in order to accommodate a partner's job (Burch, 1985: 26).

Acquiring a wage often means acquiring more power and more assistance in the household, but lower female wages help ensure that domestic labour and domestic power are still not equally shared. Some women do manage household finances but this is most likely to happen in low income households where there are few choices to be made about paying relatively fixed expenses. In households with higher incomes, husbands tend to manage the money if their wives do not have paid work. When wives in such families are employed, "either a joint management system or an independent system" is more likely but it should be remembered that these wives very often have relatively high professional salaries (Edwards, 1984: 151).

Lower female wages, combined with women's domestic responsibilities and the limited public support for childcare services (see Status of Women Canada, 1986), also mean that women usually "have a greater financial stake in marriage than do men" (Ehrenreich, 1983: 8). Those Canadian mothers without access to a male wage have a one in two chance of being poor. "One in ten Canadian families is headed by a lone parent woman, and 50% of these women are supporting their families on incomes that are below Statistics Canada low-income cut-off lines" (Statistics Canada, 1985b:2). In Australia as well the number of female headed one parent families has been growing and they "are the family type most likely to be suffering economic deprivation" (Institute of Family Studies, 1985: 11). However, Australian government programs in the early 1980s helped keep the proportion of such families living below the poverty line lower than in Canada (Institute of Family Studies, 1985: 14).

Although women's low wages make them more financially dependent on marriage, falling real wages and rising unemployment have forced many men to rely more on female earnings. Estimates in both countries suggest that poverty in husband-wife families would have increased by at least 50 percent if women had not entered the labour force (National Council of Welfare, 1979: Table 3; Edwards, quoted in Cass, 1985: 10). Between 1971 and 1981, the income of Canadian wives "was the significant factor in preventing family income from declining in real dollars" and family economic resources continue to deteriorate. "By 1979-81, increases in wives' income were no longer able to offset the decline in husbands' average income" (Pryor, 1984: 102). Reflecting these changes, poverty amongst couples with children has been rising sharply in both countries during the 1980s (Institute for Family Studies, 1985: 14; National Council of Welfare, 1985: 18). At the other end of the scale, the real economic gains made by some women and their marriage to men with professional or managerial jobs has helped to at least maintain the position of high income families and to ensure that inflation does not reduce their purchasing power (Rashid, 1986).

Rising female participation in the labour force and higher education has done more than shift the economic base and the allocation of power and tasks within households. It has also contributed to changing patterns in age at first marriage. While in 1971 close to two-thirds of Australian women between the ages of 20 and 24 had been married, fewer than half of this age group had been married by 1981 (Institute for Family Studies, 1985: 5). In Canada, the 1981 average age of brides and grooms was 24 and 26 respectively, a full year older than the average age recorded for both sexes in 1971 (Statistics Canada, 1985: Table 8).

Rising female labour force participation may also have contributed to the greater decline in female than in male marriage rates. With jobs, women have more choice about marrying. In 1970, there were about 70 marriages for every 1,000 unmarried Canadian males and females over 15 years of age. By 1982, the marriage rate had dropped to 51 for women and 56 for men (Statistics Canada, 1985: Table 8). Similar patterns appear in Australia. The decline for both sexes may also reflect the growing skepticism about the benefits or stability of marriage and the increasing possibility of purchasing many of the services previously provided mainly in the home (see Breton, 1984).

Fertility Patterns

Rising female labour force participation is related as well to declining fertility rates. While participation rates have been going up, fertility rates have been going down. "Canadians now have fewer children, later in their lives and more may choose to forgo parenthood altogether" (Romanuic, 1984: 7). Similar patterns appear in Australia. In both countries, most families now have only one or two children. Most mothers are in their mid-twenties when their first child is born and, if they have a second child, it is usually born before the mother is thirty, although there has been a slight increase in the fertility rates for women in their early thirties. As we move into the 1980s, 15 percent of Canadian families have never had children (Statistics Canada, 1985: 4), and it seems likely that 20 percent of Australian women born in the 1950s will remain childless (Institute for Family Studies, 1985: 7). While more unmarried Canadian women are having babies, the ex-nuptial fertility rates in Australia have been declining slightly (Cass, 1983: 178). But in both countries the number of children born outside marriage remains small and does little to make up for the decreasing numbers of children born within marriages (Romaniuc, 1984: 60).

"It is well documented that there is an inverse relationship between female educational attainment, labour force participation and occupational status, on the one hand, and fertility, on the other" (Romaniuc, 1984: 66). And the evidence indicates that general economic conditions influence fertility rates as well. During the Great Depression, for example, birth rates in many areas matched those of the 1980s. Although it is clear that all these factors play a part in determining whether or not women have children and how many they have, their relative importance is difficult to determine.

At the same time as more and more women have been moving into the labour force, the time and money involved in rearing children have been steadily increasing. According to one estimate, a single child will cost, in 1986 Canadian dollars, more than $115,000 before they reach age 18. Sending that child to a local university for four years would add at least another $6,800 in books and tuition alone (Clayton and Swift, 1986: 182). Two children would cost nearly a quarter of a million dollars to support through graduation at a time when average yearly income for one-earner families was $34,460 and for two-earner families, $44,840 (Status of Women Canada, 1986: 13).

Raising children puts severe economic pressure on most families in both countries. Australian data indicate that "individual provision for children's needs results in the significant impoverishment for single-parent, mother-headed families and significant impoverishment for children who live in families" (Cass, Keens, Wyndham, 1983: 34). In Canada, "families with children have experienced a substantial increase in poverty in recent years" although childcare costs have of course not been the only factor involved in this increase (National Council of Welfare, 1985: 18).

Moreover, children's economic dependency in both countries is increasing not only with lengthening periods of schooling but also with growing youth unemployment. It is much more difficult for children to help pay their own way when summer jobs are scarce. And it is difficult for them to leave or stay away from home when unemployment is high and state support through welfare or unemployment insurance low or inaccessible. An Australian survey conducted in 1981 found that a high proportion of young people frequently returned home for economic reasons (Institute of Family Studies, 1985: 6). In Canada, more than half of the children between 20 and 24 and a tenth of those 25 and over were living in their parents' home in 1985 (Burch, 1985: 22). While in both countries children are now more likely to leave home and live independently before they marry, this does not necessarily mean that they are no longer a financial burden. Especially those who are continuing their education may still be receiving money from home.

Not only do modern children cost more money, they take more time. Fewer children do not necessarily mean less work. Researchers in Canada and Australia have documented the rapid growth of professional advice on childbearing and the emergence of a new emphasis on the crucial nature of parenting (Reiger, 1985; Strong-Boag, 1982). As early as the interwar period, women were counselled to devote more time, energy and skill to mothering (McLaren and McLaren, 1986: 27). In recent years, the pressure has intensified with the proliferation of childcare manuals, advice columns and professional services and the rising educational attainment levels of women. Childcare is becoming more time consuming as well with more complicated educational programs and after school activities. Older children do spend six hours a day for about 200 days a year in school but the increasingly complex demands children face in learning about everything from computers to

AIDS are often brought home for parents to handle. And while older children at home may require less physical care and may even help with the household chores, the tensions resulting from their struggles for independence may require enormous amounts of time and energy.

Although most experts agree that childcare requires dedication and a wide range of resources, little public support has been provided for this job. Canadian and Australian governments assume that children are primarily the responsibility of families and that the state should support children only when they are handicapped, when they have broken the law, or when families have clearly demonstrated economic need (see Status of Women Canada, 1986 and Sweeney, 1983). In both countries, very few men are allowed to take leave from their labour force jobs in order to stay home with their children. While most employed women in these two countries are eligible for brief maternity leaves, such leave merely provides time for women to physically recover from childbirth, not time to offer continuing care for children. While not attending school, most Australian and Canadian children spend at least some time each week being cared for by someone other than their mother but only a small proportion of this care is provided in publicly funded or supervised centres. In Canada, a couple with two young children in 1984 could "expect to pay approximately $6970 for full-day licensed child care" (Status of Women Canada, 1986: 15) if they could find space in such a centre. Not surprisingly, given the shortage and expense of childcare facilities as well as the emphasis on the value of family care, the majority of families make do with relatives or neighbours and juggle their work hours to provide care at home. The result, all too often, is exhausted and less than high quality care in or out of the home and high levels of tension between parents.

The problems related to the time demands of raising children are often particularly acute for female headed lone parent households. Although such families do receive some state support for childcare services and other economic needs, it is seldom enough. In both Canada and Australia, one parent families headed by women are the fastest growing family type and they are also the family type facing a dramatic decline in their economic status (Institute of Family Studies, 1985:11). These women have no husbands to share the daily parenting tasks. While state subsidies for daycare help when the children are young, there is little public support for substitute care at other times and little more to purchase it.

In spite of women's rising labour force participation and the increasing amount of time spent with others, and perhaps because of the limited public support for childcare, mothers are still the primary care givers for young children. And both parents continue to play a major role in shaping their children's lives. Indeed, this influence may be growing as offspring remain in and dependent on the parental home for more and more years. Moreover, as in earlier decades, family income in particular is "a major determinant in life-chances of the next generation" (Brewer, 1983:7) and children are still learning many of their basic values and skills at home.

Of course, even if the rising costs and time demands of child-rearing and growing female labour force participation are encouraging people to have fewer children, the reduction in fertility would have been more difficult to accomplish without relatively easy access to birth control techniques. Birth rates began to decline in Canada well before public pressure from doctors, women's groups and the obvious widespread contravention of the law forced the 1969 changes in the Canadian Criminal Code that ended the ban on the advertising and sale of contraceptives. Birth rates had even started to drop before the pill became generally available on the market in the early 1960s (McLaren and McLaren, 1986:134). But, now that information on birth control and contraceptive technology are readily available, state-subsidized family planning services exist, and legal abortions are possible, it is much easier for women and men to reduce the number of unplanned pregnancies. While a 1968 Canadian survey found that 16 percent of couples had an unintended child, a 1971 study uncovered only 11 percent and, when the study was repeated in 1976, only 7% reported unwanted births (reported in Romanuic, 1984:61). Increasingly, couples are deciding that one or two children complete their families and are having tubal ligations or vasectomies, which usually end the possibilities for more pregnancies (McLaren and McLaren, 1986:134).

Because the successful use of contraceptives requires money, time and information, however, birth control is not equally available to all groups. In Canada and Australia, the data indicate that the poor are more likely to have unplanned children (Institute of Family Studies, 1985:14 and National Council of Welfare, 1985:18-19). Education also makes a difference. The "number of unplanned pregnancies among married women declines as their level of schooling increases" (Breton, 1984:5). Cutbacks in state funding underway in both countries, and attacks on abortion legislation, may make the distribution of birth control even more unequal.

Improved birth control techniques, and better access to them, have done more than help reduce fertility rates. They have also contributed to changing sexual practices and attitudes. Better access to birth control may be a factor in the increasing number of Australian and Canadian couples who live together without a formal marriage. As the Australian National Population Inquiry points out "De facto unions are usually associated with effective contraception and therefore, with no children or with a very small family" (Cass, 1983:178). A 1982 Australian study indicated that as many as 40 percent of Australian couples had lived together before marriage (reported in Institute of Family Studies, 1985:7). Research in Canada found that about a sixth of both women and men had been involved in non-marital cohabitation by 1984 (Burch, 1985:13).

It should not be assumed, however, that co-habitation means a rejection of marriage. Although in 1981 over three-quarters of the Australian young people interviewed thought it was acceptable to live together without marrying, about 90 percent of them expected to marry at some time (Institute of Family Studies, 1985:7). In Canada, "common-law partnerships are as much a prelude to marriage as a substitute for it," with a quarter of ever-married young men and a fifth of women reporting that they married a live-in companion (Burch, 1985:15). Birth control allows both women and men to discover whether or not they are sexually and socially compatible before they commit themselves to marriage or children. In addition to trying out marriage, couples also live together without formalizing the relationship because their marital or economic situation prevents them from taking this legal step even though they define the relationship as a permanent one (see Fels, 1981:34-38).

It is difficult to tell whether or not better access to birth control encourages more short-term, extra-marital sexual relationships or discourages marriage for the sake of sex. Indeed, it is difficult to determine whether or not extra-marital sexual activities have increased. There may simply be a greater willingness to discuss sexual activity today. As Breton (1984:6) points out in his study of marriage markets, however, "the more efficient the birth control devices, the lower the price that would have to be paid for unfaithfulness." On the other hand, better contraceptives may induce some women to marry because they have greater control over pregnancies (Breton, 1984:6). While better birth control may encourage some people to avoid marriage altogether and others to have a variety of sexual partners, it necessarily provides women with more choices in all areas. For, "when contraception is inefficient, the terms of trade ruling in the marriage market for the various services traded in that market are likely to be unfavourable to women and likely to improve, *ceteris paribus*, with improvements in birth control technology" (Greton, 1984:6).

But in helping to separate sexual relationships from reproduction, contraceptives not only allow more sex outside marriage, they also help make sex within marriage more possible and pleasurable. Fewer couples need practice abstention as a means of avoiding an unwanted mouth to

191

III. Family Today

feed and personality to nurture; more women can enjoy sexual intercourse without fearing an undesired pregnancy. In her study of three generations of Canadian women, Luxton (1980:61) found that older women "described sex as a duty a woman is obliged to provide for her man" while younger women "described a considerably wider range of sexual activities." Here, too, there are class and sex differences, however. Women with high levels of formal education have better access both to contraceptives and to information on sexuality, and thus may have improved possibilities for a satisfying sexual relationship. And women continue to bear the greater burden of responsibility in spite of better birth control. Many of the working class women Luxton (1980:59) interviewed are "ignorant about their sexual needs and are terrified of getting pregnant" while new attitudes push them to "become more active, take the initiative and either have orgasms or fake them, still mostly to satisfy men" (Luxton, 1980:63).

That sexual relationships constitute an integral and central aspect of marriage even with more accessible contraceptives is demonstrated by the large number of divorce petitions that are justified on the grounds of sexual transgression or incompatibility (see McKie, Prentice and Reed, 1983:133). For the Canadian state, a sexual relationship is an essential ingredient of a legal marriage "A persistent and unjustified refusal of sexual relations by one spouse may constitute 'cruelty' as a basis for divorce" (Kronby, 1986:21). And when a woman allows a man to stay overnight, it may be used as the basis for withdrawal of state support payments, on the assumption that this practice indicates the existence of a form of common-law relationship.

At the same time as female labour force participation rates have been rising, better birth control has become more accessible, and the costs of raising children have been growing, so too has the time required for each child. As more women enter the labour force, they have less time and energy to devote to children and they are receiving little extra help from the state or from men. This is particularly the case for the growing number of women who parent alone. Values have also been changing. Couples want to give each child more, and avoid the negative consequences of large families. Women want more choices in their lives. With birth control, both men and women have more choices, not only about children but also about marriage, and their attitudes related to sex are changing. Not surprisingly, birthrates have been falling and sex outside marriage has become more acceptable. In spite of these developments however, most women and men still marry, sexual relationships continue to constitute an important ingredient in the marriage bond, most couples have at least one child, and most of these

192

children receive a significant amount of their early care from their parents and grow up in the homes of their biological parents.

Companionship

Rising female labour force participation rates are related as well to changing patterns of non-sexual relationships in families. As more women enter the market, the possibilities for both more tension and more egalitarian, companionate relationships increase.

Comparing generations, Luxton (1980;52) found that women's household workload had lightened and men's hours in paid work had decreased, leaving them more time to devote to each other and to their children. Describing their marriages as partnerships, women "seemed to share more activities with their husbands and they expect to be 'friends' with them." Affection was more visibly demonstrated and problems more openly discussed. As women increasingly enter the labour force, they also share more of the financial burden of supporting the family and more of the experiences of going out to work for pay. Women's employment may ease economic pressures on the household. In addition, their income may make more leisure activities, more domestic technology and more substitutes for domestic labour possible, freeing time for more pleasurable family pursuits.

Increasing longevity and declining fertility rates also create conditions that may encourage more companionate marital relationships. Research in Australia suggests that couples now may spend several years adjusting to each other's habits, setting up house, travelling and experimenting with different life styles and division of tasks before they have their first child (Richards, 1985:134). During this period, the economic pressures on the family are often not extremely heavy, especially when there are two full-time salaries coming into the household.

With pregnancies more likely to be planned, gestation and birth may also contribute to the feeling of partnership. Fathers increasingly are participating in childbirth classes and attending the birth. In her study of Australian-born, once-married and largely middle-class families, Richards (1985:134) found that pregnancy "was almost unanimously remembered as bringing the couple closer together" and for some, childbirth "was also a significant experience, drawing them again closer." Childbearing too may offer many opportunities for shared pleasure. With fewer children, parents may have more leisure to watch together their child take that first step, score the first goal, fall in love for the first time. As children move through adolescence and young adulthood, they may not only allow parents more time together but also provide some companionship for them as well.

Moreover, as couples have fewer children born close together, and as people in both Australia and Canada live well into old age, there are more and more years spent together as a couple after the children have become independent. Even if children born to mothers who are thirty and fathers who are thirty-three stay home until they are 25, parents still have twenty years to live together without the social and economic pressures of parenting, and often with more free time from work once their position in the market is firmly established. Unlike past generations, they have many years to enjoy the pleasures of grandparenting. Retirement, common at age 65 in both countries, permits couples to spend even more time together and with their grandchildren.

Increasing female labour force participation and fewer children may also mean that both women and men are freer to leave tension filled marriages. The children, as a result, may grow up with more complicated life styles but in less tension-ridden homes.

But, on the other hand, these processes may increase stress levels within the household and make companionship and more egalitarian relationships difficult to attain. Tension from work is often brought home and may explode into violence against spouses and children. The reported cases of violence (within families) against women, children and the elderly have been rising steadily in recent years. As with extra-marital sex, it is difficult to tell whether or not this reflects an actual increase or mainly the greater public awareness resulting from the women's movement's efforts to expose it and provide alternatives. Nevertheless, it is clear that far too many families are not "havens in a heartless world" (see Guberman and Wolfe, 1985; Windschuttle, 1980).

When women enter the market, they have two jobs to perform, less energy to handle the stress created by others, and little help in managing their own. Sheer exhaustion may push women to demand assistance with household tasks, while male attitudes, lack of training and tension from paid work may push men to resist. Even before children arrive, the division of tasks may create problems. One Canadian study revealed that, for newlyweds, issues related to responsibility for housework were a major cause of disputes (reference in Proulx, 1978:13). Low female wages also mean that in many families women's wages do little to relieve economic pressures, provide domestic appliances or substitutes for domestic chores.

The tensions and fatigue created by work in and out of the home may also mean couples are too tired or upset for sex (Luxton, 1980). Moreover, couples may juggle their paid work time in order to accom-

194

modate childcare and in the process eliminate time for each other. Interviewed for a Canadian study of working families, one woman explained that her "husband works evenings, from 5 p.m. until 1:30 or 2 a.m. My work hours are from 7 a.m. until 4 p.m. We avoid child care expenses and it gives the kids enough time to spend with both parents" but, it could be added, little time for parents to be alone (Johnson, 1986:18). A Melbourne study revealed that "decisions to do shift work were often made so that one of the parents could always care for the children," making it much more difficult for the entire family to spend time together at core periods during the day or week (reported in Brewer, 1983:25).

While Richards (1985:134) found that pregnancy often brought Australian couples closer together, the early years of parenting are by many "remembered as one of maximum strain." Time and financial demands increase, often when economic resources decline as women withdraw from the labour force or reduce their paid work hours. It is still common in both countries for women to drop out of the labour force in order to care for young children, because many want to be the primary caregiver, because many cannot afford or find quality alternative care, because it only makes sense for the person with the lowest salary to withdraw from paid work, because maternity leave is only available for a short period of time to women. But for a substantial number of the women who do quit paid work, "it is a shattering experience, bitterly remembered, to be home by yourself with a very young child" (Richards, 1985:134). Moreover, it often means that housework becomes more their responsibility. For the growing number of women who cannot or do not want to stay home with their child, the price in the overwhelming majority of cases is taking on two jobs, competing demands, often guilt and certainly fatigue.

As a woman in Richards' study explained, the problem "doesn't stop there, it goes on" (1985:286). Children growing up may also be a major source of strain and cause of disputes. In addition to the usual struggles caused by children testing their independence, tensions generated by an uncertain social and economic situation "are expressed through conflicts between mothers and their children" (Luxton, 1980:87). Fathers, too, may find their knowledge and authority challenged. And, although the children leaving home may reduce these conflicts, they may leave behind parents who find they had little in common except their children.

The growing number of single parent households face additional tensions. Time management often has to accommodate two families and two sets of relationships. Economic pressures are frequently more severe as well.

III. Family Today

Although retirement offers greater freedom and leisure for couples to spend time with each other and their children, it all too often in both Canada and Australia, means poverty, ill health and dependency. In both countries, poverty amongst the elderly has not been increasing in recent years, thanks largely to state support programs. However, "One elderly Canadian in four lived below the poverty line in 1983: and the risk of poverty was significantly higher for women than for men (National Council of Welfare, 1985:28). In Australia, 9 percent of the aged income units were counted as very poor in 1981-82 (Cass, 1984:17). Poverty increased tensions in these households, which are at the same time coping with the strain caused by adjusting to new retirement patterns and ill health. Poverty in old age also frequently means dependency on others, another source of strain.

"Although Australia is reputed to have one of the highest rates of institutional care in the world, 55 percent more elderly people live with adult children than in nursing homes or other institutions" (Kinnear and Graycar, 1983:77). And state cutbacks in Australia and Canada are placing increasing pressure on younger families to bear the responsibility for their elderly parents. Research in both countries (Heller, 1986; Kinnear and Graycar, 1983) indicates that family care means care by women. Married to men often much older then themselves, outliving men by several years, women frequently face many years caring for sick husbands and then have no one to look after them in their widowhood. When elderly parents of either spouse move in, it is the women who take on the extra load. Both the work and the changed social relationships may cause rising tensions, as children and grandparents spend too much time together and as dependency relations are reversed. The situation is further exacerbated by rising female participation rates which leave women with less and less time or energy to do the work.

Finally, continuing unemployment and the threat of unemployment may place additional pressures on families, inhibiting the maintenance of companionable partnerships. A Canadian study concludes that men without jobs feel "that their unemployment has taxed their relationships within the family — particularly the marital relationship. Relationships with parents and in-laws are also placed under strain as a result of paternal employment and the resulting shifts in roles and responsibilities within families" (Johnson and Abramovitch, 1986:ii). For some couples with a strong initial relationship, there may be benefits from additional time together. But for most, the result is often conflict. Given men's higher wages, male unemployment means a drastic decline in living standards. It also often means poor health not only for the men but also for their families, who must live under increased stress and reduced incomes. As one unemployed Australian father of three explained to researchers "My wife and I have never argued before, but lately we don't seem to do anything else. There's a lot of tension because we're worried about the kids. They've got hardly any clothing left." (quoted in Windschuttle, 1980:80). According to Australian investigations, domestic violence and divorce accompany high levels of unemployment (Windschuttle, 1980:81).

Women's unemployment may affect family tranquility as well, particularly in the many households where the women's income is essential to family survival. This may be the case not only in female-headed lone parent households and in those that hover around the poverty line but also in families that have committed themselves to monthly payments on houses and cars. Without the second income, the family's entire way of life may be under threat. Moreover, women too suffer from stress and depression with job loss, placing additional strains on family relationships.

Both tensions and possibilities for closer family relationships arise with different phases in family development, with marriage breakdown and with changing economic conditions. Rising female labour force participation, falling fertility rates and increasing longevity have helped reduce some strains and lower tensions in some households while exacerbating them in others. In most households, the benefits and strains have been different for women and men.

Marriage and the Law

In both countries, changes in the law related to marriage have reflected and influenced the changing patterns of female-male and parent-child relationships. In Canada, Judge Abella (1985:13) has pointed out that the basis of the law has "shifted from the need to preserve marriages to the need to preserve families — serially if necessary. The change has come from a recognition that saving a marriage may in fact be destroying members of the family." There has been a movement away from assigning fault in marriage breakdown and from distinguishing between children born in or out of wedlock. At the same time, there has been a movement toward equalizing rights and responsibilities within marriage. And both countries have made marital rape and violence punishable under the law.

Under the various provincial statues that cover marriages in Canada, both spouses now have a mutual obligation of financial support, a shared responsibility for children, the right to cohabit and to expect a sexual relationship (Kronby, 1986:21). According to Australian federal law which governs marriages, men and women have equal rights and

197

III. Family Today

responsibilities in maintenance, child custody and living, as well as in sexual arrangements (Scutt, 1983:237). As a result of pressure from feminists in both countries, a woman's economic contribution through her work as mother and homemaker is recognized as equal to the contribution made by a man working outside the home. Generally in Canadian marriages "each spouse is entitled to do what she or he wants with the property she or he personally acquires" although exceptions include "two sorts of provisions: those intended to protect the spouse's future rights and those enacted to protect the matrimonial home" (Dulude, 1984:13). Assets required in the marriage are shared. Similarly, in Australian law, property purchased with personal earnings or other money coming to that person alone is individually controlled while family assets are equally shared. This legislation based on the assumption of spousal independence and equality is, however, not equally beneficial to women and men.

Although new divorce laws in Canada and Australia are based on the laudable assumption that both spouses are "equally innocent victims," they too have different, and unequal, consequences for each sex. According to the 1981 amendments to the Australian Family Law Act, the only ground for divorce is "irretrievable breakdown of marriage." The main requirement is that the couple live apart for a year. Custody may be awarded to either parent or may be granted to both jointly (Morgan, 1984:61). Economic need is a major factor in the list the law provides to guide judges in the determination of maintenance. As of June, 1986, Canada has a very similar law. The federal Divorce Act "establishes only one ground for divorce: marriage breakdown, which arises as a result of adultery, cruelty or separation for a period of one year" (Kronby, 1986:xiii). Custody is now based on the doctrine of "best interest" of the child (Abella, 1985:170). In both laws, there is a new emphasis on self-sufficiency. When Canada in 1968 and Australian in 1975 introduced the first legislation to broaden grounds for divorce, the annual divorce rate jumped dramatically, as many people rushed to leave marriages that had long ceased to function. But divorce rates have not been growing significantly in recent years, and actually declined in Canada after 1983. Estimates in both countries suggest that two out of five marriages may end in divorce (Institute of Family Studies, 1985:9; McKie, Prentice and Reed, 1983:60), but only "about one in ten of ever-married Canadian males and about one in eight of ever-married females have had a legal marriage end in divorce" (Burch, 1985:ii).

As Scutt (1983:239) has pointed out for Australia, in the new laws women "are viewed as responsible to the same degree as men for their own upkeep and for that of their children, yet are not granted the social and economic equality that would allow them to fulfill that responsibil-

198

ity." Or as Abella (1985:15) has said of the Canadian legislation, "It is hard to be an independent equal when one is not equally able to become independent." It is men who have higher earnings, which permit them to acquire the personal property described in the law. It is women who have the children. When marriages break up, women in both countries suffer severe economic setbacks, setbacks which are more severe than those faced by men because women usually have custody of the children, because support payments are usually very low and are often not paid at all, because women's employment opportunities are more restricted as a result of the segregation in the market and of women's childrearing responsibilities now and in the past. And perhaps because they do not have custody of the children and because they are left in a better financial position, men in both countries are more likely than women to remarry after divorce.

With the increasing number of couples living together without going through an official marriage ceremony, "all Canadian jurisdictions have adopted measures that deal expressly with common-law spouses." If they conform to the criteria ootablished in the various provincial laws, common-law spouses qualify for many of the same rights and responsibilities as a married couple (Boivin, 1985:171). In the Yukon and in four provinces, the distinction between legitimate and illegitimate children has been abolished and in all provinces children born to unmarried women have some right to support from their parents (Boivin, 1985:181). In Australia, children of common-law marriages are legally in the sole custody of their mother although there is now some protection for women whose common-law marriages break up. Children born out of wedlock have full rights (Morgan, 1984:61). Although there is a more visible presence in both countries of homosexual unions, neither country legally recognizes such relationships or permits same sex marriages.

Laws in both countries have changed along with the emergence of a new economic reality and new family structures. Provisions reflect the growing economic strength of women, the avoidance by some of the legal marriage tie and the large number of marriages that end in divorce. They both assume and legislate equality and, while women have pushed for and benefited from these changes, the results still frequently favour men.

Conclusion

As always, economic conditions, family structures, family values and the marital system are changing. Female labour force participation rates have been rising, fertility rates have been falling and both women and men are living well into old age. Marriage and childbirth are being delayed. Fewer people are marrying, more are divorcing and living together without formalizing the union. Extra marital sexual relationships and homosexual unions are more openly practiced. Children are living longer in parental homes before they marry. As a consequence of this and of women's greater longevity, there are a growing number of single person households. Divorce and separation also mean that more people of both sexes, but especially women, parent alone. Remarriage at the same time means a growing number of blended families.

But the overwhelming majority of Australians and Canadians marry, stay married to the same person for much longer than ever before because they live longer, have at least one child and raise that child for many years in their homes. The predominate pattern is one of marriage in the mid-twenties with women marrying men a few years older than themselves, of children born a couple of years later and of childbirth completed by the time the women turns thirty. While women are increasingly staying in the market throughout their childbearing years, the scarcity of public and private support as well as preference means that a high proportion drops out of the market or takes part-time work in order to care for their children. This pattern, the continuing segregation of the market, women's and men's training, skills, and values combine to ensure that women bear primary responsibility for domestic work and take a secondary place in the labour force. As a result of this inequality and the failure of the state or men to provide adequate support, lone-parenting for women often means poverty.

After partners nurture their children through the early years, adolescence and the young adulthood years, they often still have many years together as an employed and then as a retired couple. Longevity makes grandparenting more possible; in the absence of adequate pensions, it also makes poverty more likely. And because most women outlive men and marry men who are older, widowhood is almost inevitable.

Significant class differences remain and may be exacerbated by women's labour force participation. Women's wages have, however, been the major factor keeping even more couples out of poverty. Rising female labour force participation has also increased women's strength, allowing them to demand more rights and choices in and out of marriage. It has in addition helped couples abandon unhappy marriages and has encouraged women to expose abuse. But, it should be noted, the majority of women are not abused by their spouse and men have had to make many adjustments too as more and more women enter the market.

Few of these patterns are new, except perhaps for the growing number of retired couples and of single person households. And these patterns may reflect more a restructuring than an abandonment of

200

marriage and family life. Their meanings and consequences are, however, constantly changing. And while marital systems and economic conditions are very similar in Australia and Canada, differences reflecting human choices and actions remain.

References

Abella, Rosalie Silberman
1985 "Opening Address." pp. 9-26 in Elizabeth Sloss (ed.), *Family Law in Canada: New Directions*. Ottawa: Canadian Advisory Council on the Status of Women.
Armstrong, Hugh
1979 "Job Creation and Unemployment in Post-War Canada." pp. 59-77 in Marvyn Novick (ed.), *Full Employment: Social Questions for Public Policy*. Toronto: Social Planning Council of Metropolitan Toronto.
Armstrong, Pat and Hugh Armstrong
1983 *A Working Majority: What Women Must Do For Pay*. Ottawa: Supply and Services Canada for the Canadian Advisory Council on the Status of Women.
Boivin, Suzanne
1985 "To Marry or Not to Marry? A Study of the Legal Situation of Common-Law Spouses in Canadian Law." pp. 169-194 in Elizabeth Sloss (ed.), *Family Law in Canada: New Directions*. Ottawa: Canadian Advisory Council on the Status of Women.
Boyd, Monica
1984 *Canadian Attitudes Toward Women: Thirty Years of Change*. Ottawa: Supply and Services Canada for the Women's Bureau, Labour Canada.
Breton, Albert
1984 *Marriage, Population, and the Labour Force Participation of Women*. Ottawa: Supply and Services Canada for the Economic Council of Canada (Cat. no. E-C22-177/1984E).
Brewer, Graeme
1983 *The Impact of Work on Family Functioning: A Review of the Literature*, Occasional Paper Number 3. Melbourne: Institute of Family Studies.
Burch, Thomas
1985 *Family History Survey: Preliminary Findings*. Ottawa: Supply and Services Canada (Cat. no. 99-955).
Cass, Bettina
1983 "Population Policies and Family Policies: State Construction of Domestic Life." pp. 164-185 in Cora V. Baldock and Bettina Cass (eds.),

III. Family Today

Women, Social Welfare and the State in Australia. Sydney: George Allen & Unwin.
1984 *The Changing Face of Poverty in Australia: 1972-1982.* Paper presented to the Continuing Education Seminar in the Department of Social Work, University of Sydney.
Cass, Bettina, Carol Keens, Diana Wyndham
1983 "Child-rearing: Direct and Indirect Costs." pp. 13-24 in Adam Graycar (ed.), *Retreat from The Welfare State.* Sydney: George Allen & Unwin.
Clayton, Judy and Diana Swift
1986 "When the Time Comes, Can You Give Your Kids a College Education." *Chatelaine*, September.
Dixson, Mariam
1976 *The Real Matilda: Women and Identity in Australia 1788 to 1975.* Ringwood, Victoria: Penguin.
Dulude, Louise
1984 *Love, Marriage and Money.... An Analysis of Financial Relations Between the Spouses.* Ottawa: Canadian Advisory Council on the Status of Women.
Eccles, Sandra
1984 "Women in the Australian Labour Force." pp. 80-93 in Dorothy H. Broom (ed.), *Unfinished Business: Social Justice For Women in Australia.* Sydney: George Allen & Unwin.
Edwards, Meredith
1981 *Financial Arrangements Within Families.* Research Report Commissioned by the National Women's Advisory Council, Canberra: Australia.
1984 *The Income Unit in the Australian Tax and Social Security Systems.* Melbourne, Australia: Institute of Family Studies.
Ehrenreich, Barbara
1983 *The Hearts of Men: American Dreams and the Flight From Commitment.* Garden City, New York: Anchor.
Fels, Lynn
1981 *Living Together: Unmarried Couples in Canada.* Toronto: Personal Library.
Gowland, Patricia
1983 *Women in Families: The Sexual Division of Labour and Australian Family Policy.* Melbourne: Knox Community Relations Centre.
Guberman, Connie and Margie Wolfe
1985 *No Safe Place: Violence Against Women and Children.* Toronto: The Women's Press.

Institute of Family Studies
1985 *Families and Australia's Economic Future.* Submission to the Economic Planning Advisory Council, March.
Johnson, Laura C.
1986 *Working Families: Workplace Supports for Families.* Toronto: Social Planning Council of Metropolitan Toronto.
Johnson, Laura C. and Rona Abramovitch
1986 *Between Jobs: Paternal Unemployment and Family Life.* Toronto: Social Planning Council of Metropolitan Toronto.
Kinnear, David and Adam Graycar
1983 "Non-Institutional Care of Elderly People." pp. 74-88 in Adam Graycar (ed.), *Retreat from the Welfare State.* Sydney: George Allen & Unwin.
Kronby, Malcolm
1986 *Canadian Family Law.* Toronto: Stoddart.
Leacock, Eleanor
1986 "Montagnais Women and the Jesuit Program for Colonization." pp. 7-22 in Veronica Strong-Boag and Anita Clair Fellman (eds.), *Rethinking Canada.* Toronto: Copp Clark Pitman.
Luxton, Meg
1980 *More Than a Labour of Love: Three Generations of Women's Work in the Home.* Toronto: Women's Press.
1983 "Two Hands for the Clock: Changing Patterns in the Gendered Division of Labour in the Home." *Studies in Political Economy* 12(Fall):27-44.
McKie, D.C., B. Prentice and P. Reed
1983 *Divorce: Law and The Family in Canada.* Ottawa: Supply and Services Canada for Statistics Canada (Cat. no. 89-502E).
McLaren, Angus and Arlene McLaren
1986 *The Bedroom and The State.* Toronto: McClelland and Stewart.
Meissner, Martin, Elizabeth W. Humphreys, Scott M. Meis and William J. Scheu
1974 "No Exit for Wives: Sexual Division of Labour and the Culmination of Household Demands." *The Canadian Review of Sociology and Anthropology* 12(4, Part 1, November):424-39.
Morgan, Robin
1984 *Sisterhood is Global.* New York: Anchor.
National Council of Welfare
1979 *Women and Poverty.* Ottawa: National Council of Welfare.
1985 *Poverty Profile 1985.* Ottawa: National Council of Welfare, October.

O'Laughlin, Mary Ann and Bettina Cass
1984 *Married Women's Employment Status and Family Income Distribution.* Paper presented to 54th ANZAAS Congress, May, Australian National University, Canberra.
Power, Margaret, with C. Wallace, S. Outhwaite and S. Rosewarne
1985 *Women, Work and Labour Market Programs.* Paper Commissioned by the Committee of Inquiry into Labour Market Programs.
Proulx, Monique
1978 *Five Million Women: A Study of the Canadian Housewife.* Ottawa: Advisory Council on the Status of Women.
Pryer, Edward T.
1984 *Canadian Husband-Wife Families: Labour Force Participation and Income Trends 1971-1981.* Ottawa: Supply and Services Canada (Cat. no. 71-x-512).
Rashid, A.
1986 "Labour Market Activities of High Income Families." pp. 87-113 in *The Labour Force.* Ottawa: Supply and Services Canada for Statistics Canada (Cat. no. 71-001).
Reiger, Kerren
1985 *The Disenchantment of the Home: Modernizing the Australian Family 1880-1940.* Melbourne: Oxford University Press.
Richards, Lyn
1985 *Having Families: Marriage, Parenthood and Social Pressures in Australia.* Ringwood, Victoria: Penguin.
Romanuic, A.
1984 *Current Demographic Analysis: Fertility in Canada.* From Baby Boom to Baby Bust. Ottawa: Supply and Services Canada for Statistics Canada (Cat. no. 91-524E).
Scutt, Jocelynne A.
1983 "Legislating For The Right to be Equal." pp. 223-245 in Cora Baldock and Bettina Cass (eds.), *Women Social Welfare and the State.* Sydney: George Allen & Unwin.
Statistics Canada
1985 *Women in Canada: A Statistical Profile* (Cat. no. 9-0503E). Ottawa: Supply and Services Canada, March.
Status of Women Canada
1986 *Report of the Task Force on Child Care.* Ottawa: Supply and Services Canada (Cat. no. SW41-1/1986E).
Strong-Boag, Veronica
1982 "Intruders in the Nursery: Childcare Professionals Reshape the Years One to Five, 1920-1940." pp. 160-178 in Joy Parr (ed.), *Childhood and Family in Canadian History.* Toronto: McClelland and Stewart.

Sweeney, Tania
1983 "Child Welfare and Child Care Policies." pp. 35-54 in Adam Graycar (ed.), *Retreat From the Welfare State*. Sydney: George Allen & Unwin.
Windschuttle
1980 *Unemployment*. Revised edition. Ringwood, Victoria: Penguin.

IV. The Elements of Family Life

A. Gender Socialization: Its Importance

Babies, children and even adults are socialized differently if they are female than if they are male. This difference in treatment accounts for whatever differences typically exist between women and men — as R.C. Lewontin, Steven Rose and Leon Kamin (respectively, a geneticist, a neurobiologist, and a psychologist) argue. In making this argument, these scientists review and criticize popular biological-determinist arguments which assume human nature, personality and behaviour to be fixed in the genes.

Differential treatment by sex is often not subtle, and there are many summaries of research documenting it. (Lenore Weitzman, for example, reviews this body of research — see "suggested readings.") Beyond the question of the different experiences of girls and boys is that of the effects of those experiences on personality: are girls and boys, women and men, different in abilities or orientations to the world? The answer to this latter question is not clear, but seems to be both no and yes: there are no differences in ability, but there may be subtle differences in sensitivity, motivation and orientation. Complementing experimental evidence of these latter differences are the psychoanalytical arguments made by Nancy Chodorow (see "suggested readings") and others about the child's acquisition of gender identity and sexual orientation — and the consequences in terms of the "relational capacities" of women and men. It is important to begin a look at family with a consideration of gender differences, because they infuse every element of family life. Gender is important especially because it entails a division of labour in the household and a related difference in treatment and position in the paid labour force. Indeed, what is most critical about gender is not the differences in socialization and their effects on personality but the *social significance* of sex itself: what is believed about gender differences (that is, gender ideology) and the differences in life chances, or opportunities, that men and women experience (that is, differences in social structure).

207

IV. The Elements of Family Life

Suggested Readings

Weitzman, Lenore.
1975. "Sex-role socialization: a focus on women." Pp. 157-238 in Jo Freeman, ed. *Women: A Feminist Perspective*. Palo Alto: Mayfield.
Chodorow, Nancy.
1978. *The Reproduction of Mothering*. Berkeley: University of California Press.

The Determined Patriarchy*

R.C. Lewontin, Steven Rose, and Leon Kamin

"Is it a boy or a girl?" is still one of the first questions asked about any newborn infant. This question marks the beginning of one of the most important distinctions our culture makes between people, for whether the child is a boy or a girl is going to make a profound difference to its subsequent life. It will determine its life expectancy. On average, slightly more boys are born than girls; at all ages males have a somewhat greater chance of dying than females; in Britain and the United States at the moment the average male life expectancy is about 70 years, while that of females is about 76. This means that most elderly people are women — more than three women to every man in the 85 + age group, for instance.

In Western society today, on average, men are taller and heavier than women. They have larger brains, compared to women, though not when considered in proportion to body weight. Men and women show differential susceptibility to many diseases, quite apart from the obvious, reproductive ones: men suffer more frequently in our culture from a variety of circulatory and heart diseases and some cancers; women are more likely to be diagnosed as psychiatrically disturbed and to be drugged or institutionalized as a result. Men are physically stronger in terms of performance on the sports field or track. Even though a high proportion of women are in paid labor outside the home, the jobs they do tend to be different from those of men. Men are more likely to be cabinet ministers or parliamentarians, business executives or tycoons, Nobel Prize-winning scientists or fellows of academies, doctors or airline pilots. Women are more likely to be secretaries, laboratory technicians, office cleaners, nurses, airline stewardesses, primary school teachers, or social workers.

And these differences in "chosen" profession are mirrored in school performance and the behavior of children at an early age. Boys play with cars and construction sets and cognitive board games; girls with dolls, shops, nurse's uniforms, and home cooking sets. Girls expect to be primarily homemakers, boys to be breadwinners. Fewer girls at school study technical subjects, science, or metalwork; fewer boys

---

* From *Not in Our Genes: Biology, Ideology and Human Nature.* Copyright © Steven Rose, R.C. Lewontin and Leon J. Kamin, 1984. Reprinted by permission of the authors.

IV. The Elements of Family Life

study home economics. After adolescence, girls perform worse than boys at math.

All these are current "facts," objectively ascertainable statements about our present society at this time in history. Some are seemingly facts about biology, some about society, and some about both. But how are they to be understood? What are their implications, if any, for assessing the limits to social plasticity? More than almost any other social "fact" with which this book deals, "facts" about differences between men and women in society — *gender* differences — are seemingly naturalized as manifestations of essentially biological *sex* differences, so apparently obvious as to be beyond question. And indeed for many men, such assumption — which imply that the current division of labor between the sexes in our society (a *social* division of labor) is merely a reflection of some underlying biological necessity, so that society is a faithful mirror of that biology — are extraordinarily convenient.[1]

That we live in a society characterized by differences of status, wealth, and power between men and women is abundantly clear. Just as contemporary Western society is capitalist in its form, so it is also patriarchal.[2] The division of labor between men and women is such that within productive labor men tend to predominate in the more powerful and better paid, more dominant jobs, women in the less powerful, more poorly paid, and more subordinate ones. One whole category of labor — reproductive, or caring labor — is assigned largely if not exclusively to women. Reproductive labor does not just involve the biological labor of childbearing but also the task of organizing the male worker's feeding, clothing, and domestic comfort, nursing him when sick, and so forth. In addition, there is the crucial educational-ideological role of preparing the next generation for *its* productive-reproductive labor by teaching, training, and the transmission of values. That is, either in the home or in the paid sector of the economy, women are disproportionately employed as the preparers of food, the minders and

---

[1]We would like to acknowledge our particular debt, in writing this chapter, to the feminist scholarship on which we have drawn extensively, and in particular to the critical comments on earlier drafts made by Lynda Birke, Ruth Hubbard, and Hilary Rose.

[2]Z.R. Eisenstein, ed., *Capitalist Patriarchy and the Case for Socialist Feminism* (New York: Monthly Review Press, 1979); C. Delphy, *The Main Enemy: A Materialist Analysis of Women's Oppression*, WRRC Publication no. 3 (London, 1977); M. Barrett and M. McIntosh, "The Family Wage," in *The Changing Experience of Women*, ed. E. Whitelegg et al. (Oxford: Martin Robertson, 1982); H. Hartmann, *The Unhappy Marriage of Marxism and Feminism* (London: Pluto, 1981); and A. Oakley, *Sex, Gender and Society* (New York: Harper & Row, 1972).

teachers of children, and the nurses of the sick. This division of labor is a feature not merely of Western capitalist societies but also, in varying degrees, of societies that have gone through revolutionary struggle — from the Soviet Union to China, Vietnam, and Cuba.

Why does the patriarchy persist? One possibility is that it is a historically contingent form of social organization, preserved by those who benefit from it, a consequence of human biology, just as any other social form is a consequence of that biology but only one of a range of possible social organizations available to us. Others would argue, by contrast that it is an inevitable product of our biology, fixed by the biological differences between men and women, determined by our genes.

In response to the upsurge of the feminist movement, its social and political demands, its burgeoning theoretical writing of the past decade, biological determinism has stood firm in claiming that occupying leadership roles in public, political, and cultural life goes with being male as much as having a penis, testicles, and facial hair. Women's intrusions into traditionally male preserves are fervently opposed. When simple votes of exclusion to professional male domains fail, biology is invoked. Women should not be bank managers or politicians, for example. As one American doctor put it:

> If you had an investment in a bank, you wouldn't want the president of the bank making a loan under those raging hormonal influences at that particular period. Suppose we had a president in the White House, a menopausal woman president who had to make the decision of the Bay of Pigs, which was of course a bad one, on a Russian contretemps with Cuba at that time?[3] [4]

Indeed, there is a danger in women even being in any senior position in business. A front-page headline in the *Wall Street Journal* informs us that "firms are disrupted by a wave of pregnancy at the

---

[3] Quoted by K. Paige in "Women Learn to Sing the Blues," *Psychology Today*, September 1973; According to the Alloa [Scotland] Advertiser, at the time of the Falklands/Malvinas War in 1982, Tam Dalyell, M.P., claimed that Margaret Thatcher "was not fully capable of making vital decisions like that between war and peace simply because she was a woman and like every woman was affected by the menstrual cycle."

[4] This hormonal naturalization has its reverse in the recent (1981) acquittal of two women on murder charges in Britain on the ground that they killed while suffering from "premenstrual tension — a decision welcomed by some feminist voices as liberatory and condemned by others as firmly biologistic, freeing these women while by implication oppressing all.(*Wall Street Journal*, 20 July 1981.)

211

IV. The Elements of Family Life

manager level...problems are more widespread these days because more women hold high level jobs and because pregnancies are increasing among those over 30."[5] And the article goes on to explain that male executives have to work harder at short notice because of inconsiderate attacks of pregnancy on the part of their female colleagues. Moral: Women should only be in jobs in which they can be easily replaced, such as a production line or typing pool. Ignored, of course, in such an account of the problems caused by pregnant female executives is the inconvenience resulting from the high and *unplanned* rate of coronary heart disease among male executives, which must be at least as disruptive. But that is normal.

And the conclusion is of course clear: For women to work outside the home is a mistake; bad for the economy, which must then provide and pay for welfare services which would otherwise be supplied by women's unpaid labor; and against nature, which decrees that the man should be the breadwinner, the woman the raiser of children. New Right ideology is explicit on this point, despite the fact that in both Britain and the United States at least one in six households is solely dependent on the earnings of a female breadwinner.[6]

Resurgent New Right thinking rationalizes this opposition to feminist demands still further. For Britain's National Front, the natural place of women is as much tied to *Kinder-Kuche-Kirche* as was that of their Nazi forebears. This view was echoed by Enoch Powell, an M.P. in Britain's Parliament, in debate on the Thatcher government's Nationality Bill (which creates categories of British citizenship roughly designed to make a significant proportion of black British second-class citizens). Mr. Powell, proposing that British citizenship should be passed on only through the father, explained that plans to let a child claim nationality through its mother was "a concession to a temporary fashion based upon a shallow analysis of human nature....Men and women," he went on, "have distinct social functions, with men as fighters and women responsible for creating and preserving life; societies can be destroyed by teaching themselves myths which are inconsistent with the nature of man [sic]."[7]

For biological determinists, then, gender divisions in society do indeed map onto biological, sexual ones. Not only is the division of labor

---

[5]For example, see correspondence in the *Morning Star* (London), especially letters by M. McIntosh (24 November 1982) and B. MacDermott (27 November 1982).

[6]H. Land, "The Myth of the Male Breadwinner," *New Society*, 9 October 1975; H. Rose and S. Rose, "Moving Right Out of Welfare — and the Way Back," *Critical Social Policy* 2, no. 1 (1982): 7-18.

[7]Quoted in *The Sun* (London), 18 February 1981.

given by biology, but we go against it at our peril, for it is functional. Society needs both dominant, productive men and dependent, nurturative, and reproductive women.

The biological determinist argument follows a by now familiar structure: It begins with the citation of "evidence," the "facts" of differences between men and women such as those described in the first paragraphs of this chapter. These "facts," which are taken as unquestioned, are seen as depending on prior psychological tendencies which in turn are accounted for by underlying biological differences between males and females at the level of brain structure or hormones. Biological determinism then shows that male-female differences in behavior among humans are paralleled by those found in nonhuman societies — among primates or rodents or birds, or even dung beetles giving them an apparent universality that cannot be gainsaid by merely wishing things were different or fairer. Biological laws brook no appeal. And finally, the determinist argument endeavors to weld all currently observed differences together on the basis of the now familiar and Panglossian sociobiological arguments: that sexual divisions have emerged adaptively by natural selection, as a result of the different biological roles in reproduction of the two sexes, and have evolved to the maximal advantage of both; the inequalities are not merely inevitable but functional, too.

In the present chapter we will review these apparently scientific claims to explain the current gender divisions in society and will show that they represent a systematic selection, misrepresentation, or improper extrapolation of the evidence, larded with prejudice and basted in poor theory, and that, far from accounting for present divisions, they serve as ideologies that help perpetuate them. As for biological explanations of the differences in IQ performance between races and social classes, the objective of biological explanations of present sex roles is to justify and maintain the status quo.

The Status of the "Facts"

The persistent claim of biological determinist thinking is that the social structure of contemporary Western society mirrors general social structures that are universal. At worst, because of "unnatural" liberal and radical pressure, we have fallen from some prior state of social Darwinist grace. At best, we are what we must be. Hence "facts" of the type of the first paragraphs of this chapter are given a spurious universality. Take job distribution. The present universality of women in office jobs masks the fact that until the early part of this century

213

clerking was an exclusively male preserve and efforts were made to keep women out of office work.[8] "Biological" reasons were advanced then as to why they were unfit for such labor, just as in 1978 the journal *Psychology Today* could report that "as women in general are superior in fine coordination and the ability to make rapid choices, they may for example be faster typists than men."[9] Temporal shortsightedness is matched by geographical shortsightedness; for instance, although it might seem natural that men dominate medical practice in the United States, this situation is reversed for family doctors in the Soviet Union, where the majority are women. (Of course, there family doctoring has a lower status and lower pay than in the United States, but that is a different point.)

The particular dating patterns, sexual practices, and fashion styles of 1950s American teenagers are among those most strikingly universalized by biological determinism. In a well-known study of girls who had been "masculinized" by exposure *in utero* to androgenic steroids administered to their mothers, Money and Ehrhardt define the femininity of their subjects by specific criteria, including whether they show a liking for jewelry, wear pants, manifest so called tomboyish behavior, or are more concerned about a future career than about a romantic marriage.[10] This point doesn't merely embrace the ideology of the women's magazines that provides a set of acceptable standards — stereotypes; it ignores the existence of societies in which women wear pants, or in which men wear skirts, or in which men enjoy and appropriate jewelry to themselves. The girls are being judged by Money and Ehrhardt by how well they conform to the stereotyped local image of femininity. They are shown to have been mildly willing to reject these forms — though they still expected to marry and be mothers. And this rejection — among girls who were aware of the ambiguities of their own gender labeling and the unusual attention that the researchers were paying to them as opposed to their peers — is supposed to be expressive of some universal biological determination.

Naivete in the description of human social and sexual arrangements displayed by biological determinists also characterizes the attention that sociobiologists such as Wilson, Van den Berghe, and

---

[8]J. Morgall, "Typing Our Way to Freedom: Is it True That New Office Technology Can Liberate Women?" in *Changing Experience of Women*, pp. 136-46.

[9]S. Witelson, quoted in *Psychology Today*, November 1978, p. 51.

[10]J. Money and A.A. Ehrhardt, *Man and Woman, Boy and Girl* (Baltimore: Johns Hopkins Univ. Press, 1972). Their list of criteria also includes expenditure of energy in outdoor play and games, fantasies of materialism and romance, and childhood sexual play.

others have paid to a phenomenon they regard as universally human — the "incest taboo." Yet inspection of the sociological literature, if nothing else, would soon have told them that even in present day Western societies laws against incest are no barrier to its substantial incidence.[11] [12]

This kind of thinking is redolent as much of a social as of a sexual chauvinism, a chauvinism that knows nothing except the stereotype of its own society within a very sharply delimited class border. It is a narrowness that knows neither sociology, history, nor geography. Social universals then appear to lie more in the eyes of the biological determinist observer than in the social reality that is being observed. But this is interestingly true of the apparent biological universals as well. Some are straightforward. The fact that today the life expectancy of females exceeds that of males in advanced industrial societies is very sharply affected by the dramatic decline of the death rate in or around childbirth that was so characteristic of women everywhere until the

---

[11]J. Herman, *Father-Daughter Incest* (Cambridge, Mass.: Harvard Univ. Press, 1981); L. Armstrong, "Kiss Daddy Goodnight," in *Speakout on Incest* (New York: Hawthorn, 1978).

[12]The incest taboo is one of the odder sociobiological stories.(12) The argument begins from the genetically correct statement that brother-sister matings are likely to increase the number of offspring with disabling or deleterious double recessive genes, and are therefore eugenically unfavorable. It would therefore be an adaptive advantage for such close-kin matings to be avoided. Sociobiology claims that this is indeed the case among both humans and nonhumans. The mechanism whereby we and other organisms recognise one another's genetic relatedness and hence sexual availability is unspecified; one suggestion is that the rule is "Do not mate with someone you have been brought up with." The nonhuman evidence is at best fragmentary; the prediction seems to be supported by observations of some baboon populations, and by unfortunate extrapolations from the behavior of new-hatched Japanese quail; but the common observation of fairly indiscriminate mating among domestic or farmyard animals is met by the bland assurance that such species have been peculiarized by human intervention. So far as humans are concerned, social rules of permitted and forbidden mating patterns in a large number of different societies tend to be cited. Yet even if it were true that there was a universal incest taboo that forbade genetically close marriages (which there is not), it is not possible to map social definitions of kin directly onto genetic ones; and even if it were also true that this taboo was followed in practice (which it is not), the argument makes no sociobiological sense. For if the "taboo" is indeed genetically prescribed, what need is there for mere social legislation to enforce it? A natural repugnance should require no legal shoring up in this way. Unless of course it is not that our genes inhibit us from copulating with our siblings but instead induce us to pass laws regulating such copulation.(P.L. van den Berghe, "Human Inbreeding Avoidance: Culture in Nature," *Behavioral and Brain Sciences* 6 (1983): 125-68; Also see P.P.G. Bateson, "Rules for Changing the Rules," in *Evolution From Molecules to Men*, ed. D.S. Bendall, (Cambridge: Cambridge Univ. Press, 1983).)

present century. Morbidity statistics show comparably rapid changes. In the United States and England women are steadily catching up with men in the rate of deaths from lung cancer and coronary thrombosis for instance. Less obvious are such phenomena as the secular decline in sexual dimorphism in height that has been recorded over the past century. The average male-female height difference was substantially greater a century ago than it is today in advanced industrial societies. Or take the relative performance of men and women in sport. What would have been perceived only a few decades ago as a natural and inevitable difference between men and women has steadily been eroded. Dyer looked at average male-female differences in track athletics, swimming, and time trial cycling between 1948 and 1976 and showed that in each of these three sports women's performances in relationship to men have continuously improved, and that if these changes are continued, the average female performance will equal that of males for all events currently competed for by both sexes sometime during the next century.[13]

But how important are averages anyway? The fact that today on average men are taller than women does not deny that many women are taller than many men. Average statements about populations are only made *post hoc*, that is, after we have decided on the definition of the populations being described. Thus, before we can describe differences between men and women we have to define the two populations — male and female — to be compared. It is just this dichotomization that is under discussion, though, and which we are urging cannot merely be dismissed as "natural."[14] If the dichotomization masks such overlap yet serves the social functions of pushing people into one or other of two boxes labeled "man" or "woman," then attempts to pontificate about the nature and origins of the differences are in deep trouble. "Average" statements are powerful, but they are not necessarily the most helpful ways of describing phenomena.

---

[13]K.F. Dyer, "The Trend of the Male and Female Performance Differential in Athletics, Swimming and Cycling, 1958-1976," *Journal of Biosocial Science* 9 (1977): 325-39; also see K.F. Dyer, *Challenging the Men: Women in Sport* (St. Lucia, Australia: Univ. of Queensland Press, 1982).

[14]R. Hubbard, "Have Only Men Evolved?" in *Women Look at Biology Looking at Women*, eds. R. Hubbard, M.S. Henifin, and B. Fried (Cambridge, Mass: Schenkman, 1979), pp. 7-36; R. Hubbard and M. Lowe, Introduction to R. Hubbard and M. Lowe, eds., *Genes and Gender II* (New York: Gordian Press, 1977): pp. 9-34; L. Birke, "Cleaving the Mind: Speculations on Conceptual Dichotomies," in *Against Biological Determinism*, ed. S. Rose (London: Allison & Busby, 1982): pp. 60-78; and L. Rogers, "The Ideology of Medicine," in *Against Biological Determinism*, pp. 79-93.

Furthermore, they run the danger of becoming self-fulfilling. If there are average stereotypes to which girls and boys are encouraged to conform — so that boys practice being "masculine," girls practice being "feminine" — the stereotypes perpetuate dichotomies and further enhance the appearance of being "natural."

The next step in the determinist proof of these social "facts" is to map observed social divisions onto individual psychological ones. According to their arguments, when one examines the psychology of either sex we find that women excel at certain tasks, men at others. Note that differences between the sexes in average IQ cannot be claimed, because the standard IQ tests as developed in the 1930s were carefully balanced to eliminate any sex differences that the earlier version of the tests had shown. Thus an earlier generation of determinists has neatly removed this particular weapon from patriarchy's ideal logical armamentarium. Fairweather summarized the received wisdom of the psychology of sex differences as follows:

> Females have been seen...as more receptive...within the tactile and auditory domain, although retaining particular high class discriminatory abilities such as that involving face recognition....Emotionally more dependent, they are "sympathetic" both in nature and nervous system. As a result less exploratory, they fail to develop the independence of immediate surrounds necessary for orientation in large spaces, or the manipulation of more immediate spatial relations. Cerebrally, they live with language in the left hemisphere. Males on the contrary are characterised as brashly visual, preferring simple responsive stimuli, responding best with grosser movements; fearless and independent; parasympathetic and right hemispheric; and ultimately, successful.[15]

Thus men and women have different success rates in different jobs because they are doing what comes naturally.[16]

---

[15]H. Fairweather, "Sex Differences in Cognition," *Cognition* 4 (1976): 31-280.

[16]Such naturalizing is not confined to "obvious" reactionaries. William Morris, in his anarchial vision *News From Nowhere*, describes his free society as one in which the women cook and wait upon the men at table because this is what they "naturally" enjoy. However, in Utopia men recognize the skills involved in these activities and respect the women for them. Male black-power spokesmen have been known to take a similar situation. At the 1981 Labour Party Conference, when the chairman thanked the women for their tea making, he was successfully challenged by feminists under the slogan "Women make policy, not tea."

IV. The Elements of Family Life

According to Maccoby and Jacklin, girls have greater verbal ability than boys, and boys excel in visual-spatial (mechanical aptitude) and mathematical skills and are more aggressive than girls.[17] The consequence, according to psychologist Sandra Witelson, is that there may be fewer female architects, engineers, and artists

> because such professions require the kind of thinking that may depend on spatial skills in contrast women performers (vocalists, instrumentalists) and writers are less rare. This may be because the skills involved in these talents may depend on functions women do well — linguistic and fine motor coordination.[18]

Job choices in a free society are thus merely the reading out of individual preferences — ontologically prior personal decisions based on innate psychology. The social forces driving particular "choices" — the directing influences of school and families, or the male exclusion of females from particular trades and profession — are all irrelevant. That in the United States and the United Kingdom adolescent girls do worse than boys at math is quickly taken as evidence "that sex differences in achievement in and attitudes toward mathematics results from superior male mathematical ability, which may in turn be related to greater male ability in spatial tasks."[19]

Ignoring the social and cultural pressures driving the sexes in different directions, the consistently reported driving out or putting down of girls who show interest in math leads directly to the biological explanation.[20] To come back to Witelson's examples, Virginia Woolf pointed out a long time ago that in a society in which women are denied even the privilege of space — a room of one's own — almost the only permissible skills become those that do not demand privacy or space: A writer's notebook is transportable, a painter's canvas or architect's drawing board not so. And while women's

---

[17] E.E. Maccoby and C.N. Jacklin, *The Psychology of Sex Differences* (Stanford, Calif.: Standford Univ. Press, 1974).

[18] Witelson, quoted in *Psychology Today*, November 1973, pp. 48-59.

[19] C.P. Benbow and J.C. Stanley, *Science* 210 (1980): 1262-64.

[20] The story of this exclusion has often been told. See, for example, C. St. John-Brooks, "Are Girls Really Good at Maths?" *New Society*, 5 March 1981, pp. 411-12; A. Kelly, ed., *The Missing Half: Girls and Science Education* (Manchester: Manchester Univ. Press, 1979); N. Weisstein, "Adventures of a Woman in Science," in *Women Look at Biology Looking at Women*, pp. 187-206; M. Couture-Cherki, "Women in Physics," in *The Radicalization of Science*, ed. H. Rose and S. Rose (London: Macmillan, 1976), pp. 65-75.

"accomplishments" are praiseworthy, real expertise that might challenge the male or take time away from the crucial reproductive role is not. (The new feminist scholarship has chronicled an entire history of nineteenth-century medical men and psychologists insisting on the antithesis between creative work — for instance in scholarship or science — and reproduction. Women who studied would damage their essential reproductive capacity.)[21]

But how valid are the psychological claims made by Witelson and others? Are these "differences" real, and if they are, can one ascribe causes to them? These days most researchers recognize that the differences observed between men and women, or even schoolchildren, represent the outcome of an inextricable interplay of biological, cultural, and social forces with genotype during development. So the tendency has been to seek methods to research psychological traits in younger and younger children, or even in newborns. Reviews and popular books[22] claim that even here differences are found — differences in crying, in sleep patterns, in smiling, in latencies to particular response — which lay the basis for what is to come. Yet in an exhaustive review of the literature on sex differences and performance among newborns, Fairweather was able to conclude that despite persistent claims to the contrary:

> In childhood we are left with, at most, a female propensity for precise digital movement; and on the same continuum, a male propensity for activity demanding the usage of larger musculatures and certain spatial (body-orientational) abilities which these may subserve. The rest is dilemma.[23]

In slightly older children there are

---

[21] See, for example, E. Fee, "Science and the Woman Problem: Historical Perspectives," in *Sex Differences: Social and Biological Perspectives*, ed. M.S. Teitelbaum (New York: Anchor Doubleday, 1976): pp. 173-221; J. Sayers, *Biological Politics: Feminist and Anti-Feminist Perspectives* (London: Tavistock, 1982); M.R. Walsh, "The Quirls of a Woman's Brain" in *Women Look at Biology Looking at Women*, pp. 103-26; S.S. Mosdale, "Science Corrupted: Victorian Biologists Consider the Woman Question," *Journal of the History of Biology II* (1978): 1-55; S.A. Shields, "Functionalism, Darwinism, and the Psychology of Women: A Study in Social Myth," *American Psychologist*, July 1975, pp. 739-54.

[22] For example, C. Hutt, *Males and Females* (Harmondsworth, Middlesex, England: Penguin, 1972).

[23] Fairweather, "Sex Differences in Cognition."

no substantial sex differences in verbal sub-tests of IQ
tests; in reading; in para-reading skills (Cross-Modal
matching); and in early linguistic output; in articulatory
competence; in vocabulary; and in laboratory studies of
the handling of verbal concepts and processing of verbal
materials.[24]

Differences emerge only later when the "sudden polarization of abilities in adolescence" occurs.

So the actual evidence for sex differences in cognitive behavior
among infants is slight. But even were there such evidence, what
would it prove? Is it that by going back to infancy one can study "pure,
biologically determined behavior" uncontaminated by culture? The answer is no. A child can only develop in an environment that includes
the social from the earliest postnatal moment.[25] Babies interact with
their caregivers; they are held, clothed, fed, cuddled, and talked to.
Parents are said to hold and speak to their male babies differently from
their female babies, quite apart from dressing them in blue or pink.[26]
All cultures must generate expectations of behavior among parents
and hence ensure that certain types of behavior are going to be consciously or unconsciously reinforced or discouraged from the beginning. This would be the case whether the infant was cared for by a biological parent or by surrogates. We are not trying to transfer "blame" to
the mothers. The point is that the determinants of behavior are irre-
deemably interactive and ontogenetic. However young the child that is
being studied, its behavior must be the product of such interaction. To
argue that one can divide behavior chronologically into a portion given
by biology and another given by culture is to fall into a reductionist trap
from the start. This is not to discount the importance of studying the
development of behavior in young children, which is among the most
fascinating areas of human ethology. We insist, however, that such
studies do not ask naively reductionist questions of their subject; what
is needed is as rich and interactive a methodology as the varied development of human infants themselves.

But apparent psychological differences between the sexes are
just the starting point for the biological determinist argument. If there

---

[24]*Ibid.*

[25]We do not discuss here the effects of the prenatal environment on development,
important though these may be. See L. McKie and M. O'Brien, eds., *The Father
Figure* (London: Tavistock, 1982).

[26] S. Rose, *The Conscious Brain* (Harmondsworth, Middlesex, England: Penguin,
1976).

are such differences, they must, the argument runs, reflect underlying differences in brain biology. Somehow, if the differences can be grounded in biology they are seen as more secure from environmental challenge. Again we should emphasize that as materialists we too would expect to find that differences in behavior between individual humans will prove to be related to differences in the biology of those individuals. Where we differ from biological reductionism is in refusing to accept an argument that says that the biological difference is primary and causative of the "higher level" psychological one; *both* are different aspects of the same unitary phenomenon. Differences in the social environment of an individual during development can result in changes in the biology of brain and body just as much as in behavior. So to show that there are differences between the brains of males and females on average says little about either the causes or the consequences of such differences.

But are there differences? Certainly the belief in them goes back a long way. Nineteenth-century anthropologists were obsessed with the question of the relationship between intelligence and brain size. Just as they were convinced that the white brain was better developed than the black, so the male was superior to the female. Male brains were heavier, as the neuroanatomist Paul Broca pointed out, but there were also differences in structure. According to the anthropologist McGrigor Allan in 1869, "The type of the female skull approaches in many respects that of the infant, and still more that of the lower races."[27]

Much was made of the "missing five ounces" of the female brain until it was realized that when brain weight is expressed in relation to

---

[27]E. Fee, "Nineteenth-Century Craniology: The Study of the Female Skull," *Bulletin of the History of Medicine* 53 (1979): 415-33.
The juxtaposition of sexism and racism was a characteristic feature of nineteenth-century biological determinist thinking. Charles Darwin commented that "some at least of those mental traits in which women may excel are traits characteristic of the lower races.
For the French craniologist F. Pruner, "The Negro resembles the female in his love for children, his family and his cabin...the black man is to the white man what woman is to man in general, a loving being and a being of pleasure." F. Pruner, in *Transactions of the Ethnological Society* 4 (1866): 13-33; quoted by Fee, "Nineteenth-Century Craniology."
The theme runs through much of nineteenth-century evolutionary and anthropological writing and finds a curious time echo in the contemporary suggestion by Arthur Jensen that because (he claims) spatial perception is a sex-linked ability, it can be used effectively to study the relationship of black-white gene mixing on racial differences in intelligence. See A.R. Jensen, "A Theoretical Note on Sex Linkage and Race Differences in Spatial Visualization Ability." *Behavior Genetics* 8 (1978): 213-17. *Plus ça change.*

body weight the difference disappeared or even reversed. This led to further devices such as comparing brain weight to thigh-bone weight or body height.[28] Attention was diverted to brain regions — frontal or temporal lobes, for example — as the seats of differences. It was left, to Alice Leigh, a student of Karl Pearson, in 1901, using new statistical methods, to conclude that there was no correlation between skull capacity and hence brain weight and "intellectual power."[29]

For many years subsequently neuroanatomy and neurophysiology measured no differences between male and female brains. Only with the emergence of new methodology in anatomy, physiology, and biochemistry in the 1960s and 1970s (and the rise of the new biological determinism) has the question become actively asked once more. Most attention has been devoted to the claims that there is a difference in stalled lateralization between male and female brains. As a structure the brain divides neatly into two virtually symmetrical halves, like the two halves of a walnut, the left half (hemisphere) being broadly associated with right-side-of-body activity, the right half with left-side activity. This symmetry is incomplete, however. It has been known since Broca's day, in the nineteenth century, that speech and linguistic functions are, for most people, located in a region of the left hemisphere — parts of the temporal lobe. Hence left-hemisphere strokes or thromboses affect speech, whereas equivalent right-hemisphere brain damage generally does not. The regions of the temporal lobe in the left hemisphere that apparently accommodate speech are anatomically larger than the corresponding right-hemisphere regions.

Evidence for sexual dimorphism in hemispheric size in humans has begun to appear and seems more securely grounded than earlier claims for meaningful differences in overall brain size. How such differences arise is unclear: one possibility offered by Geschwind and his colleagues is that there are interactions of the fetal brain during development with hormones such as testosterone, of which more later. It is argued that testosterone slows the growth of the left hemisphere relative to the right.[30] As is characteristic in such analyses, animal data is cited to support the case in humans; thus part of the right cerebral cortex of the rat is thicker in males, while the corresponding part of the left hemisphere is thicker in females, and these differences are modi-

[28]Mosdale, "Science Corrupted."

[29]Fee, "Nineteenth-Century Craniology;" also see D.A. MacKenzie, *Statistics in Britain, 1865-1930* (Edinburgh: Edinburgh Univ. Press, 1981).

[30]N. Geschwind and P. Behan. "Left Handedness: Association with Immune Disease, Migraine and Developmental Learning Disorder," *Proceedings of the National Academy of Sciences* 79 (1982): 5097-5100.

fied by experimentally changing the hormonal balance of the animals in infancy.

There are two major problems with interpreting the significance of such observations. The first is that of extrapolating from nonhuman to human brains. While the nerve cells — the basic units that make up the brain — and the way these cells individually work are virtually identical in organisms as diverse as sea slugs and humans, the number of cells, their arrangement, and their interconnections differ dramatically. Insects and mollusks have a few tens or hundreds of thousands of nerve cells in their central ganglia, a rat or a cat may have hundreds of millions in its brain, and humans have between ten and a hundred billion in theirs, each communicating with its neighbors by up to a hundred thousand connections. Brain weight for body weight, only a few primate species and dolphins approach this order of complexity. Further, in organisms with less complex brains most of the neural pathways are laid down — genetically specified — form rather rigid and preprogrammed connections. This invariance gives such organisms a comparatively fixed and limited behavioral repertoire.

By contrast, the human infant is born with relatively few of its neural pathways already committed. During its long infancy, connections between nerve cells are formed on the basis not merely of specific epigenetic programming but in the light of experience. The microchips in a pocket calculator and a big general-purpose computer may be similar in composition and structure, but one is a limited, dedicated piece of machinery with a fixed repertoire of outputs, while the other is vastly variable. Homologies of structure between animal and human brains are of interest, but one cannot ascribe homologies of meaning, still less identities, to their outputs on this basis alone. For instance, there is a marked sexual dimorphism in the brains of certain species, notably songbirds. The male canary has a concentration of nerve cells in a particular brain region that is lacking in the female and is associated with the generation of its song, the development of which is hormone dependent.[31] This brain region is relatively smaller in the female canary. This does not allow us to predict ways in which postmortem analysis of brains would have found differences between canaries and Maria Callas, however. Nor does it allow us to deduce where in Callas's brain her singing capacity was located. Homologies of structure between species do not mean homologies of function.

---

[31]F. Nottebohm and A.V. Arnold, "Sexual Dimorphism in Vocal Control Areas of the Songbird Brain," *Science* 194 (1976): 211-13.

IV. The Elements of Family Life

Biological determinism makes great play of the evolutionary origins of the human brain, in which certain deep structures can be shown to have first evolved in our reptilian ancestors. Maclean has spoken of the "triune brain,"[32] whose three broad divisions can be derived from humanity's reptilian, mammalian, and primate forebears. But it is absurd to conclude, as some determinist arguments seem committed to doing, that with part of our brain we therefore think like snakes.[33] Evolutionary processes are parsimonious with structures, pressing them constantly to new purposes rather than radically abandoning them. Feet become hooves or hands, but we do not therefore conclude that hands behave in hooflike ways. The human cerebral cortex evolved from a structure that in more primitive-brained forebears was largely the organ of olfaction. This does not mean that we think by smelling.

Localizing emotions and behavioral capacities has been the sport of determinism since the days of phrenology. Yet while it is clearly true that we can say of particular brain regions that they are *necessary* for given behaviors (or their expression), there is no region of the human brain of which we can say that it is *sufficient* for such functions.[34] One cannot see without eyes; one still cannot see with eyes but without the vast regions of both halves of the brain to which the eyes are connected. And the property of perception — the analysis of visual information — is not localized either to the eyes or to any particular constellation of cells within the brain; rather, it is a property of the entire eye-brain system, with its interconnecting web of nerve cells.

So the fact of anatomical differences in brain structure between males and females, itself no more and no less interesting than the fact of anatomical differences in genitalia between the two sexes, does not permit us to draw conclusions about the biological substrate or innateness of behavioral differences. Just what hemispheric differences mean is simply unknown, despite the literature of hemispheric specialization that has grown up in the past decades. It has been suggested, for instance, that paralleling the linguistic skills of the left hemisphere are spatial ones in the right; that the left hemisphere is cognitive, the right affective; that the left is linear, digital, and active, while the right is nonlinear, analogic, and contemplative; that the left

---

[32] P.D. Maclean. "The Triune Brain, Emotion and Scientific Bias," in *The Neurosciences: Second Study Program*, ed. F.O. Schmitt (New York: M.I.T. Press, 1970): pp. 336-49.

[33] For example, A. Koestler, *The Ghost in the Machine* (London: Hutchinson, 1967).

[34] This theme, of the localization fallacy, occurs again in relation to the 'site' of violent behaviour, (discussed in Chapter 7.)

is Western, the right Eastern. One prominent Catholic neurophysiologist has placed the seat of the soul in the left hemisphere. Hemispheric specialization has become a sort of trash can for all sorts of mystical speculation.[35]

And to this list of speculative differences have now been added sex differences. If men have greater spatial perceptual abilities, and women better linguistic skills, one might anticipate that men would be more "right-hemispheric," women more "left-hemispheric." But this won't do. Men are also cognitive (said to be a left-hemisphere function) and women affective (said to be a right-hemisphere function). To preserve male cognitive and spatial preeminence and yet map these onto brain structures the male brain must be described as more lateralized — each half does its own thing better; while women are less lateralized — the two halves of the female brain interact more than do those of the male. Hence men can do different types of things simultaneously whereas women can only do one thing at a time without getting confused (it is not true that Gerald Ford was female, however).

The possibilities of stereotypic speculation based on differences in lateralization are obviously immense. Witelson expresses the confusion neatly:

> For example men are superior on tests of spatial skills and tend to show greater lateralisation of spatial function to the right hemisphere. Here greater lateralisation seems to be correlated with greater ability. However, in the case of language, women, in general, are superior to men, who show greater lateralisation of language skills to the left hemisphere. Thus with language greater lateralisation may be correlated with less ability.[36]

Witelson's enthusiasm for overinterpretation of data is not unique. Even some feminist writers have adopted the lateralization argument and made it over for their own purposes. In conformity with one strand of feminist writing which, like that of masculine biological determinists, argues for essential differences between the ways in which men and women think and feel but rejoices in the superiority of the female mode, Gina argues that women should welcome the intuitive and emotional strengths given by their right hemisphere, in opposition to

[35] J. Jaynes, *The Origin of Consciousness in the Breakdown of the Bicameral Mind* (Boston: Houghton Mifflin, 1976); R.F. Ornstein, *Psychology of Consciousness* (New York: Harcourt Brace, 1977).

[36] Witelson, quoted in *Psychology Today*, November 1978, p. 51.

IV. The Elements of Family Life

the overcognitive, left-hemisphere dominated, masculine nature.[37] While we would agree that the peculiarly reductive or objectivist nature of scientific knowledge as it has developed in the context of a patriarchal and capitalist society is to be opposed, we would not accept that reductionist science is innately wired into the masculine brain.

The truth of the matter is that while the evidence for hemispheric differentiation and specialization of function is among the most intriguing of the developments in human neurosciences of the past decade, its relationship to individual differences in behavior is quite unclear, except in the case of brain damage or disease in adults, where the capacity for the plastic recovery of function is very limited. (Children show much more plasticity.) Differences in lateralization, if they exist, are not explanations for social divisions, though they provide a fertile ground for biological determinist imagination.

If biologically determined male-female cognitive differences divorced from the social framework begin to dissolve on inspection, there is one difference on which all biological determinists are agreed: men and boys are more aggressive than women and girls, a difference that appears at an early age, when it manifests itself in an activity called rough-and-tumble play[38] and continues into adulthood, where it is expressed as a need or tendency to dominate. Men may not be better than women at any particular task, but they are prepared to push and shove their way to the top more aggressively. The argument received its fullest expression in the mid-1970s in a book by Steven Goldberg, *The Inevitability of Patriarchy*.[39]

Goldberg's argument is engagingly direct: wherever one looks, in all human societies throughout all history, there is a patriarchy. "Authority and leadership are and always have been associated with the male in every society." ...Such universality must imply "the strong possibility that these may be inevitable social manifestations of human physiology." ...Attempts to create a different society must fail, as "the inexorable pull of sexual and familial biological forces eventually overcome the initial thrust of nationalistic, religious, ideological or psychological forces that had made possible the temporary implementation of Utopian ideas." ...Men always have the high-status

---

[37]Gina quoted by S.L. Star, "The Politics of Right and Left: Sex Differences in Hemispheric Brain Asymmetry," in *Women Look at Biology Looking at Women*, pp. 61-76.

[38]Rough-and-tumble play is supposedly more frequent not merely in young male humans than in young females but also in males of several other mammalian species. However, its relationship to aggression is largely inferential.

[39]S. Goldberg, *The Inevitability of Patriarchy*, 2nd ed. (New York: Morrow, 1974).

roles, not because women can't do them but because they are not "for psychophysiological reasons...as strongly motivated to attain them".

The magic lies in a "neuroendocrinological differentiation"...which gives the male a greater tendency to dominate. Men will dominate, whatever behavior this might require: "Fighting, kissing babies for votes, or whatever...it is not possible to predict what the necessary behavior will be in any given society because this will be determined by social factors, but whatever it may be it will be manifested by males." ....Domination is ensured in groups and in dyads (i.e., men want to boss other men and their female sexual partners and children). The neuroendocrinology must be very flexible if it can generate such varied expressions, of course. It is a very bold neuroendocrinologist who would want to argue that the hormonal features involved in kissing babies are identical with those involved in fighting, but Goldberg is not deterred. Everything lies in the hormones, which at a particular phase of development "masculinize" the fetal brain. The magic hormone itself is testosterone, produced by the testes, seen as the "male" hormone, whose presence around birth probably produces some change in brain mechanisms with lasting subsequent effects.[40]

And if men have this Nietzschean will to dominate, what do women have in its stead? Goldberg waxes poetic. Women's hormones provide them with "a greater nurturative tendency (i.e., they react to a child in distress more strongly and more quickly than do males)....Women's role is that of "the directors of society's emotional resources...there are few women who can outfight [men] and few who can out — argue but...when a woman uses feminine means she can command a loyalty that no amount of dominant behavior ever could." What a touching picture of Goldberg's vulnerability to seduction is thus revealed! So like the home life of our own dear nuclear family. Go against it at your peril. Women should not "deny their own nature...argue against their own juices"....In every society a basic male motivation is the feeling that the women and children must be protected. "But the feminist cannot have it both ways: if she wants to sacrifice all this, all that she will get in return is the right to meet men on male terms. She will lose"....For Goldberg, then, the interplay of "male" and "female" hormones with the brain, starting early in development, is the key to the sexual universe. However, when one comes to sort out the biology from the rhetoric, the magic power of

---

[40]Actually, Goldberg's evidence for the effect of testosterone on brain mechanism is derived in large part from studies on mice and rats.

these baby — kissing and fighting or nurturant and juicy hormones seems to fade.

The Biology of Sex

What lies behind the Goldbergian thesis of "male" and "female" hormones? A digression on the biology of sex (as opposed to gender) differences in humans is necessary here. Human sexual differentiation in embryonic development begins with the influence of the chromosome carried by the sperm. Of the twenty-three pairs of chromosomes in each body cell of a normal person, twenty-two are autosomes — nonsexual chromosomes — present in two copies in either sex. The twenty-third pair are the sex chromosomes. Normal females carry a pair of X chromosomes, while males have one X and one Y chromosome. This is achieved because all ova have a single X chromosome and sperm may carry *either* an X *or* a Y; hence the fertilized egg that results from mating will be either XX or XY depending on which sperm fertilizes the eggs. At first sight, sex differences depend on the differences between an XX and an XY. For certain single characters this may largely be the case. For instance, the absence of the second X in males means that some deleterious recessive genes whose effects would otherwise be masked are expressed; females carry traits such as color blindness or hemophilia, but they are expressed in males, as sex-linked traits. But of course during development genes interact with one another — or rather the protein products of one gene interact with the protein products of another — in complex ways, and hence autosomal and sex chromosome products will be involved mutually in the development of the organism.

Attempts are sometimes made to infer the consequence of possession of X or Y chromosomes from the study of individuals with rare chromosomal abnormalities. For instance, in Turner's syndrome one of the sex chromosomes is absent (XO); in Klinefelter's syndrome there is an extra X (XXY). Males who carry an extra Y (XYY) have sometimes been described as "supermales," and efforts have been made to prove that they have higher levels of "male" hormones or are unusually aggressive or criminally inclined. Despite a flurry of enthusiasm for such claims in the late sixties and early seventies, they are now generally discounted.[41]

---

[41]See Science for the People, ed., *Biology as a Social Weapon* (Minneapolis: Burgess, 1977).

In any event, such inferences about the role of the Y chromosome in normal development are always doomed to failure. The presence of an additional chromosome produces effects that are not merely additive or subtractive to a normal developmental program; rather, such a presence throws the whole program out of kilter. Down's syndrome,[42] for instance, is a chromosomal disorder in which there is an extra autosomal chromosome (trisomy 21), but the result of the addition is to produce an individual with a wide range of defects — retarded mental, motor, and sexual development, low IQ test scores, and some disordered physical characteristics often including webbed fingers and toes. But the disorder has some positive features as well. For example, Down's syndrome children are often conspicuously happy and friendly, with "sunny" dispositions. We should not be surprised at such complex phenotypic consequences.

The Y chromosome does play an important role during normal development in the expression of male physiological and morphological characteristics, particularly for the differentiation of the testes. During embryonic development, the primitive sex gland that develops during the first few weeks requires the presence of a Y chromosome in order to differentiate into the testis. In both sexes, hormonal secretion begins to occur. Now, contrary to the impression conveyed by Goldbergian hormonal determinism, and indeed to the naming of hormones as estrogens and androgens, such sex hormones are not uniquely male or female. Both sexes secrete both types of hormone; what differs is the ratio of estrogen to androgen in the two sexes. Hormones (gonadotropins) from the pituitary — a small gland at the base of the brain — regulate hormone release from both ovary and testis, which are then carried to other regions. The presence of both androgens and estrogens (as well as other hormones) seems to be required in both sexes to achieve sexual maturity, and both types of hormone are produced not merely by ovary and testis but also by the adrenal cortex in both sexes. Furthermore, the two kinds of hormone are chemically closely related and can be interconverted by enzymes present in the body. Estrogens were at one time prepared from pregnant mare urine, which excretes the large amount of more than 100 mg daily — a record, as Astwood puts it, "exceeded only by the stallion who despite clear manifestations of virility, liberates into his

---

[42]Down's syndrome used to be called mongolism, a reference to the naive racism of nineteenth-century clinicians who viewed idiocy in the "white races" as reflective of "throwbacks" to "more primitive" black, brown, and yellow races. Of the various terms used to classify "idiocy" in this racial typology, only "mongolism" survived for any length of time.

environment more oestrogen than any living creature."[43] Nor is progesterone — a hormone that affects the development of uterus, vagina, and breasts, which is intimately involved in the processes of pregnancy, and whose rhythmic fluctuations characterize the menstrual cycle confined to females; it is present in males at levels not unlike those of the preovulatory phase of the menstrual cycle in females. It can be a chemical precursor of testosterone.

So, insofar as sex differences are determined by hormones, they are not a consequence of the activities of uniquely male or female hormones, but rather probably of fluctuating differences in the ratios of these hormones and their interactions with target organs. Genetic sex, determined by the chromosomes, is, during development, overlaid by hormonal sex, shaped by the ratios of androgens to estrogens, and normally, though not always, appropriate to the genetic sex of the individual. Of course the hormones too are produced by gene-initiated processes but are subject to much more environmental change or deliberate manipulation, either by hormone injection or removal of the hormone-producing glands, for instance by castration in animals. Finally, in humans the cultural and social environment of sexual expectations is overlaid yet again on the chromosomal and hormonal phenomena.

From Sex to Gender

There is a conspicuous lack of relationship, in humans, between, on the one hand, levels and ratio of circulating hormones, and on the other, sexual enthusiasms or preferences. In some laboratory animals, notably the rat, there is a relatively straightforward relationship between, say, estrogen and progesterone levels and sexual enthusiasm in the female, so that injection of estrogen induces the female rat to take up a position in which she raises her rump in sexual invitation. But even in the arid environment of a laboratory cage the response of the female to hormone injection depends on her prior experience, and the relationship between hormone levels and sexual activity is even less straightforward in more complicated "real life" environments. In humans the matter is certainly much more complex. Hormone levels are not simply or directly related to either sexual enthusiasm or attractiveness to the opposite sex.

Nor do the hormonal levels or ratios have much to do with the direction of sexual attraction. It has been a popular hypothesis over

---

[43]Quoted by A.M. Briscoe in E. Tobach and B. Rossoff, eds., *Genes and Gender.* (New York: Gordian Press, 1979) vol. 1, p. 41.

some forty years that people with homosexual enthusiasms would show levels of circulating hormone more appropriate to the "wrong" sex. Lesbians, it was argued, should have higher androgen and/or lower estrogen levels than heterosexuals.[44] Yet no such relationships exist. Nor would we have expected them to: the very assumption implies a reification and biological reductionism which insists that all sexual activities and proclivities can be dichotomized into hetero- or homo-directed, and that showing one or the other proclivity is an all-or-none state of the individual, rather than a statement about a person in a particular social context at a particular time in his or her history. Of sociobiology's view of the "adaptiveness" of homosexual behavior...

The failure of simplistic attempts to associate hormone levels with sexual enthusiasm or direction led determinists to the assumption that what matters is not so much the adult hormonal level but the interplay of hormones with, for instance, the brain during development — perhaps even prenatally. The role that the steroid hormones play during early development is clearly an important one, not merely in terms of the maturation of the sex organs but also because both estrogens and androgens interact directly with the brain during crucial phases of its development. There are now known to be many regions of the brain — not just those areas of the hypothalamus most directly concerned with the regulation of hormonal release — that contain binding sites at which both estrogens and androgens become concentrated. These sites are present, and hormones become bound to them, not merely prepubertally but even prenatally; and both androgens and estrogens are bound by both males and females, though there are differences in the pattern and scale of binding between the sexes, and differences in the structural effects the hormones have on the cells to which they bind.

Until a few years ago the human brain used to be regarded as "female" until the fifth or sixth week of fetal life, irrespective of the genetic sex of the individual; in normally developing males it was believed to be then "masculinized" as a result of a surge of androgens. But "femaleness" is not simply the absence of "masculinization"; it is now clear that there is also a specific alternative "feminization" process taking place at the same time, though one should be cautious

[44]L.I.A. Birke, "Is Homosexuality Hormonally Determined?" *Journal of Homosexuality* 6 (1981): 35-49.

about accepting at face value the unitary nature of processes implied by such terms as "feminization" and "masculinization."[45]

The question is of course not simply whether or not there are hormonal differences between males and females — for clearly there are — nor whether there are small differences, on average, in structure and hormonal interactions between the brains of males and females; clearly this is also the case, though the overlaps are great. The point is the *meaning* of these differences. For the determinist these differences are responsible not merely for differences in behavior between individual men and women but also for the maintenance of a patriarchal social system in which status, wealth, and power are unequally distributed between the sexes. For Goldberg, as the propagandist of patriarchy, there is an unbroken line between androgen binding sites in the brain, rough-and-tumble play in male infants, and the male domination of state, industry, and the nuclear family. Wilson, the sociobiologist, is more cautious: Our biology directs us toward a patriarchy; we can go against it if we wish, but only at the cost of some loss of efficiency.

Differences in power between men and women are thus, for determinism, primarily a matter of hormones. Appropriate doses at a critical phase in development make males more assertive and aggressive; by contrast, they make females less aggressive, or even, in one extraordinary version of the argument, more likely to offer themselves as the victims of male violence. In a book written after a decade of working with battered women in refuges from their violent husbands and lovers, Erin Pizzey claimed that certain categories of both men and women became violence-addicted as a consequence of being exposed to violence as very young children or while still unborn.[46] Their infant brains, she speculates, came to require a regular dose of hormones which she variously suggests may include adrenaline, cortisone, and the enkephalins which can only be obtained by violent and pain-giving activities. Why on this model it is men who characteristically inflict the pain and women who characteristically are the recipients of it is not made clear. The point is again a structure of argument that (without convincing evidence) traces complex human social interactions to simple biological causes and locates them in a domain so removed from present intervention as to appear inevitable and irredeemable. The fault for male violence lies, in this view, not in the present struc-

---

[45]P.C.B. Mackinnon, "Male Sexual Differentiation of the Brain," *Trends in Neurosciences*, November 1978; K.D. Dohler, "Is Female Sexual Differentiation Hormone Mediated?" *Trends in Neurosciences*, November 1978.

[46]E. Pizzey and J. Shapiro, *Prone to Violence* (London: Hamlyn, 1982).

ture of a society that traps women into relationships of economic as well as emotional dependence, nor in the despair engendered by unemployment and the devastated inner-city environment, but in a biological victimization dependent on the contingencies of hormonal interactions with the brain at or around birth. If the fault is not in our genes, it is at best in our parents; either way the circle of deprivation visits our sins upon our children.

We do not offer to explain away violence against women by replacing biologistic fantasies by crude economic and cultural reductionism. The problem is certainly too serious for that. But the complexity of male domination defies simplistic localization to the effects of hormones in the brain of the newborn. If such a Goldbergian hypothesis were correct we might expect economic and cultural success to be a consequence of individual male aggressiveness. Yet it is not apparent that such individual aggression is the key to climbing the organizational ladder that leads particular men to become successful as entrepreneurs, politicians, or scientists. The range of economic and cultural determinants for such individual successes is far more complex, and we would doubt that we could explain the emergence of a president of the United States or a British prime minister by measuring the circulating androgen levels in the bloodstream of the contenders for such a post — or even by retrospectively speculating on the levels of these hormones in the days or months following their birth. The level of explanation that must be sought lies properly in the psychological, social, and economic domain; biologists are unable to predict the future Ronald Reagans or Margaret Thatchers from any measurement, however sophisticated, of the biochemistry of today's population of newborn infants.

The counterpart to the myth that male domination and the social structure of the patriarchy are given by male hormones is that it is female hormones that produce the nurturative, mothering activity of women — the mothering "instinct." While it is clear that only women can bear children and lactate, and that this very fact is likely to result in a different relationship between a woman and the child she has borne from that which the male parent has with the child, the implications of this, either for adult caregiving to the child or receipt of the care by the child, are quite undetermined. Not merely the range of different caregiving arrangements developed in different cultures but the quick transitions in advice given by experts to women on whether they should leave their children and enter work — as during the Second World War — or return to their "natural" nurturative activities bear witness to the fact that child-care arrangements owe more to culture than to nature. To recognize the centrality of reproductive,

233

caring labor to human society, the role of mothering,[47] does not mean that the social activity of mothering is read deterministically onto the biological fact of childbearing.

All the evidence is that human infants, with their plastic, adaptive brains and ready capacity to learn, develop social expectations concerning their own gender identity, and the activities appropriate to that gender, irrespective of their genetic sex and largely independent of any simple relationship to their own hormone levels (which can at any rate be themselves substantially modified in level by social expectations and anticipations). Psychocultural expectations profoundly shape a person's gender development in ways that do not reduce to body chemistry.

Claims for the Evolution of Patriarchy

The determinist argument does not stop however with merely reducing the present existence of the patriarchy to the inevitable consequence of hormonal balance and brain masculinization or feminization, but pushes insistently to explain its origins. For if the phenomenon exists, sociobiologists claim it must be adaptively advantageous and determined by our genes; it must therefore owe its present existence to selection for these genes during the early course of human history. Even if it were not now the case that patriarchy was the best of all thinkable societies, it must be the best of all possible societies because at some previous time in human history it must have conferred an advantage on those individuals who operated according to its precepts. This is the core of the Wilsonian thesis, just as it was of the earlier wave of pop ethology offered by, for instance, Tiger and Fox.[48]

In this thesis, the near universality of male dominance arose on the bases of the biological and social problems caused by the long period of dependency of the human infant on adult care, by comparison with other species, and of the primitive mode of obtaining food employed in early human and hominid societies — gathering and hunting. If a principal source of food was given by the hunting down of large mammals, which required long expeditions or considerable athletic prowess, even if men and women originally contributed equally to this

---

[47]M. Cerullo, J. Stacey, and W. Breines, "Alice Rossi's Sociobiology and Antifeminist Backlash," *Feminist Studies* 4, no. 1 (February 1978); N. Chodorow, *The Reproduction of Mothering: Psychoanalysis and the Sociology of Gender* (Berkeley: Univ. of California Press, 1979).

[48]L. Tiger and R. Fox, *The Imperial Animal* (London: Secker & Warburg, 1977); L. Tiger, *Men in Groups* (London: Secker & Warburg, 1969).

task, women would be disadvantaged in such hunting by being pregnant or having to care for a baby they were breast-feeding, and indeed the baby's own life would be put in danger. So there would have been pressures on the men to improve their hunting skills, and on women to stay home and mind the children. Hence, genes that favored cooperative group activities and increased spatio-temporal coordination would be favored in men though not in women; genes that increased nurturative abilities — for instance, for linguistic and educational skill — would be favored in women. A socially imposed division of labor between the sexes became genetically fixed, and, as a result, today men are executives and women are secretaries.

It is easy to see the attractions of such evolutionary just-so stories, with their seductive mixture of biological and anthropological fact and fantasy. The existence of a sexual division of labor in primitive societies is a starting point as much for purely social accounts of the origins of patriarchy (for instance Engels)[49] as for biological. What is quite uncertain on the basis of newer anthropological evidence is the extent and importance of the hunter-gatherer distinction. In terms of overall contribution to food, gathering — a predominantly female activity — rather than hunting seems to have been the more important.[50] And in any event, with the small family sizes and spaced-out births of nomadic gatherer-hunter groups in the harsh conditions of their existence, the period over which women would have been at a physiological disadvantage in participation in hunting through being at a late stage of pregnancy or early stage of child-rearing would have been small.[51]

The point, however, is not to bandy about anthropological speculation, which can seemingly be directed to suit any case, but to emphasize that the real division of labor between men and women — which appears to have lasted, with variations and exceptions, over much of recorded history — still does not require a biological determinist explanation. Nothing is added to our understanding of the phenomenon, or of its persistence, by postulating genes "for" this or that aspect of social behavior. If patriarchy can take — in the Goldbergian sense — any form from baby-kissing to crusading, the

---

[49]F. Engels, *The Origin of the Family, Private Property and the State* (New York: International Publishers, 1972).

[50]G. Bleaney, *Triumph of the Nomads: A History of the Aborigines* (Melbourne: Overlook Press, 1982); N.M. Tanner, *On Becoming Human* (Cambridge, England: Cambridge Univ. Press, 1981).

[51]N.M. Tanner, *On Becoming Human.*

leash on which genes hold culture[52] (whatever such a concept might mean) must be so long, so capable of being twisted and turned in any direction, that to speculate upon the genetic limits to the possible forms of relationship between men and women becomes scientifically and predictively useless; it can serve only an ideological interest.

From Animals to Human Beings and Back

The structure of the determinists' argument that we have discussed so far is as follows: contemporary society is patriarchal. This is the consequence of individual differences in abilities and proclivities between men and women. These individual differences are present from early childhood and are themselves determined by differences in the structure of male and female brains and the presence of male and female hormones. These differences are laid down genetically and the genes for the differences have been selected as a result of the contingencies of human evolution. Each step in this reductionist argument is, as we have seen, fallacious or merely meretricious, a sort of magical hand-waving in the absence of data. Characteristically, however, the argument takes one final step — that of analogy with other species.

Again and again, in order to support their claims as to the inevitability of a given feature of the human social order, biological determinists seek to imply the universality of their claims. If male dominance exists in humans, it is because it exists also in baboons, in lions, in ducks, or whatever. The ethological literature is replete with accounts of "harem-keeping" by baboons, the male lion's domination of "his" pride, "gang-rape" in mallard ducks, "prostitution" in hummingbirds.

There are multiple problems associated with such arguments by analogy. Many derive from a common cause, the relationship between the subjective expectations of the observer and what is observed. We can consider three general areas of difficulty. First, inappropriate labeling of behavior. For instance, many species live in multi-female, single (or few) male groups with excluded males living separately either isolated or in small bands. In such multi-female groups the male will tend to attack and drive out other conspecific males, denying them access to the females. The ethologists who observe this form of group living describe the female group as being the "harem" of the male. But the term "harem" defines a sexual power relationship between a man

---

[52]This metaphor is used by E.O. Wilson in *On Human Nature* to epitomize his view of the relationship between genes for social behavior and manifest social relations.

and a group of women that emerged in Moslem and some other societies at a particular time in human history. Harems were kept by princes, potentates, and wealthy merchants; they were the object of elaborate social arrangements; they relied heavily on the wealth of the male concerned; and they coexisted in the societies in which they occurred with many other forms of sexual relationships, including homosexuality and monogamy, if the literature of the period is to be relied upon. In what sense are the multi-female groupings among some species of deer or primates or among lions so to be regarded? Indeed, in the case of the lion grouping it is now clear that far from being "supported" by their male, it is the lionesses within the group who do the bulk of the hunting and provide most of the food.

An ethology that observes the nonhuman animal world through the lenses offered by its understanding of human society acts somewhat like Beatrix Potter; it projects, willy-nilly, human qualities onto animals and then sees such animal behavior as reinforcing its expectation of the naturalness of the human condition: Mothers are nurturative because Peter Rabbit's mother offers him camomile tea when he finally escapes being put into Mr. MacGregor's pie. In this way the behavior of nonhuman animals is persistently confused with that of humans. Inappropriate analogies make animal ethology harder to do. At the same time they form ideological refractions that seemingly reinforce the "naturalness" of the status quo in human societies.

A second problem area arises from the limited nature of the observer's account of what is happening in any social interaction. It is not merely that observed animal behaviors are inappropriately labeled; the observations themselves are partial. Studies of stalled dominance hierarchies tend to focus on a single parameter, perhaps access to food or who copulates with whom. Yet there is good evidence in several species that position along one dominance continuum — even if we accept the term — does not imply a matching position along other continua.

Studies of sexual behavior in animals are parlously distorted by the assumption, seemingly based on an almost Victorian prudery among ethologists, that the male is the main actor, heterosexual procreative sex is the only form to be considered, and the task of the female is merely to indicate willingness ("receptivity") and then lie down and think of England. Whether it is newts, ducks, or rats,[53] this androcentric fantasy works its way through the ethological literature. Only

---

[53]T.R. Halliday, "The Libidinous Newt: An Analysis of Variations in the Sexual Behaviour of the Male Smooth Newt, Triturus vulgaris," *Animal Behavior* 24 (1976): 398-414.

IV. The Elements of Family Life

relatively recently has the female's role in courtship behavior ("proceptivity") become a more acceptable field of study, and it became recognized that, for instance, among rats it is mainly the female who initiates and paces sexual contacts.[54] It is surely no coincidence that the female's role in animal courtship has been discovered at a time when a new view of women's sexual independence has become current.

Thirdly, generalizations about the universality of particular patterns of behavior are made on the basis of data derived from small numbers of observations on a tiny number of species in a limited range of environments. It is well known that the study of primate ethology was seriously led astray over many years because the observations on which theories of aggressive intraspecific competition were built were made on populations in captivity in confined zoos, while the behavior of the same species in the wild was very different.[55] The same or closely related species of primates can live in widely differing habitats, varying for instance between mountains and savanna, and between conditions of relative abundance and relative scarcity of food. Under different circumstances, their social groupings and interrelations vary markedly. And as between the many different species — for example of primates — social and sexual groupings can vary from more or less monogamous to promiscuous, from groups with no recognizable dominance to those that seem more hierarchically ordered, from those that are male — led to those that are female — led, from those with marked sexual dimorphism to those with little sexual dimorphism.[56]

To select from this enormous abundance of animal observation only those moral tales that seem to support the naturalness of particular aspects of human sexual relationships and of the patriarchy is to imperil our understanding of both nonhuman and human social biology. If the tales selected by popular ethological accounts all appear to point in a single direction, one must ask: What interest is such a selective account serving? Just as understanding the behavior of baboons or lions is not helped by spurious analogizing from that of humans, so understanding the social biology of humans is not helped by reducing it to that of baboons.

---

[54]M.K. McClintock and N.T. Adler, "The Role of the Female during Copulation in Wild and Domestic Norway Rats (rattus Norvegicus)," *Behavior* 68 (1978): 67-96.

[55]S. Zuckerman, *The Social Life of Apes* (London: Kegan Paul, 1932); C. Russell and W.M.S. Russell, *Violence, Monkeys and Man* (London: Macmillan, 1968).

[56]L. Liebowitz, *Females, Males, Families: A Biosocial Approach* (North Scituate, Mass.: Duxbury Press, 1978).

These strictures remain regardless of who makes the reduction. It is not only defenders of the patriarchy who so unabashedly naturalize the arguments for innate differences in cognition, affectual understanding, and aggression between men and women. One school of feminist writing too has argued such an essentialist position, not merely stressing the importance of feminine, rather than masculine, ways of knowing and being, but rooting them in women's biology. This is the force of the defense of the right hemisphere offered by Gina, to which we referred earlier, and it forms the basis of Firestone's argument in the *Dialectic of Sex*,[57] which sees, as does the strand of radical feminism that has followed her, the primary division in society as arising not from the division of labor by class and gender but from the biological differences between men and women.

A strand of feminist sociobiology has arisen that has centered on female rather than male evolutionary adaptation as the motor of social change during the transition from hominid to human societies. In part this focus on women has been a necessary redressing of the androcentric view offered by the dominant sociobiological strand; but to repeat the methodological errors of masculinist science in the process is to offer merely the other side of the same false coin.[58]

The essentialist argument echoes that powerful tradition in psychoanalysis which seeks the roots of differences in behavior between the sexes as lying, if not in the brain, then in the ineluctable biology of the genitalia. For the Freudian tradition it is the discovery by boys that they have a penis and by girls that they lack one that is at the heart of subsequent differences in their behaviors. But where for Freud and his followers this is the source of penis envy in girls, a feminist psychoanalytic approach offers instead the argument that it is the women's power to conceive that is central; that men, alienated from their seed at the moment of impregnation, mourn this loss thereafter and become committed to creating an external, object-centered universe of artifacts, a commitment that produces the overwhelmingly phallocentric culture of a male-dominated society.[59]

Removing the locus of male domination from the brain to the genitals and to the act of procreation does not, however, thereby avoid

---

[57]S. Firestone, *The Dialectic of Sex*; see H. Rose and J. Hammer, "Women's Liberation: Reproduction and the Technological Fix," in *The Political Economy of Science*, eds. H. Rose and S. Rose (London: Macmillan, 1974), pp. 142-60.

[58]See, for example, S.B. Ehrdy, *The Woman That Never Evolved* (Cambridge, Mass.: Harvard Univ. Press, 1981); and E. Morgan, *The Descent of Woman* (New York: Stein & Day, 1972).

[59]See, for example, J. Mitchell, *Sexual Politics* (London: Abacus, 1971).

IV. The Elements of Family Life

the methodological fallacies of seeking to reduce social phenomena to nothing but the sums of individual biological determinants, and of seeking simplistic "underlying" unitary explanations of diverse cultural and social phenomena. Where for Wilson genes hold culture on a leash, for the theorists of phallocentrism it is the penis and vagina that do so. Yet important though the male-female dialectic is, it cannot be the only, or indeed the underlying, determinant of the vast variety of human sexual and cultural forms. Not merely does such essentialism assert primacy over the struggles of class and race, but it lays claim to a universality that transcends both history and geography.

We must be more modest. We do not know the limits that biology sets to the forms of human nature, and we have no way of knowing. We cannot predict the inevitability of patriarchy, or capitalism, from the cellular structures of our brains, the composition of our circulating hormones, or the physiology of sexual reproduction. And it is this radical unpredictability that is at the core of our critique of biological determinism.

Subjectivity and Objectivity

There is one final point to be made. In this chapter we have tried to analyze the structure and fallacies of the biological determinist argument which, beginning from the indubitable fact of patriarchy in present day industrial societies, seeks to ground that phenomenon in a biological inevitability. We have insisted that although all future as well as all past forms of relationship between men and women, both individually and within society as a whole, must be in accord with human biology, we have no way of deducing from the diversity of human history and anthropology or from human biology or from the study of ethology of nonhuman species the constraints, if any, that such a statement imposes.

What can be said, however, is this: We have described the emergence of biological determinist and reductionist thinking within science as an aspect of the development of bourgeois society over the period from the seventeenth century till the present day. This society, however, is not merely capitalist but also patriarchal. The science that has emerged is not merely in accord with capitalist ideology but with patriarchal ideology as well. It is a predominantly male science, from which women are squeezed out at all levels — excluded at school, frozen out within the university, and relegated to a reserve army of scientific labor, the technicians and research assistants to be hired and fired but not to be distracted from their main task of domestic labor, of nurturing the male scientist and rearing his children.[60] The story of how these exclusions operate has been told by women many times now.[61] Exclusion has a double effect. First, it denies half of humanity the right to participate equally in the scientific endeavor. Second, the residual "scientific endeavor" that the male half of humanity is left to practice on the back of the domestic and reproductive labor of women itself becomes one-sided.

It has long been recognized by historians of science that Greek science, where theory was divorced from practice, was a peculiarly patrician form of knowledge, precisely in that those who developed it were spared the day-to-day need of practice by the existence of a slave population that did the work. It was the unifying of theory and practice offered by the coming together of science and technology in the industrial revolution that generated the specific modern form of scientific knowledge. But just as Greek science was ignorant of practice and could not advance until that unity had been built, so today's patriarchal science is ignorant of domestic and reproductive labor and — as Hilary Rose has argued — is only and can only be a partial knowledge of the world.[62]

The particular stress that patriarchal science places on objectivity, rationality, and the understanding of nature through its domination is a consequence of the divorce that the division of productive and reproductive labor imposes between cognition and emotion, objectivity and subjectivity, reductionism and holism.[63] Such patriarchal knowledge can only be partial at best; feminist critiques of male-dominated science, by reemphasizing this scientifically neglected or rejected half of the interpretation and understanding of experience are

---

[60]H. Rose, "Making Science Feminist," in *The Changing Experience of Women*, pp. 352-72.

[61]See references in note 19 above and also R. Arditti, "Women in Science: Women Drink Water While Men Drink Wine," *Science for the People* 8 (1976): 24; E.F. Keller "Feminism and Science," *Signs* 7 (1982): 589-602; A.Y. Leevin and L. Duchan, "Women in Academia," *Science* 173 (1971): 892-95; L. Curran, "Science Education: Did She Drop Out or Was She Pushed?" in *Alice Through the Microscope*, ed. Brighton Women in Science Group (London: Virago, 1980), pp. 22-41; R. Wallsgrove, "The Masculine Face of Science," in *Alice Through the Microscope*, pp. 238-40.

[62]H. Rose, "Hand, Heart and Brain: Towards a Feminist Epistemology of the Natural Sciences," *Signs* (Fall 1983).

[63]For a discussion of this emphasis on the domination of nature even in Marxist and radical thought, see, for example, A. Schmidt, *The Concept of Nature in Marx* (London: New Left Books, 1971); W. Leiss, *The Domination of Nature* (New York: Braziller, 1972).

beginning to move from the analysis of reductionism to the creation of new knowledges.[64] In the long run only the integration of both forms of knowledge — just that integration which reductionism denies is necessary and determinism denies is possible — must be our goal.

---

[64]See, for example, C. Merchant, *The Death of Nature: Women, Ecology and the Scientific Revolution* (London: Wildwood House 1980); Boston Women's Health Book Collective, *Our Bodies, Ourselves* (New York: Simon & Schuster, 1976).

B. Gender Roles

Gender roles are clearly undergoing some kind of transformation, partly as a consequence of social-structural changes but also because women collectively have fought for change. With the heightening of feminist awareness, the personal costs of women's traditional gender roles have become clear, as have the privileges attached to the traditional male role. But there were costs associated with the male "provider" role as well as benefits. Consequently, while change does mean that men must give up some personal privileges, it also brings benefits to men — as it does to women.

When assessing changes in gender roles, it is important to recognize the limitations of the concept of "role." Role refers simply to what people are doing and what they are expected to do. From that perspective, recent decades have involved an impressive degree of change. Once the issues of personal *autonomy* and *power* are introduced, however, it is not entirely clear that there has been much change. For instance, are women now able to earn sufficient income to support themselves and their children outside of marriage? Given the absence of change in women's *position* in the labour market, the answer is "no" for the majority of women. Are men who live in long-term relationships with women now assuming half of the responsibility for housework and child care? Again, the evidence is not very encouraging.

Two articles follow which open the discussion of changes in gender roles. These articles, by Barbara Ehrenreich and David Osborne, are journalists' accounts (one a book review) of the limits of the apparent changes in women's work roles. Both illustrate the barriers that women face in their attempt to fit into work worlds designed for men, and both make clear how profoundly our world is structured around a gender division of labour — between home and public workplaces, and within the home.

Suggested Readings:

On Women:
Oakley, Ann.
1981. *Subject Women*. New York: Pantheon Books. Though British, a fine text on all aspects of women's position.

IV. The Elements of Family Life

Wilson, S. J.
1982. *Women, the Family and the Economy*. Toronto: McGraw-Hill Ryerson. A Canadian review of literature on women's work and the women's liberation movement.
Adamson, Nancy, Linda Briskin, and Margaret McPhail.
1988. *Feminist Organizing for Change*. Toronto: Oxford University Press. A history of the second wave of the Canadian women's movement which discusses strategies as well as ideas.

On Men:
Ehrenreich, Barbara.
1984. *Hearts of Men*. New York: Anchor Books. An unusual account of changes in men's roles since World War II.
Kaufman, Michael, ed.
1987. *Beyond Patriarchy*. Toronto: Oxford University Press. A solid collection of writings by men about men.

Strategies of Corporate Women*

Barbara Ehrenreich

Some of us are old enough to recall when the stereotype of a "liberated woman" was a disheveled radical, notoriously braless, and usually hoarse from denouncing the twin evils of capitalism and patriarchy. Today the stereotype is more likely to be a tidy executive who carries an attache-case and is skilled in discussing market shares and leveraged buy-outs. In fact, thanks in no small part to the anger of the earlier radical feminists, women have gained a real toehold in the corporate world: about 30 percent of managerial employees are women, as are 40 percent of the current MBA graduates. We have come a long way, as the expression goes, though clearly not in the same direction we set out on.

The influx of women into the corporate world has generated its own small industry of advice and inspiration. Magazines like *Savvy* and *Working Woman* offer tips on everything from sex to software, plus the occasional instructive tale about a woman who rises effortlessly from managing a boutique to being the CEO of a multinational corporation. Scores of books published since the mid-1970s have told the aspiring managerial woman what to wear, how to flatter superiors, and when necessary, fire subordinates. Even old-fashioned radicals like myself, for whom "CD" still means civil disobedience rather than an eight percent interest rate, can expect to receive a volume of second class mail inviting them to join their corporate sisters at a "networking brunch" or to share the privileges available to the female frequent flier.

But for all the attention lavished on them, all the six-figure promotion possibilities and tiny perks once known only to the men in gray flannel, there is a malaise in the world of the corporate woman. The continuing boom in the advice industry is in itself an indication of some kind of trouble. To take an example from a related field, there would not be a book published almost weekly on how to run a corporation along newly discovered oriental principles if American business knew how to hold its own against the international competition. Similarly, if women were confident about their role in the corporate world, I do not think they would pay to be told how to comport themselves in such minute detail. ("Enter the bar with a briefcase or some files. ...Hold your head high, with a pleasant expression on your face. ...After you have ordered your

---

*Reprinted by permission of The New Republic, © 1986, The New Republic, Inc.

IV. The Elements of Family Life

drink, shuffle through a paper or two, to further establish yourself [as a businesswoman]," advises *Letitia Baldridge's Complete Guide*.)

Nor, if women were not still nervous newcomers, would there be a market for so much overtly conflicting advice: how to be more impersonal and masculine (*The Right Moves*) or more nurturing and intuitive (*Feminine Leadership*); how to assemble the standard skirted suited uniform (de rigueur until approximately 1982) or move beyond it for the softness and individuality of a dress; how to conquer stress or how to transform it into drive; how to repress the least hint of sexuality, or alternatively, how to "focus the increase in energy that derives from sexual excitement so that you are more productive on the job" (*Corporate Romance*). When we find so much contradictory advice, we must assume that much of it is not working.

There is a more direct sign of trouble. A small but significant number of women are deciding not to have it all after all, and are dropping out of the corporate world to apply their management skills to kitchen decor and baby care. Not surprisingly, these retro women have been providing a feat for a certain "I told you so" style of journalism; hardly a month goes by without a story about another couple that decided to make do on his $75,000 a year while she joins the other mommies in the playground. But the trend is real. The editors of the big business-oriented women's magazines are worried about it. So is Liz Roman Gallese, the former *Wall St. Journal* reporter who interviewed the alumnae of Harvard Business School, class of '75, to write *Women Like Us*.

The women Gallese interviewed are not, for the most part, actual dropouts, but they are not doing as well as might have been expected for the first cohort of women to wield the talismanic Harvard MBA. Certainly they're not doing as well as their male contemporaries, and the gap widens with every year since graduation. Nor do they seem to be a very happy or likable group. Suzanne, the most successful of them, is contemptuous of women who have family obligations. Phoebe, who is perhaps the brightest, has an almost pathological impulse to dominate others. Maureen does not seem to like her infant daughter. Of the 82 women surveyed, 35 had been in therapy since graduation; four had been married to violently abusive men; three had suffered from anorexia or bulimia; and two had become Christian fundamentalists. Perhaps not surprisingly, given the high incidence of personal misery, two-fifths of the group were "ambivalent or frankly not ambitious for their careers."

What is happening to our corporate women? The obvious anti-feminist answer, that biology is incompatible with business success, is not borne out by Gallese's study. Women with children were no less likely to be

246

ambitious and do well than more mobile, single women (although in 1982, when the interviews were carried out, very few of the women had husbands or children). But the obvious feminist answer — that women are being discouraged or driven out by sexism — does gain considerable support from *Women Like Us*. Many of the women from the class of '75 report having been snubbed, insulted, or passed over for promotions by their male co-workers. Under these circumstances, even the most determined feminist would begin to suffer from what Dr. Herbert J. Freudenberger and Gail North call "business burnout." For non-feminists or, more precisely, post-feminists — like Gallese and her informants — sexism must be all the more wounding for being so invisible and nameless. What you cannot name, except as apparently random incidents of "discrimination," you cannot hope to do much about.

Gallese suggests another problem, potentially far harder to eradicate than any form of discrimination. There may be a poor fit between the impersonal, bureaucratic culture of the corporation and what is, whether as a result of hormones or history, the female personality. The exception that seems to prove the rule is Suzanne, who is the most successful of the alumnae and who is also a monster of detachment from her fellow human beings. In contrast, Gallese observes that men who rise to the top are often thoroughly dull and "ordinary" — as men go — but perhaps ideally suited to a work world in which interpersonal attachments are shallow and all attention must focus on the famed bottom line.

To judge from the advice books, however, the corporate culture is not as impersonal, in a stern Weberian sense, as we have been led to believe. For example, *The Right Moves*, which is a good representative of the "how to be more like the boys" genre of books for corporate women, tells us to "eliminate the notion that the people with whom you work are your friends" — sound advice for anyone who aspires to the bureaucratic personality. But it also insists that it is necessary to cultivate the "illusion of friendship," lest co-workers find you "aloof and arrogant." You must, in other words, dissemble in order to effect the kind of personality — artificially warm but never actually friendly — that suits the corporate culture.

Now, in a task-oriented, meritocratic organization — or, let us just say, a thoroughly capitalist organization dedicated to the maximization of profit — it should not be necessary to cultivate "illusions" of any kind. It should be enough just to get the job done. But as *The Right Moves* explains, and the stories in *Women Like Us* illustrate, it is never enough just to get the job done; if it were, far more women would no doubt be at the top. You have to impress people, win them over, and in general project an aura of success far more potent than any actual accomplishment. The problem may not be that women lack the capacity for businesslike detachment, but that, as women, they can never entirely fit into the boyish, glad-handed corporate culture so well described three decades ado in *The Lonely Crowd.*

There may also be a deeper, more existential, reason for the corporate woman's malaise. It is impossible to sample the advice literature without beginning to wonder what, after all, is the point of all this striving. Why not be content to stop at $40,000 or $50,000 a year, some stock options, and an IRA? Perhaps the most striking thing about the literature for and about the corporate woman is how little it has to say about the purposes other than personal advancement, of the corporate "game." Not one among the Harvard graduates or the anonymous women quoted in the advice books ever voices a transcendent commitment to, say, producing a better widget. And if that is too much to expect from postindustrial corporate America, we might at least hope for some lofty organizational goal — to make X Corp. the biggest damn conglomerate in the Western world, or some such. But no one seems to have a vast and guiding vision of the corporate life, much less a Gilderesque belief in the moral purposefulness of capitalism itself. Instead, we find successful corporate women asking, "Why am I doing what I'm doing? What's the point here?" or confiding bleakly that "something's missing."

In fact, from the occasional glimpses we get, the actual content of an executive's daily labors can be shockingly trivial. Consider Phoebe's moment of glory at Harvard Business School. The class had been confronted with a real-life corporate problem to solve. Recognizing the difficulty of getting catsup out of a bottle, should Smucker and Co. start selling catsup out of a widemouthed container suitable for inserting a spoon into? No, said Phoebe, taking the floor for a lengthy disquisition, because people like the challenge of pounding catsup out of the bottle; a more accessible catsup would never sell. Now, I am not surprised that this was the right answer, but I am surprised that it was greeted with such apparent awe and amazement by a professor and a roomful of smart young students. Maybe for a corporate man the catsup problem is a daunting intellectual challenge. But a woman must ask herself: Is *this* what we left the kitchen for?

Many years ago, when America was more innocent but everything else was pretty much the same, Paul Goodman wrote, "There is nearly 'full employment'...but there get to be fewer jobs that are necessary or unquestionably useful; that require energy and draw on some of one's best capacities; and that can be done keeping one's honor and dignity." Goodman, a utopian socialist, had unusually strict criteria for what counted as useful enough to be a "man's work," but he spoke for a generation of men who were beginning to question, in less radical ways, the corporate work world described by William H. Whyte, David Kiesman, Alan Harrington, and others. Most of the alienated white-collar men of the 1950s withdrew into drink or early coronaries, but a few turned to Zen or jazz, and thousands of their sons and daughters eventually joined with Goodman to help create the anticorporate and, indeed, anti-careerist counterculture of the 1960s. It was the counterculture, as much as anything else, that nourished the feminist movement of the late 1960s and early 1970s, which is where our story began.

In the early years, feminism was torn between radical and assimilationist tendencies. In fact, our first sense of division was between the "bourgeois" feminists who wanted to scale the occupational hierarchy created by men, and the radical feminists who wanted to level it. Assimilation won out, as it probably must among any economically disadvantaged group. Networks replaced consciousness-raising groups; Michael Korda became a more valuable guide to action than Shulamith Firestone. The old radical, anarchistic vision was replaced by the vague hope (well articulated in *Feminine Leadership*) that, in the process of assimilating, women would somehow "humanize" the cold and ruthless world of men. Today, of course, there are still radical feminists, but the only capitalist institution they seem bent on destroying is the local adult bookstore.

As feminism loses its critical edge, it becomes, ironically, less capable of interpreting the experience of its pioneer assimilationists, the new corporate women. Contemporary main stream feminism can understand their malaise insofar as it is caused by sexist obstacles, but has no way of addressing the sad emptiness of "success" itself. Even the well-worn term "alienation," as applied to human labor, rings no bells among the corporate feminists I have talked to recently, although most thought it an arresting notion. So we are in more or less the same epistemological situation Betty Friedan found herself in describing the misery — and yes, alienation — of middle-class house-wives in the early 1960s; better words would be forthcoming, but she had to refer to "the problem without a name."

Men are just as likely as women to grasp the ultimate pointlessness of the corporate game and the foolishness of many of the players, but only women have a socially acceptable way out. They can go back to the split-level homes and well-appointed nurseries where Friedan first found them. (That is assuming, of course, they can find a well-heeled husband, and they haven't used up all their child-bearing years in the pursuit of a more masculine model of success.) In fact, this may well be a more personally satisfying option than a work life spent contemplating, say, the fluid dynamics of catsup. As Paul Goodman explained, with as much insight as insensitivity, girls didn't have to worry about "growing up absurd" because they had intrinsically meaningful work cut out for them — motherhood and homemaking.

There is no doubt, from the interviews in *Women Like Us* as well as my own anecdotal sources, that some successful women are indeed using babies as a polite excuse for abandoning the rat race. This is too bad from many perspectives, and certainly for the children who will become the sole focus of their mothers' displaced ambitions. The dropouts themselves would do well to take a look at *The Corporate Couple*, which advises executive wives on the classic problems such as: how to adjust to the annual relocation, how to overcome one's jealousy of a husband's svelte and single female co-workers, and how to help a husband survive his own inevitable existential crisis.

Someday, I believe, a brilliantly successful corporate woman will suddenly look down at her desk littered with spread sheets and interoffice memos and exclaim, "Is this really worth my time?" At the very same moment a housewife, casting her eyes around a kitchen befouled by toddlers, will ask herself the identical question. As the corporate woman flees out through the corporate atrium, she will run headlong into a housewife, fleeing into it. The two will talk. And in no time at all they will re-unite those two distinctly American strands of radicalism — the utopianism of Goodman and the feminism of Friedan. They may also, if they talk long enough, invent some sweet new notion like equal pay for...meaningful work.

Book Reviews

Women Like Us by Liz Roman Gallese. Morrow.
The Right Moves: Succeeding in a Man's World Without a Harvard MBA by Charlene Mitchell and Thomas Burdick. (Macmillan)
Feminine Leadership: Or How to Succeed in Business Without Being One of the Boys by Marilyn Loden. (Times Books)
Women's Burnout: How to Spot It, How to Reverse It, and How to Prevent It by Dr. Herbert J. Freudenberger and Gail North. (Doubleday)
Corporate Romance: How to Avoid It, Live Through It, or Make it Work for You by Leslie Aldridge Westoff. (Times Books)
The Corporate Couple: Living the Corporate Game by Peggy J. Berry. (Franklin Watts)
Letitia Baldridge's Complete Guide to Executive Manners. (Rawson Associates)

My Wife, the Doctor*

David Osborne

It is five in the morning when the beeper goes off. As I try to shake myself awake, I listen to Rose call the page number. Only an hour ago we finally retreated to the hospital's tiny on-call room, perched 16 floors above the lights of New York City. Between a cardiac arrest in intensive care, her own patients and others she is covering for the night, there has been little time for sleep.

"It's a new admission," she tells me. "Stay and sleep if you want to." She is already dressed.

"No. I'll come with you." The point of this exercise, after all, is to find out what this world of my wife's is all about. And it's clearly not about sleep.

When the elevator arrives, we stand face to face with the intern whose patient's heart stopped several hours before. "She didn't make it," he says quietly, his body slumped with weariness, his face a picture of futility. There is a moment in which no one moves, nor says anything, as if to make room somehow for this sadness, to allow death its own place in the night. "I'm sorry," Rose says softly. He nods and moves slowly past us, and we step into the elevator.

Rose's admission is in 11-A, a barrel-chested, 50-year-old man, flat on his back, in obvious pain. "I'm Dr. Osborne," she tells him. "I'll be taking care of you while you're here." He says nothing; only his eyes show his skepticism.

Seating herself by his bed, she begins her questions. "What brought you here?" ("This pain in my kidneys.") "Has this happened before?" "How often?" The answers come in one-sentence grunts.

After 20 minutes, he has had enough. "I wanna tell you something", he barks. "This is the wrong time for questions. Can't you see I'm in pain here?"

Outside, the sky shows signs of pink. I can think only of sleep. "I'm sorry," Rose tells him, matter of factly. "I know this isn't easy. But it's important, if I'm to know how to treat you. We're almost done."

"This is the wrong time," he repeats, but he answers her final questions. When she begins her physical exam I leave the room, closing the door behind me, and walk down the hall.

I am standing at the nurses' station, 30 feet away, when I hear his voice rise again. "No, I'm not gonna do that!"

---

* Reprinted by permission from *Mother Jones*. Copyright © January, 1983.

IV. The Elements of Family Life

Her voice rises in response: "Yes, you are. I have to do it."

"I'm not gonna do it!"

She is ordering him now. "You have a history of ulcers. It's very important for me to do this exam."

"No!"

"I'm not leaving this room until I finish this exam."

The voices lower, and a few minutes later Rose appears.

"The rectal?" I ask.

"Yep."

"You did it?"

A nod.

"Congratulations."

She shrugs. "Minor victories."

I met Rose almost ten years ago, when medicine was still a male preserve. The women's movement was beginning to close in, however, focusing on the inadequate, indifferent care offered by male physicians, particularly to female patients. Male-dominated medicine was hierarchical, authoritarian and insensitive, the movement argued. It concentrated almost exclusively on the defeat of disease, rarely on the maintenance of health. Women's conditions, such as menopause and premenstrual tension, were too often written off as the psychosomatic complaints of unhappy housewives. Pregnancy was treated as a medical, often surgical, problem in an alien hospital environment, rather than as a natural and healthy event to be cherished by mother and father alike. Women were too often used as guinea pigs by drug companies marketing products like DES and birth control pills without adequate testing. And first-class medical care was reserved for those who could pay first-class rates.

In the 19th century, before they were forced out of practice by male physicians, women healers were common in this country. The key to better medical care today, it was assumed by many, was their return. Women in our society are taught to be more sensitive, more nurturing, more able to deal with emotion, the logic went, and these qualities would naturally make women better physicians. "Male villians victimized female patients," Gena Corea wrote in *The Hidden Malpractice*. "Only women physicians could rescue them."

Today, 30 percent of first-year medical students are women. In some specialties, such as obstetrics and gynecology, women make up one-third of all residents and interns. Overall, the percentage of women doctors has risen from five to twelve and could reach 30 or more around the turn of the century if trends continue.

For the past ten years, as the male enclave has slowly been breached and Rose has progressed from introductory chemistry to her

252

internship, I've enjoyed a front row seat. I've lived through the years of sacrifice: the 100-hour work-weeks, the nights alone, the perpetual postponement of parenthood. I've watched my wife and her colleagues grow and change, becoming more confident, more assertive, more dynamic — but also more hardened, more harried and more technical in their approach to medicine. And I've wondered just what it all means. The medical system has been shaped over the decades by a male establishment. Women are now changing that establishment, but medicine is also changing the women who enter its privileged fold. The question, after these first ten years of insurgency, is who's winning: women or medicine?

The first step

The question has several parts. How much has the medical profession changed to make way for women? How much have women had to change to make it in medicine? And how much has the quality of medical care improved in the process?

The first question is perhaps the easiest to answer. The medical profession has clearly begun to change, though it still has miles to go. For women doctors, 1982 is light years away from 1972. Rather than being only one in 20, as they were in 1963, young women in med school now find themselves numbering almost one in three. Like it or not, the men have had to get used to having women as peers.

Ten years ago, the profession was notorious for its sexism: the men's club atmosphere of the hospital, the constant barbs aimed at the few women who dared compete, the Playboy centerfolds slipped into lecture slides. Today, men simply cannot get away with that sort of behavior.

All is not roses, however. Women physicians still work in a culture that sees doctors as 50-year-old, white-haired men who look like Robert Young. In some parts of the country progress has been slower than in others. Even on the more cosmopolitan coasts, a woman can respond to the classic "Is there a doctor in the house?" only to face a questioning stare and an angry, "I said a doctor."

"Even though women are increasing their forces in medicine," Rose says, "you still have the feeling that you're unique. It's difficult, because the odds are stacked against you; you know you essentially have to be better than your male counterpart to prove yourself.

"It's also isolating outside the hospital. Other people have a hard time dealing with you because you're a woman physician. Women who haven't chosen to pursue high-powered careers may resent it or somehow feel inadequate around you. And an amazing number of men — even men my age — don't seem to be able to cope with it. They end up ignoring the subject completely or making belittling comments. So you can't really talk about what you did today and you end up feeling very lonely. It's something that just doesn't happen to male physicians."

Another problem is the dearth of role models. There are many more woman interns and residents on hospital house staffs today, but female faculty members and private physicians (called "attendings" in a teaching hospital) are still somewhat rare. "You need to be able to see people who are 20 years ahead of you," Rose explains, "who are doing what you would like to do, who have a good marriage and children and are able to handle everything — so you can say to yourself, 'Yes, this is possible, and yes, I can do it without having my life fall apart.' But most of the attendings and faculty members I've known haven't been married, or have been divorced. I don't know of anybody who is leading the kind of life I envision for myself."

The few role models that do exist are usually at lower levels of the medical establishment. In academia, for instance, where basic medical values are formed, less than four percent of full professors are women. As recently as 1979, almost half of the medical schools surveyed had no women doctors in the dean's office. And by 1980, women chaired only two percent of all academic departments. Only three women have ever been dean of a medical school. One was a temporary appointment; another, the dean of a women's medical college.

Similar ratios are found in other leadership positions, such as the review committees of the National Institute of Health or state boards that certify physicians. In 1980, only three percent of doctors on specialty boards were women. As New York psychiatrist Alexandra Symonds puts it, "Women physicians have opened the door to service, but not to power."

Macho, macho men

One specialty — surgery — remains so clearly dominated by men that it carries a virtual No Women Need Apply sign. Outside of ophthalmology and obstetrics and gynecology, which are technically classified as surgical subspecialities, 95 percent of surgeons in the U.S. were male in 1980, the last year for which the American College of Surgeons has data. In 1980, women held only 5.3 percent of residencies in general surgery and less than one percent in many of the sub-specialties.

Surgeons have always postured themselves as the macho men of medicine, the real doctors. A surgeon has to stand over the operating table for 10 to 12 hours at a stretch, the rhetoric goes, and only a real man can be trusted with such grueling work when life and death hang in the balance. Needless to say, such attitudes do not encourage women — particularly when surgeons depend upon referrals from other physicians to get their patients.

Dr. Elizabeth Sirna, a surgical intern in New York, describes some of the other obstacles. Like most hospitals, the one in which she did her surgical rotation during medical school had only two dressing rooms: one for male surgeons, the other for female nurses. "I'd be with my surgical team going into the operating room, and we'd be discussing the case," she explains. "We'd reach the dressing room and all the men would go in, but I couldn't. So I'd miss out on a discussion of the case."

Other problems came up in the operating room. "You're in the O.R., in your greens, and this private attending surgeon who's going to evaluate you is next to you," she says. "And he bumps into you in ways that, if it happened on the street, you'd belt him."

Things only got worse when she interviewed for a residency in orthopedic (bone and joint) surgery, a field barely penetrated by women. "My interviews opened my eyes to things I just assumed did not happen anymore in medicine," she says. Out of 60 people interviewed for any one program, perhaps two or three would be female. The first question usually was, "Why do you want to be an orthopedist?" I was asked whether I was physically strong enough to set bones. I was asked about my marital status. I was asked whether I was divorced and how I felt about my divorce. I was asked whether I had children and how I would fit kids into a surgical lifestyle. I've checked with men and they don't get asked about children.

"One interviewer said to me, 'I see you were a teacher before you went to medical school. You know, being a surgeon is a lot more difficult than being a teacher. Your hours aren't nine to five.' This was after four years of medical school. I was outraged."

Many women doctors believe that women make better surgeons than men, because of their smaller hands and greater manual dexterity. Sirna had already spent four months on surgical rotation, routinely assisting in the operating room, when I asked her if she agreed. "I don't know," she answered, pausing for thought, then gazing at me. "I've never seen a woman operate."

Doctor & mother

Dr. Emily Fine is a 30 year-old obstetrician-gynecologist, her clear brown eyes belying the recent strain of a four-year residency at Yale-New

255

Haven Hospital. When I spoke with her last summer she was awaiting the birth of her second child. Two years earlier, her first child had had the honor of being the first baby ever born to an ob-gyn resident at Yale-New Haven. For Fine, however, the occasion was anything but honored.

When she announced her pregnancy, she was greeted not with congratulations but with horror. For the other residents, all working 100 hours a week, the news meant one thing above all else: longer hours while Fine was on maternity leave.

Chief residents asked her to forgo her maternity leave and use vacation time instead. "I was getting all this pressure from family and friends, who would say, 'This is your body; this is your pregnancy; you've got to take care of yourself. You're going to have this child for the rest of your life. You've got to have maternity leave and you can't feel guilty about it.' But I was also a resident and I knew what it was like to be on Monday night, Wednesday night, Saturday night and Sunday, and then have to be on that next Tuesday night instead of having a little spell. I knew what they were going through in their own minds; but on the other hand, I had to take care of myself as well."

She refused the request, finally settling for two weeks' leave, but she paid the price. "There must have been meetings constantly during my pregnancy, behind my back — 'What should we do? Should we ask her to do this?' It was always a crisis. I'd like to think that the women were terrifically supportive and the men were less supportive, but it didn't work out that way. One of the most painful experiences for me was the reaction of one particular woman friend from whom I became completely estranged because of the pregnancy."

Unfortunately, Emily Fine's story is anything but unique. The biggest problem facing women in medicine today is that they must compete in a high-pressure field structured entirely for men who have wives at home. Hundred-hour work weeks are common-place throughout medical school and residency, a time when women are in their prime childbearing years.

Forced to choose between a family and a career in which they have already invested ten years and up to $100,000, many women simply opt out of the family commitment. Female physicians are nearly three times as likely not to marry as their male counterparts, and five times as likely not to have children, according to Medical Economics. More than 20 percent of the women responding to the journal's survey were divorced or separated, compared to only four percent of the men.

Those who refuse to forgo having a family find that the decision affects every aspect of their professional lives. Unlike most men, who may mouth commitments to equality but pursue their career interests regardless of their families, women often channel themselves into specialties with shorter hours (and hence lower pay). Traditionally, they have migrated into the "three Ps," as they are condescendingly known: pediatrics, psychiatry and public health. Though more women are now entering internal medicine and obstetrics and gynecology, studies confirm that many still settle for something other than their first choice. A 1981 survey of women doctors in Connecticut, for example, found that an astounding 44 percent had changed career direction at some point, most of them because of the difficulty of managing both a family and a career.

Even when they enter the "male" fields, women are often kept marginal. They earn less, for one thing. A study done for the American Medical Association showed that in 1977, women made only 70 percent of what men in the same specialty made. Part of the reason was a shorter work week, but even when the figures were broken down by hours, women still earned only 83 percent of what their male counterparts were paid.

Proportionately, women are also less likely than men to enter academia, where national reputations are made. When they do, they not only get stuck in the lower ranks, but they also face a classic double bind documented by numerous studies: they tend to be taken less seriously by many male colleagues because of their responsibilities at home, while at the same time they are often belittled for neglecting their home and family.

Unlike other problems facing women in medicine, the family/career dilemma shows no signs of solution. No one in the field believes hospitals are going to cut down their residents' hours in the foreseeable future. And the option always mentioned for women who want children — a half-time residency — is a classic example of marginalization. After all, who in her right mind would spend six to ten years in training (after eight years of higher education), working 60 hours a week on an annual salary of $10,000, just to be able to practice her profession? Women are staying away from such residencies in droves, and with good reason. Unfortunately, the other options are almost equally grim. In the 1980s, it appears, medicine will remain the province of the compulsive, overworked American male — and those willing to imitate him.

Desensitization

The call comes in at six a.m.: a critical emergency is on the way. A young boy has been in a serious accident on the Cross Bronx Expressway. Third-year medical student Rose is on her surgery rotation. Only ten years old, the victim is in a severe state of shock, his blood pressure undetectable. Being the medical student, Rose is sent to the lab for blood.

Rose immediately asks for O-positive, the universal blood type.

"I'm sorry," the technician tells her "I can't release it without your supervisor's approval, since it's not the type he requested."

There is not time to return to the emergency room for another request. "This patient is dying!" Rose shouts.

"I'm sorry."

Rose screams at her, threatens her, says anything she can think of to get the blood. Finally the technician calls her own supervisor, and allows Rose to talk with him. He gives his O.K.

Ten minutes have elapsed by the time Rose returns to the emergency room. The director is beside himself. Though they quickly transfuse the young boy, he never regains consciousness.

That afternoon the emergency room director seeks Rose out to ask why the blood was so late. Having tried for years to get the lab moved down to the first floor to prevent such problems, he asks Rose to write out her story as documentation for his case. "I'm not saying the blood would have saved his life," he tells her. "But he would have had a better chance."

"I felt horrible," Rose remembers now, two years later. "I rethought the whole thing. Maybe I should have just grabbed the blood and run; maybe I should have yelled louder. I totally blamed myself. It took me a long time to get over that, to really feel that it wasn't my fault. But I still remember every detail of that morning."

Students enter medical school, according to one female faculty member, "with stars in their eyes." During the next eight years they go through experiences never dreamt of by the rest of us. People die in their hands. Mothers must be told that their children are dead, husbands that their wives are gone. Often working 36 hours at a stretch, interns and residents must treat abused children, wasted addicts, crumbling alcoholics.

"If I were to have an eye removed," writes Dr. Michelle Harrison, author of *A Woman In Residence*, "then I would forever be a person with only one eye. If I were to take in poison without spitting it out, I would be a poisoned person. I might survive, but I would be damaged. Medical training is no less violent than surgery or poisoning. It leaves women and men no less scarred or no less without the organs that have been removed."

Throughout the process, young men and women are molded into physicians. Needless to say, they come to resemble their earlier selves about as much as a butterfly resembles a caterpillar. Women in particular — because they often start out with more sensitivity than men — go through tremendous changes during their near-decade of training.

"Most people who go into medicine have strong feelings about helping people, very compassionate feelings," Rose explains. "But after four years of school and three or four years of training have passed, you really have to struggle hard to maintain your compassion. In teaching hospitals, you hear patients referred to all the time as 'dirtballs' or 'gomers.'" (A dirtball is a social misfit: a heroin addict, a bag person. A gomer — an acronym for "Get Out of My Emergency Room!" — is an elderly patient with little mental functioning left, a vegetable waiting to die.)

"It's difficult to maintain a sense of purpose," Rose continues, "to remember that you're actually a public servant. It's very hard to keep that in mind when all of society worships physicians and you have such enormous power. Somebody's admitted to the hospital, and you can decide whether they can get out of bed to go to the bathroom. It's very hard to keep in mind that the reason you started the whole thing was that you were concerned about humanity, and that you're there to serve people. I've seen incredible changes in people I've gone to school with or worked with on house staffs. They seem to lose sight of their original purpose. Medicine for them becomes something completely different."

"A lot of good feminine qualities do get stomped out," agrees Dr. Mary Lake Polan, an assistant professor of obstetrics and gynecology at Yale. "I think the factor that most people don't consider is fatigue. Until you've worked three nights in a row, or had a night to sleep during which you were awakened every hour by a phone call, you can't understand. That's when your empathy goes. It's not so much that they're trying to deliberately stomp it out of you. That's just the end result."

"Sometimes, people get saturated," adds Dr. Ellen Harrison, an internist on the faculty of Albert Einstein College of Medicine. "They just can't listen anymore. They see their own needs and their own convenience as coming before the patient's; as a result, they begin to resent the patient. So that when a patient is in pain, the pain is truly their pain — it's a pain in the ass."

"You see a lot of death," adds Polan. "And it's not fun. It's ugly and it smells and it sounds bad and it's frightening. So you build defenses against it, because people die on you all the time. Ultimately you have to make decisions that determine whether someone lives or dies. You get hardened."

A testimony to the power of the experiences is provided by the statistics on emotional disorders among physicians. Though no hard data is available, the American Medical Association estimates that ten percent of doctors are "impaired" by alcohol or drug abuse. Withdrawal

IV. The Elements of Family Life

from emotional ties, even with one's own family, occurs with apparent frequency. And according to several studies, suicide rates are higher among physicians than among the general population. (For women the figures are striking: the suicide rate among female doctors is at least three times higher than among other women their age, though the rate is not much higher than that for male physicians.) The most telling statistics come from the internship year: one-third of all interns experience frequent or severe episodes of emotional distress or depression, according to one study, and one-fourth of those contemplate suicide.

Why does the medical training have to be so dehumanizing? Part of it is inevitable: adjusting to a world of disease and death is never easy, particularly when one is asked to assume the responsibilities a physician must shoulder. But part of it is the schedule. No normal individual can work 100 hours a week over a long period of time without stress.

Like every other medical spouse, I despise the hours. Rose's typical work cycle begins at seven a.m. on a Monday morning, when I drop her off at the hospital. She works all day, all night (catching a few hours sleep if she's lucky) and all the next day. On Tuesday evening, when I next see her, she is exhausted; on Wednesday evening she is merely tired. Thursday she is again in the hospital all day, all night and all day Friday. After a day off on Saturday, the cycle begins again on Sunday.

Needless to say, such a schedule makes a relationship difficult. During Rose's first hospital rotation in medical school, three of the four couples we knew in her class split up, and we came close. We have since learned to make adjustments, recognizing the danger signs. But after the first six months of her internship, we are not looking forward to the next three and a half years with great enthusiasm.

Hospital administrators, on the other hand, think the hours are terrific, because interns and residents provide them with a pool of cheap labor. (Most residents gross between $4 and $5 an hour, depending upon their year.) And surprisingly, many interns and residents, including Rose, believe that their schedules cannot really be any other way. A great deal of hands-on experience is necessary for an adequate training, they argue, and the sickest patients arrive in the middle of the night. Unless you want a residency to stretch to six years, the hours must be endured.

To my mind this sounds suspiciously like the concentration camp syndrome, in which one identifies with one's oppressors simply to get through the experience psychologically. To survive a residency, in other words, it helps to believe in it. Yet, some programs do exist with only 80-hour weeks and schedules requiring an intern to be on call only every fourth night, and they seem to turn out competent physicians. I would

260

also argue for lopping a year off the entire medical school and residency process — though my wife, for one, would disagree with me.

So Who's Winning?

Are women physicians improving the quality of health care in America? Or is the socialization process so profound that by the time women are practicing physicians, they are barely distinguishable from their male colleagues?   In my conversations and reading, I have found little consensus on the question.

Certain research data does support a distinction, however.   One fascinating piece of evidence is the fact that women are sued for malpractice much less frequently than men.   Angela Holder, a counsel for medicolegal affairs and an assistant clinical professor of pediatrics at Yale, has examined the matter in some depth.   An expert on malpractice, she has not found patients any more hesitant to sue a woman if they feel they have been wronged.   But she has found a different attitude among women doctors toward their patients.

"Women physicians, because they are women, may, in fact, be more openly caring with their patients than males," she argues. "Patients who think that a doctor cares whether they live or die, get better or feel miserable are very reluctant to sue the physician if all does not go well.   This has been documented by many studies of malpractice."

According to *Medical Economics*, women in private practice also appear to spend more time with each patient than do men doctors, working about 90 percent of men's hours but seeing only about two-thirds as many patients.   And psychological studies have indicated that women have more sympathy for their patients, that they enjoy emotional involvement with them more and that they are more open to dealing with dying patients than are men (though they suffer more depression as a result).   Unfortunately, such studies are limited in scale, and they actually measure the self-images of male and female physicians, rather than the actions.   Thus it is difficult to know just what they tell us.

But if there is one specialty in which women have definitely improved patient care, it is obstetrics and gynecology.   Simply by being female, a woman doctor makes the ordeal of a pelvic exam less intimidating.   And by having experienced it herself, she tends to be more sensitive to her patients' needs.

Increased sensitivity is certainly called for.   In a study reported in a 1979 journal article, 85 percent of the women questioned reported negative feelings about their last pelvic exam, including anxiety, humiliation and dehumanization.   Forty-one percent reported negative feelings toward their physician's behavior, and 72 percent said they would never discuss their sexual concerns with their doctor.

Just five years ago, obstetrics and gynecology was much more the province of the male physician, no doubt because of the long and irregular hours required. But since 1976 the percentage of women among ob-gyn residents has jumped from 14.6 to 32.2, with no end in sight. By the year 2000, the field is likely to be dominated by women. Having seen the handwriting on the wall, male gynecologists are now scrambling for female partners. And the production-line tactics of busy gynecologists are also beginning to change.

"There's a sort of standard male phrase — 'Ah, she's a crazy lady going through menopause' or 'She's having her vapors' or 'Well, she's just a teenager; she doesn't know what she's doing,'" says Mary Lake Polan. "Male gynecologists tend to denigrate women. But you don't find that when you have women doctors. Complaints are taken seriously. Not that women are giving patients any different medical treatment, not that they sit and commiserate for half an hour, because they don't have any more time than the men do. But they listen and they take seriously women's complaints."

Others agree, but minimize the differences. "I think we've made a great deal of impact for individual patients, because now they have a choice," says Florence Haseltine, coauthor of *Woman Doctor* and a doctor herself. "But many patients are angry that we're not better than men. We're callous. We hurt them when we examine them. A lot of people have been very disappointed. I don't know what they expected of women doctors. If they expect us to say, 'Yes, you've been horribly treated, and the males did everything wrong, and now women are going to do everything right,' they're not going to get that, because we're trained the same way."

"The medical system molds you into the kind of doctor it wants," Haseltine says. "You can't go into a system trying to change it. If you become a member of it, a respected member, you might then be able to make some changes. But by that time, by definition, you've been co-opted."

"It's the classic problem — if you become part of the system, it means you had to mind your p's and q's long enough to get there."

Most of the women physicians I have interviewed tend to agree. Says Ellen Harrison: "I would like to say that women are more tuned into those values that have to do with the patient is — their emotional health as well as their physical health — and that they're less likely to see the patient as a kind of object to have tests run on. But there are so many times when the distinction cannot be made that I feel a little unfair making it. There are plenty of examples of the opposite being true."

Emily Fine relates what for her is a classic example: "This happened to a woman resident a year ahead of her, who is actually a sweet, charming person. A woman came to see her whom she had seen in the clinic two months earlier, and the woman said, 'Oh, Dr. So-and-So, how are you?' Well, she didn't remember her, even though the woman went on and on about her last visit. So finally the doctor says, 'Well, let's examine you and see what's going on.' She puts the speculum in and looks at her cervix, and then she says, 'Oh, you're Mrs. So-and-So!' She didn't remember the woman, but she remembered her cervix."

Such detachment is often the product of simple overwork. But sometimes it is sheer insensitivity. "One of the things I'm very sensitive to," says Ellen Harrison, "is that people will stand at a bedside and say things in front of a patient that they should never say. Before anyone has had a chance to sit down and discuss the diagnosis with the patient, they'll blurt out that they're ruling out cancer. Or while they're examining a patient, they'll talk across the bed about what they did that weekend."

For Harrison, part of the blame has to be placed on the training process. "The values that are rewarded in academic medicine and the things that people are judged on seem to me to be male values," she says. "You either adopt them, or you go your own way and risk not being able to get the same rewards that other people get. One doesn't get a lot of positive feedback from the chairman of the department for being compassionate. One gets feedback for going to the library and reading the literature before a conference, which means not being on the wards and not having time to talk with patients. You get credit for knowing what's in the latest medical journal article, but not for teaching people how to talk with the patients or how to think through their cases — things that are more basic but less flashy. These things have more to do with training doctors to be compassionate, thoughtful people as well as good physicians."

Will Women Fight?

Back in the 1960s a ritual debate used to occur among those young and innocent enough to dream of changing the world. Should one organize outside the system, it was asked, or should one enter the best and remake it from within? A few years later, as the women's movement grew toward maturity, a related and perhaps more intelligent question was discussed: was it enough to open the institutions of power to women or was the goal more fundamental, to transform the very nature of those institutions? And if one sought the latter, was it enough to bring women into the ranks? Would that alone bring about those fundamental changes?

Today, the medical profession offers a good model to examine. Perhaps it is too early to judge; perhaps another decade or two will yield different results. But if not, the present answers are revealing. Opening the profession to women is surely important in its own right, as are reforms to create more equality within medicine: less brutal residencies; more flexibility for women who want children; more access to child care; equal opportunity for advancement. And opening the profession has indeed improved the quality of care provided some people, in some specialities, in some cases. But if fundamental changes in the nature of medicine are the goal, a profession open to women is not enough. Basic reforms in the entire system are necessary.

Few would disagree, for example, that health care has become prohibitively expensive in this country or that physicians are overspecialized. It is equally apparent that nonphysicians, such as nurse-practitioners, physicians' assistants and midwives, should be used more widely for routine care. And anyone who has seen the waiting area of an inner-city emergency room knows that poor people in this society get second-rate medical care, regardless of Medicaid and Medicare.

Such problems cannot be solved by individual physicians; they will yield only to widespread organized efforts to restructure the entire health care system. Yet the largest and most representative organization of women physicians, the American Medical Women's Association, has shown very little interest in such a cause, concentrating its energy instead on issues related more directly to the interests of its members.

With what little power and spare time they have, women doctors will continue to concentrate on improving their own tenuous positions within the profession. Inadvertently, they may stimulate the growth of health maintenance organizations (itself a worthy goal), because women choose the fixed hours and salaries offered by such institutions more often than men, who lean heavily toward office-based practices. But as for restructuring health care delivery or fighting to improve conditions for other women in the system, whether patients or nurses, we should not expect much. "There just isn't this great bond of sisterhood," as Rose puts it. "Things are much more divided along professional lines."

Florence Haseltine doesn't see why it should be any other way. "I really don't see why people should expect women to be that much different from men, when they have a job to do," she says. "I think there's too much mythology about what women are capable of doing in terms of changing things. We are changing the profession: there are many more women; women are not being harassed as much; they're starting to hold more powerful positions. And I hope there will be more of a sense of

264

fairness in the profession as women come into more power, because women tend to expect fair play. But that's about all."

Perhaps she is right. Perhaps it is just as wrong to expect a fundamental difference between male and female physicians as it is to believe that one sex belongs in the workaday world while the other belongs at home. Whatever the case, it is apparent by now that solving the problems of female doctors will not necessarily solve those of female patients. At times the two overlap, as is often the case in obstetrics and gynecology. But at times they do not.

Put simply, the main interests of most women physicians will remain the interests of women physicians. If the goal is also to advance the interests of patients, or the humanity of medicine, women doctors will not have the time, energy or power to be more than valuable allies. In the meantime, the struggle must be waged primarily by the people who receive the care and pay the bills.

C. Sexuality and Intimate Relationships

Perhaps more than anything else, the way each of us expresses our sexuality seems natural — an innate capacity that we simply discover as we mature and form relationships. As Mariana Valverde argues, however, the heterosexuality which many of us assume to be natural is not: it is the product of a personal history, involving fairly systematic socialization.

Furthermore, sexuality and intimate relations cannot be examined without a simultaneous recognition of the significance of gender, which influences both profoundly. In a society where gender relations are still unequal, and where heterosexuality is the norm, what is eroticized is social inequality — as Valverde argues. And there are many consequences of this, some more dangerous than others.

Gender inequality affects the quality of people's sexual experience. In contexts in which people are in traditional gender roles — and the woman economically dependent on the man — the woman's sexuality can become her only resource. In turn, her position of powerlessness may encourage her to barter her sexuality for the resources the man controls. Within marriage, she may see sex as something she "owes" her husband — part of her duties as wife (Luxton 1980).

While gender inequality can thus preclude the full enjoyment of one's sexuality, there are worse consequences. The sexual abuse of girls by their fathers is one extreme distortion of the notion that men have the "right" of sexual access to female dependents.

Aside from gender inequality creating the context in which sexual relations occur, there are consequences of gender socialization for people's psyches which affect their intimate relationships. Wendy Hollway and Gad Horowitz and Michael Kaufman explore the tensions and conflicts in men's sexuality which seem inevitable "side effects" of the acquisition of male identity. These range from a fear of vulnerability, given the fragility of masculine identity and the attendant need for control, to the need to violently dominate women. For women, perhaps the most common product of socialization is insufficient aggressiveness about discovering their sexual needs and ensuring that they be met.

Other aspects of intimate relationships between men and women suffer the consequences of gender socialization and gender inequality. Below are listed some readings that explore this issue.

267

IV. The Elements of Family Life

Reference

Luxton, Meg.
1980. *More Than a Labour of Love*. Toronto: Women's Press.

Suggested Readings

On Sexuality
Valverde, Mariana.
1985. *Sex, Power and Pleasure*. Toronto: Women's Press. A sensitive and sensible feminist exploration of sexuality.
Kaufman, Michael, ed.
1987. *Beyond Patriarchy*. Some of these articles are on men's sexuality — heterosexuality, bisexuality and homosexuality.
Ehrenreich, Barbara, Elizabeth Hess, and Gloria Jacobs.
1986. *Re-Making Love*. New York: Anchor Books. An interesting interpretation of changes in sexuality since the early 1960s.

On Love
Cancian, Francesca.
"Gender politics: love and power in the private and public spheres." Pp. 193-205 in Arlene Skolnick and Jerome Skolnick, eds. 1986. *Family in Transition*. Fifth Edition. Boston: Little, Brown and Company. An argument about the feminization of love and the (ironic) consequent bolstering of men's personal power.

On Male-Female Relationships
Rubin, Lillian.
1983. *Intimate Strangers*. New York: Harper & Row. Such a perceptive description and analysis that you will give the book to your friends and lovers!

Heterosexuality: Contested Ground*

Mariana Valverde

It is not easy to write generally about heterosexuality. Relations between men and women have been subject to much scrutiny over the past twenty years and although traditional ideas and practices continue to hold sway in some quarters there are other circles in which little can be taken for granted any more. These different perspectives do not merely coexist in peaceful detente. Even if there are some "islands" of both traditionalism and feminism where people live without many direct, personal challenges to their beliefs, by and large we are all living in an ideological battlefield. The combined effect of skyrocketing divorce rates and feminist ideas has produced a counter-attack by the traditionalists, who have become increasingly shrill about the divine rights of husbands. This right-wing backlash is a desperate reaction to a situation in which the breadwinner husband/dependent wife model has become economically unfeasible for the vast majority of couples as well as emotionally unsatisfying for many women.

We live therefore in a very polarized situation, with different groups contending for the power to define heterosexuality and the family. Within each camp people strategize about how to strengthen their forces and how to improve their position on the field; they react to one another's ideology and on occasion are influenced by ideas from the "enemy" camp. All this means that, reassurances of sex and family experts notwithstanding, we cannot speak confidently about heterosexuality in general. Both the ideas about it and the corresponding sexual and social practices are quite diverse and we are in a process of struggle and change.

Furthermore, we see many gaps between theory and practice. Some women have embraced the idea of an egalitarian heterosexuality that stresses choice and creativity, but in their own lives fall into traditional gender roles which they experience as "natural." On the other hand, many women who have sincerely believed in traditional concepts of marriage are finding themselves by design or by accident in unorthodox situations that are not part of the plan. Faced with such realities as an unwanted pregnancy, a daughter who comes out as a lesbian, or a divorce, women who have led "traditional" lives sometimes show a

---

remarkable degree of flexibility and inventiveness. So we cannot assume that all women with feminist beliefs have what one might describe as feminist relationships, or that women who are married and go to church on Sundays necessarily restrict themselves to monogamous heterosexuality in the missionary position.

It might be useful first to pause and consider one of the most prevalent myths used by the anti-feminists in the ideological struggle to define heterosexuality. It is a myth that often lingers in the hearts if not the minds of feminists, and so must be explicitly refuted if we are to make a fresh start. This myth comes in many guises but the common denominator is an appeal to nature to legitimize a certain traditional definition of heterosexuality as "natural" and therefore inevitable, good, and not to be argued about or criticized. Arguments for Nature try to remove heterosexuality from the realm of politics and history and put it safely away on a high shelf marked "Mother Nature: things that just are."

An influential exponent of this argument for Nature is "America's number one counsellor," Dr. Joyce Brothers. In her 1981 book entitled *What Every Woman Should Know About Men* she blithely "deduces" the traditional nuclear family from her perception of "primitive" human life. Appealing to our stereotype of "cavemen," she writes:

> It is as if way back in prehistory Mother Nature had searched for the most effective way of protecting mothers and children. Without someone to provide food for and defend the mother and child, they were at the mercy of wild beasts and predatory males....The obvious source of protection and provisions was the male. But how to keep him around?
>
> Mother Nature's solution was sex. Sex on tap, so to speak. The day-in, day-out sexual availability of the human female created what scientists call a pair bond and most of us call love. The nuclear family was born.[1]

Let us unpack the assumptions and values contained in this unfortunately typical piece of popular "scientific" writing.

•"Mother" Nature is portrayed as a manipulative mother-in-law. This is anthropomorphism at its worst, where Nature is not only a

---

[1]Joyce Brothers, *What Every Woman Should Know About Men* (New York: Ballentine, 1981), p.178.

human female but an "old hag" who manipulates people for her own purposes.

• Men are portrayed as naturally predatory and obsessed with sex. Dr. Brothers is apparently relying here on some now-discredited anthropological studies that claimed to show it was the agressiveness and sexual jealousy of the male that pushed us along the evolutionary path and made us into a civilized species. The myth of "Man the Hunter" has been successfully challenged by feminist anthropologists and primatologists. Male anthropologists have tended to assume that for example a social system could be understood by looking at the men in the system, and that competition and aggression were "natural" and beneficial to the species. Without going into details about how this traditional view was challenged, suffice it to say that now only the die-hards in the anthropological profession would see even a grain of truth in Dr. Brothers's description.[2]

• Further, even if her description were accurate there is a logical error in her argument. If males were so predatory, why would women turn to them as the "obvious source" of protection? A pack of dogs would be much more appropriate.

• The women in Dr. Brothers's prehistory appear to have not sexual feelings but only sexual "availability." Now, given that many female primates show clear signs of sexual pleasure, and some species even exhibit what can be interpreted as female orgasms, one wonders why women in prehistory would have such a passive sexuality. But the myth is that women do not really want sex, and exchange sexual favours only for male protection, while men do not really want to nurture but will reluctantly provide protection for the sake of sex. There is a lapse here in the logic of how the nuclear family can emerge from this coming together of two such vastly different beings with such completely different purposes in mind.

• Finally, it seems clear that according to Dr. Brothers the only "natural" expression of human sexuality is monogamous heterosexuality within a nuclear family. By trying to ground her view of heterosexuality in "Mother Nature" she confines all other possibilities to the obscurity of non-natural of anti-natural human behaviour. In the rest of her book she down-plays the family and does not insist on children in the way the Pope does. But she certainly believes that real sex is heterosexual sex, and real love is heterosexual love.

---

[2]See for instance Ruth Bleier, *Science and Gender* (New York, Pergammon, 1984), especially chapter five on human evolution. See also Eleanor Leacock, "Women in Egalitarian Societies," in R. Bridenthal and C. Koonz, eds., *Becoming Visible* (Boston: Houghton Mifflin, 1977).

IV. The Elements of Family Life

This belief in the naturalness of heterosexuality is so commonly accepted that we do not even notice it...These days it is seldom articulated in its most blatant forms. But in its more sophisticated and subtle versions, which de-emphasize reproduction and stress sex itself, it continues to exercise a great deal of influence not just over our thoughts but over our very feelings. We feel it is somehow right for men and women to be attracted to one another precisely because they are men or women. We smile on young happy heterosexual couples and we attend weddings celebrations, regardless of the actual interactions between the two people in question. By contrast, we feel uncomfortable when rules about monogamy and exclusive heterosexuality are broken, and feel compelled to find explanations for why woman A has so many lovers or why man B is attracted to men. But if A and B join up as a stable, monogamous couple, then we cease to ask questions. Their relationship, like Dr. Brothers's primitive society, simply is.

One of the most crucial building blocks of the traditional view of natural heterosexuality is the idea that penises and vaginas "go together" or "are meant for each other," and that erotic attraction between men and women is only the psychological manifestation of the physiological urge to engage in intercourse. There are several problems with this view. First, it portrays men and women as the dupes of their own physiology and considers eroticism as a mere cover-up for Nature's reproductive aims. People are thus dehumanized, first by being reduced to one sexual organ and then by having those sexual organs reduced to the status of reproductive tools. Secondly, it ignores the specificity of sex by collapsing it into reproduction. This implicitly devalues not only homosexuality but all non-reproductive sexual practices. It is true that if one wants to have a child, intercourse is one of the best means. But sex research has shown that if female sexual pleasure is the aim then intercourse is a poor choice, since masturbation and lesbian sex are both much more effective. (Shere Hite for example found that only 30 percent of a large sample of women regularly achieved orgasm from intercourse, while 99 percent of the women could easily achieve orgasm by masturbating.[3]) Men, for their part, often prefer fellatio to intercourse.

This sex research ought to have demolished once and for all the myth that sexual pleasure is maximized by intercourse. And the increasing availability of birth control ought also to have helped break the bond between sex and reproduction. But people still cling to the theory that the vagina is women's "real" sex organ and the "natural" receptacle for the penis and for sperm.

Why is this?

---

[3]Shere Hite, *The Hite Report* (New York: Dell, 1976).

Well, perhaps the sexual revolution happened a bit too fast for us all. Despite our experiments in sexual practices we still keep alive the notion of intercourse as the most "natural" kind of sex, providing ourselves with a fixed point or home to which we can return. It is genuinely unsettling to watch old ideas and values go out the window. We are more comfortable adding diversions and "desserts" (as *The Joy of Sex* calls them) to our sexual repertoire than questioning the underlying assumptions of a hierarchy of sexual acts that puts regular intercourse in the role of "main dish" and everything else in the role of hors d'oeuvre. It is very important to question the division of sexual acts into "basic" or "natural" and "frills." Only after we have shaken the foundations of the old edifice will we be able to look honestly at our own sexual desires and decide what really pleases us. *The Joy of Sex* approach appears very liberated, but the way sexual acts are classified suggests that one would not want to make a whole meal out of "just" oral sex or "just" anal intercourse. The equation of intercourse with the protein in a meal is simply an ideological construct. This argument for intercourse as the real thing is based on assumptions about penises and vaginas "fitting" together. If we used our imagination, we could as easily argue that other bodily parts fit together. Try it. It's a good exercise for the imagination. Indeed, if a woman has to be told she is "infantile" and "immature" if she doesn't experience intercourse as the most natural and pleasurable form of sex, or if her privileging of the vagina is achieved only after a lengthy process of indoctrination and internalization of what being an adult woman is all about, then one must wonder how well penises and vaginas do fit together. The tired cliches used to convince us that our sexuality can be reduced to the vagina (the "lock" or the "glove") and the vagina in turn to a place for the penis (the "key" or the "hand") reveal a crucial logical fallacy, a phallocentric fallacy. The lock was made so that a key would fit into it, and has no purpose in and of itself; ditto for gloves, which make no sense if considered apart from hands. But vaginas have all sorts of purposes such as allowing menstrual blood out, and most importantly giving birth to children — that have nothing to do with the phallus. One is tempted to understand the cliches about the vagina as nothing but male jealousy and defensiveness around female reproduction. Threatened by a vagina whose darkness and wetness frightens them and whose life-giving powers both scare and mystify them, men try to ignore the independent life of the vagina and reduce it to a mere container, box, or receptacle. This interpretation has been elaborated by many feminist theorists, but first and foremost by Simone de Beauvoir, who made a detailed study of the many myths and rituals that have as their common denominator an attempt to safeguard men against the elemental powers of women's sexual and reproductive activities. She writes:

> In all civilizations and still in our day woman inspires man with horror: it is the horror of his own carnal contingence, which he projects upon her....On the day she can reproduce, woman becomes impure; and rigorous taboos surround the menstruating female....the blood, indeed, does not make woman impure; it is rather a sign of her impurity. It concerns generation, it flows from the parts where the fetus develops. Through menstrual blood is expressed the horror inspired in man by woman's fecundity.[4]

De Beauvoir further reminds us that the matter-of-fact, proprietory statements made by men about the "rightness" of intercourse sometimes conceal a deep-rooted fear of the unknown, of the supernatural, and an anxiety that the vagina is the worst possible place in which a penis might find itself.

> Certain people imagine that there is a serpent in the vagina which would bite the husband just as the hymen is broken; some ascribe frightful powers to virginal blood, related to menstrual blood and likewise capable of ruining the man's vigor. Through such imagery is expressed the idea that the feminine principle has the more strength, is more menacing, when it is intact.[5]

Men's fear of intercourse can on the one hand be traced back to these mythological fears — which are not as outdated as they might seem and exist today in such popular images as the castrating bitch, nymphomaniac, nun and Queen of the Night. On the other hand they are also rooted in the very real fear of regressing to infancy and being literally swallowed up by the Mother and sucked back into the womb.[6] Without going into detail about these fears and anxieties we can certainly conclude that having intercourse is not, for men, the matter-of-fact statement of natural possession they may claim it to be. The pornography industry may spend millions trying to convince men that

---

[4]Simone de Beauvoir, *The Second Sex*, H.M. Parshley, trans. and ed. (New York: Random House, 1974), pp. 167-169.

[5]Ibid., p. 172.

[6]See for instance Karen Horney's discussion of the "male dread of women," in *Feminine Psychology* (New York: Norton, 1967).

sex is safe and fun and unproblematic, but the image of the *vagina dentata* dies hard.

It seems to me that the male fear and envy of women's sexual and reproductive power is taken to the level of mythical misogyny when its basis in fact is not recognized. There are real differences between men and women which can give rise to reasonable curiosity and even anxiety or jealousy. For instance, a father may envy his wife's ability to nurse their child. Or a man may wonder why women seem to have a more varied sexual response. These feelings are normal and need not give rise to fearful images or serpents hidden in vaginas. But they might if they are not acknowledged, if they are repressed. It is not sexual difference itself which causes dread of women. Rather, it is the repression of one's child-like curiosity or normal wonder, coupled with the ideological attempt to assert male superiority in all areas, which produces the kind of elemental anxiety that Simone de Beauvoir describes.

Ever since Freud theorized that female childhood sexuality was first polysexual and then clitoral, we have had reasons other than our own intuition for doubting that intercourse is the *summum bonum*. In Freud's account of femininity, it is never quite clear why girls give up both their happy oral sexuality and their active clitoral masturbation in order to exclusively eroticize the vagina as a passive receptacle for the phallic King. Freud merely states that the little girl is so overwhelmed at the sight of the large penis that her own tiny clitoris seems too pitiful to bother with. "Her self-love is mortified by the comparison with the boy's far superior equipment and in consequence she renounces her masturbatory satisfaction from her clitoris, repudiates her lover for her mother....[7] And she goes on to train herself to be a happy wife and mother. Far-fetched as the concept of penis envy is, it is even more far-fetched that the girl would give up her autoerotic pleasures. Why should she? Even if the penis is larger than the clitoris, at least she has a clitoris and all the envy in the world is not going to get her a penis. And is she really a size fetishist?

Freud was keen on legitimizing passive, vaginal sexuality as woman's highest calling but could not produce a better model of how this sexuality develops. One has to wonder if the whole enterprise is not impossible. Physiological, psychological and empirical arguments can be employed to demonstrate that some or even most women do in fact like intercourse at least some of the time. But what can never be proved is that intercourse is *the* sexual act and the highest good. We know women do not experience orgasm very often if the only sex they engage in is

---

[7]Sigmund Freud, "Femininity" (from the Introductory Lectures), reprinted in A. Jagger and P. Rothenberg, *Feminist Frameworks* (New York: McGraw-Hill, 1984), P. 93.

intercourse. And theoretically, we can find no reason why girls and women would relinquish the manifold possibilities of their bodies in order to concentrate exclusively on passive, penis-vagina intercourse. (Not that intercourse *has* to be passive; but tradition equates vaginal sexuality with passivity.)

And yet, despite all the evidence gathered to prove that vaginal intercourse is not the privileged form of female sexuality, the myths and cliches live on practically undisturbed. People continue to think penises and vaginas are "made for each other," and if by chance they do other things with their respective penises or vaginas they regard it as kinky, going against nature or the norm.

In referring to Simone de Beauvoir we touched on some of the possible reasons why the idea of the penis and vagina as the happy couple *par excellence* might be so impervious to both logic and experience. One of these reasons was that the vagina, both sexually and re-productively, is simply too powerful and so must be constantly conquered by being constantly coupled. The awesome fertility goddesses of past cultures have been tamed and trivialized. They have been reduced to Playboy bunnies whose sexual parts are described as "clits" and "boxes," cutesy words which empty women's sexuality of its real power and leave the phallus holding the power monopoly.

The myth of intercourse is also sustained by the idea that all eroticism depends in an essential way on *difference*, and specifically *genital difference*. Now, this idea is not necessarily patriarchal in its form and intent, for difference does not necessarily imply subordination. There can be amiable, egalitarian difference, which is presumably what fuels eroticism among enlightened heterosexuals.

The idea of difference as erotic is so common-sense and com-monplace that we do not usually pause to criticize it. We merrily proceed to examine our own erotic attraction to individual X or type Y and come up with the "differences" that are significant. But we could just as well analyze our own attractions and non-attractions by reference to similarities.

Let me give an example. A friend of mine once said "I like men because they're so different!" So I envisaged her with a tall, muscular hunk with a masculine beard and a masculine personality. But when I met her lover he turned out to be neither tall nor muscular nor ag-gressive; rather he was androgynous both in physique and personality. So where was the big difference? (My friend, incidentally, also looks more androgynous than feminine.) Was the difference that he had a penis? But other men who were much more "different" than this guy also had penises, and my friend was not interested in them. Was it really difference that attracted her to him?

There are many criteria one could use to measure human differences: size, weight, skin colour, hair colour, race, language, age, intelligence, physical fitness, beliefs, talents, etc. If a heterosexual couple is composed of two individuals who are remarkably similar in, for example, their class backgrounds, interests, and ethnicity (as is usually the case), and who are different primarily in their gender, then one can not claim with any certainty that the key to their erotic attraction is difference. In their case gender difference has been eroticized, but so have their much more numerous non-gender similarities.

It is not my intention to argue for the intrinsic erotic appeal of similarity or difference. Some people can only get interested in partners who are basically similar to them, while others need sharp differences in order to have their erotic interest sparked. To each her own, as far as I'm concerned. The point is that I do not see any valid reason for privileging gender above all else, and then *assuming* that gender difference is essentially erotic while other differences are not. In ancient Athenian culture, for instance, adult men saw adult women primarily as reproductive partners and reserved their odes to eroticism for adolescent boys. There, age differences were eroticized as a matter of course, whereas the gender difference might or might not have been erotic.

By understanding eroticism as a force which pivots around sex and gender differences we separate the erotic realm from other aspects of human existence. Activities and relationships in which sex and gender are not major factors are perceived as non-erotic. Now, to some extent there is clearly something specific about erotic interaction that makes it distinct from the pleasure of working together with others, or of having shared family roots. However, to take this distinction for granted and to absolutize it is a mistake that reinforces certain philosophical beliefs that are simply myths. First, the separation of the erotic — as the sexual, the mysterious, the irrational, the dialectic or difference — from other aspects of human interaction fosters a view of the human self as essentially and eternally divided between Reason and Passion. Secondly, because eroticism is exiled beyond the pale of reason, the everyday life of rational interaction is de-eroticized. And finally, separating Reason from Passion constructs a realm of the instinctual to which women are largely confined.

Women have suffered from this ideological division of the passionate and the rational, as many feminists have noted and criticized. Because erotic play is thought to depend on sexual difference and on the contrast between reason and passion, erotic relations have been largely confined to relations between unequals. Reason and Passion as the male and female principles are not simply different. They are unequal within the hierarchy that prevails between them. On the other hand, relations among equals as "thinking persons" have been a priori de-eroticized, because they hinge not on difference but on a sameness in what the philosophers have called "the common light of reason." Western philosophers have argued that this commonality is the basis both of thinking itself and of democratic society. Most of them also believed women did not share fully in the light of reason and therefore could not enter into the world of politics or philosophy. But even those few who argued that women did indeed have the prerequisite rationality and personhood to enter into the realm of reason and be participants in the social contract still left untouched the basic division between the erotic and the rational. Even if women had an element of rationality, they still had to represent Mother Earth and the dark instincts. And much popular culture since the nineteenth century hinges on women's *internal* struggle between their personhood, as the desire for example to learn or succeed, and their womanhood. This struggle is often tragic because the claims of the feminine are considered to be contradictory to the claims of personhood.

Thus whether or not women were allowed some access to the realm of reason and public life, there was still a sharp separation between "human" interactions (based on male-defined equality among rational human beings as conceived on the male model) and erotic interactions based on sexual difference. The equality prevailing in the intellectual world and the marketplace was considered to be inherently non-erotic, even anti-erotic, while the unequal struggle between Reason and Passion was understood as inherently sexy. Women's confinement to the realm of the semi-rational went hand in hand with a desexualization of the world of men, politics, work, and culture. One of the reasons for this was the age-old desire to use Reason as a tool to dominate nature, subjugate the passions, and not coincidentally to put women, as those closest to nature, in their place. But certainly another reason was that to admit sexuality and eroticism into the public world would have necessarily entailed recognizing homosexuality, or at the very least homoeroticism. Thus, insofar as men and women were defined as being divided by sexual difference and so fundamentally unequal, society could not afford to eroticize equality.

A further result of this has been to create a much larger gap than necessary between heterosexuality and homosexuality. Just as we have exaggerated the role of difference in heterosexual eroticism, so too have we exaggerated the role of similarity in homosexuality. A gay man does not necessarily eroticize only his partner's masculinity. And two lesbians might have certain commonalities in bodily parts and psychological traits, but can otherwise be as different as night and day. So my point is not so much that one has to "make room for" homosexuality as an eroticism of sameness, but more fundamentally to question the very separation of sameness and difference, and the process by which we overvalue difference when theorizing about sexual attraction.

Heterosexuality is too complicated and too unpredictable to be reduced to such a simple formula as "boy meets girl," "like meets unlike," "opposites attract." Men and women are clearly different, but their attraction to one another does not necessarily depend only on that difference. And in any case they are not *opposites*. Because there happen to be only two sexes, we absolutize this fact and assume that the two sexes are opposites. Buy why? What if there were three or four sexes created through some miracle of modern science? Or if we only had two senses instead of five, would we assume that those two — sight and hearing, let's say — were "opposites"? If I have two daughters, or a daughter and a son, are they opposites of one another?

Heterosexuality cannot be free until we stop thinking in terms of "opposites" that are "drawn" to one another. Men and women are not like iron filings and magnets, keys and locks or any object in those functionalist and fatalistic metaphors that try to legitimize heterosexuality as the norm by presenting it as a fate imposed on us by Nature. Heterosexuality is not our fate. It is a *choice* that we can make — or, more accurately, it *would be* a choice if our society were more pluralistic and less rigid in its construction of sexual choices. After all, choice implies the existence of several valid options, and as long as we continue to see eroticism between the sexes as fated by some inevitable sexiness inherent in genital differences, we will have a rather impoverished experience of heterosexuality.

Even if we cannot individually transcend the naturalistic view we can still work towards a freer heterosexuality by resisting this dominant ideology and attempting to maximize the creative possibilities that do exist. One thing we could do is stop repeating the myth — which we do not really believe in anyway — that we are attracted to men "just because they are different." Our own experience tells us otherwise: we are attracted to particular men partly because their "maleness" fascinates us, but also because of certain commonalities that we share as human beings or as members of certain groups. After all, we are not attracted to *all* men (as would be the case if we were attracted to sexual difference itself). On this particular man we might find muscles and a beard sexy, but on some other man we might be repulsed by the same "differences." We are not the puppets of a Mother Nature that manipulates our desires in order to have our feminine vagina become the "receptacle" for the masculine penis. We are human beings with very complex reasons for our erotic preferences.

IV. The Elements of Family Life

In all our erotic desires and activities there is an interplay of sameness and difference, of recognition and fascination, of familiarity and strangeness. Neither difference nor sameness are per se erotic; rather it is the playful movement of and between them which creates erotic exchange. A consistent eroticism of difference would exaggerate sexual difference into a pornographic scenario where the man with the biggest cock gets the woman with the biggest breasts. And a consistent eroticism of sameness would be equally unimaginative and homogenized, with everyone so equal that we would have no reason to be attracted to one person rather than another. Thus, what we need to work toward and begin imagining is an eroticism where sameness and difference are both eroticized and valued. This can help us to both break down the walls of the ego and recognize the other as our equal while maintaining the "admiration" for otherness and difference. Perhaps the most important thing to remember is that men and women were not made for heterosexuality, but rather heterosexuality exists for men and women.

Heterosexual Sex:
Power and Desire for the Other*

Wendy Hollway

A curious thing has been happening to me with various men lately: they don't want to have a sexual relationship when I do. But men are supposed 'not to be able to get enough of it', so the common assumption goes. The most obvious explanation would be that they're just not attracted to me. Well, they are! It's curious precisely because of the strong mutual attraction. Unfortunately, I don't think it's because these are feminist-influenced, anti-sexist men throwing off their conditioning about sex; and I'd probably think it was my fault if a couple of my friends weren't experiencing the same problem — for reasons that are strikingly similar.

In this chapter, I am going to give an account of the relation between sex and power in heterosexual relationships which explains why men in certain circumstances choose to avoid sex. It has very different implications for a theory of men's power from an 'all heterosexual sex is violence' position. It does not deny men's power in heterosexual relationships. But it doesn't deny women's either: it specifies how they differ.

I think it's politically important to theorise sex and power in a different way. So first I'll give my reasons. A friend of mine was talking about the sexuality issue of *Feminist Review* (no. 11, 1982). It had sparked off all sorts of new questions and ideas for her. But why, she asked me, does feminism approach sexuality from the point of view of pornography and violence against women? It leaves out such a lot of our experience. This friend is a feminist, but not so familiar with the internal debates of the movement that she takes such positions for granted. It made me hesitate. I explained why I thought that one couldn't make a separation between sex and power. But in a way she was right. There are two issues that this equation of male power and heterosexual sex leaves out. The first is that it leaves uncontested all those subtle forms of men's power which regulate heterosexual relationships. A woman can be oppressed in heterosexual couples even if her partner has never beaten

* From *Sex and Love*, eds. Sue Cartledge and Joanna Ryan. (London: The Women's Press Ltd. 1983). Copyright © Sue Cartledge and Joanna Ryan, 1983. Reprinted by permission.

IV. The Elements of Family Life

her up, never even demanded sex when she doesn't want it. The second is that it cannot address the experience of women who seek and enjoy heterosexual sex, who are attracted to, and feel in love with, men. These women's experiences cannot be reduced to 'false consciousness' (which doesn't explain anything) nor can it be argued that they want men because they seek and enjoy domination (though some women do). I'll speak for myself: I feel equal in heterosexual sex as long as I feel equal in relationship to that man more generally. I have felt very powerful in heterosexual relationships and that has expressed itself in my sexuality. Moreover, I know that men experience me as powerful (particularly when they are attracted to me): 'too powerful' is often the message I get. But I'll come back to that question.

In summary, there is a whole area of women's experience of men in heterosexual sex which feminist theory and politics has not successfully addressed. It is almost as if the more widespread assumptions about love and sex are so taken for granted that we keep missing the basic and fundamental question: why do some of us feel so strongly about men that our feminist analysis (the oppressiveness of sexual relationships with men and all that) just does not succeed in determining our feelings and practices? And if women like me feel like that after years of struggle, what about other women that we would like feminism to speak to — women more materially dependent on relationships with men than middle-class, employed feminists?

The question of women's desire for men is a huge one. I want to focus on sex because it is such an important definer of all those intense feelings. More particularly, I want to look at why *men*[1] feel similarly intense, irrational and vulnerable, and what effects it has on their relationships with women. Feminists do a lot of talking and thinking and writing about our gender and sexuality. If we're not careful, it ends up looking as if all this desire and contradiction is part of being a woman. And that can get read back through old sexist assumptions as further 'proof' of how irrational and needy we are: woman as pathology, man as normality. It's perfectly clear to me that it's not like that at all.

What does 'sex' mean that it produces all these strong feelings of desire, jealousy, dependence, dedication and fear? How do these affect the power relations between men and women who are involved with (or

---

[1]Much more has been said about women's sexuality in relationships. My focus here is on men's. This means that there is a danger of implying that only men are subject to those feelings in relationships, and the resistances that result. I know that's not true. What is true is that their needs and desires in relationships have been camouflaged by 'knowledge' about men's sexuality and what is underneath their sexual relationship has not been scrutinised.

potentially attracted to) each other? How is it the same and different for men and women?

The sections (of this chapter) run as follows: The 'greatest need' (1) indicates the intensity of feeling that is underneath men's sexual attraction to women. In (2), I show how these feelings have been assumed to be a part of women's, not men's, sexuality. By referring to several coexisting sets of assumptions about sexuality, I show how women and and men's sexuality is differentiated in such a way that men's vulnerability is protected by displacing those feelings on to women. In (3) I use the psychoanalytic concept of defence mechanisms to explain this. In (4) I indicate an answer to why men feel so vulnerable by showing the link between men's desire for the mother and the desire for a woman. Men's power can then be seen as something not inherent, but at least in part as a resistance (5). The perception of men as powerful is also promoted by women's desire for the Other and subsequent misrecognition of men as a result of their own vulnerability and also their assumptions about gender difference. In (6) I show how men's desire for the Other/mother is particularly felt in heterosexual sex, and how they thus experience the woman involved as powerful. When in other respects a woman and man occupy equal positions (and where the man cannot compensate in other arenas, as he has been able to do traditionally), the woman may well be experienced as 'too powerful' (7). I conclude by pointing out some of the implications of the argument (8).

1. The 'greatest need'

What do men feel like when they are attracted to a woman? Is it just an urge as society would have us believe, located in their anatomy (in their erections, to be precise)? One man I talked to put it as follows. He generalises, but as men are wont to do that to protect themselves I was pretty convinced that he was talking about himself. Besides where else would he have got such knowledge? Certainly not from how men are supposed to feel:

> Martin: 'People's needs for others are systematically *denied* in ordinary relationships. And in a love relationship you make the most *fundamental* admission about yourself — that you want somebody else. It seems to me that that is the *greatest* need. And the need which, in relation to its power, is most strongly hidden and repressed. Once you've opened

yourself, once you've shown the other person that you *need* them, then you've made yourself *incredibly* vulnerable.'[2]

Because I knew Martin quite well — indeed, I'd been in the position of being very attracted to him and had experienced him as astonishingly strong, self-sufficient and independent of women — I wanted to find out more about this question of vulnerability.

> Wendy: 'Yes, I agree. But I think there's a question about how much you show yourself to be vulnerable.' Martin: 'But you *do*, just by showing that you're *soft* on somebody. When you're not *admitting* it and when you're going round looking very self-sufficient. But it seems to me when you've revealed that need, you put yourself in an *incredibly* insecure state. You've shown someone what you're like. Before you've managed by showing them only what is *publicly* acceptable. And as soon as you've shown that there is this terrible *hole* in you — that you want somebody else — then you're in this absolute state of insecurity. And you need much *more* than the empirical evidence that somebody likes you, or whatever. You become neurotically worried by the possibility that you're not accepted, now you've let them see a little bit that's you, that it'll be rejected. The insecurity gives someone else power. I don't mean any viable self-exposure, or anything like that. I just mean any little indication that you *like* the other person.'

The intensity with which Martin speaks, the implications of the terms 'love relationship', 'wants', 'incredible vulnerability'; all these suggest that he is talking about a once-in-a-lifetime love. It comes as a surprise, then, when he explains that he's not talking about a 'viable self-exposure' (a wholesale declaration of life-long love perhaps?), but rather 'any little indication that you like the other person'. And this liking is bound up with attraction: he also refers to it as 'showing you're soft on somebody'.

For me, this example — and it is by no means unique — raises two questions: First, why are the feelings — the wants and needs resulting from being attracted to someone else (in Martin's case, it was to women)

---

[2]All the quotations come from my research. (Wendy Hollway, *Identity and Gender Difference in Adult Social Relations*, unpublished PhD. thesis, University of London, 1982). Italics indicate emphasis used by the speaker. In this article I have altered the transcript slightly where it has made the meaning more clear or shortened the quote. This has meant editing out pauses and repetitions but not changing the meaning.

— so strong, so non-rational? In other words, where do they come from? Secondly what effects do those feelings have on men's relationships with women whom they're attracted to (or have a sexual relationship with)? The following two sections address these questions.

2. The sexism in assumptions about difference in women's and men's sexuality

'Sex' does not just mean one thing. In fact the significance of sexual practices is that they stand in for so much which can go unsaid or misrepresented as a result. It's rare for two people to be explicit about what they want and mean when they make love/have sex for the first time. The needs and fantasies expressed through sex make us feel too vulnerable, or too guilty maybe. Yet people assume that 'sex' is simply about bodily pleasure and doesn't *mean* anything else. This comes from the assumption which sees sexual urges as natural and direct, unmediated by social meanings. Although more recently in western culture the idea of sex as a biological urge has been applied to women s sexuality too, it is still more characteristic of views of men's sexuality (Bland and Hollway, in press).[3] So the meanings of 'sex' are different for women and men. For example, the curious phenomenon that I described at the beginning of this chapter — men refusing sex with women where there was a mutual attraction — would not have seemed so curious in the case of a woman. Men are assumed to want sex anywhere for its own sake. One man friend of mine summed up his sexuality in such terms: 'I want to fuck. I *need* to fuck. I've *always* needed and wanted to fuck. From my teenage years, I've always longed after fucking.' It would be unusual to hear a woman say that. Traditional assumptions rather place women as wanting sex within the security of married life and motherhood. For contemporary feminists it is not as clearcut as that, but for some it's still very much about relationships:

> Dot: 'The one time I did fuck with Charles, it felt really *good*, like there was an awful lot that was important going on. But I didn't have an orgasm...I had lots of highs...maybe the tension between us was too great, or something. I don't know, but I was very *turned on*. When I think about that, I get a kind of quiver which is not about how successful it was

---

[3]Lucy Bland and Wendy Hollway, 'What's natural about sexuality? The problem for feminism of biological accounts of sexuality and sexual desire', *Feminist Review*, 13 (forthcoming).

sexually — if you can separate out these things. It was...it was the idea of fucking with *him*, rather than with someone else. If I'm caught off my guard thinking about it, the image I get makes me physically shudder with excitement...It grabs me at an *uncontrolled* level. That reinforces my hunch that it's the *idea* — that it's what's invested in the *idea*. I was in love with him. It's not fucking itself, it's something to do with the rights it gave me to see myself as having a relationship with him. I didn't have any of course.'

Despite the teachings of a permissive era that sex without a relationship was fine because women could be into sexual pleasure too, Dot's sexual responses, even at the level of her physical arousal, were a product of 'being in love'. What sex meant in that case was that it gave her 'rights to a relationship'. She reflects the obsolescence of this assumption in her final comment 'I didn't have any of course'.

Despite this recognition, and her participation in 'permissive' sex while growing up, her feelings and fantasies about wanting a relationship were still aroused by having sex. Men often see women's involvement through the same lens. One man described it in the following way:

Jim: 'I remember I had a strong thing for many years that you shouldn't actually sleep with someone unless you were actually in love with them in some way. And if you did it to someone you weren't in love with it was somehow pretty horrid and pretty nasty. One reason was feeling that sex was kind of dangerous. If you had sex, it meant that you were committed in some way and I didn't want that. Also that it said something — if you *just* had sex without a relationship it was letting them down because you somehow thought that they'd expect a relationship and it was a pretty shitty thing to do to have one part of it without the other. I still feel that to some extent — that somehow it was cheapening sex. It was very prissy — that this thing was so beautiful that you couldn't actually spread it around too much.'

Despite feeling that it is prissy (and indeed it is not consistent with men's claims about sex), Jim feels that the beauty of sex had to do with it being in a relationship. He's not explicit about it, but it's fairly obvious that many men (and most likely Jim) do desperately want and need relationships with women. Yet despite sideways references to his own

286

experience of the specialness of sex within a relationship, he implies that it's *women* who want the relationship; that it's because of *women's* needs that he didn't indulge in sex without a relationship; it was *women* who wanted commitment. Why did he not want commitment? His explanation below situates the sexual relationship where it belongs for him — in the realm of 'strong emotions'. However, there too his account avoids his own strong feelings by projecting them on to the woman:

> Jim: 'I was frightened of strong emotions, that's basically it. Because I remember, again a person at school, the tremendous relief when I ended the relationship, of not actually having to carry that — of not actually having to be responsible for those things.'

> Wendy: 'And was it that the girls wanted to be more intimate?'

> Jim: 'Yeah — that really frightened me, because I was frightened of making that kind of commitment, that kind of involvement, I thought I'd be let down, because of what happened the first time, when I was so unreserved about how I felt. I think that really affected my life incredibly, that first time when I fell in love.'

> Wendy: 'Why was having a relationship with this girl such a burden?'

> Jim: 'She was very strong and very emotional — that's pejorative — but I mean she had strong reactions, so that I didn't actually feel safe that I wasn't going to be knocked out, or sucked in, by her.'

'Responsibility' turns into 'commitment' and 'commitment' turns into 'involvement'. Her involvement turns out to be his involvement. His fear of involvement is linked to the first sexual relationship he'd had, before he'd learned any defences against the strength of his feelings towards women he fell in love with/made love with. With a woman who was strong and emotional the fear was greatest, because he could not be sure of his defences, his own ego boundaries. During a different conversation, Jim used the same term 'sucked in' to refer to the pleasure, intensity and danger he felt when he made love with the woman he was in a relationship with at that time. 'Sex' is capable of meaning the same things for men as it does for women: intense feelings of involvement and need, the danger to one's separate identity; wanting to have somebody for ever and fearing that they will let you down.

However, gender makes a difference to the recognition of what 'sex' means. Men can represent themselves according to a set of assumptions in which they are not in need of a relationship — in fact, not in need of anything that would make them vulnerable. After all, according to the idea that male sexuality is a 'natural drive', men are only in need of sex and they can, supposedly, get it anywhere.

'Permissive' sexuality gave new legitimacy to men's wish to have uncommitted sex with women without feeling irresponsible. In the following extract, Sam illustrates the points that I have made above — the same slippage and projection, the fear of feeling strongly. His principle that it is all right not to feel any responsibility is legitimated by permissiveness. It is motivated by his fears of his own 'sentimentality':

> Sam: 'I'll tell you something — I don't know what it means, but I'll say it anyway. When I say to somebody, who I'm making love to, I'm close to, when I say "I love you, I love you", it's a word that symbolises letting go. The night before Carol went away, she was saying it, and then I started saying it to her, when we were making love and um, what frightens me in that word, is...it's an act of commitment. Somebody suddenly *expects* something of me. They've said something that's somehow...the first word in a long rotten line towards marriage. That when you fall in *love* you're caught up in the institution. And it's been an act of principle for me, that I can love somebody and feel *loved*, without feeling any responsibility. That I can be free to say that I love somebody if I love them. Be free to feel. I can feel it quite unpredictably. It can hit me quite unexpectedly. And I think I worry about it because I can be quite sentimental.'

To the extent that this is possible in practice, Sam can eat his cake *and* have it, so to speak. His feelings, which can hit him unexpectedly, particularly when making love, are worrying. So his wish to say 'I love you', gets projected onto her declaration, where it can be comfortably located as somebody *else* expecting something of *him*. Of course, he still wants to feel loved — isn't that the crux of the matter? — but with no strings attached.

I have referred to three different assumptions concerning sexuality in the course of commenting on the meaning in the accounts that I have used. These are (i) that men's sexuality is a natural drive with any woman as its object; (ii) that women want sex within a relationship and men can get caught in commitment; (iii) (characteristic of 1960s' 'permissiveness'), both women and men just want physical pleasure from sex and neither wants a relationship.

The point that I want to emphasise is that women and men occupy different positions in these 'discourses'.[4] In the first case men are subjects, the possessors of biological urges whose 'natural' object is women. In contrast, women are subjects of the second. According to this, they are subjects of the wants and needs for relationships, rather than one-off sexual encounters. Men experience themselves as objects of this wanting and fear being 'hooked' when they sleep with women. According to 'permissive' ideas, in principle women and men are equally subjects; that is, the assumptions are 'gender blind', they are supposedly subject to the same sexual urges and wishes not to commit themselves. In the previous analyses, I have shown how men position women as wanting commitment rather than position themselves there.

3. Defence mechanisms

Gender difference thus means that women and men experience their sexuality differently. I have shown, in the case of Jim, why he was motivated to take up this position. He was enabled to defend himself against his own strong emotions by displacing them on to the woman. This is best understood through a psychoanalytic perspective.

According to Freud, material is repressed through defence mechanisms. These do not operate only within a person, but between people. The clearest example of a relational defence mechanism is projection: the feelings which a person is uncomfortable with, and therefore cannot recognise in her/himself, are projected onto another. Jim is motivated to suppress his strong emotions and sees the woman as being the one who feels strongly, wants commitment, and so on. This makes sense of his fear of involvement (which is actually to do with getting too

---

[4]By the term 'discourse', I mean a system of statements which cohere around common meanings and values. The meaning of the term is similar to a 'set of assumptions' but the way 'discourse' has been theorised (most importantly by Michael Foucault, *The Order of Things: An Archaeology of the Human Sciences*, Tavistock, London, 1970 and *The History of Sexuality, vol. 1, An Introduction*, Allen Lane, London, 1979) emphasises how these meanings and values are a product of social factors, of powers and practices, rather than an individual's set of ideas. My use of the term here also enables me to make the link with language and grammar where people are positioned (and position others) by the use of personal pronouns in sentences. For an extended discussion of these theoretical issues see J. Henriques, W. Hollway, C. Urwin, C. Venn and V. Walkerdine, *Changing the Subject of Psychology*, Methuen, London, 1983, forthcoming.

involved) in terms of her needs. He is thus purged of his own — they have been externalised.

However, a psychoanalytic account does not draw the implications about the power differences which result from these dynamics.[5] Gender difference means that women are suitable vehicles for men's projections: they have already been constructed in such a way that they manifest the characteristics that men are suppressing. Likewise they experience themselves as wanting commitment and materially are more likely to be in the position of needing it, because this is how they have been positioned historically. Thus women's and men's positions are complementary, in the sense that these gender differences make it likely that both men and women will see men as wanting uncommitted sex and women needing committed relationships. The way that gender produces different identities leads to a collusion between women and men which makes change in these areas difficult. None the less, the effect is consistently oppressive to women: it reproduces a power difference where men are supposedly free of needs and invulnerable. Women are left carrying this for both. No wonder we sometimes feel powerless! Despite collusion, the resultant contradictions have created a significant space for change.

If men's sexuality were wholly accountable through these gender positions (subject of natural drives, object of women's wishes for commitment), why would they ever stay with women, need women, feel strong emotions, and feel lost and desperate when women leave them? The answer is that 'sex' does mean more than natural urges for men too, but their subject position in that discourse offers them the possibility of repressing their strong needs of women. They take up this position unconsciously, as the slippage from one meaning to another in Jim's account illustrated. As psychoanalytic theory would insist, the slippage of meanings, the inconsistencies and illogicalities, are not arbitrary; they are motivated. As Martin's account illustrates, they are motivated by the extreme vulnerability which is the consequence of needing a woman that much — a consequence which is not eradicated when the feelings are projected onto her.

---

[5]This tendency in psychoanalysis theory is exacerbated by the way it reduces content to process. For example, Freud emphasised that the object to which desires attach themselves or around which fantasies develop was displaced from the real object and therefore of little significance. This view fails to see the systematicity in what is projected onto whom. I believe that it is here that gender (or race or class) as a *social* system of differences is necessary for the analysis.

4. Desire for the Other is desire for the mother

We want to feel loved. Sex is just about the only practice permitted to adults where wishes for comfort, support, loving can be expressed. Lacan summed up the origin in each person's history of this desire in his phrase 'desire for the Other is desire for the mother'. It may sound a little farfetched. In the following extract, Jim's account of what he wants from a relationship with a woman makes the same point in a way which is recognisable to most of us:

> Wendy: 'What was it that you wanted out of your relationship with Jeanette?'
>
> Jim: 'Well I think support, actually. Knowing that there was somebody who was going to be on my side. That I could talk about things that were affecting me and they would automatically be important to her. And that she would be able to give me strength in that way. Very classic. Like my parents' relationship in a way. But it was me who set the agenda, set the whole thing up. I remember her saying — well I was into classical music, so Jeanette pretended she was until she got confident enough. She wouldn't actually challenge me. There's a gaze of uncritical, totally accepting love that I find really attractive. "I'll love you for ever whatever" is a really powerful gaze. And that's a mother's gaze.'
>
> Wendy: 'Is that how your mother relates to you?'
>
> Jim: 'Absolutely. Whatever I do, she'll support me, she has supported me. It's quite incredible. And that makes my relationship with her very easy.'
>
> Wendy: 'And did you get that from your father?'
>
> Jim: 'No, that was very different. Well, I always felt he loved me, definitely. But he was much more — well he got annoyed with me when I didn't do it right.'

There is no reason to suppose that this 'desire for the mother' is not the historical origin of desire for the Other in both men and women. However, according to Freudian theory, the passages of boys' and girls' entry into culture and to gender create a difference not only in the object

291

of that desire but in the intensity of that desire. Girls supposedly transfer their desire onto the father, and in doing so displace their desire for the mother, who none the less remains the primary giver of love and caring. Boys repress their desire for the mother but do not normally displace it from one gender to the other,[6] it is usually relocated with full force in the first sexual relationship that a boy has.'[7] As Jim's comments illustrate, sex is the most powerful expression of this desire — the site where men want and need most and therefore feel most vulnerable. It is not arbitrary that Jim uses the same term — 'sucked in' — to refer to his relation to women's emotionality and his feelings while making love with the woman he loved. Men 'enter' women when they make love. There is a metaphorical slippage between the womb of the mother (the ultimate in protection and security and the antithesis of separation) and the vagina, wherein they can feel engulfed in the love of the Other/mother. Women's vaginas thus can be dangerous places — dangerous because men's identity depends on separation from the mother; a maintenance of fragile ego boundaries which are most vulnerable, as Martin testified, when 'attraction' to a woman heralds desire for the Other/mother.

5. Men's power as resistance to women's power as the mother/Other

The links of meaning between the mother and the woman with whom a man has sex (or is attracted to) is significant only in so far as it has political effects. It is a mixed blessing to understand that women do in fact have power over men. One of the puzzling things about feminists' analyses is that they stress men's power and women's lack of power as if they were immutable principles. I am astonished when my mother, in her matter-of-fact, apolitical way, talks about men in terms which leave me in no doubt that she feels more powerful, competent and in control than they are. Why is it so elusive to many of the women I know? In this section, I want to suggest some answers to this question. First, men's

---

[6]This would suggest that a heterosexual man's desire for the Other is even stronger, and therefore even more threatening, than a heterosexual woman's (displaced) desire. Men's greater repression, and more driven resistance to women's powerfulness (as they experience it through their vulnerability) would make sense in this light.

[7]Several men have described to me the same phenomenon when they were young, particularly when they fell in love with older women. But there's also a danger of overgeneralising. I think many men get into relationships with women who are less experienced and less confident (apparently) than they are and, by retaining this power inequality, never experience the vulnerability. Yet they don't feel entirely satisfied and will be the ones who pull away from the relationship.

strategies of resistance to the vulnerability they feel through 'needing' a woman are precisely ways of exercising power: a power conferred on them by the positions available to men through the system of gender difference. Secondly, women misrecognise men and women because we too are subject to (sexist) assumptions in which men are produced as 'strong' and women as 'weak'.

Martin's comment in the first extract I used indicates that his way of coping with his extreme vulnerability to women he is attracted to is to put on a front in which he is strong and self-sufficient. Yet because he feels so vulnerable, he cannot believe it doesn't show ('but you do show yourself to be vulnerable, just by showing that you're soft on somebody'). As a result, he cannot see himself as others see him. However strong he appears to women, he experiences himself as dreadfully vulnerable. The meanings attached to his identity are inextricable from his desire for the Other. It is ironical that Martin is one of those men who is systematically misrecognised by women as the ideal in dependability, strength, resourcefulness and so on! Women see the facade and do not see what it is covering up, particularly if they are attracted to him. How does this misrecognition come about? In the following extract, Clare gives a graphic description of her misrecognition of Phil, the man she lived with for many years:

Clare: 'That guy! I didn't even know he was so dependent on me — I had no idea, not a clue.'

Wendy: 'That's so often the way men play it. But it's also often the way women *read* it.'

Clare: 'Oh, exactly. It's two-way. His behaviour was very stereotypical, really. He was very...I thought he was a *competent* person, but he didn't think he was at all. He was outwardly confident — domineering — which actually made me feel incredibly oppressed.'

Wendy: 'How long did it take you to realise that?'

Clare: 'Oh a long time. I didn't realise he was dependent on me till I left him — literally, I had no *idea*. And when I look back on it, I realised that I *should* have known. I realised that the signs were there, and I hadn't read them. I felt him as — dominant, and domineering and confident. And he felt *lacking* in confidence. The very signs that I took to signify confidence were actually exactly the signs of his *lack* of confidence — like talking too much, being opinionated...and things that I couldn't *bear*. And when I read it back as lack of confidence, I could see. But when I was in a situation, reading it as confidence, I could never get that. Quite a lot of things changed in our relationship. When I first met him, he had a degree and he encouraged me but I got far higher qualifications than he did. So that also made him feel unconfident. And I hadn't realised that either. We did things like — both applying for Open University teaching. I got it, he didn't. It didn't occur to *me* it was a problem. Of course it was a problem for him.'

Phil's displays are equivalent to Martin's public acceptability. True, masculinity is meant to involve being confident, dominating, self-sufficient (all the signs that Clare systematically misreads).

What is interesting is that Clare knew in retrospect that she had misrecognised Phil. However, she goes on to say that she falls into exactly the same patterns with her present man. Learning about men is not a process of rational acquisition of experience. She misrecognises the men she is attracted to (just like men misrecognise those women whom they desire). For both, recognition of their own power disappears at the advent of desire.

Clare: 'Why is it, then, that I can't get hold of that knowledge about Ken? Why can't I see it? — because I can't. I still don't feel as if I know it — I don't, not in my gut. It's very silly. It's obviously that I don't want to see it. But I am extremely powerful, when I stand back and think about it, I know that. I know where my power lies. If I were somebody else, I could see it. But I have great resistance to recognising it in myself.'

Desire produces misrecognition. Through the sense of vulnerability that it inspires, the other is seen as relatively strong. The fantasy is that he/she can fulfill those needs which, though so long repressed, go back to the infant-mother relationship. The sense of vulnerability may not itself be a sign of misrecognition of oneself, but in the way that it floods other feelings about oneself, and evidence of realistic capabilities, it creates a distortion. However, the *content* of these misrecognitions depends on gender. The way that vulnerability is a product of desire for the Other may well be the same for women and men, but the positions that can be taken up in order to resist the Other's power must be different because of gender. It is for this reason that men's and women's power in sexual relationships cannot be said to be equivalent. It is not a question of 'equal but different'.

Women's power as the Other/mother in sexual and couple relationships is politically contradictory because it motivates men's resistance. Men's experience of women's power is not equivalent to women exercising it. Ironically, it is a power that women do not necessarily recognise because of our misrecognition of ourselves and men (although unawares we may use it in the way we 'mother' men in order to keep them needing us).

6. 'Frightened of getting in deep'

Broadly speaking, the sites of men's resistance to women's power are twofold. First, traditionally, men have used the same site — sexuality — to resist the woman of their desire. By having multiple or serial sexual relationships, men dilute the power that they experience one woman having over them.[8] But it's not entirely satisfactory. As Sam said:

> Sam: 'The thing that has caused me the most pain and the most hope is the idea of actually living with Jane, and that's in the context of having tried to live with three other women before. And each time the relationship's been full of possibility. I don't want to live on my own. There's too many *things* all wrapped up in coupling. There's too many needs it potentially meets, and there are too many things it frustrates. I *do* want to have a *close, central-person* relationship, but in the past, the negative aspects outweighed the positive aspects dramatically. Or my inability to work through them has led me to run.'

He then specifies further what led him to run:

> Sam: 'I'm very frightened of getting in *deep* — and then not being able to cope with the demands the relationships's making. You see a lot of these things aren't really to do with sexuality. They're to do with responsibility.'

---

[8]Women do too, though the opportunity has not been equally available.

Whose? Isn't it the same slippage again? From responsibility to commitment to involvement to fear of being let down. Multiple or serial relationships enable men (and women) to avoid facing the fear.

Secondly, in juxtaposition to the private world of the home, which is also the site of women's sexual/mothering practices, men have asserted the superiority of their position in the public world. If they depend on women at home it is not so bad if there is always work to do which comes first, or meetings to go to, or buddies to meet in the pub. The woman's sexual power can be countered through her material dependence, or her emotional dependence, or her incompetence/ unconfidence in the 'real' world. When men are attracted to women who occupy all the same positions in the world as men do, women end up having a 'double power': there is no site of resistance for men, no place where they are uncontestably in power.

7. 'Too powerful'

So let me return to my original question and summarise my conclusions as to why (some) men avoid sex even when they are attracted to a woman. Put simply, the feelings that they are keyed into by having sex in those circumstances makes a man feel extremely vulnerable. I want to emphasise that its not the 'power' of a woman's sexuality as such. That would be to naturalise it in much the same way as many oppressive cultures do. It would also be to carry over the sexist rationalisations that men have used to claim the power of their own sexual 'drives' or their penises as natural. Rather a woman becomes the 'object' onto which older desires are hooked. The power of women's sexuality is as 'psychic' object not as real object. But in practice the two cannot be separated (until a man has either done some hard work on those feelings, or displaced them into a different object).

There are an infinite number of strategies whereby men can deal with their vulnerability. I don't want to generalise to 'all men'. Most men don't resist sex: they are too driven by their desire for the Other. Usually, as I have argued above, the power is balanced by all the other arenas in which men can so easily operate. Men's power is as 'real' objects as well as 'psychic' objects for women.

However, when none of the usual inequalities operates to produce a power which counterbalances their vulnerability, they may have to refuse a sexual relationship. The boundary is drawn to exclude sex because it is there that desire is strongest and therefore there where vulnerability and the threat of losing a separate identity is greatest. Emotional involvement is not necessarily banished with sex however. He phones up because he cannot bear to lose contact. He might need me after all. But instead, he asked me if *I'm* all right. Displacement of his needs onto the 'needy' woman convinces him he's fine and it's me who's suffering. He wants to carry on being friends (because I'm the only one 'who really understands'). Another will stand on the doorstep for half an hour (after midnight) saying 'I'm going now', but never quite bringing himself to leave. Another will reach out physically to touch me (before he's censored the spontaneous gesture), then, when I respond, he withdraws.

What is it like to be on the receiving end of these contradictions? Women have often felt that it was our madness, or paranoia, or confusion, or our failure to reach the right standards of feminity. Now at last I recognise those double messages when I receive them straight in the gut. I see it clearly: it is not that he doesn't like me or doesn't want me. But, yes, it is that he will not have a relationship with me. One tells me quite openly that it would be a disaster because he'd need me too much and then I'd go. For another, it was too good. For a third it would change everything and so he's safer with his present part-time relationship.

We must also be scrupulous in recognising how these double messages, power plays, contradictions, fears are used by us in relationships too. Desire for the Other is not only men's bane. However, there are two differences. One is that women have taken on the need to change these harmful practices more seriously than men have, and can often be very honest and courageous about them. The second is that we have never been exonerated from these needs anyway. It is only the sexism of assumptions — the way that established 'truths' about sexuality are gender-differentiated — that have provided a cover for men's actions and feelings.

It is not impossible to change these dynamics. Just because women have a head-start doesn't mean men can avoid them. Some men are strong enough in themselves not to feel engulfed by their desire for the Other/mother. I think what it takes is that every man has to 'separate' from this mother. Most don't. Rather, they displace the desire onto a safe woman 'object'. If he can make it feel that she's needier than him (not so difficult, given patriarchy) he won't even know that he's vulnerable. Well hopefully it won't escape us so easily!

8. Conclusions

The main point that comes out of this analysis is to show men's vulnerability. Many of our mothers know it. How often have we heard them say 'All men are little boys. They need mothering.' Such a recognition

297

was obviously not sufficient. However, I think that it's important that feminism reclaim this knowledge. Making political this knowledge gives us a different view of men's displays of selfsufficiency, their resistances, their distancing and rejections, their 'more important' commitments. However, the point of inserting this recognition within a feminist politics is obviously not to do what it did in my mother's generation: to keep women firmly within the domestic sphere where women's power and men's resistance goes to reproduce gender difference and women's oppression.

Changing these dynamics — both men's and our own patterns which pull us into a collusion with them — is not a simple matter of political fiat. Understanding is not synonymous with changing. One man recently, confronted with what amounts to the analysis here, acknowledged that it was very accurate, very perceptive. But it didn't make any difference. He couldn't change his feelings about it just like that: neither the desire nor the resistance motivated by the vulnerability that it produced. Changing desire is not a question of political 'will'. We have to take seriously methods such as consciousness-raising, therapy, and being open to feeling and expressing our contradictory wants and needs. Here I simply want to register that this knowledge is a necessary but not sufficient condition of changing gender difference.

I want to stress that there is a relation between knowledge and power. It is relevant for feminist politics to theorise men's sexuality as well as our own. Most particularly, it is important to understand power in such a way that our own powers become apparent to us and we are not trapped in a discourse which sees power as being solely the property of men — a possession which we can never acquire by virtue of our sex. In this chapter, I have used a notion of power which sees it as being part of all social relations. It is produced not only through differences in material resources, but in the meanings through which we understand our relationships, and in the effects of gender difference in conferring power on men. However, these meanings are multiple and contradictory. By recognising these contradictions, we are not stuck with a political analysis which sees men's power as monolithic and unchangeable and which keeps women in the victim role. Power is productive, and wherever there is power, there is resistance. Heterosexuality is a site of power and of resistance for men and for women. As women we can share and analyse our relations with men in such a way as to challenge the sexist assumptions whose effects I have shown here.

Male Sexuality: Toward A Theory of Liberation*

Gad Horowitz and Michael Kaufman

Until the early 1980s the main trend in feminist presentations of sex and sexuality had to do with sexual oppression and the degradation of women by men. Whether the issue was violence, incest, rape, pornography, or "normal" heterosexual relationship, male sexuality was cast in terms of aggression, objectification, domination, and oppression. The inescapable conclusion of such an analysis was that somehow male sexuality had to be dampened, controlled, and contained.

The converse of all this was a presentation of women's sexuality that either tended to speak of women as sexual victims and objects or that developed concepts of women's sexuality as naturally soft, nurturing, and without conflict. But in recent years a new debate has emerged on women's sexuality. A spate of new books seeks to understand the tensions inherent in female sexuality and sexual expression in patriarchal, industrial societies.[1] Carol Vance, the editor of one such book, clearly summarizes this tension:

> The tension between sexual danger and sexual pleasure is a powerful one in women's lives. Sexuality is simultaneously a domain of restriction, repression, and danger as well as a domain of exploration, pleasure, and agency. To focus only on pleasure and gratification ignores the patriarchal structure in which women act, yet to speak only of sexual violence and oppression ignores women's experience with sexual agency and choice and unwittingly in-

---

* From *Beyond Patriarchy: Essays by Men on Pleasure, Power, and Change*, edited by Michael Kaufman (Toronto: Oxford University Press 1987). Reprinted by permission of the authors and O.U.P.

[1]See for example, Ann Snitow, Christine Stansell, and Sharon Thompson, eds., *Powers of Desire* (New York: *Monthly Review Press*, 1983); Carols S. Vance, ed., *Pleasure and Danger: Exploring Female Sexuality* (Boston: Routledge and Kegan Paul, 1984); Sue Cartledge and Joanna Ryan, eds., *Sex and Love: New Thoughts and Old Contradictions* (London: The Women's Press, 1983); and Mariana Valverde, *Sex, Power, and Pleasure* (Toronto: Women's Press, 1985).

creases the sexual terror and despair in which women live.[2]

Although the feminist discussion of sexuality is making important advances, the understanding by men and women of male sexuality lags woefully behind. Even among gay men, where there has been a continuing affirmation of male sexuality, much more has been written on gay history, identity and culture than on sexuality per se.

Regardless of sexual orientation, most men harbor some confusing feelings about their sexuality. Heterosexual and bisexual men who have become aware of sexism and the oppression of women often feel caught between sexual desire on one side and a pressing confusion about forms of sexual behavior or fantasy that appear to, or actually do, oppress women. For many homosexual and bisexual men there is confusion about the conflict (as determined by our society) between their sexual desire for men and their own gender identity.

As with many questions about men we can profit from recent explorations by feminists. Our starting point can usefully parallel the approach of current writings about female sexuality: the notion of sexuality as a socially constructed system of conflict and inner tension.

Male sexuality is not simply a thing, good, bad, or otherwise. It is a terrain of tension, conflict and struggle. There are a number of internal conflicts as well as a new form of sociopolitical conflict arising from the feminist challenge to patriarchy. The interaction of these conflicts tends to produce anxiety, with guilt and confusion at one extreme and an aggravation of aggression at the other. These two extremes are expressed, at the one extreme, by the guilty feelings of many men sympathetic to feminism and, at the other, by the increase in portrayals of violence against women and perhaps of actual violence itself.[3] But the points of conflict and tension will not be reduced simply by a dampening or suppression of male sexuality or simply by the removal of pornography from newsstands. Rather the solution will be sexual liberation within societies organized to meet as full a range of human needs as possible.

In the most abstract terms, the tension within male sexuality is between pleasure and power. The pleasure is the pleasure of touch,

----

[2]Carol S. Vance, "Pleasure and Danger: Toward a Politics of Sexuality," in *Vance*, op. cit., I.

[3]It is very difficult to analyze the statistical increase in rape and wife battering over the last decade in a number of countries, because the statistics do not necessarily indicate an increase in these forms of assault but might be accounted for by the increased willingness of women to report these crimes.

sensation, fantasy, and intimacy. The realm of pleasure is ultimately
derived from the body. Power is of two sorts. First is the sheer power of
pleasure. Depending on one's feeling of guilt, there may or may not be
conflict with the experience of pleasure. But the power of male sexuality also stems from social relations of power: the social power of men
over women; the power of social constraint and socially imposed forms
of sexual repression; the social power of heterosexuality over homosexuality; the internalization of social and sexual domination in the
form of the structures of masculinity and a sense of guilt.

But of course there is no simple dualism of bodily based pleasures and socially constructed power. The pleasure of sensuality cannot be divorced from pleasures derived from relations of power, or, in
reverse, inhibitions of sensuality often relate to the existing relations of
power. Furthermore the very way our body experiences pleasure is the
result of an interaction between the body and the social world.

It is more precise, then, to speak of a series of conflicts. Our
sexuality and our sexual lives display conflicts between sexual pleasure per se, the constraints of masculinity, the oppression of women,
the repression of an innate polysexuality (that is, repression of a fluid
and wide-ranging sexuality), and a generalized fetishism of the objects
of desire.

This chapter explores a number of areas in which these conflicts
are expressed. The first section examines the split between activity
and passivity and the repression of men's innate polysexuality. The
purpose is to examine how male sexuality is constructed at the psychological level and to give us some basic concepts with which to examine
the conflicts of male sexuality. This first section concludes by sketch-
ing the outlines of a theory of male sexual liberation. The second section turns to two interlocking issues — sexual objectification and
pornography — to see whether the framework of the first section helps
us analyze some of the dilemmas and conflicts faced by men and
women as we attempt to understand and change our sexual and social
worlds.

Our overall approach is psychoanalytical. One of the great contributions of psychoanalysis is the notion that there is no such thing as
a natural form of sexuality. Sexuality is simply the capacity of humans to derive pleasure from the body. The form this takes for the
child and adult is a product of biological maturation and historical
evolution within the social and natural environments. Our reading of
psychoanalysis does not start with the individual as abstracted from
society. We start with society and the body — but a body that is part of
society. The act of creating a human being is in itself a profoundly social activity, as are the body's experiences from that moment on. Nor

301

do we start with society as abstracted from the body. Society does not exist only in structures external to the human but is embedded within the body. Society is embodied. One need look no farther than the stance of a soldier or the pose of a model to understand this latter point.

There are three problems with using the psychoanalytic model. One is a long history of superficial, sexist, conservative, and otherwise objectionable interpretations. The history of offensive ideological baggage goes back to Freud himself. We do our best to dissociate ourselves from these traditions. Second is the fact that psychoanalysis employs a complex and specialized vocabulary that must be learned to make sense of the whole approach. To make matters worse, this vocabulary itself has been subject to numerous superficial, sexist, and conservative misreadings. We will do our best to limit the use of specialized terminology and, when necessary, to introduce terms as we go along without getting bogged down in terminological debates. A final difficulty is that psychoanalysis is, more than anything, a theory of the unconscious. Many of the matters we will discuss are things that each of us has either forgotten or has never consciously known. These things are only uncovered in the course of psychological analysis, and even when uncovered they are subject to interpretation. We think the best test of the material in the first section will be its application to issues of objectification and pornography in the second. Once unconscious desire is manifested in pictures or in our conscious activities, we can begin to evaluate the usefulness of the concepts we have employed to understand the unconscious.

Activity/Passivity and Polysexuality

Body and Culture

It is not quite popular to acknowledge that human sexuality is not simply innate and natural, but rather is socially constructed.[4] Sexual desire and sexual behavior vary greatly from society to society, from epoch to epoch, and from person to person. On the other hand, sexuality has to do with the body, bodily pleasure, and physiological responses. Male sexuality may be experienced in the realm of fantasy, and the stuff of our sexuality may be unconscious and deeply repressed, but it isn't constructed out of nothing. Ultimately there is the

---

[4]This is one of the themes of many articles in the collections mentioned above, as well as in Michel Foucaul: *The History of Sexuality* (New York: Pantheon, 1978), vol. I, An Introduction.

body, a tingling in the mouth, an erection of the penis, the blush of skin, the sight of an object of desire, the pleasure of taste and sound, or a pressure on the prostate that can take your breath away. Culture does not write on a blank paper.

In order for us to meet our needs in the world our desires must be controlled, organized, and related to external reality. Innate ego capacities — our ability to perceive, to remember, to move purposefully — are the means through which the child's energies are directed out at the world. And it is this world that molds that which is biologically given in the child. This process of molding is the development of the child's ego, the child's personality.

This developmental process is one of organizing, restraining, and repressing the highly malleable energy of human desire. Whereas animal instincts are closely adapted to reality, in humans there is an "organ" of adaption to reality, the ego.[5] Human desires cannot be satisfied without the intervention of the ego. "We are," says Grene, "biologically formed to be cultural animals."[6] Our desires do not take their final form until they have been molded by culture, where biological drives become desire, wish, and pleasure.

This process of transformation is the process that Freud described as repression. The extent and quality of repression is not a biological given or a social constant but changes as societies change and evolve. More specifically, the development of civilization, says Freud, has required an ever greater renunciation of pleasure.[7] Marcuse added to Freud's formulation by drawing a distinction between basic and surplus repression. Basic repression is the renunciation or sublimation of pleasure that is necessary to survive and develop as a human being. On top of this is surplus repression, the forms of repression that increase as civilization develops.[8] This ever increasing renunciation of desire is reexperienced in the development of every human being. As we mature we bring into our developing egos the structures and demands of our society.

---

[5]Heinz Hartmann, "Comments on the Psychoanalytic Theory of the Ego" in *Essays on Ego Psychology* (New York: International Universities Press, 1964), 120.

[6]Marjorie Grene, *Approaches to a Philosophical Biology* (New York: Basic Books, 1968), 44. For Freud's analysis of the drives, see his "Instincts and Their Vicissitudes," in *Standard Edition of the Complete Psychological Works of Sigmund Freud* (London: Hogarth Press), 14:121-2.

[7]See Sigmund Freud, *Civilization and Its Discontents* (1930), trans. James Strachey (New York: W.W. Norton, 1961).

[8]See Herbert Marcuse, *Eros and Civilization* (New York: Vintage Books, 1962).

IV. The Elements of Family Life

Two immediate things concern us here. One is the split between activity and passivity and the superimposition of "masculinity" and "femininity" onto this polarity. The other is the narrowing of the vast expression of sexual desire onto genital pleasure, what Freud saw as the repression of polymorphous bisexuality.

Activity, Passivity, and Bisexuality

Freud spoke of activity and passivity coexisting in the infant. At the mother's breast, he said, the newborn is the passive recipient of the mother's activities, of her care. But the infant quickly develops the desire and ability to be an active initiator, even though its ability to carry out these activities still depends on nurturing adults. The continuing development of the ego, that is, the increased capacity to master the world, is the developing of one's activity.

As the ego develops, active and passive modes of gratification are extended into general orientations of the ego, what one might call personality types. Generally, activity is associated with an aggressive, outgoing, achieving, or doing orientation; passivity with a more pacific, receptive, being orientation. Psychoanalytic theory stresses that in the first few years of life girls and boys are both active and passive.[9]

Freud also thought that, in the "language" of the unconscious, activity and passivity are related to specific zones of the body. The mouth, anus, and vagina, although capable of being vehicles of activity, have a primarily passive character because they are receptive orifices that can be pleasurably stimulated by another organ — a nipple, thumb, finger, tongue, column of feces, penis.

Although Freud referred to certain organs as essentially active or essentially passive, he did not ignore the distinction between their physiological characteristics and the psychological characteristics that are later associated with them. For example, at the breast a child may appear to be in a state of passive bliss, but active sucking is what brings it to that state. For the newborn, and likely for some time, it is not possible to describe aims as either active or passive. The mouth and vagina may be a receptive organ, but this does not necessarily suggest exclusive passivity.

---

[9]For a detailed discussion of the problems in the psychoanalytic use of the terms active and passive, see David Rapaport, "Some Metapsychological Considerations Concerning Activity and Passivity" (1953), in *The Collected Papers of David Rapaport* (New York: Basic Books, 1967), 530-68.

Young children may not consciously understand the world, but as anyone who cares for children knows, they are, without knowing it, incredibly good judges of social and psychological relations. Thus from an early age we bring to our bodies a set of social experiences. We project onto our bodies a whole set of social meanings. In other words, while the vagina is physically a receptive organ and the penis physically an insertive one, it is only through the work of culture that these become passive and active organs. What is the combination of biological and social developments that create these equations?

Boys and girls of one to three years do not seem to experience significantly different sexual desires or gratifications. They can experience both activity and passivity, and they can be erotically interested in humans of either sex; they are essentially bisexual. Very young children are curious about human bodies but do not seem to attach any importance to sex differences.[10]

With maturation this outlook changes, particularly with a growing erotic interest in the genitals. By four or five this new genital interest is impregnated with social meaning. The boy (in a male-dominant society) unconsciously experiences the penis as representing activity. The penis becomes a phallic symbol. The corollary is that an unconscious fear of "castration" develops, a fear that is so strong only because our patriarchal and heterosexist society creates a norm in which one cannot be powerful, active, or a lover of women, without possessing a penis.[11] An antithesis is set up of phallic versus "castrated." The fear of castration is not experienced literally or consciously; rather it is a bodily image associated with a loss of activity and power. Furthermore, in societies of male domination *and* where homosexuality is repressed, most boys cannot escape this castration anxiety without giving up passivity and homosexuality. Homosexuality is equated with passivity — and therefore with castration — because in a partiarchal society men are by definition domi-

---

[10]Many references in this subsection (such as to "castration" anxiety) are to unconscious processes, associations, and knowledge. One is not aware of these mental processes. The dominance of the unconscious over one's life is much greater for children than for adults. The language of this article does not refer to the conscious experience of children. Rather they have involuntary, powerful, emotional, dreamlike images of things happening bodily to themselves.

[11]For a detailed look at the issues presented in this section see Gad Horowitz, *Repression: Basic and Surplus Repression in Psychoanalytic Theory* (Toronto: University of Toronto Press, 1977), 81-125. For Freud's views on childhood sexuality see, for example, "Three Essays on the Theory of Sexuality" (1905), in *Standard Edition of the Complete Psychological Works of Sigmund Freud* (London: Hogarth Press), vol. 7.

nant; thus love for males comes to be equated with passivity. Passivity leads to anxiety about one's masculinity, and thus it is emotionally necessary in such a society for the boy to unconsciously renounce his bisexuality.

Of course the "norms" defined here do not exist in reality. This process of repression is never complete and never without its internal conflicts and tensions. What is repressed lives on, sometimes in the form of active homosexuality or bisexuality as an adult, sometimes in the form of fantasy and dreams, and sometimes in the form of intense fear — homophobia. But what does appear to be a norm for men is the impossibility of simultaneously sustaining active and passive aims without generating conflict and fear.

What occurs, therefore, is a split between activity and passivity and then an imposition on top of it of the phallic/castrated polarity. It is this superimposition that produces "masculinity" and "femininity," which until then, says Freud, "have no psychological meaning."[12] This is the unconscious logic of patriarchy as discovered by Freud.

Even where one's parental figures depart from the patriarchal norms, the boy must experience these superimpositions because of the weight of institutions, the partriarchal family form, and a whole culture that teaches that men = activity.

Children often express their fears through games. One extremely popular game among boys (and many young men) is to tuck their genitals between their legs and out of sight, and then to parade in front of each other or in front of a mirror as a female. In a group of boys the reaction is one of glee; alone, there is amusement, fascination, and terror.

Freud's Bisexuality versus Polysexuality

In *Repression*, Horowitz uncritically accepted Freud's presupposition that sexual life *must* first be experienced by all human beings in terms of the polarity or antithesis of activity and passivity. It therefore seemed obvious that the lifting of the surplus repression of bisexuality would result in something like androgyny — men and women equally capable of both activity and passivity and of homosexual and heterosexual object choice, like the very young child. We would now take a somewhat different view and would emphasize that the salience of the issue of activity-passivity in the very young child is itself a product of surplus repression.

---

[12]Sigmund Freud, "Instincts and their Vicissitudes" (1915) in Freud, op. cit., 14:134.

Earlier in this century, anthropological research on the Trobriand Islands to the east of New Guinea showed a people with no concepts of linear cause and effect — active subject and passive object — in relationships or chronology. Trobrianders did not describe things that happened as a linear series of causes and effects. Paths were not described as leading somewhere or running to and from, but were simply *at*. While we automatically connect events or shapes with lines to indicate relation and continuity, the Trobrianders did not. For example, to us one of their villages would look like a circle of huts; they described it as an aggregate of bumps. Natural and human actions were thought to be set by tradition. But these traditions were not perceived as determining behavior; they were the pattern that indicated what the action was. For example, Trobrianders did not think of work as having a reward outside of, and subsequent to, the act. "We plan future experiences climactically, leading up to future satisfaction or meaning," writes Dorothy Lee. "None of the Trobriand activities is fitted into a climactic line. There is no job, no labor, no drudgery which finds its reward outside the act. All work contains its own satisfaction." There is no radically separate individual acting in linear time as a performer of actions upon objects and invidiously compared with other individuals in terms of the adequacy of the performance. An activity can fail, but not a person. The "outcome" of any action was already determined within an overall pattern of existence and tradition.[13]

Like that of many other tribal peoples, the language of the Trobrianders represents a different description and a different experience of reality than ours. Modern languages and modern societies are deeply imbued with notions of cause and effect and with dualisms such as subject/object and activity/passivity. This can be seen in the basic sentence structure of Indo-European languages, where there is a subject, verb, and object. Whenever anything happens, someone or something is doing something usually to someone or something.

The split between activity and passivity, so fundamental to our appreciation of masculinity and femininity, is a creation of culture and society out of the original undifferentiated unity of human *being*. Our languages and our historically evolved realities highlight and

---

[13]Dorothy Lee, *Freedom and Culture* (New York: Prentice-Hall, 1959), esp. 89-120. These studies by Lee are based on the transcripts of Bronislaw Malinowski. Although current research by feminist anthropologists calls a number of Malinowski's conclusions and techniques into question, it does not appear that these criticisms would affect his actual records of the spoken language, particularly in the matters discussed here.

IV. The Elements of Family Life

accentuate a split between subject and object and between active and passive.

Freud posited an original "polymorphous perversity" of the infant, that is, a diverse, diffused capacity for sexual stimulation and satisfaction from all of the body and its senses. Similarly, the Trobrianders conceptualized sexuality as "an aggregate of pleasurable experiences,"[14] not as a series of events leading from forepleasure to genital stimulation to climax; and not as one active person *doing* something *to* a passive person. Not even as two persons doing things to one another alternately or simultaneously.

As we mature our sexuality undergoes a biological maturation and eventually is focused on the genitals. But it is culture and cultural factors that require us to undergo a surplus repression of other sexual aims and desire.

Although Freud spoke of an original polymorphous perversity, he made little use of this notion and tended to assume a natural bisexuality structured around an active/passive split. We feel it is more useful to conceive of human sexual potential as a *polysexuality* — a fluid capacity for sexual excitation and discharge through any part of our body including the brain, with its ability to fantasize, and through the various senses, touch, taste, hearing, sight, and smell. As a capacity rather than a fixed entity, sexuality is originally formless and chaotic. The process of biological maturation narrows this original polysexuality somewhat to a greater focus on genital pleasure. It organizes sexuality around genital sexuality. This appears to be in part a biologically natural process that has much to do with the reproduction of the species. It is a part of what Marcuse called the process of basic repression.

But maturation is also a process of internalizing cultural norms. What isn't natural is the surplus repression of nongenital forms of sexual excitation and expression and of the vast range of physical pleasures that we do not even consider sexual. Within the realm of surplus repression, the notion of social construction of sexuality becomes relevant. The repression and suppression of a wide range of sexual pleasure is not necessary either for biological maturation or for the existence of human culture per se.

What is repressed in the process of maturation and the creation of gender in surplus-repressive societies is not simply bisexuality but our constitutional polysexuality. The developing child internalizes the divisions of society: masculine versus feminine, active versus passive, subject versus object, normal versus abnormal, class versus class,

---

[14]Ibid., 119.

race versus race, human versus nature, and so on. A number of things happen simultaneously to our sexuality:

1. Polysexuality is narrowed down to bisexuality, which in turn is narrowed down to heterosexuality or homosexuality (with a heterosexual norm).
2. Polysexuality is narrowed down to genital sexuality with a surplus repression of other potential forms of sexual desire and expression.
3. Through the process described above, superimposed onto the natural division between the sexes are masculinity and femininity — surplus aggression and surplus passivity.

These are all norms. When all goes "well," the construction of our sexuality is a selection of certain traits and desires through which our desires and needs can be satisfied. Our ego has to function in synchrony with our social and natural environment in order that our needs will be met. The process of ego development takes place within the norms, the categories, the requirements of a given society. But none of us is the norm because each of us has a unique developmental experience and a unique constitution. Some of us differ widely from the norm, some little. An endless number of different combinations and permutations exist for the three processes mentioned above. In the end there may be an ideological norm, but there is no "real" normal or abnormal; rather there is a range of sexual beings trying to function and find fulfillment in a surplus repressive society.

We can turn this whole process around and begin to conceive of a liberated sexuality, that is, sexuality in a non-surplus-repressive society. The sexuality free human being will not experience sexuality as either active or passive or even as *both*, but as "an aggregate of pleasurable experiences." Probably genetic and experiential differences among humans will result in the development of idiosyncracies, habits, and preferences, perhaps even exclusions of one kind or another, perhaps even options for celibacy. But these will be individualized expressions of a multivalent eros rather than compulsive responses to fear and anxiety. There will be many different kinds of sexual expression, many different communities and subcultures with different sexual practices, and freedom for individuals to change and move from one way of life to another in the course of a lifetime.

Freud believed that "progress in civilization" required surplus repression. The Frankfurt school (Adorno, Horkheimer, Marcuse), synthesizing the work of Hegel, Marx, Freud, and Weber, translates

309

"progress in civilization" as the domination of nature. In order to conquer nature, human beings had to dominate their own nature, that is, to repress themselves, to transform themselves into instruments of warfare and labor, to split activity and passivity. Passivity was equated with nature and assigned to women. The *domination* of external nature, of internal nature (sexuality), of women, and of passivity in males are all aspects of an integral process of surplus repression.

Nature is now more than conquered; it is laid waste. It is time for what Marcuse calls a "reconciliation with nature." This means the end of surplus repression and the reclamation of the polysexuality of men and women. It means radically new relations of economic, political, and social organization. Neither women nor men can do it alone. New forms of human association involving both sexes and all sexual orientations can be developed only by men and women struggling together. In its present patriarchal form, male sexuality tends to be the *result* of containment and moral (anti-sexual) reformation. New forms of human sexual association must involve not the containment or the moral reformation of the sexuality of males, but its liberation.

Zones of Sexual Conflict

The development of masculinity is the development of a surplus-active character type. This implies a repression of passivity. But in our lives a tension between the two continues to exist, even if this tension is disguised and its forms differ widely. One simple example shows how deeply instilled this tension is. One man we know is concerned about his automatic need to operate in a directive, active fashion in relation to women. Nothing he does seems to reduce the tension of this need. For example, if he walks ahead of a woman through a door or along a narrow path he feels he is leading the woman. If he follows, he is aware of "being a gentleman" he feels he is "letting" the woman go ahead. The active/passive split forms the structure of our psychic reality and determines the categories through which we perceive the world and our activities within it. If such is the tension in so simple an act as walking through a doorway, think of the tremendous forces at work in sexual attraction and relationships.

The analysis in the first section of this article of the repression of polysexuality and the active/passive split can be extended to help us grapple with a number of zones of sexual contradiction and conflict for men in our society. The following are a few comments on two zones of conflict: the sexual objectification of women and heterosexual pornography.

310

Sexual Objectification

Sexual desire always has an object. The object may be oneself, it may be another, it may be of a part of another, or it may be a thing. But as we develop and as our ego builds a capacity to meet our needs in the world around us, desire becomes attached to specific objects. The object may be pleasing for its sight, its touch, its taste, its sound, or its smell.

Insofar as the objects of desire are other people, a few things happen. To some extent, particular attributes are abstracted from the total person. For the newborn baby the breast and the voice of the mother represent the whole. Later in life, whether the object of our choice is heterosexual or homosexual, the presence or absence of certain physical characteristics determines whether we will be sexually attracted to a person. The presence of a vagina or a penis is the bottom line across which all but the bisexual dare not step. In other words the part comes to represent the whole. This tendency of the part to represent the whole is also seen in patriarchal societies in the fanatic psychological and cultural investment of energy onto a relatively small and tender bit of tissue that dangles between a man's legs.

Not only the genitals or breasts but any part of the body can come to represent the whole. Further boundaries of sexual attraction are established by a number of secondary sexual characteristics. The touch of relatively hairless skin will excite one man while the feel of a rough beard will do the same for another. And because we do not go around without clothes, even when it would be comfortable to do so, it is usually these secondary sexual characteristics that become the daily currency that represents the whole. The function of fashion, makeup, body language, and what we do with our voices is to accentuate selectively or subdue a number of these secondary characteristics.

Object love is the basic way that our sexuality is expressed. This is intrinsic to the functioning of the human ego. Our ability to experience a part of the body as representative of the whole results from the inherent nature of the unconscious. But beyond these intrinsic features, the shape that object love takes is a product of particular cultures and personal experiences.

One reason why parts of the body come to represent the whole is the repression of polysexuality. With physical maturation, successive zones of the body become the site of particularly intense physical and psychological excitation. The pleasure of a part (part of one's own body or part of another) captures the pleasure of the whole. This is the result of basic repression. In itself this is not a bad thing, so long as the

311

whole person doesn't disappear in the process. The incomparable thrill and excitement attached to particular parts of our bodies or of another's body need not be denigrated. Male or female, if one can touch one's tongue against a lover's nipple or penis or clitoris and for a brief moment through contact with that protuberance capture the vastness of our desire and of our lover's desire, this is clearly a great conquest for human sexuality. This is part of the grandeur of human sexuality as opposed to the simple reproductive instincts of our animal cousins.

But superimposed on this is the surplus repression of nongenital forms of sexual desire. Surplus repression takes place increasingly as civilization "progresses" and this repression is recapitulated in the development of the individual. The primacy of genital sexuality lowers the value of other forms of sexual desire to the extent that they can only exist as elements of "forepleasure" or become taboo or are not seen as sexual at all. The outcome is the fracturing of the whole person into component parts and processes, some of which come to capture all of the sexual energies and desires of a person.

The effect of all this is pernicious as can be seen in the form taken by heterosexual male attraction to women. Even aside from this fracturing, in a society dominated by men, women become socially defined in terms of their reproductive and sexual capacities. Not defined as the brains or brawn of society, there are its reproductive core, its nurturers, its singing flesh. Combined with the tendency of the unconscious to represent the whole by a part, certain physical properties not only are objects of individual sexual desire but are invested with the society's whole definition of women.

The nature of this process and its effects on male sexuality can best be understood by using the psychoanalytic notion of "fixation" and the psychoanalytic and Marxist notions of fetishism. The fixation — an intense preoccupation and focus on certain activities or parts of the body — is a result of a developmental process in which interest and attention have moved from one thing to another and in which earlier delights are incompletely repressed. Some fixations have to do with particular pleasurable or frightening experiences or objects that simultaneously provide some form of sexual satisfaction and that give reassurance in the face of some anxiety or fear.[15]

Fetishism is the endowment with sexual significance of an inanimate object or a part of the body not normally considered an erotogenic zone. When this reaches neurotic proportions, a person

---

[15] See Otto Fenichel, *The Psychoanalytic Theory of Neurosis* (New York: W.W. Norton, 1945), 65-6, 327.

does not experience sexual excitement except as focused on, or in the presence of, that object. This sort of fetishism is almost entirely a phenomenon seen among men. Psychoanalytic investigation suggests that the fetish usually has the unconscious significance of the penis. The symbol, usually developed from childhood experiences, is a response to castration anxieties, in particular the perception that women do not have penises. A part of the woman's body or apparel — classically feet, hair, shoes, or an article of clothing — takes on the significance of the "missing" penis. The *unconscious* "discovery" of this missing penis (that is, of the object so highly valued in patriarchal society) reduces "castration" anxiety — that is, the fear of losing activity and power.

Although Freud discussed fetishism and fixation as neurotic symptoms, the concepts can be used (particularly in conjunction with the discussion in the first section above) to understand "normal" masculine sexuality. Although this discussion could apply with only a few modifications to homosexual masculine sexual desire, we will limit ourselves here to heterosexual attraction.

The heterosexual male fascination with women's bodies represents a number of things. There is a continuing desire to reexperience our first object of love and physical contact. In fact, our original model of object love was with a mother from whom we were inseparable. The fascination is insatiable. It is as if we cannot get enough of the object of desire. In the language of the unconscious this desire to take in, to "get enough of," is ultimately based on experience at the breast. (The process is partially different for a woman because she is that object of primal desire both in her developed ego and in her physical being.)

The fascination with women's bodies also relates to castration anxiety. The sight of a woman confirms that one is a man. If the root fear of male psychological development is castration, then it follows that as adults we will be fixated on the object of fear, those beings who are without penises. In a society of male domination, the common object (women's bodies) of a common fear (castration) of the dominant group (men) becomes a generalized fetish. As pointed out above, to be a sexual object is not necessarily objectionable. But here the sexual object becomes sexual fetish.

There are two final aspects of this fixation. One is a fascination with what the male has repressed in achieving masculinity. The surplus repression of passivity takes with it the repression of softness and receptivity. Part of the fetishistic fascination with the female body is with what we have lost.

In a society with a heterosexual norm, the fascination with the object of sexual desire takes the form, for the majority of men, of an in-

313

tense, eroticized, ever-present attraction to women. The development of masculine sexuality, with its prerogative of an active sexual orientation, makes this attraction socially acceptable, indeed, socially celebrated except in the most sexually repressive cultures and subcultures. It is the social norm for men to be sexual actors. In itself there is nothing wrong with that; the problem has to do with the repression of a corresponding sexual activity for women, the loss of men's passivity, and the distortion that sexual attraction and sexual activity undergo in a surplus repressive, patriarchal society. But in spite of these things, one component of what is commonly called the objectification of women is the celebration of sexuality and sexual attraction.

The fixation on and fetishism of women's bodies is a socially constructed psychological form. As a social norm, the objectification of women's bodies represents a progressive distancing from the total personality of the woman. The tendency of patriarchy to reduce women to reproductive and sexual functions is mirrored on the psychological level in the construction of masculinity. The tendency of the unconscious to represent the whole by a part is frozen and the parts *become* the whole. The appreciation of women takes the frozen form of the appreciation of women's form. First women are reduced to their reproductive and sexual functions, and then they are reduced to either one or the other. This is the familiar dualism of mother and whore. And in between, the category of virgin is so highly charged in part because it is the only point where the dualism is overcome, or better, it is the point which symbolizes both potentials.

Finally, as a socially mediated fixation that is abstracted from real women, the fascination is with a mythologized being, a collection of parts, a fiction, a mythical part that represents a mythical whole.

In short, what is loosely called men's objectification of women is actually the combination of a series of factors in apparent contradiction. The components so far identified are:

• men's object love for women and the human capacity to represent the whole by a part;
• fascination with what we have repressed (passivity, softness, receptiveness);
• the constant (and not always wanted) intrusion of erotic stimulation into our daily lives;
• confirmation of our own manhood;
• a degradation of women through the fixation on and fetishism of women's bodies and the *reduction* of the whole to some component parts.

314

Voyeurism and Pornography

In a capitalist society, a society of commodity production and acquisition, objects of desire become commodities. Wherever it can, capitalism produces objects for sexual consumption and objectifies the subjects of sexuality in order to sell other products.

Marx spoke of the fetishism of commodities. Capitalism breathes illusory life into things. Commodities — the products of social production — are "endowed with a life of their own, [they] enter into relations both with each other and with the human race." The social relations among humans that produce commodities appear, not as a "social relation between persons and social relations between things."[16] The fetishism of commodities is in part a process of mystification. But as Norman Geras points out, it is also a process of domination.[17] In a society organized not just around but *for* commodity production, the products of human labor control the lives of the producer. "The definite social relations between men themselves...assume here, for them, the fantastic form of a relation between things."[18] Commodity fetishism is mystification, but it also reflects the real life domination of humans by commodities.

This combination of mystification and domination is seen in pornography. Pornography is a prevalent commodity within which sexual objectification is expressed. Like any commodity, pornography presents strong elements of mystification and domination. A form of sexual representation, pornography — by the nature of the commodity form but also as a result of the fixation and fetishism described above — represents distorted and mystified forms of the objects it depicts. But it also accurately portrays the real-life domination of women by men.

As an artifact of a capitalist, patriarchal society, pornography captures a number of the conflicts and contradictions of that society. In an exaggerated and stylized manner, the function and form of pornography depict and portray the conflicts surrounding sexual objectification described above.[19] Of the many questions that relate to

---

[16]Karl Marx, *Capital*, trans. Ben Fowkes (New York: Vintage, 1977), 1:165-6.

[17]Norman Geras, "Marx and the Critique of Political Economy," in Robin Blackburn, ed., *Ideology in Social Science* (London: Fontana/Collins, 1972), 287.

[18]Marx, op. cit., 165.

[19]We are indebted to various contributions in the collection *Women Against Censorship*, edited by Varda Burstyn (Toronto: Douglas and McIntyre, 1985), for a number of the observations in these paragraphs. Particularly relevant to the issues addressed here were the essays by Sara Diamond, "Pornography: Image and

the issue of pornography, one interests us here. Why is heterosexual pornography so attractive to so many men? Our emphasis will be on forms of visual representation.

Pornography is a brash statement of male power, of the sexual availability of any woman to any man, of women defiled and·even dismembered. As a statement of fetishism, of mystification and domination, pornography reflects and reinforces negative images of women.

The great majority of pornographic images contain this content, and when they do not, the immediate context (the magazine, the porn theatre) and the social context induce these meanings. These contexts are ones of male collusion (in public or in private) in the oppression of women.

These meanings and contexts seem to be one reason for men's attraction to pornography. But in a sense the answer so far begs the question. Why, after all, should these meanings be attractive to men?

As we saw above, the construction of masculinity is inseparable from the repression of bisexuality and passivity. Masculinity is inseparable from a projected, adored, despised, and feared femininity that exists as its opposite. As discussed by Kaufman elsewhere in this volume[20], masculinity is a fiction in the sense that it is not what it pretends to be: biological reality. It is the ideology of patriarchal, surplus-repressive society captured in the personality of the individual. Because of its real-life distance from biological reality (that is, maleness), masculinity is an elusive and unobtainable goal. From early childhood, every male has great doubts about his masculine credentials. Because one facet of masculinity is the surplus repression of passivity, the confirmation of masculinity can best be found in the trials of manhood (war, fighting, or more refined forms of competition) and in relation to its mirror opposite, femininity. The portrayal of femininity, that is, women in a passive, dominated position in relation to men, is a relatively easy confirmation of one's own masculinity. One reason why the images of pornography are so appealing is that they confirm that one is masculine, which confirms, in gender-based social orders, that one is male.

All this is another way of saying that the fascination with pornography results from the fixation, not only on the object of sexual

Reality" (40-57); Myrna Kostash, "Second Thoughts" (32-9); Ann Snitow, "Retrenchment Versus Transformation: The Politics of the Antipornography Movement" (107-20); and Varda Burstyn, "Political Precedents and Moral Crusades: Women, Sex and the State," (4-31).
[20]Michael Kaufman, "The Construction of Masculinity and the Triad of Men's Violence," in Beyond Patriarchy.

desire, but also on the object of fear, and this fixation has to do with "castration" anxiety. Needless to say, the viewer of pornography is not conscious of this anxiety.

But while all pornography (immediately or in its context) includes this form and function, it also contains elements that stand in contradiction to sexual repression. The contradiction is to sexual repression both in the sense of social standards and in the sense of the repression of passivity and polysexuality.

In terms of sexual repression in the immediate, social sense, pornography contains elements of sexual celebration. Ann Snitow and others have pointed out that pornography sometimes includes (along with its oppressive features) elements of play, of "thrilling (as opposed to threatening) danger," of defiance, of childlike freedom. For many, particularly the young, pornography is one of the few sources of sexual information.[21] It has become a rather stale joke to say that *Penthouse* is beginning to resemble a gynecology text, but where else can most boys or young men see what a vulva looks like: of course the sexual information is distorted (particularly the information on sexuality as distinguished from anatomy, although even this is partially distorted), but we are talking here about the contradictory aspects of pornography.

Another part of the attraction of pornography is the attraction to what is socially taboo. Of course the taboo material is expressed in the language of what is not taboo: male dominance and female subservience. But again we are dealing with contradictory images.

Understood in terms of the surplus repression of passivity and bisexuality, pornography has a number of attractive features to men. We noted above that one feature of the male objectification of women is a fascination with what we have lost in the process of masculine development: passivity and receptiveness and all their associated features — softness, the feeling of being loved and adored, and so forth. Pornography represents a yearning for and fascination with those lost qualities. This is true both in what is depicted and in the action of viewing pornography.

The sexual pleasure of looking is one of the most basic of passive-receptive sexual activities. Freud, primarily an observer of adults rather than infants, read back onto infant sexuality from the repressed memories of adults and children. But observe a baby. She or he spends long moments staring, taking in the world, wrapped up in the pleasure of visual sensation. Along with activities of the mouth, seeing is a primary way that the baby takes in the world.

---

[21]Snitow, op. cit., 114-16.

IV. The Elements of Family Life

Viewing pornography, like the act of voyeurism, is a regression, a regression to an earlier moment, to an aspect of our polysexual disposition that has undergone surplus repression. "The human child," writes Fenichel, "goes through a prolonged phase of dependence [which] is gradually supplanted by activity; the memory of it, however, always admits of the recurrence of a regressive longing for substituting the earlier receptivity for activity."[22]

And it is the male, in male-dominated societies, who has undergone a surplus repression of passive aims. This repression does not destroy the passive aims (for they are intrinsic to the organism), but it forces them into disguised, distorted, derivative challenges. Pornography not only presents a passive, receptive object to marvel at; it offers a form of sexual pleasure in which men can be passive and receptive (to the image, to the object of desire). In a real-life situation, with real contact with a woman in her full subjective, directive, active presence, passivity would arouse all sorts of anxieties. And of course part of what allows the passive pleasure of viewing pornography is that the object is often portrayed as passive and unthreatening. In terms of the repression of bisexuality, because the focus of our passive attention has no penis, it is not threatening. In terms of social power, the viewer also retains his dominance.

Of course the pornographic image varies widely. Much pornography shows an active, sexually aggressive, vampish woman. Some shows the subjection of men: the classic photo of a man under her stiletto heel. Both images provide a safe portrayal of female activity in the context of male passivity, either as viewer or as an object in a picture. But as noted by Mariana Valverde, in this case the presentation of female activity and male passivity is just the surface appearance. "In fact what is going on is that the male camera eye is creating a version of female active desire (as an evil form of desire, vampire-like), and then proceeding to appropriate that representation of female desire. This is best seen in so-called lesbian porn, which is unintelligible unless we understand that masculine desire is intent on appropriating not just women's bodies but women's own active desires."[23]

For some men passivity in face of the pornographic picture can still be threatening, so insecure is their purchase on maleness, so great is the unconscious tug of repressed passivity or repressed homosexuality or both, so great is their surplus aggressiveness. In this case pornography is pleasurable only if it portrays the active and explicit

---

[22]Fenichel, op. cit., 468.

[23]Mariana Valverde, personal communication. We would also like to thank her for her comments on an earlier draft of this paper.

domination of women through images of bondage, torture, even murder. In the language of the unconscious, the dismemberment of the women (the dismembered, that is, "castrated" object) is the only thing that can quiet one's anxiety and increase one's self-esteem.

There are many economic and social reasons for the current proliferation of pornography. But what is the psychological basis of this trend? The desires expressed by looking at pornography are insatiable, not only because sexual desire itself is insatiable, but because pornography in itself cannot provide an integrated expression of passive and active sexual aims. Pornography proliferates as profit-makers see they have an insatiable market. The more you look the more the passive, receptive urges are restimulated, looking becomes ever more intense, and the aims become ever more insatiable. Viewing pornography is ultimately an unfulfilling activity. It leads to greater frustration and to grater tensions between activity and passivity. And all this leads to the increasing tendency for pornography to portray sadistic actions.

It becomes sadistic because looking provides insufficient mastery of thc object of desire. Part of the pleasure of looking is a regression to the omnipotence of childhood. The visual taking in of the object is not only passive: it is a mastery of the object because by looking, knowledge is acquired. For the unconscious, knowledge is power. As noted above, the viewer of pornography is looking for more than a pleasurable object of desire: he is looking for confirmation of his masculinity and confirmation that what he fears cannot be true, that castration is not a possibility. These are very contradictory desires, which in themselves fuel the insatiable desire. As long as the object of view remains partially unknown, the male childhood castration fears are not confirmed. The more clothes are removed and the more is seen, the more there is that has to be seen to find out that what he fears (castration) is not really true. At a certain point nothing more can be shown: already women's legs are pulled apart at ridiculous angles to show "everything." And thus the only thing left is to increase one's surplus aggressiveness (as a defense against the much feared equation of passivity with castration) and to pull the woman apart — figuratively in depictions of explicit domination or literally in snuff movies.

The proliferation of pornography is also what Marcuse called a "repressive desublimation." Over the past fifteen years there has been a certain freeing of instinctual energies occasioned by the spread of effective means of birth control, by the rise of feminism and women's activity, by the development of gay and lesbian pride, by the rejection of lifelong monogamy and premarital virginity, and by the rejection of the most blatant forms of social sexual repression, particularly in the advanced capitalist countries. But in our societies that nevertheless remain authoritarian and surplus-repressive, these released energies are channeled into distorted and unsatisfying forms in order to perpetuate the overall regime of surplus repression.

Since pornography functions to meet a number of contradictory needs and demands created by a society of surplus sexual repression and commercialization, the mere censorship of pornography will do next to nothing to reduce the degradation of women in all its myriad forms. Viewing pornography does not create the problem, it represents and in some sense helps perpetuate the problem. And the problem described here is not only the degradation of women but also the surplus repression of the full range of sexual desires, activities, and aims. The root of the problem is a patriarchal, profit-oriented, commodity-producing, surplus-repressive culture that represses polysexuality and superimposes masculinity and femininity onto the dualism of activity and passivity; such are the ultimate sources of the sexual degradation of women and the surplus repression of all humanity.

The struggle against such an imposing problem has many fronts. One is the struggle against sexist representation and spectacle. As representations of a problem they codify, symbolize, make tangible, and help propagate the problem. Strategies that demonstrate opposition and rage are far different from state censorship. This opposition must be combined with sexual education that is antisexist and prosex (without, of course, socially imposing sexual activity as a mark of normality). Active opposition and education must be combined with support for alternatives on the visual and personal fronts.[24]

Pornography represents the problem. But in a very distorted way it also represents the solution. In a distorted and oppressive manner it demonstrates that men's passive aims do not disappear, that polysexual urges do not disappear, that there remains in men a deep longing for the free and full expression and celebration of sexual desire. To say the least, pornography is not this full expression and celebration. But what do we expect from a patriarchal society of generalized commodity production?

And this leads us back to the essential problem. The solution to the problems presented in the discussion of objectification and pornography are to be found in the broad struggle against a patriarchal, surplus-repressive, class society. The prehistorical foundations of these structures are scarcity and the struggle to tame nature.

---

[24]See Varda Burstyn, "Beyond Despair: Positive Strategies," in Burstyn op. cit., 152-80, for a discussion of some aspects of the struggle against forms of sexist representation and the sexual exploitation of women.

For the first time in human history humans have the capacity to step beyond societies of scarcity. This certainly does not mean a future where machines continue to run amok and environmental pillage continues along its perilous course. Of necessity, the struggle will be an integrated one against all forms of sexual, class, gender, and human oppression informed by a keen ecological sensitivity. The goal is liberation and integration: social, political, economic — and sexual.

D. Having Children

While contraception has been practiced throughout human history (Gordon 1976), women's control over reproduction greatly increased in the 1960s, with the widespread availability of "the birth control pill." American women gained easy access to abortions after their legalization in 1973; despite their continued illegality here, middle-class women in central Canada were increasingly able to procure them (Collins 1982), while working-class women and those in more remote regions await the aftermath of the 1988 Supreme Court decision to gain access to abortion facilities. This generally increased availability of the means of contraception coincided with a growing desire on the part of women and men to plan when to have children and how many children to have. Today, most people feel that they have choice about whether or not and when to have children.

Having children is complicated, however, because in this society raising children is no easy matter. Consequently, one must be very careful about characterizing the situation as one of "choice." For instance, it is still hard for many women to imagine living their lives without children: the social identification of womanhood with motherhood has a dogged persistence, despite apparent changes in gender roles. But socialization and social norms are not the only things that push women towards motherhood. Perhaps more important are the limited options women face with respect to occupations — aside from motherwork — that bring recognition and genuine satisfaction (see the Ehrenreich article). This is not to say that there aren't strong positive reasons for having children: the personal rewards are such that millions of generations of women have done so, despite knowledge about contraception. Nevertheless, women today are also aware that the cost of having children is significant because child care is still largely a privatized responsibility. The barriers that stand in the way of women combining a career and child rearing are considerable. So, most women have children, but face the need for an individual solution to the problems posed by child-care needs and the necessity for most women to work outside the home.

Meanwhile, the process of conceiving and bearing a child has acquired a complexity that is new in the past decade. "In vitro" fertilization, involving the fertilization of an egg outside the womb and its subsequent implantation back in the womb, testifies not only to the aggressiveness of medical science but also to the strength of the desire for children on the part of some couples: the process is painful, costly, and uncertain, with worldwide success rates averaging around 13 percent (Eichler 1988: 284). The technique raises the possibility for parents to hire a woman to carry "their" child, and also allows selection of the sex of the child. "Surrogate motherhood" — involving the purchase of a woman's body to bear another couple's child — is now occurring, amidst tremendous controversy. The article by Gena Corea (a chapter from her book, *The Mother Machine*) develops a provocative criticism of surrogate mothering. The other issue of importance to child bearing is the way in which child birth itself is organized in our society. Only recently, advocates of home birth and the use of midwives are combating the long history of increased medical control over the delivery process. While the question remains about the medical implications of home vs. hospital delivery for the health of the child and the mother, it is clear that highly medicalized deliveries (i.e., those involving much technology and the liberal use of drugs) adversely affect women's adjustment to the baby and her new role (Oakley 1980).

References

Collins, Larry.
1982. "The politics of abortion: trends in Canadian fertility policy." *Atlantis* 7, 2: 1-20.
Eichler, Margrit.
1988. *Families in Canada Today*. Second Edition. Toronto: Gage.
Gordon, Linda.
1976. *Woman's Body, Woman's Right*. New York: Grossman.
Oakley, Ann.
1980. *Women Confined*. Oxford: Martin Robertson.

Suggested Readings

Eichler, Margrit.
1988. *Families in Canada Today*. Second Edition. Chapter 8. Toronto: Gage. An impassioned criticism of the new reproductive practices by a Canadian sociologist.
Petcheskey, Rosalind.
1985. *Abortion and Woman's Choice*. Boston: Northeastern University Press. A very intelligent discussion of the history of fertility control, current contraceptive practices, and the issue of abortion.

Surrogate Motherhood:
Happy Breeder Woman*

Gena Corea

Tom, a Moslem from Lebanon, married Jane, an infertile American woman. Jane wanted to adopt a child but Tom did not. He wanted to father his own. While the Vietnam war raged, he got an idea. Maybe he could find a woman who would agree to be inseminated with his sperm, bear the baby and turn it over to him and Jane. He knew many men were dying in Vietnam, leaving widows with children, and thought one of those widows, needing money for her children, might do it. "The Lord intended women to have children and I thought maybe one would want to do what came naturally and maybe help somebody else out while helping herself and her family," Tom recalled (Keane, 1981, pp. 20-30).

In September 1976, Tom and Jane contacted attorney Noel Keane in Dearborn, Michigan, to discuss Tom's idea. After that meeting, they read a newspaper account of a man who had hired a blond office worker to bear a child for him. The last of his family line, the California man wanted a child to carry on his name. So he had placed an ad for a woman in *The San Francisco Chronicle* ("Childless husband with infertile wife wants test-tube baby. English or Northwestern European background. Indicate fee and age.") The office worker had just borne him a daughter for a fee of $7,000.**

Keane now knew what to do for his clients. He ran ads for a surrogate mother in several Michigan college newspapers. Seeing the ad, a reporter called, interviewed Tom and Jane and wrote a story. In response to the ad and the newspaper story, two hundred people wrote to Keane. (One was a man volunteering the use of his 27-year-old girlfriend. "She smokes cigarettes but she doesn't drink or take drugs," he wrote.)

Keane eventually found a surrogate (breeder) for Tom and Jane. Moreover, he had queries from new clients who wanted breeders and, soon, an invitation to appear on Donahue, the national television show. After that appearance, his business accelerated as viewers who

---

* Excerpt from *The Mother Machine* by Gena Corea. Copyright © 1985 by Gena Corea. Reprinted by permission of Harper & Row, Publishers, Inc.
**The man stated that he still wanted a son. "I can't afford it right now," he said, "but I may try again."

wanted to use a breeder or to be one called him. He made many more appearances on Donahue as well as on other programs, continuing to do so long after the thrill of television celebrity had worn off. "I now went on shows like Donahue for a simple reason," he wrote. "Other than placing classified ads, the only effective way of finding surrogate mothers was through television and news articles" (Keane and Breo, 1981, p. 173).

Keane began to refer to the sale of breeder women as a "movement," a "cause," and to himself as a "pioneer" and a "champion" of breeders, whom he called "surrogate mothers."

In the next few years, others quickly jumped into the act, setting up some sixteen surrogate mother, or breeder, businesses across the country. Many were launched by physician-attorney teams, others by those who spoke of their backgrounds vaguely. One had previously worked for "a major insurance company." Another told me that he had made motion pictures, designed buildings and served as a consulting engineer for missile programs.

The firms opened up in: Louisville, Kentucky, 1979; Philadelphia, Pennsylvania, Hollywood, Los Angeles, and Malibu, California, 1981; Chevy Chase, Maryland, Denver, Colorado, and Tulsa, Oklahoma, 1982; and Columbus, Ohio, Tempe, Arizona, Springfield, Massachusetts, New York, New York, Lincoln, Nebraska, Norfolk, Virginia, Northridge and Costa Mesa, California, 1983. By May 1983, an estimated seventy-five to one hundred babies had been born to breeder women nationwide.

John Stehura, president of The Bionetics Foundation, Inc., which helps arrange surrogate pregnancies, fears that hiring surrogates is too financially burdensome for middle-class American couples. But this burden may be lifted. He thinks the price paid to women for reproductive services will come down once surrogate motherhood is more commonplace. The industry can then go to poverty-stricken parts of the country where half the current $10,000 fee may be acceptable, he told me in an interview.

The development of embryo transfer technology may bring the price down still further. Today's surrogate mother contributes half the baby's genes through her egg. Consequently, those hiring a breeder want her screened carefully for physical, intellectual and racial traits. But once it is possible to have what Stehura calls an "authentic" surrogate — a woman into whom an embryo is transferred and who herself contributes none of the child's genes — clients will find the breeder's IQ and skin color immaterial.

The genetic makeup of the woman is "much more important right now because she contributes 50 percent of the child, but in the future, it's going to be zero percent," Stehura said. He is monitoring the progress of embryo transfer technology so that once a dozen or so babies have been created, he will be ready to step in with his service.

Another surrogate firm run by attorney William Handel in North Hollywood is also planning to arrange the transfer of embryos into surrogate mothers. Noting that he keeps in contact with practitioners in the reproduction field, Handel told me in 1982 he was certain experimental work in this area was currently going on at IVF clinics connected with hospitals.

...the Monash University IVF program in Australia has already established one viable pregnancy by transferring an embryo conceived with a donor egg. This is one procedure that could be used with surrogate mothers.

Once embryo transfer technology is developed, the surrogate industry could look for breeders — not only in poverty-stricken parts of the United States, but in the Third World as well. There, perhaps one tenth the current fee could be paid women, Stehura replied: "Central America would be fine." It is "inevitable" that the United States go to other parts of the world and "rely on their support" in providing surrogates, Stehura thinks. Comparing the United States to the city and Central America to the country, he pointed out that "the cities are always supported by the country."

An "authentic" surrogate from the Third World won't even need to be very healthy. "The mother could have a health problem which could be quite serious," he said. "However if her diet is good and other aspects of her life are O.K., she could become a viable mother for a genuine embryo transfer."

Using Third World women as surrogates, Stehura maintained, would benefit them because the women would earn money with which to raise their other children.

Media helped create the phenomenon of surrogate mothering (often termed surrogate "parenting," a word choice that obscures the fact that we are talking here only of female breeders). "The true fathers of the surrogate-mother story, perhaps, are the Phil Donahue Show and People magazine," Keane wrote.[1]

---

[1]NBC's *America Alive* was one show that helped promote the practice, staging one of television's cheaper moments. Keane brought a client couple with him onto the show and NBC insisted that, as a precondition of their appearance, a potential surrogate appear with them. It was staged as a dramatic moment, a sort of "This Is Your Life," Keane recalled. The volunteer surrogate, a beautiful blond woman, came on stage to confront the couple who had never seen her before. The impression was given that she would be the husband's breeder. However, some time later, off-camera, she stated that she had a heart murmur and declined to be impregnated.

IV. The Elements of Family Life

The pattern set early on has continued through the present. Those who, like Keane, have an economic motive for promoting surrogate motherhood are generating the news about it. They go on television and explain why trafficking in breeder women is noble. What sociologist John Dollard wrote of defensive beliefs used to justify oppressive practices applies as well to the rationale these proponents offer for their businesses. This rationale stresses a partial and inadequate element in the situation (the suffering of infertile couples) and obscures a clear vision of the actual social forces. Certain facts about surrogate motherhood are highlighted in media discussions while others are buried.

Although entrepreneurs in the surrogate industry emphasize the unhappiness of infertile couples in justifying their practices, in fact not all are confining their advocacy of surrogate motherhood to the infertile. Sometimes the "empty arms" the firms are attempting to fill belong not to barren women, but to single men, or fertile women, or couples with adopted children. Some proponents of surrogate motherhood are making a conscious political decision not to highlight these other potential employers of surrogates at a time when they need public approval of the procedure in order to get laws passed legalizing it.

Keane annoys some of his colleagues by being quite open about the other employers of breeders. He wrote: "Single men are increasingly seeking surrogate mothers as a solution to having children without romantic entanglements." For men who want a chid but not a wife, surrogate motherhood offers a "dramatic option," Keane believes. Now a man can go out and have a child any time he wants. "And if he prefers to have a boy, there's a 75 to 85 percent probability we can arrange it by separating the sperm before insemination," Keane claimed (Krucoff, 1980).

Keane says he works with single men now. At least two breeders have already birthed children for separated or divorced men (Parker, 1982; Donahue, #02033). Single women are also seeking breeders, Keane maintains.

He sees nothing wrong with using breeders for women who are perfectly fertile and he may do so in the future. If a fertile woman chooses to have children by a breeder, Keane is willing to represent her if he already has enough surrogate mothers for the infertile.

Alan A. Rassaby, research fellow in the Centre for Human Bioethics at Monash University in Melbourne, also defends the use of surrogates for career-related reasons, stating that a busy female executive's or model's need for a surrogate may be just as great as that of an infertile woman. Unfortunately, he added, one can expect the career woman to be discriminated against in times of "scarce resources" (the "resources" being women's bodies).

Unlike Keane, other surrogate entrepreneurs frown on the use of surrogates for fertile women and require proof that clients are married and that the wife cannot bear babies. Because they are more selective than Keane and exercise greater control over surrogates and clients, some of Keane's competitors imply that their businesses are more reputable than his. They are critical of the fact that he is willing to accept a wide variety of clients — single men,[2] transsexuals (one, to date), and, in the future, fertile women. They are not criticizing Keane's ethics, but rather his poor political strategy for winning public acceptance of, and favorable legislation regarding, surrogate motherhood.

As I write, there are no laws in the country on surrogate motherhood. But there are statutes against baby-selling and these statutes could cause surrogate firms trouble. Until laws are passed legalizing surrogate motherhood, any public indignation aroused over the practice could threaten the emergence of this "whole new sector of the economy," as *The New York Times* referred to it (November 1980). Adoption agencies, the Catholic church and Concerned United Birthparents (a group of women who, years earlier, had given up their babies for adoption and suffered greatly from it) have opposed surrogate motherhood at public hearings.

"Keane will take anybody who walks in the door," William Handel, of Surrogate Parent Foundation, told me. He disapproved: "It's kind of a hard thing to say morally, because these are not necessarily my morals, but considering his position, I think that simply for political and P.R. reasons, you've got to play it very conservatively and very safe. It's difficult to take potshots at someone who's doing this for a married couple who cannot have children. But it's easy to criticize someone who's doing it for a gay single male, which he takes on all the time." (In fact, Keane says he has never dealt with homosexuals but "would consider them on a case-by-case basis" [Miller, 1983].)

Handel said he was not morally opposed to using surrogates for gay men. Two such men, physicians with high incomes in a stable relationship, asked him to arrange a birth for them. He declined. He is

---

[2]Harriet Blankfield, head of the National Center for Surrogate Parenting, also accepts single men as clients. She feels she would be open to a discrimination suit if she did not. "Our policy is that we will accept a couple or a single male provided that person or persons pass the screening of the potential parents," she said in an interview, adding that some single men had already been accepted.

trying to get some favorable legislation on surrogate motherhood passed, he explained, and so he runs his business conservatively.

"I told them it was a political choice I was making not to take them on. Chances are that the two of them would have made phenomenal parents."[3]

In Michigan, state legislator Richard Fitzpatrick, who introduced the second legislation in the country on breeder women, made "a conscious decision for political purposes" to apply his legislation only to married couples and not to single men seeking breeders. He did this, he stated, because "it is a highly sensitive and controversial issue enough as it is without getting into other aspects. Even those who strongly support it understand that the most important thing right now is to get the concept of surrogate parenting into the law" (Gaynes, 1981).

In addition to the fact that infertile couples are not the only ones purchasing the services of surrogate mothers, there is another fact media discussions of surrogate motherhood bury: adoption agencies do have children that infertile couples could adopt. Those who defend the use of breeder women mention, in passing, that these children are not the "right kind," and therefore couples have little alternative but to hire (white) breeders.

"While there are plenty of babies to adopt, they are not, quote, 'desirable' babies, if that's the right word to use," Dr. Michael Birnbaum of Surrogate Mothering, Ltd., in Philadelphia told me. "There are plenty of babies of mixed racial background. There are plenty of babies with handicaps, but most couples want a perfect baby if they're going to adopt it, and those kind of babies are hard to come by."

Harriet Blankfield of the National Center for Surrogate Parenting in Chevy Chase, Maryland, told me that most of the infertile couples she personally knew were not interested in adopting an older child or a handicapped child. She added: "When it came to wanting a child — no matter how desperately they wanted a child — they didn't

---

[3]Dr. Michael Birnbaum of Surrogate Mothering Ltd. thinks that within five to ten years, his firm might change its policy restricting the use of surrogates to married couples. "At this point now," he told me in an interview, "we recognize that we're kind of a trailblazer. This is a new idea and I think that we have a responsibility to those who will come after us to set the right tone in the beginning. To open this up to single couples or to a guy who wants his own kid or whatever — and we've had a couple of requests like that — I just don't think is appropriate. Give us five or ten years to work out the ethics, if that's the right word, and then I think it might be open to anybody who wants to participate. But I think in the beginning, when you've got a new idea in medicine, you've always got to be a little conservative until you do work the bugs out."

want to take what they would consider second-best....That may not be a good term but that, verbally, is how they felt emotionally."

I raise this issue not to argue that these couples should adopt special-needs children (feeling as they do, it is likely that both they and the children would be harmed by such an arrangement), but rather to point out that the desire to nurture a child for its own sake is not their prime motivation. They want only a child that meets certain specifications.

The child here is viewed as a commodity. Dr. Richard Levin of Surrogate Parenting Association in Louisville has referred, perhaps jokingly, of the baby as a "product" and Keane refers to the child as an "investment." (Keane wrote: "How can the husband be sure he is indeed the father of his 'investment' short of isolating the surrogate from other male contacts?" [Keane, 1981, p. 265]. Levin said that surrogates in his program must agree to paternity testing to ensure that the baby was fathered by his client and not the surrogate's husband. "We only take the real product," he said [Donahue #04150].)[4]

A main function of the genetic, medical and psychological screening of surrogates is to ensure quality control over the product the breeders will produce. "Do you get to choose blue eyes, brown eyes?" television host Phil Donahue asked Keane. "As a matter of fact, they [the couple] do," Keane replied. "They take portfolios that are available on each surrogate and it lists the characteristics." Keane adds that they can and do find out the surrogate's IQ.

The view of baby-as-commodity came into sharp focus in the Stiver-Mallahoff case. In January 1983, a surrogate mother delivered a defective product — a baby with a small head, probably indicating mental retardation — and all parties involved initially rejected the baby and announced it would be put up for adoption. The baby had a strep infection and the man who contracted for the child's birth — Alexander Mallahoff of Queens, New York — instructed the hospital to "take no steps or measures to treat the strep infection or otherwise care" for the child, according to an affidavit filed by Lansing General Hospital in a successful effort to secure a court order allowing it to treat the child.

---

[4]In view of such language, the questions one attorney poses are relevant: "Is the contract in which the host has agreed to carry the fertilized egg and turn over the child in the nature of an adoption or a kind of predelivery contract for a commodity? Does dealing in embryos in this fashion result in a sort of 'futures' market that should be controlled by a government agency something like the U.S. Securities and Exchange Commission?" (Schroeder, 1974).

IV. The Elements of Family Life

On the Donahue television show, Ray Stiver of Lansing, Michigan, husband of the surrogate, Judy, charged that Mallahoff "asked the hospital to put this baby to sleep, and then he asked my wife to start over and make a new one for him. It's just like buying a defective piece of merchandise." Mallahoff denied that he had done this.

Mallahoff contended that he was not the child's father and blood tests proved him right. Under intense and degrading questioning on national television as to exactly when she had had intercourse with her husband following the artificial inseminations, Judy Stiver said she had abstained for at least thirty days after, but had not been told it was necessary to abstain before, when the pregnancy might have occurred. The Stivers, after learning on camera that Ray was the child's father (the blood test results were called in to the television show), said they would take the baby. Mallahoff had said that if the child proved to be his, he might put him up for adoption but that if it had been normal, he would have taken the baby.[5]

In those cases in which a married couple is involved, why would an infertile wife agree to her husband's artificial impregnation of another woman? There are several explanations....

Moreover, for many women, the alternatives to childrearing look dismal. One woman who obtained a child through a surrogate explained: "All I ever wanted from life was to get married and have children." Then she had a hysterectomy at 25 (Keane, 1981, p. 58). She had worked in banks but could not imagine doing that for the rest of her life. "There's got to be more," she said, believing that "more" was a child. (Similarly, Lesley Brown, mother of the first test-tube baby, had worked in a factory wrapping cheese and could not bear the prospect of spending the rest of her days in the factory.)

Sociologist Hanmer believes there is another motive: it is socially structured so that, for many women, the only way she can get affection is to have children. "Children love you," she observes. "It's actually possible for women to have love relationships with children. It's extremely difficult to have them with men."

Fear of abandonment can be another motive for a woman agreeing to the insemination of a surrogate. Consider Tom and Jane, the pseudonymous clients of Noel Keane seeking a surrogate. Jane explained that she had wanted children ever since she was a little girl who played with dolls. Her husband came from a Lebanese culture

---

[5]I compiled this list of foreground questions from television programs concerning surrogate motherhood and from the writings of Keane, George Annas and Barbara Katz.

where children were prized as a symbol of manhood and her unsuccessful attempts to conceive a child had shaken her marriage "to its foundation" (Keane, 1981, p. 13). When a woman like Jane "chooses" to hire a surrogate mother, then we must ask what happens to her if she does not choose this. It may mean that her husband will leave her.

Fear of social ostracism and emotional and economic abandonment does seem to have motivated the West Indian woman who traveled by bus from New York to Detroit in an unsuccessful attempt to hire a surrogate through Keane. Married to a Nigerian, she would soon be moving to his country. She feared that, under pressure from his relatives, her husband would divorce her for her failure to bear him a child (Fleming, 1978).

We watch a series of women appear on television to explain that they want to be surrogate mothers, that they are giving the gift of life and helping infertile couples, and that we, the public, need to be educated as to the nobility of the transaction between couple and surrogate. We like these women. They are kind and intelligent. Lawyers, psychiatrists and physicians appear on television with the women and present what they call a discussion of the issues raised by surrogate motherhood:

Should the breeder be married or single? Should she have had other children or none? Should the couple meet the breeder? What kind of counselling should be done with the couple? The surrogates? What records should be kept? What if the breeder refuses to give up the baby? Can the surrogate be forced to have an abortion if the fetus is found to have Down's syndrome? Can the natural father require the breeder to undergo an amniocentesis? Can the breeder sue the father for damages arising from the pregnancy? If the couple divorces before the baby is born, who is responsible for the baby? Is the child illegitimate? Can the sperm donor deny the breeder an abortion? What if the couple dies before the child is born? If a breeder is being paid for bearing a baby, does control over the child revert to her in the wake of missed payments?

These questions keep our eyes focused on the foreground. But, as with all these technologies, there is something more going on than an attempt, motivated by compassion, to fill the empty arms of childless couples with babies. That "more" is in the background.

In surrogate motherhood, the woman is again seen as the vessel for a man's seed, just as she was under Aristotelian/Thomistic biology. According to Aristotle, woman merely supplied matter which the active male principle formed and molded into a human being. Men played the major role in reproduction while woman served as the passive incubator of his seed. That Aristotelian biology was back became clear to me when, in 1980, it was revealed that Joseph Orbie, a single, 30-year-old man, was looking for a surrogate mother who would bear him a son. He planned to hire a sex predetermination researcher who would attempt to remove the X sperm from his semen and inseminate the breeder with the remaining Y sperm (Donahue, #07290).

...producing sons for men has been a prime function of woman. Now, through technology, men may someday be able to employ her for his purpose with minimal human involvement. Like the surrogate who would lay on the examining table at a sex predetermination clinic to be inseminated with Orbie's processed, supposedly male-engendering sperm, women can serve as mere vessels for the incubation of men's sons. Though they supply the eggs (at this point, still) and nurture their babies within their bodies, their connection to the child is not acknowledged. They are to disappear after the child's birth, leaving the man as the parent. In fact, under proposed legislation in Michigan, the child of a surrogate mother would be considered not her child, but the offspring of both the man who provided the sperm and the man's wife.

That the surrogate mother is viewed as a vessel for the man's seed is evident from the language consistently used to describe her. The women are referred to as inanimate objects — incubators, receptacles, "a kind of hatchery" (Schroeder, 1974), rented property, plumbing — and they have come to speak of themselves in this way.

Though the babies born to surrogate mothers to date have all been their own children, conceived with their own eggs, the women often maintain that they are not. Some of the surrogate applicants Dr. Parker interviewed asserted that their babies belonged to the adoptive couples and they denied the possibility that they might feel any loss when they gave up their infants. Among the reasons the women gave for not expecting any emotional involvement with their babies, Parker reported, were "I'm only an incubator," and "I'd just be nest-watching" (Parker, 1983). A psychotherapist who worked with Handel in California said the attitude of many surrogates she interviewed amounted to: "I'm not the mother" (Krier, 1981).

One surrogate mother told me: "I never looked at the baby as my baby. It was their baby. I just felt like I was doing like my chickens do. I was just hatching it and all the other chickens would take care of it."

References to the woman's body as property are common. For example, Sanford Katz, professor at Boston College Law School and chair of the American Bar Association's Family Law section, commented: "I wouldn't consider this [surrogate motherhood] buying a baby. I'd consider this buying a receptacle" (*NYT*, 1980, May). A

Corea: Surrogate Motherhood

Western Journal of Medicine article referred to the surrogate as "the woman attached to the rented womb" and to her child as "her tenant" (Karp and Donahue, 1976).[6]

Advocates of surrogate motherhood often bring up the biblical story of Abraham, Sarah and Hagar like a trump card, implying that the practice is ancient, God-endorsed and, therefore, moral.

> Now Sarah Abraham's wife bare him no children; and she had an handmaid, an Egyptian, whose name was Hagar. And Sarah said unto Abraham, Behold now, the Lord hath restrained me from bearing: I pray thee, go in unto my maid; it may be that I may obtain children by her. (Genesis 16:1-2)

Sarah allowed Abraham to take concubines for his sperm to be reproduced in the world, Raymond explains. Today the Judeo-Christian tradition that a woman was valued insomuch as her ability to reproduce, has become medicalized so that it is incarnate in technology. This enhances the ethic that if a woman cannot reproduce naturally, Raymond adds, she must do it in some other way. Now the woman might take the egg of another woman into her body or — with surrogate mothering — not even bear the child.

"It is almost like allowing your husband to take a concubine so that his issue may be reproduced in the world," Raymond said. "That is, to me, the overriding ethnic: that his issue may be reproduced. It's the same old story, only this time it's made much more possible by biomedicine."[7]

---

[6]In an editorial on the case of Denise Thrane, a surrogate mother who refused to give up her baby to James and Biorna Noyes, the couple that had contracted with her for it, *The New York Times* commented that Baby Thrane was "residing in a rented womb." It added: "Mr. and Mrs. Noyes may have lost the lease on the womb; their lawyer seems something less than a crack real estate agent; and Mrs. Thrane is claiming her property" (NYT, April 1981). (Thrane kept her baby.)

[7]Two points here. 1. According to surveys, many Korean women today would allow their husbands to take a concubine if they were sonless — from 41 to 68 percent of rural women and 25 to 27 percent of Seoul women, depending on the study (Williamson, 1976, p. 95). 2. It might be argued that AID is for women what surrogate motherhood is for men. But when a married woman is artificially inseminated with donor sperm, the overriding ethic is not that her issue be reproduced in the world. It is an attempt to produce a child who appears to outsiders to be the husband's issue. This is done by matching the sperm donor as closely as possible to the husband.

While there is a centuries-long tradition asserting the centrality of a man's issue there is no comparable tradition concerning a woman's issue. We do not now, and never have had, complex social, legal and economic structures that place the

IV. The Elements of Family Life

It is often asserted that the person benefiting from the surrogate mother's "gift" is the infertile wife, not the husband. For example, Alan Rassaby asserts that satisfying the desires and needs "of a number of women" would be the primary benefit of surrogacy (Walters, 1982, p. 104).[8] Despite this reversal, the statements of Keane, Levin and their clients make it clear that Raymond is right: the overriding ethic is that the man's issue may be reproduced in the world.

Take the case of surrogate Elizabeth Kane (a pseudonym). She told a television audience that she was willing to accept any health risks involved in the pregnancy. "I felt that strongly about giving a baby to another woman that needed one. It was a gift that I had to give at any cost." Earlier she explained: "I had wanted to have another baby for a women for ten or twelve years because I had always felt...an empathy for women with empty arms" (Donahue #12170).

But the woman who received Kane's baby did not have "empty arms." She and her husband had a three-year-old adopted son. The husband explained that they sought a surrogate because another adoption would have been difficult and because "we wanted, if possible, to have a child that was biologically related to me." He *thanked* his wife for "suggesting and initiating and supporting me [my emphasis] in doing this thing." Asked how she thought Kane could give up the baby, the wife, in her reply, indicated that the child was really for her husband: "I think she was just doing it as a gift of love, you know, for mankind. You know, she had some feelings as to how a person, like, in my situation would feel not being able to have a child and knowing how my husband wanted one so deeply."

Alice Baker (pseudonym) will also be bearing a child for a couple who is not childless. Baker, a 30-year-old woman in Alexandria, Indiana, with four children of her own, was attempting, at the time of our interview in December 1982, to become pregnant for a couple who already had an adopted girl. (She had earlier borne a baby for a couple who adopted a child during her surrogate pregnancy.)

---

quality of a man's life in serious jeopardy if he fails to impregnate his wife and ensure the reproduction of her issue. For example, we have no history of laws stating that a woman may divorce her husband if he fails to impregnate her but that he has no right to divorce her on grounds of infertility.

While a single or lesbian woman is inseminated, that insemination takes place within a specific social context, one which has never held, through its laws, customs or ideology, that a woman's issue must be reproduced in the world.

[8]Rassaby, mentioning the Genesis story, also refers to Sarah who "sought to satisfy her desire for maternity through her maid-servant Hagar." As though Sarah were laboring under no imperative to provide Abraham with his issue!

Levin's statements too reveal that the surrogate "gift" is more to the husband than the wife. Conceding that childless couples could adopt an older or handicapped child or a child of another race, he adds: "But these people want a child related to them, who will carry on their [i.e., the husband's] bloodline. The women often say, 'I want my husband's baby even if someone else carries it'" (Krucoff, 1980).

Keane, too, revealed that the underlying ethic is that a man's issue might be reproduced. When his policy of screening the surrogate mother but not the father was criticized, he observed: "Well, I'll say every man has a right to reproduce himself" (Donahue #02033).

The clients of breeder firms also make it clear that Raymond's analysis is on target. For example, Mrs. Wallace, a woman whose fertility had been destroyed by an IUD-induced infection, said that a surrogate mother was her only hope for her "to have my husband's child" (Donahue #04150).[9]

Sometimes the wife already has children by a previous marriage but, because of a subsequent loss of fertility, cannot provide her second husband with children of his own. One woman, after bearing two children, had a hysterectomy and later remarried. She and her husband sought a surrogate. After meeting the surrogate, the wife said: "I felt so bad that I couldn't give my husband a child — but now I can" (Krucoff, 1980).

Keane's clients included couples in similar situations. Keane relates the story of a male client who was obsessed with having a child while his wife, who had diabetes and kidney problems, seemed unenthusiastic. It was a full-time job for her to care for herself. Despite that, the husband insisted that he wanted to hire a surrogate mother. About two weeks after the couple contacted Keane, the wife left her husband. Keane reported: "She left a note saying that she could not stand the pressure being put on her to have a child" (Keane, 1981, p. 138).[10]

---

[9]Other examples abound in Keane's book. With a tone of amusement, Keane tells the story of Olive May who was 60 years old and obsessed with providing a child for her husband who was 40 (p. 139). Also see the stories of Lorelei and John, p. 167, and Stefan and Nadia, p. 221. Another client (not described in Keane's book) explained: "It may sound selfish, but I want to father a child on my own behalf, leave my legacy. And I want a healthy baby. And there just aren't any available. They're either retarded or they're minorities, black, Hispanic....That may be fine for some people, but we just don't think we could handle it." (Annas, 1981).

[10]For example, see stories of Bridget and Bill, p. 45, and Nancy and Andy, p. 180 (in *The Mother Machine*).

IV. The Elements of Family Life

Since no laws exist on surrogate motherhood, it is uncertain whether courts will hold the contract between a man and breeder woman valid. Perhaps they will not; statutes against baby-selling seem to prohibit paying women to bear babies.[11]

When Surrogate Parenting Inc. opened in 1979 in Louisville, it stated that Kentucky law allows the payment of a fee to a surrogate mother, an interpretation of the law that state attorney general Steven Beshear brought a civil action to enjoin Richard Levin's corporation from engaging in its business but has not pressed the suit since then. Surrogate Parenting Inc. has continued operating and even expanded into the international field, matching American breeders to couples in France, Canada, Mexico and Australia.

Those running surrogate businesses want laws passed explicitly legalizing their practices. Some are working closely with legislators to write those laws. "We're actively involved with Assemblyman Mike Roos in developing a surrogate parent law," attorney William Handel of Surrogate Parent Foundation in North Hollywood, California, told me. He added later: "We helped write the legislation so it's got everything we want in it."

The first legislation on surrogate motherhood was introduced to the Alaska house of representatives in April 1981. Nine states are now considering such legislation.[12] To date, none has passed any. A number of proposed laws constitute a massive move against women's civil rights. They would establish unprecedented medical and state control over the woman's body, would attempt to make the contract between man and woman binding, and would give the sperm donor a greater right to the child than the mother. For example, proposed legislation in Michigan would give the sperm donor and his wife full rights to the child immediately upon birth.

---

[11]Some argue that hiring a breeder is not baby-selling because the father is biologically related to the child and because at the time the contract is signed, the mother is not pregnant and so is under no compulsion to provide for her child. But in 1981, attorney George J. Annas pointed out that the only two legal decisions rendered on this to date rejected this argument. "Both a lower court judge in Michigan and the attorney general in Kentucky view contracts to bear a child as baby selling," Annas reported (Annas, 1981). In 1983, the Oklahoma attorney general said that state law forbids a surrogate from taking money to bear a child for adoption by someone else (SPN, 1983, Oct). In the only decision to date at all favorable to the surrogate industry, a Kentucky court ruled in October 1983 that payment for surrogates does not violate adoption law because the payment is for termination of parental rights. An appeal has been filed with the Supreme Court of Kentucky (Brozan, 1984).

[12]The states are: Michigan, California, South Carolina, Kansas, Minnesota, Oregon, New York. (Representatives in Florida and Pennsylvania are researching the area.)

The "binding contract" provision is one for which Keane and other proponents of surrogate motherhood have argued. Keane believes that women who sign a surrogate mother contract ought to be legally bound to give up their babies.

Under one draft of proposed legislation in Michigan, if a woman changes her mind, the judge of probate court holds a hearing. While the question is being decided, the rights to the child remain with the sperm donor. Unless the woman could demonstrate "by clear and convincing evidence" that her child's best interests would not be served by terminating her parental rights, the judge would enforce the contract and order the baby given to the sperm donor and his spouse. (In keeping with the notion that the baby belongs to the man who furnished the sperm, the mother would be legally prohibited from attempting to form a mother-child relationship with her baby.)

Such provisions in draft legislation worry Jalna Hanmer: "When they can legally force a woman to give up the child, then the way opens up to horrible abuse." Annette Baran, author of *The Adoption Triangle*, has a similar concern. A woman cannot know in advance how she will feel as she progresses through the pregnancy and the child's birth, Baran points out, so she must retain the right to change her mind. "You cannot indenture her and her unborn child before the fact," she said in an interview. Some surrogate mothers and applicants have never birthed a child and may be surprised by the feelings pregnancy arouses in them.[13]

One version of Michigan legislation is based on the notion that sperm donors and surrogate mothers are fulfilling comparable functions and ought to be treated comparably under the law. Under this legislation, the natural father (who furnished the sperm) and his spouse would be considered the legal biologic parents just as under the Michigan artificial insemination statute, the natural mother and her husband would be considered the child's parents.[14] Explaining the rationale behind this draft of his bill, Representative Richard Fitzpatrick

---

[13]Of 118 surrogate applicants Parker interviewed, 24 percent were single and never married. Of twenty-five women who actually became pregnant, five were single. Thirty to 40 percent of the breeders hired into the North Hollywood program are single or divorced.

[14]This is an example of what Dr. Parker calls the "consent-intent" concept of legal parenthood. He explains that, under this concept, the legal parents could be the married couple who voluntarily give informed consent to a certain reproductive procedure with the intent of assuming parental responsibility for the child. The "consent-intent" concept of parenthood would include situations involving sperm donors, egg donors and what Parker calls "womb donors," women who bear and deliver the baby (Parker, 1982).

told me: "We believe that philosophically if a man has the right to sell the use of his reproductive organs as we currently have in the law at this time — that a man can be compensated for the donation of his sperm — certainly a woman should be able to be compensated for the donation of utilization of her reproductive organs. So we go into the law and snuggle up as close as possible to all the regulations on artificial insemination in relationship to parentage, inheritance, and all that." Allowing men to sell sperm but forbidding women to sell their eggs and wombs would constitute sex discrimination against women, Fitzpatrick and others argue.

I asked feminist leader Andrea Dworkin to comment on the argument that sperm donors and "womb donors" were comparable and that forbidding women to sell their bodies constituted sex discrimination.

"I suppose if one swallows a seriousness pill and tries to take the argument on its own terms, you'd have to point out the difference between an ejaculate of the body and the body itself which seems to me something that an ancient Greek philosopher might have pointed out — so ancient is that mode of logic," she said. "It's the difference, for instance, between tears and the eye. You could collect tears in a glass but that's different from taking someone's eyes."

She continued: "there is no analogy between the sperm of a man and the womb of a woman. There is none. They are not analogous in any way. To underscore it: Not physiologically, not ethically, not reproductively, not morally, and by no means are they analogous in terms of their meaning to the integrity of the person. What this argument underscores is that men have not yet grasped that women are not baby-making machines, and that women's bodies are not commodities best suitable to be sold. There seems to be no notion of personhood and integrity that applies *a priori* to women in men's minds. Otherwise it [surrogate motherhood] would be unthinkable."

When a woman volunteers to be a breeder, advocates of surrogate motherhood assert that the woman's act is an expression of her individual will. She wants to do it; she is a free person; what right has the state to interfere with her will?

"No one is forcing a woman to enter into this contract," a spokeswoman for Assemblyman Mike Roos said in response to the objection that surrogate motherhood was reproductive prostitution. "She enters into it of her own free will for whatever reasons she wants. It's anything but prostitution. This is a woman's free choice to use her body any way she wants to. And that's what freedom is all about."

340

Corea: Surrogate Motherhood

Feminists like Andrea Dworkin do not agree that that's what freedom is "all about." They argue, rather, the legislators and those in the human breeding business are developing a specious notion of what freedom and equality are and are applying it in their proposed legislation.

Dworkin notes "the bitter fact that the only time that equality is considered a value in this society is in a situation like this where some extremely degrading transaction is being rationalized. And the only time that freedom is considered important to women as such is when we're talking about the freedom to prostitute oneself in one way or another."

She observes that the "freedom for women" argument is conspicuously absent in the speeches of establishment people when they are talking about other aspects of a woman's life. "You never hear the freedom to choose to be a surgeon held forth with any conviction as a choice that women should have, a choice related to freedom," Dworkin said. "Feminists make that argument and it is, in the common parlance, not a 'sexy' argument. Nobody pays any attention to it. And the only time you hear institutional people — people who represent and are part of the establishment — discuss woman's equality or woman's freedom is in the context of equal rights to prostitution, equal right to some form of selling of the body, selling of the self, something that is unconscionable in any circumstance, something for which there usually is no analogy with men but a specious analogy is being made."

In response to the assertion that some women want to be breeders, Dworkin argues that the social and economic construction of the woman's will is what is at issue. This will is created outside the individual. In both prostitution and surrogate motherhood, Dworkin writes, the state has constructed the social, economic and political situation in which the sale of some sexual or reproductive capacity is necessary to the survival of the woman. It fixes her social place so that her sex and her reproductive capacity are commodities.[15]

Proponents of surrogate motherhood insist that the woman's will is interior, somehow independent of, and unaffected by the culture in which she lives. When a woman sells the use of her vagina (as a prostitute) or her womb and ovaries (as a surrogate mother), they assert that these are acts of individual will.

"This individual woman is a fiction — as is her will — since individuality is precisely what women are denied when they are defined and used as a sex class," writes Dworkin. "As long as the issues of female sexual and reproductive destiny are posed as if they are resolved

---

[15]For a fuller discussion of this point, see Dworkin's powerful *Right Wing Women*.

IV. The Elements of Family Life

by individuals as individuals, there is no way to confront the actual conditions that perpetuate the sexual exploitation of women. Women by definition are condemned to a predetermined status, role, and function" (Dworkin, 1983).

One of the actual conditions that perpetuates the exploitation of woman is her economic status. In the United States, women earn 59 cents for every dollar men earn, a proportion that remains constant regardless of the woman's employment or educational level. Most women are confined to the female job ghetto — that handful of jobs in which the pay is low and there is little or no mobility. Working women, typically, are: secretaries, typists, file clerks, receptionists, waitresses, nurses, bank tellers, telephone operators, factory workers, sales clerks in department stores or cashiers in supermarkets, elementary school teachers, beauticians or cleaning women (MacKinnon, 1979). Those women who manage to avoid job ghettos encounter sex discrimination in salaries, promotions, benefits and/or sex harassment (Pearce and McAdoo, 1981).

Within such an economic world, it is hardly surprising that money motivates women to become breeders. Remember that Tom, the man who sought a breeder, was looking for a Vietnam war widow in need of money to raise her children. One man searching for a surrogate mother described the ideal surrogate as a woman who had lost her husband. "Maybe she's struggling to make ends meet and could use the money," the unidentified man told the *Detroit Free Press* (2/4/77). In fact, when the call went out in 1980 for Australia's first surrogate mother to deliver a child for $10,000, one applicant was an 18-year-old widow left penniless after her husband was killed in an accident. Another was a 23-year-old whose husband was terminally ill and who said she urgently needed the $10,000 to provide some security for her child. More than half the ninety applicants were divorced or single. They ranged in age from single 17-year-olds to a widow of 44, and included a former prostitute (ST, 12/14/80).

Dr. Howard Adelman, a psychologist who screens breeder candidates for Surrogate Mothering Ltd. in Philadelphia, told *Ob/Gyn News*: "I believe candidates with an element of financial need are the safest. If a woman is on unemployment and has children to care for, she is not likely to change her mind and want to keep the baby she is being paid to have for somebody else" (Miller, 1983).

Dr. Philip Parker indeed found that slightly more than 40 percent of the surrogate applicants in his study were unemployed or receiving financial assistance.[16]

Rich women, Keane wrote, "are not likely to become surrogate mothers" (Keane, 1981, p. 236). When Keane placed ads for surrogate mothers in newspapers, he received responses from Pocatello, Idaho, to Jacksonville, Florida, and most of the women said they need the money (*Chicago Tribune*, 12/4/77). There were plenty of women willing to reproduce for payment. At that time, Keane was under the impression that his clients could pay a fee to the surrogate. But when, after receiving a judge's opinion in March 1977, he realized that they could not, the number of volunteers dropped to almost zero (*Detroit News*, 5/4/78).

Keane could not get enough breeders if he could not pay them. He brought a lawsuit to have the payment of a fee to a surrogate mother declared legal. He lost the first round of his suit in 1980 when Wayne County (Michigan) Circuit Judge Roman S. Gribbs sided with the prosecuting attorney. That attorney had argued: "the fact remains that the primary purpose of this money is to encourage women to volunteer to be 'surrogate mothers.' Plaintiffs have initiated this lawsuit because few women would be willing to volunteer the use of their bodies for nine months if the only thing they gained was the joy of making someone else happy by letting that couple adopt and raise her child. Thus, contrary to plaintiffs' exhortations, in all but the rarest situations, the money plaintiffs seek to pay the 'surrogate mother' is intended as an inducement for her to conceive a child she would not normally want to conceive, carry for nine months a child she would normally not want to carry, give birth to a child she would not nor-

---

[16]Additional information from Parker's study of more than fifty surrogate applicants: almost 60 percent were working or had working spouses. Their incomes (actual 1980 or projected 1981) ranged from $6,000 to $55,000. (We cannot tell from the study if most incomes were closer to the $6,000 or to the $55,000.) The applicants' education ranged from "well below high school" to one woman with a bachelor's degree. Almost 20 percent of the women did not complete high school. About 55 percent either graduated from high school or received a GED. (Here, as elsewhere in his surrogate studies, Parker fails to break the figure down. If 50 percent received a high school equivalency diploma and only 5 percent actually graduated from high school, that would tell us something about the social and economic power of these women.) About 25 percent had some post-high school college courses, business school or nursing school (Parker, 1983).

mally want to give birth to, and, then, because of this monetary reward, relinquish her parental rights to a child whom she bore."[17]

Some entrepreneurs in the surrogate mother business are sensitive to the criticism that poor women, having few opportunities to earn money, would have no choice but to become breeders. Handel, for example, says that this criticism is unfounded for he does not accept indigent women into his program. The women must have good incomes before he will accept them. However, he also noted that his company is getting middle-class and working women who, with their husbands, are using the money to set up a fund to send their children to college or to make a down payment on a house.

One surrogate mother I interviewed told me she and her husband had used the money she had earned through child-bearing to keep their small trucking business going during hard times. "We own semis [tractor trailers] and right now is a bad time with Reagan," she told me. "So we used the money to help keep the trucking company going."

Judy Stiver of Lansing, Michigan, who became a surrogate for Alexander Mallahoff of Queens, New York, is an inventory clerk earning less than $5 per hour and her husband is a part-time bus driver. Stiver said she became a surrogate in order to pay off her family's bills and, possibly, take a vacation.

Who knows what pressures are being exerted and will be exerted on even middle-income women to contribute to the family income in hard times by breeding? The pressures might range from extremely subtle and nonverbal to violent. Women may themselves suggest, even enthusiastically, that they help out the family by breeding for payment, but this does not mean that in a society that defines women by their reproductive function and consistently underpays them for their labour, that the women are acting of their own "free will."

Furthermore, that indigent women are not being accepted into many surrogate programs now, as asserted, does not mean they will not be accepted in the future. As we have seen, some of the entrepreneurs are being cautious about how they run their businesses in

---

[17]Keane himself had observed: "I am sure that without the money, the response would be very few" (Shepherd, 1981). Parker, who interviewed Keane's surrogate applicants, found that of the first 125 women, about 90 percent said they required a fee to bear babies for clients. "They related a need for the money but the degree of need varied from a feeling that the money would be used to pay bills to a more urgent need for funds" (Parker, 1983).

Keane appealed Judge Roman S. Gribbs' decision. An appellate court in Michigan ruled that the couple, while having a right to use a surrogate, had no right to compensate her. The U.S. Supreme Court refused to hear the case (Brozan, 1984).

the early years when public opposition to it could prevent them from getting laws passed legalizing it. Once the laws are on the books, it will no longer be necessary to labor under self-imposed restrictions as to who can be accepted into the program. Stehura already sees it as "inevitable" that entrepreneurs will come to use poor women as surrogates and pay them as little as one tenth the current low breeder wage.

So a woman's economic status helps construct her "will" to sell her womb. So does her emotional structure. It has been engrained in women that one of the most important roles we play is tending to all others, fostering their growth and happiness. Their needs and difficulties should be our major concern and dealing with them should take precedence over other claims, including any "selfish" needs of our own. Of course nurturing is a highly valuable activity. What is wrong here is that only women — not all human beings — are supposed to engage in it and engage in it to the exclusion of other valuable activities. This is what social worker Margaret Adams terms "The Compassion Trap" (Adams, 1971). Under the social pressure to be nurturing, one single element of woman's psyche has hypertrophied while other qualities have withered.

Pharmacrats searching for surrogate mothers or egg donors exploit woman's emotional structure. They appeal on the media for compassionate women to come forward and "give the gift of life" to a sorrowing couple. They call these women "special" and praise them as selfless, loving, sensitive and big-hearted. (Even though they may, in the very next breath, call them "rented wombs" or "receptacles.") When women are called upon to relieve the suffering of others by sacrificing — even prostituting — some part of themselves, many leap at the chance out of what Adams calls the "overriding need to feel useful and wanted in a social system that in other respects does not accord women much, if any, value or opportunity for really significant participation."[18]

The social manipulation of women's psychological resources, Adams argues, has much in common with the exploitative view of women as purely sexual objects. "What I am talking about is an exactly similar process in which not physical sexual attributes, but psychological ones, are subject to similar prostitution and misuse."

The manipulation of women's psyche is an exploitation difficult to resist because it is so hard to change our emotional structure.

"The worst thing you can do to someone is mess with the core of her in some way and I think that is what is going on in the appeal to

---

[18]I am applying Adams's insights to surrogate motherhood. She does not write about this phenomenon in her article.

345

surrogate mothers," a friend told me. "You violate or exploit a person's sense of herself. I think it's the most horrendous crime against another person. Murder is a crime against the physical self but there is also a long list of crimes committed against the selfhood of women and this is one of them."

Besides a woman's economic status and her emotional structure, another condition that perpetuates her exploitation and shapes her "will" is her social status. No matter what her individual talents or her unique character might enable her to do, this social system fixes her reproductive function as primary. As bioethicist Alan Rassaby observed in a different context, society places a greater premium on a women's childbearing role than it does on her employment prospects. Given that childbearing is the prime function for which women are valued, it is not surprising that some women only feel special when they are pregnant and assert that they love reproducing. This enables some men to use what I call the "Happy Breeder" argument in explaining why women are willing to be surrogate mothers. It is comparable to the "Happy Hooker" justification for prostitution.

In a study of Keane's surrogate applicants, Parker found that some women who had already borne babies saw surrogate motherhood as a chance to earn money while enjoying a pregnancy. Parker reported that the applicants "described a feeling regarding their [previous] pregnancy that varied from a tolerable experience to the best time of their life such that they wanted to be pregnant the rest of their lives. This latter group felt more content, complete, special, adequate, and often felt an inner glow; some felt more feminine and attractive and enjoyed the extra attention afforded them" (Parker, 1983). (Since, in his study, he does not give the number, I asked Parker exactly how many of the 124 applicants had said they felt this way. He said he did not have the specific numbers and that if I were going to quote him, I could use "the term 'some.'" He added later that "a few" women said, "I feel better when I'm pregnant than when I'm not pregnant.")

In defending surrogate motherhood, other men such as Laurence E. Karp, M.D., and Roger P. Donahue, Ph.D., have asserted that some women just love to be pregnant. Much has been made of the possibility of exploiting poor women through surrogate motherhood arrangements involving embryo transfer, Karp and Donahue write. They, on the other hand, worry about denying women a livelihood through surrogate motherhood. A few women have called their offices to volunteer their services if such embryo transfer schemes should ever be carried out.

"They state that they love being pregnant and would arrange to always be in this condition if it were not for the matter of having to keep the babies," Karp and Donahue write. "They think that hiring out their uteri would be a fine way to make a living. On reflection it seems inconsistent to categorically deny such women this kind of livelihood, while we permit and even encourage people to earn money by such dangerous means as coal mining, or racing little cars around a track at 200 miles per hour" (Karp and Donahue, 1976).

Rassaby has a similar concern. Without denying that some surrogate mothers may be the victims of an unfair social order, he asserts that some women may prefer exploitation to poverty. He believes it would be "counterproductive" to deny them the "option" of exploitation (Rassaby, 1982, p. 103).

"If men generate the ethic — which I firmly believe they are doing in this case — that women are really happy when they are pregnant, that's nothing new," ethicist Dr. Janice Raymond commented in an interview. "They've said that for ages. Now they are just saying it in a different context and are zeroing in to apply it to a specific population of women — in this case, surrogate mothers."

Raymond makes a crucial point about the social construction of a woman's will: men are controlling not only what choices are open to women, but what choices women learn to want to make. Women may have a will to be pregnant, she added, but we have the potential to want other things as well. This potential is kept largely unfulfilled.

"Not only do women not go into certain things, but they don't even have the motivation to want to because the choices have been so limited," she said. "That is what I see as most drastic: not the fact that our choices are being controlled, but that our motivation to choose differently is also being controlled."

While men like Karp and Donahue assert that some women really love to be pregnant, this becomes a self-fulfilling prophecy that closes off all the other choices a woman might make. Pointing to the social forces in the background generating a woman's desire to be pregnant-all-the-time, Raymond asked: "Why aren't men — all these reproductive biologists — saying in the same breath, 'Women love to be doing science,' or 'Women love to be doing philosophy'? You never hear that. They keep beeping out those messages, 'Women love to be pregnant,' and limiting the choices for women. And women will fulfill those choices."[19]

---

[19] Of course many women do, have and always will resist their conditioning in a male-supremacist society. Nonetheless, it is nearly impossible to overestimate the effect this conditioning has on restricting, in a thousand different ways, the lives of women.

IV. The Elements of Family Life

Because the social control over a woman begins at an earlier stage than that of the woman's actual decision-making, because it begins by controlling her motivation to choose, people can argue that women freely decide to be surrogate mothers. When television host Phil Donahue raised the question of women being used as baby factories, Janet Porter, a surrogate volunteer, replied: "But a woman still has to choose to be a surrogate mother, you know. She's not gonna be hogtied and have it done to her, you know." Donahue responded: "Yes, that's true."

Both ignore the sophisticated level of control the dominant class exerts over women.

Dworkin has a final comment on this issue of "free choice." The notion that the selling of the body is the highest expression of what freedom means in a capitalist society, she said, is a grotesque application of laissez-faire principles of capitalism. The argument that a woman has an absolute right to sell her body as a commodity and that that is a cherished freedom, is also grotesque.

She added: "These are very bizarre ideas of freedom. If you read in philosophy and in history and in all of these very important male disciplines, nothing is more important than the question: What is freedom? There is never a very simple answer to it. So how come the answer is so simple when the question is asked about women? And how come it's so functional? You have all these philosophers writing tomes about what freedom is, and I think any student of philosophy will agree that no one definitively answered the question. How come with women it amounts to some answer that has to do with buying and selling?"

Parker is conducting a long-term study of breeder women. Since a researcher's values can affect the way he designs and interprets a study, Parker's values, about which he is explicit in his writings, bear scrutiny. He defends financial gain as a legitimate motive for bearing a child. There is no evidence that breeding for the purpose of earning money has any adverse consequences — psychologically, medically or legally — he asserts. Financial reward from "a grateful husband" may even be motivating some wives to bear children now, he speculates. Parker implies that both situations — wives and breeders bearing babies for money — are appropriate. Some feel that money as a motivation for producing a child degrades the whole process of procreation, he observes, and comments: "I can see no reasonable justification to force this moral tenet on the rest of society." His basic position is stated succinctly: "I believe that a married couple's use of a surrogate mother to bear the husband's biologic child falls into the category of a fundamental right." (He does not name the belief system under which one has a fundamental right to use a woman's body and spirit for one's own purposes, but I can accurately describe it as patriarchal.)

Parker defends the surrogate motherhood business by invoking his studies: "Also, I have so far found no evidence to support the notion that surrogate motherhood with or without a fee, leads to serious adverse psychological consequences and therefore (as some people feel) should be prohibited" (Parker, 1982).

I suspect Parker sees no "evidence" of harm for a reason similar to that which Thomas Aquinas cited in maintaining that it is appropriate for men to kill and eat animals. Aquinas argued: "There is no sin in using a thing for the purpose for which it is" (Singer, 1975). And animals (imperfect beings) supposedly exist for men (more perfect beings) to use. Parker, with his patriarchal values, may see no harm in using a woman for the purpose for which she supposedly is intended: reproduction. (Remember what Tom, the surrogate seeker, said: "The Lord intended women to have children and I thought maybe one would want to do what came naturally.") It does not seem to Parker to injure the integrity of a woman when she sells her body, her self, as a commodity.[20]

---

[20]Women applying as surrogates are required to undergo interviews and counselling with psychiatrists like Parker, and Parker even argues that this requirement should be enforced by law. What kind of counselling are women getting from mental health professionals who hold the common patriarchal view of them as commodities and as baby machines and who see their freedom and equality in terms of their right to sell their bodies? Parker would like to bring many more mental health professionals into the surrogate motherhood industry. Among the numerous occasions he suggests for seeking "psychiatric input" into the process are:

— A need to judge the competency of a surrogate mother who refuses to relinquish her child
— A custody battle between the biologic father and the surrogate mother
— A need to psychiatrically evaluate surrogate mothers who allege that psychiatric damages resulted from the paid-breeding experience, an allegation perhaps made in claiming workman's compensation. (Parker places quotation marks around "resulted," apparently indicating suspicion of any such allegation.)

He recommends that regulatory legislation be passed requiring surrogate applicants to submit to psychiatric interviews which, he states, will help ensure that the women give competent, voluntary, informed consent.
If Parker's recommendations were taken seriously, numerous employment opportunities would be created for psychiatrists practicing an increasingly discredited profession. Among the many books that have critiqued psychiatry and revealed sexist values within it are: Phyllis Chesler's *Women and Madness*, Mary

IV. The Elements of Family Life

Besides studying the surrogate mothers, Parker counsels them. Generally, in each surrogate firm, a psychologist or psychiatrist like Parker is involved, as well as a lawyer and a physician. (The lawyer draws up the contract. The physician examines the breeders to determine their health and fertility, inseminates those chosen, and frequently sees them for monthly check-ups until the obstetrician takes over.) The psychologist screens the breeder candidate for mental suitability and sees the pregnant breeder for counselling roughly on a monthly basis. Handel's program is slightly different. "We're the only group in the country that insists on group therapy for the surrogates," he said. (Dworkin commented: "It's like they're not going to take a chance that a woman might have an independent thought.")

Parker believes that the pregnant surrogate should be offered special prenatal classes specifically tailored for surrogates and that support groups should be organized for pregnant and postpartum surrogates. Noting that women in one support group formed a closely knit community, he added: "This feeling of camaraderie and sharing complemented and tended to support the empathetic feelings toward the parental couple." This does suggest that the benign view of breeding-for-pay is reinforced in these groups.

Annette Baran, co-author of *The Adoption Triangle*, appeared on a television program with one professional operating a surrogate business. "His attitude is that he's got them in therapy during the whole period," Baran commented. "They recite in chorus, 'We're doing something great for somebody else. We're carrying somebody else's baby.' It's really a brainwashing affair. He plays violin strings and talks about these poor [infertile] people with their only alternative today."

Those in the surrogate industry assert that the women are "giving the gift of life" and placing a baby in the "empty arms" of a childless woman. Surrogates appearing on television say the same thing. Janet Porter, for example, explained her willingness to be a surrogate in terms of her "need to give." She was happy with her own child and wanted to give to others the joy she had. (While sperm vendors rarely assert that they are selling their sperm because they want to help the infertile, surrogate mothers often say that compassion motivates them. However, about 90 percent of surrogate applicants Parker interviewed required a fee to bear a baby [Parker, 1983]. A "need to give" was not enough motivation.)

Daly's *Gyn/Ecology*, and Thomas Szasz's *The Myth of Mental Illness and The Manufacture of Madness.*

Corea: Surrogate Motherhood

Again and again in interviews, the surrogate mothers repeat the same statements: "I'm filling the empty arms of a childless woman. I'm giving a gift of love, the highest gift anyone can give. It's their child, not mine. I'm just a chicken hatching eggs."

"It's incredible," Dworkin marvels. "It's like — the gift of love, the highest gift a chicken can give?"

There may well be isolated occasions in which one woman, seeing the suffering of a friend, does truly make a gift of a child to her. That is very different from a situation in which lawyers, psychiatrists and gynecologists are forming companies for the purpose of selling women's reproductive capacities to strangers — some of whom already have children or are unwilling to nurture "second-best" children — and are appearing on the media to solicit women and create a need for this new "service." They pretend that the first, rather noble, situation is the same as their own exploitative practice and use the same vocabulary to describe both: "the gift of love."

Is it true what the surrogates predict — that they will feel only a slight sadness at giving up their babies?

Elizabeth Kane, who had referred to herself as an incubator during her pregnancy, proved to have the complicated emotions of the actual human being she is: "The first time I saw the adoptive mother hold the baby, it was thrilling," she said. "But I also went through depression — for example, on the third day in the hospital when my milk came in and the other woman was feeding the baby. And when I said good-bye to the baby, it broke my heart. I cried for weeks every Sunday because he was born on a Sunday" (Blair, 1982).

Parker interviewed twelve surrogates who had delivered babies. He found that the women expressed "transient grief symptoms" that were highly variable. "One stated that she had almost no consciously experienced feeling of loss," he wrote. "Another described one episode of deep crying, while still another related repetitive symptoms such as crying daily at the time of delivery and sleeplessness, both lasting about one month."

In writing the above section, I recalled an interview I had had with Joe, the midwestern farmer who allowed me to watch embryo transfers in cows. He told me that on his farm, they took a calf away from its mother at seven months in order to dry the mother up so she could rest and prepare to produce the next calf. The farm expected a calf a year from each cow; it was in the business of selling these calves, which would eventually be slaughtered for beef. A portion of our interview:

351

JOE: We take the calf away from her. We call it weaning. They bawl for four or five days and before you know it, why they're out in the pasture eating and they sort of have given up on their calves. Within two weeks they've just about forgotten their calves.

ME: The cows actually cry?

JOE: Yes, sure they cry. They bawl terribly. Not with tears. It's more a yelling kind of thing. No, they don't have tears to show emotions but they certainly are very vocal about it.

ME: So the cows have real emotions, then?

JOE: Not emotions like humans have. They've been seven months with this calf. They know it's their calf and this is their main job, raising their calf. They don't want to give it up. But it's not exactly the same as with humans. I suppose it is very similar. Where humans show tears and depression, with a cow it's just excitement, bawling and this type of thing.

How deep is the woman's grief when her child is taken from her? Will that grief be viewed any more seriously by men who regard the woman as a rented receptacle than the cow's grief was viewed by men who see a cow as a machine for producing marketable products, calves? Like the cow's grief, could the woman's be misread as "just excitement"? Could a woman's crying be interpreted not as an expression of sorrow, but "more of a yelling kind of thing," or, as Parker medicalized it, a "symptom"?

How sensitive is Parker to women as complex human beings when he writes that the twelve women who delivered a baby and received a $10,000 fee did not seem to have any adverse psychological consequences merely because they received a fee, and adds, as if providing evidence that paying for women's bodies can actually have a positive psychological consequence: "As a matter of fact, one surrogate expressed that spending some of the money on items for the house helped her to deal with feelings of loss" (Parker, 1982).

One feminist with whom I discussed the loss experienced by surrogate mothers commented: "It is drilled into us in every conceivable way that we women have this maternal instinct, maternal love. We are told that if we have an abortion, we'll suffer a great psychological trauma and sense of loss. Now they're saying: 'Well, as long as you know it's not yours, you can give it up. No problem.' They're conditioning women to say: 'It's not my baby. It's your baby because you paid for it.' How fast they change! They switch propaganda on us as it suits their needs."[21]

Now, if you are a breeder woman, giving up your baby can even be therapeutic. In one study (1983), Parker found that 35 percent of the women volunteering to be surrogates had lost at least one fetus or child through abortions (26 percent) or surrender of the baby for adoption (9 percent). The experience of relinquishing the baby appeared to help the surrogate deal with prior voluntary losses of a fetus or child, he maintained.

"A few consciously felt that they were participating in order to deal with unresolved feelings associated with the prior losses. The only applicant who was herself adopted had been 'forced' to relinquish her baby at age 14 and wanted to repeat the experience of relinquishment and master it."[22]

Asked if the 35 percent rate of abortion and adoption surrender differed from the rate found in a similar nonsurrogate population of women, Parker replied: "We don't know." That data is not kept, he maintained. If the percentage is similar, Parker's theory is of questionable validity.

I asked Parker how many women actually said they wanted to be surrogates in order to atone for a previous abortion or to master feelings associated with the previous loss of a child. Parker did not give me numbers. He did tell me that not all the women who had had abortions said they wanted to be surrogates as a result of those abortions. In fact he added: "Some of them totally denied that there was any causal connection." He said he thought there generally was a causal connection "even if they [the women] are not aware of it," and he would count those denying the connection among the surrogates atoning for a previous abortion. So Parker dismisses the women's own felt experience when it contradicts his theory.

I do not know the depth of grief surrogate mothers are experiencing. I do not know whether women are eagerly signing up as breeders in an attempt to benefit from the therapy allegedly anticipated in giving up their children without great pain and loss. But I do not

---

[21]Another example: When justifying embryo transfer, Dr. John Buster, a pioneer in the technology, asserted that the real mother of the child was "the woman who nurtures and shapes a child for nine months. If that isn't being a mother, what is?" (Donahue, #08223). Yet when justifying surrogate motherhood, surrogate entrepreneurs often assert that the woman who "nurtures and shapes a child for nine months" is not the real mother; she's just a living incubator. This makes the practice of taking the woman's child from her seem more palatable.

[22]Parker's use of quotation marks around "forced" seems to indicate disbelief in the woman's account of her own experience.

think we are going to find out from Parker, the man who believes that use of a woman for paid breeding is a "fundamental right" of the user.

Besides justifying surrogate motherhood as "therapeutic," Parker serves another useful function for the surrogate industry: He explains away some of the opposition to surrogate motherhood with his insights into the irrational psychology of the opponents. The strong opponents have unconscious fantasies of adultery and incest that are triggered by the concept of surrogate motherhood, he maintains. And/or, the opponents' unacceptable anger and hostility toward children may be stirred up and expressed by condemning the surrogate who will give up the child she bears. Keane wrote: "Such irrational opposition, he [Parker] says, should be identified and discredited" (Keane, 1982, p. 254).

Parker told me that whenever you separate reproduction from sex from marriage, you tend to encourage in people the onset of fantasies that make people uncomfortable, particularly fantasies about incest. Knowing that Parker emphasizes the need for studies in evaluating surrogate motherhood and that he discredits opponents of the procedure by pointing out that they have no data on which to base their criticisms, I asked him for the scientific basis for his assertion.

"That's based upon my talking with some people," he replied. "It's not a controlled study at this point, no. That's based upon my own clinical impression, talking with some people informally — some of them even during interviews...and some of it is my own speculation."

Surrogates are being paid to perform one of woman's biological functions. This is not the first such arrangement. For centuries, women were paid to nurse the babies of others. Embryologist Dr. Clifford Grobstein sees the connection between the two roles: "If a favorable ethical and social consensus develops, the role of wet nurse (which is accepted in many cultures) could probably be expanded fairly rapidly to include surrogate childbearing."[23]

Under medical control, as physician reports reveal, wetnurses were screened, inspected, controlled, devalued and viewed as cows. We will see a comparable control exercised over surrogate mothers.

First, consider the way physicians controlled wetnurses. Dr. Isaac A. Abt, who supervised wetnurses at the Sarah Morris Hospital in Chicago, reported on his experience in 1917. Maternity hospitals and foundling asylums referred women to Dr. Abt. He would inspect

[23]Wetnursing was made obsolete around 1925 with the development of an artificial breast — the baby bottle — and a substitute for mother's milk. The development of an artificial womb and placenta would make surrogate mothering obsolete.

them for milk production, squeezing the women's breasts to see if the milk shot out or only dribbled. He did not accept dribblers.

Once hired, the women moved into the hospital. They got room, board and $8 per week. They were required to do light work. Their rooms were inspected for cleanliness. Dr. Abt wrote: "The personal hygiene of the wetnurses is carefully supervised. It is insisted that they shall bathe regularly and that they shall be attired at all times in clean clothes."

The wetnurse was compelled to retire at 9 P.M. and rise at 8 A.M. During the night, she was not permitted to nurse her own baby. In the afternoon, between milking periods, she was allowed some leisure time: "During this time she may exercise or rest....If she goes out for a walk, she takes her baby with her; this precaution helps to keep her out of mischief. She is not allowed to leave the institution after dark, and is required to be in her room by 8 P.M." (Abt, 1917).

The women did not put the foster babies directly to the breast. Instead, apparently for "sanitary" reasons, they expressed their milk into sterile bottles.[24] Dr. Abt reported: "All the wetnurses milk at the same hour under the supervision of a head nurse and assistants. Thus the operation is pretty well controlled....It is necessary to exercise watchfulness in supervising the operation, because it has been our experience in times past that wetnurses have practiced deceit, either by diluting the milk or by substituting cow's milk for their own product."

Dr. Owen H. Wilson of Nashville also emphasized that the wetnurses must be watched. They have sometimes carried milk bottles in their bosoms and emptied them into the receptacles, he warned. (What must the lives of those women have been like that they were desperate enough for money to do that?)

Just as physicians controlled wetnurses, so too are controls exerted over today's breeders (see Ince, 1984). The contracts women sign with the various surrogate mothering firms are similar. Generally the woman agrees to abstain from intercourse during the insemination period to assure the man employing her that he is the father of her child. She agrees not to smoke or drink during the pregnancy and not to use any drugs, including aspirin, without the doctor's written permission. She agrees to be present for psychological counselling during the course of the pregnancy. She is contractually bound to obey all

---

[24]There is a persistent suggestion in the medical literature that wetnurses might contaminate the baby. Dr. B. Raymond Hoobler, describing his program in Detroit, declared it was often better to have the nurse live in the hospital rather than in a couple's home: "By bringing only the milk into the nursery, rather than the wetnurse, it seemed to me that the chances of introducing infections were lessened."

medical instructions of the inseminating physician and her obstetrician. Although routine obstetrical practices have been subjected to devastating critiques in government hearings and reports and numerous books, if the physician wants to use those practices on her, she must submit.[25] She agrees not to engage in any activities that would be against her doctor's advice and that — he felt — would endanger the birth.[26] (The physician who inseminates and/or conducts prenatal exams on a surrogate mother may see himself as serving the interests of the couple or lawyer who hired the surrogate mother rather than the woman herself, just as a veterinarian sometimes sees himself as serving the interests of the cow's owner rather than the cow. For example, take the case of a surrogate mother who changed her mind and refused to give up her child to Keane's clients. The surrogate, her physician wrote to Keane, had been bothered during her pregnancy by *severe* nausea and vomiting and had at one point considered an abortion. "We firmly discouraged the abortion, as the patient's agreement and responsibility [my emphasis] were thoroughly reviewed." The physician's letter, Keane wrote, "indicates he is working for the success of the arrangement.") The breeder must adhere to a strict prenatal schedule. Keane requires no fewer than one visit to the obstetrician per month during the first seven months of pregnancy and two visits — at two-week intervals — during the ninth month. Fitzpatrick, who worked with Keane on the draft, added a similar provision to his law regulating surrogate motherhood. The Michigan draft law, House Bill No. 5184, would legally bind the breeder to obey all medical instructions of the inseminating physician and the obstetrician.

"That's got to be a denial of every civil right, even under this [Reagan] government," Dworkin commented. "When you're in prison, you have more rights than that over your own body."

Also under the draft law (since superseded by another version), the surrogate would have to sign a contract agreeing not to abort the

---

[25]See Chapter 16, note 3 for a list of books and reports criticizing obstetrical practices.

[26]Alan A. Rassaby, research fellow in the Centre for Human Bioethics at Monash University, Melbourne, believes that the activities of the surrogate mother during pregnancy do need to be legally regulated. He leaves the specific nature of these regulations open but raises questions, among them, these two: Should the woman be legally prohibited from engaging in activities, such as skiing, that are potentially but not intrinsically harmful to the fetus? If a baby is born with a disability that can be directly attributed to an activity of the surrogate who was in breach of her agreement or of the law, can she be sued for negligence? (Rassaby, 1982, p. 66).

fetus unless her doctor thought that was necessary for her physical health.[27]

Handel requires that the surrogate keep his firm informed of her whereabouts at all times. Asked why, he replied: "Because she's carrying my client's child. It's nice to know where she is at all times. If she moves, we have to know. If she changes employers or insurance, we have to know. If anything traumatic happens in her family such as a death or a job loss — anything that could materially affect the contract in any way whatsoever — we have to know. If anything comes up, we deal with it. She breaches the contract if she does not tell us."

Besides being controlled, wetnurses and surrogates are devalued. Physicians and lawyers set the value of the women's services and assess it as minimal. In 1917, Dr. Arthur D. Holmes, director of a Bureau of Wetnurses in Detroit, noted: "We placed notices in the local papers and with the members of the profession, asking women who had had stillbirths or lost their babies to register at our bureau, guaranteeing them $7 a week, board, room and necessary laundry....We soon had quite a number" (Hooblor, 1017). Dr. Abt of Chicago observed: "We pay wetnurses $8 a week. We do not like to have anyone pay them more, for it is the middle and lower class people, of no great means, who need them most."

Surrogate professionals are also setting a low wage for a surrogate mother's labor. Dr. Richard Levin figures that, counting the inseminations, the nine months of carrying the child and six weeks of recovery, the woman is giving up to a year and a half of her time. (He does not mention her labor in giving birth.) "So the fee we set — $10,000 — comes out to be less than minimum wage," he states. "Less than I feel comfortable with" (Keane, 1981, p. 220). But they have a sliding scale because Levin, like Dr. Isaac Abt before him, is concerned that middle and lower classes not be priced out of surrogate services. "If a couple says they have only $3,000," Levin explains, "I ask a mother to lower her price or try to find one who is willing to do it for that amount."

Currently a surrogate receives $10,000 or less for the following: repeated artificial inseminations; time taken off from work for doctor's visits, psychological counselling and for the birth; pregnancy-induced fatigue, nausea, weight gain, discomfort, skin stretching, loss of sleep,

---

[27]However, the Supreme Court held in 1973 that the right to privacy, as protected by the Ninth Amendment, encompasses a woman's right to end her pregnancy. Whether a woman's right to have an abortion can be waived by signing a contract is not clear. Contracts between private individuals that impose unconstitutional conditions may be held invalid [Young, 1982].

altered or suspended sexual activity; possible miscarriage (several surrogates have suffered from them already); painful labor ("I thought I was going to die from the pain," Keane quotes one surrogate mother as having said.) Additionally, she runs a one in five chance of undergoing cesarean section, major surgery with a significant complication rate. (Several breeders have already been subjected to this surgery.) Many women contract infections following the surgery. The recovery period can be even longer than in six weeks.[28] The agreement Keane has the surrogate and sperm donor sign states: "The Surrogate and her Husband, if married, understand and agree to assume all risks including the risk of death which are incidental to conception, pregnancy, childbirth and postpartum complications" (Keane, 1981, p. 293).

The surrogate may also suffer from postpartum depression, a common experience among birthing women in this culture, and from any additional anguish involved in giving up a child which is in every way her child, conceived with her egg, carried in her womb, and birthed through her labor.

"The miscarriage was absolutely horrible," one surrogate mother recalled. "I was surprised at how powerful my feelings were. I mean, I had been saying to myself all along, 'it's their baby. It's Judy's baby. I am only carrying it for them.' But when I lost the baby, I was depressed for weeks. That was the beginning of the end for me and the dentist and his wife" (Keane, 1981, p. 177).

How did Handel arrive at the $10,000 figure for all this? "It's an arbitrary figure we came up with that we thought was reasonable."

Others find these conditions "reasonable":

•Under one piece of proposed legislation, if the surrogate miscarries prior to the fifth month of pregnancy, no compensation other than medical expenses will be paid. However, if she miscarries after this time, 10 percent of the fee plus medical expenses would be awarded (Gaynes, 1981).

---

[28]The first surrogate mother hired by a Philadelphia firm was scheduled for a cesarean because she had had a previous cesarean and the physician decided she would have another. There is overwhelming evidence that many women can successfully have a vaginal birth after a previous cesarean (see Nancy Cohen and Lois Estner, *Silent Knife: Cesarean Prevention and Vaginal Birth After Cesarean*, J.F. Bergin Publishers, Inc., South Hadley, Mass, 1983). But if a doctor refuses to consider it and the woman, in a contract upheld by the state, is bound to obey him, then she must submit to this major surgery.

Corea: Surrogate Motherhood

• One surrogate mother from Joppatowne, Maryland, received $3,000 when she became pregnant for a couple from Colorado. She received another $10,000 after the baby was born on March 24, 1983. Her contract stipulated that the $10,000 would not have been paid had the baby been delivered stillborn (SPN, 1983, May).

There is a sense in which wetnurses were, and surrogate mothers are, viewed as cows. In the following racist exchange between Dr. Isaac W. Faison of Charlotte, North Carolina, and Dr. Oliver Hill of Knoxville, Tennessee, in 1917, the men appear to be speaking of cattle. Dr. Faison appealed to other physicians to develop an improved artificial milk for infants. He needed the product, he said, because in his county, few white women were available as wetnurses; few bore illegitimate children. Most available women were "colored," he explained, "a race that cannot be depended on as wetnurses." Dr. Hill rushed to the defense of southern Black women as wetnurses: "They can be cultivated until they are efficient....I really think we have an advantage over you gentlemen in the Northern cities because the negros will come for a small amount of money, if you do not overpay them or pay them in advance. And if you keep them in good physical condition, they give milk of a good quality."

Earlier in the discussion, Dr. Wilson had commented: "If enough cannot be secured from one [woman], herd milk is just as good as individual." Dr. Abt also spoke of a wetnurse as one would speak of a cow: "She produces as high as 56 ounces in twenty-four hours."

In an interview with me, an obstetrician said of surrogate mothers: "They're good mothers. They get pregnant easily. They handle the pregnancy well." When he told me this, it reminded me of Joe the farmer who had essentially said the same of recipient scrub cows into whom embryos were being transferred. They were good mothers with roomy uteri and plenty of milk, he told me.

The arrival of surrogate motherhood has not aroused the "intense emotional response" artificial insemination had evoked for almost two hundred years. Physicians and lawyers had written that AID endangers "marriage, family and society," may create "an anonymous world," is "socially monstrous," and may lead to "radical revolution" in which such concepts as "father" and "family descent," lose their meaning (Rubin, 1965).

There has been no similarly frightened response to surrogate motherhood. AID had weakened men's claim to paternity; surrogate motherhood strengthens it. The practice does not endanger the patriarchal family and is not judged to be "socially monstrous." It will lead

359

IV. The Elements of Family Life

to no radical revolution — such as a return to Mother Right — in which the concept of "father" loses its meaning.

The questions prominently raised about surrogate motherhood have been merely questions of logistics: How does one best regulate it so that, for example, women are not refusing to give up their babies, thus thwarting the plans of the men who commissioned for those babies?

In January 1984, several months after our first interview, John Stehura, president of the Bionetics Foundation, informed me that he was moving into the international arena in surrogate motherhood.

"We're bringing girls in from the Orient," he said. "From Korea, Thailand and Malaysia." (He was also exploring the possibility of initiating some pregnancies in those countries and bringing just the babies to the United States, he said.)

According to the first plan, the woman would be paid nothing for her services. The couple adopting the child would provide the surrogate's travel and living expenses. Though such women receive no pay, Stehura said, they benefit from the arrangement because they get to live. "Often they're looking for a survival situation — something to do to pay for the rent and food," he said. They come from underdeveloped countries "where food is a serious issue." These countries do not have an industrial base, but they have a human base, he said. "They know how to take care of children." Since that's missing here, he added, "obviously it's a perfect match."

No women have actually been brought into the United States as of this writing. Stehura said he was negotiating details after having advertised for "girls" in newspapers in the Orient.

The international traffic in women is about to expand.

References

Abt, Isaac. 1917. "The Technique of Wet-nurse Management in Institutions." *The Journal of the American Medical Association.*
Donahue Transcript. Interview with Dr. William Shockley.
Dworkin, Andrea. 1983. *Right-wing Women.* New York: Perrrige Books.
Fleming, Susan. 1978, January 4. "Babies By Proxy: A Quandary." *Detroit News.*
Gaynes, Mindy. 1981, July-August. "Legal Questions Surround Surrogate Parenting." *State Legislatures.*

Hoobler, B. Raymond. 1917. "Problems Connected with the Collection and Production of Human Milk." *The Journal of the American Medical Association.*

Ince, Susan. 1984."Inside the Surrogate Industry." In R. Arditti, R. Duelli-Klein and S. Minden, eds., *Test-tube Women.* London: Routledge and Kegan Paul.

Karp, Laurence and Roger Donahue. 1976. Pre-implantation Ectogenesis. *Western Journal of Medicine* 124.

Keane, Noel with Dennis Breo. 1981. *The Surrogate Mothers.* New York: Everest House.

Krier, Beth. 1981. "The Moral and Legal Problems of Surrogate Parenting" *Los Angeles Times* (Nov. 10).

Krucoff, Carol. 1980. "Surrogate Parenting is Controversial Birth Technique." *Hartford Kourint.* (Nov. 9)

Mackinnon, Catherine. 1979. *Sexual Harrassment of Working Women.* New Haven: Yale University Press.

Miller, Robert. 1983. "Surrogate Parenting: An Infant Industry Presents Society with Legal, Ethical Questions.*OB-GYN News*, 18.

New York Times. 1980. "Surrogate Mothers: A Controversial Solution to Infertility." (May 17)

Parker, Philip. 1982. "Surrogate Motherhood: The Integration of Litigation, Legislation and Psychiatry. *International Journal of Law and Psychiatry*, 5.

Parker, Philip. 1983. "Motivation of Surrogate Mothers: Initial Findings." *American Journal of Psychiatry*, 140.

Pearce, Diana and Harriette McAdoo. 1981. "Women and Children: Alone and in Poverty." Pamphlet prepared for the National Advisory Council on Economic Opportunity. Washington: Catholic University Law School.

Rasaby, Alan. 1982. "Surrogate Motherhood: The Position and Problems of Substitutes." In W. Walters and P. Singer, eds., *Test-tube Babies.* Melbourne: Oxford University Press.

Rubin, Bernard. 1965. "Psychological Aspects of Human Artificial Insemination." *Archives of General Psychiatry*, 13.

Schroeder, Leha. 1974. "New Life: Person or Property?" *American Journal of Psychiatry*, 131 (May).

Singer, Peter. 1975. *Animal Liberation.* New York: Avon Books.

ST. 1980. "Volunteer Surrogates Pour In." (December 14) Sydney.

Walters, William and Peter Singer eds. 1982. *Test-tube Babies.* Melbourne: Oxford University Press.

E. Caring for Children

While popular notions about childhood have been changing for centuries, the twentieth century is remarkable for the fickleness of its "experts" on children: they seem to change their minds about what children need nearly every decade. What is especially disturbing is how weak the link is between research findings and the proclamations of these (male) child experts. Clearly, their advice to mothers has as much to do with ideas about how women should live as a sense of what children require. This was clearest in the late 1940s and the 1950s, when the experts typically proclaimed the necessity that children have a *full-time mother* in their early years, and based this claim on very poorly conducted research on institutionalized children (Wortis 1974). Recent writings by child psychologists such as Jerome Kagan (1986) provide a striking contrast to these highly ideological proclamations about children's needs: he argues that children only require care by the same people from one day to the next.

The debate about the needs of children has taken on new meaning in the last few decades, as more and more mothers work outside the home, and as the recognition of the necessity of good day care grows. Yet, there are reasons other than women's involvement in paid work for Canadians to examine carefully the way we raise children. Our growing awareness of child abuse by parents compels us to question the merits of privatized child care, in which the mother bears the primary responsibility for children. The question that arises is how work that should be highly rewarding becomes one that for many women is stressful and unrewarding. The excerpt from Adrienne Rich's book, *Of Woman Born*, presents with stark and anguished clarity the complicated feelings motherhood induced in this feminist poet. That the situation of mothers with young children is socially constructed, and stressful because of the way it is organized, is clear in this excerpt. Anthropologist Harriet Rosenberg more systematically assesses the organization of "motherwork," and locates the factors that induce stress.

References

Kagan, Jerome.
1986. "The psychological requirements for human development." Pp. 373-84 in Arlene Skolnick and Jerome Skolnick, eds. *Family in Transition*. Fifth Edition. Boston: Little, Brown & Company.

Wortis, Rochelle.
1974. "The acceptance of the concept of the maternal role by behavioral scientists: its effects on women." Pp. 360-76 in Arlene Skolnick and Jerome Skolnick, eds. *Intimacy, Family and Society*. Boston: Little, Brown & Company.

Suggested Readings

Miller, Alice.
1983. *For Your Own Good*. New York: Farrar, Straus & Giroux. An unsettling, but insightful critique of traditional methods of child rearing which aim at control; the psychic damage to children is the concern of this former psychoanalyst.

Anger and Tenderness: The Experience of Motherhood*

Adrienne Rich

Entry from my journal, November 1960

My children cause me the most exquisite suffering of which I have any experience. It is the suffering of ambivalence: the murderous alternation between bitter resentment and raw-edged nerves, and blissful gratification and tenderness. Sometimes I seem to myself, in my feelings towards these tiny guiltless beings, a monster of selfishness and intolerance. Their voices wear away at my nerves, their constant needs, above all their need for simplicity and patience, fill me with despair at my own failures, despair too at my fate, which is to serve a function for which I was not fitted. And I am weak sometimes from held-in rage. There are times when I feel only death will free us from one another, when I envy the barren woman[1] who has the luxury of her regrets but lives a life of privacy and freedom.

And yet at other times I am melted with the sense of their help-less. Charming and quite irresistible beauty — their ability to go on loving and trusting — their staunchness and decency and unselfconsciousness. I love them. But it's in the enormity and inevitability of this love that the sufferings lie.

May 1965

To suffer with and for and against a child — maternally, egotistically, neurotically, sometimes with a sense of helplessness, sometimes with the illusion of learning wisdom — but always, everywhere, in body and soul, with that child — because that child is a piece of oneself.

To be caught up in waves of love and hate, jealousy even of the child's childhood; hope and fear for its maturity; longing to be free of responsibility, tied by every fibre of one's being.

---

[1]The term 'barren woman' was easy for me to use, unexamined, fifteen years ago. It seems to me now a term both tendentious and meaningless, based on a view of women which sees motherhood as our only positive definition.

IV. The Elements of Family Life

That curious primitive reaction of protectiveness, the beast defending her cub, when anyone attacks or criticizes him — and yet no one more hard on him than I! [...]

Unexamined assumptions: First, that a 'natural' mother is a person without further identity, one who can find her chief gratification in being all day with small children, living at a pace tuned to theirs; that the isolation of mothers and children together in the home must be taken for granted; that maternal love is, and should be, quite literally selfless; that children and mothers are the causes of each others suffering. I was haunted by the stereotype of the mother whose love is unconditional; and by the visual and literary images of motherhood as a single-minded identity. If I knew parts of myself existed that would never cohere to those images, weren't those parts then abnormal, monstrous. And — as my eldest son, now aged twenty-one, remarked on reading the above passages: You seemed to feel you ought to love us all the time. But there is no human relationship where you love the other person at every moment. Yes, I tried to explain to him, but women — above all, mothers — have been supposed to love that way.

From the fifties and early sixties, I remember a cycle. It began when I had picked up a book or began trying to write a letter, or even found myself on the telephone with someone toward whom my voice betrayed eagerness, a rush of sympathetic energy. The child (or children) might be absorbed in busyness, in his own dreamworld; but as soon as he felt me gliding into a world which did not include him, he could come to pull at my hand, ask for help, punch at the typewriter keys. And I would feel his wants at such a moment as fraudulent, as an attempt moreover to defraud me of living even for fifteen minutes as myself. My anger could rise: I would feel the futility of any attempt to salvage myself, and also the inequality between us: my needs always balanced against those of a child, and always losing. I could love so much better, I told myself, after even a quarter-hour of selfishness, of peace, of detachment from my children. A few minutes! But it was as if an invisible thread would pull taut between us and break, to the child's sense of inconsolable abandonment, if I moved — not even physically, but in spirit — into a realm beyond our tightly circumscribed life together. It was as if my placenta had begun to refuse him oxygen. Like so many women, I waited with impatience for the moment when their father would return from work, when for an hour or two at least the circle drawn around mother and children would grow looser, the intensity between us slacken, because there was another adult in the house.

I did not understand that this circle, this magnetic field in which we lived, was not a natural phenomenon.

366

Intellectually, I must have known it. But the emotion-charged, tradition-heavy form in which I found myself cast as the Mother seemed, then, as ineluctable as the tides. And, because of this form — this microcosm in which my children and I formed a tiny, private emotional cluster, and in which (in bad weather or when someone was ill) we sometimes passed days at a time without seeing another adult except for their father — there was authentic need underlying my child's invented claims upon me when I seemed to be wandering away from him. He was reassuring himself that warmth, tenderness, continuity, solidity were still there for him, in my person. My singularity, my uniqueness in the world as his mother — perhaps more dimly also as Woman — evoked a need vaster than any single human being could satisfy, except by loving continuously, unconditionally, from dawn to dark, and often in the middle of the night.

In a living room in 1975, I spent an evening with a group of women poets, some of whom had children. One had brought hers along, and they slept or played in adjoining rooms. We talked of poetry, and also of infanticide, of the case of a local woman, the mother of eight, who had been in severe depression since the birth of her third child, and who had recently murdered and decapitated her two youngest, on her suburban front lawn. Several women in the group, feeling a direct connection with her desperation, had signed a letter to the local newspaper protesting the way her act was perceived by the press and handled by the community mental health system. Every woman in that room who had children, every poet, could identify with her. We spoke of the wells of anger that her story cleft open in us. We spoke of our own moments of murderous anger at our children, because there was no one and nothing else on which to discharge anger. We spoke in the sometimes tentative, sometimes rising, sometimes bitterly witty, unrhetorical tones and language of women who had met together over our common work, poetry, and who found another common ground in an unacceptable, but undeniable anger. The words are being spoken now, are being written down; the taboos are being broken, the masks of motherhood are cracking through.

For centuries no one talked of these feelings. I became a mother in the family-centred, consumer-oriented, Freudian-American world of the 1950s. My husband spoke eagerly of the children we would have; my parents-in-law awaited the birth of their grandchild. I had no idea of what I wanted, what I could or could not choose. I only knew that to have a child was to assume adult womanhood to the full, to prove myself, to be 'like other women'. [...]

I have a very clear, keen memory of myself the day after I was married: I was sweeping a floor. Probably the floor did not really need to be swept; probably I simply did not know what else to do with myself. But as I swept that floor I thought: 'Now I am a woman. This is an age-old action, this is what women have always done.' I felt I was bending to some ancient form, too ancient to question. *This is what women have always done.*

As soon as I was visibly and clearly pregnant, I felt, for the first time in my adolescent and adult life, not guilty. The atmosphere of approval in which I was bathed — even by strangers on the street, it seemed — was like an aura I carried with me, in which doubt, fears, misgivings, met with absolute denial. This is what women have always done.

Two days before my first son was born, I broke out in a rash which was tentatively diagnosed as measles, and was admitted to a hospital for contagious diseases to await the onset of labour. I felt for the first time a great deal of conscious fear, and guilt toward my unborn child, for having 'failed' him with my body in this way. In rooms near mine were patients with polio: no one was allowed to enter my room except in a hospital gown and mask. If during pregnancy I had felt in any vague command of my situation, I felt now totally dependent on my obstetrician, a huge, vigorous, paternal man, abounding with optimism and assurance, and given to pinching my cheek. I had gone through a healthy pregnancy, but as if tranquilized or sleep-walking. I had taken a sewing class in which I produced an unsightly and ill-cut maternity jacket which I never wore: I had made curtains for the baby's room, collected baby clothes, blotted out as much as possible the woman I had been a few months earlier. My second book of poems was in press, but I had stopped writing poetry, and read little except household magazines and books on childcare. I felt myself perceived by the world simply as a pregnant woman, and it seemed easier, less disturbing, to perceive myself so. After my child was born the 'measles' were diagnosed as an allergic reaction to pregnancy.

Within two years, I was pregnant again, and writing in a note-book:

November 1956

> Whether it's the extreme lassitude of early pregnancy or something more fundamental, I don't know: but of late I've felt, toward poetry — both reading and writing it — nothing but boredom and indifference. Especially toward my own and that of my immediate contemporaries. When I receive a letter soliciting mss., or someone alludes to my 'career', I

have a strong sense of wanting to deny all responsibility for
and interest in that person who writes — or who wrote.

If there is going to be a real break in my writing life,
this is as good a time for it as any. I have been dissatisfied
with myself, my work, for a long time.

My husband was a sensitive, affectionate man who wanted children and
who unusual in the professional, academic world of the fifties — was
willing to 'help'. But it was clearly understood that this 'help' was an act
of generosity; that his work, his professional life, was the real work in the
family; in fact, this was for years not even an issue between us. I
understood that my struggles as a writer were a kind of luxury, a
peculiarity of mine; my work brought in almost no money: it even cost
money, when I hired a household helper to allow me a few hours a week
to write. 'Whatever I ask he tries to give me.' I wrote in March 1958,
'but always the initiative has to be mine.' I experienced my depressions,
bursts of anger, sense of entrapment, as burdens my husband was forced
to bear because he loved me; I felt grateful to be loved in spite of bringing
him those burdens.[...]

By July of 1958 I was again pregnant. The new life of my third —
and as I determined, my last — child, was a kind of turning for me. I had
learned that my body was not under my control; I had not intended to
bear a third child. I knew now better than I had ever known what
another pregnancy, another new infant, meant for my body and spirit.
Yet, I did not think of having an abortion. In a sense, my third son was
more actively chosen than either of his brothers: by the time I knew I
was pregnant with him, I was not sleepwalking any more.

August 1958 (Vermont)

> I write this as the early rays of the sun light up our hillside
> and eastern windows. Rose with the [baby] at 5:30 a.m. and
> have fed him and breakfasted. This is one of the few
> mornings on which I haven't felt terrible mental depression
> and physical exhaustion.
>
> ...I have to acknowledge to myself that I would not
> have chosen to have more children, that I was beginning to
> look to a time, not too far off, when I should again be free,
> no longer so physically tired, pursuing a more or less
> intellectual and creative life....The only way I can develop
> now is through much harder, more continuous, connected
> work than my present life makes possible. Another child

means postponing this for some years longer — and years at my age are significant, not to be tossed lightly away.

And yet, somehow, something, call it Nature or that affirming fatalism of the human creature, makes me aware of the inevitable as already part of me, not to be contended against so much as brought to bear as an additional weapon against drift, stagnation and spiritual death. (For it is really death that I have been fearing — the crumbling to death of that scarcely-born physiognomy which my whole life has been a battle to give birth to — a recognizable, autonomous self, a creation in poetry and in life.)

If more effort has to be made then I will make it. If more despair has to be lived through, I think I can anticipate it correctly and live through it.

Meanwhile, in a curious and unanticipated way, we really do welcome the birth of our child.[...]

Before my third child was born I decided to have no more children, to be sterilized. (Nothing is removed from a woman's body during this operation; ovulation and menstruation continue. Yet the language suggests a cutting or burning-away of her essential womanhood, just as the old word 'barren' suggests a woman eternally empty and lacking.) My husband, although he supported my decision, asked whether I was sure it would not leave me feeling 'less feminine'. In order to have the operation at all, I had to present a letter, countersigned by my husband, assuring the committee of physicians who approved such operations that I had already produced three children, and stating my reasons for having no more. Since I had had rheumatoid arthritis for some years, I could give a reason acceptable to the male panel who sat on my case; my own judgment would not have been acceptable. When I awoke from the operation, twenty-four hours after my child's birth, a young nurse looked at my chart and remarked coldly: 'had yourself spayed, did you?'

The first great birth-control crusader, Margaret Sanger,[2] remarks that of the hundreds of women who wrote to her pleading for contraceptive information in the early part of the twentieth century, all spoke of wanting the health and strength to be better mothers to the children they already had; or of wanting to be physically affectionate to their husbands without dread of conceiving. None was refusing motherhood altogether, or asking for an easy life. These women — mostly poor, many still in their teens, all with several children — simply felt they could no longer do 'right' by their families, whom they expected to go

---

[2]Margaret Sanger, *Motherhood in Bondage*, New York, Maxwell, (Reprint 1956).

on serving and rearing. Yet there always has been, and there remains, intense fear of the suggestion that women shall have the final say as to how our bodies are to be used. It is as if the suffering of the mother, the primary identification of woman as the mother — were so necessary to the emotional grounding of human society that the mitigation, or removal, of that suffering, that identification, must be fought at every level, including the level of refusing to question it at all.[...]

Once in a while someone used to ask me; 'Don't you ever write poems about your children?' The male poets of my generation did write poems about their children — especially their daughters. For me, poetry was where I lived as no-one's mother, where I existed as myself.

The bad and the good moments are inseparable for me. I recall the times when, suckling each of my children, I saw his eyes open full to mine, and realized each of us was fastened to the other, not only by mouth and breast, but through our mutual gaze: the depth, calm, passion, of that dark blue, maturely focused look. I recall the physical pleasure of having my full breast suckled at a time when I had no other physical pleasure in the world except the guilt-ridden pleasure of addictive eating. I remember early the sense of conflict, of a battleground none of us had chosen, of being an observer who, like it or not, was also an actor in an endless contest of wills. This was what it meant to me to have three children under the age of seven. But I recall too each child's individual body, his slenderness, wiriness, softness, grace, the beauty of little boys who have not been taught that the male body must be rigid. I remember moments of peace when for some reason it was possible to go to the bathroom alone. I remember being uprooted from already meagre sleep to answer a childish nightmare, pull up a blanket, warm a consoling bottle, lead a half-asleep child to the toilet. I remember going back to bed starkly awake, brittle with anger, knowing that my broken sleep would make next day a hell, that there would be more nightmares, more need for consolation, because out of my weariness I would rage at those children for no reason they could understand. I remember thinking I would never dream again (the unconscious of the young mother — where does it entrust its messages, when dream-sleep is denied her for years?)[...]

Even today, rereading old Journals, remembering. I feel grief and anger; but their objects are no longer myself and my children. I feel grief at the waste of myself in those years, anger at the mutilation and manipulation of the relationship between mother and child, which is the great original source and experience of love.

On an early spring day in the 1970s, I meet a young woman friend on the street. She has a tiny infant against her breast, in a bright cotton sling; its face is pressed against her blouse, its tiny hand clutches a piece of the cloth. 'How old is she?' I ask. 'Just two weeks old,' the mother tells me. I am amazed to feel in myself a passionate longing to have, once again, such a small, new being clasped against my body. The baby belongs there, curled, suspended asleep between her mother's breasts, as she belonged curled in the womb. The young mother — who already has a three-year-old — speaks of how quickly one forgets the pure pleasure of having this new creature, immaculate, perfect. And I walk away from her drenched with memory, with envy. Yet I know other things: that her life is far from simple; she is a mathematician who now has two children under the age of four; she is living even now in the rhythms of other lives — not only the regular cry of the infant but her three-year-old's needs, her husband's problems. In the building where I live, women are still raising children alone, living day in and day out within their individual family units, doing the laundry, herding the tricycles to the park, waiting for the husbands to come home. There is a baby-sitting pool and a children's playroom, young fathers push prams on weekends, but childcare is still the individual responsibility of the individual woman. I envy the sensuality of having an infant of two weeks curled against one's breast; I do not envy the turmoil of the elevator full of small children, babies howling in the laundromat, the apartment in winter where pent-up seven- and eight-year-olds have one adult to look to for their frustrations, reassurances, the grounding of their lives.

But, it will be said, this is the human condition, this interpenetration of pain and pleasure, frustration and fulfilment. I might have told myself the same thing, fifteen or eighteen years ago. But the patriarchal institution of motherhood is not the 'human condition' any more than rape, prostitution, and slavery are. (Those who speak largely of the human condition are usually those most exempt from its oppressions — whether of sex, race, or servitude.)

Motherhood — unmentioned in the histories of conquest and serfdom, wars and treaties, exploration and imperialism — has a history, it has an ideology, it is more fundamental than tribalism or nationalism. My individual, seemingly private pains as a mother, the individual, seemingly private pains of the mothers around me and before me, whatever our class or colour, the regulation of women's reproductive power by men in every totalitarian system and every socialist revolution, the legal and technical control by men of contraception, fertility, abortion, obstetrics, gynecology, and extra-uterine reproductive experiments — all are essential to the patriarchal system, as is the negative or suspect status of women who are not mothers.

The institution of motherhood is not identical with bearing and caring for children, any more than the institution of heterosexuality is identical with intimacy and sexual love. Both create the prescriptions

372

and the conditions in which choices are made or blocked; they are not 'reality' but they have shaped the circumstances of our lives. The new scholars of women's history have begun to discover that, in any case, the social institutions and prescriptions for behaviour created by men have not necessarily accounted for the real lives of women. Yet any institution which expresses itself so universally ends by profoundly affecting our experience, even the language we use to describe it. The experience of maternity and the experience of sexuality have both been channeled to serve male interests; behaviour which threatens the institutions, such as illegitimacy, abortion, lesbianism, is considered deviant or criminal.

Institutionalized heterosexuality told women for centuries that we were dangerous, unchaste, the embodiment of carnal lust; then that we were 'not passionate', frigid, sexually passive; today it prescribes the 'sensuous', 'sexually liberated' woman in the West, the dedicated revolutionary ascetic in China; and everywhere it denies the reality of women's love for women. Institutionalized motherhood demands of women maternal 'instinct' rather than intelligence, selflessness rather than self-realization, relation to others rather than the creation of self. Motherhood is 'sacred' so long as its offspring are 'legitimate' — that is, as long as the child bears the name of a father who legally controls the mother. It is 'woman's highest and holiest mission', according to a socialist tract of 1914,[3] and a racist southern historian of 1910 tells us that woman is the embodied home, and the home is the basis of all institutions, the buttress of society'.[4][...]

Patriarchy would seem to require, not only that women shall assume the major burden of pain and self-denial for the furtherance of the species, but that a majority of that species — women — shall remain essentially unquestioning and unenlightened. On this 'underemployment' of female consciousness depend the morality and the emotional life of the human family.[...] Patriarchy could not survive without motherhood and heterosexuality in their institutional forms; therefore they have to be treated as axioms, as 'nature' itself, not open to question except where, from time to time and place to place, 'alternate life-styles' for certain individuals are tolerated.[...]

Most of the literature of infant care and psychology has assumed that the process toward individuation is essentially the child's drama, played out against and with a parent or parents who are, for better or worse, givens. Nothing could have prepared me for the realization that I was a mother, one of those givens, when I knew I was still in a state of uncreation myself. That calm, sure, unambivalent woman who moved

---

[3]John Spargo, *Socialism and Motherhood*, New York, 1914.
[4]Benjamin F. Riley, *White Man's Burden*, Birmingham, Alabama, 1910, p. 131.

through the pages of the manuals I read seemed as unlike me as an astronaut. Nothing, to be sure, had prepared me for the intensity of relationship already existing between me and a creature I had carried in my body and now held in my arms and fed from my breasts. Throughout pregnancy and nursing, women are urged to relax, to mime the serenity of madonnas. No one mentions the psychic crisis of bearing a first child, the excitation of long-buried feelings about one's own mother, the sense of confused power and powerlessness, of being taken over on the one hand and of touching new physical and psychic potentialities on the other, a heightened sensibility which can be exhilarating, bewildering, and exhausting. No one mentions the strangeness of attraction — which can be as single-minded and overwhelming as the early days of a love affair — to a being so tiny, so dependent, so folded-in to itself — who is, and yet is not, part of oneself.

The physical and psychic weight of responsibility on the woman with children is by far the heaviest of social burdens. It cannot be compared with slavery or sweated labour because the emotional bonds between a woman and her children make her vulnerable in ways which the forced labourer does not know: he can hate and fear his boss or master, loathe the toil; dream of revolt or of becoming a boss; the woman with children is a prey to far more complicated, subversive feelings. Love and anger can exist concurrently; anger at the conditions of motherhood can become translated into anger at the child, along with the fear that we are not 'loving'; grief at all we cannot do for our children in a society so inadequate to meet the human needs, becomes translated into guilt and self-laceration. This 'powerless responsibility' as one group of women has termed it, is a heavier burden even than providing a living — which so many mothers have done, and do, simultaneously with mothering — because it is recognized in some quarters, at least, that economic forces, political oppression, lie behind poverty and unemployment; but the mother's very character, her status as a woman, are in question if she has 'failed' her children.

Whatever the known facts,[5] it is still assumed that the mother is 'with the child'. It is she, finally, who is held accountable for her children's health, the clothes they wear, their behaviour at school, their intelligence and general development. Even when she is the sole provider for a fatherless family, she and no one else bears the guilt for a child who must spend the day in a shoddy nursery or an abusive school system. Even when she herself is trying to cope with an environment beyond her

[5] Twenty-six million children of wage-earning mothers, 8 million in female-headed households in the United States by the mid-1970s (Alice Rossi, 'Children and Work in the Lives of Women', a paper delivered at the University of Arizona, February 7, 1976).

control — malnutrition, rats, leadpaint poisoning, the drug traffic, racism — in the eyes of society the mother is the child's environment. The worker can unionize, go out on strike; mothers are divided from each other in homes, tied to their children by compassionate bonds; our wildcat strikes have most often taken the form of physical or mental breakdown.

For mothers, the privatization of the home has meant not only an increase in powerlessness, but a desperate loneliness.

Motherhood, in the sense of an intense, reciprocal relationship with a particular child, or children, is one part of female process; it is not an identity for all time. The housewife in her mid-forties may jokingly say; 'I feel like someone out of a job.' But in the eyes of society, once having been mothers, what are we, if not always mothers? The process of letting-go — though we are charged with blame if we do not — is an act of revolt against the grain of patriarchal culture. But it is not enough to let our children go; we need selves of our own to return to.

To have borne and reared a child is to have done that thing which patriarchy joins with physiology to render into the definition of femaleness. But also, it can mean the experiencing of one's own body and emotions in a powerful way. We experience not only physical, fleshy changes but the feeling of a change in character. We learn, often through painful self-discipline and self-cauterization, those qualities which are supposed to be 'innate' in us: patience, self-sacrifice, the willingness to repeat endlessly the small, routine chores of socializing a human being. We are also, often to our amazement, flooded with feelings both of love and violence intenser and fiercer than any we had ever known. (A well-known pacifist, also a mother, said recently on a platform: 'If anyone laid a hand on my child, I'd murder him.')

These and similar experiences are not easily put aside. Small wonder that women gritting their teeth at the incessant demands of childcare still find it hard to acknowledge their children's growing independence of them; still feel they must be at home, on the qui vive, be that ear always tuned for the sound of emergency, of being needed.[...]

When I try to return to the body of the young woman of twenty-six, pregnant for the first time, who fled from the physical knowledge of her pregnancy and at the same time from her intellect and vocation, I realize that I was effectively alienated from my real body and my real spirit by the institution — not the fact — of motherhood. This institution — the foundation of human society as we know it — allowed me only certain views, certain expectations, whether embodied in the booklet in my obstetrician's waiting room, the novels I had read, my mother-in-law's approval, my memories of my own mother, the Sistine Madonna or she of the Michelangelo Pieta, the floating notion that a woman pregnant is a woman calm in her fulfilment or, simply, a woman waiting. Women have always been seen as waiting: waiting to be asked, waiting for our menses, in fear lest they do or do not come, waiting for men to come home from wars, or from work, waiting for children to grow up, or for the birth of a new child, or for menopause.

In my own pregnancy I dealt with this waiting, this female fate, by denying every active, powerful aspect of myself. I became dissociated both from my immediate, present, bodily experience and from my reading, thinking, writing life. Like a traveller in an airport where her plane is several hours delayed, who leafs through magazines she would never ordinarily read, surveys shops whose contents do not interest her, I committed myself to an outward serenity and a profound inner boredom. If boredom is simply a mask for anxiety, then I had learned, as a woman, to be supremely bored rather than to examine the anxiety underlying my Sistine tranquility. My body, finally truthful, paid me back in the end: I was allergic to pregnancy.

I have come to believe, that female biology — the diffuse, intense sensuality radiating out from clitoris, breasts, uterus, vagina; the lunar cycles of menstruation; the gestation and fruition of life which can take place in the female body has far more radical implications than we have yet come to appreciate. Patriarchal thought has limited female biology to its own narrow specifications. The feminist vision has recoiled from female biology for these reasons; it will, I believe, come to view our physicality as a resource, rather than a destiny. In order to live a fully human life we require not only control of our bodies (though control is a prerequisite): we must touch the unity and resonance of our physicality, our bond with the natural order, the corporeal ground of our intelligence.

The ancient, continuing envy, awe, and dread of the male for the female capacity to create life has repeatedly taken the form of hatred for every other female aspect of creativity. Not only have women been told to stick to motherhood, but we have been told that our intellectual or aesthetic creations were inappropriate, inconsequential, or scandalous, an attempt to become 'like men', or to escape from the 'real' tasks of adult womanhood: marriage and childbearing. To 'think like a man' has been both praise and prison for women trying to escape the body-trap. No wonder that many intellectual and creative women have insisted that they were 'human beings' first and women only incidentally, have minimized their physicality and their bonds with other women. The body has been made so problematic for women that it has often seemed easier to shrug it off and travel as a disembodied spirit.

My own story, is only one story. What I carried away in the end was a determination to heal — insofar as an individual woman can, and as much as possible with other women — the separation between mind and body; never again to lose myself both psychically and physically in that way. Slowly I came to understand the paradox contained in 'my' experience of motherhood; that, although different from many other women's experiences it was not unique; and that only in shedding the illusion of my uniqueness could I hope, as a woman, to have any authentic life at all.[...]

Motherwork, Stress, and Depression: *
The Costs of Privatized Social Reproduction

Harriet Rosenberg

Introduction: The Political Economy of Pain[1]

"Mother who killed two sons says she's paid price," announced a front-page headline. In 1970 a woman smothered her six-week-old son; two years later she smothered a second infant. Both deaths were recorded at the time as crib deaths. In 1984, "frayed by more than a decade of struggling for her sanity," she said that she wanted to warn other women about the postpartum depression that led to the killings. "At the first sign of that, don't hesitate to....For God's sake, ask for help," she said. "I just wouldn't want any woman to go through what I went through" (*Toronto Star*, March 3, 1984).

Why did this happen? Such violence is usually explained in individual psychological terms: people go crazy and do violent things. Yet other violent crimes such as rape, murder, and suicide have been linked to underlying social causes. The correlation between increases in suicide rates, for example, and rising levels of unemployment (Brenner 1973, 1977, 1979) establishes a link between crisis in individual lives and crisis in an economic system. But, because childbirth and childrearing are widely considered to be a "natural" female condition,

* Reprinted from *Feminism and Political Economy: Women's Work, Women's Struggles* edited by Heather Jon Maroney and Meg Luxton. Copyright © 1987 by Methuen Publications. Reproduced by permission of Nelson Canada, 1120 Birchmount Road, Scarborough, Ontario, M1K 5G4. All rights reserved.

[1]Data for this paper were collected during visits to the Post-Partum Counselling Service (PPCS), Ministry of Human Resources, Vancouver, British Columbia, in 1980, 1981, and 1982. PPCS was founded in 1971 and has served over 1,000 women. Despite the efforts of hundreds of people, PPCS was closed by the Social Credit government of British Columbia in 1983. This paper is dedicated to Joann, Jim, Penny, Allison, and Fran, former counsellors who truly fought the good fight.

I would also like to thank the men, women, and children whom I interviewed in New York, Toronto, and Vancouver for their time and the effort they made to share their understanding of parenting with me.

Thanks, too, to Gloria Gordon, Jeanne Stellman, Lawrence Kruckman, Jan Schneider, Rayna Rapp, Joan Jacobson, Don Hale, Meg Luxton, and Richard Lee for their encouragement and suggestions.

379

the possibility of social structural origins of "postpartum depression"[2] have rarely been investigated (Friedan 1968; Oakley 1972). Rather, the dominant contemporary explanatory model, constructed and maintained by a powerful medical establishment, is explicitly asocial. It defines the emotional distress of mothers as an exclusively individual problem called "postpartum depression" and has developed a variety of individual therapies including psychoanalysis, drugs, and vitamins to deal with it. To combat the tendencies which constantly push analysis of motherhood and depression in a personalistic direction we must start with a fresh perspective — one that has both feminist and political economy underpinnings.

Producing or not producing human beings is part of the political discourse of most societies. Historically, as nation-states developed, debates about population grew with them. From the mercantilists to Malthus, demography, taxation, and militarization all became intertwined problematics (Seccombe 1983; Davin 1978). Furthermore, the institutions which turned children into soldiers, taxpayers, and workers have always been part of the public debate on how societies organize to reproduce themselves. Public funds are now seen as being legitimately allocated to these tasks, through school systems and the armed forces, for example. It is the proportions which are debated, not the appropriateness of the undertaking.

And yet the daily work of childrearing within the household/family is almost entirely eclipsed from political discussion and considered to be a private matter. The fact that motherwork is integral to social reproduction and not a personal pastime is obscured. In the public domain debates rage about sexuality, abortion, and birth control, but not about the social conditions of motherwork.

This radical separation of motherwork from social reproduction has a variety of consequences, including depression, anxiety, and violence. But if we start with the premise that the personal is political and that political economy is a significant component of even the most seemingly personal experience, we can analyze motherwork as an integral part of social reproduction.

Such an approach enables us to view postpartum depression not just as an issue of private medicine but as one of public health, and to explore the consequences of the denial of parenting as a form of social labour under capitalism. Ultimately, a central aim of the socialist feminist project is to stimulate inquiry into the deep structural links

---

[2]Based on interviews with Post-Partum Counselling Service chancelleries and interviews with adoptive parents in Toronto.

between so-called private and public spheres and to locate apparently private pain in its socio-political context.

Emotional Pain after Birth or Adoption

> When they say to me, "Oh, what a wonderful baby. How lucky you are," I look around in a daze to see who they are talking to. I'm in a fog all the time. I'm so tired I can't think straight. I hate it. I want my life back.

In Western societies between 60 percent and 80 percent of mothers have emotional problems after childbirth (Davidson 1972; Dalton 1971; Yalom 1968; Hamilton 1962; Balchin 1975; Kruckman 1980). Depression and anxiety are also experienced by women who adopt[3] and by men (Bucove 1964). About 20 percent of women continue to experience depression for many months after birth or adoption, or even occasionally throughout life (Kruckman 1980; Welburn 1980; Rosenberg 1980).

In the medical and popular literature the terms "postpartum depression," "baby blues," and "postpartum psychosis" are often used interchangeably. "Baby blues" is frequently applied to all forms of postnatal psychological problems. Ideologically dismissive, it is akin to the blame-the-victim connotation of "blue-collar blues." However, more precise medical usage distinguishes different forms of the depressed experience. More carefully defined, the term "blues" is restricted to a depressed mood and transitory tearfulness that is experienced by about 80 percent of mothers on the third or fourth day after birth. This mild postpartum depression lasts for a few hours only. Although some explanations have associated it with hormonal changes at the onset of lactation (Dalton 1971), others have pointed out that there is little cross-cultural evidence for such a claim and have argued that there is a historical link in North America between the medicalization of birth and the appearance of mild postpartum depression (Catano and Catano 1981).

At the other extreme, "postpartum psychosis" is also frequently conflated with postpartum depression, especially in medical literature. This confusion results from the fact that medical studies are frequently based on hospitalized populations. Actual psychosis is relatively rare,

---

[3]Based on interviews with Post-Partum Counselling Service counsellors and interviews with adoptive parents in Toronto.

occurring in one in a thousand cases. It is treated by psychiatric intervention, hospitalization, and electroconvulsive therapy (ECT).

There is also a "mid-range" depression which may be expressed as slow, tired, hopeless behaviour, eyes filled with unshed tears or constant crying, or by intense anxiety and frantic behaviour. In this form, feelings of anger and conflict with children or mates is common. About 65 percent of the 1,000 women who sought the services of the Post-Partum Counselling Service (see note 1) expressed fears of harming their children, although very few actually did so. Physiological symptoms like constant colds and rashes, as well as frequent accidents and alcohol and drug abuse, are all associated with this form of postpartum depression (PPCS files). It is a terrifying and debilitating experience, made all the more frightening by the fact that it is rarely mentioned. "You never hear about this," said one woman. "No one ever talks about it. Are they all lying?"

It is this mid-range form of postpartum depression which will be discussed in this paper. It is this type of depression which can be clearly seen to have social structural causes amenable to a socialist feminist political economy analysis.

Treatment: Medical Models, Feminist Models

> My doctor is very squelching. He says, "It's just cabin fever, dearie. Don't worry."

> Sometimes I think my volunteer (at Post-Partum Counselling Service) is the only person in the world who puts the mother first.

There are two competing general models for the treatment of postpartum depression. The medical model stems from an analysis of depression as an individual problem; the feminist model identifies it as a problem related to the oppressed social position of women.

Although there have been different explanations of the etiology of postpartum depression and consequently different fashions in its treatment, the medical model has consistently tried to "cure" the individual. Treatment has included the use of drugs, sleep cures, and prolonged hospitalization in the nineteenth century and electroconvulsive, insulin shock, and psychoanalytic therapies in the twentieth century (Kruckman 1980). One practitioner in the 1940s was so fond of shock therapy that he claimed a 75 percent recovery rate and was not at all alarmed by the 5 percent death rate resulting from it (Kruckman 1980). By the mid-1950s, a new psychopharmacological approach had come to dominate in research and treatment. Psychoactive drugs, often coupled with hormonal injections, were widely used by doctors claiming phenomenal success rates.

The psychoanalytic theories of postpartum depression which developed in the 1930s rested upon the normative conception that biological mothering was the essential mark of femininity. A pioneer of this approach, Zilboorg, stated that depression after childbirth was related to "symbolic castration" and was common "in narcissistic, frigid, latent homosexual women" (cited in Kruckman 1980: 8). The psychiatric literature still characterizes women with postpartum depression as infantile, immature, having unresolved conflicts with their mothers, failing to adjust to the feminine role, and having penis envy. And contemporary medical analyses continue to rely heavily on theories of biological causality (Butts 1969; Karacan and Williams 1970; Seltzer 1980).

Therapy is usually directed at the conflictual areas helping the patient accept the feminine role or express jealous feelings toward the child, occasioned by thwarted dependency needs....(Seltzer 1980: 2549)

However, the studies of hormonal and genetic causes of depression tend to be poorly designed and yield insufficient and even contradictory results (Weissman and Klerman 1977; Parlee 1980; Livingston 1976). The poor quality of research on the physiological causes of postpartum depression should not cause us to discount this line of inquiry, but should alert us to the inadequacy of relying on the simplistic, unicausal models which medical research tends to favour.

A path-breaking alternative feminist model has been developed by the Vancouver Post-Partum Counselling Service (PPCS) after over a decade of experience in working with more than a thousand women (Robertson 1980; Robertson with Howard 1980). The PPCS model is explicitly woman-centred, and looks to find the causes of depression in the structure of society rather than solely in individual pathology or hormonal imbalance.

This perspective has informed the PPCS definition of depression, the population at risk, and the organization of treatment.

Basically we redefined the term. We invented a definition separate from blues and psychosis.

A social perspective has enabled them to identify situations likely to generate postpartum depression. Since they do not see the causes of postpartum depression to be either exclusively physiological or a manifestation of failed femininity, the counsellors and volunteers at PPCS are able to respond to symptoms of depression in all new parents, including men and adoptive parents. It has also enabled them to draw a profile of the person who is most likely to get postpartum depression.

IV. The Elements of Family Life

The most striking feature of the profile is that the woman who is expected to make the most trouble-free transition to motherhood is the one who is most at risk.

The average woman seen by PPCS is twenty-seven, married, middleclass (in terms of occupation and income)[4], and has had at least two years of postsecondary education. She has held responsible paying jobs (e.g., nurse, teller, social worker, hairdresser, secretary, teacher). The pregnancy was planned. Both parents attended prenatal classes. The father was present at the delivery. The woman chose to breast-feed. No significant prior incidents of depression were found among these women. PPCS also found that there was no significant correlation between Caesarean sections and depression, although many of the mothers had negative hospital experiences.[5] Nor have they found that the supposed closeness or bonding said to be inherent in non-medicated childbirth and in breastfeeding has been a mitigating factor (Arney 1980; Robertson 1976).

The societal model used by PPCS has identified loss, isolation, and lack of social support as significant factors contributing to depres-

---

[4]Most of the women who went to PPCS are middle class in terms of income level, lifestyle, and education. The counsellors have assumed that this self-selection was an artifact of a class-based society in which middle-class people have better access to services. However, some poor women do come to PPCS. They tend to be young (late teens or early twenties) single parents on welfare. PPCS counsellors concluded that their depressions were so concretely rooted in economic and social deprivation ("Dealing with the welfare system is automatically depressing") that their situation was not technically postpartum depression.

Over the years PPCS has received letters from women across Canada in response to various radio and television broadcasts they have done. This admittedly informal and unscientific survey seems to indicate that postnatal depression does cut across geographic, occupational, and ethnic lines.

Since so little research has been done on the question of postpartum depression and class, we cannot make any assumptions about differential rates between working-class, upper-class, and middle-class women. One community study in London on depression and marriage (i.e., not specifically the postnatal period) found that, subject to equivalent levels of stress, working-class women were five times more likely to become depressed than middle-class women. Working-class married women with young children living at home had the highest rate of depression (Brown, Bhrolchain, and Harris 1975; Rice 1937).

This data should caution one against assuming that working-class women are automatically plugged into networks of support that mitigate the effects of stress and depression.

[5]J. Croke, *Postpartum Depression* (Master's thesis, School of Social Work, Carleton University, Ottawa, 1982) shows that women who have had home births are less likely to experience depression after birth. However, her sample is small and further research is needed to obtain more significant data.

384

sion. Women who have lost their connection with their paid workplace are particularly vulnerable to depression (cf. Heitlinger, *Feminism and Political Economy: Women's Work, Women's Struggles*). Some women keenly feel the loss of status as a "girl" in this youth-oriented culture, an ironic situation when we consider that many societies count motherhood to be the resolution of a crisis period and the onset of social adulthood for women (Silverman 1975). Other feelings of loss stem from the very real experience of many women who report feeling deserted by their friends and family members after the first few weeks of their child's life (Saulnier, forthcoming). They have few sources of reassurance, advice, or assistance in their work as mothers. They feel their husbands do not understand the pressures of "full-time mothering." And even men who "help," can be undermining because they define the problem solely as the woman's. They do not seem to be able to offer emotional support ("I want a hug and he vacuums the living room"). Past miscarriages, the recent or past death of a parent, or loss of emotional contact with a significant person because of illness or alcoholism can also contribute to feelings of depression.

In an overall sense, postpartum depression is an expression of social isolation accompanied by loss of personal identity, loss of confidence in one's ability to cope. To understand why this should be so, we need to look at how motherhood and motherwork are structured in our society.

Mothering as Social and Personal Work

Defining mothering as work is crucial to the PPCS strategy for postpartum depression.

It is very important for women to realize that what they are doing is work. When I talk to women, I consciously change the language I use. I talk about the job and the fact that the woman is the manager. That's one of the hardest parts about the job and it usually isn't even recognized as work — even by husbands who are "nice guys" and "help" [with housework and childcare]. They don't seem to realize that helping is not the same thing as carrying the weight of responsibility that mothers carry.

This redefinition is also a prerequisite for a feminist analysis of the political economic determinants of mothering as an aspect of social reproduction under capitalism. The overlapping organization of gender relations and the division between what are called "the public" and "the private" (or the domestic household and the economy) effectively assigns the major responsibility for the social work of reproduction to

385

women without any social recognition or social support. Geographical mobility and segmented households, combined with the ideology of family privacy, mean that women with babies get very little on-the-job training from experienced workers.

For many women, becoming a parent is often devastating and confusing because they suddenly find themselves in unfamiliar work situations. Although they have prepared for childbirth by taking classes and reading books, they suddenly find that they have not just given birth to a birth but to an endlessly demanding human being. The care of that human being is not defined as work: it is seen as a private, natural, and essentialist enterprise. When women complain or despair they are frequently told, "Well, you were the one who wanted this baby." But raising a baby is not a personal hobby like raising begonias, it is an undertaking which reproduces society as well as expressing the individual need to love and cherish children.

Examples from kin-ordered societies demonstrate that childrearing is usually viewed as being both social and personal, and most cultures have provided very rich systems of social support to new parents (Lewis 1958; Mead 1962; Oakley 1976; Bettelheim 1954; Metraux 1963; Dawson 1929; Kupferer 1965; Newman 1966). While postpartum customs and rituals may seem obscure or unusual to Western eyes, they serve the very concrete social function of making a public statement that a new birth is significant to the community as a whole and that social attention must be focused on care for the new child. In industrial capitalist societies the spotlight tends to be on the fetus, the doctor, and the technology of hospital births (Arms 1977; Jordan 1978). After a mother leaves the hospital, the thousands and thousands of socially approved dollars and hours and hours of work energy crystallized in the hospital setting evaporate. The woman is on her own: she moves from the public realm of hospital medicine to the private world of her household.

In contrast, in kin-based communities mothers can usually command social support as their right in custom and ritual. Mothers can expect kin to cook, clean, protect, and advise. A new mother may be ritually prohibited from preparing food, thus placing the onus of meal preparation on her kin (Solway 1984). In such settings new mothers are not expected to know or do everything for themselves. They are seen to be at the centre of a social drama and are understood to be entitled to help with caregiving and household tasks. The existence of amulets, special foods, and behavioural taboos constantly reinforce the sensibility that mothering is a public concern and not a private pastime.

In part these social concerns reflect fears for the health of mother and child in societies with high rates of infant and maternal mortality. Postpartum ritual is at one level a communal attempt to deal with a time of real danger for babies and mothers. But such cultural supports can persist and have other effects even when mortality rates are not obviously at issue. By maintaining these rituals communities symbolically testify to their collective responsibility for children and mothers. In one study, Mexican-American women in Chicago who adhered to customary rituals in the postpartum period had no incidence of depression (Kruckman 1980). The confidence these mothers had in the social importance of childrearing was revealed in their attitude toward the evil eye. Mothers felt that if a stranger were to look at a baby he or she must immediately touch the child to ward off the evil eye. One woman recounted how when she spied a man looking at her baby, she crossed a crowded restaurant and insisted that he touch the infant. This belief, which defines uninvolved onlookers as dangerous, presses encorporating claims which prohibit looking without touching. What may look like "superstition" to those outside the culture is actually a cultural safety-net which asserts community responsibility for infant and maternal well-being. The women in this study, unlike those that PPCS found to be vulnerable in their isolation, did not find that they had to solve all problems by themselves.

For most women in North America and western Europe, however, the capacity to override claims of social non-involvement in childcare is quite limited. Unwaged caregiving in the household is rarely recognized as either a contribution to social reproduction or as real work; rather, it is seen in essentialist biological terms for women and as a private and personal reward for waged work for men. Mothers are not supposed to need nor have the right to need, social services or social funds. Public funding for social services to alleviate the work done by mothers in households is identified as a "frill" — an unnecessary expenditure which is unwarranted, especially in times of economic decline (see Armstrong and Armstrong, *Feminism and Political Economy: Women's Work, Women's Struggles*).

Furthermore, for women who do the work of caregiving there are contradictions between the low status of the work they do and and the seemingly high status of the role.[6] "Mother," "motherhood," and

---

[6]There exists a body of literature (reviewed by Parlee 1980) which links postpartum depression to a woman's difficulty in her role as a mother. With the exception of Luxton (1980), however, there has been little discussion of the actual work that women do as mothers on a day-to-day basis.

IV. The Elements of Family Life

"mothering" are words that bring forth flamboyant, extravagant, romantic images. In contrast, the work itself includes many tasks which are not socially respected. Motherwork involves dealing with infant bodily functions: people who clean up human wastes have low status (Luxton 1983). Few jobs have this contradiction so deeply ingrained.

Equally significant to the stress of mothering tasks is the fact that many women do not really know what motherwork involves until they are faced with doing it. They have only a series of platitudes to go on, about it being "the most important job in the world." It is as if one were hired for a new job with the understanding that the job description would be so vast and so vague as to be undoable, that little assistance would be provided, and that any errors would be the employee's sole responsibility. Motherwork, like any other job, must be learned. Books and courses have become the major means of learning: for most it is an inadequate method, because it is not based on experience. There is no apprenticeship period in our society as there is in small-scale kin-ordered societies where young girls learn the ropes as caregivers to younger children. In industrialized societies, a falling birthrate has resulted in small families in which girls (and boys) grow up playing in peer-oriented, age-segregated groups. Many leave home having experienced little or no contact with newborns and infants. Said one North American mother, "When the baby was born, I knew I wasn't ready. I hadn't got through the reading list."

One should add that the experts, the writers of childrearing guides are often men who in fact rarely do the daily work of caregiving themselves.[7] ("Provide a stimulating environment for the infant but don't overstimulate him," says one TV advice-giver.) Advice-givers define the job goals, and they judge the outcome. They garner wealth, prestige, and status by explaining three-month colic, thumbsucking, and toilet training, without experiencing the day-to-day working conditions of mothers. This separation between expert and worker can lead to condescending attitudes on the part of the expert. For example, Dr. Frederick W. Rutherford, in *You and Your Baby*, has some inkling that all may not go well for mothers. He had no index entry under depression but does mention "baby blues." His advice:

Since mothering is constantly defined as a role, women who don't like to do some parts of the job may be considered crazy. See Boszormenyi-Nagy and Spark (1973) for family therapists who criticize women who do not fulfill the female domestic role, and Ehrenreich and English (1979) for criticism of the experts.

[7]See L. Bloom (1976) for a short summary of the vagaries of childcare advice from the mid-nineteenth century to the late 1960s, as well as Ehrenreich and English (1979).

If you are feeling blue, pour out your troubles to someone who will make no moral judgments, someone who will understand that *no matter how little real basis there is for your depression* you nevertheless feel it strongly, but who also knows that with a little help you will manage nicely before very long. Try not to wallow in the blues, but don't be ashamed to express your feelings. You don't have to act like a cheerful cherub when you feel like a Pitiful Pearl. (Rutherford 1971: 167; emphasis added)

To the non-worker, the pain of the worker is not quite real.

Contradictory, guilt-inducing "how-to" books, magazines, and TV talk shows cater to the isolated model of caregiving and miss the social context — people with whom to talk, ask questions, share experiences. Some doctors fill this role, but the medicalization of parenting has been a risky business for mothers. Visits to the doctor can further reinforce the isolated and individuated nature of childrearing. Medical consultations are usually brief and centre on the health of the child, not the work of childrearing or the mental health of the mother. Simple-minded measures like weight gain can become an index for whether the mother is doing a good job. The fact that the child may be gaining and the mother falling apart may not be perceived by the doctor. Furthermore, family doctors may be reluctant to raise the issue of postpartum depression because they feel that women are suggestible and will get the symptoms if the issue is discussed.

Yet women are very dependent on advice from the medical establishment. Mothers may be labelled overinvolved or hysterical, but since they so rarely have alternative methods of assessing health and nutrition matters, they must rely on their doctors. If they go outside the doctor-patient dyad, women risk criticism for listening to "old wives' tales" (i.e., other women) or for negligence (e.g., attacks on home birth). Thus the privatized, asocial model of childrearing is constantly reinforced.

Stress, Depression, Burnout

This is a very scattered job. I can't think any thoughts more than halfway. At least when my husband goes to work he gets silences.

I work 24 hours a day. He [her husband] doesn't. At night when the baby cries, he never wakes up first. I have to

389

wake him and he goes to the baby. Then he's so proud
because he let me sleep!

I wish I could remember what it felt like not to have a knot
in my stomach.

If we step back from the issue of mothers learning a new job, to the
larger context of workplace stress, we gain some useful insights into
the predicament in which many women find themselves.

The effects of stress (Selye 1980, 1975, 1956; Holmes and Rahe
1967; Lumsden 1981) on mental health are now being widely studied.
Unions representing police, firefighters, public employees, and teachers in Canada and the U.S.A. have become very concerned with psy-
chosocial stress in the workplace. Unions, employers, and courts are
increasingly reading symptoms like chronic anxiety, depression, fatigue, and substance abuse (alcohol, drugs, overeating) as signals of
strain produced on the job (Ellison and Genz 1978).

Some extreme forms of mental strain and emotional exhaustion
have been called "burn-out" (Freudenberger and Richelson 1980). It has
been argued that...any kind of frontline person-teacher, social worker,
therapist, nurse, who is at the beck and call of needy individuals is
prone to burn-out" (Murdoch 1981: 6). The literature on burnout among
professionals offers some important insights into what unwaged
mothers experience in the home. Burned-out front-line workers
complain of unrelenting demands, little time away from intense personal interaction with clients or patients, shift work, and constant responsibility for two or more things at once (Maslach and Pines 1977).
Burned-out professional childcare workers are reported to experience
feelings of "inarticulated personal distress" and fatigue as do lawyers,
psychiatrists, nurses, and clinical psychologists when faced with the
tense conditions of their jobs (Mattingly 1977; Maslach and Pines 1977;
Maslach 1976; Pines and Kafry 1978).

If they are not alerted to burnout as a potential response to these
stressors, professionals may respond by blaming themselves and seeking psychiatric help for what they perceive to be personal deficiencies.
Those who have studied this process among daycare workers, for example, argue that it is the structure and intensity of the job, and not
personal idiosyncracies, that cause some workers to develop feelings of
worthlessness. Psychiatric intervention, according to this research,
rarely succeeds unless the work situation is taken into account
(Maslach and Pines 1977).

These stressful job conditions are also true of motherwork. Most
of the psychological and physical symptoms associated with burnout

are the same as those reported by mothers diagnosed as having post-partum depression. Thus I would argue that postpartum depression, like burnout, is actually a syndrome in response to the organization of work.

Not all professionals have emotional problems; nor do all mothers. But there are times in any worker's life when job demands deplete, exhaust, and undermine. Motherwork, especially in relation to an infant, is a job of high demands. For many women it is a job of perpetual shift work — of always being on call (see Stellman and Daum 1973 on health and shift work). In that respect it is like policing or nursing, with the exception that in motherwork there are rarely shifts off. Furthermore, unlike other workers, mothers are not encouraged to separate home and work life. Since mothering is seen as a role, and not as work, mothers are supposed to always remain in character. They rarely get restorative "time outs," let alone extended vacations or sick leave. The disorientation caused by lack of sleep and the disappearance of predictable routines of eating, sleeping, and waking contribute to a "twilight zone" atmosphere. In addition, women who do motherwork also do housework and frequently must combine both jobs in a space like the kitchen that can be unsafe for infants and young children (Rosenberg 1984). Time-budget studies (Meissner et al. 1975; Proulx 1978) and case studies (Luxton 1980, 1983) tell us just how unrelenting these jobs are.

Low Control and High Demands

Those who study industrial workers argue that the most stressful job situations are not caused by high demand levels alone. Multiple demands, under the right circumstances, can create positive work experiences. It is situations of high demand combined with low levels of control in decision making that cause the highest levels of worker stress, measured in terms of exhaustion and depression (Karasek 1979). Daycare workers who feel that they have high levels of participation in their centres, or social workers who feel they participate in agency decision making, express high levels of job satisfaction (Maslach and Pines 1977; Pines and Kafry 1978).

Mental strain from high demands and low control occurs more commonly among assembly-line workers, whose movements are often rigidly contained, than it does among executives, who can set hours and control working conditions (Karasek 1979). Mothering is usually thought to be more similar to an executive job than to assembly-line work. But for many women

391

IV. The Elements of Family Life

> It's a myth that we are our bosses or that we can have a cigarette and a coffee when we want. You can't plan a thing, especially when they are young. You are lucky if you can find time to go to the bathroom. And even then, you don't go alone.

Women as mothers are like women in many other work situations: they have the appearance of wide "decision-making latitude" or control,[8] but in reality they have little power to define their work situations. Typically, women's waged work (nursing, teaching, social work, working as bank tellers, as well as pink-collar jobs) is structured by institutionalized gender hierarchies. Female teachers have responsibilities within classrooms, but major decisions are usually made by predominantly male administrators. Men supervise women in social service agencies, banks, department stores, and beauty shops (Armstrong and Armstrong 1984; Howe 1975; Bank Book Collective 1979; Tepperman 1976). Women who quit underpaid, undervalued jobs for the "freedom" of domestic work and childrearing may find themselves escaping into more of the same. They may make trivial consumer choices between brands of detergent, but ultimately they can be very

---

[8]The terms "control," "decision-making latitude," and "discretion" as used in Karasek's study deserve a closer look. Karasek based his data on male labour force statistics in the U.S.A. and Sweden. "Control" was defined through the questions in the questionnaire that received a yes answer to whether the job was at a high skill level; one learned new things; the job was non-repetitious; creative; allowed freedom; permitted one to make decisions; and to have a say on the job. These were collapsed into the definition of "control" over tasks and conduct during the day. Two measures — "decision authority" and "intellectual discretion — were selected for the study because of their similarity to other measures in the literature. Karasek argues that the literature shows that "decision authority" and "intellectual discretion" are highly correlated. He argued that highly skilled work rarely combined with low decision-making authority.

This combination may be rare in male jobs, but it is more common in female jobs, where the contradiction of high skill but low authority is built into a sex-segregated labour force. Thus female nurses, teachers, tellers, and social workers are usually in the position of knowing that male authority can override their decisions. This sexist structure, coupled with the fact that women are more vulnerable to layoffs than men, argues for more sensitive measures in aggregate data studies to pick up the special stressors to which women are subject. Furthermore, in relation to (unwaged) domestic labour like motherwork, we find the contradiction between high skill levels and low authority levels to be important. The popular myth that housewives/mothers are autonomous and have high degrees of decision-making power in their jobs is belied by their economic dependence on a male breadwinner (Smith 1973; Zaretsky 1976; Luxton 1980).

392

dependent. Women who give up waged work become financially dependent on mates; they become dependent on "expert" advice-givers; and they are tied to infant-defined schedules, the schedules of other children, and the schedule of the wage-earner.

In motherwork, one of the most devastating aspects of lack of control is the absence of feedback. The isolation of the job severely limits the feedback which is so essential to decision making. Daycare workers who work with under-two-year olds argued that isolation from adult company is what they felt most distinguished motherwork from daycare work. As one teacher said,

> Even though the job description is sometimes vague, I know I will get support and feedback from other [teachers] on how I am doing and how a child is doing. That's the big difference between us and mothers.

Some mothers have compared their isolation to being a prisoner of war. Said the nursing mother of a two-month-old whose mate was frequently absent because of job commitments,

> It's pure torture. Your street clothes are taken away and you wear a bathrobe, since all you do all day is [breast-] feed the baby. Just as you fall asleep, you are woken again. You're afraid to fall asleep anyway. What's the point? But God, the worst is that there is no one to talk to.

Strategies for Job design

Occupational health and safety research on stress and social science studies of burnout situate the problems of exhaustion and depression in the workplace. They argue that solutions are social and structural, and lie in redesigning the job to lessen demands and increase control.[9]

---

[9]Karasek (1979) argues for work teams rather than single-task assembly lines. Maslach and Pines (1977), Pines and Kafry (1978), Freudenberger and Richelson (1980), and Mattingly (1977) all include mention of techniques which can give professionals more control in their workplace, including rotations and times off from the constant face-to-face patient or client contact. Collegial support, awareness sessions, and variation in tasks are considered useful ways of restructuring work situations.

Other stress-reducing techniques operate on an individual level. They include strenuous exercise (Freudenberger 1977) and biofeedback (Greenspan 1978). These individual solutions are frequently difficult for mothers of new infants, who

IV. The Elements of Family Life

This is also true for motherwork stress and burnout, and is a solution that was first suggested by nineteenth-century feminists.

Over ninety years ago, feminist economist Charlotte Perkins Gilman wrote a short story called "The Yellow Wallpaper" ([1899] 1973). It is a nightmarish account of postpartum depression based on Gilman's own experience. Gilman's pioneering economic and architectural writings go further. They outline plans for job redesign which take up the whole question of how housework and motherwork should be socially structured, albeit from a somewhat elitist perspective (Hayden 1979). Other thinkers and activists struggled to bring housework and motherwork overtly into the public sphere through daycares and producers' and consumers' co-operatives (Hayden 1981). But by the 1930s these movements were defeated. Housework and motherwork became thoroughly identified as women's individual, private projects, and as "natural" expressions of femininity.

The reawakened women's movement of the 1960s once again introduced housework and mothering as social issues. Such a task is not easy and has led to reassessments of stereotyped patterns of the division of labour. With the exception of breastfeeding, motherwork is not sex-typed labour. Caregiving may be performed by other adults, including men, or by older children, within and outside the nuclear family unit. This work is not "help," which still pins organizational responsibility on a supposedly all-knowing mother, but rather inclines toward the development of strategies for sharing responsibility, which may require women to relinquish some of the pleasures of feeling indispensable. Said one woman,

> When it was his shift with the baby, I had to leave the house. Otherwise, I just hovered over him the whole time. He got anxious and insecure and then I'd take over. It took me a long time to let go and let him be really in charge.

Such a restructuring of jobs and responsibilities forces women and men to face very deep currents of internalized socialization about what mothers and fathers should do and how they should act. It may require constant struggle with previously unacknowledged feelings

---

may be overwhelmed by lack of energy, time, and money, and by the difficulty of finding babysitters to take over while they go out.
The mother of an infant said in this regard, "I know exactly why I didn't get postpartum depression. I bought my way out. We hired a housekeeper to come in five days a week, make meals, clean, and babysit. I went out and just sat in the library. Eventually, I got a job and felt less guilty about the housekeeper."

and fears. At times it may seem that the struggle to assign tasks fairly is just too difficult. But discussions within the household and actions which aim to deliberately involve community members (e.g., drop-in centres, paid maternity/paternity leave or paid leave for a designated caregiver, flexible work hours, choice of workplace or community daycare, babysitting exchanges, co-operative non-profit daycare and political pressure groups that lobby for the maintenance and enhancement of locally controlled social services for parents) all ultimately serve to create dense networks of involvement which can lessen the ambivalences, stresses, and burnout of motherwork.

At the level of political practice, the women's movement has provided the context for this kind of debate. Local self-help groups, such as the Vancouver Post-Partum Counselling Service, have provided immediate crisis support and have helped to reduce women's dependency on experts, enhanced self-perceptions of competence, and enabled women to break down the tendency to personalize domestic problems. Since the 1960s, the lesson of consciousness-raising groups has always been that groups of women who have shared experiences begin to see that their private pain has social roots. This type of collective experience has often served as a prelude to the formation of a variety of helping organizations, from rape crisis centres to shelters for battered wives to groups like PPCS.

However, attempts to socialize childcare outside the household — a project crucial to the redesign of motherwork and parenting — continues to meet with enormous resistance. In North America there is still much popular and official hostility to "institutionalized" daycare. While it may be tolerated for "working mothers," the idea that women who do not work for wages should have access to publicly funded childcare arrangements raises even stronger negative reactions.[10] The intensity of the "fight for good day care," defined as top quality, universally accessible, twenty-four-hour-a-day and community controlled (Ross 1979), illustrates that redesigning the job of parenting is deeply ideological, because it challenges the essentialist ideologies of "the nuclear family" and "motherhood," and the allocation of resources and funds.[11] But such struggles — economic, ideological, and political

---

[10]When I proposed this solution to a group of previously quite sympathetic upper-middle-class women, they balked. Said one woman, "Sure, it sounds like a good idea, but our husbands would never give us the money. It'll never work."

[11]In Toronto, it now seems that over $225 million of public funds will be allocated for a domed sports stadium. This money could provide more than 10,000 new daycare spots for five years. A group of anti-dome pro-daycare fathers demonstrated in opposition to the project but met with little success.

IV. The Elements of Family Life

— are necessary to dismantle the crazy-making structures of privatized motherwork and in its place to create the social job of caregiving.

References

Arms, Suzanne. 1977. *Immaculate Deception*. New York: Bantam

Armstrong, Pat and Hugh Armstrong, 1984. The Double Ghetto: Canadian Women and their Segregated Work. rev. ed. Toronto: McClelland and Stewart.

Armstrong, Pat and Hugh Armstrong. 1987. "Looking Ahead: the Future of Women's Work in Australia and Canada." In *Feminism and Political Economy: Women's Work, Women's Struggles*. Toronto: Methuen.

Arney, W. R. 1980. "Maternal Infant Bonding: the Politics of Falling in Love with Your Child." *Feminist Studies* 6, no. 3.

Balchin, P. 1975. "The Midwife and Puerperal Psychosis." *Midwife Health Visitor* 11, no. 2.

Bank Book Collective, 1979. *An Account to Settle: The Story of the United Bank Workers (SORWUC)*. Vancouver: Press Gang.

Bettleheim, Bruno. 1954. *Symbolic Wounds: Puberty Rites and the Envious Male*. New York: Free Press

Brenner, M. H. 1973. *Mental Illness and the Economy*. Cambridge MA: Harvard University Press.

Brenner, M. H. 1977. "Health Costs and the Benefits of Economic Policy." *International Journal of Health Services* 7, no. 4.

Brenner, M. H. 1979. "Unemployment and Economic Growth and Mortality." *Lancet*, March 24.

Catano J., and V. Catano. 1981. "Mild Post-partum Depression: Learned Helplessness and the Medicalization of Obstetrics." Unpublished ms., St. Mary's University, Halifax.

Dalton, Katharina. 1971. Puerperal and Premenstrual Depression." *Proceedings of the Royal Society of Medicine* 64, no. 12:1249-52.

Davidson, J.R. 1972. "Postpartum Mood Change in Jamaican Women: A Description and Discussion of its Significance." *British Journal of Psychiatry* 121: 659-63.

Davin, A. 1978. "Imperialism and Motherhood." *History Workshop* 5 (Spring): 9-65.

Dawson, W.R. 1929. *The Custom of Couvade*. Manchester: Manchester University Press.

Ellison K., and J.L. Genz. 1978. "The Police Officer as a Burned Out Samaritan." *FBI Law Enforcement Bulletin* 47, no. 3 (March).

Freudenberger, H.J., and G. Richelson. 1980. *Burn-Out*. New York: Doubleday.

Friedan, Betty. 1968. *The Feminine Mystique*. New York: Dell.

Gilman,Charlotte Perkins. [1899] 1973. *Women and Economics*. Edited by Carl Degler. New York: Harper Torchbooks.

Hamilton, J.A. 1962. *Postpartum Psychiatric Problems*. St. Louis MO: C.V. Mosby.

Hayden, D. 1979. "Charlotte Perkins Gilman and the Kitchenless House." *Radical History Review* 21:225-47.

Hayden, D. 1981. *The Grand Domestic Revolution: A History of Feminist Designs for American Homes, Neighbourhoods and Cities*. Cambridge: MIT Press.

Holmes, T., and R. Rahe. 1967. "The Social Adjustment Rating Scale." *Journal of Psychosomatic Research* 1, no. 2.

Howe, Louise Kapp. 1975. *Pink Collar Workers*. New York: Avon Books.

Jordan, Brigitte. 1978. *Birth in Four Cultures: A Cross-cultural Investigation of Childbirth in Holland, Sweden and the United States*. Montreal: Eden Press.

Karacan, I., and R.L. Williams. 1970. *Current Advances in Theory and Practice Relating to Postpartum Syndromes*. Psychiatry in Medicine 1:307-208.

Karasek, R.A. 1979. "Job Demands Job Decision Latitude, and Mental Strain: Implication for Job Redesign." *Administrative Science Quarterly* 24:285-308.

Kruckman, L. 1980. "From Institutionalization to Self-Help: a Review of Postpartum Depression Treatment." Chicago: School of Public Health, University of Illinois Medical Center. Photocopy.

Kupferer, H.J.K. 1965. "Couvade: Ritual or Illness?" *American Anthropologist* 67:99-102.

Lewis, O. 1958. *Village Life in North India*. Urbana: University of Illinois Press.

Livingston, J.E. 1976. *An Assessment of Vitamin B_6 Status in Women with Postpartum Depression*. M.Sc. Thesis, Department of Medical Genetics, University of British Columbia.

Lumsden, 1981. "Is the Concept of 'Stress' of Any Use, Anymore?" In *Contributions to Primary Prevention in Mental Health*, ed. D. Randall. Toronto: Canadian Mental Health Association.

Luxton Meg, 1980. *More Than a Labour of Love: Three Generations of Women's Work in the Home*. Toronto: Women's Press.

_____. 1983. "Two Hands for the Clock: Changing Patterns in the Domestic Division of Labour." *Studies in Political Economy* 12.

397

IV. The Elements of Family Life

Maslach C. and A. Pines, 1977. "The Burn-out Syndrome in the Day Care Setting." *Child Care Quarterly* 6, no. 2 (Summer): 100-113.

Mead Margaret, 1962. "A Cultural Anthropological Approach to Maternal Deprivation." In *Deprivation of Maternal Health Care: A Reassessment of its Effects*, ed. World Health Organization. Geneva: WHO.

Meissner M. et. al., 1975. "No Exit for Wives: Sexual Division of Labour and the Cumulation of Household Demands." University of British Columbia. Photocopy. *Canadian Review of Sociology and Anthropology* 125, no. 4, part I (November).

Metraux A., 1963. "The Couvade." In *Handbook of South American Indians*, Vol. 5, ed. J.H. Stewart. New York: Cooper Square.

Newman Lucille, 1966. "The Couvade: A Replay to Kupferer." *American Anthropologist* 68.

Oakley, Ann. 1972. *Sex, Gender and Society*. London: Temple-Smith

Oakley, Ann.1976. *Housewife*. Harmondsworth: Penguin.

Parlee, M.B. 1980. "Psychological Aspects of Menstruation, Childbirth and Menopause." In *Psychology of Women: Future Directions Research*, eds. J.A. Sherman and F.L. Denmark. New York: Psychological Dimensions.

Pines, A. and B. and Kafry. 1978. "Occupational Tedium in the Social Services," *Social Work* (November) 499-508.

Proulx, M. 1978. *Five Million Women: A Study of the Canadian Housewife*. Ottawa: Advisory Council on the Status of Women.

Robertson, J. 1976. "The Abusive Parent: A Different Perspective." *Canada's Mental Health 24*, no. 4 (December): 18-19.

Robertson, J. 1980. "A Treatment Model for Post-Partum Depression." *Canada's Mental Health* (Summer).

Robertson, J. with A. Howard. 1980. *The Post-Partum Counselling Service Manual*. British Columbia: Ministry of Human Resources.

Rosenberg, Harriet. 1980. "After Birth Blues." *Healthsharing* (Winter): 18-20.

Rosenberg, Harriet. 1984. "The Home is the Workplace." In *Double Exposure: Women's Health Hazards on the Job and at Home*, ed. Wendy Chavkin. New York: Monthly Review Press.

Ross, Kathleen Gallagher. 1979. *Good Day Care: Fighting for It, Getting It, Keeping It*. Toronto: Women's Press.

Rutherford, F.W. 1971. *You and Your Baby: From Conception Through to the First Year*. New York: Signet.

Seccombe, Wally. 1983. "Marxism and Demography." *New Left Review* no. 137.

Seltzer, A. 1980. "Postpartum Mental Syndrome." Canadian Family Physician 26 (November): 1546-50.

Selye, Hans. 1956. *The Stress of Life*. New York: McGraw-Hill.

Selye, Hans. 1975. "Confusion and Controversy in the Stress Field." *Journal of Human Stress* 1, no. 2.

Selye, Hans. 1980. Preface to *Selye's Guide to Stress Research*, Vol 1. New York: Van Nostrand Reinhold.

Silverman, S. 1975. "The Life Crisis as a Social Function." In *Toward an Anthropology of Women*, ed. Rayna Reiter. New York: Monthly Review Press.

Solway, J. 1984. "Women and Work Among the Bakgalagadi of Botswana." Paper presented at the Canadian Ethnology Society, Montreal.

Stellman, Jeanne M. and S. Daum. 1973. *Work is Dangerous to Your Health*. New York: Vintage.

Tepperman, J. 1976. *Not Servants, Not Machines*. Boston: Beacon Press.

Weissman, M.M. and G. Klerman. 1977. "Sex Differences and the Epidemiology of Depression." *Archives of General Psychiatry* 34 (January): 98-111.

Welburn, V. 1980. *Postnatal Depression*. Glasgow: Fontana.

Yalom, D.I. 1968. "'Postpartum Blues' Syndrome." *Archives of General Psychiatry* 18: 16-27.

F. Housework

Like child care, housework is essential work. But like child care, it is organized in a problematic manner. The privatization of the work necessary to maintain people (such as meal preparation), and its attachment to women, was not a necessary situation. Indeed, in the early part of the twentieth century, when household appliances were being marketed, there were feminist proponents of the collectivization of housework (e.g., meal preparation, laundry, child care) (Hayden 1981). Nevertheless, there were strong privatizing forces at work: families' desires for a home that would be a "haven in a heartless world"; the already-entrenched responsibility of women for the care of children, and the closely associated desire to do a good job; the search for profits by large companies that recognized that selling an appliance to every household would be more lucrative than selling industrial appliances to commercial facilities, etc.

The isolation of privatized housework compounded economic need to drive many married women into the labour market. Once there, the problem of who would do the housework presented itself. While some of the work is being collectivized, in a commercial form (e.g., restaurant meals, fast foods, frozen prepared dinners), the majority of Canadians now acknowledge that it is unfair for the woman to continue to be responsible for the housework that remains. In fewer cases, men are actually taking on more of the responsibilities and the work. Meg Luxton describes the changes that a small number of Flin Flon couples are making; while exploring some real changes, she uncovers resistance to change.

Reference

Hayden, Dolores.
1981. *The Grand Domestic Revolution*. Cambridge: MIT Press.

Suggested Reading

Luxton, Meg.
1980. *More Than a Labour of Love*. Toronto: Women's Press.

Two Hands for the Clock: Changing Patterns in the Gendered Division of Labour in the Home*

Meg Luxton

> When I first got a job, I just never had any time, what with looking after the children and the housework. But now my husband has started to help me. He cooks and picks up the kids and is even starting to do other stuff! What a difference! Before, I used to feel like the second hand on the clock — you know, always racing around. Now, with his help, it feels like there are two hands for the clock — his and mine — so I get to stop occasionally.

More and more married women with young dependent children are employed outside the home. Studies conducted in the early and mid-1970s suggested that when married women took on paid employment, their husbands did not respond by increasing the amount of time they spent on domestic labour. These studies reached the general conclusion that married women were bearing the burden of the double day of labour almost entirely by themselves.[1]

Underlying women's double day of labour is the larger question of the gendered division of labour itself. The gendered division of labour, and particularly women's responsibility for domestic labour, have been identified as central to women's oppression in the capitalist societies as a whole, and specifically to women's subordination to men within families.[2] Women's changing work patterns have posed

---

* Reprinted from *Studies in Political Economy*, Fall 1983, No. 12. Reprinted by permission.

This article reports the results of research carried out in Flin Flon, Manitoba in 1981. All the quotes cited in the paper without references are from interviews conducted as part of that research.

[1] Heidi Hartmann, "The Family as the Locus of Gender, Class and Political Struggle: The Example of Housework," *Signs* 6:3 (Spring: 1981), 377-86.

[2] Rayna Rapp, "Family and Class in Contemporary America: Notes Towards an Understanding of Ideology," *Science and Society* 42 (Fall 1978), 278-301; Michelle Barrett, *Women's Oppression Today* (London 1980); Michelle Barrett and Mary MacIntosh, *The Anti-Social Family* (London 1983).

sharply questions about domestic labour — What is actually being done in the home? Is it sufficient? Who is actually doing it? Who should be doing it? This in turn has raised further questions about the existing unequal power relations between women and men.

In the paid labour force, some women's groups, particularly within the union movement, have organized campaigns centred on such specific issues as equal pay and equal access to jobs. Their efforts are a challenge to the existing divisions of work between women and men.[3] Such changes in the definition and distribution of women's work raise the question of whether or not attitudes toward the gendered division of labour in the family household are also being challenged. Has there been any comparable redefinition of men's work roles? And further, has there been any redistribution of work inside the family household? As women learn to drive electrohauls, shovel muck, and handle the heat of coke ovens, are men learning to change diapers, comfort an injured child, or plan a week's food within the limits imposed by a tight budget?

A recent Gallup poll on the sharing of general housework is suggestive. The poll, conducted across Canada in August 1981, reports that during the years 1976 to 1981, Canadians changed their opinions substantially about whether husbands should share in general housework. When asked the question, "In your opinion, should husbands be expected to share in the general housework or not?" 72 per cent responded "yes" in 1981 as compared with 57 per cent in 1976. Only 9 per cent (11 per cent of all men and 7 per cent of all women) replied that men should not share the work.

However, changes in attitudes do not necessarily indicate changes in behaviour. The Gallup poll goes on to suggest that there has apparently been little change in what husbands do. It also implies that women and men disagree on the extent to which men are helping regularly with housework, while in 1981, 47 per cent said they did. By contrast, in 1976, 33 per cent of women polled said men regularly helped while in 1981, 37 per cent of women polled said men regularly helped.[4]

---

[3]For example, see Deirdre Gallager, "Getting Organized in the CLC," and Debbie Field, "Rosie the Riveter Meets the Sexual Division of Labour," in *Still Ain't Satisfied: Canadian Feminism Today*, eds. Maureen Fitzgerald, Connie Guberman, and Margie Woolf (Toronto 1982).

[4]Canadian Institute of Public Opinion, *The Gallup Report* (Toronto, 7 October 1981), 1-2.

Flin Flon Revisited

In 1976-77 I investigated women's work in the home through a case study of one hundred working-class households in Flin Flon, a mining town in northern Manitoba[5] Fives years later, in 1981, I carried out a follow-up study to discover whether or not changes had occurred over the preceding five years. As Flin Flon is a small, fairly remote, single-industry town, it is not a Canadian pace setter. Changes occurring in Flin Flon probably indicate more widespread developments. While this case study does not dispute the finding of earlier studies (that when married women get paying jobs they continue to do most of the domestic labour), it does suggest that the situation is considerably more complex than had previously been perceived. It illustrates some of the factors underlying the emergence of the different patterns of attitudes and behaviours reflected in the Gallup poll. It also shows that in some working-class households, important changes in the division of labour are beginning to occur, as women exert pressure on their husbands to take on more domestic labour.

In the first study, I interviewed women of three generations. The first generation set up households in the 1920s and 1930s, the second in the 1940s and 1950s, and the third in the 1960s and 1970s. With just a few exceptions, women of the third generation were the ones with young children under the age of twelve. Just over half the women interviewed had held paid work outside the home for some period after their marriage. None of them, however, had worked outside the home while their children were young. Most had worked for pay before their children were born, but then had not worked for pay again until their children were of school-age. Regardless of whether or not they held paid jobs outside the home, these women identified themselves primarily as housewives and considered domestic labour their responsibility. They generally maintained that they did not expect their husbands to help with domestic labour. Those few men who did some work were praised as wonderful exceptions.

In the follow-up study I sought out only women of the third generation and was able to locate forty-nine of the original fifty-two. In striking contrast to the previous study, I found that these women, all of whom had children twelve years of age or less, were for the most part working outside the home for pay. Over half of these women had pre-school children, and nineteen had had another baby between 1976 and 1981. Despite their continued child care responsibilities, forty-four

---

[5]Meg Luxton, *More than a Labour of Love: Three Generations of Women's Work in the Home* (Toronto 1980).

women had full-time employment. Of these, fourteen said they would prefer to be in the home full-time; nine said they would prefer part-time paid work; and almost half (21) said they were satisfied with the situation they were in. Four women had part-time paid work. Of these, two were satisfied while one wanted, but had not yet been able to find, a full-time paid job. One wanted to return to full-time domestic labour, but could not afford to quit her job. Only one woman was still working full-time in the home and she said she was there by choice.

What emerged from the interviews was that regardless of whether or not they wanted to be employed, these women were changing their identification of themselves as being primarily housewives. As one of the women who was working for pay full-time, but who wished she could stay at home, put it:

> I am a housewife. That's what I always wanted to be. But
> I have also been a clerk for four years so I guess I'm one
> of those working mothers — a housewife, a mother and a
> sales clerk.

Given the demands of their paid work, these women were forced to recognize their domestic labour in some way. Both interviews and time budgets showed that the attitudes women have towards their work responsibilities (both paid and domestic) affect the way they reorganize domestic labour. A key factor was the extent to which they are willing to envisage a change in the gendered division of labour inside the family household.

Labour-force participation did not necessarily reflect their approval of "working mothers." In 1981 all of the women were asked what they thought about married women who had dependent children and who worked outside the home. Seven flatly opposed it under any circumstances, although all of them were in that situation. Nine did not think it was right for them personally, although they felt such a decision should be made on an individual basis. Eight women said it was fine if the woman needed the money, although they opposed mothers working outside the home for any other reasons.[6]

---

[6]The problem here, however, lies in trying to determine what constitutes economic need. All of these women (24) maintained that they were working outside the home for economic reasons, because their families needed the money. In all likelihood, this is true. However, it may be that these women, like most employed housewives who have been studied, also have non-economic reasons for accepting paid employment. Economic necessity is a more socially legitimated reason and some of these women may be dealing with the contradictory feeling they have toward their

In contrast, over half of the women interviewed (25) maintained that mothers with dependent children had every right to work outside the home if they wanted to. Many of them (14) went further and argued that it was better for mothers to be working outside the home. For these women, economic need was only one of several valid reasons that women would take paid employment.

There was a direct correspondence between the attitudes these women expressed toward paid employment for mothers and their views on the gendered division of labour in the home. All of the women were asked who they thought should be responsible for domestic labour. Their responses show three distinct strategies in balancing the demands of domestic labour, paid employment and family. I have identified these distinct positions, based on their conceptualization of appropriate gender relations, as follows:

1. separate spheres and hierarchical relations;
2. separate spheres and co-operative relations;
3. shared spheres and changed relations.[7]

1. *Separate Spheres and Hierarchical Relations*

Seven respondents (14 per cent) advocated a strict gender-based division of labour. They flatly opposed women working outside the home because doing so would both violate women's proper role and detract from their ability to do domestic labour. These women argued that men, as males, were breadwinners and were "naturally" also house-

---

family obligations and their pleasure in employment by convincing themselves and others that they are only working because they "have to."

[7]There were no obvious sociological factors that might explain the differences in opinion and behaviour. While a large-scale survey might reveal correlations between these different strategies and such factors as political or religious affiliation, ethnicity, and husbands' attitudes, at least among this group of women, and given the available data, no such patterns emerged.

It is also important to point out that while these three approaches are typical, they are not the only available options. Some women have fully egalitarian relations with the men they live with; others live alone or with other women.

A creative strategy was developed by one couple (not included in the study). The man worked a forty-hour week in the mines; the woman was a housewife. They determined mutually what work she was responsible for during a forty-hour week. She did child care while he was at work, as well as heavy cleaning and certain other chores. The rest of the domestic labour — child care, cooking, cleaning, laundry, shopping — they divided equally between them. As a result, each worked a forty-hour week at their own work and shared all remaining labour.

hold or family heads. Women were to be subordinate to their husbands — this was described by several women as "taking second place to my husband." They argued that women's wifely duties included acquiescence in relations to their husband's demands and putting their families' needs before their own. These women maintained that they themselves held paid jobs outside the home only because their earnings were crucial. They intended to stop work as soon as the "emergency" was over.

They insisted that their paid work must never interfere with their ability to care for their husbands and children or to run their households. Because they assumed that domestic labour was entirely women's responsibility, they did not expect their husbands to help. They maintained that boy children should not be expected to do anything at all around the house and argued that they were teaching their girl children domestic skills, not because the mothers needed help, but as training for the girls' future roles as wives and mothers. Accordingly, these women sustained the full double day of labour entirely by themselves.

To deal with the contradiction between their beliefs and their actions, these women worked even harder at their domestic labour. In what appears to be a rigorous overcompensation, they actually raised their standards for domestic labour. They were determined to behave as though paid work made no difference to their domestic performance. Many of them insisted, for example, that every evening meal include several courses made from scratch as well as home-made desserts.

As a result, these women set themselves up in a never-ending vicious circle and ran themselves ragged. Their fatigue and resulting irritability and occasional illnesses only served to convince them that their original prognosis was correct: paid employment is bad for women and harmful to their families.

2. Separate Spheres and Co-operative Relations

Seventeen women (35 per cent) said that women and men are different. Each gender moves in a separate sphere and marriage, in uniting a woman and man, requires co-operation between the two spheres, with each person pulling his or her own weight. These women considered it acceptable for women to "help out" by earning money when necessary but, they argued, women's real work was in the home.

There were two identifiable currents within this general position. Nine women advocated full-time domestic labour for themselves though they agreed that might not be the best option for all women. These women maintained that they should not be working outside the home because they thought it interfered with their family responsibilities. While they were more flexible in their attitudes than those in the first group of women, they argued generally for the maintenance of the gendered division of labour. Particularly in their childrearing attitudes and behaviour, they adhered to a strict notion that boys should not be expected to engage in domestic labours while girls should be encouraged to do so.

Like the first group of women, these women also did most of the domestic labour on their own. Their way of trying to cope with the enormous strain this created, however, was to ease up their standards for domestic labour. They were much more willing to purchase "convenience foods" or to eat in restaurants. They talked about doing less around the house and about feeling vaguely disappointed that they could not keep their place nicer. They were, however, prepared to accept that they could not work outside the home and continue to do full-time domestic labour as well.

Taking a slightly different approach, eight women stated that paid work was acceptable for women with children, if the woman's income was necessary for her household economy. While these women also indicated that they were in favour of maintaining a traditional gendered division of labour, they often engaged in contradictory practices. They would argue that domestic labour was women's work, but in day-to-day activities they frequently asked their husbands to lend a hand, and they all expected their boy children as well as the girls to learn and take on certain domestic tasks.

To a large extent, it appears that the discrepancy between their beliefs and their behaviour lies in an experienced necessity. Unlike those who argued for hierarchical relations, these women were unwilling to become "superwomen." They acknowledged the pressures on them and were willing to ask for help. The extent to which they asked for, and received, assistance varied from household to household. In most cases, children had assigned chores such as washing the dishes or setting the dinner table which they were expected to do on a regular basis. Husbands were not assigned regular jobs but were usually expected to "lend a hand" when they were specifically asked.

3. Towards Shared Spheres and Changing Relations

Twenty-five women — just over half the sample (51 per cent) — stated that regardless of necessity, women with young children had the right to paid employment if they wanted it. For them, wives and husbands were partners who should share the responsibilities for financial support and domestic labour. They supported the idea of changing the division of labour and in practice they were instituting such changes by exerting increasing pressure on their husbands and children to redistribute both the responsibility for, and the carrying out of, domestic labour. As it is these women who are challenging the existing ideology and practice of the gendered division of labour, and especially the place of women and men in the family home, I want to look more closely at the changes they have enacted in the last five years.

A Redistribution of Labour Time

While the women who argued for separate spheres were defending a gendered division of labour within the household, statements made by the third group reflected the trends indicated in the Gallup poll. When these twenty-five women were asked in the 1976 study if they thought husbands should help with domestic labour, most agreed that they did not expect their husbands to do anything, although six said their husbands actually did help. By 1981, however, they unanimously insisted that husbands should help out and all said their husbands did some domestic labour on a regular basis.

An examination of time budgets for these households shows that men have in fact increased the amount of time they spend on domestic labour. By themselves, the figures seem to be quite impressive; men increased their domestic labour time from an average of 10.8 hours per week in 1976 to 19.1 hours in 1981 — an increase of 8.3 hours.

By contrast, in 1976 full-time housewives spent an average of 63 hours per week on domestic labour while women working a double day spent an average of 87.2 hours per week working, of which 35.7 hours were spent on domestic labour. In 1981, women doing both jobs averaged 73.9 hours per week of which 31.4 hours were spent on domestic labour. This is a decrease of only 4.3 hours per week. While one would not expect a direct hour for hour substitution for one person's labour for another, there is a discrepancy between the increase in men's work and the relatively insignificant reduction in women's work. Women on an average were spending 12.3 hours a week more than men on domestic labour. Furthermore, there is a discrepancy between the women's insistence that domestic labour should be shared equally and the actual behaviour of household members. These discrepancies generate considerable tension between wives and husbands — tension

410

which reflects the power struggle inherent in the redistribution of domestic labour.

Women and Men's Domestic Labour

The women who want their husbands to be more involved have developed a variety of strategies and tactics with which to get the men to take on more work. These range from gentle appeals to fairness or requests for assistance to militant demands for greater (or equal) participation. In a few cases, women discussed the situation with their husbands and they mutually agreed on a sharing of tasks that both partners considered fair and reasonable. In the majority of cases, however, negotiations appeared to be out of the question. Instead the couples seemed locked into tension-generating, manipulative power struggles.

For the women, the impetus to change comes first from the pressures of their two jobs. It is fuelled further when they compare their experiences with those of their husbands. Some contrasted their own working time at home with their husband's leisure time.

> I come home from work dead tired and I still have to cook and be with the kids and clean up. And he just lies around, drinking beer, watching TV and I get so mad, I could kill him.

Others compared the standards their husbands expected from their wives with those the men held for themselves. They noted that when living alone, some men kept their households immaculately clean; others lived in a total mess. Whatever their standards for themselves, when the women were around, men changed their behaviour, altered their expectations and pressured the women to meet male standards.

> When my husband is on his own, he's quite happy to live in a pig sty. Mess doesn't bother him. But the minute I get back he insists that he can't live in the house unless it's spotless.
>
> Before we were married he lived on his own and his place was so clean and tidy. But as soon as we got married, he somehow never felt he could clean up. It was all up to me.

Despite the obvious interest these women have in redistributing domestic labour, and despite their motivating anger, there are numerous forces operating which make it difficult for women to insist that their spouses actually share the work.

Because inequalities in the division of labour are based on male power, when woman demand equalization of the work, they are challenging that power. Some women were afraid that if they pushed for more male participation, they would provoke their husbands' anger and rage. At least one woman said her husband had beaten her for suggesting he help with domestic labour.

While there is evidence to suggest that when women have paid employment they increase their own power in marriage, all of these women earned considerably less than their husbands. As a result, the men retained economic power (bread-winner power). Men can also use their greater earnings as a justification for not doing domestic labour. They often argued that with their earnings they discharged the responsibility to the household. Under present circumstances it is up to the individual women to initiate changes in the patterns of domestic labour. For many, economic dependency makes it difficult to challenge their husbands.

Furthermore, the actual task of getting men to do domestic labour is often difficult. If women want their husbands to begin doing domestic labour, they must be prepared to take responsibility not only for overcoming male resistance but also for helping the men overcome both the accumulated years of inexperience and the weight of traditional assumptions about masculinity. Generally, the women assumed that their husbands were unfamiliar with domestic labour and therefore neither knew what needed doing nor had the necessary skills to carry out the work. Taking on this training of resisting and unskilled workers is often in itself an additional job.

When men do start doing domestic labour, women begin to lose control. Domestic labour has traditionally been the one sphere of female control and power. For most women, the kitchen is the closest they ever come to having a "room of one's own." It is difficult for many women to relinquish this, particularly if they are not compensated for that loss by gains made elsewhere — for example in their paid work. While the women were uniformly pleased that their husbands had increased their contribution, they were troubled by the way domestic labour was being redistributed.

Men and Domestic Labour

That men increase the amount of time they spend on domestic labour does not in itself convey much about changing work patterns. Most significantly, it was still assumed that women were primarily responsible for domestic labour and that men were "helping out." When women do domestic labour they often juggle several tasks at once. Once of the ways that men have increased the amount of time they spend on domestic labour is by taking over some of that simultaneous work. Many women reported that their husbands were willing to watch the children while the women prepared dinner or did other household chores. While such actions obviously relieved some of the pressures and tensions on women, they did not reduce the amount of time required of women for domestic labour.

Often when men (and children) took on certain tasks, they ended up generating even more domestic work. A number of women indicated that their husbands cooked, but when they did so they seriously disrupted the orderliness of the kitchen, emptying cupboards to find something and not putting things back or using an excessive number of dishes in the preparation. Another commonly cited example was that when men agreed to look after the children, they actually paid more attention to their visiting friends or the TV. Unattended, the children ran "wild" through the house so that when the woman returned she had to spend a great deal of time tidying the house and calming the children. Further, many women pointed out that getting their husbands to do domestic labour required a considerable amount of their time and energy. Sometimes, women argued, it took more work to get the man to do the work than it did to do the work themselves.

Furthermore, men tended to take over certain specific tasks which had clearly defined boundaries. They did not take on the more nebulous, on-going management tasks and they rarely took responsibility for pre-task planning. For example, a number of men did the grocery shopping on a regular basis but they insisted that the woman draw up the basic list of things needed. Some men would do the laundry, if all the dirty clothes were previously collected and sorted and if the necessary soap and bleach were already on hand.

A recurring theme throughout the interviews was that men preferred jobs that involved working with machinery. A number of men were willing to do the vacuuming because they enjoyed playing with the vacuum cleaner. One woman described how her husband had refused to cook until they purchased a food processor. After that he was forever reading the recipe book and planning new techniques for meal preparation. Several women noted that their husbands had increased their participation in meal preparation after they bought microwave ovens.

IV. The Elements of Family Life

The redistribution that is occurring is selective. The husbands tend to take the path of least resistance. The trend has been for men to take on those tasks that are the most clearly defined, or sociable and pleasant ones, while leaving the more ill-defined or unpleasant ones to the women. Repeatedly women noted that their husbands had taken on reading the children a bedtime story and staying with them until they fell asleep, thus "freeing" the women to wash the dishes and tidy the kitchen. Men were often willing to feed their infant children or take older ones to the park, but on the whole they would not change soiled diapers or wash their children's hair. They would wash the dishes but not the kitchen floor or the toilet. One man would vacuum the living room rug but refused to do the stairs because they were too awkward.

A number of women expressed concern about this pattern. They noted that when men took on the more pleasant aspects of domestic labour, they were left with the most onerous and boring tasks. They were particularly concerned when the man took on more of the play-time with children. As one woman expressed it:

> I'm really glad he's spending more time with the children. They really enjoy it. But it's beginning to make me look like the meany. Daddy plays with them and tells them stories and other nice things while I do the disciplining, make them wash up, tidy their toys and never have time to play because I'm cooking supper.

One of the most significant transformations of men's involvement in domestic labour has been in the area of child care. While most fathers have always spent some time with their children, particularly with older children, increasingly they are doing more of the day-to-day caregiving, especially with younger children. Perhaps the most significant change of all has been with the birth process itself.[8] In 1976 only 4 out of 25 men had been present at the birth of at least one of their children. However, of the babies born between 1976-1981, 10 of the 19 new fathers had been present at the birth (and only 2 of these were of the original 4). The wives indicated that they felt very strongly that having their husbands involved in the birth also drew the men into the whole process of pregnancy, child birth and infant care. Men who were willing to attend the birth were subsequently more inclined to get

---

[8]It seems to me that the involvement of men in the actual birth of their children is of enormous significance — something which has not yet been appreciated, or studied.

414

up at night with the baby, to take over certain feedings and to be generally more involved with their small babies.

Despite this very promising shift, women were still responsible for overall child care. All twenty-five women said it was up to them to arrange day care for their children when they worked outside the home. If the child care arrangements fell through on any particular day, it was the woman who had to get time off work to stay home, although this can in part be explained by her lower pay and in part by his unavailability when underground.

Furthermore, men "babysat" their own children — something that women never did. The implication of this typical reference was that the children were the responsibility of the mother, and the father "helped out." This attitudinal difference was often carried out in behaviour as well. Women repeatedly described situations where men would agree to watch the children, but would then get involved in some other activity and would ignore the children. As children grew up, they learned from experience that their mothers were more likely to be helpful, and so they would turn to the woman rather than the man for assistance, thus actively perpetuating the traditional division of labour.

The ambivalent and often reluctant way in which these men have moved into domestic labour reflects a combination of valid reasons and invalid excuses. In "The Politics of Housework," Pat Maindari describes with biting sarcasm the various forms of male resistance developed in response to a wife's attempt to share housework:

> (Husband): "I don't mind sharing the work, but you'll have to show me how to do it."
> Meaning: I'll ask a lot of questions and you'll have to show me everything every time I do it because I don't remember so good. And don't try to sit down and read while I'm doing my jobs because I'm going to annoy the hell out of you until it's easier to do them yourself.[9]

Flin Flon women described various forms of male behaviour that were obviously intended to resist attempts to draw them into domestic labour. The majority of resisters took a subtle approach (passive resistance) similar to the ones satirized by Maindari. One woman described how their kitchen sink was directly in the centre of the kitchen counter. Normally the draining board sat on the left-hand side and the dirty dishes were stacked on the right. Her husband maintained he

---

[9]Pat Maindari, "The Politics of Housework," in *Sisterhood is Powerful*, ed. Robin Morgan (New York 1970), 449-51.

was unable to do the dishes as he was left-handed and the sink was designed for right-handed people. Some women talked suspiciously of the way household machinery "broke down" when their husbands tried to use it. Several women told of incidents where their husbands agreed to do the work but then repeatedly "forgot" to do it, complained when the women "nagged" them about it, and finally told the women to do it themselves if they did not like the way the men did it. One man explained his position quite clearly:

> Look, I'm not interested in doing stuff around the house. I think that's her job, but since she's working she's been on my back to get me to help out so I say "sure I'll do it." It shuts her up for a while and sometimes I do a few things just to keep her quiet. But really, I don't intend to do it, but it prevents a row if I don't say that.

For men to take on domestic labour meant that they had to give up some of the time they had previously spent on their own enjoyments. Within certain limits this may not be much of a sacrifice, but at some point a man's increasing involvement in domestic labour starts eroding his ability to engage in other activities he values highly. There is a substantial difference between washing dishes and watching TV, and in having to come home early from drinking with one's mates at the pub because one has to cook dinner.

Because the majority of men have, until recently, not been expected to do domestic labour, they have not been taught either implicitly, the way girls learn via their dolls and play kitchens, or explicitly, through "helping" mother or in home economics classes. As a result, they often lack knowledge and are unskilled and awkward. Working at a job for which one is ill-prepared often generates feelings of anxiety, inadequacy and incompetence which are easily translated into a generalized reluctance to continue the job.

Some men expressed a willingness to do domestic labour but they were afraid that if it were publicly known that they did "women's work," they would be subjected to teasing and ridicule. One man, for example, quite enjoyed doing the vacuuming. However, there were no curtains on the windows, so the interior of the house was visible from the street. As a result, he did the vacuuming on his knees so that no one would see him! Other men were willing to do tasks inside the house but steadfastly refused to do those tasks that were "women's work" outside in public (hanging washing on the line, for example).

This fear of public ridicule was illustrated by two neighbours. Both families visited together frequently, and the men were friends.

They also did a considerable amount of cooking and cleaning. Both, however, insisted that their wives not let the other couple know of the extent to which the men did domestic labour. The fear of public ridicule may reflect a deeper fear. When wives insist that men move into an area that has traditionally been defined as "women's work," men face a challenge to their conventional notions of femininity and masculinity. This may arouse deep psychological and emotional resistances, and stimulate anxiety and fear.

Because most couples are unable to negotiate openly a redistribution of labour, they often get locked into tension-producing manipulations. This was illustrated rather graphically by the story one woman told about how she "got" her husband to do the laundry.

She began by explaining that she felt it was only right that he do some of the domestic labour once she started working full-time outside the home. She asked him to help her and he agreed in principle, but he did not do anything. When she asked him to do things like cook supper or wash the dishes he would regularly say that he was going to, but then he would put it off indefinitely so that he ended up doing it all. She decided that she needed to teach him to do one specific task on a regular basis. Laundry, she estimated, would be an appropriate job for him, so she figured out what the discrete tasks involved in doing the laundry were.

The first day she left the laundry basket of sorted clothes sitting at the top of the basement stairs. As he was going down to his work-room she asked him to take the laundry down and put it on top of the machine. She repeated this several times until he automatically took the basket down without being asked. "Once he had done that a few times I knew he'd taken it on regular so I was ready to move on to the next step." She then asked him, as he went down with the basket, to put the laundry into the machine. Once that was learned, she asked him to put in the soap and turn the machine on.

> Finally it got so he would regularly carry the laundry
> down, put it in and turn it on. I never even had to ask
> him. So then I began getting him to pick up the dirty
> clothes.

Eventually, after more than six months of careful, though unstated strategizing on her part, the man was doing all the work involved in laundry. "Now he does it all regular. I think I will train him to do the dishes next."

While neither of them discussed what was going on, the husband by participating in the process gave his tacit acceptance of the new division of labour. However, because the work was being redistributed by manipulation rather than negotiation, the process only served to exacerbate the already existing tensions between the spouses. It did not engender greater respect or affection between the two. By "tricking" her spouse, the woman had relieved some of the burden of her work but she was contemptuous of him for the way he took it over:

> What a fool. If I'd have asked him, he would have refused. If I'd begged and pleaded he would have said he'd do it if he knew how, but would have said he didn't know how and so couldn't. So I fooled him and now he does it. But the whole thing's really stupid.

For his part the husband refused to discuss what was occurring. The wife's interpretation was bitter:

> Things are changing in our life. My job has forced us to do things differently. But he will not talk about it. So I play tricks and hate him and I think he must resent me — but I don't know because he won't tell me. So things change but I don't know what it means. Sometimes I think men are really stupid, or they hate women or at least there's no point trying with them.

Conclusion

This case study suggests that changing patterns of paid employment are creating a crisis in the way labour is currently distributed and accomplished in the family household. It illustrates the ambiguities reflected in the Gallup poll findings and shows that these ambiguities arise from serious problems in the way domestic labour is changing. It also suggests that ideologies of "family" are very strong and play a central part in the way most people organize their interpersonal relationships and their domestic lives.

Because people tend to evaluate their experiences in light of existing social explanations and ideologies, the response of Flin Flon women can be set in a broader context. The three perspectives expressed reflect ideologies which are currently prominent.

Those women who put forward a "separate spheres and hierarchical relations" position were defending the traditional conservative view which locates women inside the family, subordinates women's

418

interests to men's, and places priority above all on the preservation of the breadwinner husband/dependent wife nuclear family.

Because the beliefs these Flin Flon women held conflicted directly with the activities they engaged in, they were compelled to mediate the contradiction. Their attempts to defend a strict gendered division of labour forced them deeper into the hardship of the double day. Their actual experiences highlight the conditions under which support for right-wing "pro-family" reform movements is generated, for in their opinion, it is their paid work that creates the problem.

Those women who argued for "separate spheres and co-operative relations" were expressing a classic liberal view of appropriate female/male relations in the family. This "different but equal" perspective echoes the maternal feminism of some early twentieth-century theorists. It is also found in many sociologists of the family such as Young and Wilmott, who argue that marriages are now symmetrical or companionate.[10]

Those women who argued for "shared spheres and changing relations" were expressing contemporary feminist views which hold that the existing gendered division of labour is a major factor in women's oppression. In challenging the way work is divided in the home, they are questioning the existing relationships between women and men, and between children and adults. Discussing existing family relationships, Hartmann has argued that "Because of the division of labour among family members, disunity is thus inherent in the 'unity' of the family."[11]

This study suggests that a large-scale social transformation is occurring as traditional patterns are eroding and new ones are emerging, but to date the change has been acted out on the level of the individual household, and may, in the short run, be intensifying family disunity. What emerged from these interviews was the total isolation both women and men felt. Women involved in active, collective organizing to change the division of labour in the paid work-force have the women's liberation movement, the trade union movement, Status of Women committees, and sometimes the law and other organizations or institutions such as the Human Rights Commissions, to back them up. In contrast, women challenging the gendered division of labour in the home do so on an individual basis. Similarly, there is a complete lack of social and material support for men with regard to domestic labour. Very few unions have won paternity leave, for example, so it is

---

[10]Nellie McClung, *In Times Like These* (1915; Toronto 1972); Michael Young and Peter Willmott, *The Symmetrical Family* (London 1973).

[11]Hartmann, "Family as the Locus," 379. (See n. 1 above.)

very difficult for new fathers to get time off work to be with their new children. This makes it very difficult for men actually to take equal responsibility for their infants.[12] Accordingly, any man who takes on domestic labour places himself at odds with current social practices. It takes a certain amount of self-confidence and courage to do so.

As a result, the majority of respondents implied that they considered that the changes in their domestic division of labour were specific to their individual households. They perceived these changes not as part of a large-scale transformation in the patterns of work and family life, but as a personal struggle between them and their spouse. Such a perception only exacerbated the tensions between women and men.

As material conditions change and new ideologies emerge, many individuals and families are floundering, trying to decide what they want, how to get it, and most problematically, how to resolve conflicts between various possibilities and needs. There are currently no social policies or clear-cut, developing social norms to provide a context in which individuals can evaluate their own actions. Instead, there are several contending ideologies and related social movements, such as the "pro-family" movement.[13] While these movements articulate positions on what female/male relations should entail, they rarely organize to provide support for women to achieve the desired end. The current situation is thereby generating a great deal of confusion and often pain and interpersonal conflict, especially between women and men.

Finally, this study demonstrates that until the exclusive identification of women with domestic labour is broken, there is no possibility of achieving any kind of equality between women and men. If the necessary labour is not redistributed, women end up with a dramatically increased work load. Unlike earlier studies, the findings of this research suggest, that despite all the problems, some working-class women are contesting male power and challenging male privilege and some men are responding by assuming more responsibility for domestic labour.

---

[12] In Quebec the unions of CEGEP teachers have won paternity leave. This has made it possible for some men to take equal responsibility for infant care.

[13] Susan Harding. "Family Reform Movements: Recent Feminism and Its Opposition," *Feminist Studies* 7:1 (Spring 1981), 57-75.

V. Trouble Spots in Family Life

A. Two-Job, Dual-Career Marriages

Those of us who believe that gender roles have so changed that women now face virtually the same opportunities as men are most surprised when we attempt dual-career, or even two-job, marriages. At least, if and when we have children, we cannot help but be dismayed at the obstacles that women face in trying to combine family and career. In fact, the society we live in is still profoundly organized around basic gender divisions.

Neighbourhoods in North America are built in a way that fails to incorporate commercial and public services into blocks of housing, and thus establishes the need for the services of a housewife (Hayden 1984). Privatized housework and child care assume the full-time housewife. Without large-scale state provision of quality child-care facilities, couples are usually forced to sacrifice the career or job of one parent to the needs of the child, at least in the first year of the baby's life. Whatever arrangements parents make, it seems necessary that either the baby's needs or the mother's needs (or a bit of both) must suffer because of the absence of flexible work hours, the organization of career expectations on the male model, the absence of community assumption of some of the responsibility for young children, etc. The excerpt from journalist Caroline Bird's *The Two-Paycheck Marriage* discusses some of the problems that couples who attempt two-job, and especially two-career, marriages must face.

References

Hayden, Dolores.
1984. *Redesigning the American Dream*. New York: Norton.

The Two Career Collision Course*

Caroline Bird

If her Age Thirty Crisis is the Baby Panic, his is the Bind of the Two Person Career. Successful male careers have so often involved the support of an unofficial Second Person — a supportive wife who frees him to give everything to his work — that many careers have come to require this backup. At the beginning, while they are establishing their competence, two-career couples need no more help from each other than college roommates. But as soon as they get into serious career politics and need a Second Person, they find there is a limit to what they can do to back each other up.

This is the bind. She sees it first. She may say she needs a wife, but all she has is a husband, and everyone knows that husbands don't do the work of corporate, political, or academic wives.

He has a wife, so it takes him a little longer to see that the rules of the career game have been made by men married to Second Persons. He may not see the bind until something happens to show him that his own wife isn't doing what those men's wives do.

For a rising marketing manager, it was having to meet his boss at the London airport with a cheap canvas duffel bag for luggage. He had decided to go on the spur of the moment and couldn't find his suitcase. His wife was in a plans board meeting at her advertising agency, but he made them call her out to the phone. "Oh my God," she said. "I never got around to unpacking it. It's in my station wagon full of my summer clothes. Darling, I can't leave and I can't talk now. Just go out and buy yourself a new one." By that time the only store open was the corner drugstore.

It dawned on him, at that moment, that a vice-president of marketing should have instant access to a suitcase that was not full of somebody else's summer clothes. He was right.

Career Rule One says that the First Person of the career couple doesn't have to worry about the logistics of food, clothing, or shelter, while working. Food, clothing, and shelter are to be as available as water from the kitchen tap. Wherever the careerist labors, at home or at work, meals appear whenever he is hungry. Dirty clothes pick themselves up

---

* From *The Two Paycheck Marriage* by Caroline Bird. (New York: Rawson, Wade Publishers, 1979). Copyright © 1979. Reprinted by permission.

and hang themselves pressed and cleaned in the closet, and plumbing emergencies are strictly for somebody else. The only maintenance time he is expected to take is for matters requiring his physical presence, such as visits to doctors, lawyers, dentists, barbers, or for civil duties such as voting and serving on juries.

Career couples may start to live by the "roommate test" devised by Sandra and Daryl Bem, psychologists from Stanford University. Home chores are divided on the basis of personal preference, hired out to a paid helper, or simply left undone. But as careers advance they both have to find ways to meet the competition from men who have Second Persons managing the home front. Rather than admit they have any "outside" commitments, they may have to keep their attempts at equality a secret. She may feel, for instance, that she has to bend over backward to disprove the suspicion that she is staying at home for family duties, and he may not wish to have it known he has to leave early to do the marketing or pick up a child from the sitter.

An accountant discovered the bind when he was offered a partnership in a growing firm in Phoenix, Arizona, but realized there would be no job available for his wife there. And it said right in their personally written marriage contract that neither would take a job in a place where an equally good opportunity could not be found for the other. It hadn't worried him at the time, because accountants can always find work anywhere — but not an opportunity like this one!

Career Rule Two says that the First Person of the career must be ready to work whenever and wherever it best serves the career. A growing number of young career couples agree to go where the best opportunity offers, whether for the wife or the husband, but this always means violating this Career Rule for one of them. A computer specialist agreed always to follow his wife, on the ground that it was easier for him to find work than for her. A wife with a Ph.D. in nuclear physics, on the contrary, agreed to go wherever her husband, a chemist specializing in law, could find work in his esoteric specialty.

The career needs of a wife can handicap the career mobility of a man in exactly the same way that women traditionally have been handicapped by the presumption that they will always follow their husbands. The experience of Joseph Juhasz, professor of psychology, suggests that the handicap may be more severe for a husband because it is less expected. When Bucknell University refused to hire his wife, he followed her to the University of Colorado at Boulder. Eventually he landed a job in her new location, but only after being snubbed by her new colleagues and suspected by prospective employers. No one believed that a competent man would quit to follow his wife.

A real career means frequent moves on short notice as opportunities arise. Many organizations groom their promising candidates for promotion by giving them short-term experience all over the country. Those who refuse seldom get another chance. Big companies expect a candidate for promotion to be ready to take on the challenge of a new job in another city with little or no time out for the work of moving there.

This is hard on women officers, who seldom have a "corporate wife" to do the packing and relocating. It is particularly hard on a single mother being groomed for promotion, because she has no one to house-hunt for her in the new location or even to watch her children while she attempts to do it for herself. But a candidate whose wife is not a Second Person may be even worse off than a single mother if his wife has a serious career commitment in the area he is being asked to leave.

There are a number of bases on which the couple can make the decision. They can maximize immediate money earnings: if there's no good job for her, they won't go. They can maximize career opportunity: if his prospects are much greater than hers, she'll go. They can refuse any change unless both stand to profit equally.

As the proportion of two-career families increases, bureaucracies may find it harder to groom promising candidates this way. But in spite of public criticism they are not changing very fast. A man with a career wife continues to be at a disadvantage. In the economic recession of the late 1970s, bureaucracies were not hurting for talent. For every middle manager who refused a move, five others were eager to go.

Career Rule Three says that the First Person of the career has a cheering section at home, and there's a reason why. If a dedicated professional is to be coolly objective, he is going to need to get his own emotional support off the job, preferably from someone who won't set up a second set of waves. A career wife may want to give this support, but finds the timing awkward. She may not be available just when her husband badly needs relaxation, recreation, or simply a friendly ear.

Career couples can buck each other up, but they can also buck each other down. This is what happened to an accountant on the day he was promoted to head of his department. The news thrilled him, but it scared him, too. On the way back to his office he avoided the curious inquiries of the colleagues he would soon have to supervise and thought only of what his wife would say when he told her the good news that night. But when he got home he found she had been so badly humiliated during her day at the office that he felt his good news would make her feel even worse. He hid the split of champagne he had brought home to celebrate and settled down to listen. After hours of assuring her that a job didn't matter all that much, he found himself believing his own words and losing enthusiasm for his own recent triumph.

V. Trouble Spots in Family Life

Employers count on continuing enthusiasm in candidates for promotion, and they recognize the importance of dependent wives in maintaining it. "I'd gone up in the corporation as far as I could go as a single man," an executive vice-president confessed to John Cuber, author of *The Significant Americans.* "Why they are so prejudiced in favor of married men, I'll never know. Maybe it's those psychological adjustment guys in Personnel."

Salesmen need so much emotional support from home that companies woo their wives with presents and trips. At conventions, they may offer wives tips on how to help their husbands get ahead. Much of the advice draws heavily on the crude flattery advocated by the "true womanhood" cults: "Don't nag," one lecturer advised, and, "watch your figure." Since affirmative action, convention programs for "wives" have been renamed programs for "spouses," but no counterpart books or programs school company husbands in fulfilling the supportive role.

This does not mean, however, that emotional support is not going to be demanded of *him*. According to psychiatrist Ruth Moulton, successful women need unusual emotional support from men, and the Henning and Jardim study of managerial women bears her out. A wife with a rising career may have been launched by a supportive father or mentor and expect the same continual encouragement from a husband. Moulton found successful women patients often used their husbands as sounding boards and support systems for advice about how to handle difficult men, approval of their papers, help with framing letters and coaching about every move ahead. Husbands may have encouraged them in the beginning, but eventually they felt used, bored, and resentful. Moulton goes on to say that a wife denied emotional support at home is tempted to look for it on the job from a boss, colleague, or even a subordinate on the job.

"Somehow, I never got down to finishing the book," a professor explained when he lost out on tenure. "When Joan wasn't working she could run down references in the library for me. She was always available for typing and reading. But when she went to work she lost interest in my project — and so did I. When the time came for tenure review, I just didn't have the publications for the promotion."

Career Rule Four says that the First Person of a successful career gets direct assistance in his work from an unpaid Second Person at home. For those now at the top, it began innocently enough. An ambitious young husband brought work home. His young wife was not only eager to share his work, but she was also the only other person with a financial interest in it. She typed, filed, kept books, checked facts, answered phones, made appointments. Later on she listened, learned, entertained, made friends who could help. Her unpaid work may have been the most profitable use of her time. According to an analysis made by Lee Benham, an economist at Washington University in St. Louis, a woman's college education does more to raise the income of her husband than it does to increase the income she can earn herself.

As the career advanced, so did the staff work for which there was as yet no money. Ministers' wives kept church books. Doctors' wives relayed critical messages. Political wives distributed leaflets, organized meetings, knocked on doors, stuffed envelopes. The wives of authors typed, checked facts, edited, listened.

"I was at the typewriter from 9 p.m. to 1 a.m. every night for a year, while he slowly dictated to me," Jane Cheney Spock told a reporter of her life while her husband was writing his famous manual, *Baby and Child Care*. "Sometimes I'd say, 'That's not clear,' and I did quite a lot of changing of expressions and other things that weren't clear. I consulted all kinds of doctors about what should be in the book on the various diseases. Some of the doctors didn't approve of Ben, so I had to woo them. In those days, there were eight different formulas, and I tested them again and again to make sure they worked, and I found that one, given out by New York Hospital, didn't work. The nipples clogged up."

At first, her help merely saved money. But a wife who has typed, filed, listened, coached, advised, remembered, and answered the phone for decades develops uniquely relevant skills and knowledge that the First Person can't buy in the open market. This is what happens to women like Madeline Steingut, wife of the veteran Speaker of the New York State Assembly who sat in on so many political huddles in Albany during the twenty-six years her husband was in the New York State Assembly that she became a force in New York State politics.

At the very top, the work of a wife can become a full-time executive responsibility. Elizabeth Lyman, wife of the President of Stanford University, traveled with her husband, raised funds, made speeches, spoke out on public issues, and assisted him by entertaining nearly fifty groups in the course of an academic year. To do all this, she kept a full-time secretary, a house manager, a custodian, and a caterer busy assisting *her*.

Rosalynn Carter is a textbook example of the increasingly important work done by a career man's Second Person. Like many wives of small businessmen, she started doing the books at the Carter warehouse when her husband left the Navy to run that business. When he went into politics, she became an aide, a campaigner, and a public relations adviser.

In 1978, Rosalynn Carter was supervising research on issues the President assigned her from her own office in the working quarters of the White House. She attended Cabinet meetings because, "If I didn't,

427

there's no way I could discuss things with Jimmy in an intelligent way." These discussions were not conducted casually, but at weekly working lunches reserved for Mrs. Carter on the President's tightly programmed schedule.

The Carters believe in the two-person career. They think they can strengthen family life in America by encouraging other couples to follow their example. Like Mrs. Carter, Second Lady Joan Mondale has been given a White House office, a staff, and specific responsibilities for relations with the arts community. In 1977, at least three wives of high-ranking Presidential aides had quit jobs as schoolteachers to do volunteer work from offices in the White House. Even after her separation from political adviser Hamilton Jordan, Nancy Jordan continued to work a full day as an aide in the West Wing, where large groups are received.

Anne Wexler, wife of Joseph Duffey, head of the National Endowment for the Humanities, expressed the Carter philosophy shortly before she was appointed to the White House staff. "It's easy for us because we both work and the children are grown. But there must be great strains and pressures when only one member of the family is involved in something like this — the other one must feel left out."

The Carters had reason to worry about the health of the two-person career. In 1978, Second Persons were growing restive and a few were striking out for careers of their own. Even southern wives grew uppity. In Alabama, the former wife of Governor George Wallace talked of running for Governor. In Georgia, the divorced wife of Senator Herman Talmadge used all she had learned as a Senator's wife to run for Congress herself, but lost. The Spocks were divorced, and in an interview with *The New York Times*, Jane Spock attributed the breakup to his lack of recognition for her work on the baby care manual that had made him a household word.

In spite of the example of the Carters, the two-person career was not attracting the sophisticated young college graduates who were seeking fame in Washington. These young couples wanted it all, and "all" meant two *equal* careers.

The Cool Supercouples

Almost everyone applauded their ambition, but people asked how long a husband and wife could keep their separate careers as well as each other. It was a good question.

Ten years out of college, the promising dual-career couples dwindle down to a precious few.

Some are no longer married.

Some are still married but only one has a career. Usually it's the wife who drops out, and when the career that remains is his, there's no public relations problem. She's having a baby or keeping house or into volunteer work. Husbands who drop out have a harder time explaining themselves. They may be described as going to school, starting a business, or "taking time off to think things out."

The couples who wanted everything, who survive with both careers growing into their forties or fifties, are very special people. First off, they have double luck: if it's a first marriage, their careers have paced each other. Next, they are personally cool, because for both of them work comes first: however much they may think of each other, each has to be able to keep going for weeks on end without daily doses of love and affection. Another point is that the kind of work they do has to make it possible for them to help in each other's careers or keep out of each other's working lives altogether. Finally, they are human dynamos, compulsive planners, and time misers. But when they have to choose, work wins out over friends, family, leisure — even children.

They are Cool Supercouples because work defines the terms of their marriages. Work brings them together, keeps them together, or separates them. A working relationship may even last longer than the marriage. It is surprising how many of the stablest two-career marriages are between people in the same occupation or on the same professional network.

Entertainers marry entertainers. "With our crazy hours, you can't marry anyone else," say Eli Wallach, award-winning star of the film *Baby Doll*. He met his wife, Anne Jackson, when both were in a Tennessee Williams play and they now have three children. They like to spar with each other. "I've looked at Anne up on a 40-foot screen in bed with another man and not many husbands have to cope with that," he once boasted.

"I welcome *vive la difference*, all right," she retorted. "But what I don't like is if he's making more money than I am."

There are academic couples like the sociologists Peter Rossi and Alice Rossi. He's an opinion research specialist. She's an innovator in the sociology of women. Or academics Robert Whitman and Marina von Neumann Whitman: both are professors at the University of Pittsburgh. He took a leave from his job as head of the English department to join her in Washington when she went there to serve on the President's Council of Economic Advisers.

There are literary couples operating their separate typewriters together like Eleanor Clark, author of *The Oysters of Locmariaquer*, and her Pulitzer Prize-winning husband, Robert Penn Warren. Joan Didion was writing her fastidious novel, *A Book of Common Prayer* while her husband, John Gregory Dunne, was writing his own novel, *True Confessions*, which became a national best-seller. They edit each other's work, but he admits she's the better pencil editor.

There are media couples, like Jo Moring, news director of NBC Radio Network and Jerry Moring, news manager of WNBC-TV in New York who each have a phone beside their bed so that both can call their newsrooms at the same time.

Marrying a fellow professional is a career stimulant. Learning and teaching sharpens the skills of both. Each has an in-house resource for work problems. Sociologists married to other sociologists actually have been found to publish more papers than sociologists married to people who aren't in the field.

In work that depends on the exchange of information such as fashion, news, entertainment, publicity, research, and publishing, a spouse in the business can double the flow of vital gossip. Married competitors have more to gain by exchanging information than they have to lose by divulging an occasional "secret." As in the nineteenth-century marriages of property, a mutual economic interest stabilizes these unions.

Although a high proportion of women doctors and lawyers are married to fellow professionals, the wives are not apt to be as distinguished or as active as their husbands. In politics, where a Second Person is practically indispensable, it is hard to find couples whose careers have been separate, equal, and successful. There never had been a married couple serving in Congress until 1976, when Congresswoman Martha Keys, of Kansas, and Indiana Congressman Andy Jacobs fell in love and married while both were serving together on the powerful House Ways and Means Committee. Neither constituency was entirely happy about the marriage. In 1978, he was reelected, but she was defeated.

Work is so important to Cool Supercouples that a direct conflict of interest may end an otherwise satisfactory marriage. This is what happened to a couple who married while getting their graduate credentials in urban planning. After graduation, their best job offers took them to different cities. Both liked their jobs. During two years of commuting it gradually dawned on them that they never would be able to live together because they both couldn't be city manager of the same city and neither would be happy doing anything else. They divorced to leave each other free to make other commitments, but the divorce brought them closer — it took all the strain out of the relationship. They continued to spend weekends together, making love and talking shop.

430

The opposite is even more common. A couple drawn together by their work marry, only to discover that their working relationship was happier than their marriage relationship. They divorce, but continue collaborating. Television's Sonny and Cher Bono resumed acting together for a time after their divorce when they found they couldn't hold their ratings with separate acts.

"We've kept the best part of our marriage, which was working together," a former wife said of her business partner and former husband. "The divorce got rid of the worst, the emotional problems."

Some Cool Supercouples are in entirely different but quality absorbing careers. They preserve their marriages and both careers by keeping them strictly separate. Former Congresswoman Bella Abzug's husband is a stockbroker famous for his refusal to talk to reporters. "Nah, if you want a statement," he tells them, "ask Bella." The husbands of political women like Gloria Schaffer, Connecticut Secretary of State, or Frances T. Farenthold, once candidate for Governor of Texas, appear in newspaper writeups only as "businessmen."

Few people know that Charlotte Curtis, editor of the powerful Op Ed page of *The New York Times*, is married to a surgeon who practices in Columbus, Ohio. The marriage is so private that she doesn't even list herself as married in *Who's Who in America*. "It works," she says, "because neither of us has ever had to play a role. He is a man who works. I am a woman who works. It never occurred to me to pull him away from the job he loves any more than he wanted me to quit *The New York Times*." They get together weekends in the home they maintain in New York, the home they maintain in Columbus, or in a hotel in Washington, halfway between.

Like many professional couples, both Curtis and her husband work such long hours that it isn't a hardship to live in different cities. He has to be in the operating room at eight in the morning and doesn't get home until after eight at night, so even if she lived in Columbus all the time, she wouldn't see much more of him than she does now.

Cool Supercouples have a limited capacity for anything that is not work-related. They talk shop at home. They talk shop at parties. If they take a vacation, they go where they can go on talking shop: the Hamptons on Long Island for artists, publishers, media people; Cape Cod for the doctors and psychiatrists. Some never take vacations at all. Charlotte Curtis once left her typewriter at home for a week of sunning with her husband in the Caribbean, but she wound up writing in longhand.

Those who come close to "having everything" become compulsive about time and canny about priorities. They may spend all the money they make on the logistics of making it.

431

V. Trouble Spots in Family Life

The first year John Sawhill was president of New York University, every member of the family was being maintained in a separate place. Their son was at prep school. Isabel Sawhill was working in Washington at the Urban Institute, and living alone during the week in their Georgetown house, while a male house manager ran the president's residence for John in New York. When Isabel and her husband gave a party in New York, all she had to do with it was to catch the Eastern Airlines shuttle from Washington in time to arrive with the guests.

One rising young corporate manager with a new baby thinks that entertaining for business at home is an idea cooked up by stay-at-home wives who want to feel important. "No one below the president level is set up to impress other people with the quality of their housekeeping and it really isn't necessary," she scoffs. "If I have to impress someone I'll take them to a restaurant or the theater."

Couples who have everything put a lot of energy into planning their lives. They attack every new day as if it were a suitcase that has to be repacked so that you can get one more thing into it. What goes is spontaneity. In a smoothly run dual-career home, the order of the day is posted in a visible place, such as the refrigerator door, and deviations are avoided because they involve multiple phone calls. There is no margin for emergencies and no room for impulsive gestures in a home that does not have a Second Person. Some couples even make appointments for lovemaking.

Social life is the first thing to go from the schedule. "There isn't any way to produce at this pace and have much of a social life," Dr. Virginia Johnson, of the Masters and Johnson sex research team told a reporter.

Career couples may look as if they are socially active. They sound as if they go everywhere, know everybody, make all the parties. But what goes on at these parties sounds very much like work. Doctors, lawyers, politicians, communications executives, and other people in the so-called "contact" industries spend all their time selling themselves, sounding out ideas, and digging for information that can help them. The people they keep seeing shift kaleidoscopically from rivals to allies. Even when they become friends, they talk primarily business. Frequently they get no further into each other's lives than perfunctory bulletins about how well their children are doing at school.

They may be proud to have "real," "old," or "outside" friends, but even when they cherish them, they very seldom have time to keep up with their lives.

Cool Supercouples often say that they are "each other's best friend," but if they are in different fields, often they don't have time to go to each other's parties. Charlotte Curtis has friends her husband never has met, and he has friends that she never has met.

Not only are parties politicized, but even sports and hobbies. Business organizations maintain memberships in athletic clubs so that their executives can play squash and tennis with clients. As part of his 1978 campaign to woo Congress, President Carter invited rebellious young members of the House to play tennis with him.

Cool Supercouples do relax, but their idea of relaxation is to work under relaxing circumstances. They buy a country hideaway, not for the outdoor activities it provides, but in order to have a place to work in peace and quiet on weekends. The fact is that an advancing career is so exciting that nothing else is anywhere near as much fun.

Cheerfully, they cooperate in the popular pastime of putting their lifestyle down. They complain of lack of time for the reading and thinking that would make them more productive — but they manage to do it. They complain of fatigue, but they look good and their health is superb. For some people, uphill is comfortable all the way.

But not for very many. Most people want rewarding work, but this does not mean that they regard their work as their main source of satisfaction.

For most couples, two lifelong careers are as restrictive as the traditional lockstep. But even these couples can have more of what each of them wants most if they know what it is they want, and they are willing to make tradeoffs to get it. And two paychecks enable them to choose the tradeoffs most comfortable for them.

Alternatives

The most common solution for the Age Thirty Bind is for her to trade in her *career* for a *job* that allows her to do the work of the Second Person and have children while she's doing it. This classic solution works well for most couples. His career pulls ahead so fast that she "naturally" falls into the role of support. When he has an important meeting, she cancels commitments that would interfere with it. If they are just a little bit tactful, they may not have to admit that she really has given up the race for the top. *One Career, His* works fine at age thirty, but if she has put aside career aspirations she merely puts the crisis on ice for a decade.

There are other possibilities. A great deal of the strain can be relieved if there is only one career in the family at a time, but it doesn't always have to be *One Career, His*. *One Career, Hers* gives him some of the options enjoyed formerly only by affluent home-makers. Warm Supercouples who want both career and more time with each other can eliminate the need for a Second Person by working together in *One Career, Theirs*.

None of these arrangements need be permanent. A versatile couple can take turns in career involvement or trade a few years of Cool Supercoupling for a mid-life sabbatical of *No Career* life.

One Career, Hers

Society doesn't always disapprove of *One Career, Hers*. She gets permission for a career if she is married to a man who can't have one. She actually is encouraged to aspire if her husband is disabled, unemployed, a student, or retired. She's not supposed to enjoy this good fortune, of course, and she has to be prepared to give it up gracefully. Breadwinning wives of students have to be particularly careful to extinguish any long-term ambitions they may acquire while earning.

The happiest "permission" is the retirement of a husband. Careers start later in life for women, and if the husband is older, her career may bloom just about when his is over. The Perrys shifted His Career to Hers so naturally that they didn't realize they were doing it. Jack was a promotion man who was glad to retire from the job, but he missed daily lunches with his contacts in the media. Hanging around the house, he got interested in his wife's hobby of matching rare china. Phyllis had long had a home-based business helping people fill out incomplete sets of Haviland. Listening to her problems, he could see human-interest feature stories, which he began to peddle to his old press friends. It was fun to lunch with them as he had always done, and a relief to have a story that wasn't about the old company products. Soon Phyllis was flooded with inquiries both from buyers and sellers. To get more stock, they took trips to small towns where antique china still can be bought. They exhibited at antique shows, put ads in trade papers, and Jack kept the feature stories going. The business grew so large that Phyllis had to rent a shop. Within two years, the income from the shop plus Jack's Social Security had exceeded Jack's earnings before retirement.

But the best thing about the business was what it did to their marriage. The promotion work that had taken him away from Phyllis for so many years now brought him closer to her. A booster by temperament and by calling, Jack thoroughly enjoyed his new role as supportive Second Person.

A rare form of arthritis was the "permission" which enabled the Stintons to discover that role reversal fitted their temperments. It struck, by sheer accident, just when he needed his hands for his first big construction contract.

434

Bird: The Two Career Collision Course

It had taken Walt a long time to get started in life. After high school, he "goofed around and played tennis" before trying college, then quit for a hitch overseas with the Seabees, then came home to putter around the big old house in which he had grown up with five brothers and sisters. He liked farming, but he had no illusions about it. He knew that his mother and father would never have been able to rear their big family on the apples and milk they produced. As a child, he had watched them take turns commuting 100 miles to graduate work in the city that had qualified his mother to be a librarian and his father to be superintendent of schools.

Everyone thought that Nancy was the making of him. A shy slip of a girl — Walt's mother was afraid, at first, that she wouldn't stand up for herself — Nancy was a math major with a good job in the multinational corporation headquarters near the Stinton farmstead. To catch up with Nancy, he cashed in his G.I. benefits on a B.S. in "electronic engineering." It was a new field, and to Walt it sounded ideal. You had to have a college degree and work for a big company, but you were really a very highly paid electrician with freedom to move around from place to place. But it was a narrow specialty, and big companies didn't need any more when he got out. He drifted back to construction work while waiting.

Meanwhile, Nancy kept on getting raises. She was an ideal First Woman for her company's affirmative-action program. Shy, young, tenacious, quietly assertive, she blossomed under encouragement. Walt worried about the traveling she had to do, but she worried about the growing income gap between them. "You could be a contractor on your own," she suggested.

Easygoing, friendly Walt was a natural-born salesman. With Nancy's sharp eye on the estimates, he more than broke even on the trial year they had set for it. When he landed two sizable contracts they resolved the Baby Panic in favor of a baby. Both mothers were delighted. Now Walt would shape up. Privately, they congratulated each other on the way Nancy had handled what could have been a delicate situation. And both thought how well he coped when arthritis struck.

Walt had surgery on his hands just before Nancy had the baby. The specialists said it was a success. He'd be able to do normal things, like driving a car, but he wouldn't ever be able to handle power tools or do the strenuous work of construction. When the bandages came off, he couldn't grab anything, not even a pot, so for the first time in her married life, Nancy had to do all the cooking when she brought the baby home from the hospital.

Her six weeks of maternity leave expired before Walt's stitches were out, so she had to bathe the baby early in the morning before she went to work, but soon he was able to get the baby's dinner ready so that Nancy could have the fun of feeding her as soon as she walked in the house at night. Walt took the baby everywhere, tossing her lightly and confidently over his massive shoulder, his thick hand spanning her little back.

When Walt was better, they started thinking about what he might find to do. The vocational counselor they enlisted gave Walt aptitude tests. For company, Nancy took them, too.

The results were a surprise. They showed that the temporary situation was actually ideal for them. Nancy looks like a slightly compulsive schoolteacher, but the Strong-Campbell Interest Inventory which has been purged of sex bias disclosed that she was really a manager and planner. She liked to create structures, not work in those already set up by others.

Walt, on the other hand, liked the structured work that is closely related to homemaking — the indoor, clean-hands, routine, housekeeping-type jobs. The occupations toward which his interests pointed, the counselor told them, were military, headed by "policeman"! He had liked the structured life of the Seabees, where people do what they are supposed to do. And he scored much higher than Nancy on liking for office *practices*. It was the nine-to-five *schedule* against which he had rebelled. And though their mothers wouldn't believe it, the tests showed Nancy less interested in the domestic arts than most women, while Walt's interest topped the scale for men.

And that is the way it is going to be for the foreseeable future. Walt's love is old houses, so they've bought one that looks like the farmhouse in which he grew up. He'll have to hire manual labor, but he'll be on hand to direct the work of restoring it.

Walt can't stop talking about the house. "It's a Dutch Colonial authentic with '1734' on the barn. It will take years to get it in shape, but it's a real beauty. We have three acres so I have apple trees and a garden. It's surrounded by cornfields but twenty minutes nearer her work. And the fellow next door raises buffaloes, real buffaloes like you find on old nickels. What a place to raise a family!"

The way inflation and exurban real estate values have been trending, it may be the very best use he could make of his time.

The Stintons are ideally situated for lifestyle pioneering. They are both rather conventional people who didn't set out to prove anything by their so-called "role reversal." They don't know what strains they might be feeling if Walt's arthritis had not excused him from the career commitment he *didn't* want while giving her permission to become the executive she *did* want to be.

436

Bird: The Two Career Collision Course

Fewer, newer, and much more suspect are the careers of women who have no excuse for overshadowing the careers of their husbands. Most of the married women in *Who's Who in America* have husbands who are not listed in their own right, including anti-feminists Phyllis Schlafly and Marabel Morgan, author of *Total Woman.* Schlafly's husband is a lawyer who inherited money. Charles Morgan is a tax attorney in the Miami firm of Peters, Maxey, Short and Morgan, who looks after the money his wife has made explaining how she saved their marriage by deferring to him.

A man who gives up his own career for his wife's can expect raised eyebrows — and so can his wife. Friends thought Joe was crazy to stay on in the Air Force to send Marcia to law school. People close to them told them right to their faces that she'd divorce him when she became a lawyer and started making money.

Instead, they are closer than before. They've become, as she puts it, "grooved into each other, like puzzle pieces." He helps her do research, gets books for her in the library. She bounces ideas off him. He's listened to so many cases now for so long that he comes up with ideas about them himself. He helped furnish her office, knows the people she works with, goes with her to the evening affairs to which lawyers bring their wives, and whenever he can get off work, he goes to court to watch her in action.

Neither of them liked their jobs when they married, but Joe didn't mind the life of a sergeant in the Air Force as much as some of the other fellows. He'd beef, but he'd go along.

Not Marcia. "I don't want to be a secretary to a lawyer," she would fume. "I want to be a lawyer myself." She talked about it and he talked about it and they finally decided that she should try.

Quitting to go to law school cut their income almost in half, so they both had to do odd jobs to earn the money for her tuition. They did anything they could find. Janitor work. Yard work. Car fixing. When she had to study, he did her odd jobs as well as his — three jobs in all. And he learned to do things around the house he had never done before. When exams came, he did the cooking, paid the bills, cleaned the house, gave her a massage, listened to her tell him all about torts.

It sometimes made her feel edgy. When the money for food went for law books, she'd sometimes pick a quarrel with him over money. She hated feeling guilty about spending thousands of dollars all on herself. "But look, honey," he told her, "it's not my money, it's our money, and we're doing what we want." Inside, she wasn't at all sure that she would have done the same thing for him. Toward the end, when she couldn't cram for exams and work, too, he re-enlisted in the Air Force to get the bonus that paid her last year's tuition.

437

V. Trouble Spots in Family Life

Now that she's through the bar and working, she urges him to think of what would really make him happy. He could get out of the Air Force. Go back to school. Start an electronics shop with the skills he developed in the Air Force. Be his own boss. But he's not letting her rush him. He's building a boat. He takes every day as it comes. He likes living with Marcia because she's where the action is. What he really wants out of life is to make her happy and that's a big load for her to bear.

Marcia feels guilty. What makes it work? "A lot of talking," she says, "a lot of talking." She works at keeping communications open. To pay him back, she's trying to learn enough about electronics so she can understand what *he's* up against. She'd like to lavish luxuries on him. "If he wanted to go to Alaska," she says, "I'd send him." At home, there's no question about who does the housework these days. She does it.

She reads women's magazines to learn about new ways to pamper him. One of the ways is breakfast. She slips out of bed before he's awake in the morning to make herself pretty. Then, when breakfast is halfway made, she wakes him so he can get himself cleaned up, too. And even if she has to be in court at 10 o'clock, they always have a leisurely breakfast and exchange the day's schedule. "It makes me cuddly inside to think of him during the day and know what he's doing," she says. A nice thing about the morning is that he has to leave ahead of her, so she doesn't have to leave him at home with the breakfast dishes.

They've resolved the bind of the Two Person Career. Whatever he chooses to do when he's out of the Air Force, One Career, Hers is comfortable for both of them.

Sensitive, idealistic men have always had vocational problems. When they marry the assertive women who seem to attract them, they often have marital problems as well. The Dees could have looked like characters in this standard situation if Lila's public relations business did not support Jerry in the full-time volunteer work affluent wives often do. Because he's a man and a minister's son, Jerry has been able to mobilize the conservative business community behind urban redevelopment. Her best clients were men they met through his church and community involvement.

Neither expected this outcome. Like many ministers' sons, Jerry decided he didn't want to be poor, so he went to Harvard Business School. Thoughtful, sober, a top student, he was snapped up by an international company and sent to their branch in Ohio. A Harvard professor's daughter, Lila had worked in public relations in college and was slated for promotion, and was sure she would find something in Ohio for her to do.

Ohio was culture shock. Lila canvassed every sizable employer in the small city. No jobs. Nobody wanted a Vassar graduate, even as a secretary. Some local company presidents she wrote to had never heard of public relations and others said they didn't need it. Respectfully, literately, Lila demurred. A few finally allowed her to do for nothing some of the projects she suggested. By the end of the second year business was so good that she was hiring other similarly stranded college-educated wives to help her. But by this time Jerry was so disenchanted with his job that he thought of going back to New York.

Corporate life, Jerry had discovered, was not as portrayed in Harvard Business School cases. Told to represent the company in the community, he brought back suggestions for pollution controls, a day-care center for children of workers, and increased contributions to local charities. When his suggestions were ignored, he spent more time with the board members of local charities than he did with his colleagues in the company. His shift to community service enabled him to do more of the work he really wanted to do.

One Career, Hers gives a work-committed woman the advantages enjoyed by traditional work-committed men. The difficulty of finding a husband for the arrangement has been greatly exaggerated. Some men are talented and enthusiastic Second Persons and many more are happy to be relieved of the responsibility of First Career Person if the relief can be accomplished with reasonable tact.

Role reversal marriages yield unexpected fringe benefits. The first is that the partners have to think about each other and take special care of their relationship. Second Person Husbands can't be taken for granted like Second Person Wives. Then, too, the hostile curiosity of outsiders draws them closer: they are two against the world. But the most important dividend is the strength any marriage gains from a more equal division of power than is possible when the traditional head of the household provides all the money and sets all the rules.

Working Together

Most couples meet through their work, and almost all of them wonder how it would be to work as well as to live together.

But that's nepotism, and most employers won't let them do it. Rules against nepotism sometimes prevent couples from marrying for fear of losing their jobs. In the past, the wife was almost always the one who lost out, but since the women's movement, conflicts of interest are no longer automatically resolved in favor of the husband. Some civil rights lawyers think that Title VII of the Civil Rights Act of 1964 forbids an employer to reject an applicant because of the job held by the applicant's spouse, and the national Plan of Action, adopted by the National Women's Conference in Houston, endorses this interpretation.

Companies that try to live up to the spirit of non-discrimination on the basis of marital status have found themselves hiring couples, many of them newly minted MBAs, who have met and married in college and have looked for jobs from the same few prime employers of their specialties. Couples are beginning to appear in management-training programs of corporations as well as in law and accounting firms. According to Eugene Jennings, professor of management at Michigan State University, they have caused so many "problems" that some companies are quietly trying to avoid hiring any more of them.

More subtle, and much more dangerous are the conflicts of interest that arise when husband and wife are employed by competitors. Since it may be illegal to discriminate against applicants on the basis of spouse's occupation, employers are very careful how they question them. According to a business magazine, a personnel man for an oil company asks things like, "Are you familiar at all with the oil business?" in hopes of trapping the applicant into saying, "My husband has worked in it for fifteen years," if that happens to be the case.

Feminist men concerned about equal opportunity for women sometimes lean over backward to reverse the presumption that a husband's interest is overriding. One lawyer refused to represent a client who wanted to sue a foundation, because his own wife sat on the foundation's board. "People might think she could be influenced," he said. The appearance of favoritism caused a husband to turn down a sales job with the supplier of a company for which his wife was purchasing agent.

Some couples try to solve the problem by not talking shop at home. In 1978 Marcia Grace, a creative group head with the advertising agency, Wells Rich Greene, was married to Roy Grace, creative director at a competitive agency, Doyle Dane Bernbach. According to *The New York Times*, they have a "gentle-person's agreement" to hold out trade secrets from each other. "If it's really privy," says Ms. Grace, "I mentally shred it."

In book publishing, so many executives are married to each other that it's virtually impossible to worry about conflicts of interest. Agents marry editors. Editors marry publishers. Sally Richardson, director of subsidiary rights for St. Martin's, is married to Stewart Richardson, editor-in-chief of Doubleday. They both read manuscripts in bed. The time they discovered they were reading separate copies of a manuscript up for auction, they agreed not to talk about it.

Employers are less tolerant in fields where patent rights control millions of dollars. An old company executive discovered the career price he was paying for his wife's job when his boss wouldn't let him take papers home because his wife, also a geologist, could read the blueprints.

The way around nepotism is to go into business together. This used to be the universal pattern and millions still do it. Most farms are still run by a husband and wife, and "Mom and Pop" stores still require two to make both ends meet. Plumbers and electricians expect their wives to do the books as well as the dishes. Businessmen who marry their secretaries can't always afford to retire them. Sometimes the unpaid supporting spouse is a husband. Opera star Shirley Verrett is only one of the many highly paid women whose husbands take care of their business affairs.

But working *for* a spouse is not what most couples want. Wives who do the books, answer the phone, or otherwise backstop their husbands resent the slave labor. Many of them wrote us to complain that they never had any money of their own and were shortchanged on vacations, Social Security, and other benefits that automatically would have gone to a worker who was paid. One told us a tale of literal slavery. She worked for her husband, she wrote, only because he threatened to beat her up if she looked for a paying job elsewhere.

Working with a spouse as an equal partner is something else. It sounds as if it would solve all the other ways in which jobs get in the way of family life. Working together attracts couples frustrated by employers who send them to different cities, put them on schedules that eat up the time they could spend together, discriminate against one or the other on the basis of their marital status, or unwittingly pit them against each other.

The dream is widespread. A couple blocked by antinepotism rules in rising in the management of the staid conglomerate for which both work, plan to continue drawing their salaries until they have enough money saved up to quit, open a bookstore on Cape Cod summers and spend their winters reading in Florida.

An academic couple commuting to their weekend marriage from appointments in different cities have vowed eternal togetherness once their present contracts are fulfilled. They are going to resign from their respective faculties, say good-bye to faculty politics, and set up their own research service on the West Coast.

Stephen and Babs took the plunge when she became pregnant with their first child. They had talked for years about going into a printing business together. He worked in production at the advertising agency where she was a junior copywriter. They knew the costs of getting out leaflets, mailing pieces, catalogues, brochures, and they knew they could cut those costs by doing the designing themselves and contracting the work directly to the shops Stephen knew. If they built up a clientele and made money, they could start up a shopping center newspaper throwaway, or they could become printing consultants, like a couple they knew, or could even publish specialized books.

The baby brought the plan to action because Babs wanted to nurse the baby without quitting work and it would be easier to do if she could make her own hours. So she sketched a new business announcement card with a stork in one corner and sent it out to all the business people they thought might have jobs for them. They had a little money saved up. Stephen's father, a printer, lent them more. To save money, they planned to work out of their apartment until they broke even.

At first, all was chaos. Babs brought the baby home to an apartment piled high with cartons of stock for their first orders. Bills, orders, letters, and scribbled notes of phone messages littered the kitchen and the bathroom. Still holding the baby, Babs found a place to sit down and cry. Stephen was contrite. He moved out the cartons, picked up the papers. And while the baby settled into her eating and sleeping habits, Babs found time to sketch layouts on the drafting board they set up in a corner of the living room.

The first year was a roller coaster ride. Some weeks absolutely nothing happened. The phone didn't even ring. They sat terrified, watching the bank balance melt. Then there'd be a flood. More work than the two of them could handle. Should they hire help? At the end of the year they netted out about what they had earned between them at the agency. They had worked longer hours — they thought they had, at least — and sometimes under pressure, but they had goofed off a lot, too, sometimes when they wanted the time.

They celebrated breaking even by renting a cheap office and hiring a babysitter so Babs could get away from the apartment three afternoons a week. Next year was better.

Printing isn't the only service that Mom and Pop can deliver cheaper and better than large organizations with high overload. Employment agencies, editorial services, research services, legal work, counselling services, accounting services, advertising, promotion, public relations are possibilities. Also, landscaping, dog grooming, catering, travel agencies, plant shops. All the many different franchise businesses, from McDonald's to the dry cleaners, are good possibilities if you have the money to buy them.

If Babs and Stephen had wished to bring up their baby in a closely knit rural community they could have teamed her writing and his printing to run a small-town weekly newspaper. The income isn't big, but the life is attractive, and many can be bought at affordable prices.

There are as many reasons for husbands and wives who are doctors and lawyers and accountants to go into partnership together as there are for professionals who do not happen to be spouses to do so. Charlotte and Bob Herberg bought *Southwestern Art,* a museum publication, in Austin, Texas, because they wanted to broaden its editorial appeal. Dr. Elizabeth Goessel and Dr. Colter Rule share an office on the ground floor of the Park Avenue building in which they share a marriage several floors above. They also share research in biofeedback as a technique for reducing disease-causing stress.

Those who aren't willing to go into business together have a harder time working together. An advertising agency or a law firm occasionally will assign married professionals on the staff to the same project, but most employers try to keep their work as separate as possible. Couples who want more time off the job individually sometimes have been able to persuade an employer to let them share the same job for one pay-check, on the theory that two minds on a task are worth the bookkeeping costs of carrying an extra name on the payroll. This gets around the problems of nepotism, too.

Shared appointments are attractive to small, liberal arts colleges because they widen the range of talents without adding jobs to the faculty. In the science building of little Hampshire College, in western Massachusetts, one door reads BEV AND FRED HARTLINE, GEOPHYSICS, another AL AND ANN WOODHULL, BIOLOGY, and a third KURTISS AND COURTNEY GORDON, ASTRONOMY.

A faculty wife hit on the idea of a joint appointment when she and her husband decided that neither of them wanted to work full time while their children were small. Under the arrangement they made with a small Midwest college, her husband stayed home in the morning while she taught a course in women's studies. After lunch, she stayed home while he taught two courses in his field, religion.

Everyone gained something slightly different. The college gained a new course and a role model of sex equality for students on their small campus. She solved her problem of babysitting and continued to use her Ph.D. in education without working full time. Her husband enjoyed the letup from the job pressure of a full-time teaching load and the improvement in family life that went with it, but the enduring benefit to him was professional. He felt the arrangement advanced his career because it gave him more time for research.

Her husband thinks it gets a little too close at times. He wonders whether the intimacy of working in the same institution and knowing the same people makes it harder for them to develop new interests and grow. But she doesn't see this as a problem. Individuals vary in their needs and, indeed, their tolerance for constant companionship.

The danger of too much togetherness looms larger for couples who share the same duties. Ann and Michael Coburn, the first married couple to be ordained as Episcopal priests, schedule their work as assistant to the rector of the St. James Episcopal Church in Danbury, Connecticut, so that only one of them works at a time. They also try to schedule one day a week to spend together alone. Parishioners think they have the perfect marriage but they say they have to work at it. "People can have more equal marriages," Ann says, "but whether they can handle the idea of team-work is another question."

Teamwork, of course, is what's involved when a husband and wife share exactly the same duties. So far, only a few of the job-sharing experiments have involved husbands and wives, and in spite of government and foundation funded projects to promote the idea, job-sharing between unrelated persons who want part-time work has not proved the solution to the demand for flexible hours.

On balance, working together cannot be whole-heartedly recommended for every couple. Those who succeed differ widely in how they manage it. Some couples in business together try to reproduce the arms-length division of labor of traditional organizations: he is boss on new business, for instance, while she rules over the checkbook. Others talk everything through and make all their decisions together. Some couples have rules about talking business at dinner. Others are resigned to talking about nothing else. A freelance writer who works with her husband thinks that the working partnership is better if it preceded the marriage. One thing seems sure. A couple working together has *more* of a marriage. More to talk about. More to share. More to fight about. And more testing of the weak areas of the relationship. If it's good, it can be very good. If it's bad it can end in a divorce that involves all areas of life, or a marriage maintained for the sake of the business.

Resolutions to Mid-Life Crisis

When a couple hits 40, the partners begin moving in opposite directions. With the kids out of the way, sex and career turn up for her, but they level off and start declining for him. The stage is set for marital disaster.

Successful or not, the bloom is off his career. He begins to wonder whether it was worth the blood it has cost him, whether there's something more to life. If he's bored, he thinks of changing jobs. Or women. A younger woman, eager and new, who takes him back to his twenties, when sex was endless and effortless, and he wanted it more than she did. His own wife knows too much, needs too much.

If she took career time out for the children and never made it all the way back, she may look for something radically new. She may experiment sexually with other men or even with women. Or file charges of

444

sex discrimination against her employer. Join a political movement. Get religion. Nag her husband to go to a marriage counselor, or join a sensory-awareness group.

Statistics of the 1970s showed how often the scenario ended badly. Newly divorced women looked for jobs and became unemployment figures. They inundated the community colleges set up to train high school graduates. So many of their students were older women with children that day care became a burning issue on many campuses.

Literate, restless, well enough off, for the most part, to buy a book or magazine, take a course, or even pay a counselor, these "mature women returning to the labor force" were a luscious market for entrepreneurs in publishing, education, social work, and the so-called "helping professions."

Foundations, states, the Federal government and universities spent money to teach the returning women how to look for a job, how to assess their aptitudes, how to train for a skill, how to write a resume, what to say on a job interview, how to dress for success, how to feel about themselves, how to be assertive but not aggressive, and generally how to radiate the job confidence that most of them did not feel. Profit and nonprofit, it was a growth industry of the decade, an industry based on the fraudulent, cruel, and counter-productive premise that there was something a mature woman could do to put her back on the career ladder she left to rear children.

They took courses and they read the books, but most of them continued to be unemployment statistics or discontented workers in dead-end jobs. I could think of only one honest thing to say to an audience of returning women who expected me to tell them how to get paid what they were worth: If you don't land a job that utilizes your talents, it's not your fault.

Returning women can find jobs, but they are the wrong age and sex for the careers they really want. They can't change their age or sex, but they can help change the male career timetable. And some of them were doing it. All over the country, couples were challenging the male career timetable. Some of them were writing cheerful alternatives to the midlife crisis scenario.

Dan and Julie headed off the crisis because they saw it coming and switched roles in time. He knew something was wrong when he urinated blood in the lavatory of a plane. It wasn't really kidney trouble, as the hospital first thought. Dan is a psychologist who was retained by corporations to advise their salesmen, and he now thinks it was his body's rebellion against the traveling that was taking him away from Julie and the children. At the time he thought he was dying. When he recovered, he resolved not to spend one more day of his life traveling. He made one more trip, then quit, cold turkey.

They had started out, after college, to be equal. Dan had done his diapering and getting up in the night with their first baby, but when the second baby came, Julie dropped out of medical school and went domestic. Dan began to make money and spend more and more time away for his company. He'd be off for three weeks and then back again only long enough to quarrel and make up with her. Once he took her along, but it made her feel worse to see the fun he was having some of the time on his trips while she was stuck at home taking care of the children. That made him feel more guilty. When they got home, he was so close to the breaking point that he blew up at her for breaking a glass. A week later he was in the hospital.

The breakdown was the beginning of insight for both of them. At first, he was manic. He talked about being born again. They'd sell everything and go to California. He'd go into private practice and spend all his time at home with the family. "But you can do that right here," Julie reasoned. "If you want more time with the children, you can take them over. Maybe they'll take me back at medical school."

Miraculously, her old medical school was willing to take her back. It was being sued by a woman who claimed she had been excluded on the basis of her sex. Julie had made an exceptional record so she made a convenient double token: older than the conventional medical student and the mother of school-age children, too.

When they started their new life of role reversal, staying home seemed at first like a much needed vacation. He spent a lot of time getting acquainted with the kids. He liked the idea that he was the one to do the nitty gritty things, like making them pick up their rooms. And he learned to cook. He'd alternate between the good stuff and just throwing pizzas at the family. Gradually, he began to see a few clients at the house.

Scheduling his new life was a problem. He'd drive the kids to school, go swimming at the Y, and then come home to read the paper and drink coffee for about an hour, like a housewife goofing off. He'd go on cleaning binges. He refinished the piano and coached the soccer team at his children's school.

When the novelty wore off, and before his practice built up, he had time to monitor his feelings about eventually becoming the househusband of a doctor. "Sometimes I felt threatened, sometimes I didn't," he recalls. "The medical parties were the worst. The women thought that what I was doing was great, but the men, especially the older men, would just look at me funny and say, 'Oh, you're taking care of the house.' When I could feel the fast track she was on I would make more effort to develop my private practice."

It wasn't a steady thing, the way he felt. "Sometimes I would cook a real good dinner and was keeping it warm when she called at 6:30 to say she would be home at 7:30, and then at 7:20 to say she wouldn't be home until nine, and I would continue to keep it warm and be supportive when she came in. And other times I'd just get fed up and furious and put everything in the refrigerator and take the kids and go out and forget her. I had to find some kind of balance with that."

More money made things better. When his practice improved, and she began to draw a paycheck as a resident, they moved into a condominium and hired a cleaning service. Dan was glad to give up the drudgery and isolation of housework, but he has turned it to career advantage in counselling women patients.

There are no models for their reversal of direction, so they have to do a lot of talking about it. They know that there is only one solution to the midlife career crisis, and that is to help each other switch directions. He has to help her find ways to resume the career she shelved while she helps him pick up the family involvement and personal development he shelved during the work-intensive phase of the male career timetable.

Julie is exceptional: she had a well-defined career goal and was able to get back on the track. But when she starts to practice, she will face the temptation to overcommit herself that led to his breakdown and they hope his experience can help her avoid it. She knows the toll of living vicariously through the family and she is helping him avoid it.

They talk a great deal about dividing their time between the personal and professional sides of their lives. One plan is to set aside an evening a week for each other, another for the children, and another that *each* family member can use for her/or himself.

Reversal of direction is easier if both plan and prepare for it during their thirties. The wife of a college professor became interested in speech therapy when one of her children was slow in talking. Tuition at the university was free for wives, so she started taking psychology courses on the subject as they were offered. By the time her children were in school, she was ready to take the graduate course leading to a professional degree in speech therapy. She thinks she has become a better therapist of young children herself. Her practice at the clinic fits in with the academic schedule of her husband, an experimental physicist. Her exposure to his work has interested her in the relatively unexplored "hard science" of phonometrics, the measurement of variations in speech sounds.

Some couples are able to make the shift of career involvement without dramatic outside upheavals. Most of their friends think that

Davis still is the First Career Person in the family, and that Melissa is just spending a little more time on the travel agency she started with a friend as a lark when their children were in school. The fact is that the boom in travel has expanded their business so fast that Melissa now puts in long, exhausting hours as she and her partner cope with the problems of growth. Meanwhile only Davis, Melissa, and a few top officers of his company know that he has gone as high as he's going to go on the corporate totem pole. He'll always have a job there, but they'll move him sideways in the future, not up.

It was hard to take in the beginning. Some of the men who lost out on the last round developed psychosomatic symptoms. One separated from his wife. Several others quit. Davis and Melissa saw the blocked career as an opportunity for Davis to develop the sides of his life that had been neglected while he was bucking for promotion.

He's staying on, but he's shifting gears at the office. He's using the support of a familiar job and work schedule to steady his change of direction, and the company is helping him. He is finding new, non-competitive ways to help younger men on the job. He takes over high-level public relations chores like talking at length with distinguished visitors the president of the company can see for only a moment of greeting. He's been told to represent the company informally in local affairs. With company approval, for instance, he is using his engineering background to work on environmental issues facing the local county council. These varied assignments make it easy to come in late and go home early.

Home is now where the action is for Davis. He has learned to cook gourmet dishes. He is building a greenhouse for the plants Melissa is now too busy to nurture. The environmental issues he has studied for the county council have interested him in the local wildlife. He and his high school son are taking a census of the animals in a threatened stretch of woodland near their home. And for the first time in his life he is taking music lessons.

Other, more radical solutions to the midlife career crisis are being mulled by couples who haven't reached it yet. Some Cool Supercouples are talking about a midlife career shift they could make together. This means piling up money while both are too busy to spend it, then taking a few years off to start slower, less-demanding occupations that allow them to develop new interests and talents.

One very successful couple is saving the wife's entire salary against his fiftieth birthday. On that day, she will give up her $50,000-a-year salary and he will cash in his share of the group medical practice which is bringing them an income many times that much. She plans to teach. He's going to write a novel. Their children will be out of college,

448

so they could travel if they felt like a change of scene to go with the change of pace.

A plan that is getting a great deal of attention, but so far little actual implementation, is a midlife career sabbatical during which one or both take a few years off from one career for a noneconomic pursuit. The problem is not financial, but re-entry. Working couples can take turns supporting each other while one takes time out, but it is hard to get back to a career without falling back a number of steps on the promotional ladder.

Companies such as IBM, Xerox, Wells Fargo, and Lederle Laboratories have at times experimented with a corporate version of the academic sabbatical. In order to attract scientists from prestigious universities, they have offered some high-ranking professionals paid leaves of absence during which they are encouraged to explore interests totally unrelated to their work. Some have become social workers or fund raisers for their favorite causes. Others have traveled and studied. One scientist spent his year off studying oriental religions in India. The theory is that the time out is an investment in human capital which will yield dividends in higher levels of productivity when the professional goes back to his profit-oriented work.

Couples are just beginning to explore the more obvious of the options two paychecks afford. Some discover them by accident, when she becomes the temporary or permanent breadwinner. Others plan them. Either way, couples discover that her job makes it possible for both to do work they like better than the work they are doing, to alternate work and leisure, to invest their time in causes, hobbies, leisure, their children, or each other.

Ideally, husband and wife gain equally. But there is a curious paradox. Women most often *initiate* a variation in the standard male career timetable, *but men are most often the winners*, because they never before have been able to opt for anything but paid achievement as a life commitment. Men always have had the right to choose how they earn, but they are only beginning to claim the right to choose between paid and unpaid work that the women's movement has won, in principle at least, for women.

The potential for human satisfaction staggers the mind. "Let us suppose," wrote Midge Miller, Wisconsin state legislator and feminist, "that we were to suggest a method for decreasing early deaths from heart attacks and other tension-related illness in middle-aged men.

"Suppose this plan would also make education more relevant and help young people continue their education without an accumulation of debt.

449

V. Trouble Spots in Family Life

"Suppose it would give young children more time with both parents, help women find more satisfaction in their lives and enable them to support themselves when necessary.

"Suppose this plan would help elderly and disabled persons enjoy life more, make further contributions to society and provide themselves a better standard of living without damaging their health.

"There is no doubt that liberals and conservatives alike would respond. Well, we can develop such a plan if we find the means for breaking certain rigid work patterns developed during the industrial revolution. We are overworking some, while depriving others of the opportunity to make a living."

What will the world be like when widespread claim of these options really breaks the lockstep of family and career? Nobody really knows. The experiments of a minority are already changing the meanings of work and love. Ahead — and soon — are new ways of working, a new kind of "family," and basic changes in what men and women expect from each other.

B. Divorce

The importance of family relationships to our lives and even to our identities is clear to those of us who experience separation and divorce. The disintegration of intimate relationships — however troubled they may have been — shakes people's foundations thoroughly. When studying divorce, it is tempting to conclude that its distress is simply a product of "human nature." Yet, a good case can be made that the breakup of an intimate relationship is particularly anguishing in a society where people are not part of tight-knit communities, and in fact are often quite isolated. Many people, especially men, rely on one close relationship to meet all of their needs for intimacy and friendship. This partly explains why so many people who have divorced remarry — and why men do so more quickly and in larger numbers than women.

The article by Anne-Marie Ambert and Maureen Baker represents a thorough discussion of divorce and its aftermath by two Canadian sociologists. They explore the causes of the relatively high divorce rates, the gender differences in coping with life after divorce, and the effects of divorce on children. Janice Drakich, then, takes up an issue recently made controversial by some groups of divorced men: the common practice of granting the custody of young children to their mothers.

Suggested Reading

Weitzman, Lenore.
1985. *The Divorce Revolution*. New York: The Free Press. A thorough examination of the consequences of the new divorce laws for men, women and children.

Marriage Dissolution*

Anne-Marie Ambert and Maureen Baker

Introduction

Until 1968 divorce was something that did not happen in one's own family — it was something embarrassing that afflicted Americans, not Canadians. Indeed, legal divorce was practically unheard of in Canada before World War II. But, one year after the grounds for divorce were extended, the divorce rate in Canada had already more than doubled. A mere ten years later, in 1978, the rate was six times what it was in 1968. Now a recent report from statistics Canada is telling us that people who get married in the 1980s have a high probability of divorcing. What has been happening to Canadian marriages in the past fifteen years?

Table 1. Incidence of Divorce in Canada by Year:
Frequencies and Rates (per 100,000 population)

Years	Frequencies	Rates
1921	558	6.4
1931	700	6.8
1941	2,462	21.4
1951	5,270	37.6
1961	6,563	36.0
1968	11,343	54.8
1969	26,093	124.2
1970	29,775	139.8
1971	29,685	137.6
1976	54,207	235.8
1978	57,155	243.4
1979	57,474	251.0
1980	62,019	259.0

Sources: From Statistics Canada, July, 1977. *Vital Statistics*, vol. II, *Marriages and Divorces 1975*, pp. 28-29, Ottawa; also, statistics for 1976 and 1977 from an advance bulletin from Statistics Canada, Dec. 4, 1978, p. 6; statistics for 1978 from another advance bulletin from Statistics Canada, Sept. 4, 1979, p. 10; also D.C. McKie et al., 1983. *Divorce: Law and the Family in Canada.* Statistics Canada.

---

* From *The Family: Changing Trends in Canada* ed., Maureen Baker. Reproduced by permission of McGraw-Hill Ryerson Limited.

V. Trouble Spots in Family Life

First of all, it should be pointed out that the Canadian divorce rate is still moderate by international standards. Most western industrialized countries have also been experiencing rising rates of divorce. The American divorce rate in particular has soared from 1960 to 1980 and has become one of the highest in the world. The divorce rate in the Soviet Union has also risen. The reasons for rising rates of separation and divorce are similar in all these industrialized countries.

Table 2. Crude Divorce Rates in Several Industrialized Countries: 1980 (per 1,000 population)

Japan	1.22
France (1979)	1.59
Sweden	2.41
Canada (1979)	2.51
England and Wales	3.01
USSR	3.50
United States	5.19

Source: United Nations Department of International and Economic and Social Affairs Statistical Office. *Demographic Yearbook 1980*. Copyright United Nations (1980 and 1982). Reproduced by permission.

Causes of High Divorce Rates

Among social researchers there is a considerable amount of agreement about why divorce is so prevalent. At a societal level, divorce is a by-product of the individualistic and hedonistic mentality of the technological era. It is the mark of the "me" generation. The emphasis is on self-fulfillment, personal freedom, and enjoyment. Other-orientation and couple-orientation are not stressed in the family as much as in the past. A climate of moral liberalism has made divorce more acceptable and encouraged narcissistic tendencies by such slogans as "Do your own thing." At the same time, religion has seen its sphere of influence drastically reduced in matters concerning family and personal life. The sanctity of marriage has been eroded and has been replaced by a more personal, legalistic and secular view of the marital relationship.

Our technological society has also offered us more life-style alternatives, from more effective birth control devices to laundromat and catering services. Some of these changes have enabled more women to enter the paid labour force. Indeed, the employment of married women is seen by several researchers as one of the most important variables in the recent upsurge in divorce rates (Becker, 1981), and it therefore deserves additional comment.

Studies have found that employed married women consider divorce as an option more often than unemployed married women (Huber and Spitze, 1980; Albrecht and Kunz, 1980) and that women who can be independent financially initiate the decision to separate more often than women who need their husbands' financial support. Moreover, Ross and Sawhill (1975) have found that women's divorce rates increase with each additional thousand dollars they earn. There are also indications that once divorced, high-income women are less likely to remarry (Edwards, 1967; Renne, 1971). Ambert (1983) investigated this relationship further and found that high-income divorced women said they wanted to remarry as often as low-income women but felt less social and financial pressure to do so. Fairly typical of separated high-income women was a thirty-eight-year-old executive who was involved in a serious relationship for over a year. Marriage was being considered, but she added that she was "very cautious because I could have so much to lose." Low-income women saw the situation quite differently: They felt they had everything to gain by remarrying.

Advocates of the ideology that women should stay at home will feel vindicated by these results. However, we should point out that more women than men had to remain in unhappy marriages in the past because they had no other alternative. Currently, the choices for both parties are closer to being equalized. This is not a positive change only if one operates under the assumption that women should suffer failed marriages more than men do.

Along with these contributory variables, the past decades have witnessed a drastic shift in the acceptance of divorce as a fact of life. For instance, a Canadian public opinion poll in 1943 showed that 24 percent of the respondents felt that divorce laws were too harsh. But in 1966, 60 percent of the respondents were in favour of relaxing divorce laws (Pike, 1975). We have come to accept divorce in a more liberal way because its typical consequences are now less catastrophic. The social costs, and perhaps even the psychological costs, have become less onerous. As Bernard phrases it, "Social costs act selectively; when they are low, they release more people into the divorce population; when they are high, they release few" (1971:97).

V. Trouble Spots in Family Life

The Double Standard of the Divorce Act of 1857

> The conception of divorce as a penalty for matrimonial misbehaviour was reflected in its consequences. A guilty wife could not claim maintenance after divorce and the innocent spouse had the better claim to the custody of the minor children of the marriage. In some legal systems the guilty spouse was liable to forfeit all or part of the financial benefits derived from the marriage, and in most, a husband who obtained a divorce on the grounds of adultery from his wife was entitled to damages from her paramour. Many systems prohibited a spouse who had committed adultery from remarrying or from remarrying within a certain period or from marrying his or her paramour.
>
> Law Reform Commission of Canada 1975c:1

Source: D.C. McKie et al., Divorce: *Law and the Family in Canada* 1983. Statistics Canada. Reproduced by permission of the Ministry of Supply and Services.

Although there is disagreement among researchers on this point, the relaxation of divorce laws could have contributed to a rise in divorce (Stetson and Wright, 1975). If we return to Table 1 we see how a dramatic increase in divorce rates followed the liberalization of Canadian laws in 1968. There are two immediate reasons for this upsurge. In previous years a divorce was very difficult to obtain, and in provinces such as Quebec one could be obtained only through the federal parliament. Divorce therefore may have been beyond the reach of those with less money. After 1968, as these people filed for divorces, the backlog was cleared and divorce rates more than doubled. But this does not mean that a relaxation of divorce laws increased marital dissolution. Indeed, it is quite likely that a large proportion of the increase in the divorce rates was actually due to couples who were in fact already separated or who were living together unhappily, hoping that the proreform lobby would bring about a change in the legal practices. Therefore, when the Divorce Act passed, many people legalized their separations or "emotional divorces."

In themselves easier divorce laws probably do not contribute significantly to higher divorce rates. Rather, the societal variables we have already touched on increase the demand for divorces and herald the introduction of more liberal laws. Both the higher rates of divorce and the less rigorous laws are the result of the socio-economic forces we have already described. However, the variables contributing to a high divorce rate create a social climate wherein couples who are not happy together will divorce rather than remain married. They may work even less hard at maintaining their marriage than in a society which is less individualistic, less hedonistic, more family oriented, and where marriage is still viewed as sacred.

In addition to these societal factors, there are personal causes of divorce. For instance, studies have found that couples who marry in their teens, especially if the wife is premaritally pregnant, run a greater risk of being maritally unhappy and of divorcing (Lee, 1977). Other personal variables correlated with high rates of divorce are alcoholism, brief acquaintance, and dissimilarity of social class, age, and education.

Divorce and Marital Happiness

Although divorce rates have soared, they do not represent an adequate picture of marital happiness. We cannot know from rates of divorce whether people are more or less happily married than fifty years ago. In retrospect, the social situation up until World War II seems to have been less complicated, more moral, and certainly more bound by religious and social restrictions. Conjugal roles were more clearly delineated, and sexual compatibility was less important than reproduction: There was far less introspection about the personal aspects of one's marriage. People were more solidly and securely married than today, but we do not know if security increased happiness.

Do high divorce rates automatically mean that marital happiness is uncommon? Studies of married persons generally indicates that the quality of marriage varies with gender, the stage in the life cycle, the number of children, and the couple's level of education. In an unpublished Canadian study of 102 separated and divorced persons, nearly one-third reported that, on the whole, eliminating the last two years of their marriages, their relationships had been above average in terms of happiness. At the other extreme, about 40 percent of the subjects reported unhappy marriages. While there is definitely a relationship between marital unhappiness and divorce, the relationship is far from clear. Many unhappy people stay together while some happily married people eventually divorce. In the separate research of Ambert (1983) and Baker (1980), in-depth interviews pointed to a few reasons why people who claimed to have had happy marriages eventually divorced.

Firstly, it was apparent that some people divorce for the wrong reasons. These divorces resulted from circumstances which had little to do with the relationship: problems at work, mid-life crises, or continuing emotional problems. Under such circumstances, feelings of dissatisfaction are generalized to the marriage. The person may even come to believe that the problem lies in the marriage itself and that, by leaving the marriage, things will return to normal.

For instance, when asked who was to be blamed for the demise of his marriage, a remarried man said: "Me, no question about that. I threw away a perfectly good marriage. I got out of my marriage rather than reorient my general life goals. I projected onto my marriage my general dissatisfaction — I was so self-centered and distraught by my problems at work."

A separation or divorce follows with a temporary feeling of well-being which is rapidly replaced, in some cases, by deeper despair as one realizes that the problems are still there. In fact, after the separation the problems may be aggravated by loneliness, loss of financial resources, and estrangement from children.

Another path from a fairly happy marriage to divorce is what could be called "taking a risk," and usually takes the form of adultery. An affair may begin suddenly or unexpectedly during a business trip or as a result of a long friendship. The person has not been actively seeking the opportunity but does not turn it down once it presents itself. Because the marriage is secure the husband or wife sincerely believes that there will be no consequences, but in some cases there are. The new companion may take up a great deal of time or seem to meet personal needs that had been forgotten during the marriage. The relationship becomes more involved and a divorce follows. Both ex-spouses are often shocked by the rapidity with which this scenario unfolds and, more often than not, the unfaithful spouse does not remarry the person with whom he or she was having the affair.

Marital unhappiness does not necessarily lead to divorce, nor does marital happiness always guarantee marital stability — a topic which is neglected in the research literature. Nor do we subscribe to the popular belief that to have an affair outside of one's marriage means the marriage is not a good one. To be realistic, any marriage is a human relationship and, as such, is rarely perfect. Therefore something, however small, is always lacking in any marriage, as in any relationship. We have studied marriages which were considered very good and in which adultery took place for no other reason than that the opportunity presented itself: nothing was amiss in the marriage. The idea that this cannot happen is a romantic myth not supported by research evidence. However, there are other kinds of marriages in which something is indeed missing, and this lacuna does lead to adultery.

Marital Stability and Unhappiness

As there are couples who are happily married but eventually divorce, there are many couples who remain together despite their unhappiness with each other. Some are waiting for a suitable time to part, such as when the children have grown up. Others wait until they have a career secured or money saved. Many people delay until they develop another relationship before they seek a divorce from their spouse.

The reasons why unhappily married couples do not divorce is as interesting as why others seek legal termination of their marriages. However, researchers have focused on those who seek divorces because it is easier to find and to interview such a sample. Many people stay together because of religious convictions, since some established churches do not permit divorce or remarriage after divorce. However, the fear of social censure seems to be just as compelling a reason to remain married. In particular, those who live in small, cohesive communities may remain married even though they are emotionally divorced from their partners.

Unemployed women may stay in unhappy marriages because they cannot afford to live on their own and support their children. Others fear the consequences of a drastically reduced income after divorce. Some men fear the effects of high child-support payments and the division of property on their own life-styles and business ventures.

For Interest What Has Been Said

> It does not much signify whom one marries, as one is sure
> to find the next morning that it is someone else.
> Samuel Rogers

> When two people are under the influence of the most vio-
> lent, most insane, most delusive, and most transient of
> passions, they are required to swear that they will remain
> in that excited, abnormal, and exhausting condition con-
> tinuously until death do them part.
> George Bernard Shaw

> When a girl marries, she exchanges the attention of many
> men for the inattention of one.
> Helen Rowland

V. Trouble Spots in Family Life

The chain of wedlock is so heavy that it takes two to carry it
— sometimes three.
                              Alexandre Dumas

Above all, it would seem that many couples remain together because they are used to each other. They are part of a pair. Separating might actually be more painful than remaining together. Marriage to one particular person has become a habit one cannot abandon. There is the matter of stability and the difficulty of throwing away so much security for the unknown. And finally, couples who are unhappy remain together because of a lack of more attractive alternatives. The perceived lack of alternatives may be financial and/or human. As Levinger has well explained it, the external attractions are not sufficiently strong to overcome the internal pull in such situations.

We met a couple who had remarried after a three-year separation and a few months of divorce. She was ten years older than he. She explained why she accepted him back. "In the first place, he had left me...not for another woman, but just because he was tired of it all. He is a big child and he found out that he couldn't live with other women because they wanted him to take care of them. He was used to being taken care of....At first, when he left, I was thrown in quite a state of panic. I had never been on my own with four children....The first thing he did was to buy an adult condo and a Ferrari sports car. We had had money, but with four children and two expensive life styles, it was worrisome....I come from a country where people didn't use to marry for love but for familial reasons. He left me and that left me nowhere. Do you think I could ever remarry? No. I am 55. Besides, I prefer to have him here where I can control the finances than having him squander our money away."

Therefore, in contradiction to what we have been taught about marriage, some couples divorce even though they had a relatively happy marriage while many other couples who are relatively unhappy remain together. These ambiguities stem from the nature of the institution of marriage. It is unfortunate, however, that we have no direct research literature on unhappily married couples who choose to remain together.

The Decision to Separate

In the literature on divorce there has been controversy concerning who makes the decision to separate. In Canada wives tend to be the petitioners for divorce in approximately 60 percent of the cases. But petitioning for divorce is a legal act that takes place after someone has decided to dissolve the marriage.

In the first study on this topic, Goode (1956) found that ex-wives reported to have been the first ones to suggest divorce. This finding seemed paradoxical since women are often considered to be more marriage and family-oriented than men. Women are also more likely to bear total responsibility for the children once the marriage is dissolved. They have less money than men, lower-paying jobs, and fewer alternatives to meet people of the opposite sex (Baker, 1980). Why then would they be the first to suggest divorce? Goode provided the following explanation for this apparent paradox:

> We suggest, then, that in our society the husband more frequently than the wife will engage in behavior whose function, if not intent, whose result, if not aim, is to force the other spouse to ask for the divorce first. Thereby the husband frees himself to some extent from the guilt burden, since he did not ask for the divorce. A by-product of this process frees him still more: the wife's repeated objections to this behavior will mean that there are family squabbles, and one almost constant result of repeated family squabbles is a lessened affection between husband and wife. In particular, of course, these squabbles mean that the husband can begin to think of himself as also aggrieved, as also sinned against.
>
> Source: *Women in Divorce* by William J. Goode (Copyright 1956 by The Free Press, a Corporation) pps. 136-137.

In accordance with the American studies, we found that women were the ones both to initiate discussion of divorce and to keep up the discussion. But, in contradiction to American studies (Goldsmith, 1980), the final decision tended to be more often a masculine or a joint one than a feminine one. Moreover, both ex-husbands and ex-wives agreed on their reports of the decision-making process.

How can we reconcile these results with those of the few American studies done on the topic? First, the conflicting findings may simply be a result of the type of sample involved and/or of the fact that what holds for the United States does not necessarily apply to Canada. Or it may be that the way in which decision-making was measured differed in the Canadian studies. Ambert used a three-step process which corresponds more closely with reality than the one-step question used in the United States: People do not usually decide to divorce one minute and leave the house the next. The process of deciding often drags on for years. But,

461

during the Ambert study, the subjects spontaneously offered assessments such as "She left"; "She decided to leave"; or "She told me to leave." Such assessments occurred during the nonstructured part of the interview. Yet, when faced with the three-step decision-making process, many respondents concluded that while the wife had suggested separation, the husband had decided upon it. This apparent contradiction is easily resolved when we realize that the person who raises the issue in discussion may not be the person who actually makes the final decision.

The research of Baker reinforces Ambert's findings. In Baker's study (1980) both women and men agreed that women initiated the decision to separate. However, after further probing, it became obvious that women had first brought the issue out into the open but usually in response to what they saw as serious problems in the behaviour of their husbands. For example, one woman asked her husband to leave after many years of his alcohol and drug abuse. Another told her husband to leave when he had a blatant affair with her best friend. Wives seemed to be more articulate than husbands concerning problems in their relationships. Husbands were either unaware of the fact that their marriages were dissolving or unwilling to discuss the decline of the relationship with their wives. However, many husbands behaved as though subconsciously they wanted out of the relationship but did not want to take the responsibility for suggesting separation. Instead they encouraged their wives to initiate the separation.

The reason why women more often than men initiated the discussion on separation and insisted on pursuing it was that they had not wished to separate but merely hoped to resolve the problems in their marriages. Subconsciously husbands may have reached what Federico (1979) calls the Point of No Return in the marriage earlier than wives. When this point is reached, willing to recognize his Point of No Return "will engineer the same outcome indirectly" (Federico, 1979:98). This implies that the decision to separate is the result of a complex series of subtle negotiations and often remains subconscious until one partner articulates it as a last plea. After trying various methods of accommodation such as improving her physical appearance, expressing affection, discussing problems with her husband, using a third party to mediate, withdrawing, and quarreling, a wife may try the last resort: "If we don't get along we may as well divorce." Separation may follow even though it is not the wish of the one who first suggested it.

While more women desert now than in the past, our research does not corroborate journalistic impressions that women leave their husbands and children as often as, or more often than, men do. However, women definitely seem to initiate discussions of separation more often than men and become petitioners more often then men.

Support Networks and Marriage Dissolution

Once the separation is effected, how do the individuals cope? One aspect of this coping which has undergone much current study is that of social support. In a Canadian study by Baker (1983), patterns of social and emotional support were examined for 150 separated and divorced men and women. While men relied on both sexes to help them through the crisis of separation, women turned mainly to their female friends and relatives. Mothers, sisters, and female friends provided companionship, child care, and emotional support which proved invaluable, especially in the early months of separation. Men's helping networks involved friends of both sexes, but male subjects more often praised the assistance of their female friends. In some cases, men relied on a friend's wife rather than on the friend himself and suggested that women were more empathic and willing to discuss the intricacies of the dissolution of a marriage. Men also changed their friends with greater ease after marital separation, choosing to associate with single or divorced people.

The sex role socialization of women, their training in nurturance, and their greater availability made them important informal resources in assisting people through the personal crisis of separation. Although neither male nor female subjects said that they first turned to professionals for assistance or even that professionals were most helpful to them, about one-third of the sample sought professional help at the most critical or traumatic time of their marriage dissolution. In Baker's study there were no statistically significant sex differences in seeking professional help, yet women were far more likely than men to report emotional problems at all stages of marriage dissolution.

Women's closer ties with their families of origin and the fact that they usually receive custody of the children means that they rely more heavily on family for emotional and material support after separation. Custody means that the woman often becomes the link between the children and both the paternal and maternal grandparents. If the grandparents come to visit the children, they see the children's mother in the process. Consequently, divorced women are seen mainly in their family role as mothers. On the other hand, men are more likely to live alone, less likely to need financial assistance from their parents, and are more often seen outside the role of father. In short, the transition from married to single life is more rapid and complete for men.

V. Trouble Spots in Family Life

Women's lower incomes force them to rely on sporadic support payments from their ex-husbands, welfare, or money borrowed from their parents. Reliance on financial assistance from others often increases dependence and reduces self-esteem. Receiving assistance in the form of shared accommodation, help in paying for groceries, free baby-sitting, or borrowed money from parents increases women's obligations to family and makes it more difficult to develop a new self-image and a single life-style. By staying within the family or maintaining long-term relationships with friends, women are often subtly pressured into a more conservative, family-oriented life-style than separated men. The sexual double standard discourages many women from breaking outside of this closed network and reduces their opportunities to develop new relationships.

Divorce and Emotional Problems

Studies from various statistical sources unanimously indicate that divorced persons have higher rates of treatment for emotional problems than married, widowed, or never-married persons (Bloom et al., 1979; Gove, 1979). Recent studies have uncovered rates of psychiatric care as high as 40 percent among divorced men and women (Bloom et al., 1979; Wallerstein and Kelly, 1980).

Rates of psychiatric care, suicide rates, accident rates, and postmarital stress are generally higher for men than for women (Ambert, 1980; Gove, 1970), although women more readily report emotional problems. (These studies do not contradict the fact that Baker [1983] found no statistically significant gender differences in consultation with professionals after separation. Included in her list of professionals were marriage counselors, lawyers, and clergy in addition to psychiatrists. Other studies usually only measured psychiatric consultation.) However, a controversy remains about the differential impact of separation and divorce on men and women. Studies based on self-report data usually indicate that separated and divorced women report more problems with depression (Baker, 1980; Belle, 1980), especially divorced women with children at home and a low income (Goldman and Ravid, 1980:49). But depression is only one type of emotional problem, and it is also possible that men fail to report their depression.

Ambert (1982) found that separated and divorced mothers with custody were less happy in their parental role than custodial fathers. The levels of satisfaction of the mothers were partially affected by financial insecurity. Moreover, the children of low-income mothers were much more difficult to handle at all ages than those of higher-income mothers and even than those of custodial fathers, who generally had higher incomes. Therefore, on a wide range of situations, the daily life of separated and divorced mothers is much more stressful than that of their ex-husbands. Other Canadian studies (Schlesinger, 1979a; Nelson, 1981) have corroborated these results.

However, the life of the divorced man is stressful in different ways. Among divorced couples with children, only about 13 percent of the fathers receive custody of their children. It is also more common for the husband to leave the marital home first and to leave his wife and children in the marital home. Without his children the husband often experiences intense loneliness, which he often deals with by a series of social and sexual encounters and rapid remarriage. The fact that men remarry sooner than women after divorce may indicate that they experience more difficulty than they are willing to admit in living on their own (Baker, 1983).

Several theories have attempted to explain the high rates of emotional problems among the separated and divorced. The reaction or stress theory argues that separation and divorce are emotionally exhausting and highly stressful life events. The loss of a marital partner, the loss of contact with children, reduced financial circumstances, lack of sexual contact, and single parenting severely tax most people's emotional resources. One problem with this theory is that it does not adequately explain why men have higher rates of treatment for psychiatric disorders when it is women who more often experience a shortage of money, retain custody of the children, must re-enter the labour force, have more problems finding new partners after separation, and report more emotional problems.

Bernard (1972) has suggested that marriage as an institution has been more advantageous to men than to women because it provides men with nurturance, physical care, and domestic services. As housewives and mothers, women are trained to respond to the needs of others, and their domestic services allow their husbands to pursue occupational goals and leisure activities free from the responsibilities of child care and household maintenance. After separation the husband loses both nurturance and services. Most men have not been socialized to obtain emotional support from other men. Instead they turn to women for close friendship and empathy (Baker, 1984a). Because men have not been socialized to express their emotional concerns as openly as women, they often do not seek help until their problems have reached serious proportions. On the other hand, women talk out their postmarital problems with their girlfriends, their sisters, and their mothers, and deal with their stress in more constructive ways. This may explain men's higher rates of psychiatric care: They seek formal help while women are able to make use of personal networks.

Another theory states that divorced people experience more emotional problems because within marriage those with emotional problems are likely candidates for divorce (Rushing, 1979). This would explain higher rates of emotional problems among divorced people but would not adequately explain why women report more emotional problems and men are treated more for psychiatric disorders after divorce. In interviews with forty-nine ex-couples, Ambert found that more of the men who were in treatment after separation had been in treatment during their marriages. If replicated on larger samples, such data would indicate that emotional problems in married men may be more related to marriage dissolution than similar problems in married women. The in-depth material of Ambert's study led to the hypothesis that men who suffer from emotional problems have more difficulty maintaining a stable marriage than other men or even women with emotional problems. However, we would need a longitudinal study involving control groups to more adequately explore this apparent relationship. Divorced men who were in treatment for emotional problems also had a lower remarriage rate than women with emotional problems when they were reinterviewed two years later. However, there was no difference in remarriage rate among treated and untreated women. The problems men experienced in marriage and in remarriage when they had emotional problems seemed to be compensated for by a higher socio-economic status. The men with higher incomes who were treated were more likely to remarry than men with lower incomes who were also treated. This exploratory study suggests that both gender and income are important variables in the relationship of emotional problems to marital stability.

Children and Divorce

What effect, if any, does divorce have on children? Researchers' opinions have fluctuated on this issue. Ten or twenty years ago, it was believed that divorce was very detrimental to children. Then other researchers began pointing out that remaining in an unhappy but stable home was even more harmful to children than marriage dissolution (Hess and Camara, 1979; Johnson and Lobitz, 1974; Oltmanns et al., 1977).

There are several good reviews of the impact of marital dissolution on children from a psychological point of view (Hetherington et al., 1978; Luepnitz, 1979). In these studies the consensus is that, in the short run, few children are untouched by divorce, but that over 50 percent of the children of divorced parents are undistinguishable from others five years later. It is emphasized that children of divorced parents have a better prognosis when the custodial parent is emotionally stable, provides love and a structured life, and when the noncustodial parent maintains a regular relationship with the children and is supportive of the custodial parent.

There are also strong indications that the socio-economic situation of the postdivorce family is a very important determinant of the impact of divorce on children (Colletta, 1979). It is generally agreed, although practically no socio-psychological data exist on this, that after separation, the ex-spouse's standard of living is lower than it had been, and that this difference is much more acute among women, especially mothers with the custody of their children (Arnold, 1980; Baker, 1980; Bane 1976). Many of these mothers become poor, have to go on welfare, and move to poorer neighbourhoods with sub-standard housing. The family's entire life-style is negatively affected. Therefore, it is quite possible that situations which have hitherto been believed to be consequences of divorce are actually consequences of a roduced standard of living. In order to verify this hypothesis we would need to study and compare families of divorce who lose their standard of living with others who retain it. It may be that it is not so much the father's absence which causes problems but rather the deteriorated social status that accompanies such an absence.

As indicated in a previous section, Ambert found important differences in the overt, observable behaviour of the children of lower-class and middle-to-upper-class custodial mothers. In another study of a large and representative sample of all the in-school teenagers in Montreal, Ambert and Saucier also found that there were many variables on which adolescents from divorced families scored significantly lower than children from intact families, while the scores for adolescents from widowed families were generally intermediate. Some of the differences they found were related to academic success and expectations for the future — all of which were lower among children of divorce (Ambert and Saucier, 1983). However, they have not yet carried out the analysis by social class.

At least one study has found that proportionally fewer adults with high educational attainments came from one-parent homes than from legally intact homes (Duncan and Duncan, 1969). Therefore, we would expect that one long-term consequence of parental divorce when the custodial parent has a lowered standard of living is a lower educational achievement and less employment success. Generally speaking, low standards of living do not promote attitudes which are favourable to learning, school, and schoolwork; schoolwork benefits from a stable family environment, parental guidance, and space. Overcrowding, improper nutrition, noise, and lack of discipline will tend to lead children into the streets and not into books and formal education. On the other hand, one could hypothesize that custodial mothers who are above the poverty level may stress education, especially for their daughters, as they do not want their children to repeat their own mistake. Such mothers also may motivate their children, especially their daughters, as a form of vicarious compensation.

Studies also indicate that boys are more adversely affected by parental strife and separation than girls (Hetherington and Parke, 1979; Rutter, 1971). Some of our own results corroborated these findings, although there were many exceptions. How can we explain this gender differential? At the intuitive level we could expect that girls would be more affected because they are more dependent upon the home environment than boys. Yet the reverse occurs. One reason may be that children need a same-sex adult role model more than a cross-sex one. Most children live with a custodial mother, and many children of divorce see their fathers rarely or strictly within an artificial context (restaurants, outings, movies). Male children more than female children are deprived of a same-sex role model. Indeed, studies of boys reared by custodial fathers have shown that they had a better self-esteem than boys reared by a custodial mother, and the reverse occurred for girls.

A second and complementary reason for more adverse effects of divorce on male children may be found in those results by Wallerstein and Kelly, (1980) which showed that custodial mothers were more affectionate toward their daughters and more thoughtful of their needs than they were of their sons'. Daughters were more adequately mothered (or parented) than were sons. Finally, sons often give a more difficult time to their mothers than daughters do, which may explain in part why mothers may be more solicitous about their daughters. Boys may need a stronger authority figure than girls, and the structure of the average divorced family does not always provide this figure.

It has been thought that, as more children experience divorce, they will suffer less because they will not feel so different from other children. Yet Wallerstein and Kelly did not find that knowing other children in the same situation made such a difference. The loss of one parent, the presence of a stressed parent, and a diminished standard of living make a stronger impression on children than the fact of whether or not they have peers in the same situation. Peers in the same situation may be helpful during part of the school period, but such peers do not make up for the difficulties inherent in parental separation, especially not in early childhood when peers are less important than parents.

Remarriage

Because three-quarters of divorced men and two-thirds of divorced women eventually remarry, we have to consider remarriage as the most important path after divorce. Throughout this discussion it has been obvious that research on divorce is still in its infancy. More questions remain unanswered than have been explored. The situation is even more acute concerning remarriage and familial recombination or reconstitution.

While divorce may be a growth experience for the unhappily married couple, we have seen that, in the short run, it can be detrimental to children. Similarly, while remarriage is the goal of most divorced persons, it is sometimes problematic for children, especially for teenagers. The literature indicates that young children suffer more from parental divorce than teenagers do. Children are often too young to understand the situation clearly and less detached from their parents than adolescents, who are striving for independence and are more peer-oriented (Kalter and Rembar, 1981). Thus they have alternatives which young children do not have (Steinberg, 1982).

If the custodial parent is to remarry, the young child generally adapts better to the situation than the adolescent. The young child is more willing to establish an affectionate relationship with the step-parent, who may interfere with freedom and impose a life-style which the teenager is not eager to accept. Friction between step-parent and adolescent is more likely than with a young child, who may eagerly accept one more person to love.

Unpublished research by Ambert suggests that children over the age of ten sometimes sabotage their parent's remarriage. However, in order to study this phenomenon more systematically we would need information on remarriages which are successful compared to those that are not. Presence of children, age and gender of the children are key variables that should be investigated. Even though few adolescents go about destroying their parent's remarriage, the fact remains that remarriage is a far more complex situation when children are involved than when they are not. Not only do more individuals have to adjust to each other but the emotional atmosphere itself is more complicated. Also, when children are present the ex-spouse probably remains more in evidence than when there are no children, and this often becomes a source of friction for the entire family. This situation may be particularly difficult when only one ex-spouse remarries. Especially if the husband remarries first, his new marriage may bring about a renewal of hostilities with his children's mother; in addition, the new wife and the ex-wife may be competing for the same financial resources. But many men are actually relieved when their ex-wives remarry since they no longer have to make alimony payments and may be able to use the remarriage as a reason for decreasing child support.

Other variables that should be studied in the context of the stability of second marriages are: age, social class and financial responsibilities, the age difference between the spouses, the effect of the first marriage, and the social network. A greater proportion of remarriages than of first marriages involve a large age discrepancy, especially men marrying much younger women who have never been married before (McKie, 1983). Such a situation will lead to a much greater proportion of married couples who are at different stages in their life cycles. The older man is generally established in his work, has had children, and has been married before. In comparison, the younger woman has had no children and may want some later; she may not yet have had a chance to test herself on the labour market and, later, may wish for greater independence to do so. When they are both older, the man will enter retirement before his second wife. How will they cope with his status as a senior citizen? Might not the younger woman wish for a younger husband at that point? Might not the older man envy his younger wife's employment status?

When asked to compare his two marriages, one man explained that his first marriage probably had been a better one. "I am concerned about the much younger age of my second wife and the fact that she wants a second child. I only want one, no more." He also felt that temperamentally he was better suited to his first wife. "It was easier to get along with one's wife ten years ago because there were fewer ideological pressures from outside the marital unit." He added that he did not feel as secure in terms of raising his daughter from his second marriage as he felt about his older daughter.

American statistics inform us that remarriages are somewhat more vulnerable to divorce than first marriages. Since second divorces are on the rise in Canada, we may one day come to experience a series of marriages or serial monogamy as a commonplace. Ambert (1983) found that individuals who divorce many times were less stable than other divorced persons, were more likely to have been in treatment for emotional problems, and also tended to be deserters. In the case of men, they are described by their ex-wives as immature and cruel. Moreover, a California study indicated that remarried persons were less happy with their remarriages than those who were in first marriages (Renne, 1971).

Certainly we would expect that the divorce rate would be higher among second marriages because of the simple fact that people who object to divorce for moral or religious reasons are excluded from the sample of remarried people. But in addition to this, the problems of the

470

reconstituted family seem to be somewhat different and potentially more serious than those of first marriages. The presence of ex-husbands and ex-wives can complicate the new marriage. Additional sets of grandparents and other relatives can be intrusive. Many divorced men are sending money to their ex-wives and children as well as supporting their new families. This puts considerable financial pressure on both families. The children from two families are bound to experience problems of adjustment. These different problems of second marriages and reconstituted families are just beginning to receive serious attention from researchers (Messinger, 1976; Gross, 1981).

Conclusion

In this chapter we have presented current information on divorce and have emphasized the roles played by men, women, and children. Although marriage dissolution is a fascinating realm of study and has many practical implications for social welfare as well as social science theory, research is still not very advanced in this field. In the United States, where the topic has been researched more thoroughly and over a much longer period than in Canada, researchers have been fortunate to have a journal specifically entitled *Journal of Divorce*, which was first published in 1976. In Canada published research on separation and divorce is scarce and focuses largely on statistical correlates of high divorce rates. Researchers must often send their material south of the border to get it published.

Although the American divorce and remarriage rates are much higher than Canadian rates, we can learn from a comparison of the few Canadian studies with the abundant American research on the experiences of the separated and divorced. Separation seems to be a stressful life event for most people, even more stressful than legal divorce. The decision to separate is usually made tentatively over a period of years and often culminates when the partner who does not want to separate brings the topic into the open. Men often leave the marital home first and leave their wives with the children. Both partners experience financial difficulties, but women's incomes are considerably lower than men's, even though they usually retain custody of the children. Although the courts often order ex-husbands to pay child support, many men default after a year or two. This creates financial hardship not only for the ex-wife but also for the children. A reduced standard of living may be one of the most important aspects of divorce for children, although they are also affected by the emotional state of the custodial parent, their own understanding of the break-up, the relationship

V. Trouble Spots in Family Life

between their parents, and the quality of their own contact with the noncustodial parent. Although there has been a slight increase in joint custody of children after divorce, this seems to be practised mainly by middle- to upper-class people. Many working-class men give up their children to their ex-wives, not knowing that they have any custodial rights. Despite the fact that the new family law states that custody decisions should not be based on gender, there has been little change in patterns of custody over the past twenty years. Men still lose their children after separation.

As divorce and remarriage become more common in Canada, attitudinal change will also continue. Rather than a life-long commitment, marriage is becoming a life-style which alternates with periods of single-parenting or nonfamily living. The Law Reform Commission has already made significant changes in the division of family assets after divorce. Marriage counselors are retraining as separation and divorce counselors. Feminists are encouraging women to become self-supporting and to plan their education, their careers, their pension plans, and their marriage contracts for the possibility of living alone. Schools are becoming more aware of the need for programmes oriented to children of working and separated parents.

But despite the fact that rates of separation and divorce are higher than they have ever been in Canada, many people remain optimistic about the desirability of marriage and family living. The high rates of remarriage may indicate several different things. They suggest that people divorce in order to search for better marriages and not because they despair of marriage altogether. This implies that our standards for the quality of married life may be rising. But high rates of remarriage may also indicate that living alone in a couple-oriented society is socially and financially very difficult. The pressures to remarry are strong, especially for the single parent on a low income or the noncustodial parent who is lonely. Regardless of which interpretation of rising remarriage rates we wish to accept, we cannot fail to come to the conclusion that marriage and family living are still popular and satisfying institutions for most Canadians.

References

_____. 1983. "Separated Women and Remarriage Behavior: A Comparison of Financially Secure Women and Financially Insecure Women.' *Journal of Divorce* 6:43-54.

_____. 1983. "Divorce: Its Consequences and Meanings." In K. Ishwaren, ed. *The Canadian Family*, pp. 289-300. Toronto:Gage.

_____. 1984a. "Women Helping Women: The Transition from Separation to Divorce." *Conciliation Courts Review* 22(1):53-63.

Albrecht, S.L. and Brusegard, D.A., eds. 1980. *Perspectives Canada III*. Ottawa: Statistics Canada.

Ambert, Anne-Marie and Saucier, J.-F. 12984. "Adolescents' Academic Success and Aspirations by Parental Marital Status." *Canadian Review of Sociology and Anthropology* 21(1):62-74.

Ambert, Anne-Marie. 1982. "Differences in Children's Behavior Towards Custodial Mothers and Custodial Fathers." *Journal of Marriage and the Family* 44:73-86.

Arnold, R 1980. Separation and After: A Research Report. Ontario Ministry of Community and Social Services (mimeographed).

Baker, Maureen. 1980. "Support Networks and Marriage Dissolution." Unpublished report to the Faculty of Social Work, University of Toronto.

Bane, M.J. 1976. "Marital Disruption and the Lives of Children." *Journal of Social Issues* 32:109-120.

Belle, D. 1980. "Who Uses Mental Health Facilities?" In M. Guttentag, S. Salasin, and D. Belle, eds. *The Mental Health of Women*. New York: Academic Press.

Bernard, Jessie. 1971. *Remarriage: A Study of Marriage*. New York: Russell and Russell.

Bloom, B.L.; White, S.W.; and Asher, S.J.. 1979. "Marital Disruption as a Stressful Life Event." In G. Levinger and O. Moles, eds. *Divorce and Separation*. New York: Basic Books.

Colletta, N.S. 1979. "The Impact of Divorce: Father Absence or Poverty." *Journal of Divorce* 3:27-35.

Duncan, B. and Duncan, O.D. 1969. "Family Stability and Occupational Success," *Social Problems* 16:273-285.

Edwards, John N. 1967. "The Future of the Family Revisited." *Journal of Marriage and the Family* 29:505-511.

Federico, J. 1979. "The Marital Termination Period of the Divorce Adjustment Process." *Journal of Divorce* 3:93-106.

Goldman, N. and Ravid, R. 1980. "Community Surveys: Sex Differences in Mental Illness." In M. Guttentag, S. Salasin, and D. Belle, eds. *The Mental Health of Women*. New York: Academic Press.

Goldsmith, J. 1980. "Relationships Between Former Spouses: Descriptive Findings." *Journal of Divorce* 4:1-20.

Goode, William J. 1956. *Women in Divorce*. New York: The Free Press.

Gove, W.R. 1970. "Sex, Marital Status, and Psychiatric Treatment: A Research Note." *Social Forces* 58:89-93.

Gross, P. 1981. "Kinship Structure in the Remarriage Family." Paper delivered at Annual Meeting of Canadian Sociology and Anthropology Association, Halifax.

Hess, R.D. and Camara, K.A. 1979. "Post-divorce Family Relationships as Mediating Factors in the Consequences of Divorce for Children." *Journal of Social Issues* 35:79-86.

Hetherington, E.M. and Parke, R.D. 1979. *Child Psychology: A Contemporary Viewpoint*, 2d ed. New York: McGraw-Hill.

Hetherington, E.M.; Cox, M.; and Cox, R. 1978. "The Aftermath of Divorce." In J.H. Stevens, Jr. and M. Mathews, eds. *Mother/Child, Father/Child Relationships*. Washington, D.C.: The National Association for the Education of Young Children.

Huber, Joan and Spitze, Glenna. 1980. "Considering Divorce: An Expansion of Becker's Theory of Marital Instability." *American Journal of Sociology* 86(12): 75-89.

Johnson, S.M. and Lobitz, C.K. 1974. "The Personal and Marital Adjustment of Parents as Related to Observed Child Deviance and Parenting Behaviour," *Journal of Abnormal Child Psychology* 2:193-207.

Kalter, N. and Rembar, J. 1981. "The Significance of a Child's Age at the Time of Parental Divorce." *American Journal of Orthopsychiatry* 51:85-100.

Lee, G.R. 1977. "Age at Marriage and Marital Satisfaction: A Multivariate Analysis with Implications for Marital Stability." *Journal of Marriage and the Family* 39:493-504.

Luepnitz, D.A. 1979. "Which Aspects of Divorce Affect Children?" *Family Coordinator* 28:79-85.

McKie, D.C.; Prentice, B.; and Reed, P. 1983. *Divorce: Law and the Family in Canada*. Ottawa: Ministry of Supply and Services.

Messinger, L. 1976. "Remarriage Between Divorced People With Children from Previous Marriages: a Proposal for Preparation for Remarriage." Journal of Marraige and Family counselling April:193-200.

Ollmanns, T.F.; Broderick, J.E.; and O'Leary, K.I. 1977. "Marital Adjustment and the Efficacy of Behavior Therapy with Children." *Journal of Consulting and Clinical Psychology* 45:724-729.

Pike, R. 1975. "Legal Access and the Incidence of Divorce in Canada: A Sociohistorical Analysis." *Canadian Review of Sociology and Anthropology* 12:115-133.

Renne, K.S. 1971. "Health and Marital Experience in an Urban Population." *Journal of Marriage and Family* 33:338-350.

Renne, K.S.. 1971. "Health and Marital Experience in an Urban Population." *Journal of Marriage and the Family* 33:338-350.

Renne, K.S.. 1971. "Health and Marital Experience in

Ross, H.L. and Sawhill, I.V. 1975. *Time of Transition: The Growth of Families Headed by Women*. Washington, D.C.: The Urban Institute.

Rushing, W.A. 1979. "Marital Status and Mental Disorder: Evidence in Favor of a Behavioral Model." *Social Forces* 58:540-556.

Rutter, M. 1971. "Parent-Child Separation: Psychological Effects on the Children." *Journal of Child Psychology and Psychiatry* 12:233-260.

Steinberg, M.E. 1982. "Une Étude de la Relation entre l'Androgynie Psychologique et l'Adaption Post-Divorce dans des Familles d'Enfants de Quatre à Sept Ans." Unpublished Doctoral Dissertation, Université de Montréal.

Stetson, D.M. and Wright, G.C., Jr. 1975. "The Effects of Laws on Divorce in American States." *Journal of Marriage and the Family* 37:537-547.

Wallerstein, J. and Kelly, J.B. 1980. *Surviving the Breakup: How Children and Parents Cope with Divorce.* New York: Basic Books.

In Whose Best Interest?
The Politics of Joint Custody

Janice Drakich

When the nuclear family dissolves through separation or divorce, courts of law reconstitute family relationships by awarding the custody of children to mothers, or fathers, or both parents. Custody embraces the sum of parental rights with respect to the physical, moral, and emotional well-being of the child, including personal care and control (Parry, Broder, Schmitt, & Saunders 1986, p.101). The granting of these parental rights to both parents — joint custody — is a new practice in Canada and the subject of this paper.

The underlying guiding principle in the award of custody is "the best interests of the child." Sole custody with preference toward the mother has been the predominant form of child custody since the end of the 1920's (Boyd 1987). This custodial arrangement is increasingly being challenged in Canada with arguments that "joint custody" is a better arrangement than sole custody (see Roman and Haddad, 1978 for the typical argument; Henderson 1988). Proponents believe that joint custody is in the best interests of children and parents in almost all cases (Henderson 1988). Opponents argue that joint custody can only be in the best interests of children and parents in a limited number of cases and under specific conditions.

The debate and politics surrounding joint custody will be examined against the historical background of custody determinations and the contemporary political and social climate. The benefits and risks of joint custody will be assessed from a review of the social science and legal literature. A brief history of the trends in Canadian custody determinations will be presented taking into account impinging social-structural and ideological factors. Following the history discussion, the argument challenging sole custody will provide the backdrop for an explanation of what joint custody means, how it works and the answer to the question — In whose best interests is joint custody?

History of Child Custody Awards in Canada

> AND WHEN THEY HAD BROUGHT A SWORD BEFORE
> THE KING, HE SAID, "DIVIDE THE LIVING CHILD IN
> TWO, AND GIVE HALF TO ONE AND HALF TO THE
> OTHER." BUT THE WOMAN WHOSE CHILD WAS
> ALIVE, SAID TO THE KING, "I BESEECH THEE, MY
> LORD, GIVE HER THE CHILD ALIVE AND DO NOT
> KILL IT." BUT THE OTHER SAID, "LET IT BE NEITHER
> MINE OR THINE, BUT DIVIDE IT." (1 Kings 3)

The parable of King Solomon points to the dilemma facing the courts in awarding custody. In contested custody cases, the competing requests of the parents must be balanced against the interests of the child. The current reality of custody options — sole custody or joint custody — is echoed in the biblical mothers' statements.

Unlike King Solomon, Canadian judges have always been guided by statute or case law in their custody determinations. Canada inherited British Common Law and accepted the reasoning of the English courts in awarding custody in the nineteenth century. Under British Common Law, men — husbands and fathers — were the absolute and undisputed heads of the household. Both in law and tradition, men had complete and unquestioned authority over their wives and children. In the event of divorce, "the father was considered the parent naturally endowed to have custody of the children" (MacDonald 1986, p. 10). According to Backhouse (1981, p.216), the judicial approach in the early nineteenth century was to treat the "father's rights to custody as virtually absolute."

One of the best known cases illustrating the indisputable right of the father to his children is the English case of *R* v *De Manneville* in 1804. In this case, the mother petitioned for custody of her eight-month-old baby after leaving her husband because of his cruelty. The judge refused the mother's petition for custody and denied her access or visitation. The father was awarded custody despite the fact that the child was still breast-fed and that the father's cruelty was proven to have caused the marital breakdown. This case clearly demonstrates that fathers had the indisputable right to the "natural possession" of their children. It further suggests that neither the ability to care for the child nor the degree of attachment felt by the father were relevant to the custody determination. The immutability of the father's custodial right can be seen in a 1824 English case. The mother was denied custody of her child "although the father was in prison and his mistress, who provided child care, brought the child to him for visits" (Polikoff 1983, p.186).

Mothers had absolutely no rights to their children. Upon divorce, mothers faced the loss of custody and the real possibility that they would never see their children again. Master Sergeant Talfourd, a British barrister, summarized the powerlessness of women in child custody laws in the nineteenth century:

> By the laws of England, the custody of all legitimate children from the hour of their birth belongs to the father. If circumstances however urgent should drive the mother from his roof, not only may she be prevented from tending upon the children in the extremity of sickness, but she may be denied the sight of them; and, if she obtain possession of them by whatever means, she may be compelled by writ of habeas corpus to resign them to her husband or to his agents without condition — without hope. (Chesler 1986, p.3)

The changing social landscape in the nineteenth century challenged the common-law right of fathers to their children. The industrial revolution and the entrenchment of the separation of work into two spheres — women's work in the home and men's paid work outside of the home — contributed to changes not only in the role of women but also in their image as mothers. Further, the transformation in family relationships to an emphasis on mutual affection and sentimentality gave the family a psychological and emotional dimension within which parents assumed responsibility for their children's emotional and physical well-being (Anderson 1987). Perceptions of childhood were also changing. Childhood began to be seen as a distinct stage of development during which time children needed constant care, attention, and love (Aries 1962; Anderson 1987). As men left the home to work for wages, women were left with the responsibility for child care (Cook & Mitchinson 1976). Mothers were increasingly seen as central to their children's development.

The gentle erosion of fathers' automatic right to their children in Canada can be traced to the lawyers' arguments and the judge's decision in the Ontario case of *The Queen* vs. *James Baxter*. In Toronto in 1846, James Baxter, the father of a six-month-old girl and a man alleged to be intemperate and violent, requested that the court order the infant to be taken from the mother and delivered to him. The judge in this case awarded custody to the mother noting that "the child was an infant of very tender age: not more than seven months old, requiring the tender loving care of a mother, and whose health if not its life might be endangered by depriving it of care and of natural food which the mother supplies to it" (Backhouse 1981, p.218). This case did not immediately cause a landslide of decisions in favour of mothers. Rather, as Boyd (1987) poignantly reveals, mothers began to receive custody in cases where the father had character or personality flaws and the mothers themselves strictly conformed to the expectations of nineteenth-century womanhood and motherhood. In the Baxter case, for example, the father was alleged to be intemperate and violent. The mother's reputation was not discredited and she had returned to her father's home after the separation. While changes in societal attitudes toward childhood, nurturance and the role of the mother were beginning to influence the judiciary in the mid-nineteenth century, the judiciary was still not convinced that mothers had rights to custody.

In 1855, legislation was passed in Canada that gave the court the discretion to award custody to a mother of infant children up to the age of 12 in cases where the judges saw fit (Backhouse 1981, p.219). This legislation did not deny the father's ownership of the child. It simply recognized the fact that men do not possess the biological equipment necessary to breast feed. Moreover, it reflected the gender ideology of that time, which held that men did not have the innate psychological disposition to nurture, and the cultural norms that precluded fathers' participation in the care of young children (MacDonald 1986, p.10).

The cases that follow this legislation in the ensuing sixteen years reflect the reluctance to award custody to mothers. Backhouse (1981) suggests that visible shifts in judicial perceptions of parenting did not occur until the 1880's. The decisions in Ontario courts in the cases of *Re Ferguson* in 1881, and *Re Murdoch* 1882 illustrate "a departure from the notion of quasi-property paternal rights over children" (Backhouse 1981, p.230) and the emerging concept of "the best interests of the children." By the end of the nineteenth century, the common-law practice of awarding custody to the father was eroding. While mothers were given custody, it is important to recognize that custody was awarded in cases where the fathers were morally delinquent and where maternal custody was viewed to be in the interest of the child's welfare, particularly in the case of very young children.

Systematic research on custody in twentieth-century Canada has yet to be done. However, the major shifts in judicial thinking have been identified in a number of works (Boyd 1987; Mayrand 1985; Abella 1981).

Drakich: The Politics of Joint Custody

Fathers' automatic right to custody was struck down in 1925 by legislation that granted mothers and fathers equal entitlement to custody. In an effort to balance parents' equal entitlement to custody, or from the pressure of pro-children advocates, or simply because of changing attitudes and perceptions, judges increasingly focused on the welfare of the child in custody determinations. One legal translation of the welfare of the child in the twentieth century was the "tender years doctrine." The "tender years doctrine" articulates the belief that children under seven need their mothers more than their fathers to develop emotionally and physically. An Ontario court in 1933 suggested the "tender years doctrine" as a general rule of common sense in awarding custody of children under the age of seven (Abella 1981, p.14). The "tender years doctrine" was buttressed by the elevation of motherhood to a sacred profession. Judges and lawyers gave some of the finest eulogies to motherhood. MacDonald (1986, p 1?) provides examples of such statements.

> It is not for a Court to rend the most sacred ties of nature which bind a mother to her children, except in extreme cases.

> There is but a twilight zone between a mother's love and the atmosphere of heaven.

Mothers were assumed to have greater ability than fathers to parent and nurture. Moreover, the recognition, especially in Freudian psychology, of the mother's role in childhood development influenced the belief that young children were better off with their mothers. From 1933 to the 1970's, the "tender years doctrine" guided judicial decisions and consequently mothers were the preferred custodial parent. The "tender years doctrine" is no longer a legal doctrine, but is still applied as a common sense rule (Boyd 1987, p.9).

In the late 1970's, the "tender years doctrine" was supplanted by "the best interests of the child" doctrine. Justice Mayrand (1981, p. 160) suggests that the judgements of the Supreme Court of Canada in two custody cases in 1976 established the "paramountcy (sic) of the child's welfare in considering to whom custody should be granted." "The best interests of the child" became the single criterion in custody determinations with the passage of the Family Law Reform Act in Ontario 1978 and remains the single standard in both federal and provincial legislation (Abella 1981). The basis of custody determinations in the

481

twentieth century went from common-law paternal rights to the doctrine of "tender years" and finally to the current doctrine of "best interests of the child." Both of the latter two doctrines favoured the mother — the primary caregiver of children — as the custodial parent.

Considering contemporary attitudes toward motherhood, it is surprising to learn that mothers enjoyed the preference of the courts in custody cases for fewer than fifty years in Canadian history. Recent challenges in Canada to maternal preference in custody indicate moreover, that the situation may change again.

The Current Challenge to Maternal Preference

Evidence of women's increased labour force participation and allegations of men's increased participation in the household are used to challenge the maternal preference in custody determinations. It is argued that the maternal preference was formulated at a time when women's primary role was that of homemaker and that changes in women's roles have rendered the maternal preference an anachronism (Miller 1979). Using the ideology of gender equality, it is argued that fathers as well as mothers are capable, competent parents. Alleging discrimination against men in current custody awards, and borrowing from the experience in the United States, the custodial arrangement of joint custody has been proposed. The next section will examine the issue of joint custody in Canada and the supporting argument which is couched in the discourse of equality and the standard of "the best interests of the child."

In 1985, the federal government was considering changes to the *Divorce Act* of 1968. The reforms were intended to ensure that both men and women were given equal rights and obligations, to reduce the hostility between divorcing couples, to consider alternatives to the adversarial system, and to consider joint custody of children after divorce. A lobby was mounted by groups — particularly Fathers' Rights Groups — advocating a statutory preference/presumption in favour of joint custody, which amounts to imposing joint custody in situations where one or both parents do not agree to it. In other words, a "presumption" of joint custody is *involuntary* joint custody of children after divorce. Considerable debate ensued over proposals to make joint custody the preferred disposition of child custody disputes (National Association of Women and the Law 1985). In the end the decision was made to retain the principle of the "best interests of the child" and to make joint custody an option rather than a presumption under Section 16 (4) of the *Divorce Act* of 1985.

Advocates of joint custody continue to lobby for a presumption of joint custody. In the province of Ontario in 1987 and 1988 there were two initiatives by private members of the provincial parliament, Mr. O'Connor and Dr. Henderson, to introduce a presumption of joint custody as an amendment to the Children's Law Reform Act, 1980. The arguments in favour of a presumption of joint custody at first are appealing and even seductive. The argument favouring joint custody usually begins by claiming that fathers are discriminated against in child custody cases. It claims further that the current adversarial approach to custody makes one parent the winner and the other the loser. Since mothers typically are granted custody, fathers are usually viewed as losers in custody battles and are relegated to the status of visitor in the lives of their children.

After reviewing the problems with the current system, the advocates claim that joint custody will solve the problems experienced by children and mothers as well as fathers, in the divorce/custody process. It is argued that joint custody allows "moms" and "dads" to continue to share the decision making and responsibilities concerning the children after divorce. In sharing these responsibilities, both parents will continue to have contact with their children after divorce. The proponents of this position, citing the research of Wallerstein and Kelly (1980), maintain the necessity of continued parental contact for children's positive emotional adjustment after divorce. They argue that continued contact is in "the best interests of the child."

The appeal of joint custody and its uncritical acceptance is cause for concern. Joint custody is now a statutory preference or presumption in the majority of states in the United States. The American experience of joint custody and the research on it enjoins us to critically examine the application and the politics of joint custody. The next section presents the arguments and the research used to assess joint custody to be the ideal custodial arrangement and to support the legislation of a presumption of joint custody. These arguments and the research will be critically examined in a later section of the paper that discusses the reality and application of joint custody.

V. Trouble Spots in Family Life

Joint Custody: The Ideal Arrangement Argument

The argument in favour of joint custody is premised on the popular misinterpretation that joint custody means shared physical and legal custody. Joint legal custody refers to the equal rights of both parents to make decisions about the child's education, health care, residence, religious training, and discipline. Joint physical custody refers to parental sharing of the day-to-day responsibilities of childrearing. The application and practice of joint custody do not usually include both aspects. However, the belief that joint custody is both equal sharing of the physical care of the child and joint decision-making — in other words, co-parenting — represents an appealing solution to custody disputes. It conforms to our sense of equity by removing the alleged gender discrimination in the courts. It obviates the necessity for judges to possess the wisdom of Solomon, and avoids the unpleasantness of awarding sole custody to only one of the parents. Not surprisingly, joint custody has been promoted as the panacea for the emotional and developmental problems that divorce is assumed to create for children. Its advocates offer six consequences of joint custody that would benefit mothers, fathers and children.

First, it is argued, joint custody promotes continued contact with both parents after divorce. Research on sole-custody arrangements suggests that children desire frequent contact with the noncustodial parent (usually the father) and are disappointed with infrequent contact. And, according to the evidence, the frequency of children's contact with their noncustodial father in sole-custody arrangements decreases over time (Wallerstein & Kelly 1980; Heatherington, Cox & Cox 1978). Proponents conclude that joint custody is a legal prescription for equal contact, which would remedy the problem of decreased visitation in sole custody cases.

The second benefit is assumed to follow from the first benefit. This position maintains that children's emotional adjustment and development will be facilitated through the equal contact resulting from joint custody. And preservation of children's relationships with both parents appears to be central to their post-divorce adjustment. Wallerstein and Kelly's (1980) examination of the effects of divorce on children found that children adjusted positively to divorce when they had frequent interaction with both parents. It has been argued that children in sole-custody arrangements are unable to maintain their attachment to both parents because they are often placed in a position of having to choose, or take sides with one or the other parent. It is believed that the

484

stress of choosing between parents is diminished when children are shared equally with respect to rights and responsibilities. And the children's observations of their parents' joint decision-making will decrease the harmful consequences of divorce.

A third expected benefit of joint custody is that shared physical custody will alleviate the burden that mothers, as sole custodial parents, experience. Proponents argue that after divorce mothers with sole custody are overburdened with the day-to-day care of their children. Miller (1979, p.364) states that "joint custody allocates to the father a more equitable share of the child rearing burden, and eases the abnormally heavy burden on sole custody mothers." The impression is that shared physical custody gives fathers more responsibilities and mothers more free time.

A fourth presumed benefit is that as a result of shared post-divorce parenting, the relationship between the mother and father will improve. "The need to reach an agreement on all major child rearing decisions, combined with equalized parental power, fosters an atmosphere of detent rather than hostility" (Miller 1979, p.364). The belief is that continuing contact for the purpose of decision-making brings harmony to the embittered relationship between divorced parents.

A fifth possible benefit is that the non-custodial parent, again usually the father, will experience less distress and enjoy higher self-esteem under joint custody. It is argued that sole custody has negative effects for the noncustodial parent. Fathers report emotional distress as a result of decreased contact with their children and from their status as marginal parent (Grief 1979).

Finally, it is assumed that joint custody will lead to greater voluntary compliance with financial support orders. Proponents attribute the high rate of default on child-support orders to the discrimination practiced by the courts and the obstruction of access rights under sole custody.

The early research on joint custody was extremely favourable and fueled the joint custody argument. Mothers, fathers, and children were thriving, it seemed. Steinman (1981) reported that joint custody allowed mothers to relinquish their full-time mothering roles to pursue their careers and adult social life. For fathers, joint custody was a way to maintain contact with their children, to fulfill their role as fathers, and consequently to feel good about themselves — according to the research. Both mothers and fathers were apparently able to diminish their sense of loss and personal failure, and preserve their self identities as parents and adults within a joint custody arrangement. Grief (1979) found that fathers were less depressed and more satisfied with their post-divorce relationships. Abarbanel (1979) found that parents were satisfied and children were successfully adjusting to the divorce because they had a sense of being loved and wanted by both parents. These findings are impressive and lead one to believe that joint custody is the solution for post-divorce families.

Joint Custody: A Caveat to the Ideal Arrangement Argument

A superficial review of the benefits apparent in the early research on joint custody suggests that a joint custody arrangement is more favourable than marriage itself! Perhaps the appeal of joint custody is that it is better than the marriage that preceded it, or at least that it re-produces marriage and family after divorce. Miller (1979, p.365) even cites a case of a joint custody arrangement that was so co-operative and successful that the couple remarried.

Upon closer inspection, however, it is clear that the advantages of joint custody depend on a number of factors. A successful joint custody arrangement requires two important ingredients: parents who have voluntarily entered into the arrangement and parents who are atypical divorcing couples. The subjects in the studies with very positive results were parents who had *voluntarily* chosen joint custody as their way of life after divorce. These parents had a history of co-operation, communication, mutual respect, and commitment to their children. Moreover, they were atypical divorcing couples in that these feelings of mutual respect and communication survived the divorce. They were highly motivated to work together and to sacrifice to make the arrangement successful. This research suggests that joint custody is a viable arrangement when parents voluntarily choose it and make it work.

Proponents of *involuntary* joint custody misuse and misrepresent these research findings by generalizing the benefits of voluntary joint custody to the arrangement itself and by ignoring the qualifiers identified in the research. The joint custody arrangement described by its proponents is the romanticized post-divorce structure of the family. The degree of fit between this romanticized ideal and the reality of joint custody is not examined. Recent evidence suggests that the fit is poor.

The Fit Between the Ideal and the Reality of Joint Custody

The popular notion of joint custody as shared legal and physical custody reflects only the minority of joint custody arrangements. For the most part, a joint custody arrangement involves the sharing of legal custody, but one parent — usually the mother — has physical custody. This arrangement is virtually indistinguishable from maternal sole custody with liberal access to the father. When physical custody rests with the mother, the mother is still as responsible for the day-to-day care of the children as she was prior to the divorce. Weitzman (1986) studied post-divorce families in California over a ten year period and found that most men did not want custody of their children. One question she was interested in was whether fathers who did not have custody were satisfied with their visitation schedules after divorce. She found that 70 per cent of noncustodial fathers preferred to see their children less often than they actually did, while the remaining 30 per cent liked things the way they were. Not *one* father indicated a desire to see his children more. This should not be surprising if we consider the facts.

Women have traditionally been the primary caregivers of children. Childcare is women's responsibility, not men's. While the media and anecdotal accounts suggest that men are embracing the responsibilities of fatherhood, research does not support this impression. Granted, co-parenting does exist for some men. For the majority of men, however, their role as father in the intact family involves very little caregiving. Men have not assumed an equal share in child-care (Armstrong and Armstrong 1987). In fact, recent research indicates that men continue to do little with respect to child care or housework (Michelson 1985; Statistics Canada 1985; Connelly & MacDonald 1983; McFarlane 1975; Meissner, Humphreys, Meis & Scheu 1975). There is no reason to believe that men who did not assume child care responsibilities during marriage will be transformed into "mothers" upon the award of joint custody. Courts can order co-parenting but parents must make it a reality. In those cases where co-parenting did not exist during the marriage, a court order cannot make it happen. The fact that most of the joint custody awards in the United States and Canada are joint *legal* custody and not joint *physical* custody (California State Senate 1987; Richardson 1988) reflects the lack of interest, desire or ability of fathers to share in the day-to-day child care responsibilities.

Aside from the issue of a father's willingness or ability to co-parent, there are other factors that militate against successful post-divorce co-parenting. The absence of co-parenting prior to divorce clearly predicts problems in co-parenting after divorce. Even if one lives in eternal hope of change, a change to effective co-parenting after divorce is possible only in the absence of interparental conflict. Steinman (1981) states that the major undertaking in joint custody is for parents to put aside their marital and divorce-engendered anger. Evidence suggests that benefits from continued contact with both parents occur only when parents are co-operative. Heatherington, Cox and Cox (1978) found that a high level of conflict negates the generally positive effect of frequent visitation by noncustodial fathers. Thus, the argument for joint custody rests on shaky ground when the nature of the relationships of most divorcing parents is taken into account.

For most couples, conflict is inherent in the divorce and the post-divorce process. To expect co-operation between divorcing couples who were unable to maintain their marriage may be unrealistic. In the context of hostile or warring parents, conflict rather than co-operation increases (Steinman, Zimmelman & Knoblauch 1984). Differences of opinion in childrearing, among other joint decisions, have dangerous consequences for children. Heatherington, Cox and Cox (1978) found that children in high-conflict intact and divorced families had more adjustment problems than children in low-conflict families. The researchers conclude that interpersonal conflict may affect the post-divorce adjustment of the children more than the structure of the family. This conclusion is further supported by a number of studies that have shown that children living in conflict-ridden nuclear families are more poorly adjusted than children living in well-functioning, single-parent families (Clingempeel and Reppucci, 1982). Thus, interparental conflict destroys the advantages of continued contact, and makes co-parenting difficult if not impossible. It would seem that the requirement of co-operation in joint custody is inherently contradictory to the reality of the relationships between divorcing couples. A large study of divorce mediation in Colorado found that fully half of joint custody awards had been changed because they were found to be unworkable by the parents (Pearson & Thoennes 1984). Another study showed no differences in a comparison of joint- and sole-custody arrangements with respect to levels of conflict or hostility between couples (Luepnitz 1982).

Another concern about contact in joint custody was voiced by Goldstein, Freud and Solnit (1973). The authors argue that children cannot maintain close emotional ties with both divorced parents, and that visitation rights are artificial and disruptive in a child's life and therefore not in the best interests of the child. Continuity of care with one parent is essential, they argue, and they go so far as to recommend that visitation rights be suspended altogether.

In the majority of post-divorce cases, the standard of living decreases severely for women and increases substantially for men (Weitzman 1985; Richardson 1988). The economic consequences of divorce are detrimental to children and their relationships with their parents. Wallerstein and Kelly (1980) found that the sharp decline in income disrupted children's lives, forced residential moves, and decreased daily contact with the custodial mother. Mothers after divorce are overwhelmed with the responsibility of becoming economically independent, maintaining the children and the home, and facilitating the post-divorce adjustment. In Canada, in 1985, 60.4 percent of female headed single-parent families were poor (National Council of Welfare 1987). Finnbogason and Townson (1985) reviewed existing empirical literature, and found that in Canada default rates on maintenance payments were in excess of 50 percent. They state that the "Law Reform Commission of Canada" estimates the true rate to be as high as 75 per cent. The magnitude of default bodes ill for the commitment of fathers to their children after divorce. The premise that "the best interests of children" involves joint custody is suspect in light of the high level of fathers' noncompliance to child-support orders.

Proponents of joint custody argue that fathers default on support payments because of custodial mothers' obstruction of fathers' access rights. The argument contends that with joint custody fathers will willingly make support payments and significantly lower the volume of maintenance order defaults (Lamb, 1987). However, a study of maintenance defaulters conducted by the Alberta Institute of Law Research and Reform in 1981 found no relationship between satisfaction with access and payment status (National Association of Women and the Law 1985). Non-custodial fathers who had no visitation/access problems were as likely to default on support payments as fathers with such problems. Further, Pearson and Thoennes (1984) found in their examination of custody arrangements and support payments in the United States that neither voluntary nor imposed joint custody arrangements resulted in greater compliance with support orders compared to sole-custody arrangements. So, the evidence appears to contradict the assumed benefit of support compliance in joint custody situations. Moreover, it is interesting to note that both in the United States and Canada researchers (Weitzman 1986; Grief 1985; and Richardson 1988) found that the complaints surrounding access/visitation are more commonly voiced by mothers who are disappointed with the infrequence of father visitation than from fathers complaining about inaccessibility to their children.

The potential and real disadvantages of joint custody, as outlined above, demand careful consideration before awarding joint custody and particularly before moving toward a presumption of joint custody (involuntary joint custody) in Canada. The available research on *involuntary* joint custody points to its potential harm. Steinman, Semmelman and Knoblauch (1985) studied voluntary and imposed joint custody families in San Francisco. They found that *none* of the court influenced [mediated] or imposed joint custody arrangements examined were successful. Children in these arrangements were more likely to be stressed or severely at risk of major emotional disturbances. Similarly, parents in imposed joint custody arrangements were unable to set aside their feelings of hostility. The relationship typically involved lack of respect or trust for their ex-spouses as individuals and as parents. The intense conflict between the parents interfered with their acting in accord with the needs of their children. Current research conducted by researchers at the Centre for the Family in Transition (1988) in California suggests that *involuntary* joint custody does not promote child adjustment post-divorce. Researchers found that children who had more frequent access to both divorced parents were more emotionally troubled and behaviourally disturbed.

Carefully reviewing the research on joint custody should lead to disenchantment with this arrangement. Such has been the case in the United States. In 1980 California was the first state to enact a joint custody statute. In less than a decade, the California State Senate struck a task force to examine its experience with joint custody. Its report, published in June, 1987, indicated that joint custody is "a complicated arrangement and takes special parents and children to make it work," and that to fail to "appropriately evaluate parents and children results in inappropriate awards or mediated agreements of joint custody that are harmful to children." In response to this re-examination, the Senate Task Force on Family Equity Report (California State Senate 1987) has recommended amendments to California's joint custody legislation that take into account the parenting skills and co-parenting abilities of the parents.

In Whose Best Interests?

There is no doubt that the concept of joint custody has an overwhelming appeal. The appeal lies in its rhetoric of gender equality, co-parenting and "best interests of the child." An understanding of joint custody, however, must be located in the reality of the post-divorce family and not in its fabrication. Research has shown that joint custody can work if parents enter the arrangement voluntarily with mutual respect, a willingness to cooperate and communicate, and a commitment to the child and to co-parenting. Joint custody does not work, if those ingredients are absent. And when joint custody does not work it is the children who most suffer the consequences. Considering the potential harm to children, it is alarming that Fathers' rights groups continue to lobby for a presumption of joint custody. In this final section of the paper, the question that will be addressed is "who is best served by a presumption of joint custody?"

As we have seen, when the intact family is dissolved, the typical arrangement after divorce is that children live with their mothers and visit with their fathers. This arrangement is usually made with the mutual consent of both mothers and fathers. In fact, in 85.6 per cent of cases women receive custody (McKie, Prentice & Reed 1983). When custody is contested by the father, nearly half are awarded sole custody (Richardson 1988). However, very few fathers request custody.

The reality of the high percentage of awards to mothers is a result of the fact that mothers perform the childrearing in our society. This is recognized by fathers and the courts. An argument could easily be made that the maternal preference evident in the courts in the last half of this century has not been a preference at all but a reality-based custody decision that conformed to the "best interests of the child" standard. Men are not and have never been primary child caregivers. Fathers alleging sex discrimination in custody awards shift the focus away from parenting to the sex of the parent — in other words, they turn attention from the "best interests of the child" to the best interests of the non-custodial parent. Awarding custody to the parent that has been and will continue to be the primary caregiver would logically appear to be a custody award that is "in the best interests of the child."

While it is alleged that *involuntary* joint custody will produce two primary caregivers — fathers and mothers — the experience with voluntary joint custody indicates that this result is unlikely. Morris (1988, p. 19) studied a sample of typically middle-class, professional Canadian parents who had legal or de facto joint custody arrangements.

491

She found that mothers continued "to assume more responsibility for coordinating the routines of their children, even when in the other home." The co-parenting aspect of joint custody is left up to the parents to work out, which normally results in an arrangement *identical to sole maternal custody*. Even in voluntary joint custody arrangements continued contact or co-parenting is not guaranteed. It is unrealistic to believe that it can be imposed by legislation.

Joint custody defined and practiced as joint legal custody raises the question of what fathers' rights groups really want in their lobby for a presumption of joint legal custody. If they want the positive results demonstrated in the research, these can only be realized by actual sharing of day-to-day responsibilities and decision-making within a co-operative context. Evidence indicates that *most men do not want to have these responsibilities for their children* (NAWL, 1985). In this case, it would appear that the application of joint legal custody considers only the best interests of the non-caretaker parent, usually the father. Legal recognition of his authority over his children may serve to raise his self-esteem and control, but what does it do for children? Moreover, parental rights, without parental responsibilities, calls into question the justice and equity of the control of the absent parent over the primary caregiver's decisions.

Those parents who mutually want a joint custody arrangement can have it. Who, then, are the parents that are lobbying for a pre-sumption of joint custody? Clearly, those parents are the ones who do not have custody and who are unable to reach a mutually agreeable ar-rangement with their ex-spouse. Embittered by their divorce experience and frustrated by the uncooperative nature of the relationship with their ex-spouse, these parents have sought redress through the courts. Joint custody is seen by them as the solution. Considering the research that has been reviewed in this paper, joint custody holds false promises as the solution. Furthermore, parents engaged in a hostile, warring relationship are, as we have seen, likely to harm the child emotionally and psychologically. That parents are willing to place children in the middle of their battlefields, speaks volumes to the question of whose best interests are served by joint custody. Joint custody has become the politicization of the conflict between divorcing mothers and fathers. To debate fathers' rights over the rights of children is to move us back in time to a paternal presumption rather than forward.

Movement toward a presumption of joint custody must be put on hold in Canada until there is empirical support for it. To frame social policy and write legislation on the basis of emotionally appealing rhetoric and selected studies based on unrepresentative samples is to place our children at risk, and in Wallerstein's words, "to experiment with the children of this country" (Polikoff 1985, p.4). The social science researchers who study the consequences of divorce (Heatherington, Wallerstein, Weitzman, and Steinman) have all made strong public statements against *involuntary* joint custody. Each one agrees that joint custody is an ideal solution for ideal parents, but that it is not for every divorcing couple. Nor is it in the best interests of all children. To impose joint custody on couples where one or both parents are opposed is truly to divide the child in half. To establish joint custody as an arbitrary standard of what constitutes the best interests of the child is to preclude an informed, factual determination of the question in the case of each child.

Bibliography

Abarbanel, Alice
1979 "Shared Parenting After Separation and Divorce: A Study of Joint Custody." *American Journal of Orthopsychiatry* 49 (2) 320-29.
Abella, Rosalie Silberman
1981 "Family Law in Ontario: Changing Assumptions." *Ottawa Law Review* 13 1-22.
Anderson, Karen
1987 "Historical Perspectives on the Family." Pp. 21-39 in K. Anderson et al. (eds.) *Family Matters*. Toronto: Meuthuen Publications.
Anderson, Karen, Armstrong, H., Armstrong, P., Drakich, J., Eichler, M., Guberman, C., Hayford, A., Luxton, M., Peters, J., Porter, E., Richardson, C.J., & Tesson, G.
1987 *Family Matters*. Toronto: Methuen Publications.
Ariès, Phillipe
1962 *Centuries of Childhood: A Social History of Family Life*. New York: Vintage Books.
Armstrong, Pat and Hugh Armstrong
1987 "The Conflicting Demands of 'Work' and 'Home.'" Pp. 133-40 in K. Anderson et. al. (eds), *Family Matters*. Toronto: Methuen Publications.
Backhouse, Constance B.
1981 "Shifting Patterns in Nineteenth-Century Canadian Custody Law." Pp. 212-48 in David H. Flaherty, (ed.) *Essays in the History of Canadian Law*, Vol 1. Toronto: The Osgood Society.

V. Trouble Spots in Family Life

Boyd, Susan
1987 "Child Custody, Ideologies and Female Employment." Paper presented at the National Association of Women and the Law Biennial Conference. Winnipeg, Manitoba, 1987.
Center for the Family in Transition
1988 Summary of Centre for the Family in Transition research presented at the 65th Annual Meeting of the American Orthopsychiatric Association, March 30, 1988.
Chesler, Phyllis
1986 *Mothers on Trial: The Battle for Children and Custody*. New York: McGraw-Hill Book Company.
Clingempeel, Glenn W. and Reppucci, N. Dickon
1982 "Joint Custody after Divorce: Major Issues and Goals for Research." *Psychological Bulletin* 9(1) 102-127.
Connelly, M. Patricia and Martha MacDonald
1983 "Women's Work: Domestic and Wage Labour in a Nova Scotia Community." *Studies in Political Economy* 10 (Winter) 45-72.
Cook, Ramsey and Wendy Mitchinson
1976 *The Proper Sphere*. Toronto: Oxford University Press.
Finnbogason, Eva and Monica Townson
1985 "The Benefits and Cost Effectiveness of a Central Registry of Maintenance and Custody Orders." Status of Women Canada. Minister of Supply and Services Canada.
Goldstein, J., A. Freud, and A. Solnit
1973 *Beyond the Best Interests of the Child*. New York: The Free Press.
Grief, Judith Brown
1979 "Fathers, Children and Joint Custody." *American Journal of Orthopsychiatry* 49 311-319.
Heatherington, E., M. Cox, and R. Cox
1978 "The Aftermath of Divorce." In J. H. Stevens Jr. & M. Matthews (eds.), *Mother-Child, Father-Child Relationships*. Washington, D.C.: National Association for the Education of the Young.
Henderson, J.
1988 "Two Parents are Better than One." *Globe and Mail*, Tuesday, May 10.
Lamb, Louise
1987 "Invountary Joint Custody: What Mothers will Lose if Fathers' Rights Groups Win." *Herizons* (Jan/Feb) 20-23, 31.
Luepnitz, Deborah Ann
1982 *Child Custody: A Study of Families after Divorce*. Toronto: Lexington Books.

MacDonald, James
1986 "Historical Perspective of Custody and Access Disputes." Pp. 9-22 in Ruth S. Parry et al. (eds.), *Custody Disputes: Evaluation and Intervention.* Toronto: Lexington Books.
Mayrand, Albert
1983 "The Influence of Spousal Conduct on the Custody of Children." Pp. 159-73 in Rosalie S. Abella and Claire L'Heurent-Dube (eds.), *Family Law: Dimensions of Justice.* Toronto: Butterworths.
McFarlane, Bruce
1975 "Married Life and Adaptions to a Professional Role: Married Women Dentists in Canada." Pp. 359-66 in Pavez S. Wakil (ed.), *Marriage, Family and Society.* Toronto: Butterworths.
McKie, D.C., B. Prentice, and P. Reed
1983 *Divorce: Law and the Family in Canada.* Ottawa: Statistics Canada, Research and Analysis Division.
Meissner, Martin, Elizabeth W. Humphreys, Scott M. Meis and William J. Scheu
1975 "No Exit for Wives: Sexual Division of Labour and the Culmination of Household Demands." *The Canadian Review of Sociology and Anthropology* 12 424-439.
Michelson, William
1985 "Divergent Convergent: The Daily Routines of Employed Spouses as a Public Affairs Agenda." *Public Affairs Report* 26 (4) 1-10.
Miller, D.
1979 "Joint Custody." *Family Law Quarterly* 13 345-412.
National Council of Welfare
1987 "Progress Against Poverty." Ottawa: National Council of Welfare.
National Association of Women and the Law (NAWL)
1985 A submission to the Senate Standing Committee on Legal and Constitutional Affairs — Bill C-47: Joint Custody, Child Support, Maintenance Enforcement, and Related Issues. Ottawa: National Association of Women and the Law.
Parry, Ruth S., Elsa Broder, Elizabeth A. G. Schmitt, Elisabeth B. Saunders, and Eric Hood
1986 *Custody Disputes: Evaluation and Intervention.* Toronto: Lexington Books.
Pearson, J., and N. Thonnes
1984 "Mediating and Litigating Custody Disputes: A Longitudinal Evaluation" *Family Law Quarterly,* 17 497-524.

V. Trouble Spots in Family Life

Polikoff, Nancy
1985 *Brief of Amicus Curiae.* Court of Appeals of Maryland, No.12, *Taylor* v, *Taylor*.

Polikoff, Nancy
1983 "Gender and Child-Custody Determinations: Exploding the Myths." Pp. 183-202 in Irene Diamond (ed.), *Families, Politics, and Public Policy: A Feminist Dialogue on Women and the State.* New York: Longman, Inc.

Richardson, C. James
1988 *Court-Based Divorce Mediation in Four Canadian Cities: an Overview of Research Results.* Ottawa: Minister of Supply and Services, Canada.

Roman, M. and W. Haddad
1978 *The Disposable Parent.* New York: Holt Rinehart and Winston.

California State Senate
1987 Senate Task Force on Family Equity

Statistics Canada
1985 Women in Canada: A Statistical Report. Ottawa: Supply and Services Canada (Cat. no. 89-503E).

Steinman, Susan
1981 "The experience of children in a joint custody arrangement: A report of a study." *American Journal of Orthopsychiatry*, 51 (3) 403-14.

Steinman, Susan B. and S. E. Semmelman and T. M. Knoblauch
1985 "A Study of Parents Who Sought Joint Custody Following Divorce: Who Reaches Agreement and Sustains Joint Custody and Who Returns to Court." *Journal of the American Academy of Child Psychiatry* 24(5) 554-62.

Wallerstein, Judith S. and Joan B. Kelly
1980 *Surviving the Breakup: How Children and Parents Cope with Divorce.* New York: Basic Books.

Weitzman, Lenore
1986 *The Divorce Revolution: The Unexpected Social and Economic Consequences for Woman and Children in America.* New York: The Free Press.

C. Domestic Violence Against Women and Children

When women and children are victimized in the relationships that we expect to afford them nurturance and support, we are justifiably horrified. And it is difficult to rationally analyze the situation. Nevertheless, it is necessary to understand *why* such violence is occurring in order to take steps, collectively and individually, to prevent its perpetuation.

Fortunately, sociologists have sufficient analytical skills and knowledge to understand much about the causes of domestic violence. It is fairly clear, in fact, that precisely those factors that define family life today are chiefly responsible for the violence directed at women and children: the intensity of family relationships, especially those between lovers; the privatization of family life, which entails both heavy responsibilities and little outside support or relief for parents; gender socialization and men's characteristic need for control; the locus of much of our living in the small, private home, which produces a need for the control of young children; and the "sanctity" of "the family."

The article by Rebecca and Russell Dobash describes the circumstances surrounding violence against women, and begins to elaborate some of the factors causing such violence. Susan Cole's article discusses the causes of child abuse, focusing especially on the importance of the cultural context and gender socialization.

Suggested Reading

Miller, Alice.
1983. *For Your Own Good.* New York: Farrar, Straus, Giroux. This impassioned critique of traditional child-rearing practices goes a long way towards explaining the psychological causes of domestic violence.

The Violent Event*

Rebecca and Russell Dobash

The beginning of the violent episode [...]

The events described to us were almost always preceded by a verbal confrontation relating to ongoing aspects of the marital relationship, with the husband or wife making demands on their partner or complaining about various transgressions. The majority of these arguments were not trivial but centred on long-standing contentious issues. Whether it was the first, worst, last, or typical violent incident described by the women, the majority of the disputes that preceded the violence focused on the husband's jealousy of his wife, differing expectations regarding the wife's domestic duties and the allocation of money. This pattern also emerged concerning the most frequent source of confrontations throughout the couple's married life. 44 per cent of the women reported sexual jealousy (almost always unfounded) as the major source of altercations, followed by disagreements relating to money (16 per cent) and the husband's expectations regarding the woman's homemaking (16 per cent).

Sources of Conflict

Many of the women we spoke to told us of similar reactions from their husbands. One woman described how her husband...was jealous from the very beginning of their marriage.

> From the very start he's always been jealous, if he seen me even speaking to a neighbour and it happened to be a man, it didn't matter if he was nine or ninety, 'what are you talking to him for, What can you have to talk to him about?' I mean, you could just be passing the time of day with somebody.[...]

Other women reported that their husbands instigated arguments regarding domestic duties, such as housekeeping or child-minding activities.

---

* From *The Changing Experience of Women* ed., Elizabeth Whitelegg. (London: Basil Blackwell, 1982). Reprinted by permission.

V. Trouble Spots in Family Life

One woman recounted an argument over food preparation when discussing what usually happened before an assault:

> I would be in bed and if he was in that kind of mood, he would pull the bedclothes off and say. 'Get out of that fucking bed. Come on, get out and get me something to eat'. He might start on about my family or friends — it could be anything that would set him off — he would say: 'Pull your face straight, you miserable bugger', or 'There's never anything in this bloody house to eat. Is that all you've got?' I said we might have a bit of boiled ham or something. He said: 'Right, put that on a sandwich.' Or if there's cheese, 'There's never anything but bloody cheese, cheese, cheese, cheese, all the time.' So you'd get it, and then I might just answer back, and I'd say: 'Well it's good enough for me, cheese, and it's good enough for the children. What's wrong with a cheese sandwich?' It would start off with him being angry over trivial little things, a trivial little thing like cheese instead of meat on a sandwich, or it might be the way your face just looked for a second at him, or something, and then he'd just give you one across the face, always across the face.

The other common focus of disputes leading to attacks was the expenditure of money. The women told us that their requests for housekeeping money and their husband's expenditure of money on his individual pursuits, such as a night out at the pub or gambling, led to verbal confrontations and violence. In describing the last time her husband used violence against her, one woman recalled the specific verbal exchange about money that led to the attack.

> Well, I had friends in and he went away out and he came in the scullery and says to me: 'Can I get ten bob for the bookies?' And I says to him. 'I've no got very much money.' So he went out and there was nothing said. The next thing my sister saw him walking back in the living room and she says to me: 'He is coming back in, and he's in a hell of a temper. You can see it on him.' So the next thing we heard the scullery getting smashed up, you see, so I went in and I says to him: 'What's wrong?' 'Don't you f — ing ask me what's wrong,' he says. I says: 'What is it? What have I done? So he slapped me across the face.

500

Although confrontations usually precede violent attacks, confrontations do not necessarily involve verbal exchanges. Some of them may involve only a one-word or one-sentence accusation made by either partner, which is immediately followed by a punch or a kick; other violent events begin without any words having been uttered.

The following account illustrates a violent reaction regarding food preparation that began without a verbal confrontation.

> He had come home from work and he'd been drinking. He was late and I'd started cooking his meal, but I put it aside, you know, when he didn't come in. Then when he came in I started heating it because the meal wasn't ready. I was standing at the sink, and I was sorting something at the sink, and he just came up and gave me a punch in the stomach. I couldn't get my breath. He'd punched me and the wind was knocked out of me. I just sort of stood there, and I couldn't get my breath. I held on to the sink for ages, and the pain in my stomach and trying to get my breath, and that was the first time I remember that he ever touched me. It was only because his tea wasn't ready on the table for him.

Men who repeatedly attack their wives often do so because they perceive, as in the preceding example, that their wives are not providing for their immediate needs in a manner they consider appropriate and acceptable. These chastisements are sometimes not prefaced by an argument.

[The following quotation demonstrates] the reaction of men who thought that their needs and desires should take precedence over those of all other members of the family.

> We were having a birthday party and my father was there. Well, I had my son blow out the candles and make a wish and then help make the first cut. I had him give the first piece to my father because he had to go to work. My husband stormed out of the house. He came back loaded that night simply because my father had the first piece of birthday cake instead of him. That was the first time he broke my wrist.[1]

---

[1] R.J. Gelles (1974) *The Violent Home: A Study of Physical Aggression Between Husbands and Wives.* Beverly Hills: Sage, p.139.

The antecedents of this episode related to the failure of the wife to meet her husband's perceived immediate needs, a failure that threatened his conception of himself as the head of the household.

The specific factor or factors preceding the violence may seem insignificant and the violent response totally unrelated to the context in which it occurs when the confrontations are analyzed without due consideration of the ongoing relationship. It is imperative, therefore, that we seek an understanding and explanation of verbal encounters preceding violent episodes in the wider patterns of subordination and domination in the marriage and in the expectations of the men and women involved. In a violent episode it is not necessarily the specific issue that is being contested but the relationship between the husband and wife. Couples usually argue over the same issues during their marriage and though these problems may not explicitly arise prior to a violent episode, they are the background factors that shape the marriage and its violence.

The husbands of the women we interviewed, did not like their actions, opinions, and beliefs questioned during a verbal confrontation and quickly responded to such challenges with force. Women were required to agree with their husbands and accept their position of authority regardless of its merit. If they did not, they might be summarily silenced through the use of force.

> We were having an argument about something. I think it was money. I'm no exactly sure but probably because we didn't have the money for him to go out — that was what usually caused all the arguments. It was the first time he really hit me. It wasn't just a slap, you know, he didn't give me a black eye at first, but it was really a sore one, you know, a punch. Before then he used to shout and bawl messages, you know; I wouldn't answer back, didn't open my mouth. I used to just sit there or go and wash the dishes or something. But this time I started shouting back at him and that was it. He got angry and made a dive for me and started thumping me about.

The verbal exchange and efforts to avoid violence

When and if a verbal exchange preceded the episode the women often attempted to alter the seemingly inevitable course of events by trying to reduce the potential for violence. The primary, and one would think potentially the most successful technique is withdrawing from the situation. This opportunity is usually denied the women. Withdrawing from a potentially violent situation within the home is very difficult for a woman: there is no safe place to go in the home; children have to be attended to; and the husband might very well block her exit. A second alternative, is agreement with the accusations that the aggressor is making.[...] A woman who agrees, either truthfully or falsely, to her husband's accusations regarding her supposed infidelity or failure to meet his need may actually guarantee a violent punishment.[...]

Women attempt to avoid or divert the violence by other means: they try to reason with their husbands or they seek an alternative, non-violent solution during the verbal confrontation. Some try to withdraw from the argument by not arguing. Other women take the opposite tack and attempt to point out injustices in their husband's claims or put their own point of view. On some occasions such efforts to avoid violence are successful: 'Well, if I thought I had time, you know, I'd sort of slowly back down, and sort of, you know, overcome the situation by changing the subject into something else. But other times, well, usually, I didn't, and I got it'

Regardless of the reaction from the woman she usually is unable to avoid or prevent a violent response. Almost 70 per cent of the women told us that arguments with their husbands nearly always, or often, ended in an attack. The verbal confrontations were usually short, most lasting less than five minutes. Only a very few women on very infrequent occasions responded to their husband's verbal aggression by initiating violence.

The nature of the violence and the reactions of women

The men usually employed various forms of violence but on occasion a man would use only one type of physical force as the following example illustrates:

> Well, he just started shouting and bawling and then he just called me names, you know, swearing at me. And he started hitting me, punching me. He kept punching my face all the time — it was my nose. And he wouldn't let me sit down or anything. He made me stand in the middle of the floor. He wouldn't let me go into bed and I was screaming and he just kept punching my face. He'd walk away, maybe go into the kitchenette, come back, and have another punch at me.... All night. I wasn't to sit on the chair or the floor, I was to stand there. He fell asleep and I bent into bed and he woke up in the morning and he asked me what had happened to my face because my nose was all swollen and bruised. I told him

503

it was him, but he didn't say anything. Then that night he came back and thumped me again, and it was just the same routine.

This account illustrates that being punched can mean much more than one might envisage. Many men use their feet in attacks on their wives, Commonly, the woman is pushed or punched to the floor and then severely kicked in the head and body.[2]

The dynamic aspects of violence to wives cannot be captured in a gross quantitative manner. Only in the first assault in a marriage, is the violence usually of a singular nature, such as one slap or punch. In the majority of incidents men use various forms of violence, as the following incidents reveal:

He punched me, he kicked me, he pulled me by the hair. My face hit a step. He had his bare feet, you know, with being in bed, and he just jumped up and he pulled on his trousers and he was kicking me. If he had his shoes on, God knows what kind of face I would have had. As it was I had a cracked cheek bone, two teeth knocked out, cracked ribs, broken nose, two beautiful black eyes — it wasn't even a black eye, it was my whole cheek was just purple from one eye to the other. And he had got me by the neck and, you know, he was trying, in fact, practically succeeded in strangling me. I was choking, I was actually at the blacking-out stage. I was trying to pull his fingers away, with me trying to pull his fingers away, I scratched myself, you know, trying to get his fingers off. He hit me and I felt my head, you know, hitting the back of the lock of the door. I started to scream and I felt as if I'd been screaming for ages. When I came to he was pulling me up the stair by the hair. I mean, I think it was the pain of him pulling me up the stair by the hair that brought me round again. I can remember going up the stair on my hands and knees and the blood — I dinnae know where it was coming from — it was just dripping in front of my face and I was actually covered in blood. I just got to the kitchen door and he just walked straight to his bed. I just filled the sink with cold water, put a dish towel in it, and held it up to my face. I remember I went through to the living room and I fell asleep and I woke

---

[2]Kicking and standing on women was practised with hobnail boots in Yorkshire during the late nineteenth century and was called 'purring'.

up in the morning with this matted dish towel and, God I
couldn't move. There wasn't a bit of me that wasnae sore.

As these examples illustrate, men who attack their wives often use
extreme force and they do not restrain themselves because they are attacking a woman.

The response of women [once violence begins]

Regardless of the severity of the attacks, women usually report that they
seldom attempt to respond to violence with force. Often it is impossible to
retaliate. The superior strength of men allows them to immobilize their
wives' hands and/or feet or enables them to force the woman down to the
floor or against a wall. As one woman told us: 'I'd have loved to have been
able to hit him back, but I just couldn't bring myself to do it. In fact, I
was in situations that I couldn't hit back. In fact, the only thing I've done
is bit his finger.'
The percentage of women in our study who attempted to hit back
was about the same whether it was the first, worst, or last violent
episode. When we asked about their typical response only a very small
number (four women out of the entire group) said that they always tried
to hit their husbands back. The majority said they never (33 per cent) or
seldom (42 per cent) attempted to use force. The remaining 24 per cent of
the women attempted to use force on a few occasions.
The majority of the women we interviewed responded to a violent
attack by remaining physically passive. Women learn that it is futile to
attempt to match the physical force of their husbands and try primarily
to protect themselves during attacks. Two women summed up the experience of most of the women: 'Well, I didn't try to hit him back. It just
got worse if I did.' 'I just tried to defend myself, got my arms up to save
myself.' A woman who reported receiving only one black eye in all of the
attacks she experienced during her married life indicated that this was
because she learned to protect herself: 'Just the one, and I never got a
black eye again. It was always, I held my hand up to my face. That's the
first thing I ever done as soon as he made a move, you know,
automatically.' Another common response was to scream or cry but this
reaction often led to even greater violence. One woman described how she
learned that it was always best to remain silent and passive.

I found out the best way not to get him into a tirade would
be not to cry out loud, do you know what I mean, not to cry
out. I know it sounds silly, but if you can just think to

505

> yourself, 'I'm going to get two or three and then he'll stop,'
> that wasn't bad. He could just stop after two or three, but he
> wouldn't if you cried out or you protested.

Screaming and crying was likely to arouse the curiosity of outsiders, who usually did not intervene but who might learn that the public image of the husband as a decent, upstanding fellow was not the same as his private behaviour. Not only do men who attack their wives not like their opinions and desires to be questioned or thwarted, they also do not like their wives to resist punishment. Women are supposed to accept physical abuse because their husbands feel that it is justified.

Physical injuries

The physical consequences of violent events were often visible on the faces and limbs of the women we interviewed. It is difficult to appreciate the seriousness of the injuries received in a particular assault or from repeated attacks over a period of several years. The women reported that the usual assault resulted in bruising of the face, limbs, or body. The bruises ranged from minor discolourations of the skin to severe contusions requiring weeks to heal. Bruising usually was coupled with other injuries such as cuts to the face or body, abrasions, torn hair and fractures.[...]
Women are sometimes knocked unconscious.[...]
One woman described the result of a particularly brutal attack during most of which she was unconscious.

> He grabbed me from the chair, dragged me into the sitting
> room, to the hall, pulled me halfway up the stairs, then
> pulled me back down and started to kick and stand on me.
> And that was in front of his own mum. I was knocked out
> with the first couple of blows he gave me. He was ham-
> mering into something that was just like a cushion on the
> floor. I had a broken rib, broken leg on the right side, two
> front teeth knocked out, burst chin — I've still got the scar
> — I had five stitches, and a broken arm on the right side.

The multiple injuries sustained by this woman were rather unusual. However, nearly 9 per cent of the women reported receiving fractures or losing teeth at some time during their married life.
The injuries often required medical attention and even hospital-ization. Nearly 80 per cent of the women reported going to a doctor at

least once during their marriage for injuries resulting from attacks by their husbands; nearly 40 per cent said that they sought medical attention on five separate occasions. Many women thought they required medical care but were prevented by their husbands from seeking such attention. The women we interviewed suffered serious woundings, innumerable bloodied noses, fractured teeth and bones, concussions, miscarriages and severe internal injuries that often resulted in permanent scars, disfigurement and sometimes persistent poor health.

Physical injuries are often coupled with serious emotional distress. Many women are chronically emotionally upset and/or depressed about the attacks and the prospects of the next one. For some women the emotional distress is so severe that medication and even hospitalization become necessary. "Just bang, bang, bang, and me heart used to be going fifty to the dozen. And I used to be shaking like a leaf [days after the attack]. But I hadn't to show him this,[...] I was always terrified. My nerves were getting the better of me in the finish, you know. I was getting so I used to shake through bloody fear. He knew this and I think he loved this."

Presence of others during an altercation

Violent events like the ones described in the foregoing accounts usually occur in the home but this does not necessarily mean that they are not observed by others. We found that 59 per cent of the first violent incidents did occur without anyone observing them, but over 75 per cent of the women reported that the last attack was observed by at least one other person, usually their children. Over the course of a violent marriage there was an increase in the probability that others would be present during an assault. This pattern is not surprising: young married couples are usually childless or have only infant children, who are not thought of as observers, but as the children grow older, it is very difficult for them to avoid witnessing attacks. A majority of women (59 per cent) reported that the children usually were present during an assault, and it was not unusual for some children almost always to observe attacks on the mother.

The reactions of the children were varied. Many of the younger children were frightened, and unable to comprehend what was occurring — 'they just sat quiet,' — but some young children comprehended and reacted: 'Donna used to get hysterical. The wee soul, she'd only be about six and one-half, and she would say, 'come on, dad, you're going to be good and you're not going to fight with mum tonight. Please, dad, you promised'. As the children grow older, they occasionally attempt to intervene either physically or verbally.[3] Beatings are sometimes witnessed by friends or relatives, who, like the children, react in various ways. The woman's friends or relations are much more likely to intervene than the husband's friends or relatives:

[For example.]

> *And whenever he's hit you in front of people, what have they usually done?*
>
> Well, actually his friend, he sort of said, you know: 'Come on, get a hold of yourself.' This sort of thing. They didn't really tell him off. They didn't want to quarrel with him, too, but they sort of said: 'Get a grip on yourself'. You know, 'Leave her alone' and that. Mostly when I was pregnant, you know. They'd pull him back, but they never actually fought with him because of it.
> They told him to calm down.
>
> *And how do you think these outsiders felt about you, seeing you getting battered?*
>
> I think they were just more embarrassed than anything else that they happened to be there at the time.
>
> *And do you think they felt sorry for you and reckoned — did they want to get involved?*
>
> I don't think they wanted to get involved at all. I mean most of his friends anyway was doing the same things to their wives. I mean Bruce used to give his wife knockings as well.

As described in the above account, the usual response of friends and relatives is simply to do nothing or to tell the husband to stop. Very rarely do friends or relatives attempt physically to intervene in the violence.

Pleas from outsiders seem to make very little difference: 'They used to tell him to stop but he didn't take any notice'. Outsiders may actually touch off or aggravate an assault. If a woman were to question her

---

[3]See Gelles. op. cit. p. 33 et seq. Also see J. R. Hepburn (1973) 'Violent behaviour in interpersonal relationships'. *Sociological Quarterly* 14 (Summer) pp. 419-29, and H. Toch (1969) *Violent Men: An Inquiry into the Psychology of Violence*, Chicago: Aldine.

husband's actions or his supposed rightful authority over her in front of friends or relations, he might consider this a double affront. Not only had she questioned his authority, but she had rebuked him in front of others, a double humiliation. In describing the first violent attack one woman told us about this type of confrontation. Her husband had invited another couple to visit them, but instead of coming directly home from work to help entertain the guests he stopped at a friend's home. When he arrived home with his friend, his wife protested about his late arrival — both in front of his friend and within hearing distance of the visiting couple. He responded by telling her to 'mind her own business. I do what I like'. When she complained that he was inconsiderate, he punched her against the wall and knocked her unconscious. This happened 'simply because I chastised him and there was somebody there in the sitting room.'

Though outsiders do at times inhibit a violent attack, the presence of an audience prior to or during such an episode may help escalate the assault. This depends upon the man involved, the nature of the verbal exchange with his wife, and the orientation of the outsiders to violent behaviour.[4] The presence of others during a verbal altercation is most likely to precipitate violence if the potential aggressor perceives the observers as supportive of his actions or if, as in the example cited above, he feels humiliated in their eyes.

After the violent event

Reaction

After an assault, the typical reaction of both the man and the woman is to remain in the home. Almost all of the women (90 per cent) reported that usually they remained in the house and were unable to do anything immediately after an attack.

> I didn't do anything about it. After he hit me I just cried and tried to keep quiet, hoping he would calm down.

> I just used to sit and cry because I know for a fact that if you start hitting back then you'll get more hitting back, you see. So I just sort of sat back and took it all.

---

[4]Faulkner's work on violence among ice hockey players illustrated a situation in which a supportive audience reinforced and indeed demanded the use of physical force. See R. Faulkner (1973) 'On respect and retribution: toward an ethnography of violence'. *Sociological Symposium* 9 (Spring) pp. 17-35.

A considerable proportion of the women we interviewed (20 per cent) also indicated that their husbands forcibly kept them from going out. A few women discussed extreme restraints upon their mobility: 'Before he went to work in the morning he would nail the windows shut, and padlock the doors from the inside'.[5] Husbands might physically prevent their wives from leaving the house even to seek help or medical assistance, but usually women were restrained by verbal threats of retaliation.

Women sometimes responded to a violent attack by attempting to placate their husbands: 'I used to ask him if he wanted something to eat. Or I wouldn't say anything, you know, sort of try and get him to cool down more or less'.

Immediately after an attack husbands tended to do nothing, to ignore the act, or to behave as if nothing had happened. Almost 80 per cent of the men usually acted in this manner.

> He just sat and read and that. He didn't talk. We didn't talk to one another.

> He went to sleep. Mind you, he was tired [from beating her]. I've no doubt that he was physically worn out. He was exhausted.

> He didn't feel anything. Most peculiar, [he] just starts talking to you, you know, as long as you're doing as you are told.

The second most common response of the husband following the attack was to go to a pub or just out to cool off.

Feelings about the violence

The feelings and emotions expressed by the women we interviewed were complex. Women usually felt very upset after a violent episode, and these feelings persisted for several days and sometimes weeks afterward: 'I was very upset about it. I mean, I had never seen anything like this

---

[5]S. Eisenberg and P. Micklow (1974) 'The assaulted wife: Catch 22 revisited. (an exploratory legal study of wifebeating in Michigan)'. Mimeograph, University of Michigan Law School. Also available from Rutgers University School of Law, 180 University Avenue, Newark, N.J. 07102.

happening. I'd never experienced violence in a home. I was pretty upset about it. I was crying all the time'. This account aptly describes the typical reaction of over 65 per cent of the women. Women also felt shocked, frightened, ashamed, bitter, and angry after an assault: 'Oh, I was frightened, you know, I was terrified, miserable. I was always sitting on an edge waiting for him to get to sleep.'

A woman often feels angry after a violent event because her husband ignores her feelings and concerns, because he reacts to her protestations with violence, because a special event such as Christmas or a child's birthday has been spoiled, or because he has shamed her by attacking her in front of friends or relatives. In our study intense anger was most likely after the worst assault since it was typically both humiliating and severe.

Men may also feel angry after a violent episode, but unlike the women their anger is a continuation of the feelings that gave rise to the verbal confrontation and not a response to the attack. However, men usually act, or at least appear to act, blase after attacking their wives and express little or no remorse. The husbands of the women we spoke to very rarely apologized or showed contrition immediately following an assault.

If there was any expression of remorse or contrition it usually occurred early in the marriage and after the first violent incident: Over 35 per cent of the men apologized after the first attack, whereas only 14 per cent did so after the worst attack. The bulk of the men typically acted as if nothing had happened. Whether it was the first, worst, or last assault, they very rarely expressed any remorse or regret, and if they did apologize it was usually after a few days or weeks. Only a small percentage (8 per cent) of the husbands almost always expressed remorse immediately following the violent event; 22 per cent usually expressed regret after a few days.

On a few occasions men showed their contrition by doing something for their wives such as helping with the dishes. One woman described how her husband used this technique several weeks after a violent attack.

> Oh, he was sorry. He tried to make it up you know. He would help me do things in the house that week, which he never did. And when it came up for New Year he was saying, 'Oh, wait and I'll clean this. I'll do that'. I think that was his way of trying to say he was sorry.

However, whether it was the first, worst, or last violent attack, expressions of regret or contrition, apologies or helpful behaviour were not

511

typical of the men. Instead, they rarely or never expressed remorse or contrition regarding their violent actions.

> No. he didn't apologize. He never said he was sorry. I used to say to hint sometimes 'Do you not feel sorry about it' and he'd say: 'No, I'd never say I was sorry because if I was I wouldn't do it in the first place'. He always said that.

> I never recall him having any remorse whatever, never recall him ever coming to see me and saying, well honey,' put his arm around me and say 'I'm sorry.

Not only did most husbands fail to apologize or show regret after a violent attack, they often continued to argue with, or to act aggressively towards their wives, demanding that she do something for him, threatening to bring in a third party who he thought would take his side and condemn his wife, or threatening to put her out of the house.

> Oh, I've seen it after he'd maybe stopped the hitting — the actual hitting would maybe go on for ten minutes or something — but then he would sit and go on for hours. And you're sitting there in a cold sweat waiting on whatever else is going to happen. I couldn't talk, my mouth was shut. I would just sit and he'd maybe make me do things, you know, break something and say: 'Right, sweep that up'.

Men also attempt to rationalize their violent behaviour by denying responsibility for the assault or by arguing that their wife's actions or inactions provoked them.

> He'd always just deny it or say it hadn't happened or say it had been an accident. Even to this day he'll argue: 'I never hit you when you were pregnant. That's a lie. That's the last thing in the world I'd do'. He still insists he's not a violent man. He'll say: 'That's one thing I hate is a man that hits a woman'.

> He would always make out it was my fault. If I hadn't said this or if I hadnae done that, it would never have happened. He always claimed that I provoked him. It was always I provoked him.

Although most men were not drunk when they attacked their wives (30 per cent of the men in our police sample were described as intoxicated and 25 per cent of the women described their husbands as often drunk at the time of an incident), some of the men who had been drinking denied that they had hit their wives or maintained that they were not responsible for the beating because they were intoxicated.

> He always says that he never hit me, but I know that he knows because sometimes he says things about it.

> He would say: 'Look, this isn't me, it's the drink that is making me act this way'.

Men who have only had a small amount to drink and could in no way be considered drunk also use alcohol as an excuse. Women, too, may use their husband's drinking (of even minimal amounts) as a means of making sense of the violent behaviour and of placing blame upon something 'outside' the marital relationship.[6]

Thus, men deny responsibility for their violent acts by asserting that their wife's arguing or perceived inappropriate behaviour led them to behave in a violent manner.[7]

Accusations which place the blame upon the victim, may lead a woman to express shame or guilt regarding the violent event. In our study this was especially the case after the first attack since it was seen as a blemish on the marriage. One of the women we interviewed told us that after the first assault she 'was ashamed. I didn't want anybody to know, I was hoping the neighbours hadn't heard'. Women often feel that if only they would try harder, keep the house cleaner, or cook better, then maybe their husbands would not beat them. Some women even apologize to their husbands for supposedly provoking the violence.

Violent incidents are very rarely discussed by husbands and wives. Usually no explicit effort is made to effect a reconciliation and reconstitute the relationship or to explore and resolve the conflicts that keep surfacing. Couples usually just drift back together again.

---

[6] See Gelles, op. cit. pp. 113-18 for a discussion of the role of alcohol in violent events and C. H. McCaghy (1968) 'Drinking and deviance disavowal: the case of child molesters.' *Social Problems* 16(1) pp. 43-9, for an example of the use of alcohol in disavowing responsibility for a socially unacceptable form of deviance.

[7] G. W. Sykes and D. Matza (1957) 'Techniques of neutralization: a theory of delinquency'. *American Sociological Review* 22, pp. 667-70, considered several techniques that adolescents use in dealing with their feelings regarding delinquent acts: two of these are 'denial of responsibility' and 'denial of the victim' in blaming the victim.

V. Trouble Spots in Family Life

> I just went about my business normally, It was just a case of
> talking and no more, like, 'What are you wanting for
> breakfast? What are you wanting for your tea?' And he
> wouldn't say what he wanted, 'Just anything will do.' It was
> just talking and answering and no more.[...]

Despite this pattern of letting things ride, women do make it very clear
to their husbands that they are upset and dissatisfied with the pattern of
violence and with the marriage. It is erroneous to assume because the
couple does not talk about the violence that women accept it.[...]

Rights, authority and violence

We conclude from the experiences of the women we interviewed that
husbands believe that their wives cannot and should not make certain
claims upon them. Claim making is not a two-sided process. Men who use
violence consider it their right and privilege as men and as heads of
households to make claims of their wives; if their demands are not met,
as in the cases of the timing of meals or of responding to sexual advances,
the woman may be punished. Conversely, the man does not believe that
his wife can make such strong claims relating to his actions: he considers
her claim-making to be extraordinary and inappropriate and she might
be silenced through the use of force.

Violent men often view other people as objects to be exploited in
their attempts to meet their own needs. They elevate the fulfilment of
their personal desires to the status of a 'natural law', operating on the
premise that their own welfare is of primary and exclusive concern to
others. In arguments and confrontations preceding their use of violence
these men rarely note or admit to the discontent of the other person and
to their concerns and needs, and this is especially true in relationships
with women.

This predisposition is not evident only in men who attack their
wives. Many men in Western society learn to expect that their wishes
and concerns come first, that because they are males and heads of
households they have certain prerogatives and rights that supersede
those of women — especially in the family where the rights of males over
females are clearly defined from a very early age. The difference between
violent men and other males is that the former are prepared to use
physical means to enforce or reinforce their own views. When men do use
force to chastise and punish their wives for failing to live up to their
unilateral standards, they can be very violent indeed.

In summary, the violent episode most often is preceded by a short verbal confrontation, although some prefatory arguments may be intermittent and last several hours. The altercations relate primarily to the husband's expectations regarding his wife's domestic work, his possessiveness and sexual jealousy, and allocation of the family's resources. The verbal confrontation may be initiated by either the husband or the wife, but it is usually initiated by the husband. When a husband attacks his wife he is either chastising her for challenging his authority or for failing to live up to his expectations or attempting to discourage future unacceptable behaviour. Men use diverse and often severe forms of physical force. The usual method of attack is slapping, punching, and kicking, which results in bruises, lacerations, and fractures, some of which require medical treatment and even hospitalization. Men commonly fail to react to the consequences of their violent actions — ignoring the violence and acting as if nothing had happened. Although some men eventually may apologize they very rarely do so immediately following an attack. The majority do not express any contrition whatsoever and often deflect the blame for their violent actions onto their wives. Women, on the other hand, do not ignore the violence but they must remain in the home, often detained by the husband or because they have few places to go. Generally, women feel shattered, frightened, ashamed, and angry. Emotions of this nature may continue for days or weeks after the attack.

Child Battery*

Susan G. Cole

Sitting in the gloom of her kitchen, Eleanor wished for the moment of peace to last. There had been so few of them since she had married Bob, and even fewer since Jimmy had been born three years ago. With Bob, it was those eruptions of violence that disturbed what she had hoped would be a blissful domestic environment. And now Jimmy wouldn't stay still for a second, except for this brief one.

She wished for more friends too, and for more to do.

She also wished for more light, but she had resigned herself years ago to the fact that her house would not be a replica of those bright spacious sunny ones she used to admire in *Better Homes and Gardens*. Her home simply wasn't better than average, and she didn't even have a garden. But now, wait, two minutes. She closed her eyes and transported herself to a garden where she contentedly weeded and pruned.

Suddenly, there was a piercing scream. It tore through her reverie so violently that her fist came down on the table, and half startled, half angry, she went to Jimmy. He had broken his truck.

"Stop it," Eleanor warned, but Jimmy only howled. She shook him. Jimmy's eyes widened as he tried to catch his breath. He screamed louder. "It's only a truck, a toy," she fumed. How could he worry so much about a small truck giving out, when her entire life had been given up to him? She wrenched the truck out of his hand and walked away. But now he wanted it back, broken or not. And she gave it to him. Only she didn't give it to him, she threw it at him. It struck the boy on the side of his head, where he began to bleed, all over his clothes, on the carpet, on the towel she held against him as she tried to make it better.

With the possible exception of sexual abuse, the battery of children has to be the criminal act in our society met with the most shock and anger. It seems almost inconceivable that parents could harm their children, that they would place them on hot stoves to punish them for wetting diapers, that they would bludgeon them with telephone re-

* From *No Safe Place: Violence Against Women and Children*, ed. by Connie Guberman and Margie Wolfe. Copyright © 1985 by Connie Guberman and Margie Wolfe. Reprinted by permission of the Women's Press, Toronto.

ceivers, that they would break their arms, bang their heads against walls, that these actions could be taken against children as young as four months old, and that reports of the abuse are increasing in numbers.[1] Many people are particularly confounded by the physical excesses of mothers who are not supposed to be this way, and who seem to be the living embodiment of the rejection of the female principle, the one that says that women are consistently more nurturing, more loving — naturally so — more likely to salvage a society steeped in a grotesquely violent media and headed inexorably for nuclear annihilation.

History tells us that our own apparent dismay about child abuse is relatively new. Euthanasia was an accepted practice for unwanted children in most ancient civilizations. Children were also sold into slavery, a practice still going on in poverty-stricken countries where another child can be a liability, rather than a welcome addition to a family. Not until the nineteenth century were laws created in the Western world to keep children out of the work force where they were exploited as wage-slaves and made to work in conditions that posed a danger to their safety. Elsewhere, young girls, especially, are still sold into sexual slavery or traded for goods and favours to men who can offer both. There was a time when even animals had better protection. Mary Ellis has become the classic case. She was regularly beaten by her parents in the 1870s and was rescued in 1874 by representatives of the Society for the Prevention of Cruelty to Animals. There was no such thing as the Society for the Prevention of Cruelty to Children at the time.

The extent of society's neglect and exploitation of children can be accounted for by the fact that children had the legal status of property and property only.[2] Although, in contemporary society, we tend to view children as more valuable than property or commodities, the basic status of children has not changed all that much. We still think we own our children. We still believe they reflect on our own person, rather than express any personal integrity of their own: many people have children expressly for these ego-laden reasons. Children still barely have enough credibility to have their testimony taken seriously in a court of law; the credibility of children is extremely low, especially in

---

[1]In her article "The Battered Baby Syndrome," in *Violence in Canada*, edited by Mary Alice Beyer Gammon (Toronto: Methuen, 1978), Gammon describes reports as having increased in Ontario by 52.5 percent between the years 1972 and 1976 (p. 94).

[2]Kathleen Lahey, "Research on Child Abuse in a Liberal patriarchy," in *Taking Sex into Account*, ed. Jill McCalla Vickers (Ottawa: Carleton Univ. Press, 1984), pp. 160-61.

North America where children tend to be more sheltered than children brought up anywhere else in the world. Yet, with all of this "protection," they remain remarkably vulnerable.

It is probably safe to say that the practice of child abuse does not have the same social approval per se as it may have had in the past. Still, the statistics are distressing. In the United States,[3] approximately 3 out of 100 children are kicked, bitten, or punched by a parent each year. And 8 out of 100 children will experience this kind of treatment at some time before the age of 16.[4] The injuries are sometimes fatal. Why does the abuse persist? How does the syndrome begin?

Before we explore the question of how and why child battery occurs, it is crucial to examine three main elements of modern society that guarantee that the abuse will continue. They are the sanctity of the family; the extent to which violence and authoritarianism receive constant approval within the context of a patriarchal society; and the ways in which all of us underestimate the links between "soft-core" abuse[5] — verbal outbursts, the odd yank of an arm, all of these expressions of parental power — and the "hard-core" abuse that sometimes leads to murder.

Like any other crime that takes place in the home, the statistics documenting the incidence of child abuse are likely not that accurate and represent a lower incidence than actual abuse. Child abuse takes place in private, and the privacy accorded to the family protects the perpetrators most effectively. The federal Criminal Code still exonerates child batterers from criminal liability if, according to the parent, the purpose of the battery was to discipline the child.[6] The privacy of

---

[3]Unfortunately, the American data overwhelms Canadian statistics. We do have some, based on reports of various Children Aids Societies, but Canadian researchers, among them Mary Van Stolk, author of *The Battered Child in Canada* [(Toronto: McClelland and Stewart, 1978), p. 3], agree that an accurate statistical picture is difficult to obtain. Further references to Van Stolk appear in the text.

[4]Richard Gelles, "A Profile of Violence toward Children in the U.S.," in *Child Abuse: An Agenda for Action*, eds. George Gerbner, Catherine Ross, and Edward Zigler (New York: Oxford Univ. Press, 1980), p. 87. Further references to this work appear in the text.

[5]"Hard core" and "soft core" are terms coined in Mary Van Stolk's book. I have used them here knowing they evoke the issue of pornography, pornography being the arena in which these terms are normally used. They help to make the connection between violence in the home and our pornographic culture.

[6]Section 43 of the Criminal Code reads: "Every school teacher, parent or person standing in the place of the parent is justified in using force by way of correction towards a pupil or child as the case may be, who is under his care, if the force does not exceed what is reasonable under the circumstances." Note the use of the legal language "correction" and not, say, protection from danger.

the family — which the state violates only grudgingly when it moves in to interview — has made it almost impossible to apprehend the real violence taking place within it. Some of what we know about wife assault applies to child abuse, only the players are slightly different. Whereas men who batter are often protected by police officers who refuse to interfere in a "domestic dispute" because a man's home is his castle, a doctor treating a child's injuries often prefers to take the case at face value, rather than invade the sanctity of the family and traditional authority by asking questions about how the injury was caused. Should the doctor ask, s/he would prefer to believe the parent's often flimsy explanation rather than interfere with the parent's control over her or his child (Van Stolk, p. 38).

Neighbours seldom want to interfere with the kind of parenting going on next door. For that matter, how could a neighbour, or any other concerned observer, be sure that the discipline being carried out so audibly next door is that much different or more extreme than the discipline that is part of everyday life in a family. This is a society that gives enormous reinforcement to the uses of coercion and force when disciplining children, and only within the last decade has there been any legal proscription against corporal punishment in the schools.

Barbara Pressman in her book *Family Violence: Origins and Treatment*, makes persuasive presentation of the extent to which we approve of violence in society and explains that parents are getting and giving double messages about it. She points to the American Commission on the Causes and Prevention of Child Abuse which cites the statistic that half the adults in America approve of teachers striking students when there is proper cause and that being noisy can be counted as one of those proper causes according to 28 percent of the sample. If property had been damaged by the child, 67 percent of the adults would approve, and 84 percent, a startling number, would approve of corporal punishment if the child had hit someone. What this means is that an overwhelming majority of parents agreed that it is all right for a larger, more powerful person, the school authority, to strike the child, even to show that hitting is bad. "The lesson," Pressman writes, referring to what the child learns from what the parents approves, "is not that hitting is inappropriate, but that physical strength and power are the appropriate means of controlling behaviour."[7]

The power hierarchy and the expression of that power by those at the top — through violence, apparently sanctioned by many adults —

[7]Barbara Pressman, *Family Violence: Origins and Treatments*, (Guelph, Ont.: Children's Aid Society and Family Counselling Services/Univ. of Guelph, 1984), pp. 96-97. Pressman quotes Lewis Harris' poll taken in 1968.

guarantee that child abuse will go on. Almost concurrent with the report of the American Commission on the Causes and Prevention of Child Abuse, Voice of Women, monitoring the two Canadian television networks for a 30-hour period, noted that in that time frame 249 violent conflicts were shown, totaling 1 every 7 minutes.[8] A random sampling of the products of culture — Rambo plotting revenge in Vietnam, Conan the Barbarian flexing fearsomely — shows a preoccupation with violent acts that are heroic and, according to the pornographer who brought us SNUFF *et al.*, erotic. The idea that violence is abhorrent in a sexist, capitalist society is wishful thinking at best. John P. Spiegel, the Director of the Lemberg Center for the Study of Violence summed it up best: "Violence is not an instinct. It isn't pressure that comes from within that has to be released. It is a cultural style."[9]

We also know that many child abusers were themselves battered as children.[10] It is relatively easy to understand how victimization at an early age can lead a person to batter his or her own children: battery becomes the model for discipline and the terror that goes with it is perpetuated by a parent who thinks that developing an atmosphere of fear is the only way to get a child to do what s/he is told. It does not help that total obedience remains the standard for what defines a good child. A quiet child is assumed to be good, instead of, say, passive and acquiescent. A noisy child is considered bad instead of, say, active and curious. For the most part, parents receive no alternative to punitive and authoritarian practices to keep the "bad kids" in line. Many of the batterers who were themselves the recipients of harsh disciplinary punishment believe somehow that the experience was good for them.

We live in a society that has conceived and carried out full-scale wars, perhaps the plainest evidence of our collective acceptance of violent solutions to the problem of conflict. And we are growing less, not more, sensitive to how violence really feels. Recent data indicates that prolonged exposure to explicit violence (and explicit sexual violence, though this is not relevant here) desensitizes viewers to the harm

---

[8]These statistics are taken from an unpublished paper by L. Swift, prepared by the Edmonton Branch of Voice of Women in 1969. For an extensive and very useful discussion of violence and television and its effects on children, see George Gerbner's "Children and Power on Television," in *Child Abuse*.

[9]J.H. Pollack, "An Interview with Dr. John D. Spiegel: What You Can Do to Help Stop Violence," *Family Circle*, Oct. 1968, p. 79.

[10]There are many who have discovered this, especially Ray Helfer and C. Henry Kempe. Helfner edited the book *The Battered Child* (Chicago: Univ. of Chicago Press, 1980), which is something of a primer and is now in its third edition. But another good source comes from M.J. Paulston and P.R. Blake, "The Abused, Battered and Maltreated Child: A Review," *Trauma*, 9, No. 4 (Dec. 1967), 56-57.

caused by the violence.[11] We ought to wonder what the connection is between that tendency and the one Mary Van Stolk describes when she talks about how parents who batter tend to underestimate the extent of the force they are using (p. 115).

This last fact, the trend toward underestimating how much force we use, is relevant to all of us who have either had children or had any contact with them. Before we smugly disdain child abusers for their absence of "control," we should take into account our own experiences. Anyone who has had to sit with a youngster for more than an afternoon may herself comprehend how quickly the breaking point approaches. How many times have we hollered at a child without having any idea how terrifying the experience may be for that person? How many of us have yanked a kid's arm to stop that child from picking up an object s/he may have dropped? Why do we think that this kind of "controlling behaviour" is significantly different from the actions of the child abuser? Because we do it for the child's good? That is precisely what many child batterers argue. Many researchers have devised a spectrum of child abuse that begins with verbal and emotional outbursts — the kind many of us have all the time — and escalates to hard-core battery and sometimes murder. In a way, we are all complicit in the hard-core abuse as long as we shrug off our own soft-core excesses.

Given our definitions of what a good child is, given the reinforcement of harsh disciplinary measurers, given the inundation of media endorsing violent behaviour, given the extent to which most of us have become desensitized to violence just by seeing the nightly news, given the fast-blurring line between soft- and hard-core abuse, which fades precisely because we are all desensitized in this culture, it is a wonder that the incidence of child abuse is as infrequent as it is. From a feminist perspective, the numerous conditions under which anyone can scream at a child, shake a child, pull him, push her, precisely because we are in positions of power in relations to children, should be recognized as, if not abusive, then at least too close to abusive for comfort.

---

[11]Dr. Ed. Donnerstein's work on explicit violence and pornography is crucial in this area. In testimony given at hearings on pornography in Minneapolis, Donnerstein summarized his research, saying, "Subjects who have seen violent material or x-rated material see less injury to a rape victim than people who have not seen these films." Public Hearings on Ordinances to Add Pornography as Discrimination against Women, Committee on Government Operations, City Council, Minneapolis, Minn., 12-13 Dec. 1983. *Transcript, I*, 37-38 (unpublished).

To appreciate how close we come to being abusive to our children merely in the course of our daily parenting, is to begin a process of understanding how child abuse works. The line between soft-core abuse — yelling, dominating, using our children as extensions of our own egos — and the hard-core violence that maims and injures is a very slender one. What is crucial is that each of us as parents has the power to damage our kids, whether we use that power or not. Thus, the *carte blanche* of parents has to be questioned and challenged. Moreover, as we will discover, the fact that some parents do graduate from soft-core power-plays to hard-core violence is explained by social forces.

Still, it is the most vicious type of child-beating that is the subject here, the kind that inflicts physical injury on the child. It used to be that this kind of child battery was assumed to be committed mostly by women, but newer data suggests that women do not necessarily beat their children more than men do. At this point, we should be prepared to say that women and men beat their children in equal numbers (Van Stolk, p. 6). But the similarities end there. In a sexist society, men batter their children because they have power. Women batter their children because they have little power, except the power they can exercise over their children.

The adage "a man's home is his castle" is still relevant in most North American families. Regardless of what traditionalists and some segments of the child-protection movement say, a man who batters his children is not evidence of a family falling apart, he is evidence that the family remains the locus of male power which stays protected and intact. Child abuse occurs in families whose hierarchies are only marginally more extreme than that of the average family.[12] Men are on top and children are on the bottom, and so children become especially vulnerable to the actions of an abusive father.

The particular conditions in which the father might find himself are relevant only to a point. It is true that financial stress, for example, is sometimes a factor contributing to child abuse (Gelles, p. 97). But this kind of stress does not get acted out on a child in a total vacuum. Power is the key. If the family structure did not give the father the power to batter his children and, crucially, to get away with it, he would not beat them, regardless of the state of his finances.[13] The missing link between financial stress and child abuse is self-esteem.

---

[12]"Clearly, the more inequality in the home, the greater the risk of severe parental violence" (Gelles, p. 102).

[13]Gelles makes a point of saying that "...it would be a mistake to infer that poverty is the sole cause of violence" (p. 97).

V. Trouble Spots in Family Life

Financial problems and their blow to the ego conflict strongly with that power afforded to fathers and to their self-perception as the embodiment of parental authority. And, when a father's self-esteem is damaged, he will be more inclined to exercise his authority, to let everyone know who is running the show.[14] How many times have you heard of situations in which mothers, unable to say no, direct children to their fathers who have no difficulty laying down the law? Mom is soft, Dad is tough as nails, a disciplinarian who believes he is not fulfilling his role as a parent unless he throws his weight around.

It is not as if he gets no reinforcement for what he is doing. He is just being a regular fellow, trying to adjust to what is expected. Read a portrait of the typical child abuser: hard-hearted, no nurturing sense, inarticulate and unable to express feelings, controlling, intimidating, able to back up his demands with the threat of physical force.[15] It sounds more like James Bond than anyone else. And, while it is true that the male abuser, who is often unemployed (Gelles, p. 97) and a substance abuser (Van Stolk, p. 9), does not exactly have the ideal curriculum vitae, his personality is the model for our cultural standards of masculinity.

Researchers looking at the child-abuse syndrome avoid this kind of analysis assiduously, or so it seems. They insist that something is going terribly wrong when a father abuses a child,[16] not that the universe is unfolding in the way that patriarchal norms are established. We live in a society where men have power in the family. We live in a society where violence is a cultural style. We also live in a society where violence is a cultural style belonging especially to men. Very

---

[14]Gammon's article "The Battered Baby Syndrome" traces and charts an interactional model of child abuse developed through the work of S. Wasserman, David Gil, and Richard Gelles, which incorporated frustration and self-esteem as factors in child abuse (pp. 104-05).

[15]This is a composite portrait of mine based on a number of readings. "Hard-hearted" refers to Van Stolk's claim that parents do not "feel" anything when they beat their children (p. 16); "No nurturing sense" refers to the inability to create the parent/child bond, a feature of Brandt Steel's "Psychodynamic Factors in Child Abuse," in *The Battered Child*, pp. 49-85; "controlling and intimidating" refers to the tendency already mentioned of child abuses to be harsh disciplinarians who need to express their own authority. Finally, I think that men's greater size and the extent to which they are taught as young boys to use their bodies, afford them the ability to back up their demands with physical force.

[16]See the work of Brandt Steele and J.H. Pollack, in particular their "A Psychiatric Study of Parents Who Abuse Infants and Small Children," in *The Battered Child*. The work of Serapio Zalba, such as "Treatment of Child Abuse," in *Violence in the Family*, ed. Suzanne K. Steinmetz and Murray A. Straus (New York: Dodd Mead, 1975), is also key in this area.

little work has been done to make the connections between society's expectations of men — that they be predisposed to a *machismo* celebrated relentlessly in everything from organized sports — where assault is encouraged and made entertaining, sometimes part of the rules of the game — to pornography where violence is eroticized and fused with male sexuality, and to violence in the home. In turn, male violence reinforces for children all the rigid sex-roles that contributed to the violence in the first place.

The attitude that men have an inherent right to power and its expression is already well on its way to development when young boys know enough to separate themselves from trivial "girlish" pastimes; when Clint Eastwood becomes a role model; when men learn that wives are supposed to cater to their needs; and when they open their eyes wide enough to see the products of a seven-billion-dollar pornography industry[17] that lets them buy access to female sexuality. The ways in which male power can be exercised are intensely promoted by the media, so that it is unlikely that men will know an alternative to power-tripping and a preoccupation with violence. They may never know what nurturance feels like. This means that especially well-socialized men are bound to be disasters around children.

Children, by their nature, grate on the nerves of strict disciplinarians, who are accustomed to getting their way and to maintaining control over situations. A child's spontaneity will aggravate a man who does not want any interruptions in his neatly ordered life. A child's curiosity will annoy a man who believes he knows everything and who therefore has no patience with someone, even a child who does not. A child is loud, bad news for a man who likes to choose who will make noise and when. A child's playfulness is trivial to a father who takes everything seriously, especially his own power. Children are demanding, they have needs, something men are taught to monopolize. Sometimes children distract mothers from meeting fathers' needs. In short, children get in the way. A father's pre-violent resistance to a child almost guarantees that the child's demands will grow louder and that the situation will escalate to become violent. Although all of this sometimes applies to the female child abuser, it is not, as we will see later, the main dynamic at work in the case of female child batterers.

We can learn a great deal about fathers battering children from what we know about wife assault. The same power men have over women, and the fact that they batter because they are permitted to do so, applies to fathers and children as well. Sometimes the connection

---

[17]See "The Place of Pornography," *Harper's*, Nov. 1984, p. 31.

between child assault and wife assault is painfully close. In 20 percent of the situations in which men are beating their children, they are beating their wives as well.[18] Battery of children often begins at pregnancy when one outburst can damage two victims (Van Stolk, p. 6).

The anger men feel toward their pregnant wives and their children-to-be is often related to their inability to cope financially with an addition to the family. As we will see further on, access to the freedom to choose pregnancy would probably make for fewer abused children, but it is not clear that a potentially abusive father would agree to the termination of a pregnancy if his assent reflected his own inability to support a family. There are many factors to be weighed here. As long as men are the heads of families and wield power in the traditional family's unequal context, they will not likely concede personal failure and agree to their wives having abortions. Instead, the wives will have children and the husbands will continue to believe that they have a right to beat all the family members, that this is, in fact, expected of them and that their world will fall apart if they do not.

Researchers, both those who accept the psychopathological model and those who understand that social factors are important, will accept many explanations for why men beat their children except for the obvious one that men have power, especially in the family and need to have it reinforced even if the ones they are supposed to be caring for are hurt by it. Similarly, the literature on female battery rings false to the feminist ear. Sometimes the researchers, Ray Helfer and C. Kempe among them, will be relatively generous and attribute the batter to the mother's batter as a child. But, most of the time, the literature, especially that espousing the psychodynamic and psychopathological approaches to child abuse, reeks of assumptions of what is "natural" among women.[19] Seldom does the research address the social context that sets women up for profound disappointment in their lives as mothers. The result is an unsympathetic view of the female child batterer as monster, not only because she beats her children, but because, in so doing, she subverts mother nature.[20] This is an especially biased

---

[18]Testimony of Douglas J. Besharov, Director, National Center on Child Abuse and Neglect, before the House of Representatives Committee on Science and Technology, 14 Feb. 1978. Transcript, pp. 17-18.

[19]This is essentially the substance of the psychopathological model for child abuse as expressed by Zalba and others. This was the first clinical approach to child abuse and crucially centres on a blame-the-victim model, and was done at a time when women were assumed to be major perpetrators of violence against children.

[20]Edward Zigler, author of "Controlling Child Abuse: Do We Have the Knowledge and/or the Will?", in *Child Abuse*, agrees: "The notion that child abusers lack maternal instinct has reinforced the anger and revulsion associated with child

view compared to the view of the male child batterer who is working out the experience of his battery as a child, often at the hands of yet another "unnatural" woman, his mother. In seeking a more sympathetic approach to child battery in the hands of women, I am not suggesting that women do not hurt their children when they beat them, or that the abuse should be excused. What is at issue here is the tendency among researchers to bring their own sexist values to the investigation, so that men are "excused" (read: it was their mother's fault) and women are villified (read: they are sick and unnatural).[21]

What gets left out is this: for adult men, adult life at the top of the family hierarchy is the payoff; to abuse is their right. For women, adult life at the bottom is a trauma; to abuse is relief, even if the feeling is only temporary and overwhelmed by consuming guilt.

Brandt Steele, a psychologist, attributes female battery of children to the breakdown of the mother's ability to mother a child. He refers, throughout his work, to the distortion of her deep, sensitive, intuitive awareness and response to the infant's conditions and needs, and to her desire that her children satisfy *her* needs.[22] Why does he call these expectations unreasonable? Why is he so surprised that women expect that children will do something for *them* and that that is what children are there for? Society, until recently rocked by the demands and insights of the women's movement, insisted that child-rearing was the *only* way a woman could fulfill herself in life. Why should we be so surprised that women want to get something out of it?

Child abusers come from all backgrounds (Van Stolk, p. 7). Regardless of class, female abusers share a feeling of being imprisoned by their roles as mothers.[23] This is a role women are encouraged to enjoy lest they lose economic support from a man and lose status as human beings. One family planning counselor described how pregnant teenagers believe that the only way they could achieve status or value as human beings was by becoming a mother.[24] A lot of work is done to convince women that they are supposed to like the role and that childbirth is the ultimate achievement. It starts when little girls play

---

abuse" (p. 4). Indeed, the book *Child Abuse* is a collection of essays designed to further a "social," rather than an "individual," approach.

[21]Kathleen Lahey's "Research on Child Abuse in a Liberal Patriarchy," in *Taking Sex into Account*, synthesizes the research and describes its biases.

[22]Steele, "Psychodynamic Factors in Child Abuse," in *The Battered Child*, pp. 49-85.

[23]Murray Straus, "Family Patterns and Child Abuse in a Nationally Representative American Sample," *Child Abuse and Neglect*, 3 (1979), 213-25.

[24]Susan G. Cole, Interview with Elizabeth Parker, Director Family Planning Service, Toronto, 4 June 1981.

with dolls and the socialization continues relentlessly as magazines for home-makers pour on the positive reinforcement for the creative act of housekeeping and child-rearing. What the researchers who examine the "breakdown of mothering" fail to note is that many women are in the home via the coercion of social conditioning and that, if this conditioning were not so effective, many women who have no desire to care for children would not be in positions to have them. In other words, sexism's excessive — and false — advertising for the value of the nuclear family and the relative roles within it has a great deal to do with creating the battered-child syndrome.

No, say the exponents of "defective socialization," whose ideas harken back to the idea "Why can't she just be a good mother like everybody else?" which trivializes women's real experience in the world. Feminists might argue the opposite, that child abusers have been socialized too well. Entirely prepared for a blissful life in which motherhood will empower them, many women are led into situations where there is little satisfaction, and even less power. This means that, like well-socialized men, well-socialized women will be disasters around children. Children will become the scapegoats, the only ones with less power than the angry women who are supposed to care for them.

Having been prepared for heaven on earth in the home, the well-conditioned woman proceeds with her life as prescribed only to discover that babies do not give unconditional love, they cry a lot instead. They do not obey on command because they appreciate what their mothers have done for them; they just demand more and more. They do not wet their diapers at convenient times or bellow for food on cue. There is little financial reward for the job and even less mobility. For women who have been told only the upside of the housewife's story, the real experience of motherhood makes for an alienation that is profound. And there is no escape, either for the mother or the child. To leave the baby alone is to neglect it, and to be guilty of what is called soft(er) abuse. To stay is to make the child vulnerable to a rage that, in spite of *how* it is vented, comes from somewhere legitimate.

Still, Steele, and other exponents of psychodynamism, wonder how it is that child abusers do not affect the child-mother bond so important to child-rearing. Mary Van Stolk, wisely questions the practice of wrenching children away from their mothers at birth to be put in the more "expert" care of medical doctors, thus pointing out the contradiction between society's expectations of mothers and the actions of society's institutions (p. 45).

But few observers have ever suggested that the child-mother bond may not exist because of the women's experience during pregnancy, or because that woman may never have wanted the child in the first place. It may be that the abuse of the child begins in pregnancy when women consume alcohol or drugs that put the foetus at risk. What addicts women to alcohol? we should be asking. What makes them have to avoid reality? What about the child battery that begins when a husband beats his spouse? What we know about battering husbands is that their assault grows more vicious when the victim is pregnant.[25] She is held responsible for the child; her pregnancy is her failure and bodes for the imminent failure of the father to provide for his family. Consider then, if a woman's pregnancy provokes a violent attack from her husband, what attitudes she may develop toward the child? Is it not possible that she could blame the child for the assault or lash out at it?

Is this a wanted child? Rarely, except in feminist literature, has the fact that women do not control their reproductive choices ever been linked to the incidence of child abuse. While it is true that many battering parents want their children, they want them to be other than the way they are. Many battering parents never wanted their babies and considered them burdens from the beginning.[26] When a couple is unable to afford a child, they should have the choice as to whether or not they should have the child. If a woman in a battery situation leaves herself more vulnerable to a brutal attack, she should have the option of terminating her pregnancy. Many will argue that abortion is the ultimate in child abuse. But this romanticization of the foetus makes it impossible to mitigate the misery battered women often experience in pregnancy and consigns an unwanted child to what could be a childhood in hell.

And what about a woman's hellish life within the family? Freedom to choose pregnancy does not entail only choosing when to cope with having a child and terminating the pregnancy when times demand it. Reproductive freedom is real when pregnant women have the self-determination to walk out the door of a batter situation and have the resources to keep their children and rear them. But these circumstances do not occur frequently, and women, whether battered or "just" controlled, find themselves locked into situations which they do not feel they can change.

---

[25]This is based on my interviews with assaulted women prepared for "Home Sweet Home?," an article I wrote for *Still Ain't Satisfied! Canadian Feminism Today*, ed. Maureen FitzGerald, Connie Guberman, and Margie Wolfe (Toronto: Women's Press, 1982), pp. 55-67.
[26]This is Mary Van Stolk's explanation for the abuse of the foetus in vitro via alcohol and drug abuse (p. 45) in *No Safe Place*.

V. Trouble Spots in Family Life

A study by Murray Straus in 1979 surveyed families with children between the ages of one and a half and five years and puts the matter into perspective. Straus discovered that what really caused women to lose control was closely associated with the female sex roles. So now consider a typical portrait of the conditions of a female child abuser: responsibility for toilet-training; for training children to eat and to sleep on command (infants tend to be recalcitrant on all three counts); too much housework, marital disharmony, isolation in the house, financial worries. This could be almost *any* woman. Most of these conditions are going to be factors in the lives of housewives unless child-rearing and housework are shared in the home. As for financial worries, these are epidemic among women, who made 60 cents on the male dollar;[27] who work part-time when they would rather have full-time employment;[28] who, if they are sole-support mothers, can expect social assistance programs that still leave them short of the poverty line since their benefits are only 63 percent to this line.[29]

The point here is this: the conditions of men and women within a patriarchal society set both sexes up so that abuse of their children is actually quite likely. Men, socialized to hide their feelings of love and encouraged to express their dominance, take seriously their roles as authoritarians in the family. The fact that violence is the culturally acceptable way for men to express their power leads to the child-abuse syndrome. Women, on the other hand, discover the false promise of life within the nuclear family and, out of frustration, lash out in socially sanctioned ways — physical punishment — at the only ones more vulnerable than themselves. The family institutionalizes it all, for as the family is the locus of male power, it is also the locus of female powerlessness.

More crucially, this could happen to anyone. The tendency among observers of child abusers is to identify them as anomalies — people out there, not people like ourselves. But we are all socialized intensely to conform to male and female sex roles. We are all part of the social order's cultural style of violence, especially when it comes to our children. None of this would persist as it does unless children remained as devalued as they are. Physically attacking them, subjecting them to emotional abuse, allowing our frustration to come out at them, keeps children in their place as likely targets. If you are a woman who

---

[27]Strause, pp. 213-25.

[28]Most recent data from Statistics Canada.

[29]According to the most recent data from Statistics Canada, 72 percent of women work part-time and over half of those would prefer a full-time job.

has heard her child whine too much and has let go with a torrent of verbal abuse — even "shut up" at the top of your lungs — then you know what I am talking about.

As consciousness of the existence of the child-abuse syndrome has increased, professionals who have contact with children have been encouraged to improve their process of identifying abuse. Under the auspices of various provincial child-abuse programs, handbooks have been developed for physicians to assist in the first phase of combatting child abuse — the detection phase. Through these handbooks, medical doctors have been encouraged to recognize the symptoms and to take a more proactive role in dealing with patients and with their parents. Many doctors have resisted, in keeping with the Western medical model which addresses the injury itself and not the conditions that precipitated it. But their associations have supported the new initiatives. Teachers too have taken a stronger stand. In light of new policies generated within their federations, they face the risk of losing their jobs if they fail to report suspected instances of child abuse.

In the meantime, in the post-detection phase, the Children's Aid Societies have remained entrenched in their process of trying to maintain the nuclear family at all costs. Certainly the CAS has become more aware of and has taken action on the need for better housing and for community day care that is accessible, but still, CAS principles have centred around preserving the family, the institution whose protection often perpetuates the conditions that engender child abuse in the first place. The issue is not only that the CAS parachutes into homes, removing children, bringing them back, removing them again in a dizzying yoyo effect, but also that actions of CAS workers affect men and women differently.

This should not come as a surprise since an abusive mother's relationship to her child is different from an abusive father's. Children are often in the way of their abusive fathers, while children are often the very essence of the identity of their abusive mothers. Women who beat their children *do* love them and lose something precious when a child is being taken away from them. An abusive mother has a great deal at stake in her children, possibly too much, which is often the very difficulty that she acts out through violence. When a woman subsumes her identity in her children, when she attacks them because their "naughtiness" reflects badly on her, when she can have no identity without her children, she crumbles when they are no longer there.

If the mother is the abuser and the CAS worker removes the child, the separation from the mother is traumatic and usually rein-

531

V. Trouble Spots in Family Life

forces her lack of self-esteem. If she is in a battery situation with her husband, the consequences can be especially damaging when the actions of the state seem to sanction his abuse of her. If she cannot take care of the child, to the extent that the CAS has to race in to the rescue, then the husband's abuse of the mother receives justification.

Jeffrey Wilson, a family lawyer and one of Canada's most eloquent and effective advocates of children's rights, agrees that maybe the movement has gone too far, that no one is considering the needs of parents, that the courts are entirely unsympathetic to the experience of women who are at the bottom of a rigid hierarchy that makes it impossible for them to recover their children once they have been forced to give them up.[30] At least abusive fathers, if they want to see their children, have more resources to hire legal counsel and, regardless, do not share the feeling that without children they have no identity.

We have to be very careful as we argue that social structures and patriarchal institutions operate to condemn men and women equally to becoming abusive parents; only one half of the argument, the half about women, is likely to get heard. Women have less clout in the legal system and less credibility with government agencies in a sexist society. We may be very clear about how male sex roles automatically cast men as child abusers, but the more we say that the conditions of women, the way we are defined — targeted for abuse, denied freedom of choice over who we can be and over our reproduction, denied economic parity with men — forecasts the battery of children, the more we have to guard against the agents of the state and those of other repositories of power identifying *all* women as unfit mothers and acting accordingly. Kathleen Lahey put it this way:

> I suspect that even if [the] point is that vast institutional changes have to be made if life is to be safe for women and thus for children [this approach] will be taken as simply saying that women are not fit mothers. And that is only a short step from saying that male members of the state, who are the policy makers anyway, are better able to decide how children are to be raised and by whom. The whole concept of fitness for mother-hood plays directly into the hands of judges and legislators who would thus be able to resolve the patriarchal impulse toward control over women and reproduction.[31]

---

[30]The New Democratic Caucus, *The Other Ontario: A Report on Poverty in Ontario* (Toronto: New Democratic Caucus, June 1984), p. 17.

[31]Susan G. Cole, Interview with Jeffrey Wilson, Toronto, 7 Oct. 1984.

In December 1983, the Standing Committee on Social Development submitted its report on child abuse to the Ontario Legislature. The report focused solely on legislative approaches to the problem, and the legislative options consistently dealt with the safety of the child. There was virtually no mention of root causes of child battery, no analysis of the social forces that perpetuate it, and only a passing, seemingly pop-psychological reference to the absence of touch in the child-rearing practices of the abusers or to the batterers' unrealistic expectations of their children.

This is the kind of report we usually toss aside as either superficial or too legislation oriented to be of much use, except that the report did make one small suggestion about which preventative measures might be considered in the future. Kathleen Lahey's fears of state excesses might be all too well founded. The report referred to testimonies of witnesses who stressed the need for an effective screening system during prenatal and postnatal periods to help detect cases that pose a high risk of child abuse. In some hospitals in England every pregnant woman who is admitted to give birth is assigned a nurse or social worker who counsels and determines whether she is a high-risk individual. If a high- or moderate-risk situation is detected, contact is maintained with the family for six months.[32]

What is a high-risk case? One public health official testified that the failure of the mother to touch or cuddle her baby ought to be a crucial indicator.[33] When what? and says whom? Remove the child? On what basis? This notion of prescreening is as close as the report comes to discussing ways of preventing abuse (the rest prevents re-abuse) and evokes the spectre of the state and its mechanisms swooping in to decide who and how children should be reared, exchanging the hardship of the child for the hardship of the parent. Feminists must begin to make some crucial distinctions. We have to accept that the privacy in the home and the family is not sacred and support a physician or teacher who identifies a case of child abuse and does something about it. At the same time, we have to establish that prescreening is state intervention in the extreme, approximates a new eugenics, and approaches totalitarianism.

The government's approach has been consistent in recognizing that the safety of the child comes first, and this is a priority with which it is too difficult to argue. But patriarchal institutions, and by that I mean government agencies and hospitals and the medical establish-

---

[32]Lahey, p. 116.

[33]Standing Committee on Social Development, *Second Report on Family Violence: Child Abuse* (Toronto: Government of Ontario, Dec. 1983), p. 11.

ment generally, seem to be unable to deal with this priority without appropriating all reproductive functions as well as women's lives in general. It is not only prescreening for child abuse that has to be examined here, but that recommendation, whether accepted or not, combined with paternalistic abortion laws, proscriptions against midwifery, and persecution of anyone who wants to give birth other than in a hospital. Power is power no matter where it is applied, and feminists have to be vigilant, questioning at all times the state's motives and increasing clout in the area of reproductive choice.

The feminist agenda also has to include the provision of an integrated strategy for dealing with and understanding child abuse. The strategy must centre on the roots of women's oppression and the essential oppression of sex roles so as to make comprehensible the battery of children at the hands of their parents. First, we have to understand that beating up children is consistent with what is expected of fathers who conform to sex-role stereotypes, and we have to use that consciousness to alter our expectations of what men should be. Care for children, real care for children, must cease being divorced from traditional male activity. Right from the time they are boys and sneer at the idea of playing with dolls, men have resisted caring for children.

Second, the glorification of the nuclear family has got to stop. Too many women are lied to about what family life will be like for them and, because they believe this is their only choice, they blame themselves for their grief and frustration and cannot imagine changing their lives. Indeed, the nuclear family has to be exposed for what it is — a dangerous place for women and children. Traditionally the privacy of the family has been sacrosanct. Now we know that keeping family matters private has protected the perpetrators of violence within it. As long as the family remains hierarchical, with fathers on the top, they can exercise their authority through brutality, and mothers try to gain authority in the same way. As long as total authority is vested in parents, children will be vulnerable to attack: neighbours will mind their own business while the "discipline" is being meted out; family members will be discouraged from talking about it; the exlusivity of the family will continue to isolate its members, especially mothers, from contact with other people or from activities not related to child-rearing.

The entire structure of child-rearing has to change. Every child should be a wanted child. This is not to say that mothers who beat their children do not love them, but rather, that a child who is born by choice is less likely to be kicked in utero by the father and even less likely to be viewed as an "enemy," as Mary Van Stolk describes the feeling,[34] once it has been brought into the world. If any woman had the freedom to choose, the incidence of child abuse would go down; if better and affordable day care were available so that women were more mobile in their everyday lives, then the conditions referred to by researchers as "stress" and "frustrations" would surely abate.

If financial stress is among these conditions, then the re-allocation of resources is also in order. This redistribution of wealth is relevant, not only to reduce the disparity between poor, middle-income, and wealthy families, but to reduce the disparity between men and women as well. Women must be paid equally for work of equal value; the benefits to sole-support mothers have to increase. Most important, the means of making mothering and child-rearing — women's work — values in our society must be developed. Would a father taking care of children not feel less disgusted with the job if he did not have contempt for what women do? And what is a fit mother in our society but one who chooses to consign herself to hundreds of hours of work a week with no pay and with few immediate rewards?

Finally, we must come to grips with the fact that the celebration of violence is our cultural style; that capitalism and sexism depend on the maintenance of power over others — over women and children in particular; that power and who has it is related to the incidence of child abuse; that men and women know few other ways to exercise that power without using force and intimidation over their own children and, in the case of husbands, over their wives as well. A redistribution of wealth is crucial, but so is a redistribution of power. As it stands, children do not have a choice. We need to take them more seriously, and we need to recognize our own complicity in the child-abuse syndrome. Each of us has been impatient with a child; we've wished for blessed relief from their constant demands; we consider vacations an escape from them; we've yelled, pulled, and yanked at them, when they have not the slightest opportunity of fighting back and achieving self-determination. We use their dependence on us as a means of justifying our power over them. All of this devalues them.

If children had more power, they would be less vulnerable. They would not be made scapegoats for violence at the hands of women who, as it is, can lash out at no one else. If women had more power, if they had more life choices, they would not be shunted into the home where isolation and disappointment foster the frustration that triggers a violent attack on their children. If men had less power, if fathers were not expected to mete out physical punishment in the name of authority, if violent and aggressive behaviour were not so quintessentially male in

---

[34]Standing Committee on Social Development, p. 11.

the patriarchal scheme of things, so many children would not be ter-
rorized by parental abuse. In short, change the power dynamics in society, and there will be fewer beaten children.

Further Reading

Books

Camden, Elizabeth.
If He Comes Back He's Mine. Toronto: Women's Press, 1984.
Gerbner, Beroge, Catherine J. Ross, and Edward Zigler, ed.,
Child Abuse: An Agenda for Action. New York: Oxford Univ. Press,
1980.
Pressman, Barbara.
Family Violence: Origins and Treatments. Guelph, Ont.: The City of
Guelph, Children's Aid Society and Family Counselling Services/Univ.
of Guelph, 1984.
Van Stolk, Mary.
The Battered Child in Canada. Toronto: McClelland and Stewart,
1978.

Articles

Beyer Gammon, Mary Alice.
"The Battered Baby Syndrome: A Reconceptualization of Family
Conflict." in *Violence in Canada.* ed. Mary Alice Beyer Gammon.
Toronto: Methuen, 1978, pp. 93-11.
Lahey, Kathleen.
"Research on Child Abuse in a Liberal Patriarchy." *In Taking Sex into
Account.* Ed. Jill Vickers. Ottawa: Carlton Univ. Press, 1984, pp. 156-
84.
Straus, Murray.
"Family Patterns — Child Abuse in a Nationally Representative
American Sample." *Child Abuse and Neglect*, 3 (1979), 213-25.